The Official
World Wildlife Fund Guide to
Endangered Species of North America

Volume 2

Birds

Reptiles

Amphibians

Fishes

Mussels

Crustaceans

Snails

Insects & Arachnids

BEACHAM PUBLISHING, INC.
WASHINGTON, D.C.
CHARLES COUNTY COMMUNITY COLLEGE
LA PLATA, MARYLAND

The Official
World Wildlife Fund Guide to
Endangered Species of North America

Managing Editor
David W. Lowe

Editors
John R. Matthews
Charles J. Moseley

World Wildlife Fund Consultants
Richard Block
Julia A. Moore
Lynne Baptista

Photo Editor
Charles J. Moseley

Book and Cover Design
Amanda Mott

Map Production
Steven K. Shahida

Editorial Assistant
C. Peter Kessler

Production
Nancy Gillio
Patricia Price

Originating Editor
John R. Matthews

Library of Congress
 Cataloging-in-Publication Data
The Official World Wildlife Fund Guide to Endangered   Species
 of North America / editors. David W. Lowe, John R. Matthews,
 Charles J. Moseley.
  Includes bibliographical references.
   Includes index and appendices.
   Describes 540 endangered or threatened species, including
 their habitat, behavior, and recovery.
   1. Nature conservation—North America. 2. Endangered
 species—North America. 3. Rare animals—North America. 4.
 Rare plants—North America. I. Lowe, David W., 1951- II. Mat-
 thews, John R., 1937- . III. Moseley, Charles J., 1946- . IV.
 World Wildlife Fund.
QL84.2.035   1990   574.5'29'097—dc20   89-29757
ISBN 0-933833-17-2

Printed in the United States of America
First Printing, January 1990

Contents
Volume 2

Color Photo Credits — Volume 2

Cover Photos
American Peregrine Falcon
Little Kern Golden Trout
San Joaquin KIt Fox
San Francisco Garter Snake
—Susan Middleton with David Liittschwager

Page C-1
American Peregrine Falcon — Susan Middleton with
   David Liittschwager
Hawaiian Hawk — Robert J. Shallenberger
Masked Bobwhite — C. Allan Morgan
Attwater's Prairie Chicken — C. Allan Morgan
Audubon's Crested Caracara — Lee Kuhn

Page C-2
Hawaiian Stilts — Robert J. Shallenberger
Hawaiian Common Moorhen — Robert J. Shallenberger
Mississippi Sandhill Cranes — Donna Dewhurst
Hawaiian Coot — Robert J. Shallenberger

Page C-3
Florida Scrub Jay — Lee Kuhn
Whooping Cranes — C. Allan Morgan
Nihoa Finch — Robert J. Shallenberger
Least Bell's Vireo — B. "Moose" Peterson

Page C-4
Green Sea Turtle — C. Allan Morgan
Ringed Sawback Turtle — Roger W. Barbour
Desert Tortoise — Susan Middleton with David
   Liittschwager

Page C-5
San Francisco Garter Snake — Susan Middleton with
   David Liittschwager
Blue Tailed Mole Skink — C. Kenneth Dodd, Jr.
Atlantic Salt Marsh Snake — Robert S. Simmons
Eastern Indigo Snake — Ray E. Ashton, Jr.
Concho Water Snake — Robert and Linda Mitchell

Page C-6
Mona Ground Iguana — C. Kenneth Dodd, Jr.
Blunt-Nosed Leopard Lizards — Susan Middleton with
   David Liittschwager
Golden Coqui — George Drewry
Puerto Rican Crested Toad — David M. Dennis

Page C-7
Houston Toad — C. Allan Morgan
Wyoming Toad — LuRay Parker
Maryland Darter — Roger W. Barbour
Santa Cruz Long-Toed Salamander —
   Ray E. Ashton, Jr.
San Marcos Salamander — Robert and Linda Mitchell

Page C-8
Gila Trout — John N. Rinne
Shortnose Sturgeon — Jim Couch
Little Kern Golden Trout — Susan Middleton with
   David Liittschwager
Devil's Hole Pupfish — Thomas M. Baugh
Unarmored Threespine Stickleback —
   B. "Moose" Peterson

Page C-9
Okaloosa Darter — Roger W. Barbour
Snail Darter — Roger W. Barbour
Watercress Darter — Roger W. Barbour

Page C-10
Oahu Tree Snails — William P. Mull
Endangered Freshwater Mussels —
   A. E. Spreitzer/OSU Mus. Zool.
Flat-Spired Three-Toothed Snail — Craig W. Stihler

Page C-11
Oahu Tree Snails — William P. Mull
Valley Elderberry Longhorn Beetle — Richard A.
   Arnold
Tooth Cave Ground Beetle — Robert and Linda Mitchell
Delta Green Ground Beetle — Richard A. Arnold
Kentucky Cave Shrimp — Chip Clark
California Freshwater Shrimp — Susan Middleton with
   David Liittschwager
Bay Checkerspot Butterfly — Noel LaDue

Page C-12
Pawnee Montane Skipper Butterfly — Paul Opler
Schaus Swallowtail Butterfly — Thomas C. Emmel
Palos Verdes Blue Butterfly — Richard A. Arnold
San Bruno Elfin Butterfly — Richard A. Arnold
Lange's Metalmark Butterfly — Richard A. Arnold
Tooth Cave Spider — Robert and Linda Mitchell
Bee Creek Cave Harvestman —
   Robert and Linda Mitchell

Ready Reference Index for Volume 2
(Refer to Volume 2 Index for listing by Scientific Names)

BIRDS (Page 561)

Common Name	Scientific Name	Page

REPTILES (Page 719)

AMPHIBIANS (Page 783)

FISHES (Page 801)

MUSSELS (Page 955)

CRUSTACEANS (Page 1023)

The Official
World Wildlife Fund Guide to
Endangered Species of North America

BIRDS

Nihoa Millerbird
Acrocephalus familiaris kingi

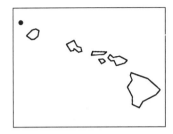

Robert J. Shallenberger

Status . . . . . . Endangered
Listed . . . . . . March 11, 1967
Family . . . . . . Muscicapidae (Thrush)
Description . . . Small, secretive thrush, gray-brown above, white below.
Habitat . . . . . . Nihoa; dense shrubs.
Food . . . . Insects.
Reproduction . . Clutch of 2 eggs.
Threats . . . . . . Limited range.
Region 1 . . . . . Hawaii

Description

The inconspicuous Nihoa millerbird is dark gray-brown above and buff-white below; it has a dark, thin, warbler-like bill. Its name, "millerbird," is derived from its habit of preying on the larger miller moths.

It was discovered in 1923 by Alexander Wetmore. A related species, the Laysan millerbird (*Acrocephalus f. familiaria*) was discovered on Laysan in 1891 but became extinct by 1923.

Behavior

The millerbird is secretive, running, hopping, or flying about in the underbrush, and rarely leaving cover. It is sedentary and sel-dom moves more than 20 meters (65 ft) out of its home territory, usually an area of about 0.2 to 0.4 hectares (0.5 to 1.0 acres). Millerbirds are insectivorous, gleaning prey from leaves, stems of bushes, leaf litter, and from the soil surface. Although little is known of its breeding behavior, it is thought to nest between January and May and lay a clutch of two eggs.

Habitat

Nihoa Island is a 62-hectare (156-acre) remnant of a volcanic cone in the northwestern Hawaiian island chain. It has steep slopes, rocky outcroppings, well-developed valleys, and precipitous cliffs on the west, north, and east. The topography is quite rugged, although the maximum elevation is only 277 meters (910 ft.). The millerbird prefers areas of dense shrubs where it can forage and build low nests.

Historic Range

The Nihoa millerbird is endemic to the island of Nihoa. Early estimates placed the number of millerbirds between 100 and 200. More reliable census techniques used during the 1960s and 1970s estimated a population that ranged between 200 and 600 birds.

Current Distribution

The Nihoa millerbird remains restricted to Nihoa Island, which is about 400 kilometers (250 mi) northwest of Oahu, Hawaii. The island's carrying capacity is considered to be 600 birds, and a 1986 estimate of the millerbird population was 577. No attempts have been made to establish the millerbird on any of the other islands of the northwestern chain.

Conservation and Recovery

The Nihoa millerbird, like other island birds, is highly susceptible to outside disturbance of any kind. If an introduced predator, such as the rat, became established, it could devastate bird populations. Avian diseases, brought in from outside by migrating birds, could also pose a serious threat to the millerbird. These factors need to be monitored closely and immediate action taken to counteract their effects.

Because the population is small and highly concentrated, a severe hurricane or a tidal wave could decimate the millerbird on Nihoa. Therefore, a Fish and Wildlife Service (FWS) recovery team is examining the possibility of translocating the millerbird to other islands.

The island of Nihoa is a part of the Hawaiian Islands National Wildlife Refuge administered by the FWS. Landing on the island or entering surrounding waters is prohibited, except by special permit. Permits are typically granted only for research purposes.

Bibliography

Berger, A. J. 1981. *Hawaiian Birdlife*. University of Hawaii Press, Honolulu.

Scott, J. M., *et al.* 1988. "Conservation of Hawaii's Vanishing Avifauna." *Bioscience* 38(4):238-253.

U.S. Fish and Wildlife Service. 1984. "Recovery Plan for the Northwestern Hawaiian Islands Passerines." U.S. Fish and Wildlife Service, Portland.

Contact

Regional Office of Endangered Species
U.S. Fish and Wildlife Service
Lloyd 500 Building, Suite 1692
500 N.E. Multnomah Street
Portland, Oregon 97232

Office of Environmental Services
U.S. Fish and Wildlife Service
300 Ala Moana Boulevard
P.O. Box 50167
Honolulu, Hawaii 96850

Yellow-Shouldered Blackbird

Agelaius xanthomus

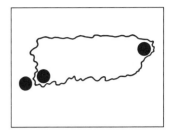

Bruce A. Sorrie

Status . . . . . . Endangered
Listed . . . . . . November 19, 1976
Family . . . . . . Icteridae (Blackbird)
Description . . . Blackbird; dark gray with yel-
low shoulder patch.
Habitat . . . . . Variety of wooded and wet-
land areas.
Food . . . . Insects, some plant material.
Reproduction . . Clutch of 2 or 3 eggs.
Threats . . . . . Habitat destruction, nest
parasitism.
Region 4 . . . . Puerto Rico

Description

The yellow-shouldered blackbird, similar to the better-known red-winged blackbird (*Agelaius phoenicus*) of North America, is about 18 to 23 centimeters (7 to 9 in) in length. Adults are predominately dark to neutral gray, with a yellow shoulder patch, usually edged with a narrow white margin.

There are two subspecies of the yellow-shouldered blackbird: *A. xanthomus xanthomus*, known only from Puerto Rico and Vieques islands, and *A. x. monensis*, which is restricted to Mona and Monito islands.

Behavior

Yellow-shouldered blackbirds are monogamous and pair six to ten weeks before breeding. Males establish and defend limited territories around nesting sites, which the females also defend after nests are constructed. Breeding begins in April or May and appears to be triggered by the onset of spring rains. Clutch sizes are two or three. Only the female incubates and broods, although both sexes bring food and clean the nest. Incubation lasts 12 to 13 days and the nestling period ranges from 13 to 16 days. This blackbird usually nests in colonies. It feeds primarily on insects but will eat some plant material such as cactus fruits.

Habitat

The yellow-shouldered blackbird is known to nest in eight different habitat types: mangrove pannes and salinas (coastal mangrove zone), offshore red mangrove cays, black mangrove forest, lowland pastures, suburbs (a university campus), coconut and royal palm plantations, cactus-scrub, and coastal cliffs. On Mona Island, it nests on pinnacles along the coast.

Historic Range

In the mid-1800s the yellow-shouldered blackbird was abundant in the San Juan area of Puerto Rico, and as late as the 1930s the bird was still common in lowland areas. After this time, there was no available information until 1972, when numbers were estimated at about 2,400 individuals in three principal population centers: coastal southwestern; coastal eastern Puerto Rico; and Mona Island.

Current Distribution

The largest population, numbering slightly more than 400, is centered in coastal southwestern Puerto Rico in an area from Ensenada to Punta Guaniquilla. A smaller population at Roosevelt Roads Naval Station, near Ceiba in eastern Puerto Rico was hit by Hurricane Hugo in 1989. It is not yet clear whether any survived. Other sites throughout the island probably total fewer than 100 individuals. The total current population is about 720 birds. The Mona Island race consists of about 220 individuals.

Conservation and Recovery

Since the turn of the century sugar cane cultivation and housing development have transformed extensive areas of Puerto Rico into unsuitable habitat for the blackbird. By 1968 only about 25 percent of the blackbird's original feeding and nesting habitat remained undisturbed.

The introduced rat (*Rattus rattus*) and the mongoose (*Herpestes auropunctatus*) are widespread in lowland areas, and as a result

blackbirds have been forced to nest on small islands, in cactus and palm fronds, or on steep cliffs, out of reach of the predators. The aggressive, cavity-nesting pearly-eyed thrasher (*Margarops fuscatus*) displaces the blackbird in some suitable habitat. Nest parasitism by shiny cowbirds is the most critical limiting factor for the blackbird. The shiny cowbird has become one of lowland Puerto Rico's most common birds and is now found spreading throughout the West Indies.

A zoning plan was established for the Roosevelt Roads Naval Station in 1980 to minimize the impact of base activities on the blackbird, and since 1977, 96 nest boxes have been placed in the Boqueron State Forest. The Cabo Rojo National Wildlife Refuge Youth Conservation Corps has been active in the recovery effort, building nest boxes and cowbird traps. These programs appear successful. The Mona Island race receives complete protection within the Department of Natural Resources' Mona Island Refuge.

Bibliography

Post, W. 1981. "Biology of the Yellow-Shouldered Blackbird (*Agelaius*) on a Tropical Island." *Bulletin of the Florida State Museum, Biological Sciences* 26(3):125-202.

U.S. Fish and Wildlife Service. 1983. "Yellow-Shouldered Blackbird Recovery Plan." U.S. Fish and Wildlife Service, Atlanta.

Contact

Regional Office of Endangered Species
U.S. Fish and Wildlife Service
Richard B. Russell Federal Building
75 Spring Street, S.W.
Atlanta, Georgia 30303

Caribbean Field Office
U.S. Fish and Wildlife Service
P.O. Box 491
Boqueron, Puerto Rico 00622

Puerto Rican Parrot
Amazona vittata

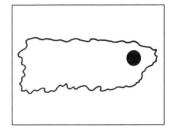

Luther C. Goldman/USFWS

Status . . . . . . Endangered
Listed . . . . . . March 11, 1967
Family . . . . . . Psittacidae (Parrot)
Description . . . Green parrot with red fore-
head and blue wings.
Habitat . . . . . Mature forests.
Food . . . . Fruits, seeds, and leaves.
Reproduction . . Clutch of 4 eggs.
Threats . . . . . Habitat destruction, collectors.
Region 4 . . . . Puerto Rico

Description

The brightly colored Puerto Rican parrot is about 30 centimeters (12 in) long. It is mostly green with a red forehead, blue wing feathers, and flesh-colored bill and feet. It is closely related to the Jamaican black-billed parrot (*Amazona agilis*) and the Hispanolian parrot (*A. ventralis*).

Behavior

Puerto Rican parrots, which reach sexual maturity at three to five years, form stable pair bonds. Mates stay together throughout the year, except when the female is nesting. The male then assumes full foraging duties. The Puerto Rican parrot is a deep forest bird that nests in tree cavities and tends to use the same tree year after year.

The female lays from two to four eggs, which she incubates for about 26 days. Young parrots hatch nearly naked and with closed eyes. After about a week, the female resumes foraging duties with her mate, browsing on fruits, seeds, and leaves for part of the day. Chicks fledge at about nine weeks of age.

Habitat

Present habitat of the parrot is sheltered deep within the largest remaining area of essentially unmodified forest on Puerto Rico. The parrot is critically dependent on mature, large-diameter trees to provide cavity nesting sites that have been in continuous use for decades.

The tabonuco tree (*Dacryodes excelsa*), used both as a nesting site and as a food source, grows mainly at elevations under 600 meters (2,000 ft). Laurel sabino (*Magnolia splendens*) and nuez moscada (*Ocotea moschata*) grow in the upper forests now used by the parrots. The primary nesting tree in recent decades has been the palo colorado (*Cyrilla racemiflora*).

The current parrot habitat on Puerto Rico is not the preferred one. When lowland habitat was destroyed, parrots retreated to the upper forest area. Although parrots previously migrated seasonally to lowland forests, they now seldom leave the western edge of the forest to forage in the lowlands and are restricted to the sierra palm and palo colorado zones in the Caribbean National Forest.

Historic Range

This parrot was once abundant on the island of Puerto Rico and was also found on the islands of Culebra, Vieques, and Mona. Historic population figures are highly speculative, but may have exceeded a million birds. The population probably remained reasonably stable until the 16th century when European settlement began.

Current Distribution

By the early 20th century the species had disappeared from all of the offshore islands and was restricted to five known areas on the mainland of Puerto Rico. By about 1940 the only remaining population was in the Luquillo Mountains, including the Caribbean National Forest of eastern Puerto Rico, the largest area of remaining native vegetation. In 1989 fewer than 100 parrots survived— about 43 in the wild and 52 in captivity.

Conservation and Recovery

The destruction of the island's native forests has been the major factor in the historic decline of the Puerto Rican parrot. By 1912 the island was more than 80 percent deforested; and by 1922 only about 8,097 hectares (20,000 acres) of the Luquillo Mountains remained forested.

In recent decades the forests have revived. Currently, more than 40 percent of the island is wooded, and woodland acreage has doubled in the Luquillo Mountains. But it will take many more decades for trees to mature to the point that they provide natural cavities for parrot nests.

The Puerto Rican parrot suffers from both high rates of mortality and low reproduction. Current habitat in the Luquillo Mountains has a much wetter climate than the parrot's historic range. Protection from rain is a major factor in choosing nest cavities. In addition, hurricanes can cause severe parrot decline, not only through physical battering, but also by destruction of nesting trees and damage to food supplies.

In late 1989, Hurricane Hugo battered the eastern end of Puerto Rico. Surveys taken following the storm indicated that only about half of the island's wild parrots survived. Daily counts varied from a low of seven to a high of 23, indicating that the birds were moving around a great deal, probably in search of food.

Nest robbing by humans to obtain cage birds has been another major cause for parrot decline in this century. There is evidence that some nest cavities were cut open and nest trees were cut down to obtain nestling parrots. Parrots have also been shot as a crop pest and hunted as a game bird.

The long-term, continual habitat decline is due to many interacting causes. Since recreational areas have been constructed in the Caribbean National Forest, there has been a dramatic increase in visitors to the area. Selective logging of mature trees has changed the character of significant areas of the forest.

The Puerto Rican parrot probably owes its continued survival to the fact that most of its remaining habitat is owned by the U.S. Forest Service. The Caribbean National Forest, comprising 11,269 hectares (27,846 acres) in the Luquillo Mountains, was declared a wildlife refuge in 1946. Four known breeding pairs in the wild produced a total of 21 eggs in 1987. Of these, 11 hatched. Three chicks were removed for the captive breeding program. In 1989, nine chicks were hatched, but only five fledged.

The Puerto Rico Field Station's Luquillo Aviary has collected a captive population of over 52 birds, including six captive-bred chicks produced in 1989. In addition, biologists have "double clutched" two of the wild nests to increase egg production. This procedure involves removing the first clutch of eggs from a nest and transferring them to an incubator. The nesting female then lays a second clutch which she incubates. In 1987 this technique was used on two of the four active nests. The captive parrot flock will provide the birds to establish a second wild population in the Rio Abajo forest on the western end of the island.

Bibliography

U.S. Fish and Wildlife Service. 1987. "Recovery Plan for the Puerto Rican Parrot, *Amazona vittata*." U.S. Fish and Wildlife Service, Atlanta.

Wiley, J. W. 1980. "The Puerto Rican Amazon (*Amazona vittata*); Its Decline and the Program for Its Conservation," In R. F. Pasquier, ed., *Conservation of New World Parrots*. International Council for Bird Preservation.

Contact

Regional Office of Endangered Species
U.S. Fish and Wildlife Service
Richard B. Russell Federal Building
75 Spring Street, S.W.
Atlanta, Georgia 30303

Caribbean Field Office
U.S. Fish and Wildlife Service
P.O. Box 491
Boqueron, Puerto Rico 00622

Cape Sable Seaside Sparrow
Ammodramus maritimus mirabilis

USFWS

Status	Endangered
Listed	March 11, 1967
Family	Fringillidae
	(Finches and Sparrows)
Description . . .	Short-tailed sparrow; greenish gray and white; streaked breast; yellow between eyes and beak.
Habitat	Salt marsh.
Food	Insects, seeds.
Reproduction .	Clutch of 3 or 4 eggs.
Threats	Habitat alteration.
Region 4	Florida

Description

The Cape Sable seaside sparrow, similar to other subspecies of seaside sparrows, is a small, short-tailed bird, mostly greenish gray above, with a white breast that is lightly streaked with brown. It has a yellow lore patch (the area between the beak and eye). The Cape Sable seaside sparrow was discovered by A. W. Howell in 1918. Before being relegated to subspecific status, it was well known as the most recently discovered bird species in the continental United States.

This sparrow has also been classified as *Ammospiza maritimus mirabilis* in the scientific literature.

Behavior

The Cape Sable seaside sparrow is nonmigratory. Males remain on or near their breeding territories year round and defend areas used for breeding, nesting, and feeding. The defended territory is a nest-centered area smaller than the breeding-season home range.

Females lay a clutch of three or four eggs, which are incubated 12 or 13 days. The newly hatched young spend about 11 days in the nest, then are active on the ground but unable to fly. They are tended by their parents for up to 20 additional days, after which they are capable of flight.

Habitat

Nesting habitat for the Cape Sable seaside sparrow is marsh with moderately dense, clumped grasses and enough open space among the stems to permit movement. Such habitat is subject to occasional flooding, which can be a major cause of nest loss.

Historic Range

Seaside sparrows are widespread along the salt marshes of the Atlantic and Gulf coasts of North America from Massachusetts to Texas. The Cape Sable subspecies occurs only in extreme southern Florida and is isolated from breeding populations of other seaside sparrows. Populations have been documented in four broadly defined locations: Cape Sable, southern Big Cypress Swamp, Ochopee, and Taylor Slough.

Current Distribution

The Cape Sable seaside sparrow remains widely distributed over a large area of extreme southern Florida and continues to occupy much of its historic range. A 1981 census found sparrows at 278 of 864 sites surveyed. At present, sparrows appear to be rare or absent from the Cape Sable and Ochopee areas. The greatest number—a minimum of 6,600 birds—were found in the Big Cypress Swamp and Taylor Slough in the East Everglades.

In the Big Cypress Swamp, sparrows are now found in the area north and west of Shark Slough, between the coastal cordgrass marsh and the saw grass marshes of the Everglades. Unlike the Ochopee area, the frequency and extent of recent fires here did not greatly affect the sparrow habitat. Recent surveys indicate that sparrows are well dispersed over an area from south of the Loop Road into the headwater marshes of coastal rivers.

Taylor Slough and nearby areas support a substantial population of sparrows, estimated at 3,700 birds by a 1981 census.

Conservation and Recovery

Unlike most other seaside sparrows, the Cape Sable subspecies is adapted to a habitat that undergoes periodic fires. The timing of the burns is important, however. Those occurring late in the dry season, during and immediately after nesting, threaten eggs and newly fledged young. If burned too frequently, an area may never support a vigorous population of nesting sparrows.

The most immediate threat to the Cape Sable seaside sparrow is posed by alteration of the East Everglades, the only part of its range not under Park Service management. There, residential development, lowered water levels, and changes in vegetation may make the area unsuitable for nesting habitat.

According to the Fish and Wildlife Service Recovery Plan, management options for the sparrow's essential habitat include purchase and management of habitat by state or federal agencies, or zoning changes, instituted by counties, to prohibit development. Historic water levels should also be maintained.

Bibliography

Quay, T. L., and E. Potter, eds. 1983. *The Seaside Sparrow: Its Biology and Management.* Occasional Papers of the North Carolina Biological Survey, North Carolina State Museum.

U.S. Fish and Wildlife Service. 1983. "Cape Sable Seaside Sparrow Recovery Plan." U.S. Fish and Wildlife Service, Atlanta.

Werner, H. W. 1975. "The Biology of the Cape Sable Sparrow." Report. U.S. Fish and Wildlife Service. Everglades National Park, Homestead, Florida.

Contact

Regional Office of Endangered Species
U.S. Fish and Wildlife Service
Richard B. Russell Federal Building
75 Spring Street, S.W.
Atlanta, Georgia 30303

Florida Grasshopper Sparrow
Ammodramus savannarum floridanus

Michael F. Delaney

Status	Endangered
Listed	July 31, 1986
Family	Fringillidae
	(Finches and Sparrows)
Description . . .	Short-tailed sparrow, mostly gray and black, streaked with brown.
Habitat	Poorly drained, frequently burned-over scrub land.
Food	Insects, seeds, berries.
Reproduction .	Clutch of 3 to 5 eggs.
Threats	Agricultural development.
Region 4	Florida

Description

The Florida grasshopper sparrow is a short-tailed bird, about 13 centimeters (5 in) long. Darker in color than related subspecies, it is mostly black and gray, streaked with brown on the nape and upper back. Adults have whitish, unstreaked front parts with some buff on the throat and breast. In juveniles the breast is streaked. The stripe over the eye tends to be ochre, and the bend of the wing is yellow; the feet are flesh colored. There are no marked sexual differences.

The Florida grasshopper sparrow gets its common name from its weak song, which resembles the buzz made by grasshoppers.

Behavior

Like other grasshopper sparrows this species probably produces a clutch of three to five eggs. The incubation period is about 12 days; young fledge in nine days. The grasshopper sparrow forages on the ground for insects, seeds, and berries. It is nonmigratory.

Habitat

The Florida grasshopper sparrow inhabits stunted, scrubby growths of saw palmetto, dwarf oaks, bluestems, and wiregrass, which are maintained by periodic fires. Areas of low, sparse growth, rather than sod-forming grasses, are needed for nesting. Common shrubs of the habitat include pawpaw, dwarf oak, gopher apple, and St. John's wort. Common grasses and herbs include pineland threeawn, bluestems, flat-topped goldenrod, beak rushes, pipewort, and yellow-eyed grass.

Historic Range

Grasshopper sparrows are found throughout much of temperate North America. The Florida subspecies, though, is limited in range and is geographically isolated from other subspecies. It is adapted to scrub habitat in Florida's south-central prairie region.

Current Distribution

Surveys conducted between 1980 and 1984 estimated an adult population of less than 250 birds at nine widely scattered Florida sites—in southern Osceola, southern Polk, northern Highlands, western Okeechobee, and western Glades counties. Populations occur at the Three Lakes and Fisheating Creek wildlife management areas (Osceola and Glades counties), at the Avon Park Bombing Range managed by the Air Force (Highlands County), and at other sites on private land.

Conservation and Recovery

The prairie region of south-central Florida has increasingly been converted to pasture to the detriment of the grasshopper sparrow. This sparrow will nest in improved pastures where some native vegetation remains. But when pastureland is stripped of shrubs and saw palmetto, the bird is driven out.

Much of the land within the range of the Florida grasshopper sparrow is contained in a few large, private ranches, and many landowners are unaware of the sparrow's existence. Recovery of the bird could be helped if ranchers adapted their pasture management practices to the sparrow's nesting cycle. For example, the sparrows currently occupy several pastures that are managed by periodic winter burns. By avoiding the nesting season, winter burns do not adversely affect sparrow populations. Rather, they improve the habitat by maintaining the prairie scrub community at an early successional stage.

The Air Force's Avon Park Bombing Range is one of the more valuable pieces of real estate in Florida in terms of wildlife management. The Range contains over 100,000 acres with an estimated 5,000 acres of increasingly rare scrub habitat, rich in native wildlife. The land not only shelters the grasshopper sparrow, but other Endangered and Threatened species as well. The Air Force has already begun consultations with the Fish and Wildlife Service to determine a productive management plan for scrubland under its authority.

Bibliography

Delany, M. F., and J. A. Cox. 1985. "Florida Grasshopper Sparrow Status Survey." Report, U.S. Fish and Wildlife Service, Jacksonville, Florida.

Kale, H. W., II. 1978. *Rare and Endangered Biota of Florida*; Vol. 2, *Birds*. University Presses of Florida, Gainesville.

Contact

Regional Office of Endangered Species
U.S. Fish and Wildlife Service
Richard B. Russell Federal Building
75 Spring Street, S.W.
Atlanta, Georgia 30303

San Clemente Island Sage Sparrow

Amphispiza belli clementeae

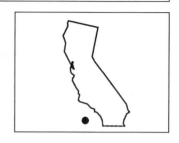

U.S. Navy

Status	Threatened
Listed	August 11, 1977
Family	Fringillidae (Finches and Sparrows)
Description	Large-bodied sparrow, gray and black.
Habitat	Scrub vegetation.
Food	Seeds, small invertebrates.
Reproduction	Clutch of 3 eggs.
Threats	Reduced food supply.
Region 1	California

Description

The San Clemente Island sage sparrow is gray with black streaks on its sides and a single black spot on its chest; it has dark cheeks, dark streaks on the sides of its throat, and a white line over the eyes. Length averages 17 centimeters (7 in). In 1898, R. Ridgway separated the San Clemente from the mainland races because of its larger body size and bill.

Behavior

The non-migratory San Clemente Island sage sparrow is essentially a ground dweller. It uses the shrub canopy for feeding, protection, roosting, song perches, and nesting.

Nests are usually constructed fairly close to the ground in dense foliage.

Breeding habits are similar to its mainland relatives. The sage sparrow nests from mid-March through mid-June. Although clutch size averages four eggs in the mainland races, the island subspecies produces only three eggs. Eggs are incubated for 13 to 14 days; juveniles molt in late summer.

The diet of mainland birds consists of a variety of seeds and other plant material as well as invertebrates, and the island species is thought to have similar feeding habits.

Habitat

The San Clemente Island sage sparrow is restricted to moderately dense, dry scrub areas along the west coast of the island. This plant community occurs only at lower elevations on the island, and consequently the sparrow rarely strays further than 30 to 40 meters (100 to 130 ft) above sea level. This habitat, a type of maritime desert scrub, supports a mixture of low-growing, dry-season deciduous shrubs, predominantly box thorn, ragwort, and cactus.

Historic Range

The San Clemente Island sage sparrow is restricted to San Clemente Island, California, where early 20th-century ornithologists viewed it as a conspicuous element of the island's fauna.

Current Distribution

A 1976 survey projected the San Clemente Island population to be 112 birds, and the adult-to-juvenile ratio suggested a stable or slightly expanding population. A more recent study (1986) indicated a somewhat larger and stabilized population of 176 to 213 pre-breeding and 264 to 296 post-breeding birds.

Conservation and Recovery

Possible reasons for the overall decline of this sparrow are: a reduced food supply; habitat destruction by feral pigs and goats; and competition with other birds, such as the white-crowned sparrow, house finch, or horned lark, which all partially overlap the sage sparrow's range. The sage sparrow appears unable to effectively use marginal habitat. Predation may also be a significant factor, although no direct evidence has been reported. Some possible predators are feral cats, island fox, kestrels, northern harriers, and barn owls.

The island is administered by the Navy, which has developed a management plan to preserve the native wildlife. A program to remove introduced feral cats, goats, and pigs from the island is already underway and will help to reestablish this species. Revegetation of bird habitat will require planting of maritime sage scrub associates on hills and knolls where wind dispersal of seeds is likely.

Bibliography

Grinnel, J., and A. H. Miller. 1944. "Distribution of the Birds of California." *Pacific Coast Avifauna* 27.

Johnson, N. K. 1972. "Origin and Differentiation of the Avifauna of the Channel Islands, California." *Condor* 74:295-315.

U.S. Fish and Wildlife Service. 1984. "Recovery Plan for the Endangered and Threatened Species of the California Channel Islands." U.S. Fish and Wildlife Service, Portland.

Contact

Regional Office of Endangered Species
U.S. Fish and Wildlife Service
Lloyd 500 Building. Suite 1692
500 N.E. Multnomah Street
Portland, Oregon 97232

Natural Resources Office
Staff Civil Engineer (18N)
NAS North Island (Building 3)
San Diego, California 92135-5018

Laysan Duck
Anas laysanensis

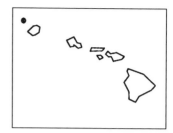

D. B. Marshall

Status . . . . . . Endangered
Listed . . . . . . March 11, 1967
Family . . . . . Anatidae (Ducks and Geese)
Description . . . Dark, reddish brown duck, irregular white patch around the eye.
Habitat . . . . . . Dense vegetation near water.
Food . . . . . . Insects, crustaceans.
Reproduction . Clutch of 3 or more eggs.
Threats . . . . . Low numbers, limited range.
Region 1 . . . . Hawaii

Description

The Laysan duck, which has also been known as the Laysan teal, is a dark, reddish brown duck, 41 centimeters (16 in) long, resembling a female mallard. Its dark plumage is accented by bright purple-green patches bordered with white on the forewing. First-year birds have white eye-rings; older birds develop a more extensive irregular patch of white that extends toward the back of the head. Feet and legs are bright orange in males, duller in females. Bill color is the easiest way to distinguish the sexes. Males have a blue-green bill with black spots along the top of the upper beak; females have a dull, brownish yellow bill with black spots along the lateral borders of the upper mandible.

Behavior

The Laysan duck is primarily insectivorous, feeding on brine flies, cutworm larvae, miller moths, and small crustaceans. Birds nest from February through August, although most eggs are laid between May and late July. Clutch size is three or more eggs.

Habitat

Laysan ducks are usually found in the lagoons, tidal pools, and marshes of the island. During hot, clear weather, the birds seek cover by mid-morning in dense stands of *Pluchera*, *Ipomoea*, and *Sicyos*, remaining there until the temperature cools in the early evening.

Historic Range

The species was first reported in 1828 on both Laysan and Lisianski Islands. Since then it has been seen only on Laysan Island and has always been rare.

Current Distribution

The Laysan duck is found on the 423-hectare (1,020-acre) Laysan Island, the largest of the northwestern Hawaiian Islands, situated 1,135 kilometers (710 mi) northwest of Kauai and about 560 kilometers (350 mi) southeast of Midway Island. The island is part of the Hawaiian Islands National Wildlife Refuge and is under the jurisdiction of the Fish and Wildlife Service.

The Laysan duck came close to extinction in the early part of this century. Between 1910 and 1920 the population hit a low of about 20 birds. As of 1989, the population is holding stable at about 500. Several hundred Laysan ducks are held in breeding facilities throughout the world.

Conservation and Recovery

In 1890 rabbits were introduced to the island and rapidly destroyed the island's vegetation. Loss of ground cover laid bare the topsoil, which was subsequently eroded by wind and rain. This ecological disaster resulted in extirpation of the Laysan millerbird, the Laysan rail, and the Laysan honeycreeper. The Laysan duck and the Laysan finch (Endangered) barely survived. When the rabbits were eliminated in 1923, plant life on the island began to recover. Present conditions are thought to approximate those prior to the introduction of rabbits.

During the late 1950s a captive propagation program was developed as a backup against natural or human-caused disasters. Ducks were taken from Laysan Island and sent to the Honolulu Zoo for acclimatization before being shipped to various zoos and game bird breeders around the world. Breeding stock was sent to the New York Zoological Park, the San Diego Zoo, the Wildfowl Trust in England, the San Antonio Zoological Gardens, and Tracey Aviary. Many zoos and breeding farms now raise Laysan ducks in captivity, and a bird exchange program is encouraged to prevent close inbreeding.

Because of its limited distribution on Laysan Island, the Laysan duck will always be considered a vulnerable species. Laysan Island is managed as part of the Hawaiian Islands National Wildlife Refuge and has been designated as a Research Natural Area under the International Biological Program. The island is being considered for inclusion in the National Wilderness Preservation System. Presently, only scientists are permitted access to the island.

Bibliography

Berger, A. J. 1981. *Hawaiian Birdlife*. University of Hawaii Press, Honolulu.

Moulton, D. W., and M. W. Weller. 1984. "Biology and Conservation of the Laysan Duck (*Anas laysanensis*)." *Condor* 86:105-117.

U.S. Fish and Wildlife Service. 1982. "Laysan Duck Recovery Plan." U.S. Fish and Wildlife Service, Portland.

Contact

Regional Office of Endangered Species
U.S. Fish and Wildlife Service
Lloyd 500 Building, Suite 1692
500 N.E. Multnomah Street
Portland, Oregon 97232

Office of Environmental Services
U.S. Fish and Wildlife Service
300 Ala Moana Boulevard
P.O. Box 50167
Honolulu, Hawaii 96850

Hawaiian Duck
Anas wyvilliana

Robert J. Shallenberger

Status	Endangered
Listed	March 11, 1967
Family	Anatidae (Ducks and Geese)
Description	Waterbird with dark brown plumage.
Habitat	Wetlands, mountain streams.
Food	Snails, insects, plant matter.
Reproduction	Clutch of 2 to 10 eggs.
Threats	Habitat loss, hunting.
Region 1	Hawaii

Description

Also known by the Hawaiian name "koloa," the Hawaiian duck is a dark brown mallard, probably evolved from stray migratory ducks that remained in Hawaii as year-round residents. In general, mallards range from 52 to 71 centimeters (20 to 28 in) in body length, although the Hawaiian duck is noticeably smaller than its mainland counterpart. Unlike the mallard, both sexes of the Hawaiian duck are similar, resembling a dark female mallard. The larger male typically has a darker head and neck, and an olive-colored bill; females have orange bills.

The Hawaiian duck is closely related to the Laysan duck (*Anas laysanensis*) and the Mariana mallard (*A. oustaleti*). The species was first described in 1852 and, since then, has been variously classified as a subspecies of either the mallard or the New Zealand gray duck. The American Ornithologists Union now lists it as a full species.

Behavior

The Hawaiian duck is typically found alone or in pairs, although larger numbers of birds occasionally congregate around a rich food source. It is very wary of outside disturbance, particularly when nesting or molting. It feeds on snails, dragonfly larvae, earthworms, grass seeds, and other plant matter. While a strong flyer, it does not range far from its narrowly defined home territory and rarely moves between islands.

Nests are built on the ground near water at any time of the year; peak breeding season is from December to May. The female lays a clutch of two to ten eggs, which she incubates for about 30 days. Most chicks hatch during April, May, and June.

Habitat

The Hawaiian duck adapts to a wide range of wetland habitats, including freshwater marshlands, flooded grasslands, coastal ponds, streams, mountain pools, mountain bogs, and forest swamps from sea level up to an elevation of 2,500 meters (8,000 ft).

Historic Range

The Hawaiian duck was known from all the main Hawaiian islands except Lanai and Kahoolawe. Although there are no estimates of the original population, it is likely that this bird was once fairly common.

Indiscriminate hunting in the late 1800s and early 1900s took a heavy toll on the Hawaiian duck, whose numbers fell drastically until mid-century. In 1949, only about 500 birds remained on Kauai, an unknown number on Niihau, and about 30 on Oahu. It was then considered only an occasional visitor to the island of Hawaii and had been eliminated from Maui and Molokai. It was apparently extirpated on Oahu in 1960 when Kaelepulu pond, the last nesting site on the island, was modified as part of a housing development. By the 1960s the Hawaiian duck was found only on Kauai.

Current Distribution

The Hawaiian duck has been reintroduced to the coast of the island of Hawaii from Hawi south to Paauilo. A natural population on Kauai has remained stable. Estimates from the mid-1960s indicated approximately 2,000 to 3,000 birds, mostly in remote, mountainous stream areas. A population of about 50 birds has been established on Oahu in typical waterfowl wetland habitat. Recently over 300 birds were released on Oahu at Kawainui Marsh, Naupia Ponds, Waimea Falls Park, and Hommaluhia Park.

Conservation and Recovery

Many factors have contributed to the Hawaiian duck's decline, but the loss of wetland habitat is the primary cause. Wetlands —natural sites such as coastal plain wetlands and artificial sites such as pond-like taro fields—once provided an abundance of habitat for island waterbirds. In 1850 dry sugarcane cultivation began to replace taro fields, reducing the wetland acreage. Today only about 500 acres remain in taro or other wetland crops throughout the islands.

Recently, residential development has encroached into these areas and continues slowly but steadily to eliminate wetlands. Today, much of the wetlands of the islands has been drained, filled, and developed.

To further complicate the matter, introduced plants have made strong inroads in the remaining wetlands, forcing out native plants. Species such as California grass, water hyacinth, and mangrove out-compete native species and eliminate open water, exposed mudflats, or shallows.

On Kauai, where most Hawaiian ducks are found, few lowland marsh habitats remain. On Oahu populations are found at James Campbell National Wildlife Refuge, Punahoolapa Marsh, and the prawn ponds adjacent to the wildlife refuge, but predators in these areas are a major limiting factor. Good habitat is useless if mongooses or feral cats are present.

Hunting of waterfowl was stopped on Kauai in 1925. Active conservation began in

1952 when Kanaha Pond on Maui was designated as the first state waterfowl sanctuary.

Research on endemic waterbirds began in 1962 with a study of the Hawaiian duck on Kauai, supported by the World Wildlife Fund. In 1972, the first national wildlife refuge for waterbirds was acquired in Hanalei Valley, on Kauai. Since that time, four additional wetland refuges have been established: Huleia, along the Huleia River on Kauai; Kakahaia on Molokai; Pearl Harbor on Oahu; and the James Campbell National Wildlife Refuge on Oahu.

Although the Kauai population of Hawaiian duck, which exceeds 2,000 birds, is self-sustaining, Fish and Wildlife Service goals for delisting the species call for self-sustaining populations of 500 birds on Oahu and the island of Hawaii.

Bibliography

Berger, A. J. 1981. *Hawaiian Birdlife*. University of Hawaii Press, Honolulu.

Paton, P. W. C. 1981. "The Koloa (Hawaiian Duck) on the Island of Hawaii." *Elepaio* 41(12):131-133.

U.S. Fish and Wildlife Service. 1985. "Recovery Plan for the Hawaiian Waterbirds." U.S. Fish and Wildlife Service, Portland.

Contact

Regional Office of Endangered Species
U.S. Fish and Wildlife Service
Lloyd 500 Building, Suite 1692
500 N.E. Multnomah Street
Portland, Oregon 97232

Field Office of Endangered Species
U.S. Fish and Wildlife Service
300 Ala Moana Boulevard
P.O. Box 50167
Honolulu, Hawaii 96850

Florida Scrub Jay

Aphelocoma coerulescens coerulescens

Lee Kuhn

Status	Threatened
Listed	June 3, 1987
Family	Corvidae (Crows and Jays)
Description	Crestless jay with blue wings and tail, a blue-gray back, and gray breast.
Habitat	Thickets of scrub oaks.
Food	Omnivorous; lizards, acorns.
Reproduction	Clutch of 3 to 6 eggs.
Threats	Beachfront development.
Region 4	Florida

Description

The Florida scrub jay is an isolated subspecies of the more common scrub jay (*Aphelocoma coerulescens*). This crestless blue bird, about 30 centimeters (12 in) long, has blue wings and tail. A necklace of blue feathers separates its gray throat and gray underparts. A white line over the eye often blends into a whitish forehead. The long tail is loose in appearance.

Behavior

The scrub jay has a life span of ten years or more, mates for life, and has sedentary habits. It rarely breeds when it first reaches maturity; instead, a young bird remains with its parents as a "helper" for several years. (Males may remain as long as six years). As the family group enlarges, the territory grows. A male helper may then claim part of the enlarged area for his own breeding territory. The female deposits a clutch of three to six small, spotted eggs. The incubation period is 15 to 17 days; young fledge in about 20 days.

The scrub jay is omnivorous, eating almost anything it can catch. Diet mainstays are lizards and arthropods in spring and summer, and acorns in fall and winter. It has been observed to perch on deer to remove ticks.

Habitat

Scrub jays prefer dense thickets of scrub oaks less than 3 meters (10 ft) in height, interspersed with bare sand for foraging and burying acorns. Scrub jays rarely reside in habitat with more than 50 percent canopy cover that is taller than 3 meters.

The Florida scrub jay lives only in the Florida scrub habitat, which grows over fine, white, well-drained sands. This type of sand occurs along the present coastline of Florida, and on island dunes deposited when sea levels were higher. The most commonly occupied habitat is oak scrub, consisting of a single layer of evergreen shrubs, usually dominated by three species of oak—myrtle oak, sand live oak, and Chapman oak.

Historic Range

Scrub jays have been reported in the past throughout the Florida peninsula, from Gainesville south.

Today, the scrub jay has been completely eliminated from Broward, Dade, Duval, Pinellas, and St. Johns counties, and numbers have been drastically reduced elsewhere throughout its historic range. The total population has probably decreased by at least half over the last century.

Current Distribution

The scrub jay is widely distributed in the western United States, but the Florida subspecies is restricted to scrub areas of peninsular Florida. The most important dune systems within its range occur along the Atlantic coastal ridge (Volusia and Brevard counties), on Lake Wales Ridge (Polk and Highlands counties), and in Ocala National Forest (Marion, Putnam, and Lake counties).

Total Florida scrub jay population was estimated in 1984 at between 15,000 and 22,000 birds, most of which are on public lands.

Conservation and Recovery

The major cause of the jay's population decline is habitat destruction. Many tracts of habitat, particularly along the coast, have been cleared for beachfront hotels, houses, and commercial developments. Interior scrub along the Lake Wales Ridge has been cleared for citrus groves or housing. Altogether, the acreage of scrub jay habitat has decreased by at least 40 percent. Development trends in Florida will continue to diminish scrub jay habitat for many years to come. At the present rate of development, it has been predicted that by the early 1990s only a few Florida scrub jays will remain.

Fortunately, the largest population of scrub jays occurs within the Merritt Island National Wildlife Refuge and the Kennedy Space Center. The refuge has begun a program of controlled burning of all scrub on its land, which should maintain suitable habitat. Scrub jay habitat on other public lands in Florida will need to be managed to maintain the low-growing scrub oak and bare sand that the jays need for survival.

Bibliography

Cox, J. A. 1984. "Conservation and Ecology of the Florida Scrub Jay." Dissertation. University of Florida, Gainesville.

Kale, H. W., II. 1978. *Rare and Endangered Biota of Florida*; Vol. 2, *Birds*. University Presses of Florida, Gainesville.

Woolfenden, G. E., and J. W. Fitzpatrick. 1984. "The Florida Scrub Jay." In *Monographs in Population Biology No. 30*. Princeton University Press, Princeton.

Contact

Regional Office of Endangered Species
U.S. Fish and Wildlife Service
Richard B. Russell Federal Building
75 Spring Street, S.W.
Atlanta, Georgia 30303

Aleutian Canada Goose
Branta canadensis leucopareia

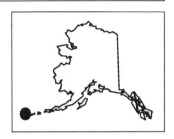

Roy Lowe/USFWS

Status	Endangered
Listed	March 11, 1967
Family	Anatidae (Geese and Ducks)
Description	Small goose; brownish gray above with black head and neck.
Habitat	Wetlands.
Food	Marsh vegetation, grain, insects.
Reproduction	Clutch of 6 eggs.
Threats	Predation.
Region 1	California, Oregon (wintering range)
Region 7	Alaska (breeding)

Description

The Aleutian Canada goose is a smaller subspecies of the common Canada goose. Length is between 56 and 109 centimeters (22 and 43 in). Plumage is brownish gray above. The head and neck are black, with a white "chin strap." Breast is paler brown and undertail feathers are white. Nearly all Aleutian geese have a white ring at the base of the neck.

The Aleutian race is characterized by an abrupt forehead, cheek patches separated by black feathers, and a narrow, dark border beneath the white neck ring. It is difficult to differentiate the Aleutian Canada goose from similar subspecies, such as the cackling Canada goose (*Branta camademsis minima*). A cackler generally has darker edgings on its breast feathers, giving it a slightly darker appearance than an Aleutian.

Behavior

Because breeding areas in the Aleutian Islands are remote, the Aleutian Canada goose has not been extensively studied. In most respects it is similar to other subspecies of Canada geese. The Aleutian is gregarious in non-breeding season, often gathering in flocks of several hundred. It is thought to mate for life, with ganders defending mates from other males. The nesting season varies according to latitude and weather. The female lays a clutch of about six eggs and incubates them for 28 days. As soon as chicks hatch, the mother leads them to water. The family group swims together with the gander leading and the mother bringing up the rear.

The Aleutian feeds on marsh vegetation, eel grass, and algae. During migration, it has been known to glean harvested grain fields. During the breeding season, it feeds on water plants, insects, and crustaceans.

Habitat

On the islands where they breed, Aleutian Canada geese prefer inland areas, such as meadows and marshes, but will also nest near inlets and bushy areas near the sea. When migrating, they frequent marshes, meadows, and grain fields where they feed on corn and other grains left behind by mechanical harvesting techniques.

Historic Range

Aleutian Canada geese once bred from the eastern Aleutian Islands to the Kuril Islands and were most abundant in the western Aleutians. The original breeding range included most of the larger Aleutian Islands from the Islands of Four Mountains to Attu Island and Bering Island. Aleutian Canada geese historically wintered in Japan and in North America, from British Columbia to California.

Current Distribution

The main breeding population of Aleutian Canada geese, estimated at about 300 breeding pairs in 1982, is on Buldir Island in the western Aleutian chain. A remnant breeding population of unknown size was discovered in June 1982 on Chagulak Island in the Islands of Four Mountains. Aleutians now winter mostly in California. The largest recorded number, about 2,700 birds, was

seen in California in 1981 and was more than triple the 1975 population count.

Breeding populations of Aleutian Canada geese have been ·reestablished on Agattu, Nizki, and Amchitka Islands.

Conservation and Recovery

The major cause of Aleutian goose decline was the introduction of Arctic foxes (*Alopex lagopus*) into the breeding range by the Russian-American Company during the 1830s. Buldir Island—the main breeding island today—is one of the few Aleutian islands without a fox population. The geese have also been hunted by humans while nesting, during migration in Alaska, and on their wintering grounds. Some Aleutian geese were domesticated by the island natives.

In 1965, the Aleutian Islands National Wildlife Refuge staff completed a program to eliminate foxes from Amchitka Island. Since then, foxes have been eliminated on Agattu, and trapping programs were initiated on the islands of Alaid, Nizki, and Kanaga.

Various attempts to breed Aleutian Canada geese for reintroduction to the wild produced mixed results. In 1971 the first release of captive-bred geese on Amchitka failed to establish a breeding population. In 1974, 41 captive-bred geese were moved to the western Aleutians and released on Agattu Island. Four pairs nested, two successfully, and five goslings hatched. Two of these tagged geese were recaptured in California later the same year.

In 1980, in an attempt to improve reproductive success, wild adult males captured on Buldir were paired with adult captive-reared females. The pairs were allowed to produce and raise their own young at propagation facilities on Amchitka Island. Natural young were supplemented with foster young, and during the winter of 1980-1981, 18 migrated south to Oregon and California. Using another reintroduction strategy, naturalists captured 60 wild geese on Buldir and released them on Agattu to establish a breeding population there.

In 1982, because of rising costs and the mixed success of captive-breeding, all captive Aleutian geese were released on Agattu, and the captive-breeding program was phased out. Only wild birds are now used in transplantation efforts.

An encouraging year for the recovery effort was 1987. It was confirmed that relocated birds were indeed returning to Agattu to breed, a major milestone. For the first time in decades, Aleutian geese were found nesting on Nizki Island, site of a 1981 release of captive-reared birds. Field biologists have relocated 60 adults and 76 goslings from the island of Buldir to Amchitka Island, hoping to establish yet another breeding population there.

Bibliography

Bent, A. C. 1912. "Notes on Birds Observed During a Brief Visit to the Aleutian Islands and Bering Sea in 1911." *Smithsonian Miscellaneous Collection* 56(32):1-29.

Jones, R. D. 1963. "Buldir Island, Site of a Remnant Breeding Population of Aleutian Canada Geese." *Wildfowl Trust Annual* 14:80-84.

Temple, S. A., ed. 1978. *Endangered Birds: Management Techniques for Preserving Threatened Species.* University of Wisconsin Press, Madison.

U.S. Fish and Wildlife Service. 1982. "The Aleutian Canada Goose Recovery Plan."U.S. Fish and Wildlife Service, Anchorage.

Contact

Regional Office of Endangered Species
U.S. Fish and Wildlife Service
1011 E. Tudor Road
Anchorage, Alaska 99503

Hawaiian Hawk
Buteo solitarius

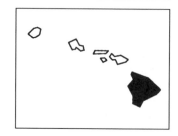

Robert J. Shallenberger

Status	Endangered
Listed	March 11, 1967
Family	Accipitriidae
	(Hawks and Eagles)
Description . . .	Bird of prey; dark phase, entirely dark brown; light phase, dark brown with white underparts.
Reproduction	Clutch of 1 egg.
Habitat	Lowland forests.
Food	Birds, small mammals.
Threats	Nest disturbance, habitat loss.
Region 1	Hawaii

Description

The Hawaiian hawk, whose Hawaiian common name is the "io," is a broad-winged hawk with light and dark color phases occurring in about equal numbers. Average body length is 46 centimeters (18 in) for females and 39 centimeters (16 in) for males. Dark phase adults are dark brown all over, appearing black in the field. Immatures have a tawny mottling on back and breast. Light phase adults have a dark brown head and a brown mottled back; the chest and belly are white with brown flecking on the margin. Light phase immatures are brown-bodied with a buff white head and mottled chest. Immatures of both phases have bluish green ceres (the membrane at base of upper beak), legs, and feet.

Behavior

The Hawaiian hawk is a strong flier and often soars on thermal currents above the slopes of Mauna Loa and Mauna Kea volcanoes. When hunting, it prefers to perch in a tree and swoop down on rodents, other small animals, and birds. The Hawaiian hawk vigorously defends its nest and will attack any other hawk, owl, or even human that ventures too near. A mated pair tends to use the same nest year after year, adding to it each new season until it grows very large (sometimes 40 inches across and 30 inches deep). Juveniles move into territories of their own in late fall and early winter.

Hawaiian hawks breed at three or four years of age. Birds nest from March through September. The female usually lays a single egg in late April or early May and does most of the incubation. The egg hatches after about 38 days. The female then develops a low tolerance for the male and often keeps him at a distance. For four to five weeks, the male hunts alone and returns to the nest with food. Careful parental care leads to a high fledgling success rate. Chicks fledge at about nine weeks but remain dependent for several months—a long time in comparison with other hawks.

Habitat

The Hawaiian hawk is the only hawk native to the Hawaiian islands. It is found from near sea level to an elevation of 2,600 meters (8,500 ft) and is more abundant in windward than in leeward forests. It avoids dry scrub areas and prefers either open savanna or denser rain forest. The species adapts well to agricultural habitats—papaya groves, macadamia nut orchards, and sugarcane fields—that are bounded by large trees.

Historic Range

Early European explorers found the Hawaiian hawk on the island of Hawaii, where it was common in some localities. It has been sighted occasionally on the islands of Kauai, Oahu, and Maui, but is known to breed only on Hawaii.

Current Distribution

The distribution of the Hawaiian hawk has not changed, but its numbers have declined. Within Hawaii Volcanoes National Park, hawk numbers have been recorded for over 40 years. In 1968, the population reached its low, estimated at several hundred birds. Currently, the population appears stable at about 2,000 birds.

Conservation and Recovery

The Hawaiian hawk was once thought to be a guardian spirit that watched over the older families of Hawaii. Eventually, the hawk itself came to need protection from the drastic decline of its forest habitat. Most lowland forests have been converted to agricultural or urban uses. Non-native plants dominate much of the island below 800 meters (2,600 ft), while upper-elevation forests have been logged and subsequently converted to pasture.

Field studies during the early 1980s were the first systematic attempt to document the habitat and behavior of the Hawaiian hawk. These studies found that the hawk's only true predators were human. For years, illegal shooting took its toll, but this seems to have abated. A more serious problem is harassment of nesting hawks. When nesting birds are disturbed repeatedly, incubation or feeding is disrupted, causing young to starve or leave the nest prematurely. Frequently disturbed nests are often abandoned by adults.

Because its population has stabilized, the outlook is bright for the Hawaiian hawk, so long as efforts continue to arrest forest decline and to preserve high quality habitat on the island.

Bibliography

U.S. Fish and Wildlife Service. 1984. "The Hawaiian Hawk Recovery Plan." U.S. Fish and Wildlife Service, Portland.

Contact

Office of Environmental Services
U.S. Fish and Wildlife Service
300 Ala Moana Boulevard
P.O. Box 50167
Honolulu, Hawaii 96850

Ivory-Billed Woodpecker
Campephilus principalis

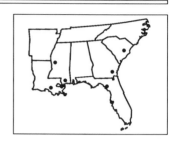

Arthur A. Allen/Cornell Lab. of Ornithology

Status	Endangered (possibly extirpated from U.S.)
Listed	March 11, 1967
Family	Picidae (Woodpecker)
Description . . .	Large woodpecker; red crest in males, black in females.
Habitat	Large tracts of old-growth, bottomland forests.
Food	Engraver beetle larvae.
Reproduction .	Clutch of 2 or 3 eggs.
Threats	Logging, habitat destruction, hunters.
Region 4	Southern U.S.

Description

The ivory-billed woodpecker, the largest of the North American woodpeckers, is about 50 centimeters (19.5 in) in length. Males have a red crest, which is all black in females. Both sexes have a black crown and forehead and a white stripe on the sides of the head, which extends down the neck and joins midway down the back. Ivory-bills have extensive white patches on the trailing edge of the wings in flight. Immatures are duller black and lack red on the crest.

Behavior

For nesting, the ivory-billed woodpecker excavates cavities in trees—a live ash, hackberry, or sweetgum, and sometimes a dead oak or royal palm. Most nest cavities are ex-cavated about 9 meters (30 ft) off the ground. The female lays a clutch of two or three eggs which are incubated for about 20 days. Young fledge in about 35 days. The ivory-bill forages on the larvae of engraver beetles, which bore just under the bark of dead or dying trees, by tearing away the bark to get to the beetles.

Habitat

The ivory-billed woodpecker requires large tracts of forest to survive—up to 810 hectares (2,000 acres) for each pair. In the U.S. the species inhabited bottomland, cypress swamps, and uncut long-leaf pine forests, but its specialized feeding habits restricted its occurrence. Stands of dead or fire-killed trees provided the best foraging areas. A remnant population, recently rediscovered in Cuba, inhabits an extensively logged pine forest on the eastern end of the island.

Historic Range

This species once ranged from north Texas and Oklahoma across the southern states to North Carolina and was considered fairly common in at least seven states—Alabama, Florida, Georgia, Louisiana, Mississippi, South Carolina, and Texas. The last confirmed ivory-bill was observed in the mid-1940s in a mature forest in northern Louisiana (Tensas River National Wildlife Refuge).

Current Distribution

The ivory-billed woodpecker is considered possibly extirpated from the U.S. The 1970s brought a few unconfirmed reports of ivory-bills, but many researchers now believe these sightings may have been of the similar pileated woodpecker (*Dryocopus pileatus*). The ivory-bill can be distinguished by its larger size, the all black crest of the female, and what appear as white shields on the lower back of perched birds.

Conservation and Recovery

The reasons for the decline of ivory-bills are the loss of habitat to logging and of mature birds to overhunting. In 1989 the Fish and Wildlife Service (FWS) funded a "last effort" survey to determine if ivory-bills still exist in the U.S. Dr. Jerome A. Jackson of Mississippi State University has initiated a survey in hope of finding a reclusive population. Recent studies suggest that several remote areas may still harbor ivory-bills. These include: the Atchafalaya Basin (Louisiana), Santee River (South Carolina), Altamaha River (Georgia), Yazoo River (Mississippi),

Pascagoula River (Mississippi), and the Suwannee, Withlacoochee, and Ochloconee rivers (Florida). The survey is scheduled to conclude in 1992.

If you think you have seen an ivory-billed woodpecker, the FWS requests that you: note common field characteristics—size, coloration, and vocalizations; photograph the bird or record the bird's sounds; locate the exact site on a map; and contact Dr. Jackson at Mississippi State University (601/325-3120).

Ornithologists suspected that ivory-bills would be found in the remaining forests of eastern Cuba. In 1986, researchers there confirmed sightings of male and female ivory-bills. The size of this population is unknown, but, given the bird's habitat requirements, it is probably very small. If the Cuban population survives, the largest North American woodpecker might someday be reintroduced to the U.S.

Bibliography

Short, L. L. 1982. *Woodpeckers of the World.* Delaware Museum of Natural History, Greenville.

Short, L. L. 1985 "Last Chance for the Ivorybill." *Natural History* Aug:66-68.

Short, L. L., and J. F. Horne. 1986. "The Ivorybill Still Lives." *Natural History* July:26-28.

Contact

Regional Office of Endangered Species
U.S. Fish and Wildlife Service
Richard B. Russell Federal Building
75 Spring Street, S.W.
Atlanta, Georgia 30303

Puerto Rican Nightjar

Caprimulgus noctitherus

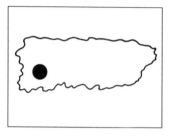

Cameron B. Kepler

Status	Endangered
Listed	June 4, 1973
Family	Caprimulgidae (Nightjar)
Description . . .	Darkly mottled, nocturnal bird with a white throat band.
Habitat	Dry, lowland, semi-deciduous forests.
Food	Insects.
Reproduction	Clutch of 2 eggs.
Threats	Predation, deforestation, human encroachment.
Region 4	Puerto Rico

Description

The Puerto Rican nightjar, also known as the Puerto Rican whip-poor-will, is a robin-sized nocturnal bird, 24 centimeters (9.6 in) long, with long bristles around its bill. It has a fluffy plumage mottled with dark brown, black, and gray; a white band across the throat; and white spots at the end of the tail.

The Puerto Rican nightjar is a tropical species, similar to the mainland whip-poor-will (*Caprimulgus vociferus*) but smaller and darker. Some ornithologists consider the Puerto Rican nightjar a race of the mainland species rather than a separate species. The nightjar's song, however, is quite different. Nocturnal bird songs are important in court-ship and mating and help maintain repro-ductive isolation between closely related species.

Behavior

Nightjars capture insects in flight, foraging from regular perch sites. The nightjar is thought to breed from May through July. It does not build a nest but lays eggs in leaf litter under bushes in the shelter of overhanging trees. Like other members of its family, it probably raises two broods each year. Clutch size is two eggs, and incubation lasts about 19 days. Young birds wander from the nest by the third day after hatching and are able to fly by the 14th day. Adults abandon the nesting site after chicks have fledged.

Habitat

The Puerto Rican nightjar has been found only in dry, mixed deciduous and evergreen forests, where there is a closed tree canopy. In Puerto Rico, these forests, which support abundant insects, are restricted to the lower limestone and serpentine slopes and coastal plains of the island.

Historic Range

The nightjar is native to the lower elevation forests of Puerto Rico.

Current Distribution

The Puerto Rican nightjar is currently limited to three areas in the southwestern part of the island: Guanica Forest with about 400 breeding pairs; the Susua Forest with about 100; and the Guayanilla Hills with about 50 pairs.

Conservation and Recovery

The introduction of the mongoose (*Herpestes auropunctatus*) to Puerto Rico in 1877 initiated the decline of the Puerto Rican nightjar. The mongoose is an extremely efficient predator of ground-nesting birds and reptiles. Deforestation of Puerto Rico's lower elevations accelerated the decline of the species, bringing it to the brink of extinction. Less than 3 percent of its historic habitat remains in undisturbed condition. The expanding human population of Puerto Rico continues to threaten the small tracts of nightjar habitat that remain.

Past conservation of the nightjar has been incidental to other conservation efforts. Current population sites within the Susua and Guanica state forests and within forest reserves assure minimal future habitat modification. The Guanica Forest has been recognized as part of the international network of Biosphere Reserves by UNESCO, emphasizing its ecological importance.

Bibliography

Bond, J. 1961. *Birds of the West Indies*. Houghton Mifflin Company, Boston.

Kepler, C. B., and A. K. Kepler. 1973. "The Distribution and Ecology of the Puerto Rican Whip-poor-will, an Endangered Species." In *Living Bird, Eleventh Annual*. Cornell Laboratory of Ornithology, New York.

Reynard, G. B. 1962."The Rediscovery of the Puerto Rican Whip-poor-will." *Living Bird* 1:51-60.

U.S. Fish and Wildlife Service. 1984. "Puerto Rican Whip-poor-will Recovery Plan." U.S. Fish and Wildlife Service, Atlanta.

Contact

Regional Office of Endangered Species
U.S. Fish and Wildlife Service
Richard B. Russell Federal Building
75 Spring Street, S.W.
Atlanta, Georgia 30303

Caribbean Field Office
U.S. Fish and Wildlife Service
P.O. Box 491
Boqueron, Puerto Rico 00622

Piping Plover
Charadrius melodus

Status	. . . . . .	Endangered in Great Lakes watershed.
		Threatened elsewhere.
Listed	. . . . .	December 11, 1985
Family	. . . .	Charadriidae (Plover)
Description	. . .	Short-billed, compact shorebird.
Habitat	. . . .	Beaches, sand bars.
Food	. . . . .	Marine crustaceans, shellfish, insects.
Reproduction	.	Clutch of 4 eggs.
Threats	. . . .	Habitat disturbance.
Region 3	. . .	Great Lakes
Region 4	. . .	Atlantic and Gulf Coasts
Region 5	. . .	Atlantic Coast
Region 6	. . .	Northern Great Plains
Canada	. . . .	Ontario

James P. Mattsson/USFWS

Description

The piping plover is a stocky, short-billed shorebird, 17 centimeters (6.8 in) long. Both sexes are similar in size and color. In breeding plumage plovers are pale beige above and white below, with a black chest band and crown patch. The bill is orange, tipped with black, and the legs are bright orange. In winter, piping plovers lose their black markings; the bill is all black, and leg color fades to yellow.

The American Ornithologists' Union recognizes two geographically separate subspecies of the piping plover: *Charadrius melodus melodus* and *C. m. circumcinctus.* Recent scientific studies, however, have detected little or no difference between the groups, and the Fish and Wildlife Service (FWS) treats these two "subspecies" as distinct breeding populations of the same species—one on the Atlantic coast of North America, the second scattered from the northern Great Plains into Canada.

A close relative of the piping plover, the snowy plover (*C. alexandrinus tenuirostris*) was surveyed in 1988 in the western United States to determine its status as a future candidate for listing.

Behavior

The piping plover is one of the earliest migratory birds to return to New England beaches, often arriving in early March. Characteristically, it darts across the sand on its stilty, orange legs, stopping suddenly to stab with its sharp beak, before darting off. Because its coloration blends so well with sand beaches, its distinctive "piping" call—peep-lo!—is often heard before the bird is seen.

Breeding season for piping plovers is from late March to August. During the courtship ritual, the male flies in figure-eights. On the ground it puffs up its feathers, and struts and whistles around the female, stretching its neck and stamping its feet. When nesting, a mated pair scoops out a depression on the beach above the high tide line, sometimes lining it with small stones, shells, or driftwood. The female lays four pear-shaped, buff-colored, white eggs, marked with small spots of dark brown or black. Both parents normally incubate the eggs for about 30 days. The well-camouflaged young leave the nest a few hours after hatching—as soon as their down is dry—and begin to feed on their own. Family groups stay together for about a month until the chicks fledge.

The piping plover's diet consists mainly of crustaceans, mollusks, and other small marine creatures, supplemented by insects. The Endangered least tern (*Sterna antillarum*) is a known breeding associate of piping plovers on the northern Great Plains and Atlantic coast.

Habitat

The piping plover nests on sand or pebble beaches, typically associated with large bodies of water. When nesting inland, the plover seeks out small islands and flats along major river systems or finds undisturbed spots, such as abandoned gravel pits or salt-encrusted spits along alkali lakes.

Birds from the northern Great Plains and Great Lakes winter along the Gulf coast. Populations that breed along the Atlantic coast winter from North Carolina south-ward, occasionally in the Bahamas and West Indies. Little is known of the piping plovers' habitat requirements on their wintering grounds. The FWS is currently working with state biologists to study wintering populations.

Historic Range

In 1804, the explorers Lewis and Clark observed the plover on sandbars in the Missouri River between Iowa and Missouri. At the turn of the century, the plover was described as common in Nebraska, breeding along the Platte River and on the Loop River northwest of Grand Island. Uncontrolled hunting led to depletion of these breeding populations. As human disturbance of nesting areas increased, the piping plover retreated northward into Canada and along the northern Great Lakes.

In 1912 the bird was a common summer resident along the Lake Michigan shoreline in Illinois, but it no longer breeds there. In Michigan, the plover declined to a 1984 low of only 13 pairs. At Long Point, Ontario, a large population was reduced to zero by the late 1970s.

The Atlantic coast population has also experienced serious decline, principally because of increased beachfront development and recreational use. For example, the number of breeding pairs on Long Island, New York, declined from over 500 in the 1930s to a current population of about 100. Nesting is increasingly confined to rare undisturbed stretches of beach.

Current Distribution

In 1980, 900 pairs of piping plovers were estimated to breed along the Atlantic coast from Newfoundland to North Carolina. A 1986 census estimated 550 pairs along the

U.S. Atlantic coast, and 240 pairs in eastern Canada. Over 80 percent of the breeding population nests in Massachusetts, New York, New Jersey, and Virginia.

Inland, an unknown but small number of piping plovers is found in northeastern Montana and along the Missouri River system in the Dakotas and Nebraska. Around the Great Lakes, where the species is listed as Endangered, populations are at critical lows: in 1988, 24 pairs of plovers were found in Lake of the Woods, 22 in Minnesota, and two in Ontario.

In Canada the species is most numerous in Saskatchewan, but in Manitoba only 20 percent of historic nesting sites are currently in use.

Conservation and Recovery

Protected by the Migratory Bird Treaty Act, the bird recovered from the effects of hunting during the 1920s, only to fall prey to a range of other manmade and natural factors.

Much of the decline of this ground nester has been caused by human disturbance of its habitat. Beachfront development and recreation along Great Lakes and Atlantic coast beaches has expanded greatly. Home building and road construction have destroyed suitable nesting habitat outright. Swimmers and beach hikers disturb plover nests and disrupt incubation. Unleashed pets on the beaches kill plover chicks and destroy eggs. Accumulation of debris and garbage has attracted such predators as foxes, wild dogs and cats, opossums, skunks, and rats.

Inland populations declined when large-scale water control projects along major rivers drastically altered plover breeding habitat. The few remaining river islands that would be suitable for nesting are now used for recreation. Human disturbance in the form of off-road vehicles is even reaching into the remote, sparsely populated alkali wetland country of the Dakotas, Montana, and Saskatchewan. Natural predators, such as the raccoon and the gull, have greatly expanded their ranges since the 1940s, increasing plover chick and egg mortality.

The FWS Recovery Plan for the Atlantic coast population sets a goal of increasing the population to 1,200 breeding pairs. If this number can be maintained for five consecutive years, the bird would be considered for delisting. To accomplish this FWS naturalists are continuing to monitor population trends through yearly surveys. Individual nesting sites have been examined and management programs established for sites on public land. Additional sections of beach in wildlife refuges may be declared "off limits" for the plover breeding season, a step already taken for some beaches in Massachusetts, Rhode Island, Connecticut, New Jersey, and Virginia.

Efforts to reduce nest disturbance by pedestrians, off-road vehicles, and predators have included fencing, limiting recreational use, rerouting off-road vehicles, enforcing pet leash rules, removing litter and garbage, and removing predators. In addition, an existing public information program is being expanded to alert beach dwellers and recreational users to possible harm they can cause the piping plover. As part of this program, public service announcements will be made on local television and radio stations in Nebraska to alert the public to the presence of plovers on the Platte River. Plover alert posters will be displayed in businesses that sell recreational equipment and all-terrain vehicles.

The Canadian Wildlife Service has offered to cooperate with the FWS to preserve populations on the Great Lakes and elsewhere. The piping plover is listed as Endangered by

Canada's Committee on the Status of Endangered Wildlife.

Bibliography

Cairns, W. E., and I. A. McLaren. 1980. "Status
of the Piping Plover on the East Coast of
North America." *American Birds* 34: 206-208.

Graham, F., Jr. 1986. "Cry of the Plover."
Audubon 88(3):12- 17.

Haig, S. M., and L. W. Oring. 1987. "The Piping
Plover." In R. L. Di Silvestro, ed., *Audubon
Wildlife Report 1987*. Academic Press, New
York.

U.S. Fish and Wildlife Service. 1988. "Atlantic
Coast Piping Plover Recovery Plan." U.S. Fish
and Wildlife Service, Newton Corner, Massachusetts.

U.S. Fish and Wildlife Service. 1988. "Great
Lakes and Northern Great Plains Piping
Plover Recovery Plan." U.S. Fish and Wildlife
Service, Twin Cities.

Contact

Regional Office of Endangered Species
U.S. Fish and Wildlife Service
One Gateway Center, Suite 700
Newton Corner, Massachusetts 02158

Regional Office of Endangered Species
U.S. Fish and Wildlife Service
Federal Building, Fort Snelling
Twin Cities, Minnesota 55111

Masked Bobwhite
Colinus virginianus ridgwayi

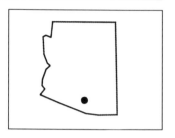

C. Allan Morgan

Status	Endangered
Listed	March 11, 1967
Family	Phasianidae
	(Pheasants and Quail)
Description . . .	Mottled, reddish brown quail with a cinnamon breast and black head.
Habitat	Semi-arid and desert grasslands, desert scrub.
Food	Seeds, plants, insects.
Reproduction	. Clutch of 5 to 15 eggs.
Threats	Livestock grazing, fire suppression, predators.
Region 2	Arizona
Mexico	Sonora

Description

The masked bobwhite is a quail with a short tail and plump body, ranging from 22 to 27 centimeters (9 to 11 in) in length. Males are characterized by a cinnamon breast, black head and throat, and a varying amount of white above the eye. Females lack the black head and cinnamon breast, but instead are a mottled brown above, with a buff head and white breast. Females are essentially indistinguishable from the Texas bobwhite (*Colinus virginianus texanum*) found in subtropical Texas and Tamaulipas, Mexico.

Behavior

The bobwhite is a seasonally gregarious bird, gathering into social groups called "coveys." Broods of five to fifteen young form the nucleus of the cool weather covey. Unproductive adults and young separated from other broods may join, but covey size rarely exceeds 20 birds. Masked bobwhites usually remain in coveys until late June, when mating bonds form, and pairs gradually separate from the covey to nest.

Breeding season, heralded by the "Bob-whoit!" call of the male, begins with July rains. Birds build their nests on the ground and require thick cover for concealment; therefore, nesting may be delayed until sufficient ground cover has developed. If rains are delayed or absent, masked bobwhites may not nest that season. Chicks begin to hatch in late July and may continue to hatch until early November.

The masked bobwhite feeds on a variety of legume and weed seeds during the fall, winter, and early spring; and plant material and insects in summer and early fall.

Habitat

Masked bobwhite habitat extends through open grasslands, across semi-arid desert scrub, and into desert grasslands at the extreme northern edge of its range. Grass and weed cover is seasonal; trees and bushes vary in composition and density from site to site. In the southern and eastern portions of the Sonora savanna grassland, an enormous variety of thorny scrubs and trees are present. At the northern limits, mesquite is present throughout. Habitat elevation rises from 150 to 1,200 meters (500 to 4,000 ft) above sea level. Freezing temperatures are infrequent, and almost never last more than 24 hours. July through September rainfall averages 25 centimeters (10 in).

Historic Range

The masked bobwhite has always been restricted to the level plains and river valleys of Sonora, Mexico, and extreme south-central Arizona. The eastern and southern distribution of the masked bobwhite is limited by the merging of Sonoran savanna grassland with the more dense Sinaloan thorn-scrub. To the west and northwest a decrease in summer precipitation excludes bobwhites from the desert scrub communities of the Central Gulf Coast, Lower Colorado River, and Arizona Upland subdivisions of the Sonora Desert. The northern limit of historic masked bobwhite range is defined by the Altar and Santa Cruz Valleys of Arizona.

Current Distribution

By the turn of the century the masked bobwhite was eliminated from southern Arizona

when native grasslands were depleted by cattle grazing. As cattle ranching spread throughout Sonora after 1930, the masked bobwhite began to disappear from there also. Because of the bobwhite's secretive nature, its current population distribution in Mexico is hard to estimate, and no recent population counts are available.

Conservation and Recovery

Grazing cattle and other livestock remove grasses and forbs from the land, depriving the masked bobwhite of nesting habitat, cover, and food. Depletion of ground cover prevents brushfires, allowing woody plants to invade and gradually take over the grasslands, forcing out the masked bobwhite. The woody habitats are then occupied by bobwhite relatives—the scaled quail, Gambel's quail, or the elegant quail.

From 1937 through 1950, unsuccessful attempts were made to reintroduce the masked bobwhite to Arizona and New Mexico and to restore populations in Sonora. Pen-raised captive birds or wild Mexican bobwhites were released in unsuitable habitats, outside of their historic range, and did not survive.

A recovery program for the masked bobwhite began in 1966, when a successful captive breeding program was established at Patuxent, Maryland. This captive colony now produces 3,000 chicks each year under carefully supervised conditions. Through the 1970s, biologists, trying to pinpoint suitable habitat, released these pen-raised birds to the wild at different locations in Arizona; most birds disappeared within two months, due to coyote predation. Efforts gradually narrowed to the Altar Valley's privately owned Buenos Aires Ranch, which seemed to provide ideal masked bobwhite habitat. In 1985, the Buenos Aires Ranch was acquired by the

Fish and Wildlife Service and became the Buenos Aires National Wildlife Refuge.

Current reintroduction techniques have become more sophisticated. Patuxent-raised chicks are returned to the wild in family groups under the tutelage of "foster parents," usually wild male Texas bobwhites that have been sterilized. These foster parents teach the released birds essential survival skills.

Although the long-term success of these efforts depends as much on weather cycles as on chick survival rates, biologists feel that they are on the right track with the masked bobwhite. The captive bobwhite release program will run for five years (1985-90) at the Buenos Aires National Wildlife Refuge, followed by a two-year evaluation period. The goal, as set forth in the Recovery Plan, is to establish a self-sustaining population in Arizona within ten years, thus reversing a trend that drove the masked bobwhite out of this country more than 80 years ago.

Bibliography

Banks, R. C. 1975. "Plumage Variation in the Masked Bobwhite." *Condor* 77:486-487.

Johnsgard, P. A. 1973. *Grouse and Quails of North America.* University of Nebraska Press, Lincoln.

Phillips, A., J. Marshall, and G. Monson. 1964. *The Birds of Arizona.* University of Arizona Press, Tucson.

U.S. Fish and Wildlife Service. 1984. "Revised Masked Bobwhite Recovery Plan." U.S. Fish and Wildlife Service, Albuquerque.

Contact

Regional Office of Endangered Species
U.S. Fish and Wildlife Service
P.O. Box 1306
Albuquerque, New Mexico 87103

Puerto Rican Plain Pigeon

Columba inornata wetmorei

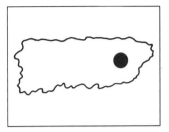

James Wiley

Status	Endangered
Listed	October 13, 1970
Family	Columbidae (Doves and Pigeons)
Description	Large, plump-bodied, blue-gray dove.
Habitat	Varied.
Food	Plant matter.
Reproduction	Clutch of 1 egg, up to 3 broods per year.
Threats	Nesting disturbance, hunting.
Region 4	Puerto Rico

Description

The Puerto Rican plain pigeon is a large-bodied bird (38 cm; 15 in) that resembles the common city pigeon or rock dove. At a distance it appears pale blue-gray overall. The head, hindneck, breast, and part of the folded wing are colored with a red-wine wash. When folded, the wing shows a white leading edge; in flight, it forms a conspicuous wing bar. Legs and feet are dark red. The female is slightly smaller and duller than the male. Juveniles are browner overall, with pale wing margins and dark eyes.

The plain pigeon is thought to represent a fairly recent island adaption of the red-billed pigeon (*Columba flavirostria*) or its close relative, Salvin's pigeon (*C. oenops*), found in Central and South America. Three races of the plain pigeon are recognized: the Cuban plain pigeon (*C. inornata inornata*); the Jamaican (*C. i. exigua*); and the Puerto Rican (*C. i. wetmorei*).

Behavior

The plain pigeon breeds throughout the year, with peaks in late winter and early spring. The male defends a territory year round against other males. A mated female selects a nest site within the male's territory. Both sexes construct a flimsy platform of twigs to serve as a nest. The female lays a single egg, which she incubates for about 14 days. Chicks fledge after 23 days and are dependent on adults for the next few days. A pair may produce up to three eggs per year. Males and females brood and care for hatchlings in shifts.

Adult pigeons congregate in small flocks during the height of breeding season and may form larger flocks for roosting and feeding in the fall. The plain pigeon feeds on a wide variety of plant seeds and fruits, including royal palm, mountain immortelle, West Indies trema, and white prickle.

Habitat

The plain pigeon is adapted to a range of habitats. In the past, it has nested in wetlands, lowland forests, or cultivated mountain areas, including upland coffee plantations. Within its remaining range on Puerto Rico, it prefers to nest in bamboo groves or among hardwoods in canyons.

Historic Range

The species has been rare in Puerto Rico since at least the early part of this century. It was reported near extinction in 1926 and was subsequently considered extinct until rediscovered in 1963 near the town of Cidra, Puerto Rico.

Current Distribution

The only confirmed population of the Puerto Rican plain pigeon occurs in the east-central part of the island near Cidra and the neighboring towns of Cayey, Caguas, Comerio, Aguas Buenas, and Aibonito. Estimates indicate that the population declined to a low of about 75 birds by 1977. In 1988, about 150 pigeons were thought to survive.

Conservation and Recovery

The once common Puerto Rican plain pigeon suffered a severe population decline when extensive tracts of island forests were cleared during the 19th and early 20th centuries. Unregulated hunting accelerated the rate of decline. Because the plain pigeon flocks seasonally, it provides easy prey for hunters. This now rare pigeon was reportedly sold for food as recently as 1961.

The plain pigeon has been unable to replenish its population because of a high rate of nesting failures, caused primarily by human disturbance. Nesting sites are interspersed between villages and urban areas; some birds literally nest in the backyards of new homes. People disturb breeding birds, molest nesting birds, and steal squabs from nests.

A captive breeding program, begun in 1983, produced a total of 47 squabs by the end of 1988. The next step in this recovery effort will be a release of captive-bred pigeons to establish a second population at the Rio Abajo Commonwealth Forest located near the center of the island.

Bibliography

U.S. Fish and Wildlife Service. 1982. "Puerto Rican Plain Pigeon Recovery Plan." U.S. Fish and Wildlife Service, Atlanta.

Contact

Regional Office of Endangered Species
U.S. Fish and Wildlife Service
Richard B. Russell Federal Building
75 Spring Street, S.W.
Atlanta, Georgia 30303

Hawaiian Crow

Corvus hawaiiensis

USFWS

Status	Endangered
Listed	March 11, 1967
Family	Corvidae (Crows and Jays)
Description	Large crow; dark, sooty brown with a long pointed bill.
Habitat	Open forests and pasture.
Food	Omnivorous.
Reproduction	Clutch of 1 to 5 eggs.
Threats	Very low numbers.
Region 1	Hawaii

Description

The Hawaiian crow, known in Hawaiian as "alala," is a large, sooty brown bird, which appears almost black; its stocky body measures 48 centimeters (19 in) in length. The bill is long and thick. This species has also been classified as *Corvus tropicus*.

Behavior

The Hawaiian crow is more secretive than the common American crow and is usually heard before it is seen. Immature birds reach sexual maturity in their second or third year. Breeding pairs nest from March through July. Clutches consist of one to five eggs, but recently few young have survived to fledge.

Although omnivorous, the Hawaiian crow usually feeds on the fruits of trees and shrubs.

It forages for insects among leaf litter and sometimes extracts nectar from flowers. Other foods include mice, small lizards, and the young of small birds.

Habitat

The Hawaiian crow is usually found in higher elevation ohia (*Metrosideros collina*) or mixed ohia and koa (*Acacia koa*) forests that have an understory of other native shrubs and plants. These produce fruit for the crow's diet. The Hawaiian crow prefers open forests or groves bordering pasture. It avoids more dense, closed forests. Originally, habitat elevation ranged from 305 to 2440 meters (1,000 to 8,000 ft). By the 1940s the crow's range had become greatly reduced to a narrow, discontinuous belt between 760 and 1,830 meters (2,500 and 6,000 ft).

Historic Range

This species is known only from the island of Hawaii. Its breeding range was historically restricted to the forests of the slopes of the Hualalai and Mauna Loa volcanoes. At the turn of the century, the Hawaiian crow occupied all of its known range and was considered abundant. The Hawaiian crow declined steadily since this time, until by the 1970s fewer than 150 crows survived on the island.

Current Distribution

The outlook remains grim for the Hawaiian crow. Sometime in the early 1980s the species suffered a serious population crash. A 1986 estimate placed the number of Hawaiian crows in the wild at 12. In the spring of 1987 researchers were only able to locate two crows.

Recovery and Conservation

No single reason for the drastic population decline of the Hawaiian crow has been determined, and prospects for its recovery are considered slim. Increased human settlement in the Kona districts and changes in land use have been cited as a cause. It is also clear that crows were widely hunted. The birds have been legally protected from hunting since 1931, however, and the population did not rebound as was anticipated.

Browsing and grazing by cattle, horses, sheep, and goats have caused significant changes in native forests and may be a factor in the abandonment of some sections of the crow's range. Again, researchers were puzzled by the fact that, during the 1970s, crows inhabited some tracts of highly modified pastureland, yet seemed absent from nearby, relatively pristine forests.

Generally low breeding productivity may have triggered the most recent population crash. Studies over the last decade have determined that, on average, less than a single young fledged per nest. Causes of this reproductive failure seem to be a combination of poor hatchability of eggs, predation by rats or mongooses, avian diseases, and a declining food supply as many native food plants are crowded out by non-native vegetation.

The Olinda Endangered Species Breeding Facility on the island of Maui is struggling to keep alive a captive breeding population of less than ten birds. The difficulties of captive breeding are exacerbated by the low number of individuals and the very limited gene pool. Unfortunately, in June 1987, a fertile female died of egg-impaction. In early 1988 a fertile egg was hatched, and the young crow fledged. This marked the breeding program's first unequivocal success.

Bibliography

Baldwin, P. H. 1969. "The Alala (*Corvus tropicus*) of Western Hawaiian Island." *Elepaio* 30(5):41-45.

Berger, A. J. 1981. *Hawaiian Birdlife*. University of Hawaii Press, Honolulu.

U.S. Fish and Wildlife Service. 1982. "Alala Recovery Plan." U.S. Fish and Wildlife Service, Portland.

Contact

Regional Office of Endangered Species
U.S. Fish and Wildlife Service
Lloyd 500 Building, Suite 1692
500 N.E. Multnomah Street
Portland, Oregon 97232

Office of Environmental Services
U.S. Fish and Wildlife Service
300 Ala Moana Boulevard
P.O. Box 50167
Honolulu, Hawaii 96850

Kirtland's Warbler
Dendroica kirtlandii

Michigan Natural Features Inventory

Status	Endangered
Listed	March 11, 1967
Family	Emberizidae; Subfamily Parulinae (Wood Warbler)
Description	Small songbird; blue-gray above and yellow beneath.
Habitat	Thickets of young jack pine.
Food	Insects, tree sap, berries.
Reproduction	Clutch of 3 to 5 eggs.
Threats	Habitat loss.
Region 3	Michigan

Description

Kirtland's warbler is a songbird, 15 centimeters (6 in) long. It is blue-gray above and yellow below, with coarse spotting on the breast and sides. Males have a black spot on the cheek, which in females is gray. The warbler has a white eye ring which is broken by a dark eye line.

Behavior

This warbler builds its nest on the ground beneath pine trees. The nest is constructed of strips of bark, grass, and other fibers, and is usually lined with finer grasses, pine needles, and hair. Clutch size is three to five eggs, which are white, speckled with brown. It is the only blue-gray warbler that wags or bobs its tail as it walks on the ground.

In migration, the bird travels a direct route between its nesting grounds in Michigan and its wintering range in the Bahamas and Dominican Republic, entering and leaving the U.S. along the North and South Carolina coasts.

Habitat

Ideal breeding habitat for Kirtland's warbler consists of homogeneous thickets of five- and six-year-old jack pines interspersed with grassy clearings. Such a habitat is created and maintained by intense and periodic brushfires. The warbler requires enough ground cover to conceal its nest but shies away from areas that are overgrown. When deciduous trees begin to dominate an area, the warbler moves out. A tract of jack pine must be at least 32 hectares (80 acres) and preferably larger to attract Kirtland's warbler.

Nesting habitat is also limited to a specific soil type. With one or two exceptions all nests have been found on Grayling sand, a poor soil that is extremely porous. The porosity of the soil allows rainwater to drain away quickly without flooding warbler nests. Grayling sand occurs in 29 counties of the lower Michigan peninsula, corresponding closely with naturally occurring stands of jack pine.

At its wintering grounds in the Bahamas, Kirtland's warbler occupies low, broadleafed scrub, which is the prevailing habitat there.

Historic Range

The narrow habitat requirements of the Kirtland's warbler have always restricted its range. Presumably the bird nested in the conifer zone on the sandy outwash plains in the wake of the Wisconsin Ice Sheet. This conifer zone was a narrow strip across the north-central states, and the amount of suitable habitat at any one time was probably small. The few specimens taken east and west of the present migration path suggest the possibility of former nesting grounds in Minnesota, Wisconsin, and Ontario. Recent studies have identified stray male warblers at jack pine tracts in Wisconsin and Minnesota, but there is no evidence of nesting.

In 1951, on the hundredth anniversary of its discovery, the Kirtland's warbler became the first songbird to have its entire population censused. Researchers found 432 singing males, which suggested a total population of about 1,000 birds.

Current Distribution

A Kirtland's warbler nesting ground was discovered in 1903 near the Au Sable River almost on the boundary of Crawford and Oscoda counties, Michigan. Fully 90 percent of all the nests found since that time have been located in this area. During surveys in the 1970s, virtually all nesting was in Crawford, Oscoda, and Ogemaw counties. These counties have thousands of acres of natural jack pine forest on Grayling sand.

In 1986, 210 pairs were censused, but there was a noticeable and unexplained decline to 167 pairs in 1987. In 1989, the population had increased slightly to about 200 pairs.

Conservation and Recovery

Forest fire control has greatly reduced the size and frequency of burns in the Au Sable River watershed to the disadvantage of the warbler. Also, forest management has encouraged the replacement of jack pines with red pines or hardwoods, further reducing habitat. Currently, only about 1,820 hectares (4,500 acres) are suitable for breeding birds, which is a substantial reduction from the 6,070 hectares (15,000 acres) available in the 1950s and 1960s. This is probably the most important reason for the overall decline in numbers.

In 1957, the Michigan Department of Natural Resources set aside three tracts of 10.3 hectares (25.4 acres) each to be managed for the benefit of the Kirtland's warbler. In two of these, jack pine was planted in a special arrangement to leave numerous clearings. These tracts have succeeded in attracting nesting warblers.

At about the same time, the U.S. Forest Service set aside a management area of more than 1,620 hectares (4,000 acres) in the Huron National Forest in Oscoda County for the warbler. Management practices have included burning and planting in an effort to provide ideal nesting habitat. The birds have returned to these sites year after year.

A second limiting factor is parasitism by the brown-headed cowbird (*Molothrus ater*). This bird lays its own eggs in the warblers' nests. Cowbird chicks hatch first and outcompete warbler chicks for food. In the 1970s, cowbirds reduced warbler egg production by at least 40 percent and in some years almost completely wiped out their reproductive effort.

Since the early 1970s, Fish and Wildlife Service personnel have been trapping and removing cowbirds. By 1980, they had relocated some 40,000 cowbirds, significantly decreasing the impact of parasitism. Kirtland's warbler has not recovered as quickly as hoped, however, suggesting that other unknown factors are at work.

In 1987, the breeding area of Kirtland's warbler was photographed from the air to assist the recovery team in planning. Actual nesting sites will be compared with potential sites to determine other habitat features that seem critical for nesting. In addition, recent captures have shown that many warblers stay in the nesting range later into the fall than previously believed. As some activities, such as rabbit hunting, logging operations, and seismic surveying, are currently allowed in the habitat area after August 15, an effort will be made to extend prohibitions until September 15.

Bibliography

Mayfield, H. F. 1963. "Establishment of Preserves for the Kirtland's Warbler in the State and National Forests of Michigan." *Wilson Bulletin* 75:216-220.

Orr, C. D. 1975. "1974 Breeding Success of the Kirtland's Warbler." *Jack-Pine Warbler* 53:59-66.

Radabaugh, B. E. 1974. "Kirtland's Warbler and Its Bahama Wintering Grounds." *Wilson Bulletin* 96:374-383.

Shake, W. F., and J. P. Mattsson. 1975. "Three Years of Cowbird Control: An Effort to Save the Kirtland's Warbler." *Jack-Pine Warbler* 53:48-53.

U.S. Fish and Wildlife Service. 1976. "Kirtland's Warbler Recovery Plan." U.S. Fish and Wildlife Service, Twin Cities.

Contact

Regional Office of Endangered Species
U.S. Fish and Wildlife Service
Federal Building, Fort Snelling
Twin Cities, Minnesota 55111

Northern Aplomado Falcon
Falco femoralis septentrionalis

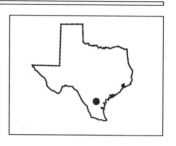

Steve Dobrott

Status	Endangered
Listed	February 25, 1986
Family	Falconidae (Falcon)
Description	Raptor with boldly marked head, gray back, and long, banded tail.
Habitat	Open rangeland, savanna, grasslands.
Food	Birds, insects, rodents, other small animals.
Reproduction	Clutch of 2 or 3 eggs.
Threats	Habitat degradation, pesticides.
Region 2	Arizona, New Mexico, Texas
Mexico	Veracruz, Chiapas, Campeche, Tabasco

Description

The northern aplomado falcon is a distinctive bird of prey; adults are distinguished by dull red underparts, a gray back, a long and banded tail, and a striking black and white facial pattern. The aplomado falcon (*Falco femoralis*) has been divided into three subspecies. The northern aplomado is the largest of the three, displaying a body length from 38 to 42 centimeters (15 to 16.5 in) and a wingspan from 102 to 122 centimeters (40 to 48 in). This is intermediate in size between the American kestrel and peregrine falcon.

The two other subspecies—*F. f. pichinchae* and *F. f. femoralis*—are found south of Central America and can be distinguished from the northern aplomado falcon by different dimensions, by the configuration of the abdominal bands, and by the relative darkness of their plumage.

Behavior

Aplomado falcons are predatory and feed on birds, insects, rodents, small snakes, and lizards. Although the bird feeds heavily on insects, smaller birds make up over 90 percent of the diet in terms of bulk. The northern aplomado falcon typically glides horizontally from tree perches in pursuit of small birds and insects. The approach ranges from a slow flapping flight to a full-powered sprint. Males and females sometimes hunt together; while the male hovers overhead, the female pursues the prey by hopping along the ground. Aplomado falcons have occasionally been observed stealing prey from other birds—a practice known as kleptoparasitism.

These falcons do not construct their own nests but must depend on the availability of platforms and nests constructed by other hawks, ravens, or jays. In eastern Mexico, falcons nest during the dry season from January to June, producing eggs throughout this time. Most clutches of two or three eggs are laid in March through May. In the U.S., most egg-laying was recorded in April or May. The incubation period lasts about a month; nestlings fledge within 40 days of hatching and remain dependent for another month.

Habitat

This falcon prefers open rangeland and savanna—semi-arid grasslands with scattered trees and scrub growth. Associated trees are the oaks, acacias, or palms. In the U.S., the species was found in the coastal prairies along sand ridges, in woodlands along desert streams, and in desert grasslands with scattered mesquite and yucca. In central Mexico the falcon has been found in open pine woodland.

Historic Range

The aplomado falcon has a wide geographic distribution that includes most of South America and parts of Central America. It has ranged into the desert grasslands and coastal prairies of the southwestern U.S.

The northern subspecies was first described from a specimen taken in 1887 near Ft. Huachuca, Arizona. The breeding range of this subspecies extended from Guatemala through central Mexico into southeastern Arizona, southern New Mexico, and southern Texas. Although the northern aplomado nested occasionally in New Mexico until

1952, it disappeared from most of its U.S. range by 1940.

In Mexico, the breeding range encompassed the states of Tamaulipas, Chiapas, Campeche, Tabasco, Chihuahua, Coahuila, Sinaloa, Jalisco, Guerrero, Veracruz, Yucatan, and San Luis Potosi. In Guatemala, the subspecies was found along the Pacific slope of the Central American cordillera.

Current Distribution

This falcon has been extirpated as a breeding species from the United States. It nests regularly only along the Gulf Coast of Mexico in portions of northern and central Veracruz, northern Chiapas, western Campeche, and eastern Tabasco. Population estimates are unavailable, but the species is considered uncommon and declining in its home range. The status of the Central American population is unknown.

Conservation and Recovery

Habitat degradation is probably responsible for the disappearance of the subspecies from the United States. Thousands of acres of grassland habitat have been lost in this century because of a natural climatic drying trend and by conversion of prairie to agricultural uses. Much of the open grasslands of Arizona, New Mexico, and the Texas coastal plain have been gradually overgrown by shrubs and small trees; denser vegetation makes it difficult for the falcon to take its prey. In many places, permanent desert streams have been channelized and riparian habitats eliminated with catastrophic effects on local fauna. Along the coast, grazing cattle have damaged or destroyed wetlands where many bird species historically bred. A decline in numbers of smaller birds has meant a decline in falcon prey.

Pesticide use in the U.S. probably contributed to the overall degeneration in habitat quality. Although now banned in the U.S., the pesticides DDT and DDE continue to be used in Mexico. During a recent survey, falcons in Veracruz were found to be severely contaminated by pesticides. These pesticides disrupt the falcon's reproduction by causing extreme eggshell thinning. Nestings in Veracruz in the 1960s and 1970s have been observed to fail due to eggshell breakage during incubation. Experiences with the peregrine falcon show that pesticide contamination can lead to severe, rapid population declines.

Efforts are underway to reintroduce the northern aplomado falcon into its historic range in the southwestern U.S. In 1983, the Peregrine Fund established a captive breeding population with seven birds at its facility in Santa Cruz, California. The hatching success rate has been poor, but through 1988 over 20 young had been reared.

Potential reintroduction sites have been surveyed. In Arizona, scientists have examined the Ft. Huachuca Military Reservation, the Research Ranch near Elvin, the San Pedro River National Wildlife Refuge (NWR), and the Santa Rita Experimental Range southeast of Tucson. In Texas, suitable habitat exists at the Laguna Atascosa NWR, the King Ranch near Kingsville, and the Attwater Prairie Chicken NWR near Eagle Lake. Researchers are examining sites on the White Sands Missile Range and on the Animas NWR in New Mexico.

The Peregrine Fund released nestlings at the King Ranch and at Laguna Atascosa in 1985, 1986, and 1987, with some success. Scientists hope to improve the chances of these reintroduction efforts by using wild-caught nestlings from Mexico, as well as propagated birds.

While assisting the reintroduction effort, the Fish and Wildlife Service (FWS) plans to recommend that suitable habitat in the southwestern U.S. be protected through acquisition or negotiation. Proper management techniques will need to be applied to maintain and restore a healthy grassland ecosystem. Such techniques would include prescribed burns and brush removal.

The goal of the draft Recovery Plan is to achieve a self-sustaining population of at least 100 breeding pairs in the U.S. If this goal is reached and maintained for three years, the FWS will consider reclassifying the falcon to Threatened. The goal, however, is many years away.

Achieving a stable population of at least 200 breeding pairs in Mexico may require the elimination of DDT and DDE within the breeding range of the falcon.

Bibliography

Hector, D. P. 1980. "Our Rare Falcon of the Desert Grassland." *Birding* 12(3):92-102.

Hector, D. P. 1989. "Northern Aplomado Falcon Recovery Plan [Technical/Agency Review Draft]." U.S. Fish and Wildlife Service, Albuquerque.

Kiff, I. F., *et al.* 1978. "Eggshell Thinning and Organochlorine Residues in the Bats and Aplomado Falcons in Mexico." *Proceedings of the 17th International Ornithological Congress.* 1978:949-952.

Contact

Regional Office of Endangered Species
U.S. Fish and Wildlife Service
P.O. Box 1306
Albuquerque, New Mexico 87103

American Peregrine Falcon
Falco peregrinus anatum

Arctic Peregrine Falcon
Falco peregrinus tundrius

American Peregrine Falcon   Susan Middleton

Status	Endangered (American peregrine) Threatened (Arctic peregrine)
Listed	October 13, 1970
Family	Falconidae (Falcon)
Description . . .	Medium-sized raptor; dark above, streaked light below with black head and nape.
Habitat	Nests on cliffs and buildings.
Food	Birds.
Reproduction . .	Average clutch of 4 eggs.
Threats	Pesticides.
All Regions . . .	Entire continental U.S.

Description

The Peregrine falcon is a fast-flying bird of prey. It is 38 to 53 centimeters (15 to 21 in) long and has a wingspread of about 1.4 meters (3.75 ft). In flight it shows sharply pointed wings and a narrow tail. The peregrine is dark slate above with a broad black mustache and a black cap and nape. It has a white throat and upper breast. The tail is lightly banded. Immature birds are dark brown above, heavily streaked below. The Arctic subspecies is paler overall and has whiter underparts. Immatures have a pale brown forehead and a thinner mustache on the side of the head.

Throughout the world, numerous peregrine falcon subspecies, including the Eurasian peregrine (*Falco peregrinus peregrinus*), are Endangered.

Behavior

Peregrines normally breed at about three years of age. By mid-March birds begin pairing; eggs are laid in early April in the south and late April in the north. Clutch size is three to four eggs, which are incubated by both sexes for about 33 days. Males provide most of the prey during incubation. Young peregrines fledge in mid-June to mid-July and remain with parents for several additional weeks.

Peregrines travel up to 11 kilometers (7 mi) from their nest site to hunting areas, flying at speeds in excess of 96 kilometers per hour (60 mph) They prey on a wide variety of birds, striking victims from above with their talons after a high-speed dive.

Little is known about post-breeding movement, but peregrines are occasionally reported within their breeding range throughout the winter near large rivers or waterfowl refuges such as Monte Vista and Bear River National Wildlife Refuges in southern Colorado and northern Utah.

Habitat

Peregrines are found in a great variety of hunting habitats, such as grasslands, meadows, and open country. They prefer cliffs for nesting sites; reintroduced birds now regularly nest on high-rise buildings and bridges in metropolitan areas.

Historic Range

Historically, peregrines have ranged throughout the world, wherever prey has been abundant. In North America the American peregrine nested from central Alaska across north central Canada and south to Central Mexico. The Arctic peregrine nested from northern Alaska to Greenland. Both subspecies winter in South and Central America. The American peregrine also winters along the Pacific coast from British Columbia southward.

The species has been present in the U.S. for at least 30,000 years. Fossil remains have been found at the LaBrea Tar Pits in California, where Pleistocene remains are believed to range from 5,000 to 40,000 years in age. Peregrine remains have also been found in Indian caves and middens.

Historic records indicate that the peregrine has been only locally common throughout the United States. In the 1930s and 1940s there were at least 210 active nests and about 350

pairs throughout the eastern U.S. By the mid-1960s the peregrine was extirpated from the East as a breeding species. All breeding pairs in the East since the 1960s are the result of an ambitious effort to reestablish the species through the release of captive-bred birds.

In 1973 it was estimated that there were between 250 and 350 active aeries (nests and broods) in the western U.S. As of 1983, somewhat more than 200 of these aeries survived.

Current Distribution

The peregrine falcon has been successfully reestablished as a breeding species in the eastern U.S. and populations have increased throughout the western U.S. and in Alaska. According to the Peregrine Fund there are at present about 100 breeding pairs of peregrines in the East, about 18 in the Midwest, and around 400 in the western U.S.

Populations of the Arctic peregrine have also increased in recent years. It is believed that by the mid-1970s, the number of nesting pairs had decreased some 30 percent from an estimated historic high of 150 pairs. Surveys in Alaska during 1989 documented 85 nesting pairs, leading to an estimate of at least 150 to 175 actual breeding pairs. According to the Fish and Wildlife Service (FWS), the Arctic peregrine falcon population continues to increase and is approaching its historic level. The FWS is currently evaluating whether to remove the Arctic peregrine from the list of Threatened and Endangered species.

Conservation and Recovery

The increased use of pesticides, especially DDT, after 1950 was the major cause of peregrine decline in the U.S. DDT causes eggshell thinning in many birds, and was the major cause of low peregrine reproduction.

Although banned in the U.S. in 1972, DDT is still used in many parts of the world.

Because the range of the peregrine includes the entire continental U.S., the FWS has developed regional recovery plans. The eastern-region plan is concerned with reestablishing the extirpated population; the West Coast plan is concerned with protecting existing aeries; and the Rocky Mountain/Southwest plan is aimed at reintroduction of the falcon in the northern Rocky Mountain states, augmenting existing pairs with introduced peregrines in the central Rocky Mountain states, and monitoring and protecting the species in the southwestern states.

Recovery efforts also concentrate on expanding the captive breeding and release program. Captive breeding technology is now well beyond the experimental stage. A large breeding stock of American peregrine falcons is available, and extensive release programs are in operation. The principal propagation center in the East has been the Peregrine Fund at Cornell University. Peregrines were produced there from 1973 through 1985. In 1986, the captive flock was moved to Boise, Idaho, where it continues to provide young for release in the eastern U.S.

The Peregrine Fund, a private conservation organization dedicated to saving the species, has released about 3,000 captive-bred peregrines since the early 1970s. Federal and state agencies, together with private conservation groups such as the Peregrine Fund, have initiated release programs throughout the country. While most reintroductions have taken place in wilderness areas, some have taken advantage of the peregrine's ability to nest on bridges and urban high-rises. Captive-bred birds have been released in a number of U.S. cities, including Milwaukee, Wisconsin; Salt Lake City, Utah; Albany, New York; and Baltimore, Maryland. Five

baby peregrines were sent to anesting box on top of the Guardian Building in Detroit as part of the reintroduction effort in the Midwest.

Peregrines have also been found nesting on top of the Throgs Neck bridge on Long Island, New York. The presence of these urban raptors often stimulates local interest in preservation and passing motorists occasionally tie up traffic to rescue a fallen nestling.

Bibliography

Cade, T. J. 1982. *The Falcons of the World.* Cornell University Press, Ithaca, New York.

Craig. G. 1986. "Peregrine Falcon." In R. L. DiSilvestro, ed., *Audubon Wildlife Report 1986.* National Audubon Society, New York.

Ratcliffe, D. A. 1980. *The Peregrine Falcon.* Buteo Books, Vermillion, South Dakota.

U.S. Fish and Wildlife Service. 1987. "Revised Peregrine Falcon, Eastern Population Recovery Plan." U.S. Fish and Wildlife Service, Newton Corner, Massachusetts.

U.S. Fish and Wildlife Service. 1982. "Pacific Coast American Peregrine Falcon Recovery Plan." U.S. Fish and Wildlife Service.

U.S. Fish and Wildlife Service. 1984. "American Peregrine Falcon Recovery Plan (Rocky Mountain/Southwest Population)." U.S. Fish and Wildlife Service. Denver.

U.S. Fish and Wildlife Service. 1982. "Recovery Plan for the Peregrine Falcon—Alaska Population." U.S. Fish and Wildlife Service.

Contact

Regional Office of Endangered Species
U.S. Fish and Wildlife Service
One Gateway Center, Suite 700
Newton Corner, Massachusetts 02158

Regional Office of Endangered Species
U.S. Fish and Wildlife Service
Lloyd 500 Building, Suite 1692
500 N.E. Multnomah Street
Portland, Oregon 97232

Hawaiian Coot
Fulica americana alai

Robert J. Shallenberger

Status	Endangered
Listed	October 13, 1970
Family	Rallidae (Rails and Coots)
Description	Slate-gray waterbird with a white frontal shield.
Habitat	Wetlands.
Food	Aquatic plants, crustaceans, insects.
Reproduction	Clutch of 4 to 6 eggs.
Threats	Habitat loss.
Region 1	Hawaii

Description

The Hawaiian coot is a subspecies of the American coot, a common North American waterbird. The Hawaiian coot is smaller in body size, 33 to 40 centimeters (13 to 16 in) in length, and has dark slate-gray plumage and conspicuous white undertail feathers. The bill extends up the front of the head to form a prominent white frontal shield. In a small number of Hawaiian coots (15 percent) the frontal shield is red. The sexes are alike in appearance. This bird is known by the Hawaiian name "alae ke'o ke'o."

Behavior

The coot nests in ponds and reservoirs, irrigation ditches, and openings among marsh vegetation. Nesting occurs mostly from March through September and appears to be triggered by local habitat conditions, such as water levels. Some breeding occurs year round. The coot builds its nest from aquatic vegetation, anchoring it to clumps of emergent plants. Nests may occasionally be free floating. Clutch size averages between four and six eggs. Incubation lasts from 23 to 27 days. Chicks leave the nest soon after hatching.

Coots often build additional false nests near the actual nest and use these as loafing or brooding platforms. Coots prefer to feed close to nests but will fly long distances when food is scarce locally. They dive for food or forage in mud and sand, feeding on seeds and leaves of aquatic plants, snails, crustaceans, small fish, tadpoles, and insects.

In general, coots are noisy and aggresively territorial. The male reacts first to drive other coots away, but in his absence the female will confront intruders. Confrontation sometimes leads to outright violence. Coots rapidly charge across the water with wings flapping and attempt to upend an intruder by rearing back, grabbing at the neck with one clawed foot and striking out with the other, all the while making sharp jabs with the bill. The winner of the contest will then attempt to hold the other bird under water. This sharply anti-social behavior explains the use of the colloquialism—"old coot"—to describe a misanthropic person.

Social conflict, however, is tempered by the coot's large repertoire of displays employed to communicate non-hostile intentions. It signals with body posturing, the positioning of tail feathers or wings, and the angle of the neck feathers. When aroused it can inflate its frontal sheild, and when threatened by predators or human intruders, it erects its feathers to appear much larger than it is.

Habitat

Hawaiian coots inhabit a variety of freshwater and brackish wetlands, including lakes, tidal ponds, and marshes where vegetation is interspersed with open shallows. Coots generally prefer more open water than gallinules, particularly for feeding, but some plant cover is necessary for protection from predators. Coots nest only where water levels are stable and will avoid salt water. Pristine habitat may support as many as 24 coots per hectare (10 per acre) during the non-breeding season. Most suitable wetlands are near the coastline below 200 meters (660 ft) in elevation.

Historic Range

This species was once found on all the larger Hawaiian islands except Lanai and Kahoolawe, which apparently lacked suitable waterbird habitat.

Current Distribution

Coots are most numerous on Oahu, Maui, and Kauai. Censuses from the late 1950s to the late 1960s indicated a population of less than 1,000. Since then populations have gradually increased to an average of 1,840 birds, as surveyed from 1980 through 1986.

Conservation and Recovery

Loss of both natural and cultivated wetland sites, such as taro fields, has been the primary cause for the decline of the coot and other Hawaiian waterbirds. Once a staple of Hawaiian agriculture, wet taro fields have nearly all been replaced by dry sugarcane fields. Today only about 200 hectares (500 acres) of taro or other wetland crops remain on the islands. Other wetlands have been filled to construct hotels and other commercial and residential development. Encroaching non-native plants, such as California grass, water hyacinth, and mangrove, have degraded remaining wetlands.

A century ago, Hawaii's endemic waterbirds were nominally protected by the law because of their role in controlling army worms, an agricultural pest. In 1952 Kanaha Pond on Maui was designated as the first state waterfowl sanctuary.

In 1972 the first national wildlife refuge for waterbirds, consisting of 371 hectares (917 acres), was acquired in Hanalei Valley on Kauai. Since that time, four additional wetland refuges have been established: Huleia, along the Huleia River on Kauai; Kakahaia on Molokai; Pearl Harbor on Oahu; and the James Campbell National Wildlife Refuge on Oahu. These refuges have enabled the Hawaiian coot to stabilize its population.

Bibliography

Byrd, G. V., *et al.* 1985. "Notes on the Breeding Biology of the Hawaiian Race of the American Coot." *Elepaio* 45(7):57-63.

Ehrlich, P. R., D. Dobkin, and D. Wheye. 1988. *The Birder's Handbook: A Field Guide to the Natural History of North American Birds.* Simon and Schuster, New York.

Ripley, S. D. 1977. *Rails of the World.* David R. Godine, Boston.

Ryan, M. R., and J. J. Dinsmore. 1980. "The Behavioral Ecology of Breeding American Coots in Relation to Age." *Condor* 82:320-327

U.S. Fish and Wildlife Service. 1985. "Recovery Plan for the Hawaiian Waterbirds." U.S. Fish and Wildlife Service, Portland.

Weller, M. W. 1980. *The Island Waterfowl.* The Iowa State University Press, Ames.

Contact

Regional Office of Endangered Species
U.S. Fish and Wildlife Service
Lloyd 500 Building, Suite 1692
500 N.E. Multnomah Street
Portland, Oregon 97232

Office of Environmental Services
U.S. Fish and Wildlife Service
300 Ala Moana Boulevard
P.O. Box 50167
Honolulu, Hawaii 96850

Hawaiian Common Moorhen
Gallinula chloropus sandvicensis

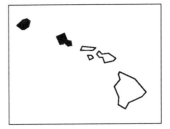

Robert J. Shallenberger

Status	Endangered
Listed	March 11, 1967
Family	Rallidae (Rails and Coots)
Description	Black waterbird; slate-blue beneath.
Habitat	Wetlands.
Food	Algae, insects, mollusks, aquatic plants.
Reproduction	Clutch of 6 or more eggs.
Threats	Habitat loss, predation.
Region 1	Hawaii

Description

Also commonly known as the Hawaiian gallinule, the Hawaiian common moorhen is a medium-sized waterbird, 30 to 35 centimeters (12 to 14 in) long. It is black above and slate-blue below with white dashes along the flank and white markings beneath the tail. Legs and feet are yellowish green with a red band (garter) around the upper leg. Sexes are similar in appearance. This waterbird is a subspecies of the common moorhen of North America and Eurasia. It is non-migratory and presumably originated from stray migrant mainland birds that colonized Hawaii. The Hawaiian name for the moorhen is "alae'ula."

Behavior

The reclusive moorhen generally nests in shallow water in areas of dense emergent vegetation. Plant tops are folded over and interwoven to create a platform nest. Although some breeding occurs year round, most nesting activity is from March through August, keyed to water levels and plant growth. Average clutch size is about six eggs but can be as high as 13. Chicks swim away from the nest shortly after hatching but depend upon the parents for several weeks.

The moorhen is an opportunistic feeder whose diet can include algae, aquatic insects, mollusks, seeds, and other plant matter.

Habitat

The Hawaiian moorhen nests and feeds in a variety of wetland habitats—freshwater ponds and reservoirs, marshes, taro patches, and beside streams or irrigation ditches—where there is dense vegetation. Salt or brackish water is generally avoided for nesting sites. Most of the moorhen's habitat occurs below 125 meters (400 ft) elevation.

Historic Range

In the 1800s, this waterbird was considered common on the main Hawaiian Islands, except for Lanai and Kahoolawe. By 1947 its status was precarious. Populations on Hawaii and Maui had been extirpated, and the Oahu population nearly so. Surveys in the 1950s and 1960s estimated that no more than 60 birds survived.

Current Distribution

Today the population numbers over 750 birds. About 500 are found on Kauai among taro fields on the Hanalei National Wildlife Refuge and in a bulrush marsh near the community of Paradise Pacific. About 250 birds are found on James Campbell National Wildlife Refuge and among the Haleiwa lotus fields on Oahu. A small population has recently been reintroduced to Molokai.

Conservation and Recovery

Loss of wetlands is the primary cause of the moorhen's overall decline. Historically, both natural coastal plain wetlands and flooded taro fields provided an abundance of habitat for waterbirds. As early as the 1850s significant losses in habitat began as dry crops, such as sugarcane, began to replace taro. Today, only about 200 hectares (500 acres) of

agricultural wetlands remain. Large tracts of natural wetlands were filled or drained to support development. Many former moorhen sites are occupied by hotels, commercial complexes, housing, and recreational facilities.

Non-native plants, such as California grass, water hyacinth, and mangrove, have been introduced into wetlands to the detriment of native plants. In most cases, introduced plants cannot be used by the moorhen. Mongooses and feral cats have preyed upon moorhen young and eggs.

In 1972 the first national wildlife refuge for waterbirds, consisting of some 371 hectares (917 acres), was established in Hanalei Valley on Kauai. Since then, four additional wetland refuges have been created: Huleia along the Huleia River (Kauai), Kakahaia (Molokai), Pearl Harbor, and the James Campbell National Wildlife Refuge (Oahu). Other wetlands are protected by conservation agreements. These refuges have been instrumental in enabling the moorhen population to return to its current levels.

Bibliography

U.S. Fish and Wildlife Service. 1985. "Recovery Plan for the Hawaiian Waterbirds." U.S. Fish and Wildlife Service, Portland.

Contact

Regional Office of Endangered Species
U.S. Fish and Wildlife Service
Lloyd 500 Building, Suite 1692
500 N.E. Multnomah Street
Portland, Oregon 97232

Office of Environmental Services
U.S. Fish and Wildlife Service
300 Ala Moana Boulevard
P.O. Box 50167
Honolulu, Hawaii 96850

Whooping Crane
Grus americana

C. Allan Morgan

Status	Endangered
Listed	March 11, 1967
Family	Gruidae (Crane)
Description . . .	Large wading bird with white plumage except for black primaries on wings; red facial skin.
Habitat	Wilderness wetlands.
Food	Crabs, clams.
Reproduction . .	Clutch of 2 eggs.
Threats	Diminished habitat.
Region 1 . . .	Idaho
Region 2 . . .	Texas, New Mexico
Region 6 . . .	Colorado, Utah

Description

The long-legged whooping crane is the tallest North American bird. Males stand 126 centimeters (4.5 ft) tall and weigh about 7.3 kilograms (16 lbs); females weigh slightly less. Adult "whoopers" are white overall, except for red facial skin on the crown and side of the head. Black wing primaries are prominent in flight. The bill is dark gray, becoming lighter as the breeding season approaches. Legs and feet are usually black. The whooping crane's closest relatives in North America are five races of the sandhill crane (*Grus canadensis*).

Behavior

The whooping crane is thought to reach sexual maturity between four and six years of age. It is a monogamous bird that forms a lifelong pair bond with its mate. Toward the end of winter, pre-mating behavior begins with an increase of dancing displays and a loosening of territoriality. Pairs begin arriving at the breeding grounds in late April, returning to the same nesting site year after year.

In late April or early May, the female lays two eggs, which are olive-buff and covered with dark, purplish brown blotches. Both parents share in the month-long incubation. The male sits on the nest during the day, the female at night. After a chick hatches, the family group stays close to the nest for about 20 days.

Whoopers migrate southward from mid-September, flying by day and stopping to feed and rest at night. By mid-November cranes have arrived at the wintering grounds, where they remain for six months. Until January, cranes feed almost exclusively on blue crabs foraged from flooded tidal flats and sloughs. By then, most flats and sloughs have drained, and cranes move into shallow bays and channels to forage on clams and an occasional blue crab. Whoopers swallow clams and small blue crabs whole. They carry larger crabs ashore and peck them into small pieces.

The whooping crane is extremely wary of intruders during breeding season and has a very low tolerance for human presence. Whoopers are noted for being easily disturbed by passing aircraft, but there is some evidence that the skittish birds are becoming more tolerant.

Habitat

Nests are constructed in dense emergent vegetation, which grows in marshes, sloughs, prairie potholes, or along lake margins within large, undisturbed tracts of wilderness. Bulrush (*Scirpus validus*) is the dominant plant. Cattail, sedge, musk-grass, reed bentgrass, spike rush, and other aquatic plants are also common. Currently used nesting habitat is poorly drained and interspersed with numerous potholes, most with a soft loamy bottom. Potholes are separated by narrow ridges, which support an overstory of black spruce, tamarack, and willow.

The crane's wintering grounds are salt flats, marshes, and barrier islands along the Texas coast. Marsh plants are dominated by salt grass, saltwort, popping cane, glasswort, and sea ox-eye. Inland margins of flats are dominated by Gulf cordgrass. Upland portions of the wintering habitat include sandy and gently rolling terrain, covered with live oak and redbay or long-stemmed grasses.

Historic Range

The whooping crane once ranged over most of North America, from the Arctic coast south to central Mexico, and from Utah east to New Jersey, South Carolina, and Florida. Within historic times, the breeding range extended northwest from central Illinois through Iowa, Minnesota, North Dakota, southern Manitoba and Saskatchewan, to the general vicinity of Edmonton, Alberta. Breeding populations of whooping cranes were gone from the north-central U.S. by the 1890s.

The principal historic wintering grounds were the tall grass prairies of southwestern Louisiana. Besides winter migrants, this region supported a small nonmigratory population around White Lake that was depleted by a severe storm in 1940. The last crane there was taken into captivity in 1950.

Whoopers wintered along the Gulf coast in Texas and northeastern Mexico, primarily in the Rio Grande Delta, but also in the interior tablelands of western Texas and high plateaus of central Mexico, areas shared with sandhill cranes.

Current Distribution

The last known nesting area for the Canadian population of whooping cranes is the Wood Buffalo National Park (Northwest Territories), between the headwaters of the Nyarling, Sass, Klewi, and Little Buffalo rivers. This population numbered 138 birds in 1989. Their wintering grounds are along the southern coast of Texas—the Aransas National Wildlife Refuge (NWR), Matagorda Island, Isla San Jose, portions of the Lamar Peninsula, and Welder Point (on the east side of San Antonio Bay).

A small breeding population of whooping cranes (15 to 20) has been introduced into the Gray's Lake NWR in Idaho. This population winters in New Mexico at the Bosque del Apache NWR and near Chihuahua, Mexico.

Experimental breeding populations are kept at the Patuxent Wildlife Research Center at Laurel, Maryland; at the International Crane Foundation in Baraboo, Wisconsin; and at the San Antonio Zoo. Including captive birds, the total population of the whooping crane is only about 300.

Conservation and Recovery

Conversion of the midwestern prairie pothole habitat to hay and grain fields rendered most of the whooping crane's original breeding range unsuitable, while increased human disturbance forced it from remaining nesting sites. From the 1870s to the 1920s, uncontrolled hunting took a large toll of whooping crane populations. When hunting was eventually stopped, cranes confronted a new threat—collision with power lines, which became the leading cause of whooping crane death.

Establishment of the Wood Buffalo National Park in 1922 by the Canadian government inadvertently assisted conservation of the whooping crane. The crane's breeding grounds within the park were not discovered until 1954. In 1937, the Aransas Wildlife Refuge in Texas was established to secure one of the last viable whooping crane wintering areas. These wintering grounds were initially damaged by oyster dredging (now prohibited) and are now suffering from slow but constant erosion.

An ongoing captive propagation effort was intensified in 1966 when the Patuxent Wildlife Research Center was established at Laurel, Maryland. Patuxent has propagated a captive flock, which numbers around 30. Eggs from this flock, as well as some collected from the Canadian population, have been added to sandhill crane nests at Gray's Lake NWR. The eggs are incubated and hatchlings raised by sandhill cranes, which serve as foster parents. When these whoopers reach sexual maturity, they form pair bonds with their own kind and reproduce.

In 1983, the Fish and Wildlife Service (FWS) recovery team began a survey of potential reintroduction sites in the eastern U.S. and has now narrowed the field to two prime candidates: southern Georgia's Okefenokee Swamp, and Florida's Kissimmee Prairie. Captive reared whoopers will be introduced into one of these areas, using techniques that have been proven in work with Mississippi sandhill cranes. The FWS expects to begin establishing an eastern population sometime in 1991.

The Canadian Wildlife Service published its Whooping Crane Recovery Plan in 1988; the plan complements FWS efforts and sets up the first recovery team ever organized for an endangered species in Canada. In cooperation with researchers at the Patuxent Wildlife Research Center, Canada plans to establish its own captive breeding population in 1990.

Bibliography

Allen, R. P. 1952, 1956. *The Whooping Crane.* Research Report Number 3, (and supplement) National Audubon Society, New York.

McNulty, F. 1966. *The Whooping Crane.* Dutton, New York.

U.S. Fish and Wildlife Service. 1986. "Whooping Crane Recovery Plan." U.S. Fish and Wildlife Service, Albuquerque.

Contact

Regional Office of Endangered Species
U.S. Fish and Wildlife Service
P.O. Box 1306
Albuquerque, New Mexico 87103

Mississippi Sandhill Crane
Grus canadensis pulla

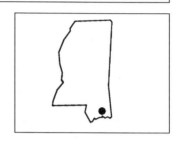

Donna Dewhurst/USFWS

Status	. . . . .	Endangered
Listed	. . . . .	June 4, 1973
Family	. . . .	Gruidae (Crane)
Description	. . .	Large wading bird; gray with red patch on crown.
Habitat	. . . . .	Wetlands.
Food	. . . . .	Omnivorous.
Reproduction	.	Clutch of 1 or 2 eggs.
Threats	. . . .	Habitat reduction.
Region 4	. . . .	Mississippi

Description

The sandhill crane is a large wading bird, between 86 and 121 centimeters (34 and 48 in) tall, with a wingspread up to 2.1 meters (7 ft). Like other cranes it is characterized by its long legs, neck, and bill. Adult coloring is mostly gray with dark legs and a bald, red crown and forehead. Immature birds have a tuft of feathers over the tail and no red markings. The Mississippi subspecies is visually distinguished from other sandhill cranes by its darker color.

Behavior

The sandhill crane feeds on reptiles, amphibians, insects, and aquatic plants. In winter it will feed in harvested grain fields. The sandhill crane flies with its neck ex-tended and with a slow wingbeat that has a distinctive flip on the upstroke. It is a gregarious bird, flying and roosting in groups. Courtship displays are elaborate and include grass tossing, loud calling, bowing and leaping, and running with outspread wings. After pairing, cranes select a breeding territory for courtship, mating, and nesting. Pairs defend a territory from other cranes and tend to use the same site year after year. Territory sizes vary greatly between 36 and 202 hectares (90 and 500 acres). Clutch size is one or two eggs, which hatch around May. Cranes will often nest again if a first nesting attempt fails.

Habitat

Mississippi sandhill cranes nest in open savannas, swamp edges, young pine plantations, and along the edges of pine forests where rainfall drainage forms shallow wetlands. Trees associated with this habitat include longleaf pine, slash pine, and bald cypress. Shrubs include gallberry, wax myrtle, black gum, sweet bay, and yaupon.

Historic Range

Small populations of sandhill cranes were once found in widely separated areas along the Gulf coastal plain of Louisiana, Mississippi, Alabama, and Florida. Cranes may have bred in the savannas just east of the Pascagoula River in Mississippi in the early part of the century. Population in the late 1920s was estimated to be about 100 cranes.

Current Distribution

The Mississippi sandhill crane is now confined to an area of southern Jackson County, Mississippi, extending from the Pascagoula River west to the Jackson County line. The southern limit is Simmons Bayou and the northern is an east-west line about four miles north of Vancleave. Part of this area is within the Mississippi Sandhill Crane National Wildlife Refuge. The main winter roost is in the Bluff Creek, Bayou Castelle, and Paige Bayou marshes. The 1983 population in the wild was estimated to be about 40 individuals. By 1989, the population had climbed to about 60 cranes, mostly through the introduction of captive-bred cranes.

Conservation and Recovery

By the early part of this century, the majority of the Gulf coast's old-growth longleaf pine forests had been harvested. In the 1950s timber companies established pine plantations in the area, greatly changing the natural growth patterns of native vegetation. Drainage ditches, access roads, and fire

breaks were added, eliminating large areas of crane habitat. Three east-to-west highways cross the crane's present range, including Interstate Highway I-10. These highways increase habitat disturbance and have encouraged commercial and residential development of portions of the crane's remaining habitat. Hurricanes periodically sweep through the region, bringing heavy rains and flood tides that destroy nests and drown chicks.

The Nature Conservancy initiated establishment of the crane refuges by acquiring a tract of 692 hectares (1,709 acres), which was then augmented by further purchases and donations. The Mississippi Sandhill Crane National Wildlife Refuge, administered by the Fish and Wildlife Service, now totals nearly 7,285 hectares (18,000 acres).

In spite of this protection, the wild population has been unable to naturally increase the size of the flock. For unknown reasons, newly hatched cranes exhibit an abnormally high mortality rate. When researchers discovered that removing one egg from a two-egg nest did not diminish the overall survival rate of chicks and fledglings, they began taking second eggs to bolster the captive propagation program. Since 1966, an average of three eggs per year have been collected from the wild and incubated at the Patuxent, Maryland, wildlife facility to create a captive flock of breeding cranes. In 1989 the captive flock totaled 28 cranes. Each December about ten captive-reared cranes are released on the refuge. The success of this effort has been crucial for the survival of the Mississippi sandhill crane. The long-term goal for recovery is to establish a stable population of at least 100 cranes, including 30 breeding pairs.

During the 1970s, litigation over construction of an I-10 interchange and closure of thousands of acres of refuge land to deer hunters generated a great deal of local hostility toward the crane. Recipes for cooking sandhills were published in local newspapers. Since then, resentment has cooled, and public opinion seems to be coming around to the crane's side. The City of Gautier police department recently adopted the Mississippi sandhill crane as its emblem, which is prominently displayed on the sides of its cruisers.

Bibliography

Aldrich, J. 1972. "A New Subspecies of Sandhill Cranes from Mississippi." *Proceedings of the Biological Society of Washington* 85(5):53:70.

U.S. Fish and Wildlife Service. 1984. "Recovery Plan for the Mississippi Sandhill Crane, *Grus canadensis pulla*." U. S. Fish and Wildlife Service, Atlanta.

Valentine, J. M. 1981. "Breeding Ecology of the Misissippi Sandhill Crane in Jackson County, Mississippi." In J. C. Lewis, ed., *Proceedings of the 1981 Crane Workshop*. National Audubon Society, Tavernier, Florida.

Valentine, J. M., and R. E. Noble. 1970. "A Colony of Sandhill Cranes in Mississippi." *Journal of Wildlife Management* 34:761- 768.

Contact

Regional Office of Endangered Species
U.S. Fish and Wildlife Service
Richard B. Russell Federal Building
75 Spring Street, S.W.
Atlanta, Georgia 30303

California Condor
Gymnogyps californianus

Glen Smart/USFWS

Status	Endangered (Extinct in the wild)
Listed	March 11, 1967
Family	Cathartidae (New World Vulture)
Description	Large vulture; dark plumage and a naked, orange head.
Habitat	Isolated rocky cliffs.
Food	Carrion.
Reproduction	Clutch of 1 egg.
Threats	Low numbers.
Region 1	California

Description

California condors are among the largest flying birds in the world. Adults weigh approximately 9 kilograms (19.8 lbs) and have a wingspan up to 2.75 meters (9.1 ft). Adults are black except for white underwing linings and edges. The head and neck are mostly naked; the skin on the neck is gray, grading into shades of yellow, red, and orange on the head. Males and females cannot be distinguished by size or plumage.

Birds need five or six years to attain adult characteristics. Sub-adults go through a "ring-neck" stage, lasting from two to four years, during which the neck is ringed by feathers, the head is grayish black, and the wing linings are mottled. Immatures gradually acquire adult coloration.

The California condor is a member of the family of New World vultures (Cathartidae), a family of seven species that includes the closely related Andean condor and the turkey vulture.

Behavior

The California condor feeds on the carcasses of deer, elk, pronghorn, and smaller mammals. Livestock carcasses constituted a major food source that became increasingly important as other prey species declined. Adult California condors have no known natural enemies and can live as long as 45 years. They are capable of sustained flight speeds of between 70 and 95 kilometers per hour (45 and 60 mph) and may fly up to 225 kilometers (140 mi) a day between roosts and foraging grounds.

Condor pairs begin mating and selecting nesting sites in December, although many pairs wait until late spring. The female condor lays a single egg, which is then incubated by both parents for about 56 days. Condors sometimes lay a second egg to replace an egg that is lost or broken. Both parents share in daily feeding for the first two months and then decrease the frequency of their visits to the nest. The chick fledges at about six months of age but does not become fully independent until the following year. Parent birds sometimes continue to feed the chick even after it has begun its own flights to foraging grounds. Birds reach sexual maturity at about eight years of age.

Immature condors are especially mobile. In one year an immature condor fitted with a radio transmitter foraged and roosted in five different California counties in both the coastal and inland mountain ranges. Because of the long period of parental care, it has been assumed that condor pairs nest every other year. This pattern seems to vary, however, depending on the abundance of food and on the time of year that the nestling fledges.

Habitat

The California condor nests in caves, crevices, and potholes in isolated rocky cliffs of the Pacific Coast and Transverse mountain ranges. It roosts in dead snags or tall open-branched trees near important foraging grounds. The condor commonly perches until mid-morning, preening and grooming itself. It then soars off in search of carrion, returning to the roost site in the late afternoon.

Most condors forage in open grassland and oak-savanna habitats, primarily in the foothills surrounding the southern San Joa-

quin Valley. To ensure easy take-off and approach, the condor requires fairly open terrain for feeding. Condors regularly locate food by the presence of other birds, such as eagles and ravens.

Historic Range

The fossil record of the California condor goes back 100,000 years and indicates that the species once ranged over much of western North America, from British Columbia to northern Baja California, and east along the coast to Florida. Condors nested in west Texas, Arizona, and New Mexico until about 2,000 years ago. Condors lived in the Pacific Northwest until the 1800s, and in northern Baja California until the early 1930s.

Current Distribution

By the 1960s the California condor population had declined to no more than 60 birds. By the early 1980s only about 25 birds survived. Currently, no California condors are living in the wild.

Conservation and Recovery

Causes of condor decline have been diverse and difficult to document. It appears that most are related to mortality factors, such as poisoning, shooting, and collisions with power lines, rather than reproductive failure. Records suggest that the condor's nesting success over the past 40 years has been about 50 percent, which compares favorably with several other species of vultures that are not endangered.

The use of pesticides and other poisons in California has certainly contributed to condor mortality. Because it feeds on carcasses, the condor often ingests the poisons that killed the prey, such as DDT, cyanide, or strychnine. Condors have been known to suffer from lead poisoning after ingesting pellets from animals killed by hunters. Levels of ingested poisons may not be fatal to adults but will kill chicks and immature birds.

The first organized effort to protect the California condor began in 1937 when the Sissquoc Condor Sactuary was established in Santa Barbara County. A second, larger sanctuary was established in 1947 in Los Padres National Forest in Ventura County and now consists of 21,450 hectares (53,000 acres). But these and subsequent private, state, and federal efforts—expanding legal protection, closing nesting sites to the public, restricting road and air traffic near nesting sites, setting up new sanctuaries—did little to stem condor decline.

In 1978 a panel appointed by the American Ornithologists' Union and the National Audubon Society recommended an aggressive program of trapping condors for captive breeding and telemetry studies. A condor research center was established in 1980.

Telemetry studies in the early 1980s revealed that all remaining condors in the wild at that time belonged to a single breeding population. In 1982, eight of these condors were brought into captivity to join a condor that had been in the San Diego Zoo since 1967. Six fledglings were taken captive in 1983 in an attempt to stimulate second nestings in the wild.

When four of the last five California condor breeding pairs in the wild disappeared for unknown reasons over the winter of 1984-1985, the Fish and Wildlife Service decided to capture the last wild birds for the captive breeding program. This drastic and controversial action was considered necessary to prevent extinction of the species. Many scientists were of the opinion that more remained to be done in the field and that capture of the wild birds was premature. It was also a con-siderable gamble because no chicks had yet been hatched in captivity.

The last free-flying condor was captured on the Bitter Creek National Wildlife Refuge in 1987, bringing the total known population to 27 birds—14 birds in special breeding facilities at the San Diego Wild Animal Park, and 13 at the Los Angeles Zoo.

In April 1988, the first condor chick ever conceived in captivity was hatched in an incubation chamber at San Diego Wild Animal Park. The chick was named Molloko, a Maidu Indian word meaning "condor." A second captive-bred chick was successfully hatched at the San Diego facility in April 1989, and additional fertile eggs are being incubated.

Naturalists hope that this signals a turning point in their efforts to save the California condor. Eventually, captive-bred birds will be returned to suitable habitat in the wild. The release schedule will depend on the success of captive breeding efforts and finding a correct reintroduction strategy. Reintroduction experiments are now under way in southern California, using captive-bred Andean condors.

Bibliography

Ogden, J. C. 1985. "The California Condor." In R. L. Di Silvestro, ed., *Audubon Wildlife Report* 1985. National Audubon Society, New York.

U.S. Fish and Wildlife Service. 1984. "Revised California Condor Recovery Plan." U.S Fish and Wildlife Service, Portland.

Contact

Regional Office of Endangered Species
U.S. Fish and Wildlife Service
Lloyd 500 Building, Suite 1692
500 N.E. Multnomah Street
Portland, Oregon 97232

Bald Eagle
Haliaeetus leucocephalus

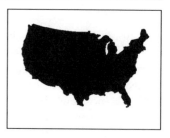

Frank J. Gallo

Status	Threatened (Michigan, Minnesota, Oregon, Washington, Wisconsin) Endangered (Other continental U.S.) Unclassified (Alaska)
Listed	March 11, 1967
Family	Accipitriidae (Eagles and Hawks)
Description	Dark brown with white head and tail; massive yellow, hooked bill.
Habitat	Mature conifer forests near open water.
Food	Fish, small mammals, carrion.
Reproduction	Clutch of 2 eggs.
Threats	Pesticides, shooting, human encroachment.
All Regions	United States
Canada	Western provinces

Description

The bald eagle is a large, majestic bird of prey, with a barrel-shaped body between 80 and 100 centimeters (32 and 40 in) long, and a wingspan that reaches 2.3 meters (7.5 ft). Adult birds are dark brown to black with a white head and tail. The massive, hooked bill and legs are yellow. Immature birds, which are dark brown with mottled white wings, are often mistaken for golden eagles. Immatures gradually acquire the distinctive white head and tail in their fourth year.

Behavior

The bald eagle feeds primarily on fish but will also eat rodents, other small mammals, and carrion. The bald eagle circles when hunting, scanning the ground with its sharp eyesight and swooping suddenly to take its prey. Adopted as the national bird in 1782 because of its fierce, independent demeanor, the bald eagle is actually rather timid.

Bald eagles are thought to mate for life. They display a spectacular courtship ritual that includes high speed dives and descending somersaults; mating birds often lock talons in mid-air. After pairing, the birds construct a nest in the fork of a tall tree or on a cliffside, often as high as 21 meters (70 ft) off the ground. The nest is a massive structure of sticks, branches, and foliage, and is lined with a deep layer of finer materials. Used and added to year after year, nests can grow to enormous sizes. One 19th-century nest in Ohio measured 3.7 meters (12 ft) deep and 2.7 meters (9 ft) in diameter.

Females lay a clutch of two eggs as early as October in southern breeding areas and as late as mid-March in the north. Both parents incubate the eggs for about 35 days and share feeding duties for about three months until the chicks can fly and hunt on their own. The adult eagles then drive fledglings from the nest.

Most bald eagles in Canada and the northern U.S. move south in the fall. As a result, thousands are present in the lower 48 states from November through March. The National Wildlife Federation, which conducts an annual count, reported in 1988 that there were 11,241 wintering bald eagles throughout the country, mostly in the West and Midwest. At night groups of these wintering birds gather in communal tree roosts, which, like nests, are used in successive years.

Habitat

Bald eagle habitat varies greatly throughout its range. Generally, nesting eagles are associated with mature, secluded forests (particularly conifers) where there are flowing streams, areas of open water, and abundant fish. Eagle nests have been found in various mature trees, such as ponderosa and loblolly pines, cottonwoods, oaks, poplars, and beech.

Historic Range

Records show that bald eagles once nested in most of North America—in Canada, Alaska, and at least 45 of the lower 48 states. In some states, decline in the numbers of nesting bald eagles was already well under way in the 19th century. In other states, significant decline probably did not occur until the 1940s.

Current Distribution

Alaska is home for the largest population of bald eagles in North America, an estimated 30,000 individuals. Another large population, claimed by some researchers to approach the Alaskan population in size, breeds in Canada's western provinces. These populations are considered stable and healthy.

In the lower 48 states, 2,440 breeding pairs nested in 1988, according to the Fish and Wildlife Service (FWS). The greatest concentrations are found in the Pacific Northwest, the upper Great Lakes, Florida, and around the Chesapeake Bay.

Of the 696 breeding pairs in the Pacific Northwest, the largest number is found in Washington (305 pairs). There, bald eagles nest on the San Juan Islands and the Olympic Peninsula coastline. In Oregon 150 pairs nest in the Klamath Basin, near lakes in the high Cascades, and along the coastline and the lower Columbia River.

In the northern and Great Plains states (New England west to Colorado and Utah) 1,011 pairs nested in 1988, principally in Minnesota, Wisconsin, and Michigan. The bald eagle population in the Southeast (531 pairs in 1988) is concentrated in Florida (399). Around the Chesapeake Bay, 181 pairs nested in Maryland, Delaware, and Virginia.

Conservation and Recovery

In the 1940s, after a long and steady decline in bald eagle numbers caused by shooting, alteration of habitat, and human encroachment into the wilderness, the pesticide DDT was introduced into the environment. Pesticide residues worked their way up the food chain and accumulated in the tissues of larger predators. Some birds, including the peregrine falcon and the bald eagle, began laying eggs with abnormally thin shells. These eggs were unable to bear the weight of the incubating adult birds and broke. The bald eagle suffered an abrupt population crash and disappeared from many states. By 1981, occupied nests were known in only 30 states, and about 90 percent of nesting pairs were concentrated in just ten states.

Between 1960 and 1973 nesting bald eagles disappeared from 18 of 44 Michigan counties. The Chesapeake Bay population fell from 150 pairs in 1962 to about 85 pairs in 1970. Nesting pairs disappeared from the upper portions of rivers and were greatly reduced at the upper end of the bay. Bald eagles were once common nesters along the Atlantic coast from the Chesapeake Bay to the Florida Keys, but by the late 1970s the Florida population alone was secure, and that had been reduced by half.

When DDT was banned in the U.S. in the early 1970s, the eagle's reproduction at once began to improve. Recovery was assisted by intensive efforts by federal agencies that included systematic monitoring, enhanced protection, captive breeding, relocation of wild birds, and a far-flung publicity program. State agencies became increasingly involved through tax-funded programs to monitor eagle nests and assist reintroduction projects. The Nature Conservancy and the National Wildlife Federation acquired important nesting sites and wintering habitat, and actively pursued conservation agreements with landowners. The combined efforts paid off.

By 1980 and 1981 the nesting population in the lower 48 states had doubled. The rebound has continued so strongly that the FWS is currently in the process of reclassifying part or all of the bald eagle populations in the lower 48 states from Endangered to Threatened.

In recent years, the relocation of wild chicks has been widely used to help the bald eagle recolonize its former range. Chicks are taken from nests in Alaska or Canada and released in states with few nesting eagles. Relocation has succeeded in many states, including Pennsylvania, New York, and Indiana, and has enabled the FWS to end its bald eagle captive breeding program.

Although the bald eagle seems well on the way to recovery, it still faces a number of threats. Illegal shooting is the most frequently recorded cause of eagle mortality, although the rate of shooting deaths has declined in recent years. The National Wildlife Federation offers a $500 reward for information leading to the conviction of persons shooting eagles. Some birds continue to die from lead poisoning contracted by feeding on pellet-killed carrion.

Collision with power lines and electrocution are other causes of bald eagle mortality. To counter these, power companies, particularly in the Northwest, have begun extensive design changes aimed at reducing eagle deaths. In recent years, privately sponsored rehabilitation facilities have been established to treat injured eagles and return them to the wild.

In addition to population increases, the return of bald eagles to abandoned breeding grounds gives conservationists reason to cheer. In 1987, a bald eagle nest in Tennessee produced young for the first time since breeding eagles disappeared from the state decades ago; in 1989 there were 11 active nests in Tennessee. And that same year saw the first recorded instance of bald eagles nesting in Kansas.

The recovery of the bald eagle has not occurred without controversy, however. In December 1988 the General Accounting Office issued a study that was sharply critical of the management of the federal Endangered Species Program. The study concluded that the FWS and the Interior Department concentrated an undue amount of resources into the recovery of several high-profile species, such as the bald eagle and the black-footed ferret, while ignoring many species of plants and animals that have less public appeal but are more immediately in danger of extinction. The highly publicized recovery of the bald eagle was an effort, concluded the report, to indulge public tastes at the expense of scientific priorities.

The FWS is in the process of downlisting the bald eagle, which should encourage a restructuring of priorities and a reapportioning of resources. There is little doubt that the success story of the bald eagle will strengthen the hand of the FWS as it shifts its attention to lesser known or appreciated species that are threatened with extinction.

In June 1989, the Interior Department created a new wildlife refuge for the Florida panther and other endangered species in south Florida. The 12,140-hectare (30,000-acre) Florida Panther National Wildlife Refuge is adjacent to the Big Cypress National Preserve and provides protected habitat for the Endangered wood stork (*Mycteria americana*), Everglade snail kite (*Rostrhamus sociabilis plumbeus*), red-cockaded woodpecker (*Picoides borealis*), peregrine falcon (*Falco peregrinus anatum*), and eastern indigo snake (*Drymarchon corais couperi*), as well as the south Florida bald eagle population.

Bibliography

Dunstan, T. C. 1978. "Our Bald Eagle: Freedom's Symbol Survives." *National Geographic* 153(2):186-199.

Fischer, D. L. 1985. "Piracy Behavior of Wintering Bald Eagles." *Condor* 87:245-251.

General Accounting Office. 1988. "Endangered Species: Management Improvements Could Enhance Recovery Program." GAO/RCED-89-5. General Accounting Office, Washington, D.C.

Green, N. 1985. "The Bald Eagle." In R. L. Di Silvestro, ed., *Audubon Wildlife Report 1985*. National Audubon Society, New York.

Contact

Regional Office of Endangered Species
U.S. Fish and Wildlife Service
Lloyd 500 Building, Suite 1692
500 N.E. Multnomah Street
Portland, Oregon 97232

Regional Office of Endangered Species
U.S. Fish and Wildlife Service
P.O. Box 1306
Albuquerque, New Mexico 87103

Regional Office of Endangered Species
U.S. Fish and Wildlife Service
Federal Building, Fort Snelling
Twin Cities, Minnesota 55111

Regional Office of Endangered Species
U.S. Fish and Wildlife Service
Richard B. Russell Federal Building
75 Spring Street, S.W.
Atlanta, Georgia 30303

Regional Office of Endangered Species
U.S. Fish and Wildlife Service
One Gateway Center, Suite 700
Newton Corner, Massachusetts 02158

Regional Office of Endangered Species
U.S. Fish and Wildlife Service
P.O. Box 25486
Denver Federal Center
Denver, Colorado 80225

Kauai Nukupuu
Hemignathus lucidus hanapepe

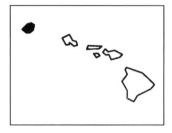

H. Douglas Pratt

Status	Endangered
Listed	March 11, 1967
Family	Fringillidae; Subfamily Drepanidinae (Hawaiian Honeycreeper)
Description	Honeycreeper with long downcurved bill; male olive above with yellow head; female green-gray above.
Habitat	Dense, wet forest.
Food	Insects and larvae.
Reproduction	Clutch size unknown.
Threats	Low numbers, deforestation, predation.
Region 1	Hawaii

Description

The rare Kauai nukupuu, a honeycreeper about 14 centimeters (5.5 in) long, has a downcurved, sickle-shaped bill up to 3 centimeters (1.2 in) long. The upper mandible is twice the length of the lower. The male is olive above with a yellow head and underparts. The female is gray-green above. Both sexes have a black lore patch (the area between the bill and the eye).

Discovered on Kauai by S. B. Wilson in 1887, the Kauai nukupuu is one of three subspecies of *Hemignathus lucidus*. The Maui subspecies, *H. l. affinis*, survives in small numbers. The race on Oahu, *H. l. lucidus*, is extinct.

Behavior

The nukupuu gleans caterpillars, insects, and larvae from tree trunks and branches. Nothing is known of its breeding biology.

Habitat

Kauai, the fourth largest of the Hawaiian Islands, has a land area of 143,240 hectares (553 sq mi). The highest peaks—Kawaikini (1,573 m; 5,243 ft) and Mt. Waialeale (1,544 m; 5,148 ft)—are found near the center of the island. Dominant native trees are the ohia (*Metrosideros collina*) and the koa (*Acacia koa*). Mixed ohia-koa forests are found on about 34,400 hectares (85,500 acres). The island's volcanic slopes and plateaus are checkered with eucalyptus and pine plantations.

The Alakai Swamp, at 1,200 meters (4,000 ft) elevation, is the primary habitat of the nukupuu. Annual rainfall is between 380 and 508 centimeters (150 and 200 in) along the Wainiha Pali (cliff) on the east, but only 127 centimeters (50 in) on the western side next to the Waimea Canyon.

Historic Range

The nukupuu, found on both Kauai and Hawaii, has always been extremely rare. It was considered scarce in the late 19th century, and only four sightings have been made in this century.

Current Distribution

The nukupuu is known to nest in koa trees in the Kokee area and along both sides of the Waimea Canyon on Kauai. It was recently reported from Kohala Mountain on the island of Hawaii where it had not been seen since the 1800s. Nukupuu's close relative, *H. l. affinis*, inhabits the upper northeast slope of Haleakala on Maui. A recent estimate placed the total number of surviving birds of both subspecies at less than 50.

Conservation and Recovery

Deforestation of Kauai was rapid and severe in the early part of this century when land was cleared for agriculture, and forest bird populations declined in direct proportion. Stands of native forest trees are now concentrated at higher elevations and in remote interior valleys. Only about half of the remaining forest is considered undisturbed.

Rooting, browsing, and trampling by feral pigs and goats have been recognized as problems since the 1930s. The activities of these animals are detrimental to most native plants and encourage the establishment of non-native, weedy varieties.

Predation by the introduced black rat undoubtedly threatens the rare nukupuu and other endangered Hawaiian forest birds. This rat is found on almost every forested mountain on Kauai and is able to climb trees in search of eggs and young birds. A number of recent sightings have fueled fears that another efficient bird predator—the mongoose—is becoming established on the island.

In 1964, 4,023 hectares (9,940 acres) of the Alakai Swamp were set aside to establish the Alakai Wilderness Preserve. This preserve encompasses the nukupuu's primary habitat. The Fish and Wildlife Service Recovery Plan identifies an area of about 7,890 hectares (19,500 acres) that is considered essential for the survival of forest birds on Kauai. Most of this area is currently under control of the Hawaii Division of Forestry and Wildlife.

Bibliography

Scott, J. M., *et al.* 1988. "Conservation of Hawaii's Vanishing Avifauna." *Bioscience.* 38(4):238-253.

U.S. Fish and Wildlife Service. 1983. "Kauai Forest Birds Recovery Plan." U.S. Fish and Wildlife Service, Portland.

Contact

Regional Office of Endangered Species
U.S. Fish and Wildlife Service
Lloyd 500 Building, Suite 1692
500 N.E. Multnomah Street
Portland, Oregon 97232

Office of Environmental Services
U.S. Fish and Wildlife Service
300 Ala Moana Boulevard
P.O. Box 50167
Honolulu, Hawaii 96850

Akiapolaau
Hemignathus munroi

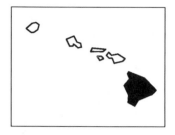

H. Douglas Pratt

Status	Endangered
Listed	March 11, 1967
Family	Fringillidae; Subfamily Drepanidinae (Hawaiian Honeycreeper)
Description	Honeycreeper with a long sickle-shaped bill; males are green with yellow head and underparts; females entirely greenish yellow.
Habitat	Ohia-koa and mamane-naio forests.
Food	Insects.
Reproduction	Few young.
Threats	Deforestation, predators.
Region 1	Hawaii

Description

The akiapolaau is a chunky-bodied honeycreeper, about 14 centimeters (6 in) long and weighing about 29 grams (1 oz). The green-backed male has a yellow head and underparts. The female is a uniform greenish yellow. The species has a unique bill, consisting of a long sickle-shaped upper mandible and a short, straight lower one. This species was originally classified as *Hemignathus wilsoni.*

Behavior

The akiapolaau moves along the main trunk and branches of forest trees gleaning beetle larvae and other insects from the bark. To get at its food, the akiapolaau holds its beak open and chisels at the bark with its stout lower mandible. It then picks out exposed insect larvae with the curved upper mandible. The breeding biology is largely unknown. Only two akiapolaau nests have ever been found, both abandoned before completion. Nests were discovered in October and February, but males have been heard singing virtually year round. These facts suggest that the species has a prolonged breeding period, but individual birds nest infrequently. Akiapolaau have been observed in stable social groups of three (two adults and one young).

Habitat

The akiapolaau inhabits mixed forests of ohia (*Metrosideros collina*) and koa (*Acacia koa*), where it shows a preference for koa, Hawaii's most common native forest tree. Part of the population also inhabits mamane (*Sophora chrysophylla*) and naio (*Myoporum sandwicense*) forests. This species has not adapted to any varieties of non-native trees.

Historic Range

Restricted to the island of Hawaii, the akiapolaau was formerly found throughout the native forest above 400 meters (1,300 ft). It was once common on the eastern slopes of Mauna Loa and the northeastern slopes of Mauna Kea. Habitat elevation ranges from 1,200 to 2,200 meters (4,000 to 7,300 ft).

Current Distribution

The akiapolaau survives in two widely separated populations along the Kona Coast on Mauna Loa and Mauna Kea, where it is locally common in higher-elevation ohia-koa forests and rare elsewhere. The most recent Fish and Wildlife Service (FWS) estimate places the population at about 1,500.

Conservation and Recovery

Most native forests on the island of Hawaii have been cleared and the land converted to agricultural or urban uses. Surviving upper-elevation forests have been much reduced by logging and conversion to pasture. In addition, forest acreage has been lost because of a widespread dieback of ohia. Dieback of these trees continues between the elevations of 760 and 1,830 meters (2,500 and 6,000 ft), primarily in the Hilo, Kau, Olaa, and Waikea areas. Reasons for the dieback are unknown, but it has been accompanied by a decline in native bird populations.

Also, several bird predators have been introduced to Hawaii including the domestic cat, Polynesian rat, black or roof rat, Nor-wegian rat, mongoose, and the common myna. These predators probably severely limit the akiapolaau's reproduction.

The FWS Recovery Plan for the akiapolaau and similarly threatened forest birds explores ways to stem dieback of koa trees and to reclaim forest habitat. Primary goals are to restrict grazing animals, remove exotic predators and competitors, revegetate with native plants, and establish essential habitat areas as sanctuaries.

In 1985, the FWS, together with The Nature Conservancy of Hawaii and the state, acquired 3,360 hectares (8,300 acres) of native forest on the island of Hawaii. This purchase is considered the first step in the establishment of the Hakalau Forest National Wildlife Refuge, designed primarily to preserve forest bird habitat. The refuge is situated on the northwestern slope of Mauna Kea and contains some of the most pristine koa-ohia forests remaining on the islands. A 162-hectare (400-acre) parcel was acquired in 1988 by The Nature Conservancy and sold to FWS for inclusion in the refuge.

Bibliography

U.S. Fish and Wildlife Service. 1982. "The Hawaii Forest Bird Recovery Plan." U.S. Fish and Wildlife Service, Portland.

Contact

Regional Office of Endangered Species
U.S. Fish and Wildlife Service
Lloyd 500 Building, Suite 1692
500 N.E. Multnomah Street
Portland, Oregon 97232

Field Office of Endangered Species
U.S. Fish and Wildlife Service
300 Ala Moana Boulevard
P.O. Box 50167
Honolulu, Hawaii 96850

Kauai Akialoa
Hemignathus procerus

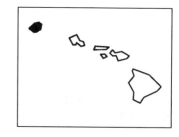

H. Douglas Pratt

Status	Endangered (possibly extinct)
Listed	March 11, 1967
Family	Fringillidae; Subfamily Drepanidinae (Hawaiian honeycreeper)
Description	Honeycreeper with a long downcurved bill; male olive-yellow, female green-gray.
Habitat	Dense, wet ohia forests.
Food	Nectar, insects.
Reproduction	Unknown.
Threats	Critically low numbers.
Region 1	Hawaii

Description

The Kauai akialoa is a honeycreeper about 20 centimeters (8 in) in length. It has a sickle-shaped bill often well over 5 centimeters (2 in) long. The male is olive-yellow above and yellow below; the female is green-gray above. Both sexes have a black patch between the eye and bill.

Behavior

The akialoa moves along tree bark, foraging for insects. It also feeds on ohia and lobelia nectar. Its breeding biology is unknown. The closely related *Hemignathus obscurus* produces two young in late June and nests in koa trees.

Habitat

Kauai, the fourth largest of the Hawaiian Islands, has a land area of 143,240 hectares (553 sq mi). The highest peaks—Kawaikini (1,573 m; 5,243 ft) and Mt. Waialeale (1,544 m; 5,148 ft)—are found near the center of the island. Dominant native trees are the ohia (*Metrosideros collina*) and the koa (*Acacia koa*). Mixed ohia-koa forests are found on about 34,400 hectares (85,500 acres). The island's volcanic slopes and plateaus are checkered with eucalyptus and pine plantations.

The Alakai Swamp, an area of dense ohia forest at 1,200 meters (4,000 ft) elevation, is the primary habitat of the akialoa and other island forest birds. Annual rainfall is between 381 and 508 centimeters (150 and 200 in) along the Wainiha Pali (cliff) on the east, but only 127 centimeters (50 in) on the western side next to the Waimea Canyon.

Historic Range

The akialoa is restricted to the island of Kauai, where it was once relatively abundant. Three other akialoa subspecies, which once inhabited the other large islands, are extinct.

Current Distribution

The Kauai akialoa may now be extinct. It was considered the most common forest bird on the island in the late 19th century, but by 1928 it was gone from the outer forest. The akialoa was last seen in 1965, and none was found during surveys from 1968 to 1973 and in 1981. If the akialoa survives, the population is estimated at less than ten birds.

Conservation and Recovery

Little is known about the reasons for forest bird decline throughout the Hawaiian Islands, and especially on Kauai. Although severe forest bird decline occurred on many of the islands during the 19th century, primarily because of deforestation, the most drastic decline on Kauai occurred during the first 30 years of this century.

Many acres of forest have been cleared for agriculture and pasture. Grazing animals have been introduced, and some types have adapted to the wild. Alien plants, insects, and diseases have spread aggressively. In addition to competition with exotic species, the akialoa must also compete with other native birds, and contend with rats and other introduced predators. Natural variations in food supply—the dramatic seasonal variation in the ohia blossoms—also affects the akialoa.

In 1964, 4,023 hectares (9,940 acres) of the Alakai Swamp were set aside to establish the Alakai Wilderness Preserve. The Fish and Wildlife Service (FWS) Recovery Plan identifies an area of about 7,890 hectares (19,500 acres) that is considered essential for the survival of forest birds on Kauai. Most of this area is currently under control of the Hawaii Division of Forestry and Wildlife.

In its recovery plan for Kauai forest birds, which includes the Kauai akialoa, the FWS notes the imminent danger of extinction for many Hawaiian native birds. It recommends establishment of a captive propagation program and sperm bank as a last-ditch attempt to save as many as possible. For the Kauai akialoa such efforts may be too late.

Bibliography

Berger, A. J. 1981. *Hawaiian Birdlife*. University of Hawaii Press, Honolulu.

Huber, L. N. 1966. "Observation of Akialoa, Field Notes. Alakai Swamp, Kauai, March, 1965." *Elepaio* 26(8):71.

Scott, J. M., *et al.* 1988. "Conservation of Hawaii's Vanishing Avifauna." *Bioscience* 38(4):238-253.

U.S. Fish and Wildlife Service. 1983. "Kauai Forest Birds Recovery Plan." U.S. Fish and Wildlife Service, Portland.

Contact

Regional Office of Endangered Species
U.S. Fish and Wildlife Service
Lloyd 500 Building, Suite 1692
500 N.E. Multnomah Street
Portland, Oregon 97232

Office of Environmental Services
U.S. Fish and Wildlife Service
300 Ala Moana Boulevard
P.O. Box 50167
Honolulu, Hawaii 96850

Hawaiian Stilt
Himantopus mexicanus knudseni

Robert J. Shallenberger

Status	Endangered
Listed	October 13, 1970
Family	Recurviostridae (Stilt)
Description	Black and white wading bird with long, pink legs.
Habitat	Wetlands.
Food	Worms, crabs, insects, small fishes.
Reproduction	Clutch of 4 eggs.
Threats	Habitat loss, predation.
Region 1	Hawaii

Description

Known on the islands as "ae'o," the Hawaiian stilt is a slender, long-legged wading bird with an average height of about 40 centimeters (16 in). It is black above (except for the forehead), white below, and has distinctive pink legs. Sexes are distinguished by back color (brownish in females, black in males) and voice (female call is lower than male). The Hawaiian stilt is derived from mainland black-necked stilts that colonized Hawaii centuries ago. In the Hawaiian subspecies, black extends lower on the forehead and around the sides of the neck, and the bill, tarsus (lower leg), and tail are longer.

Behavior

The Hawaiian stilt is an opportunistic feeder that eats a wide variety of aquatic organisms—worms, small crabs, insects, and small fishes. It defends a narrow territory around the nest, which is a simple scrape in the ground. Nesting season extends from March through August. Females lay a clutch of four eggs, which are incubated for 24 days. Chicks stray from the nest within 24 hours of hatching but may remain with both parents for several months.

Habitat

The Hawaiian stilt nests in fresh or brackish ponds, mudflats, and marshlands. It prefers small, sparsely vegetated islands in shallow ponds but will also use dry, barren areas near shallow water. On Kauai, stilts have successfully used man-made, floating nest structures. Often nesting and feeding areas are widely separated, and stilts fly between them daily.

Stilts will feed in freshwater or tidal wetlands. Loafing areas are generally mudflats, mats of pickleweed, or open pasture where visibility is good and predators few. Suitable stilt habitat is generally below 150 meters (500 ft) in elevation.

Historic Range

The Hawaiian stilt was once locally common on all the major Hawaiian islands, except Lanai and Kahoolawe, where wetlands are scarce. In the 1940s, the stilt population had declined to about 300 birds.

Current Distribution

The stilt is still present on all islands of its historic range; about 65 percent of the population is found on Maui and Oahu. Population counts over the last 25 years have fluctuated from a low of 253 (1960) to a high of 1,476 (1977). While some fluctuation is probably natural, indications are that the population has stabilized between 1,000 and 1,500 birds.

Conservation and Recovery

Natural coastal plain wetlands and artificial sites, such as flooded taro fields, once provided an abundance of habitat for waterbirds. When crops grown in dry fields began to replace taro in the 1850s, wetland acreage began a steady decline. Today, many wetlands have been filled, farmed over, or built over with hotels, industrial sites, housing, and other developments.

Introduced plants have degraded some remaining wetland habitat. Species such as California grass, water hyacinth, and mangrove often out-compete native plants, eliminating open water, exposed mudflats, and shallows. Predators are considered a major limiting factor of waterbird populations.

The best approach for conserving the Hawaiian stilt is to preserve remaining wetlands and rehabilitate degraded areas. Sanctuaries are very important. Kanaha Pond and Kealia Pond were the first state sanctuaries on Maui. In 1972, 371 hectares (917 acres) were acquired in Hanalei Valley on Kauai for the first national wildlife refuge. Since that time, four additional wetland refuges have been established: Huleia, along the Huleia River on Kauai; Kakahaia on Molokai; Pearl Harbor on Oahu; and the James Campbell National Wildlife Refuge on Oahu.

As with other Endangered Hawaiian waterbirds, the Fish and Wildlife Service has set a recovery goal of achieving a self-sustaining population of 2,000 birds. When stilt populations reach that level for three consecutive years, the service will consider reclassifying the Hawaiian stilt as Threatened.

Bibliography

Berger, A. J. 1981. *Hawaiian Birdlife*. University of Hawaii Press, Honolulu.

U.S. Fish and Wildlife Service. 1985. "Recovery Plan for the Hawaiian Waterbirds." U.S. Fish and Wildlife Service, Portland.

Contact

Regional Office of Endangered Species
U.S. Fish and Wildlife Service
Lloyd 500 Building, Suite 1692
500 N.E. Multnomah Street
Portland, Oregon 97232

Office of Environmental Services
U.S. Fish and Wildlife Service
300 Ala Moana Boulevard
P.O. Box 50167
Honolulu, Hawaii 96850

San Clemente Island Loggerhead Shrike

Lanius ludovicianus mearnsi

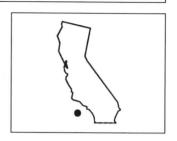

U.S. Navy

Status	Endangered
Listed	August 11, 1977
Family	Laniidae (Shrike)
Description	Gray above, white below with a black mask.
Habitat	Open country with scattered trees.
Food	Insects and other small invertebrate and vertebrate species.
Reproduction	Clutch of 4 to 7 eggs.
Threats	Low numbers, loss of habitat, predation.
Region 1	California

Description

The San Clemente Island loggerhead shrike is a medium-sized bird, about 22 centimeters (9 in) in length. Plumage is gray above and white below, with a black mask. The black wings and tail are marked with patches of white. The San Clemente shrike is classified as a distinct subspecies of the mainland loggerhead shrike based upon a smaller body size, a smaller foot, shorter wing and tail, darker plumage, and larger bill.

Behavior

Shrikes are efficient, search-type predators that forage from elevated perches for a diversity of prey, ranging from land snails to small mammals, with insects being the most common prey. Lacking the talons of raptors, shrikes kill or stun prey with their strong beaks. They have acquired the nickname "butcher birds" by their habit of impaling prey on large thorns or barbed-wire fences before eating them. They also store prey in this manner for future meals.

Although little is known of the specific life history of this subspecies, it is probably similar to that of mainland loggerhead shrikes. Mainland shrikes occupy separate breeding and winter territories. In much of California, particularly southern and central coastal regions, shrikes are nonmigratory.

March and April are prime nesting months. Shrikes build their nests in small trees or shrubs at or below a height of about 6 meters (20 ft). Both sexes participate in the care and feeding of the young and sometimes the male shares incubation tasks. Clutch size is from four to seven eggs, and incubation averages about 14 days; young fledge after about three weeks.

Habitat

Loggerhead shrikes are usually found in open country with scattered trees and low scrub, which can provide an adequate supply of prey, a selection of elevated perches, and sufficient roosting and nesting cover.

Historic Range

Loggerhead shrikes occupied a major portion of San Clemente Island in the early 1900s, nesting primarily at Pyramid Cove (extreme southern coastline), Northwest Cove, and midway along the eastern shoreline. Accounts of early observers imply that the island supported a considerable and widely dispersed shrike population.

Current Distribution

All observations since the 1960s document a marked decrease in the shrike population. A year-long study in the 1970s determined that only about 30 shrikes inhabited the island. The 1989 population estimate, provided by the Navy's Natural Resource Office, is 12 to 20 birds.

Today, loggerhead shrikes are restricted primarily to higher elevations on the eastern part of the island. In fall and winter, solitary shrikes are seen on the island's uppermost mesas. Shrikes currently use only the island canyons where sufficient ground cover exists for nesting.

Conservation and Recovery

The decline of the shrike population on San Clemente Island is due to the large feral goat population. Severe grazing and browsing by goats radically altered vegetation character-istics on the island, eliminating nesting and roosting habitat and exposing birds to increased predation, primarily from feral cats.

Competition from other species may also be a factor in the shrike's decline. Shrikes may be displaced by kestrels, which greatly outnumber them and share similar food and nesting preferences. The island's kestrel population has increased while the shrike population has declined.

According to the Fish and Wildlife Service, recovery for the San Clemente loggerhead shrike will require revegetation with maritime sage scrub to provide suitable nesting habitat. Woodland nesting habitat could be expanded, especially at the upper ends of large canyons where open foraging habitat is near. Since historic accounts do not indicate an extensive woodland, reforestation of San Clemente Island will not be attempted.

Bibliography

Johnson, N. K. 1972. "Origin and Differentiation of the Avifauna of the Channel Islands, California." *Condor* 74:295- 315.

Morrison, M. L. 1980. "Seasonal Aspects of the Predatory Behavior of Loggerhead Shrikes." *Condor* 81:297-300.

U.S. Fish and Wildlife Service. 1984. "Recovery Plan for the Endangered and Threatened Species of the California Channel Islands." U.S. Fish and Wildlife Service, Portland.

Contact

Regional Office of Endangered Species
U.S. Fish and Wildlife Service
Lloyd 500 Building, Suite 1692
500 N.E. Multnomah Street
Portland, Oregon 97232

Natural Resources Office
Staff Civil Engineer (18N)
NAS North Island (Bldg 3)
San Diego, California 92135-5018

Palila

Loxioides bailleui

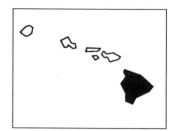

H. Douglas Pratt

Status	Endangered
Listed	March 11, 1967
Family	Fringillidae; Subfamily Drepanidinae (Hawaiian honeycreeper)
Description	Large, gray finch with a yellow head and dark mask.
Habitat	Mamane forests.
Food	Mamane seeds, insects.
Reproduction	Clutch of 2 eggs.
Threats	Habitat decline, predation.
Region 1	Hawaii

Description

The palila is one of the Hawaiian finches, the largest birds among the honeycreepers. It is between 15 and 17 centimeters (6 and 6.5 in) long and weighs about 50 grams (1.8 oz). This thick-billed bird has a golden-yellow head, gray back, and whitish abdomen. The bill itself is dark, and a black mask (lore patch) runs from the bill to the eyes. Females and juveniles have more subdued coloring than males. This species was formerly classified as *Psittirostra bailleui*.

Behavior

The nesting season of the palila begins in late spring and lasts five or six months. These monogamous birds defend a small territory around the nesting tree and forage over a larger area. Females construct nests on horizontal branches of the larger mamane (*Sophora chrysophylla*) and naio (*Myoporum sandwicense*) trees from grasses and large dead twigs, and line them with lichens and rootlets.

The female usually lays two brown-splotched white eggs, which are incubated for 18 days. The palila will often renest if a first effort in the early part of the season is unsuccessful. Parents care for the young and feed them mamane seeds and insects for about a month until they fledge. The young move with the parents in a family group for an extended period of time.

Habitat

Palila depend on the mamane-naio forest ecosystem for all their feeding and nesting needs and concentrate in areas where large mamane trees carry fully developed green pods.

Historic Range

Palila were formerly found throughout the higher regions of the island of Hawaii, in the north and south Kona districts, the Hamakua district on the eastern slope of Mauna Kea, and the mamane and naio forests on the southern and western slopes of Mauna Kea.

Current Distribution

The palila is now confined to the mamane-naio forests of Mauna Kea above 1,830 meters (6,000 ft), inhabiting a small portion of what appears to be suitable forest habitat.

In 1988, biologists from the Patuxent Wildlife Research Center's Hawaii Research Station and state personnel conducted a comprehensive survey for the palila on the slopes of Mauna Kea. Riding an upward trend, the population was estimated to be 4,300. In 1989, however, a follow-up census revealed that the population had decreased by almost 20 percent to about 3,500 birds.

Conservation and Recovery

Until now, little research has been done to discover the reasons for palila decline. Although forest habitat seems adequate to support a healthy population, the mix of forest plants has changed over the years and may be affecting the palila in ways that are not understood. Weather may account for palila decline in some years. Rains are infrequent but usually heavy, and if they occur when the adult is away from the nest, young may die. Predators, such as the tree-climbing roof rat, cats, and mongooses, have increased in number. Because palila nests are usually placed

on horizontal branches, both the cat and rat have easy access to them.

A full-scale radio telemetry study was begun in 1988 to determine this bird's habitat selection and use, daily movement patterns, and home range. Findings from this research should fill in many of the blank spaces in our knowledge of the palila.

Bibliography

U.S. Fish and Wildlife Service. 1978. "Palila Recovery Plan." U.S. Fish and Wildlife Service, Portland.

Scott, J. M., *et al.* 1984. "Annual Variation in the Distribution, Abundance, and Habitat Response of the Palila." *Auk* 101:647-64.

Van Riper III, C. 1980. "Observations on the Breeding of the Palila *Psittirostra bailleui* of Hawaii." *Ibis* 122:462-75.

Contact

Regional Office of Endangered Species
U.S. Fish and Wildlife Service
Lloyd 500 Building, Suite 1692
500 N.E. Multnomah Street
Portland, Oregon 97232

Field Office of Endangered Species
U.S. Fish and Wildlife Service
300 Ala Moana Boulevard
P.O. Box 50167
Honolulu, Hawaii 96850

Akepa
Loxops coccineus ssp.

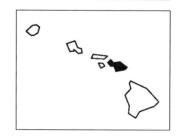

H. Douglas Pratt

Status . . . . . . Endangered
Listed . . . . . . October 13, 1970
Family . . . . . Fringillidae; Subfamily Drepanidinae (Hawaiian Honeycreeper)
Description . . . Small honeycreeper with a long, notched tail; males bright red-orange or yellow.
Habitat . . . . . Closed-canopy forests.
Food . . . . . . Insects.
Reproduction . Clutch of 3 eggs.
Threats . . . . . Deforestation, disease.
Region 1 . . . . Hawaii

Description

The akepa is a small finchlike bird with a long notched tail; body length is from 10 to 12 centimeters (4 to 5 in) and weight about 10 grams (0.35 oz). Two akepa subspecies are listed as Endangered: the Hawaii akepa (*Loxops coccineus coccineus*), and the sub-species found on Maui (*L. c. ochraceus*). Hawaii akepa males are bright red-orange with brownish wings and tail, while females are gray to green with considerable yellow, especially on the breast. Both sexes have yellow bills. The Maui akepa has a gray bill; males are orange or yellow.

Behavior

Akepas, which are often seen in small flocks, keep mostly to the forest canopy where they forage for insects. Only three

akepa nests have ever been discovered, all in natural ohia (*Metrosideros collina*) or koa (*Acacia koa*) tree cavities up to 15 meters (45 ft) above the ground. These active nests of the Hawaii akepa were discovered in March and May; one had three eggs and fledged two young in June. No nests of the Maui akepa have been discovered. The akepa feeds on caterpillars and spiders, occasionally visiting ohia and other flowers for nectar.

Habitat

The akepa inhabits the closed canopy of upland mixed ohia and koa forests where it gleans insects from foliage and flowers.

Historic Range

The Hawaii subspecies has never been collected outside the island of Hawaii. It was formerly widespread, and in the early 1900s was described as abundant in parts of Kona, Hilo, and on Kohala Mountain.

Considered abundant on Maui before 1900, the Maui akepa went into a sharp decline in the 20th century. Between 1900 and 1980 only six sightings were reported, all within two miles of Pohaku Palaha at the upper junction of Kipahulyu Valley and Haleakala Crater.

Current Distribution

Current populations on the island of Hawaii are on the eastern slopes of Mauna Kea, eastern and southern slopes of Mauna Loa, and the northern slope of Hualalai, at an elevation of 1,500 meters (4,900 ft). Total akepa species (including the subspecies on Oahu) has most recently been estimated at about 15,800 birds.

During a 1980 study, only eight Maui akepa were recorded on Maui, leading to a population estimate of 230 for the entire island.

Conservation and Recovery

Avian diseases have been responsible for the historic decline of many native Hawaiian birds, including the akepa. Avian pox and avian malaria came to the island in the 1820s with introduced mosquitoes (*Culex quinquefasciatus*). Forest bird populations above 1,500 meters (4,900 ft), where mosquitoes are less abundant, have a lower incidence of disease. Other introduced insects, such as parasitic wasps and predaceous ants, have eliminated many native insects which once served as food for native birds.

The most immediate threat to the akepa is the continued degradation of its remaining habitat. Upper elevation koa forests on Hawaii have been drastically reduced through logging and subsequent conversion to pasture. Animal grazing and browsing have severely modified the forests that

remain. The wetter forests are subject to rooting by feral pigs, which spread the seeds of exotic plants such as banana poka (*Passiflora mollissima*) and strawberry guava (*Psidium cattleianum*) in their feces after ingesting the fruits.

Widespread dieback of ohia, Hawaii's most common native forest tree, has modified large portions of habitat on the island of Hawaii, and additional areas may be threatened. The causes for the death of this tree are not known. Dieback continues between the elevations of 760 and 1,830 meters (2,500 and 6,000 ft), primarily in the Hilo, Kau, Olaa, and Waikea areas.

An additional threat to the akepa is predation. Several potential bird predators have been introduced to Hawaii, including the domestic cat, Polynesian rat, black or roof rat, Norwegian rat, mongoose, and common myna.

Recovery of the akepa and similar birds largely depends on habitat conservation and restoration. In late 1985, the Fish and Wildlife Service (FWS), The Nature Conservancy of Hawaii, and the state purchased a total of 3,360 hectares (8,300 acres) of native forest on the island of Hawaii. This marked the first phase of the proposed establishment of a 13,560-hectare (33,500-acre) Hakalau Forest National Wildlife Refuge on the northwestern slope of Mauna Kea. The refuge is designed primarily to preserve the habitat of endangered forest birds and contains some of the best preserved koa-ohia forests remaining on the islands. Another 162-hectare (400-acre) parcel was acquired in 1988 by The Nature Conservancy and sold to the FWS for inclusion in the refuge.

Since the akepas, as well as other forest birds, are in danger of extinction while recovery efforts are studied and implemented, the FWS is exploring the possibility of captive propagation. The ultimate goal of such a program would be the creation of a captive flock to furnish birds to supplement wild populations. Little is known, however, about the ability of Hawaiian forest birds to live and breed in captivity. To test the feasibility of captive propagation, the FWS began a trial program in cooperation with several U.S. zoos. In late 1988, 15 pairs of a non-threatened honeycreeper, the common amakihi (*Hemignathus virens*), were sent to participating zoos to determine if the birds can live and breed in captivity. If successful, this effort will provide essential information on how to manage a captive propagation program for the rarer Hawaiian forest birds.

Bibliography

Amadon, D. 1950. ''The Hawaiian Honey-creepers (Aves, Drepanididae).'' *Bulletin of the American Museum of Natural History* 95(4).

Sincock, J. L., and J. M. Scott. 1980. ''Cavity Nesting of the Akepa on the Island of Hawaii.'' *Wilson Bulletin* 92:261-263.

U.S. Fish and Wildlife Service. 1982. ''The Hawaii Forest Bird Recovery Plan.'' U.S. Fish and Wildlife Service. Portland.

U.S. Fish and Wildlife Service. 1984. ''Maui-Molokai Forest Birds Recovery Plan.'' U.S. Fish and Wildlife Service. Portland.

Contact

Endangered Species Field Office
U.S. Fish and Wildlife Service
Lloyd 500 Building, Suite 1692
500 N.E. Multnomah Street
Portland, Oregon 97232

Office of Environmental Services
U.S. Fish and Wildlife Service
300 Ala Moana Boulevard
P.O. Box 50167
Honolulu, Hawaii 96850

Poo-uli
Melamprosops phaeosoma

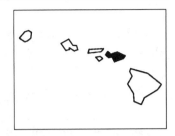

H. Douglas Pratt

Status	Endangered
Listed	September 25, 1975
Family	Fringillidae; Subfamily Drepanidinae (Hawaiian Honeycreeper)
Description	Brown honeycreeper with buff underparts and a black face mask.
Habitat	Ohia forests.
Food	Insects, larvae.
Reproduction	Unknown.
Threats	Habitat degradation, predation, disease.
Region 1	Hawaii

Description

Not discovered until 1973, the poo-uli, or black-faced honeycreeper, is a chunky, short-tailed forest bird about 14 centimeters (5.5 in) long. It is brown above and has a prominent black face mask, a white throat, and a thick, black bill. The underparts are buff washed with brown.

Behavior

Creeping along tree bark, the poo-uli forages for snails and beetles, but will feed on a variety of insects and larvae. It often forms small feeding groups with the Maui parrot-bill and the Maui creeper. Nothing is known of its breeding behavior.

Habitat

Poo-uli are associated with closed-canopy ohia forest with a dense shrub understory.

Historic Range

Past distribution of the poo-uli is largely unknown because of its recent discovery. It was found on Maui in an area of about 61 hectares (150 acres) on Haleakala volcano between the upper forks of Hanawi stream. It undoubtedly had a wider distribution in the past. Bones tentatively identified as poo-uli were found in a lava tube on the southwest slopes of Haleakala in 1982.

Current Distribution

The poo-uli occurs only on Maui. All recent observations have been between 1,440 and 1,720 meters (4,800 and 5,400 ft) elevation just east of Hanawi. The species has only been seen three times during recent bird counts, but because it is inconspicuous, it may be more common than these few sightings would indicate. In 1986 it was estimated that the poo-uli population stood at about 140 birds.

Conservation and Recovery

Large tracts of forest on Maui, especially on the dry leeward slopes, have been cleared for agriculture, and fire was commonly used by Polynesians to burn forest tracts to maintain pili grass used for housing thatch. European settlers eliminated all dry forest on Maui up to at least 1,500 meters (5,000 ft) for ranching pastures. By the turn of the century, almost all forest except the very wet ohia forest in the windward mountain sections had been eliminated.

Degradation of remaining forests continues. Browsing and rooting feral goats, pigs, and axis deer trample or uproot many native plants, leaving the habitat open to invasion by non-native plants. The combined impact of feral mammals and exotic plants has changed the species composition, distribution, and densities of native plants on which forest birds depend. The Fish and Wildlife Service (FWS) Recovery Plan focuses on controlling the number of feral animals and on eliminating introduced plant species.

The State Reserve system holds and actively manages about 30 percent of the remaining forest resources on the island. Since the poo-

uli, as well as other forest birds, exists in such a small population, the FWS is currently testing the feasibility of captive propagation of endangered forest birds. Little is known about the ability of Hawaiian forest birds to live and breed in captivity.

Bibliography

Berger, A. J. 1981. *Hawaiian Birdlife*. University of Hawaii Press, Honolulu.

Casey, T. L. C., and J. D. Jacobi. 1974. "A New Genus and Species of Bird from the Island of Maui (Passeriformes: Drepanididae)." *B.P. Bishop Museum Occasional Papers* 24(12):215-226.

Scott, J. M., *et al.* 1988. "Conservation of Hawaii's Vanishing Avifauna." *Bioscience* 38(4):238-253.

U.S. Fish and Wildlife Service. 1984. "The Maui-Molokai Forest Birds Recovery Plan." U.S. Fish and Wildlife Service, Portland.

Contact

Regional Office of Endangered Species
U.S. Fish and Wildlife Service
Lloyd 500 Building, Suite 1692
500 N.E. Multnomah Street
Portland, Oregon 97232

Office of Environmental Services
U.S. Fish and Wildlife Service
300 Ala Moana Boulevard
P.O. Box 50167
Honolulu, Hawaii 96850

Kauai o'o

Moho braccatus

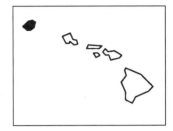

Robert J. Shallenberger

Status	Endangered (possibly extinct)
Listed	March 11, 1967
Family	Meliphagidae (Honeyeater)
Description	Brown-bodied forest bird with black head, wings, tail, and feet.
Habitat	Dense, wet forests.
Food	Lobeli and ohia nectar, insects.
Reproduction	Unknown.
Threats	Low numbers, habitat degradation, predation.
Region 1	Hawaii

Description

The Kauai o'o (also known as "a'a") is a honeyeater, and like others in this group has a characteristic tongue adapted for feeding on nectar. It is typically between 19 and 21.5 centimeters (7.5 and 8.5 in) long and has a black head, wings, tail, feet, and bill. Abdomen and undertail are brown; thighs are yellow.

The o'o is the last representative of the family Meliphagidae in the United States.

Behavior

Because the bird has been rare for decades, little is known of its habits or behavior. The adult bird feeds on nectar of the lobeli and ohia, spiders, moths, and crickets. The bird is secretive, and few of its nests are found. A tree-cavity nest, containing two young, was located in late May during the early 1970s.

Habitat

The island of Kauai is the fourth largest of the Hawaiian Islands. The highest peaks, near the center of the island, are Kawaikini at 1,573 meters (5,243 ft) and Mt. Waialeale at 1,544 meters (5,148 ft). The dominant native trees are ohia (*Metrosideros collina*) and koa (*Acacia koa*), which are found primarily in the Kokee area and along the Waimea Canyon. The island supports many large eucalyptus and pine plantations.

Historic Range

The honeyeaters belong to a large family of birds, which are widely distributed in Australia, Micronesia, and central Polynesia. Four of the five species of honeyeaters native to Hawaii are extinct.

The o'o was common throughout the island of Kauai in the late 19th century but rare by the 1920s.

Current Distribution

The Alakai Swamp, at 1,200 meters (4,000 ft) elevation, is the primary remaining habitat of the o'o. In 1973, there were fewer than 100 surviving birds, and a 1981 survey found only two o'o. Extinction is a virtual certainty for this species, if it has not already occurred.

Conservation and Recovery

Deforestation of Kauai was rapid and severe in the early part of this century when land was cleared for agriculture, and forest bird populations declined in direct proportion. Stands of native forest trees are now concentrated at higher elevations and in remote interior valleys. Only about half of the remaining forest is considered undisturbed.

Rooting, browsing, and trampling by feral pigs and goats have been recognized as problems since the 1930s. The activities of these animals are detrimental to most native plants and encourage the establishment of non-native, weedy varieties. Hunting is used to control populations of feral pigs and goats, and several attempts have been made to remove pest plants on trails leading into the Alakai Swamp and other undisturbed forest areas. Predation by the introduced black rat and the spread of avian diseases have undoubtedly contributed to the loss of the o'o.

In 1964, 4,023 hectares (9,940 acres) of the Alakai Swamp were set aside to establish the Alakai Wilderness Preserve. This preserve encompasses the o'o's primary habitat. The Fish and Wildlife Service Recovery Plan identifies an area of about 7,890 hectares (19,500 acres) that is considered essential for the survival of forest birds on Kauai. Most of this area is currently under control of the Hawaii Division of Forestry and Wildlife.

Protection and rehabilitation of forest habitat will certainly help remaining forest bird populations, but most biologists consider these actions too late to save the oo from extinction.

Bibliography

Scott, J. M., *et al.* 1988. "Conservation of Hawaii's Vanishing Avifauna." *Bioscience* 38(4):238-253.

U.S. Fish and Wildlife Service. 1983. "Kauai Forest Birds Recovery Plan." U.S. Fish and Wildlife Service, Portland, Oregon.

Contact

Regional Office of Endangered Species
U.S. Fish and Wildlife Service
Lloyd 500 Building, Suite 1692
500 N.E. Multnomah Street
Portland, Oregon 97232

Office of Environmental Services
U.S. Fish and Wildlife Service
300 Ala Moana Boulevard
P.O. Box 50167
Honolulu, Hawaii 96850

Molokai Thrush
Myadestes lanaiensis rutha

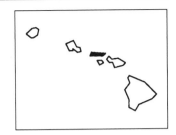

H. Douglas Pratt

Status . . . . . . Endangered
Listed . . . . . . October 13, 1970
Family . . . . . . Muscicapidae; Subfamily
Turdinae (Thrush)
Description . . . Heavy-bodied thrush, brown
above, gray below.
Habitat . . . . . . Ohia forest.
Food . . . . Fruits, berries, insects.
Reproduction . . Unknown.
Threats . . . . . Deforestation, feral animals,
disease.
Region 1 . . . . Hawaii

Description

The Molokai thrush is a fairly large, heavy-bodied bird, about 18 to 20 centimeters (7 to 8 in) long. Adults are dark brown above and gray below; immatures are spotted below. The Hawaiian name for this thrush is olomao, and it is also commonly known as the Lanai thrush. This species was originally classified as *Phaeornis obscurus rutha*.

Behavior

The Molokai thrush is a reclusive bird that usually keeps beneath the forest canopy. It feeds on fruits, berries, and insects. Its breeding biology is unknown, but a closely related bird on the island of Hawaii, the omao (*Phaeornis obscurus obscurus*), constructs a bulky nest of branches, fern fronds, mosses, and leaves. Clutch size is one or two eggs.

Habitat

The island of Molokai, 61 kilometers (38 mi) long and 16 kilometers (10 mi) wide, lies 14.5 kilometers (9 mi) northwest of Maui in the Hawaiian Islands. It is formed of two volcanoes; the oldest, Puu Nana, lies in the rain shadow of the larger eastern volcano, Kamakou. Kamakou reaches a height of 1,491 meters (4,970 ft); its northern face is precipitous. Erosion within the two major northern valleys, Pelekunu and Wailau, has completely encircled a rugged plateau—Olokui—with 610-meter (2,000-ft) cliffs. This forested plateau is the most isolated and pristine land in the main Hawaiian Islands. The

Molokai thrush is found in a wet, montane ohia forest with a dense understory of mosses, vines, and tree ferns. Habitat elevation is above 1,200 meters (4,000 ft).

Historic Range

This species was once very common throughout Molokai and was regularly collected by scientists in the 19th century. During the 20th century the species declined rapidly, and, until surveys on Molokai in 1979 and 1980, there were only two reported sightings.

Current Distribution

At present, the Molokai thrush is restricted to the Olokui Plateau between Kamakou Peak and Pepeopae Bog. The population was estimated at 19 birds in 1986.

Conservation and Recovery

European settlement of Molokai eliminated all dry forests on the south coast up to at least 900 meters (3,000 ft), converting most of the land to pasture. By the turn of the century, only the very wet, mountainous ohia forest remained, and many native Hawaiian birds had vanished.

Although deforestation has stopped, habitat destruction continues. Browsing and rooting by feral goats and pigs and axis deer have disrupted the growth of native vegetation, allowing non-native plants, including strawberry guava, blackberry, New Zealand flax, and various gingers, to invade. The original ground cover has drastically changed in composition, distribution, and density. Many native forest birds have been unable to adapt to these conditions, and populations have declined.

Avian pox and malaria, spread by introduced mosquitoes, have played a large role in the decline of many native Hawaiian birds. Most remaining birds live at higher elevations where the mosquito density is low. Scientists are now concerned that a temperate-zone subspecies of the night mosquito (*Culex pipiens pipiens*) may become established at higher elevations and further spread avian diseases.

The first effort to conserve native birds was made in 1903 when the State Forest Reserve system was created. The protection of watershed was the primary concern, and reserve management included fencing out cattle, hunting of feral animals, and the reforestation of denuded areas with exotic trees. The State Reserve system holds and actively manages about 30 percent of the remaining forest resources on the island.

Bibliography

Scott, J. M., *et al.* 1988. "Conservation of Hawaii's Vanishing Avifauna." *Bioscience* 38(4):238-253.

U.S. Fish and Wildlife Service. 1984. "The Maui-Molokai Forest Birds Recovery Plan." U.S. Fish and Wildlife Service, Portland, Oregon.

Van Riper, C. III, and J.M. Scott. 1979. "Observations on Distribution, Diet, and Breeding of the Hawaiian Thrush." *Condor* 81:65-71.

Contact

Regional Office of Endangered Species
U.S. Fish and Wildlife Service
Lloyd 500 Building, Suite 1692
500 N.E. Multnomah Street
Portland, Oregon 97232

Office of Environmental Services
U.S. Fish and Wildlife Service
300 Ala Moana Boulevard
P.O. Box 50167
Honolulu, Hawaii 96850

Large Kauai Thrush
Myadestes myadestinus

H. Douglas Pratt

Status	Endangered
Listed	October 13, 1970
Family	Muscicapidae; Subfamily Turdinae (Thrush)
Description:	Large-bodied thrush; brown above, mottled gray below; short, broad bill.
Habitat	High elevation forests.
Food	Fruit, insects.
Reproduction	Unknown.
Threats	Low numbers, predation, disease.
Region 1	Hawaii

Description

Known in Hawaiian as "kamao," the large Kauai thrush is about 20 centimeters (8 in) long. It is dull brown above with a brown forehead. Its gray breast is faintly mottled. The bill is short and broad.

Behavior

The large Kauai thrush feeds primarily on fruit and occasionally on insects. Breeding habits are thought to be similar to those of the related omao, which lays a clutch of one or two eggs that hatch in May or June. All Hawaiian thrushes are accomplished singers and practice their art dawn or dusk from the tops of dead trees. Hawaiian thrushes have a habit of shivering their wings while perched.

Habitat

In the past, the large Kauai thrush inhabited all of the island's forests, but it is now found only at higher elevations where the largest tracts of wet ohia forests remain. Deforestation of the island was rapid and severe in the early part of the century when land was cleared for agriculture. The area of undisturbed native forest now totals only about 16,190 hectares (40,000 acres).

Historic Range

The large Kauai thrush was the most common forest bird on the island of Kauai during the 19th century but vanished from the outer forest by 1928. Its decline has continued throughout this century. Of the six species of native Hawaiian thrushes, three are extinct, and the Kauai and Molokai species are nearly so. The omao (*Myadestes obscurus*), which occurs on Hawaii, is still common.

Current Distribution

The large Kauai thrush is now confined to the forest of the Alakai Swamp. In 1973 the number of large Kauai thrushes was estimated at about 340, but by 1986 the population had plummeted to only 24 birds.

Conservation and Recovery

Avian pox and malaria, spread by introduced mosquitoes, have been a major factor in the decline of many native Hawaiian birds. Most remaining birds live at higher elevations where mosquito populations are low. Scientists are now concerned that a temperate-zone subspecies of the night mosquito (*Culex pipiens pipiens*) may become established at the higher elevations and carry diseases to the remaining forest birds.

Predation by the introduced black rat is undoubtedly a factor in the decline of the large Kauai thrush. It is found on almost every forested mountain on Kauai and is able to climb trees in search of eggs and young birds. Researchers fear that another introduced bird predator, the mongoose, may soon gain a foothold on the island.

In 1964, the Alakai Wilderness Preserve, consisting of 4,022 hectares (9,939 acres), was established to protect forest birds on Kauai. The Fish and Wildlife Service (FWS) Recovery Plan for forest birds identifies an area of 7,892 hectares (19,500 acres) on the island as essential for the survival of these species. Most of this area is currently administered by the Hawaii Division of Forestry and Wildlife.

Since the large Kauai thrush and other forest birds could easily go extinct while recovery efforts are studied and implemented, the FWS is experimenting with captive propagation of endangered forest birds. The ultimate goal would be to create a captive flock to furnish birds to supplement remaining wild populations. Little is known, however, about the ability of Hawaiian forest birds to live and breed in captivity.

To test the feasibility of captive propagation, the FWS has begun a trial program in cooperation with several U.S. zoos. In late 1988, 15 pairs of a non-threatened honeycreeper, the common amakihi (*Hemignathus virens*), were sent to participating zoos to determine if the birds can live and breed in captivity. If successful, this effort will provide essential information on how to manage a captive propagation program for the rarer Hawaiian forest birds.

Bibliography

Berger, A. J. 1981. *Hawaiian Birdlife.* University of Hawaii Press, Honolulu.

Pratt, H. C. 1982. "Relationships and Speciation of the Hawaiian Thrushes." *The Living Bird* 19:73-90.

Scott, J. M., *et al.* 1988. "Conservation of Hawaii's Vanishing Avifauna." *Bioscience* 38(4):238-253.

U.S. Fish and Wildlife Service. 1983. "Kauai Forest Birds Recovery Plan." U.S. Fish and Wildlife Service, Portland.

Contact

Regional Office of Endangered Species
U.S. Fish and Wildlife Service
Lloyd 500 Building, Suite 1692
500 N.E. Multnomah Street
Portland, Oregon 97232

Office of Environmental Services
U.S. Fish and Wildlife Service
300 Ala Moana Boulevard
P.O. Box 50167
Honolulu, Hawaii 96850

Small Kauai Thrush
Myadestes palmeri

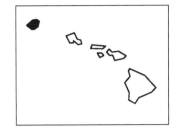

H. Douglas Pratt

Status	. . . . .	Endangered
Listed	. . . . .	March 11, 1967
Family	. . . . .	Muscicapidae; Subfamily Turdinae (Thrush)
Description	. . .	Rare thrush, brown above, gray below, white abdomen and eye ring.
Habitat	. . . . .	Stream banks in high elevation forests.
Food	. . . . . .	Fruit, insects.
Reproduction	. .	Clutch of 2 eggs.
Threats	. . . . .	Low numbers, habitat disturbance, disease.
Region 1	. . . . .	Hawaii

Description

The small Kauai thrush is about 18 centimeters (7 in) long. It is dull brown above, gray below, and has a white abdomen and eye ring. Legs and feet are pinkish tan. Both the large and small Kauai thrushes are known as "kamao" on the island.

Behavior

The secretive small Kauai thrush spends most of its time under vegetation along streambanks, feeding on insects and fruit. The first nest of the small Kauai thrush was discovered in 1982 and contained two young.

Habitat

This species has always been restricted to dense ohia forests in the Alakai Swamp. Although much of the rest of the island was deforested in the first half of the century, the Alakai Swamp remains one of the least disturbed natural areas of Kauai. The area of undisturbed native forest on Kauai now totals about 16,190 hectares (40,000 acres), concentrated at higher elevations and in remote interior valleys.

Historic Range

The small Kauai thrush was considered the rarest of the Hawaiian thrushes. At the turn of the century, the large Kauai thrush was 100 times more common on the island.

Current Distribution

The small Kauai thrush remains a resident of the Alakai Swamp. A survey conducted between 1968 and 1973 put the number of birds at 177; current estimates are essentially unchanged.

Conservation and Recovery

Always rare, the small Kauai thrush has declined because of a number of factors, including the encroachment of non-native plants into the habitat. Avian pox and malaria have devastated bird populations at lower elevations, and scientists are now concerned that a temperate subspecies of the night mosquito (*Culex pipiens pipiens*) may become established at higher elevations and spread the diseases there.

Predation by the introduced black rat is undoubtedly a factor in the decline of the small Kauai thrush. This rat is found on almost every forested mountain on Kauai and is able to climb trees to search out eggs and young birds. Recent sightings suggest that it is only a matter of time before another efficient bird predator, the mongoose, gains a foothold on the island.

In 1964, the Alakai Wilderness Preserve, consisting of 4,022 hectares (9,939 acres), was established to protect forest birds on Kauai. The Fish and Wildlife Service (FWS) Recovery Plan for forest birds identifies an area of 7,892 hectares (19,500 acres) on the island as essential for the survival of these species. Most of this area is currently administered by the Hawaii Division of Forestry and Wildlife.

The FWS is exploring the feasibility of captive propagation for endangered forest birds to stave off extinction. The goal of such a program would be to create a captive flock that could be used to supplement remaining wild populations. It is not known, however, whether the Hawaiian forest birds will live and breed in captivity.

In late 1988, 15 pairs of a non-threatened honeycreeper, the amakihi (*Hemignathus virens*), were sent to several participating zoos on the mainland to determine the birds' response to captivity. If successful, this effort will provide essential information on how to manage a captive propagation program for the rarer Hawaiian forest birds.

Bibliography

Kepler, C. B., and A. K. Kepler. 1983. "A First Record of the Nest and Chicks of the Small Kauai Thrush." *Condor* 85:497-99.

Pratt, H. C. 1982. "Relationships and Speciation of the Hawaiian Thrushes." *The Living Bird* 19:73-90.

Scott, J. M., *et al.* 1988. "Conservation of Hawaii's Vanishing Avifauna." *Bioscience* 38(4):238-253.

U.S. Fish and Wildlife Service. 1983. "Kauai Forest Birds Recovery Plan." U.S. Fish and Wildlife Service, Portland.

Contact

Regional Office of Endangered Species
U.S. Fish and Wildlife Service
Lloyd 500 Building, Suite 1692
500 N.E. Multnomah Street
Portland, Oregon 97232

Office of Environmental Services
U.S. Fish and Wildlife Service
300 Ala Moana Boulevard
P.O. Box 50167
Honolulu, Hawaii 96850

Wood Stork
Mycteria americana

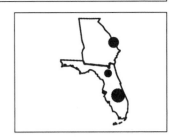

Lee Kuhn

Status	Endangered
Listed	February 28, 1984
Family	Ciconiidae (Stork)
Description	Large, long-legged wader; white with black flight feathers; bald gray head; stout downcurved bill.
Habitat	Wetlands.
Food	Fish, amphibians.
Reproduction	Clutch of 2 or 3 three eggs.
Threats	Loss and alteration of wetlands.
Region 4	Florida, Georgia, South Carolina

Description

The wood stork is a large (102 cm; 40 in), long-legged wading bird with an unfeathered gray head and a stout downcurved bill. It has a wingspan of 155 centimeters (61 in). Plumage is white with black flight feathers and tail. Immature birds have a feathered head, which, along with the neck, is grayish brown. Like a crane, the wood stork flies with the neck fully extended, but it perches in trees, which cranes will not do. The wood stork is the only species of true stork breeding anywhere in the U.S.

Behavior

Wood storks prefer to nest in the tops of large cypress trees growing in water. They are highly gregarious; as many as 25 nesting pairs have been observed in a single tree. The nest, which is added to each year, is a flimsy platform of twigs and sticks lined with finer materials.

The average wood stork clutch size is three eggs. When the young hatch, they are scantily covered with down and are reared in the nest. If food is scarce because of drought, colonies often fail to breed. If rains are too heavy after the onset of breeding, colonies may abandon the eggs.

The wood stork is largely mute. It feeds primarily on small fishes. The stork gropes in shallow water with an open beak, which it snaps shut when it feels its prey. Because feeding success improves with age and experience, young birds must spend twice as long foraging as mature birds.

Habitat

The wood stork usually nests in cypress and mangrove swamps along rivers and streams or adjacent to shallow lakes. Ideal foraging habitat is shallow wetlands that flood in the spring, producing an increase in the fish population. With the onset of summer the ponds begin drying up, concentrating fish for the catch. These drying periods typically correspond with the height of the nesting season.

Historic Range

Historically, wood storks bred throughout the states along the Gulf of Mexico, from Texas to Florida, and along the Atlantic coast from Florida to South Carolina. The post-breeding summer range extended north to Arkansas, Tennessee, and North Carolina. Wood storks have been sighted incidentally as far north as Montana, Wisconsin, and New York.

Researchers estimate that in 1930 there were about 60,000 wood storks in the U.S. breeding population (40,000 adults and 20,000 non-breeding immatures). Censuses in 1960 located 10,060 breeding pairs. Between 1960 and 1975 the U.S. breeding population declined 41 percent—to 5,982 pairs. This decline continued until 1980, when the number of breeding pairs stabilized at about 4,800.

Other breeding populations from Mexico to South America appear stable and are not endangered. Wood storks from the Mexican west coast are regular post-breeding migrants in California and Arizona; those from rookeries in eastern Mexico are seen in Texas and Louisiana.

Current Distribution

Breeding populations in the United States are restricted to Florida, southeastern Geor-gia, and South Carolina. Major rookeries are concentrated on the Florida peninsula and extreme southeastern Georgia. Estimates of the breeding population have held fairly steady since 1980. In 1986 the National Audubon Society estimated that there were 5,850 breeding pairs in U.S. rookeries.

Conservation and Recovery

Although many of the wood stork's breeding sites in southern Florida remain largely undisturbed, nesting attempts in these areas have failed repeatedly in recent years because of inadequate or insufficient foraging habitat. Suitable foraging areas in south Florida have decreased by about 35 percent since 1900 due to wetlands alteration, such as construction of levees, canals, and floodgates.

The traditional rookeries in south Florida—Everglades National Park, and the National Audubon Society's Corkscrew Swamp Sanctuary—are secure in the sense of being protected from disturbance, but nearby foraging areas have been drastically modified by residential and commercial development. Nesting success then depends on feeding areas that are far from the rookeries. For this reason none of the wood stork rookeries can be called truly "secure."

Raccoon predation has also been a problem at central Florida rookeries. In 1981, raccoons destroyed all 168 wood stork nests at a rookery in Hillsborough County when water levels dropped low enough under nest trees to provide access for the predators.

When the wood stork was officially listed as Endangered, the Department of Energy (DOE) was forced to examine the environmental impact of operating a nuclear reactor on the Savannah River, south and east of Augusta, Georgia. A way was devised to prevent thermal pollution of the river, but reactor operation was expected to raise water levels downstream to the point that the foraging habitat would be unusable by wood storks. The DOE agreed to construct an artificial foraging area to replace the habitat that would be lost when the reactor came on line.

The site selected for the artificial habitat was Kathwood Lake, a dry lake bed at the National Audubon Society's Silverbluff Plantation Sanctuary near Jackson, South Carolina. The U.S. Fish and Wildlife Service, National Audubon Society, the DOE, the Soil Conservation Service, Auburn University, the Savannah River Ecology Lab of the University of Georgia, and a major area contractor (E.I. du Pont de Nemours) all worked together to design and build the habitat, which was completed in 1986. In July, the wading lake was stocked with fish from the Orangeburg National Fish Hatchery, and local storks discovered it soon after. Within a week, over 70 storks were actively foraging in the lake.

Many private land owners and public land managers have since requested details of the Kathwood Lake design in order to reproduce it in their own areas. This successful collaboration is serving as a model for other attempts to provide wood stork foraging habitat.

In June 1989, the Interior Department created a new wildlife refuge for the Florida panther and other endangered species in south Florida. The 12,140-hectare (30,000-acre) Florida Panther National Wildlife Refuge is adjacent to the Big Cypress National Preserve and provides protected habitat for the Endangered Everglade snail kite (*Rostrhamus sociabilis plumbeus*), bald eagle (*Haliaeetus leucocephalus*), peregrine falcon (*Falco peregrinus anatum*), and eastern indigo snake (*Drymarchon corais couperi*), as well as the wood stork.

Bibliography

Kushlan, J. A., and P. C. Frohring. 1986. "The History of Southern Florida Wood Stork Population." *Wilson Bulletin* 98:368-386.

Ogden, J. C. 1985. "The Wood Stork." In R. L. Di Silvestro, ed., *Audubon Wildlife Report 1985.* National Audubon Society, New York.

Ogden, J. C., and B. W. Patty, 1981. "The Recent Status of the Wood Stork in Florida and Georgia." Technical Bulletin WL5. Georgia Department of Natural Resources/Game and Fish Division, Atlanta.

Ohlendorff, H. M., E. D. Klaas, and T. E. Kaiser. 1978. "Organochlorine Residues and Eggshell Thinning in Wood Storks and Anhingas." *Wilson Bulletin* 90(4):608-618.

U.S. Fish and Wildlife Service. 1986. "Recovery Plan for the U.S. Breeding Population of the Wood Stork." U.S. Fish and Wildlife Service, Atlanta.

Contact

Regional Office of Endangered Species
U.S. Fish and Wildlife Service
Richard B. Russell Federal Building
75 Spring Street, S.W.
Atlanta, Georgia 30303

Hawaiian Goose

Nesochen sandvicensis

Robert J. Shallenberger

Status	Endangered
Listed	March 11, 1967
Family	Anatidae (Ducks and Geese)
Description	Heavily barred gray-brown goose; black face, cap, and hindneck; black bill and feet.
Habitat	Sparsely vegetated volcanic slopes.
Food	Green vegetation, small berries.
Reproduction	Clutch of 1 to 6 eggs.
Threats	Loss of habitat, predation, low reproduction.
Region 1	Hawaii

Description

The Hawaiian goose, or "nene," ranges between 56 and 102 centimeters (22 and 40 in) in length, about the size of the common Canada goose. It has a blunt, triangular, black bill and a black face, cap, and hindneck. The side of the neck is buff and darkly furrowed. The gray-brown body and wings are heavily barred. The nene has also been described in the scientific literature as *Branta sandvicensis.* It is the state bird of Hawaii.

Behavior

The nene typically reaches sexual maturity after two years. Nesting season is from October through February. Geese tend to nest in the same area year after year, often in a "kipuka" (an island of vegetation surrounded by barren lava). Average clutch size is four eggs, which are incubated for 30 days. If a first attempt fails, geese will not usually renest that season. During the breeding season, non-breeding birds form loose flocks within the nesting areas.

Young nene, being flightless, are extremely vulnerable to predators for about 11 to 14 weeks after hatching. Family groups flock soon after young are able to fly and remain in the breeding grounds for about a month. They then wander freely in search of foraging areas. Nene feed on green vegetation and berries of native plants, such as ohelo (*Vaccinium* ssp.), kukaenene (*Coprosma ernodeoides*), pukiawe (*Styphelia tameiameiae*), and ulei (*Osteomeles anthyllidifolia*).

Habitat

The Hawaiian goose nests in areas of rugged lava flow among upland scrub, grasses, and herbs. Unlike other geese, it does not require open water but will swim where water is available close to the nests. During the non-breeding season the nene feeds in pastures dominated by introduced grasses.

Historic Range

Before the European discovery of Hawaii in 1778 by Captain James Cook, it is estimated that about 25,000 Hawaiian geese inhabited the islands. The population began to decline about 1800, and the bird was soon extirpated from lowland areas. A population on Maui became extinct before 1890. By 1944 most remaining birds were concentrated at higher elevations in the Hualalai-Puuwaawaa region on the island of Hawaii. By 1952 the total population had plummeted to a low of about 30 birds.

Current Distribution

The nene survives on Hawaii on the upper slopes of Mauna Loa at elevations above 1,500 meters (5,000 ft) and on Kilauea at slightly lower altitudes. On Maui, a reestablished population is found above 2,100 meters (7,000 ft) near the center of the island. As of 1982 a total of 1,800 captive-reared geese had been released on both Hawaii and Maui. Although the propagation and release program has failed to establish self-sustaining colonies, it has enabled the wild nene population to hold steady at about 400 birds.

Conservation and Recovery

Hunting, egg collecting, and predation have contributed to the historic decline of the nene. Reduction of habitat and a scarcity of native food plants are probably the main reasons for its continued difficulties. Poor reproduction in the wild has kept the nene from replacing its losses. Only about 50 percent of adult geese breed each year, and gosling mortality is high.

Since 1949 the state of Hawaii has operated a propagation program to release geese into the wild from stocks raised in captivity at Pohakuloa, on the island of Hawaii. In the early 1950s, the Severn Wildfowl Trust in England began rearing the birds and distributing them to zoos and aviaries; the Trust has also released captive-bred geese on Maui.

In 1972 the Fish and Wildlife Service initiated a nest enclosure project at the Hawaiian Volcanoes National Park on Hawaii. Pairs of wing-clipped adult birds are confined to wire enclosures that provide semi-natural, predator-free conditions. Their offspring are then permitted to leave the pens to occupy adjacent habitat, which has been rehabilitated and replanted with native food plants. At Haleakala National Park on Maui, a similar program is underway.

Bibliography

Kear, J., and A. J. Berger. 1980. *The Hawaiian Goose: An Experiment in Conservation.* Buteo Books, Vermillion, South Dakota.

U.S. Fish and Wildlife Service. 1983. "The Nene Recovery Plan." U.S. Fish and Wildlife Service, Portland.

Contact

Office of Environmental Services
U.S. Fish and Wildlife Service
300 Ala Moana Boulevard
P.O. Box 50167
Honolulu, Hawaii 96850

Eskimo Curlew
Numenius borealis

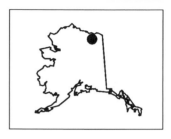

Don Bleitz

Status	Endangered
Listed	March 11, 1967
Family	Scolopacidae (Sandpiper)
Description	Long-legged wading bird; dark brown with a pale throat and long, downcurved bill.
Habitat	Open tundra, tidal marshes.
Food	Insects, snails, berries.
Reproduction	Clutch of 3 or 4 eggs.
Threats	Low numbers.
Region 7	Alaska

Description

Also known as the doughbird or prairie pigeon, the Eskimo curlew is the smallest of the American curlews, measuring about 36 centimeters (14 in) in total length. It is a long-legged wading bird with a plump body that is dark brown above and lighter below. The throat is white or pale buff. The upper breast is streaked with dark brown and the under-wings are reddish brown, with darker bars. It has a long, black, downcurved bill; dark brown eyes; and grayish blue legs. Both sexes appear alike.

Behavior

Birds breed and nest when they return from their wintering grounds in late May or June.

Nests are usually a hollow in the ground lined with leaves or straw and are difficult to locate. The camouflaged eggs are brownish green to blue. Clutch size is three to four eggs. Curlews forage in wetlands on insects, snails, and berries.

Habitat

Eskimo curlews nest in wetlands north of the tree line in open tundra, and in tidal marshes near the Arctic Ocean. Their winter habitat is on the pampas of Argentina.

Historic Range

Historically, the Eskimo curlew bred in the northern Mackenzie District of Canada and along the Alaskan coast. In late summer, curlews migrate to Argentina, mostly flying over open ocean from Labrador to South America. Some few were known to fly south over the Great Plains to the Texas coast. On their northward migration, they could be seen in Texas and Louisiana in early March, then along the Mississippi, Missouri, and Platte River valleys.

Current Distribution

The Eskimo curlew was considered possibly extinct until a recent flurry of sightings in the central and southern U.S. and in Canada. In May 1981, 23 Eskimo curlews were observed on Atkinson Island, Texas. In April 1987, one bird was sighted in a meadow along the Platte River in Nebraska, and in May at least two more were reported from the Texas coast. In late May 1987, Canadian Wildlife Service personnel discovered an Eskimo Curlew nesting in northern Canada. It is believed that the breeding population is between 100 and 150 birds.

Conservation and Recovery

The Eskimo curlew was already rare in the early part of this century and has been seen only occasionally since that time. Hunting during migration may have been partly responsible for the bird's decline, but disease or predation are probably more significant factors. None of these factors can be verified, because this rare species has not been sufficiently studied. Nor have recovery strategies been devised, since the bird both nests and winters far from normal human encroachment.

In response to recent sightings, shorebird specialists from the U.S. and Canada gathered at a meeting of the American Ornithologists' Union to discuss the plight of the curlew. These specialists recommended immediate protection and management of known stopover areas along the Eskimo curlew's migration routes. The Fish and Wildlife Service is in the process of forming a recovery team to plan the conservation effort for the Eskimo curlew. The team will include representation from the Canadian Wildlife Service and the International Committee for Bird Preservation.

Bibliography

Blankinship, D. R., and K. A. King. 1984. "Probable Sighting of 23 Eskimo Curlews in Texas." *American Birds* 38: 1066-1067.

Gollop, J. Bernard. 1988. "The Eskimo curlew." In W.J. Chandler, ed. *Audubon Wildlife Report 1988/89*. Academic Press, San Diego.

Greenway, James C. 1958. *Extinct and Vanishing Birds of the World*. American Committee for International Wild Life Protection, New York.

Contact

Regional Office of Endangered Species
U.S. Fish and Wildlife Service
1011 E. Tudor Road
Anchorage, Alaska 99503

Hawaii Creeper

Oreomystis mana

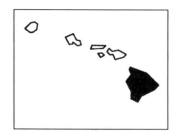

H. Douglas Pratt

Status	Endangered
Listed	September 25, 1975
Family	Fringillidae; Subfamily Drepanidinae (Hawaiian Honeycreeper)
Description . . .	Small honeycreeper; olive green above, yellow-brown below; white throat.
Habitat	Ohia and koa forests.
Food	Insects, larvae.
Reproduction . .	Clutch of 2 eggs.
Threats	Deforestation.
Region 1	Hawaii

Description

The Hawaii creeper is sparrow-sized, up to 13 centimeters (5 in) long and weighing about 14 grams (0.5 oz). It has a thick, pale, slightly curved bill. Plumage is predominantly olive green on the back and yellow-brown below. The throat is white. Field identification is complicated by the creeper's similarity to the amakihi, Hawaii akepa, and Japanese white-eye. This species was previously classified as *Loxops mana*.

Behavior

The Hawaii creeper is usually solitary but is sometimes found in small family groups. It gleans insects from tree bark. Little is known of its breeding biology and natural history.

The clutch size is probably two eggs, which are laid in a nest built in the crotch of a limb or between the bark and trunk of the koa tree. Active nests have been found in January and February.

Habitat

The creeper prefers mixed ohia (*Metrosideros collina*) and koa (*Acacia koa*) forests where it feeds on insects gleaned from the trunks and branches of trees. Beetle larvae make up a large part of its diet. Habitat elevation is usually above 1,070 meters (3,600 ft).

Historic Range

The Hawaii creeper was formerly found in the ohia and mixed ohia-koa forests throughout the island of Hawaii. It was common in the Kona and Kau districts, as well as in the forests above Hilo.

Current Distribution

Presently found throughout upper-elevation native forests on the eastern coast, the Hawaii creeper is locally rare to common on Keauhou Ranch and on the eastern slopes of Mauna Loa. It is rare on the western coast. The most recent population estimate (1986) for the Hawaii creeper is 24,780 birds.

Conservation and Recovery

Like many of Hawaii's forest birds, the Hawaii creeper declined due to deforestation of the islands. Hawaii's forests have been drastically reduced by logging and the subsequent conversion of land to crops and pasture. Today, most forest areas below 800 meters (2,600 ft) have been converted to agricultural or urban uses. Wetter forests on the island are subject to rooting by feral pigs, which uproot native plants and spread the seeds of competing exotic plants, such as banana poka and strawberry guava.

Widespread dieback of ohia, Hawaii's most common native forest tree, has recently modified large tracts of forest on the island of Hawaii, and additional areas may be threatened. Research is under way to determine whether this dieback is a recurrent natural phenomenon. Dieback continues between the elevations of 760 and 1,830 meters (2,500 and 6,000 ft) primarily in the Hilo, Kau, Olaa, and Waikea areas.

In addition to habitat loss, the Hawaii creeper and other forest birds are vulnerable to avian pox and malaria that are spread by mosquitoes. Mosquitoes were first introduced to the islands in the 1820s. Loss of native birds is especially evident at lower elevations where mosquitoes are most numerous. Other introduced insects, such as parasitic wasps and predaceous ants, have eliminated many native insects, which served as food for the creeper.

Recovery of the Hawaii creeper and other forest birds depends on the preservation and restoration of a large, contiguous tract of native forest habitat. In 1985, the U.S. Fish and Wildlife Service, together with The Nature Conservancy of Hawaii and the state Department of Land and Natural Resources, purchased 3,360 hectares (8,300 acres) of native forest as the first phase in a proposed 13,560-hectare (33,500-acre) Hakalau Forest National Wildlife Refuge. Designed primarily to preserve the habitat of endangered forest birds, the refuge is located on the northwestern slope of Mauna Kea. In 1988 another 162 hectares (400 acres) was added to the refuge.

Bibliography

Scott, J. M., S. L. Conant, and H. D. Pratt. 1979. "Field Identification of the Hawaiian Creeper on the Island of Hawaii." *Western Birds* 10:71-80.

U.S. Fish and Wildlife Service. 1982. "The Hawaii Forest Bird Recovery Plan." U.S. Fish and Wildlife Service, Portland.

Contact

Regional Office of Endangered Species
U.S. Fish and Wildlife Service
Lloyd 500 Building, Suite 1692
500 N.E. Multnomah Street
Portland, Oregon 97232

Field Office of Endangered Species
U.S. Fish and Wildlife Service
300 Ala Moana Boulevard
P.O. Box 50167
Honolulu, Hawaii 96850

Crested Honeycreeper
Palmeria dolei

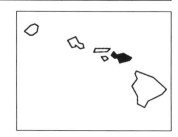

H. Douglas Pratt

Status	Endangered
Listed	March 11, 1967
Family	Fringillidae; Subfamily Drepanidinae (Hawaiian Honeycreepers)
Description . . .	Honeycreeper; primarily black with orange nape and bushy crest.
Habitat	Ohia forests.
Food	Nectar.
Reproduction . .	Unknown.
Threats	Habitat destruction, predation, disease.
Region 1	Hawaii

Description

At about 18 centimeters (7 in), the crested honeycreeper is the largest of the subfamily Drepanidinae on Maui. It is primarily black and in poor light appears entirely black. The dark feathers are tipped with gray on the breast and throat, off-white on the wing and tail tips, and orange over most of the body. The bird has a prominent orange nape and ragged, white crest. The thighs, orange or yellowish, can be very conspicuous in some light. Immature birds are duller and lack the orange tint and the crest. The Hawaiian name for this bird is "akohekohe."

Behavior

The crested honeycreeper feeds primarily on ohia nectar but will use a variety of other flowers, such as tree ohelo (*Vaccinium calycinum*) and akala (*Rubus hawaiiensis*), when ohia flowers are unavailable. No nests have ever been found, but the birds are thought to pair in February and March. Adults with juveniles have been seen in May.

Habitat

This species' known habitat is wet ohia forests on Maui and Molokai in the Hawaiian Islands. In 1980, 415 observations on Maui were recorded in an area of about 4,450 hectares (11,000 acres) at elevations from 1,260 to 2,130 meters (4,200 to 7,100 ft).

Historic Range

Historically, the crested honeycreeper was locally abundant on both Maui and Molokai.

It was last seen on Molokai in 1907 and was not seen on Maui between about 1900 and 1942, probably because few ornithologists looked for it.

Current Distribution

The population, now estimated at about 3,800 birds, occurs in two major groups on east Maui, separated by Koolau Gap. To the west of the gap, large numbers inhabit an area of about 1,620 hectares (4,000 acres), all privately owned. To the east the honey-creeper's range extends nearly 10 kilometers (6 mi) along a mile-wide swath of forest above 1,470 meters (4,900 ft) elevation, then south to upper Kipahulu Valley and Manawainui.

Conservation and Recovery

The Hawaiian Islands have been extensively altered by human settlement. The magnitude of ecological changes since that time is only now being appreciated. Large tracts of forest, especially on the dry leeward slopes, were cleared by the Polynesians for agriculture. European settlers eliminated all dry forest on Maui up to at least 1,500 meters (5,000 ft) for pasture. By the turn of the century, almost all forests, except the higher elevation ohia forests, were gone, and forest bird populations had declined precipitously.

In much of the remaining forests, browsing and rooting by feral goats and pigs and axis deer have seriously disturbed native plants, allowing introduced plants to invade the habitat. The combined impact of feral animals and non-native plants has changed species composition, distribution, and plant densities, and these changes affect native birds.

Avian diseases, especially pox and malaria, were spread by introduced mosquitoes, and played a large role in the decline of many native Hawaiian birds. In addition, predation and competition with introduced bird species has taken its toll of forest birds.

The State Reserve System holds and actively manages about 30 percent of the remaining forest resources of the islands, including those on Maui. The Nature Conservancy manages the Waikamoi Kamakou preserves. Haleakala National Park has implemented a program to control some exotic plants, and a portion of the Haleakala Crater district has been fenced.

Since the crested honeycreeper could easily suffer a population crash while recovery efforts are studied and implemented, the Fish and Wildlife Service is exploring the possibility of captive propagation for it and other endangered forest birds. The ultimate goal would be the creation of a captive flock to furnish birds to supplement wild populations. Little is known, however, about the ability of Hawaiian forest birds to live and breed in captivity.

Bibliography

Scott, J. M., *et al.* 1988. "Conservation of Hawaii's Vanishing Avifauna." *Bioscience* 38(4):238-253.

U.S. Fish and Wildlife Service. 1984. "The Maui-Molokai Forest Birds Recovery Plan." U.S. Fish and Wildlife Service, Portland.

Contact

Regional Office of Endangered Species
U.S. Fish and Wildlife Service
Lloyd 500 Building, Suite 1692
500 N.E. Multnomah Street
Portland, Oregon 97232

Office of Environmental Services
U.S. Fish and Wildlife Service
300 Ala Moana Boulevard
P.O. Box 50167
Honolulu, Hawaii 96850

Molokai Creeper
Paroreomyza flammea

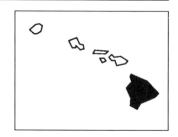

H. Douglas Pratt

Status	Endangered (possibly extinct)
Listed	October 13, 1970
Family	Fringillidae; Subfamily Drepanidinae (Hawaiian Honeycreeper)
Description . . .	Honeycreeper; male scarlet, female brown above and white below.
Habitat	Ohia forests.
Food	Insects.
Reproduction . .	Unknown.
Threats	Habitat destruction, low numbers.
Region 1	Hawaii

Description

Known in Hawaiian as kakawahie, the Molokai creeper is a small honeycreeper, about 13 centimeters (5 in) in length and weighing about 14 grams (0.5 oz). It is a slender bird with a stiff tail. Males are orange, with brown wings and tail; females are dark brownish green, washed with orange. This species has been variously classified as *Oreomystis flammea* and *Loxops flammea*.

Behavior

The Molokai creeper often hangs upside down to dig insects out of tree trunks or larger branches. Little is known of its breeding biology.

Habitat

The island of Molokai, 61 kilometers (38 mi) long and 16 kilometers (10 mi) wide, lies 14.5 kilometers (9 mi) northwest of Maui in the Hawaiian Islands. It is formed of two volcanoes; the oldest, Puu Nana, lies in the rain shadow of the larger eastern volcano, Kamakou. Kamakou reaches a height of 1,491 meters (4,970 ft); its northern face is precipitous. Erosion within the two major northern valleys, Pelekunu and Wailau, has completely encircled a rugged plateau—Olokui—with 610-meter (2,000-ft) cliffs. This forested plateau is the most isolated and pristine land in the main Hawaiian Islands and still supports populations of rare forest birds. The Molokai creeper is found in wet, montane ohia forests with a dense understory of mosses, vines, and tree ferns. Habitat elevation is above 1,200 meters (4,000 ft).

Historic Range

In the 1890s the creeper was abundant on both the windward and leeward sides of Molokai.

Current Distribution

This bird was last seen in 1963 in the rugged high country between Pepeopae Bog, Papaala Pali, and Waikolu. No creepers have been found during recent bird surveys, indicating that this species is either extremely rare or extinct. There is no current population estimate.

Conservation and Recovery

The pristine island ecosystem that existed on Molokai before the first Polynesians settled in the Hawaiian Islands is now largely gone, and the arrival of European settlers accelerated the island's conversion to agriculture. Large tracts of forest, especially on the dry leeward slopes, were cleared for agriculture by the Polynesians, and fire was commonly used to burn vast areas to maintain pili grass used for thatching houses. European settlers eliminated all dry forest on Molokai's south coast up to at least 900 meters (3,000 ft). By the turn of the century almost all forest, except the very wet ohia forest, had been eliminated. Hawaiian forest birds declined as a result.

The combined impact of rooting feral animals and invasive non-native plants has disrupted most remaining stands of native forests. The changing composition, distribution, and densities of native food plants have severely restricted the food supply of island birds.

The State Reserve system currently holds and actively manages about 30 percent of the state under forest cover, including forests on the island of Molokai. Management activities include fencing out cattle, hunting of feral animals, and reforestation of denuded areas.

Since the Molokai creeper is extremely rare, if not extinct, there is little hope that a captive breeding program will be able to save this species. But other forest bird species may be helped to survive through captive breeding, and the Fish and Wildlife Service is exploring the possibility of captive propagation for other endangered Hawaiian forest birds.

Bibliography

Berger, A. J. 1981. *Hawaiian Birdlife*. University of Hawaii Press, Honolulu.

Scott, J. M., *et al.* 1988. "Conservation of Hawaii's Vanishing Avifauna." *Bioscience* 38(4):238-253.

U.S. Fish and Wildlife Service. 1984. "The Maui-Molokai Forest Birds Recovery Plan." U.S. Fish and Wildlife Service, Portland.

Contact

Regional Office of Endangered Species
U.S. Fish and Wildlife Service
Lloyd 500 Building, Suite 1692
500 N.E. Multnomah Street
Portland, Oregon 97232

Office of Environmental Services
U.S. Fish and Wildlife Service
300 Ala Moana Boulevard
P.O. Box 50167
Honolulu, Hawaii 96850

Brown Pelican
Pelecanus occidentalis

Luther Goldman/USFWS

Status	Endangered in Texas, Louisiana, and California
Listed	October 13, 1970
Family	Pelecanidae (Pelican)
Description . . .	Large, light brown waterbird with massive bill and throat pouch.
Habitat	Coastal islands.
Food	Fish.
Reproduction . .	Clutch of 3 eggs.
Threats	Pesticides.
Region 1	California
Region 2	Texas
Region 4	Alabama, Florida, Louisiana, North Carolina, South Carolina

Description

The brown pelican is a large, diving water bird, weighing up to 3.5 kilograms (8 lbs) and having a wingspan of up to 2 meters (7 ft). It has a light brown body with a white head and neck, which are often tinged with yellow. In breeding season, the back of the neck turns dark brown and a yellow patch appears at the base of the foreneck.

The U.S. is home to two subspecies of the brown pelican: the California brown pelican (*Pelecanus occidentalis californicus*), native to the southern California coast; and the Eastern brown pelican (*P. o. carolinensis*), which occurs on the Atlantic and Gulf coasts. While generally similar in appearance, the Califor-nia subspecies is slightly larger, and shows a darker hindneck and bright red throat pouch during breeding. This red throat pouch is rare among Eastern brown pelicans.

The brown pelican is one of two pelican species found in North America. The white pelican (*Pelecanus erythrorhynchos*) winters along the southern California coast, the Gulf coast, and the Atlantic coast of Florida.

Behavior

Brown pelicans are rarely found away from salt water and do not normally venture more than about 32 kilometers (20 mi) out to sea. They feed almost entirely on fish captured by plunge diving.

Brown pelicans are colonial nesters that use small, inaccessible coastal islands as breeding sites. Nesting occurs primarily in early spring and summer. The normal clutch size is three eggs and both sexes participate in incubation. Young are born naked and helpless and acquire down after about ten days. Fledging takes place at 12 weeks. In some years, depending on water temperature and prey availability, birds disperse northward from their breeding range in late summer. Brown pelicans are only very rarely observed inland.

Many brown pelicans stay close to their nesting sites throughout the winter. A portion of the eastern subspecies migrates to Florida, the Caribbean coasts of Columbia and Venezuela, and the Greater Antilles. During cold winters, some Texas brown pelicans winter along the Gulf coast of Mexico.

Brown pelican populations fluctuate considerably from year to year and from place to place. Colonies may switch breeding sites yearly, especially in Florida where the breeding population is widely distributed. Therefore, abandonment of rookeries in one area is no indication of an overall declining population. The pelican is a long-lived species that has evolved with this boom and bust reproduction strategy.

Habitat

The brown pelican almost always nests on coastal islands, rarely more than 2 meters (6 ft) above high tide. In the eastern U.S. it uses low, sandy islands and spits or mangrove trees for nesting. Islands and spits are subject to erosion and flooding by storm and spring tides, forcing brown pelicans to constantly shift nesting sites. Florida brown pelicans nest slightly above the high tide line on islands of black, red, or white mangroves, and to a lesser extent in other trees and shrubs, including Australian pine, red cedar, live oak, redbay, and seagrape.

Historic Range

The Eastern brown pelican has nested along the Atlantic and Gulf coasts of the U.S. (from the Carolinas to Texas), the West Indies, and Central and South America. Large numbers were once found on small coastal islands in Texas, Louisiana, Florida, and South Carolina, while smaller numbers nested in North Carolina and possibly Georgia. Nesting has not been recorded in Mississippi or states north of North Carolina. In 1983 several pairs of pelicans nested on a spoil island in Alabama's Mobile Bay, the first nesting recorded in that state.

In the early 1800s, John J. Audubon estimated up to 9,000 nesting pairs in Florida; 3,000 to 6,000 pairs in South Carolina; and perhaps a hundred pairs in North Carolina. A small colony of a few hundred birds was seen sporadically in Georgia. In the past, between 10,000 and 15,000 pairs nested in Louisiana and between 1,500 and 4,000 in Texas.

Historically, up to 50,000 birds nested in Louisiana and Texas. Between 1957 and 1961, pelican populations in both states declined precipitously because of pesticide poisoning. Nesting ceased on the Louisiana coast and was very nearly eliminated on the Texas coast.

On the West Coast, the California brown pelican nests on offshore islands in extreme southern California and Baja California, Mexico. Population estimates before 1968, when regular surveys were begun, indicate that up to 2,000 pairs nested on Anacapa Island and an equal number nested on the Channel Islands. Smaller colonies have been recorded on Santa Barbara Island, San Miguel Island, and Santa Cruz. During the

1930s, another large colony, estimated at 2,500 pairs, nested on Los Coronados, near the U.S.-Mexican border. Islands in the Gulf of California have always held the largest population of California brown pelicans.

Current Distribution

During the last decade the Florida population of brown pelicans has remained stable. In 1989 about 11,500 pairs nested throughout the state in 37 active colonies, stretching from Daytona Beach on the Atlantic coast to Panama City on the Gulf of Mexico. In South Carolina two colonies support about 5,000 nesting pairs, a population at or above historic levels.

The North Carolina brown pelican population has shown an increase in recent years. There are now about five active colonies in two separate coastal areas. Biologists attribute the increase to the northward expansion of the South Carolina population, aided by the recent creation of dredge spoil islands which provide additional nesting habitat.

Along the Texas and Louisiana coast, the pesticide disaster of the 1950s and 1960s has been somewhat mitigated. The Texas population recovered from a low of less than 100 pelicans in the late 1960s to about 500 pairs in 1989. In Louisiana, where the breeding population was extirpated, colonies have been successfully reestablished using birds from Florida. Currently, the nesting population numbers over 1,000 pairs.

Annual surveys of California brown pelican populations began in the late 1960s. Current estimates indicate that the total population is about 48,500 pairs. Of this total, 3,000 pairs (6 percent) nest in southern California; 33,000 (68 percent) nest in the Gulf of California; 7,500 (15 percent) nest on islands off mainland Mexico; and 5,000 (10 percent) in southwest Baja California.

Conservation and Recovery

Pesticide pollution presented a double threat to the survival of the brown pelican—direct poisoning and impaired reproduction. Between 1957 and 1961, exposure to concentrations of the pesticide endrin almost eliminated the brown pelican as a breeding species along the Texas and Louisiana coast. Exposure to the pesticide DDT caused dramatic reproductive failure in brown pelicans on the Gulf, Atlantic, and Pacific coasts. DDT interferes with calcium formation and produces brittle, thin-shelled eggs that are easily crushed during incubation. As a result, the brown pelican was listed as Endangered throughout its U.S. range in 1970.

In the late 1960s, brown pelican populations in South Carolina declined primarily because of egg loss resulting from eggshell thinning. In California, thin-shelled eggs and other complications resulted in almost complete reproductive failure. Out of 375 nests in one colony in 1969, no young were produced. In 1970, a colony on Anacapa Island produced only a single fledgling from 552 nesting pairs. This dramatic decline was caused by the direct dumping of DDT wastes into the Los Angeles sewer system by a pesticide manufacturing plant.

In 1972 the Environmental Protection Agency placed a ban on the use of DDT in the U.S. and sharply curtailed the use of endrin. As a result, residue levels of these chemicals have steadily decreased in most areas with a corresponding rise in reproductive success for all brown pelican populations. As a result, the Eastern brown pelican populations of the Atlantic coast and the Florida Gulf coast have been removed from the federal list of Endangered Species.

Following publicity about the plight of the brown pelican, human interference in their nesting areas, by both scientists and the public, increased. Human disturbance causes adults to flush, resulting in egg breakage or an increase of predation on unguarded eggs and nestlings. Access to brown pelican colonies is now generally limited to scientific investigators and resource managers on federally owned nesting sites.

Currently, the Louisiana and Texas populations of the Eastern brown pelican and the California brown pelican remain Endangered. The California subspecies, however, has shown considerable recovery and the Fish and Wildlife Service (FWS) is now reconsidering its status. Current FWS plans are to downlist the California brown pelican from Endangered to Threatened in 1990.

Bibliography

Anderson, D. W., and J. O. Keith. 1980. "The Human Influence on Seabird Nesting Success: Conservation Implications." *Biological Conservation* 18:65-80.

Briggs, K. T., *et al.* 1983. "Brown Pelicans in Central and Northern California." *Journal of Field Ornithology* 54:353-373.

King, K. A., *et al.* 1977. "The Decline of Brown Pelicans on the Louisiana and Texas Gulf Coast." *Southwest Naturalist* 21(4):417-431.

Schreiber, R. W. 1980. "The Brown Pelican: An Endangered Species?" *Bioscience* 30(11):742-747.

U. S. Fish and Wildlife Service. 1983. "The California Brown Pelican Recovery Plan." U. S. Fish and Wildlife Service. Portland.

U. S. Fish and Wildlife Service. 1980. "Eastern Brown Pelican Recovery Plan." U.S. Fish and Wildlife Service, Atlanta.

Contact

Regional Office of Endangered Species
U.S. Fish and Wildlife Service
Lloyd 500 Building, Suite 1692
500 N.E. Multnomah Street
Portland, Oregon 97232

Regional Office of Endangered Species
U.S. Fish and Wildlife Service
Richard B. Russell Federal Building
75 Spring Street, S.W.
Atlanta, Georgia 30303

Red-Cockaded Woodpecker
Picoides borealis

Jerome A. Jackson

Status	Endangered
Listed	October 13, 1970
Family	Picidae (Woodpecker)
Description . . .	Woodpecker with white cheek patch; males with red head patch.
Habitat	Old-growth pine stands.
Food	Wood-boring insects.
Reproduction . .	Clutch of 2 to 5 eggs.
Threats	Habitat destruction.
Region 2	Texas
Region 4	Arkansas, Florida, Georgia, Kentucky, Louisiana, Mississippi, North Carolina, South Carolina, Tennessee

Description

The red-cockaded woodpecker is approximately 19 centimeters (7.25 in) long with a black and white barred back, black-flecked flanks, and black bars on its white outer tail feathers. It has conspicuous white cheeks and a black band running from the eye to the crown. The adult male has small red patches on each side of his head; females lack the red head plumage.

Because the male's red cockades are small and usually concealed beneath black plumage, adults are virtually indistinguishable in the field. Nestling and fledgling males, however, are easily distinguished, even in the nest cavity. About 15 days after birth, males develop a red oval crown patch in the center of an otherwise black crown. This coloring is retained until the first molt in the fall.

Behavior

Clans of this nonmigratory woodpecker maintain year-round territories around nesting and roost trees. A clan consists of a mated pair, the current year's offspring, and "helpers"—immature males from a previous year that aid the parents with incubation, feeding, and brooding duties.

The red-cockaded woodpecker excavates nesting cavities in living pine trees—the only excavator to use living trees exclusively.

Nesting occurs in April and May. Clutch size is from two to five eggs; incubation lasts about ten days.

Following fledging, juveniles remain in their parents' home range through the summer and into the fall. From late fall to early spring juvenile females disperse, but some juvenile males remain to become helpers. Red-cockaded woodpeckers feed on tree surface and subsurface arthropods.

Habitat

For nesting, red-cockaded woodpeckers use old-growth trees of most southern pine species, except for sand pine, spruce pine, white pine, and table-mountain pine. The woodpecker shows some preference for mature longleaf pine (*Pinus palustris*).

Many trees selected for nesting have been found to be infected by the heartwood decaying fungus (*Phellinus pini*). This decay may make it easier for the woodpecker to excavate a nest cavity. Cavity trees tend to be clustered in small groups, forming colonies of up to 57 trees. Most active colonies are found in open, park-like stands of pine with sparse hardwood midstories; red-cockaded woodpeckers will abandon nest cavities when the understory reaches the height of the cavity entrance. Pine stands with well-developed hardwood midstories seem to provide better habitat for pileated woodpeckers and red-bellied woodpeckers, species that usurp red-cockaded woodpecker nest cavities.

Historic Range

In the early 19th century John James Audubon stated that the red-cockaded woodpecker was "found abundantly from Texas to New Jersey and as far inland as Tennessee" and that it was most numerous in the pine barrens of Florida, Georgia, and South Carolina. In the early 20th century or-

nithologists still considered the bird locally common in Florida, Georgia, South Carolina, and Louisiana. About that time researchers began to notice a rangewide population decline and fragmentation into isolated local populations.

Current Distribution

A thorough census of red-cockaded woodpeckers on federal lands was conducted in 1979. In national forests in the southern U.S. slightly more than 2,100 active colonies were scattered throughout Texas, Florida, Mississippi, Alabama, South Carolina, and Louisiana. There were an additional 200 colonies on wildlife refuges in Florida, Georgia, Arkansas, Louisiana, Mississippi, North Carolina, and South Carolina, and another 340 to 400 colonies on military bases. The total on federally owned lands was about 2,700 birds. Undoubtedly there are additional red-cockaded woodpeckers on private land throughout the region.

Conservation and Recovery

Compared with many other endangered birds, the red-cockaded woodpecker is relatively abundant and widespread. However, the prospects for long-term survival are uncertain. A major portion of southern pine habitat has been cleared and converted to other uses. Stands of old-growth pine, required by the species for nesting, are scarce and declining. There are no legal requirements or incentive programs to encourage private landowners to perpetuate old-growth pine forest. There is little doubt that the total red-cockaded woodpecker population continues to decline as more nesting habitat is lost.

Since the bird's habitat requirements are well known, public lands can be managed to maintain viable woodpecker populations.

Some form of incentive will be needed to assure that private forest lands are managed to provide connecting habitat corridors between the fragmented populations on public land.

In 1987, federal biologists, in cooperation with state and local officials in North Carolina, began a program to protect cavity trees of a red-cockaded woodpecker population, estimated at 130 birds. To date, over 600 cavity trees on private land have been marked with small aluminum signs showing the bird and stating that the tree should not be cut. Because the program has been so well received, efforts are underway to expand it throughout the woodpecker's range.

Bibliography

Audubon, J. J. 1839. *Ornithological Biography.* Edinburgh.

Baker, W. W., *et al.* 1980. "The Distribution and Status of Red-Cockaded Woodpecker Colonies in Florida." *Florida Field Naturalist* 8:41-45.

Jackson, J. A. 1977. "Red-Cockaded Woodpeckers and Pine Red Heart Disease." *Auk* 94:160-163.

Jackson, J. A. 1986 "Biopolitics, Management of Federal Lands, and the Conservation of the Red-Cockaded Woodpecker." *American Birds* 40:1162-1168.

Lennartz, M. R., and R. F. Harlow. 1979. "The Role of Parent and Helper Red-Cockaded Woodpeckers at the Nest." *Wilson Bulletin* 91:331-335.

Ligon, J. D. 1970. "Behavior and Breeding Biology of the Red-Cockaded Woodpecker." *Auk* 87:255-278.

U.S. Fish and Wildlife Service. 1985. "Red-Cockaded Woodpecker Recovery Plan." U.S. Fish and Wildlife Service, Atlanta.

Contact

Regional Office of Endangered Species
U.S. Fish and Wildlife Service
Richard B. Russell Federal Building
75 Spring Street, S.W.
Atlanta, Georgia 30303

Inyo Brown Towhee

Pipilo fuscus eremophilus

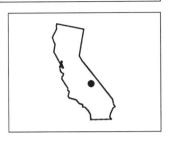

Denise L. LaBerteaux

Status	Threatened
Listed	August 3, 1987
Family	Fringillidae (Finch)
Description	Sparrowlike songbird; gray-brown above, white below.
Habitat	Scrub vegetation and open woods.
Food	Seeds and insects.
Reproduction	Clutch of 3 or 4 eggs.
Threats	Low numbers, restricted range, habitat alteration.
Region 1	California

Description

The Inyo brown towhee is a sparrowlike songbird, 17 to 19 centimeters (7 to 7.5 in) long. The bird is gray-brown above, whitish below, and has a buff throat ringed with dark streaks and a dark breast spot. The Inyo is one of several recognized subspecies of the brown towhee.

Behavior

The towhee builds cuplike nests of grass in bushes and low trees, where it lays a clutch of three or four bluish white eggs. The incubation period is 11 days; young fledge in eight days. Roger Tory Peterson describes the towhee's song as a "rapid chink-chink-ink-ink-ink . . . on one pitch." It is nonmigratory and feeds on seeds and insects.

Habitat

The Inyo brown towhee has become adapted to a rigorous desert streambank environment not fully duplicated elsewhere within the species' range. It prefers rocky canyons cut by water courses with scrub vegetation or open woodlands for foraging. It nests in dense vegetation beside springs and flowing streams.

Historic Range

The Inyo's historic range is limited to the desert riparian habitat of the Argus Mountains (Inyo County), California.

Current Distribution

The entire population of this towhee, estimated in 1987 at fewer than 200 birds, is confined to pockets of suitable habitat within the arid region south of Owens Lake and west of Death Valley. Three-fourths of the population inhabits an area about 18 kilometers (11 mi) in diameter on the China Lake Naval Weapons Center (Inyo County). The remainder inhabits land managed by the Bureau of Land Management (BLM) and a small area—77 hectares (190 acres)—of private land.

Conservation and Recovery

The Inyo's very low numbers and limited range make it extremely vulnerable, and the Fish and Wildlife Service is considering reclassifying it as Endangered. Its fragile habitat, near some of the region's few water sources, has been trampled and browsed by wild burros and horses. Cattle grazing in the area was discontinued in 1981, and 8,000 wild horses and burros were also removed. These actions appear to have made a significant difference in regenerating vegetation favored by the Inyo.

The Navy controls almost 75 percent of the towhee's habitat and will continue to remove wild burros and horses from the land. The Navy does not use the towhee habitat for weapons testing and does not anticipate any future activities detrimental to the towhee.

The BLM manages 260 hectares (640 acres) as the Great Fall Basin-Argus Mountains Area of Critical Environmental Concern and has produced a management plan for this area. Hiking, camping, hunting, and off-road vehicle use are currently permitted. Mineral exploration on public land could pose a threat through habitat disturbance. Controlling access to the habitat area and maintaining the integrity of the riparian and spring habitat is necessary to prevent further decline of the Inyo brown towhee. The BLM is

charged by law to consider the welfare of the towhee when leasing mineral rights.

Since the Inyo brown towhee has highly specific habitat requirements, any threat to the water supply or streamside vegetation could affect nesting and feeding activities.

Bibliography

Cord, B., and J. R. Jehl, Jr. 1979. "Distribution, Biology and Status of a Relict Population of Brown Towhee (*Pipilo fuscus eremophilus*)." *Western Birds* 10:131-156.

LaBerteaux, D. 1984. "Untitled/Unpublished Report on the Inyo Brown Towhee." California Department of Fish and Game, Sacramento.

Contact

Regional Office of Endangered Species
U.S. Fish and Wildlife Service
Lloyd 500 Building, Suite 1692
500 N.E. Multnomah Street
Portland, Oregon 97232

Audubon's Crested Caracara
Polyborus plancus audubonii

Lee Kuhn

Status	Threatened in Florida
Listed	July 6, 1987
Family	Falconidae (Falcon)
Description	Dark brown, crested bird of prey with a massive, bluish bill and red-orange facial patch.
Habitat	Open prairie, pastures.
Food	Carrion, live prey.
Reproduction	Clutch of 2 or 3 eggs.
Threats	Agricultural and residential development.
Region 4	Florida

Description

A unique American bird of prey, Audubon's crested caracara combines characteristics of both hawks and vultures. It is a long-necked, long-legged bird with a body length of about 60 centimeters (24 in), a wingspread of about 122 centimeters (48 in), and a 25-centimeter (10-in) tail. Mostly dark brown, the white lower parts of its head, throat, abdomen, and undertail are sometimes tinged with yellow. It has long yellow legs and a massive, bluish bill, bordered with a red-orange facial patch. Prominent white patches on the outer parts of the wings are conspicuous in flight.

John James Audubon discovered this bird in 1831, naming it *Polyborus vulgaris*. In the past it has also been known as *Polyborus plancus cheriway*, *P. cheriway audubonii*, and *Caracara cheriway audubonii*.

The crested caracara is the official bird of Mexico and appears on that country's national seal with a snake in its beak. It is known by a variety of common names, including Audubon's caracara, caracara eagle, Mexican eagle, Mexican buzzard, and king buzzard.

Behavior

The crested caracara has a voracious appetite and feeds with equal delight on carrion or living prey. Its diet includes small turtles and turtle eggs, insects, fish, frogs, lizards, snakes, birds, and small mammals. It hunts both on the wing and on the ground. Pairs will sometimes work together to bring down larger prey, such as rabbits or egrets. Caracaras are frequently seen among vultures feeding on road kills.

Crested caracaras apparently mate for life. The nest, a bulky structure of slender vines and sticks, is usually located in a cabbage palm. Peak breeding season is from January to March. Clutch size is two or three eggs and the incubation period is about 32 days. Young fledge at eight weeks of age and remain with the family group for an additional few months.

Habitat

The crested caracara is a bird of open country. Its typical habitat is dry prairie with isolated patches of wetlands. It can also be found in improved pastures and even in lightly wooded areas which have stretches of open grassland. The Kissimmee Prairie, north of Lake Okeechobee, is the center of Florida's crested caracara population. It is a low, flat, grassy plain, dotted with shallow ponds and sloughs.

Historic Range

Most caracaras are found in Central and South America as far south as Tierra del Fuego. The crested caracara is the only subspecies native to the U.S. It is found in an arc that sweeps north from Panama, through Central America and Mexico, and into extreme southern Arizona and Texas. It was once an occasional visitor to southern New Mexico and southwestern Louisiana. Isolated populations occur in Cuba and Florida.

Once a common resident in the prairie region of central Florida, the crested caracara was found from northern Brevard County south to Fort Pierce, Lake Okeechobee, and Rocky Lake (Hendry County). It was also an occasional visitor to the Okaloosa as far north as Nassau County and to the lower Florida Keys (Monroe County).

Current Distribution

The range of the crested caracara in Florida continues to shrink. Birds are now rarely found as far north as Orlando or east of the St. Johns River. The region of greatest abundance is a five-county area (Glades, De Soto, Highlands, Okeechobee, and Osceola counties) north and west of Lake Okeechobee.

The 1987 population estimate was 300 adults and about 200 immatures. This is less than one-third of the population in 1900.

Conservation and Recovery

Habitat loss is the principal threat to the crested caracara. Much of the open prairie of central Florida has been lost to agricultural and residental development. More roads and increased traffic have added to crested caracara mortality, since the bird is exposed to traffic when feeding on road kills.

The Fish and Wildlife Service is encouraging local governments and private organizations to acquire land used by the species. Continuing land development, however, raises questions about long-term prospects for the crested caracara.

Bibliography

Layne, J. N. 1985. "Audubon's Caracara." *Florida Wildlife* 39:40-42.

Contact

Regional Office of Endangered Species
U.S. Fish and Wildlife Service
Richard B. Russell Federal Building
75 Spring Street, S.W.
Atlanta, Georgia 30303

Maui Parrotbill

Pseudonestor xanthophys

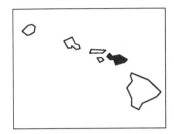

H. Douglas Pratt

Status	Endangered
Listed	March 11, 1967
Family	Fringillidae; Subfamily Drepanidinae (Hawaiian Honeycreeper)
Description	Short-tailed honeycreeper with a parrotlike bill.
Habitat	Ohia forests.
Food	Insect larvae.
Reproduction	Unknown.
Threats	Habitat alteration, predation, disease.
Region 1	Hawaii

Description

The Maui parrotbill is a chunky, short-tailed bird, about 14 centimeters (5.5 in) long. It is olive green above, yellow below, and has a prominent yellow eye stripe. A heavy, hooked, parrotlike bill gives this honeycreeper a top-heavy appearance.

Behavior

The Maui parrotbill finds and feeds on insect larvae and pupae by using its powerful bill to tear into dead wood. The parrotbill's breeding biology is unknown.

Habitat

The species is presently found only in ohia (*Metrosideros colina*) forests on Maui at eleva-

tions between 1,290 and 2,040 meters (4,300 and 6,800 ft). Formerly, it was also common in koa (*Acacia koa*) and dry lowland forests.

Historic Range

The parrotbill is known from fossil deposits on the north coast of Molokai in the Hawaiian Islands, representing a pre-Polynesian population that inhabited dry lowland forests.

Current Distribution

On Maui the parrotbill inhabits the northeastern slope of Haleakala, the 3,050-meter (10,000-ft) volcano that dominates the eastern end of the island. The center of its present range is between Puu Alaea, Kuhiwa Valley, Lake Waianapanapa, and upper Kipahulu

Valley, with a narrow extension west to near the Haleakala Ranch. Although its range extends over 13 kilometers (8 mi), the population is concentrated in an area of less than 2,025 hectares (5,000 acres). A 1980 population estimate of 500 is not believed to have changed significantly.

Conservation and Recovery

Large tracts of forest, especially on the dry, leeward slopes, were cleared for agriculture by the Polynesians, and fire was commonly used to clear forests to maintain the pili grass used for housing thatch. European settlers eliminated all dry forest on Maui up to at least 1,500 meters (5,000 ft) for ranch pastures. By the turn of the century, almost all forest except the very wet ohia forest on upper mountain slopes had been eliminated, and with it many Hawaiian birds.

Grazing animals were introduced on Maui over a hundred years ago and many became feral. Their rooting and trampling were recognized as problems as early as the 1930s, and a program was established to eradicate them. Hunting now controls the feral pig and goat populations.

Introduced plants, insects, and diseases have spread aggressively. Predation by introduced rats is undoubtedly a factor in the decline of endangered Hawaiian forest birds, since rats are able to climb trees in search of eggs and young birds.

Avian diseases, especially pox and malaria, were spread by introduced mosquitoes and have played a large role in the decline of many native Hawaiian birds. Most remaining birds live at higher elevations where the mosquito density is low. Scientists are now concerned that a temperate-zone subspecies of the night mosquito (*Culex pipiens pipiens*) may become established at the higher elevations and further spread avian disease.

The first effort to conserve native birds was made in 1903 with the creation of the State Forest Reserve system. Designed primarily to protect the watershed, this system nonetheless instituted practices beneficial to wildlife, such as fencing, hunting feral animals, and reforesting. The system holds and actively manages about 30 percent of the state's forests, including land on Maui.

The Nature Conservancy manages the Waikamoi Kamakou preserves, and Haleakala National Park has undertaken a program to control some exotic plants. A portion of the Haleakala Crater district has been fenced.

The Fish and Wildlife Service is currently exploring the possibility of captive propagation for Hawaiian forest birds. The goal of such a program would be the creation of a captive flock to furnish birds to supplement remaining wild populations. Little is known, however, about the ability of Hawaiian forest birds to live and breed in captivity.

Bibliography

Scott, J. M., *et al.* 1988. "Conservation of Hawaii's Vanishing Avifauna." *Bioscience* 38(4):238-253.

U.S. Fish and Wildlife Service. 1984. "The Maui-Molokai Forest Birds Recovery Plan." U.S. Fish and Wildlife Service, Portland.

Contact

Regional Office of Endangered Species
U.S. Fish and Wildlife Service
Lloyd 500 Building, Suite 1692
500 N.E. Multnomah Street
Portland, Oregon 97232

Office of Environmental Services
U.S. Fish and Wildlife Service
300 Ala Moana Boulevard
P.O. Box 50167
Honolulu, Hawaii 96850

Ou

Psittirostra psittacea

H. Douglas Pratt

Status	Endangered
Listed	March 11, 1967
Family	Fringillidae; Subfamily Drepanidinae (Hawaiian Honeycreeper)
Description	Male has bright yellow head, dark green back, light green underparts; female has green head.
Habitat	Forests.
Food	Fruits, flowers, insects.
Reproduction	Unknown.
Threats	Deforestation, disease.
Region 1	Hawaii

Description

The ou is one of the largest Hawaiian honeycreepers, measuring about 16 centimeters (6.4 in) long. Males have bright yellow heads clearly separated from dark green backs and light green underparts. Females have green heads. The distinctive parrotlike bill is straw-colored in both sexes.

Behavior

The ou's diet consists of fruits, flowers, and insects; it also feeds large numbers of caterpillars to its young. Adults seem to prefer the fruit of the ieie (*Freycinetia arborea*). Nothing is known of the breeding biology of the ou.

Habitat

The only current habitat for the ou seems to be ohia (*Metrosideros collina*) forests at middle elevations, between about 900 and 1,500 meters (3,000 and 5,000 ft).

Historic Range

The ou was common in the wet forests of Kona, eastern Hawaii, and Kohala; occasionally it was found even in drier forests.

Current Distribution

About 400 ou remain on the island of Hawaii, in mid-elevation forests east of Mauna Kea and Mauna Loa. A very few of the birds inhabit the Alakai Swamp on Kauai.

Conservation and Recovery

The main factor in the decline of Hawaii's forest birds has been deforestation. Hawaii's forests were once extensive but have been drastically reduced by logging and conversion to croplands and pasture. Today, most of the forests below 800 meters (2,600 ft) have been converted to agricultural or urban uses, and the upper elevation koa (*Acacia koa*) forests on Hawaii have been severely cutback. Grazing and browsing animals have also modified remnant forests at upper elevations.

Widespread dieback of ohia, Hawaii's most common native forest tree, has diminished large portions of ou habitat on the island of Hawaii, and additional areas may be threatened. The cause of death for many of these trees has not been determined.

In addition to deforestation, Hawaiian forest birds are very vulnerable to disease. Avian diseases—pox and malaria—spread by mosquitoes introduced to the islands in the 1820s have been the most damaging. Other introduced insects, such as parasitic wasps and predaceous ants, have eliminated some native insects that served as food for birds.

Recovery of the ou and other forest birds will depend on restoring habitat and obtaining essential habitat areas as sanctuaries. In late 1985, the Fish and Wildlife Service (FWS), together with The Nature Conservancy and the state of Hawaii, purchased 3,360 hectares (8,300 acres) of native forest on the island of Hawaii. It marked the first phase of the proposed establishment of a 13,560-hectare (33,500-acre) Hakalau Forest National Wildlife Refuge, which is designed primarily to preserve the habitat of endangered forest birds. The refuge is located on the northwestern slope of Mauna Kea and contains some of the best koa-ohia forests forests remaining on the islands. Another 162-hectare (400-acre) parcel was acquired in 1988 by The Nature Conservancy and sold to FWS for inclusion in the refuge.

Bibliography

Berger, A. J. 1972. *Hawaiian Birdlife*. The University Press of Hawaii, Honolulu.

U.S. Fish and Wildlife Service. 1982. "The Hawaii Forest Bird Recovery Plan." U.S. Fish and Wildlife Service, Portland.

Contact

Regional Office of Endangered Species
U.S. Fish and Wildlife Service
Lloyd 500 Building, Suite 1692
500 N.E. Multnomah Street
Portland, Oregon 97232

Field Office of Endangered Species
U.S. Fish and Wildlife Service
300 Ala Moana Boulevard
P.O. Box 50167
Honolulu, Hawaii 96850

Dark-Rumped Petrel

Pterodroma phaeopygia sandwichensis

Robert J. Shallenberger

Status	Endangered
Listed	March 11, 1967
Family	Procellariidae (Shearwater)
Description	Dark gray seabird with a white forehead and underparts and a short, wedge-shaped tail.
Habitat	Nests in burrows; pelagic habitat unknown.
Food	Fish, plankton, ship garbage.
Reproduction	Unknown.
Threats	Predation, disease.
Region 1	Hawaii

Description

The dark-rumped petrel, also known as the Hawaiian petrel or 'ua'u, is a seabird that averages 40 centimeters (16 in) in length with a wingspan of about 90 centimeters (36 in). It has a short, wedge-shaped tail. The upper body is dark gray; forehead and underparts are white. Wings are white below with conspicuous dark margins. Legs and feet are flesh-colored, and webs are black-tipped. The bill is grayish black, relatively short and stout, with a sharp, downcurving tip. The dark-rumped petrel is one of two subspecies; the other, *Pterodroma phaeopygia phaeopygia*, is restricted to the Galapagos Islands.

Behavior

Members of the family Procellaridae are seabirds that can glide long distances close to the surface of the water. They are good swimmers and feed on fish, plankton, and sometimes ship garbage. Petrels nest in colonies on high, barren mountain slopes, entering and leaving the colonies at night. Nesting burrows are used year after year, generally by the same pair and, if damaged, are sometimes re-excavated.

Habitat

On the island of Maui, the dark-rumped petrel currently nests above an elevation of 2,200 meters (7,200 ft), where vegetation is sparse. In Haleakala, Maui, dominant plants in nesting areas are grasses and bracken fern. Pukiawe (*Styphelia tameiameiae*) dominates in the moist habitat sites. Nesting burrows are commonly located among large rock outcrops, in talus slopes, or along edges of lava flows. Burrows are excavated to depths of 1 or 2 meters (3 to 6 ft). Dark-rumped petrels use their nesting habitat between March and November. Present nesting sites may not be preferred habitat but, nevertheless, support the last known viable breeding colonies on the island.

Historic Range

The dark-rumped petrel once nested throughout the Hawaiian islands. It spends most of its time at sea, but its pelagic range is not known. Ornithologists recognized by the 1930s that the 'ua'u was in danger of extinction.

Current Distribution

The largest concentration of dark-rumped petrel nests are in the upper elevations of Haleakala National Park on the island of Maui. This colony was estimated at about 400 nesting pairs in 1983. Remnant populations have been discovered on a number of the islands, including Hawaii and Lanai, and possibly Molokai and Kauai. A 1988 survey of two populations estimated the population at 431 breeding pairs.

Conservation and Recovery

The mongoose is probably responsible for the decimation of Hawaiian dark-rumped petrel populations. Early descriptions of petrel nesting areas indicated that their burrows were typically found between 450 and 1,500 meters (1,500 and 5,000 ft). The present higher elevation colonies are probably the upper limits of most dense predator populations. The restriction of dark-rumped petrels to higher altitudes also suggests the possibility that mosquito-borne diseases may have eliminated populations at lower elevations, as has happened with other Hawaiian birds.

Feral pigs, first introduced by Polynesian settlers and later by European explorers, became well established on all of the larger Hawaiian islands and may prey upon the dark-rumped petrel's eggs.

In an effort to conserve endangered Hawaiian birds, predator control has been underway since 1966. Both poison and trapping have been used at Haleakala National Park. Recent efforts, however, have been limited to trapping because of severe restrictions on the use of effective poisons. Currently, researchers are working to develop a highly specific poison lethal to the mongoose.

Bibliography

Scott, J. M., et al. 1988. "Conservation of Hawaii's Vanishing Avifauna." *Bioscience* 38(4):238-253.

Simmons, T. R. 1985. "Biology and Behavior of the Endangered Hawaiian Dark-rumped Petrel." *Condor* 87:229-245.

U.S. Fish and Wildlife Service. 1983. "Hawaiian Dark-Rumped Petrel and Newell's Manx Shearwater Recovery Plan." U.S. Fish and Wildlife Service, Portland.

Contact

Regional Office of Endangered Species
U.S. Fish and Wildlife Service
Lloyd 500 Building, Suite 1692
500 N.E. Multnomah Street
Portland, Oregon 97232

Office of Environmental Services
U.S. Fish and Wildlife Service
300 Ala Moana Boulevard
P.O. Box 50167
Honolulu, Hawaii 96850

Newell's Townsend's Shearwater

Puffinus auricularis newelli

T. Telfer

Status	Threatened
Listed	September 25, 1975
Family	Procellariidae (Shearwater)
Description	Medium-sized, gull-like bird, black above, white below.
Habitat	Pelagic; nests on cliffs and remote sea islands.
Food	Fish, plankton, sometimes ship garbage.
Reproduction	Clutch size unknown.
Threats	Predation, artificial lights.
Region 1	Hawaii

Description

Newell's Townsend's shearwater, also known as Newell's manx shearwater or 'a'o, is a gull-sized seabird, 30 to 36 centimeters (12 to 14 in) long with a wingspan of about 84 centimeters (33 in). Upper parts, including the crown, neck, back, wings and tail, are glossy black. The throat, breast, and wings are white. The black bill is sharply hooked at the tip. Feet are webbed and distinctly pink; toes are characteristically gray with well-developed claws adapted for burrow excavations and climbing.

The species has also been known by the scientific name *Puffinus puffinus newelli*.

Behavior

Newell's Townsend's shearwater glides long distances close to the surface of the water. It is a good swimmer and feeds on fish, plankton, and sometimes ship garbage. It nests in burrows on remote islands or sea cliffs. The nesting burrows are used year after year, generally by the same pair.

Habitat

The 'a'o uses its nesting habitat for over nine months of the year—April through November. Nest sites are typically in steep mountainous terrain between 150 and 690 meters (500 and 2,300 ft) elevation in or near dense stands of ferns. Ferns help stabilize burrows against soil erosion and offer protection from predators and the elements. Tree cover is usually moderate to light, and tree roots serve to shore up burrow entrances and discourage rooting by feral pigs.

Rainfall in nesting areas ranges from 102 to 254 centimeters (40 to 100 in) annually. The 'a'o typically requires an open, downhill flight path to get airborne and thus favors ridge crests or embankments. There may be other subtle nesting habitat requirements, such as the slope of the area, humidity, and temperature, but these remain unknown.

Historic Range

Newell's Townsend's shearwater nests and breeds only on the Hawaiian Islands. It was first described in 1900 from a specimen obtained on Maui by Brother Mathias Newell in 1894. How far the 'a'o ranges from land is unknown. Non-breeders and subadults are thought to concentrate near the equator where currents are rich with oceanic nutrients. Some 'a'o are thought to pass through the north-central equatorial region on their way to the breeding grounds.

Current Distribution

There are breeding colonies on Kauai, Hawaii, Molokai, and possibly Oahu. Recent surveys (1988) indicate at least 57 breeding pairs of Newell's Townsend's shearwaters in three populations. The 'a'o inhabits the islands from April to October and is mostly absent the remainder of the year.

Conservation and Recovery

The greatest limiting factor for 'a'o is predation by pigs, cats, black rats, and, most threatening of all, the mongoose. Already established on the other main islands, the mongoose may have reached the island of Kauai as well.

The shearwater normally flies to and from nesting grounds only after dark, and fledgling shearwaters apparently have a strong attraction to light, possibly because of a natural luminescence of their food supply or because they navigate using the reflection of the moon and starlight on the water. Man-made lighting induces night blindness, which causes shearwaters to fly into utility wires, poles, trees, and buildings. Between 1978 and 1981, more than 5,500 shearwaters fell on Kauai's highways, athletic fields, and hotel grounds.

In 1978 biologists initiated a Save-Our-Shearwater campaign. During the fall fledgling season, residents are asked to pick up fallen shearwaters and deposit them at an aid station, where injured birds are treated before being released. Without this successful program, a larger number of birds would die. Attempts to shield streetlights from directing glare upwards have not been totally effective, and research is under way to develop lights that will not attract shearwaters.

Bibliography

Scott, J. M., *et al.* 1988. "Conservation of Hawaii's Vanishing Avifauna." *Bioscience* 38(4):238-253.

U.S. Fish and Wildlife Service. 1983. "Hawaiian Dark-Rumped Petrel and Newell's Manx Shearwater Recovery Plan." U.S. Fish and Wildlife Service, Portland.

Contact

Regional Office of Endangered Species
U.S. Fish and Wildlife Service
Lloyd 500 Building, Suite 1692
500 N.E. Multnomah Street
Portland, Oregon 97232

Office of Environmental Services
U.S. Fish and Wildlife Service
300 Ala Moana Boulevard
P.O. Box 50167
Honolulu, Hawaii 96850

Light-Footed Clapper Rail
Rallus longirostris levipes

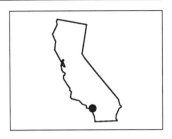

B. "Moose" Peterson

Status	Endangered in the U.S.
Listed	October 13, 1970
Family	Rallidae (Rails, Gallinules, Coots)
Description	Hen-like marsh bird with a long, slightly downcurved bill.
Habitat	Coastal salt marshes.
Food	Insects, small fish, snails, plant matter.
Reproduction	Clutch of 4 to 8 eggs.
Threats	Loss of wetlands.
Region 1	California
Mexico	Baja California

Description

The light-footed clapper rail is a compact, long-billed, henlike marsh bird, 35 to 41 centimeters (14 to 16 in) long. It has a tawny breast, a gray-brown back, vertical dusky and white bars on its flanks, and a white patch under its short up-cocked tail.

Behavior

The rail is an omnivorous forager, feeding on snails, crustaceans, insects, tadpoles, and small fish, as well as some plant matter. It is usually a year-round resident in its home marsh and is primarily sedentary.

Clapper rails nest from mid-March to mid-August, and most eggs are laid from early April to early May. Clutch size ranges from four to eight eggs, which are incubated for about 23 days. Both parents attend the nest, which is constantly incubated during daylight hours.

After the chicks hatch, the parents construct two or more brood nests out of dried cordgrass. Both parents care for the young; while one forages, the other broods the chicks. After a few days, chicks accompany adults on foraging trips.

Habitat

Clapper rails require salt-water or brackish marshes, with adequate vegetation for nesting, foraging, and cover. Nests are built under clumps of pickleweed, often placed directly on the ground or in stands of cordgrass slightly above ground level.

Historic Range

When originally described, the light-footed clapper rail ranged widely in salt marshes along the Pacific coast, from Santa Barbara County, California, to the Bay of San Quintín, Baja California Norte, Mexico. Some ornithologists, questioning the identification of birds at the lower end of the range, place the southern boundary at Ensenada, Baja California Norte. Within this range, most salt marshes along the coast at one time supported breeding populations of light-footed clapper rails.

Current Distribution

At present, light-footed clapper rails are found in 21 California marshes and at least two in Baja California. Nearly 90 percent of the U.S. population inhabits only six marshes. The greatest concentration of rails is at Upper Newport Bay in Orange County. Other locations having sizable rail populations are: the Kendall-Frost Reserve and Tijuana Marsh in San Diego County, Anaheim Bay in Orange County, and Goleta Slough in Santa Barbara County. In the early 1970s the California light-footed clapper rail population was estimated at 500 to 700 pairs. By 1986 only 143 pairs were estimated to survive within the state.

Conservation and Recovery

The major factor in the decline of the light-footed clapper rail has been the destruction or degradation of its salt marsh habitat. Dredging and filling of marshes has continued all along the California coast, particularly around San Diego, Mission Bay, and the Los Angeles-Long Beach area. In southern California only about 25 percent of the wetlands that existed in 1900 remain.

In remnant wetlands, various natural phenomena threaten the surviving rail population. Violent storms and excessive runoff can severely damage the marsh community. Nesting vegetation may be torn away or matted down so it is unusable, and nests are often lost to above-normal tides. Because most nests are built on or close to the ground, predation has contributed to the decline.

Since 1979, several marshes have been restored, and several other areas of marshland have been protected, including Anaheim Bay and Upper Newport Bay (Orange County), Goleta Slough (Santa Barbara County), South Bay Marine Reserve, Tijuana Marsh, and Kendall-Frost Ecological Reserve (San Diego County).

One recovery technique that has worked well is the provision of artificial nesting platforms. Designed to float up and down with the tides, platforms in the Anaheim Bay National Wildlife Refuge were used extensively during the 1986 and 1987 breeding seasons. Similar platforms are now being constructed at Point Magu, Carpenteria Marsh, and the Kendall-Frost Reserve, California.

Bibliography

Massey, B. W., et al. 1984. "Nesting Habitat of the Light-footed Clapper Rail in Southern California." Journal of Field Ornithology 55:67-80.

U.S. Fish and Wildlife Service. 1985. "Recovery Plan for the Light-Footed Clapper Rail." U.S. Fish and Wildlife Service, Portland.

Contact

Regional Office of Endangered Species
U.S. Fish and Wildlife Service
Lloyd 500 Building. Suite 1692
500 N.E. Multnomah Street
Portland, Oregon 97232

California Clapper Rail
Rallus longirostris obsoletus

Jack Wilburn

Status	Endangered
Listed	October 13, 1970
Family	Rallidae (Rails, Gallinules, Coots)
Description	Long-billed, henlike bird; olive-brown above with a cinnamon-buff breast.
Habitat	Saltwater and brackish marshes.
Food	Mussels, clams, spiders.
Reproduction	Clutch of 5 to 9 eggs.
Threats	Loss of wetlands.
Region 1	California

Description

The clapper rail is one of the largest species of the genus *Rallus*, measuring 32 to 47 centimeters (13 to 19 in) from bill to tail. It has a henlike appearance with strong legs, long toes, and a long bill. It has a cinnamon colored breast, dark flanks with white bars, and olive-brown upper parts.

The California clapper rail was first described as a king rail, *Rallus elegans* var. *obsoletus*, in 1834 by Ridgway, who in 1880 reclassified it as a new species of clapper rail, *R. obsoletus*. In 1926, A. J. Van Rossem combined the Pacific coast clapper rails into one species, and in 1977, S. Ripley revised the species again, identifying 24 separate sub-

species in North, Central and South America, and the Caribbean.

Behavior

The California clapper rail is secretive and difficult to flush. Once flushed, however, it can frequently be closely approached. Birds accustomed to humans, such as those at the City of Palo Alto Baylands, continue to feed despite people on nearby boardwalks. When disturbed, clapper rails usually fly only a short distance before landing.

Clapper rails nest from mid-March to July, with peaks of activity in early May and again in early July. The female lays a clutch of five to nine eggs, and both parents take turns incubating for 23 to 29 days. The eggs are light tan or buff-colored with cinnamon-brown or dark lavender spotting at the broader end.

California clapper rails feed mostly on mussels, spiders, clams, and small crabs.

Habitat

The clapper rail constructs its nest in marshlands near tidal ponds, arranging plants or drift material over the nest as a canopy. It will often construct a brood nest on higher ground to shelter the young from storm tides; this is usually a simple platform of twigs without a canopy. Marsh vegetation includes cordgrass, pickleweed, gum-plant, and salt grass. Clapper rails in the South San Francisco Bay marshes prefer to nest in stands of cordgrass but build their nests mostly of pickleweed.

Historic Range

The salt marshes of South San Francisco Bay, including portions of San Mateo, Santa Clara, and Alameda counties, once support-ed the largest populations of California clap-per rails. Smaller populations were found along western Contra Costa County, eastern Marin County, and near Petaluma (Sonoma County). Some records indicate that there may have been a sizable population in Napa Marsh in western Napa County. Marshes south of San Francisco Bay in Elkhorn Slough and others adjacent to Monterey Bay also once had small populations. The eastern limit of the historic range is believed to have been Southampton Bay (Solano County).

Current Distribution

The California clapper rail is now restricted to the San Francisco Bay ecosystem. In South San Francisco Bay, clapper rail populations are found in remnant salt marshes, such as Bair and Greco Islands (San Mateo County), Dumbarton Point (Alameda County), and Santa Clara County coastlands. In San Mateo County, rails are found as far north as San Bruno Point. Scattered individuals nest near creek mouths in northern Alameda County, western Contra Costa County, and eastern Marin County. A small breeding population may also still exist in Richardson Bay in Marin County. Other small populations are found in northern San Pablo Bay, along the Petaluma River as far north as Schultz Creek, along most major tidal marshes and creeks in Sonoma and Napa counties, and at Bull Is-land on the Napa River.

Conservation and Recovery

Around the turn of the century, indiscrim-inate hunting initiated a clapper rail decline. A newspaper account from 1897 mentions some 5,000 rails of various species killed during a single week. After the Migratory Bird Treaty Act was passed in 1913, prohibit-ing such wholesale slaughter, rails regained some of their former abundance. However, wetland destruction had begun. Marsh was lost first to agriculture, then to urban development, airports, and salt evaporation ponds.

Two hundred years ago the San Francisco Bay ecosystem contained about 734 square kilometers (289 sq mi) of tidal marsh; today, only 152 square kilometers (50 sq mi) remain. This dramatic reduction of marshland has greatly reduced the clapper rail population. One site in Suisun Marsh is largely undis-turbed and supports a healthy clapper rail population, but most marshes are degraded in one form or another. Remnant marshes in South San Francisco Bay are bounded by steep earthen levees; upper marsh vegetation has been eliminated, reducing cover for rails during winter flood tides.

Adult clapper rails are preyed upon by the northern harrier, red-tailed hawk, and the peregrine falcon (*Falco peregrinus*). Young rails and eggs are eaten by Norway rats. The horse mussel is strong enough to trap a clapper rail's foot or beak and may cause some rail deaths.

Conservation of the rail's marsh habitat has been under way for some time, mostly through land acquisition. Tracts of salt marsh in South San Francisco Bay and San Pablo Bay have been acquired by the National Audubon Society and other organizations. The California Department of Fish and Game has restored marshes in Redwood City. The U.S. Fish and Wildlife Service has established the San Francisco Bay National Wildlife Refuge, while the East Bay Regional Park District has worked to restore marshes on the Hayward shoreline.

Bibliography

Gill, R. Jr. 1979. "Status and Distribution of the California Clapper Rail." *California Fish and Game* 65:36-49.

Ripley, S. 1977. *Rails of the World: A Monograph of the Family Rallidae.* D. R. Godine Publishing, Boston.

U.S. Fish and Wildlife Service. 1984. "The Salt Marsh Harvest Mouse and California Clapper Rail Recovery Plan." U.S. Fish and Wildlife Service, Portland.

Contact

Regional Office of Endangered Species
U.S. Fish and Wildlife Service
Lloyd 500 Building, Suite 1692
500 N.E. Multnomah Street
Portland, Oregon 97232

Yuma Clapper Rail
Rallus longirostris yumanensis

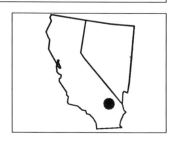

Ronald M. McKinstry

Status	. . . . . .	Endangered
Listed	. . . . . .	March 11, 1967
Family	. . . . .	Rallidae (Rails, Gallinules, Coots)
Description	. . .	Long-billed, henlike, gray-brown marsh bird.
Habitat	. . . . . .	Freshwater marshes.
Food	. . . . . .	Crayfish, fish, clams, insects.
Reproduction	. .	Clutch of about 6 eggs.
Threats	. . . . .	Loss of wetlands.
Region 1	. . . . .	California
Region 2	. . . . .	Arizona
Mexico	. . . . . .	Sonora, Baja California

Description

The Yuma clapper rail is one of seven North American subspecies of the clapper rail, which is a large, henlike marsh bird. The Yuma subspecies, which averages 36 to 42 centimeters (14 to 16 in) in length, is gray-brown with a tawny breast, a white throat and undertail, and bars across the flanks.

Behavior

The Yuma rail feeds on crayfish, small fish, clams, isopods, and a variety of insects. Most of the U.S. population remains on its breeding grounds from mid-April to mid-September. The rails then migrate south to Mexico for the winter.

Little is known of Yuma clapper rail breeding and nesting. Clutch size is thought to be about six eggs. Nests are constructed on dry hummocks or in small shrubs amid dense cattails just above water level. Two types of nests have been found: one of sticks and dead leaves, another of finer stems with dry blossoms still intact.

Habitat

In the U. S., Yuma clapper rails nest in freshwater marshes. They prefer mature stands of cattails and bulrushes along the margins of shallow ponds with stable water levels. Mexican populations prefer brackish marshes, dominated by dense stands of tall salt cedar (*Tamarix gallica*) with an understory of iodine bush (*Allenrolfia occidentalis*).

Historic Range

In general, western clapper rails range from northern California along the Pacific coast to central Mexico. The Yuma clapper rail has been sighted along the Colorado River where Nevada, Arizona, and California meet, south to Yuma, Arizona, and into Mexico. The bird probably winters in Mexico. It is thought that the Yuma clapper rail was not distributed along the Colorado River until suitable habitat was created through dam construction.

Current Distribution

A survey conducted in 1969 and 1970 estimated about 700 breeding birds in the U.S. More recent estimates put the population between 1,700 and 2,000, distributed over an area defined by the Colorado River delta (Mexico), the Salton Sea (California), Topock Marsh (Arizona), and along the Gila River to near Tacna (Arizona).

Conservation and Recovery

Water control projects on the Colorado have changed the nature of this once free-flowing river. Dams eliminated many backwaters and created new marshes and wetlands. Regulated water releases in the lower Colorado River slowed currents enough to allow sedimentation, which in turn allowed cattail and bulrush marshes to emerge. As new habitat developed upstream, the rails moved in. Salton Sea was created in 1905 when the Colorado River overflowed its banks into Imperial Valley. Protection and development of these wetlands for waterfowl management created habitat for the Yuma clapper rail. However, other suitable rail habitat has been lost through dredging and channelization projects along the Colorado River.

Although the rail population appears to be stable, its fate is tied to the various water projects along the Colorado River. The key to maintaining or expanding the rail population is maintaining early growth stages of cattail marsh by creating shallow water areas. Eventually, a mat of dead cattails forms in the shallows, providing nesting cover for rails.

Bibliography

Banks, R. C., and R. E. Tomlinson. 1974. "Taxonomic Status of Certain Clapper Rails of Southwestern United States and Northwestern Mexico." *Wilson Bulletin* 86(4):325-335.

Moffitt, J. 1941. "Notes on the Food of the California Clapper Rail." *Condor* 43:270-273.

Ripley, S. 1977. *Rails of the World: A Monograph of the Family Rallidae.* D. R. Godine Publishing, Boston.

U.S. Fish and Wildlife Service. 1984. "Yuma Clapper Rail Recovery Plan." U.S. Fish and Wildlife Service, Albuquerque.

Contact

Regional Office of Endangered Species
U.S. Fish and Wildlife Service
Lloyd 500 Building, Suite 1692
500 N.E. Multnomah Street
Portland, Oregon 97232

Regional Office of Endangered Species
U.S. Fish and Wildlife Service
P.O. Box 1306
Albuquerque, New Mexico 87103

Thick-Billed Parrot
Rhynchopsitta pachyrhyncha

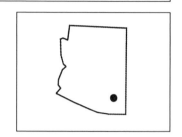

Noel Snyder

Status	Endangered
Listed	June 2, 1979
Family	Psittacidae (Parrot)
Description	Green parrot with black bill and red forehead and eyebrow.
Habitat	Conifer and mixed conifer-deciduous forests.
Food	Conifer cones, acorns, juniper berries.
Reproduction	Unknown.
Threats	Low numbers, collectors, habitat destruction.
Region 2	Arizona, New Mexico
Mexico	Sierra Madre Occidental

Description

The thick-billed parrot is mostly green with red patches on the forehead and forewing. It grows to a length of about 40 centimeters (16 in) and has a wingspan of 20 to 25 centimeters (8 to 10 in). The tail is long and pointed; the large, hooked bill is black in adults, pale in young birds. In flight a yellow stripe on the underwings is conspicuous.

Behavior

The thick-billed parrot is a strong flyer, attaining speeds approaching 80 kilometers per hour (50 mph). It makes regular flights of 10 to 20 kilometers (6 to 12 mi) searching for food. The parrot feeds primarily on conifer cones, but also eats acorns and juniper berries. It nests in naturally occurring tree cavities or abandoned woodpecker cavities.

Habitat

In 1986, a flock of thick-billed parrots was reintroduced to southeastern Arizona in habitat similar to that favored by the Mexican population. The flock was established in the Chiricahua Mountains within the Coronado National Forest at elevations between 2,000 and 3,000 meters (6,600 and 9,800 ft). The higher mountain slopes are covered with mature pine, fir, spruce, and aspen. Lower elevations are dominated by various oak species mixed with conifers. In winter, overnight temperatures can drop considerably below freezing.

Historic Range

The thick-billed parrot is principally a native of Mexico, but small populations once inhabited Arizona and New Mexico. It was a seasonal resident in the Chiricahua Mountains of southeastern Arizona. The species disappeared from the U.S. in the early 1900s, when it was hunted for food by miners and woodsmen. Much of its montane forest habitat was destroyed to provide lumber for mining operations.

Current Distribution

Thick-billed parrots are now found in the Sierra Madre of western Mexico. The small Arizona flock, now numbering about a dozen parrots, winters in the Chiricahua Mountains of southeastern Arizona within the Coronado National Forest. During the summer, the flock migrates 400 kilometers (250 mi) to the northwest to the Mogollon Rim of central Arizona.

Conservation and Recovery

Increased collection of wild thick-billed parrots for sale in the pet trade, coupled with the continued destruction of mountain forest habitat, has dimmed the prospects for the survival of the species in Mexico.

In 1986, using birds confiscated from smugglers, the Arizona Game and Fish Department, in cooperation with the Fish and Wildlife Service and the Forest Service, released 26 parrots in the Chiricahua Mountains. Some of these parrots were lost to raptors, others flew to Mexico, but about half remained in Arizona. Over the next two years, the flock established a migratory pattern, wintering in the Chiricahua Mountains and moving to the Mogollon Rim of central Arizona during the summer.

The size of the flock has remained about 12, with new releases replacing parrots lost to raptors. In 1988, two young birds, distinguished by their pale bills, were seen, indicating that at least one pair had bred successfully in the wild.

A separate release program, using captive-bred, hand-reared parrots, was not successful. On release, the parrots made no attempt to flock and, although they had been fed on pine cones for six months prior to release, did not try to feed. A captive-bred but parent-reared bird was also released with this group. It immediately joined the wild flock upon release. Future releases will be limited to parent-reared birds.

The main problem now facing the release program is obtaining a supply of parrots. Those confiscated from smugglers are often in poor physical condition, their flight feathers having been pulled or cut to prevent their escape. A number of private breeders and zoos are working to provide a steady supply of healthy thick-billed parrots, including the Jersey Wildlife Preservation Trust, the San Diego Zoo, Los Angeles Zoo, Sacramento Zoo, Gladys Porter Zoo, Arizona-Sonora Desert Museum, Bronx Zoo, and Salt Lake City Zoo. With an increased supply of captive-bred parrots, the Thick-Billed Parrot Project expects to move toward larger and more regular releases in the future.

Bibliography

Lanning, D. V., and J. T. Shiflett. 1983. "Nesting Ecology of Thick-Billed Parrots." *Condor* 85:66-73

Wetmore, A. 1935. "The Thick-Billed Parrot in Southern Arizona." *Condor* 37:18-21.

Contact

Regional Office of Endangered Species
U.S. Fish and Wildlife Service
P.O. Box 1306
Albuquerque, New Mexico 87103

Florida Snail Kite
Rostrhamus sociabilis plumbeus

P. W. Sykes/USFWS

Status	Endangered
Listed	March 11, 1967
Family	Accipitriidae (Eagles and Hawks)
Description	Slate-gray bird of prey with orange-red legs and a prominent hooked bill.
Reproduction	Clutch of 3 eggs.
Habitat	Subtropical freshwater marshes and sloughs.
Food	Apple snails.
Threats	Loss of wetlands, drought.
Region 4	Florida

Description

The Florida snail kite, also known as the Everglade kite, is a snail-eating hawk with an average body size of 43 centimeters (17 in) and a wingspan of about 120 centimeters (47 in). The adult male is slate gray, shading into black, with black wing tips and head. The slightly larger female is dark brown above with a white forehead and throat. The squared tail of both sexes is white with a broad black band and lighter terminal band. Legs are red-orange and the eyes red. Immature birds of both sexes resemble the adult female.

The snail kite is in the subfamily Accipitrainae, comprising the true kites. Four subspecies were originally recognized: the Everglade snail kite (*Rostrhamus sociabilis plumbeus*) of peninsular Florida; the Cuban snail kite (*R. s. levis*) of Cuba and the Isle of Pines; the Mexican snail kite (*R. s. major*) of eastern Mexico, northern Guatemala, and northern Belize; and the South American snail kite (*R.s. sociabilis*) of Nicaragua, Honduras, Costa Rica, and the southern coast. In 1975, the populations in Florida, Cuba, and the Isle of Pines were combined into one subspecies (*R. s. plumbeus*).

Behavior

The Florida snail kite feeds almost exclusively on one species of freshwater mollusk—the apple snail—which is found in shallow, open-water areas of the Everglades. The kite patrols low over the marsh with a great deal of wing-flapping as it searches for snails; it dives and captures snails by extending its feet before it into the water. The bird's hooked bill is ideally suited to removing the snail from its shell.

Kites nest over water in trees, shrubs, or cattails. Cattails are used when trees or shrubs are not available, and nests may fall if buffeted by winds. Although the kite can nest throughout the year, the main nesting period is from January through August. Kites reach breeding age at ten months. The usual clutch of three eggs is incubated by both parents for about 30 days. Young fledge in 23 to 28 days and are tended by both parents.

Florida snail kites are not monogamous. One of a pair will usually abandon the young about three to five weeks before its mate. Birds are gregarious and somewhat nomadic, usually dispersing after nesting.

Habitat

The kite prefers areas of shallow open water, such as sloughs and marshes, that remain wet throughout the year. The depth of the water can fluctuate as long as the bottom does not dry out. The apple snail feeds on marsh plants among sawgrass or cattails, and regular seasonal flooding is needed to sustain an adequate snail population.

Historic Range

The Florida snail kite once ranged throughout the Florida peninsula, Cuba, and the Isle of Pines in the Caribbean. The Caribbean populations are not considered in jeapardy.

Current Distribution

The snail kite nests in Lake Okeechobee's western marshes, Loxahatchee National Wildlife Refuge, the St. Johns River headwaters reservoir, lakes Kissimmee and Tohopekalig in central Florida, and the northern part of the Everglades National Park.

Wandering birds have been recorded at other sites as far north as Duval, Wakulla, and Marion counties in Florida. During high-water years, kites have been observed in the Big Cypress National Preserve. During drought years, as in 1981-1982, kites disperse over much of Florida, ranging as far north as Dixie, Marion, and Hillsborough counties in search of food sources.

Populations were estimated at 668 birds in 1984, but after the drought of 1985 only 407 birds were surveyed.

Conservation and Recovery

The main threat to the Florida snail kite is loss of its habitat and its principal food source. The draining of south Florida's wetlands for agriculture and for residential development began in the early 1900s and continues at a rapid pace today. Increased demand on the freshwater supply has lowered water levels and dried out wetlands, restricting the habitat of the apple snail, and, consequently, the snail kite.

While the kite is adapted to natural drought cycles, large-scale water control regimens worsen the effects of dry periods. Since 1925 Lake Okeechobee water levels, for example, have become more seasonal, variable, and significantly lower. Drought-flood cycles have been shortened from ten or more years to five or six years, and the snail population has declined.

Water pollution also poses a serious threat to the Florida snail kite and the apple snail. Pesticides applied from the air to orchards and fields often drift into the marsh. Toxins accumulate in the apple snail and are passed on to the kite.

Several species of introduced plants are also altering the habitat. An exotic water hyacinth that forms dense mats on the water surface makes it impossible for kites to hunt. The Australian punktree can rapidly invade snail kite habitat, changing it from open marsh to dense stands of trees.

The National Audubon Society leases about 11,330 hectares (28,000 acres) on the west side of Lake Okeechobee, containing one of the snail kite's principal nesting areas. The society has relocated kite nests to artificial nest structures to prevent loss to heavy wind and rain.

The Fish and Wildlife Service (FWS) does not believe that the Florida snail kite can ever be delisted because of the continuing loss of habitat. However, in its 1986 Recovery Plan the FWS stated that an average population of 650 birds for a ten-year period, with annual declines of less than 10 percent, would warrant reclassifying the Florida snail kite from Endangered to Threatened.

In June 1989, the Interior Department created a new wildlife refuge for the Florida panther and other endangered species in south Florida. The 12,140-hectare (30,000-acre) Florida Panther National Wildlife Refuge is adjacent to the Big Cypress National Preserve and provides protected habitat for the Endangered wood stork (*Mycteria americana*), bald eagle (*Haliaeetus leucocephalus*), peregrine falcon (*Falco peregrinus anatum*), and eastern indigo snake (*Drymarchon corais couperi*), as well as the Florida snail kite.

Bibliography

Amadon, D. 1975. "Variation in the Everglade Kite." *Auk* 92:380-382.

Beissinger, S. R., and J. E. Takekawa. 1983. "Habitat Use by and Dispersal of Snail Kites in Florida During Drought Conditions." *Florida Field Naturalist* 11:89-106.

Sykes, P. W., Jr. 1984. "The Range of the Snail Kite and Its History in Florida." *Bulletin of Florida State Museum, Biological Science* 29(6):211-264.

U.S. Fish and Wildlife Service. 1986. "Florida Snail Kite Revised Recovery Plan." U.S. Fish and Wildlife Service, Atlanta.

Contact

Regional Office of Endangered Species
U.S. Fish and Wildlife Service
Richard B. Russell Federal Building
75 Spring Street, S.W.
Atlanta, Georgia 30303

Least Tern
Sterna antillarum antillarum

Status . . . . . . Endangered
Listed . . . . . . May 28, 1985
Family . . . . . Laridae; Subfamily Ster-
             ninae (Tern)
Description . . . Graceful black and gray
             seabird with a black cap
             and nape.
Habitat . . . . . Open sandy areas along
             shores.
Food . . . . Fish.
Reproduction . . Clutch of 2 to 3 eggs.
Threats . . . . . . Channelization and dam-
             ming of rivers.
Region 2 . . . . . New Mexico, Oklahoma,
             Texas
Region 3 . . . . . Illinois, Indiana, Iowa, Mis-
             souri
Region 4 . . . . . Arkansas, Kentucky,
             Louisiana, Mississippi,
             Tennessee
Region 6 . . . . . Colorado, Kansas, Mon-
             tana, Nebraska, North
             Dakota, South Dakota

Steven W. Kress/WWF

Description

Least terns are the smallest of the terns, measuring 20 to 22 centimeters (8 to 9 in) in length and having a 50-centimeter (20-in) wingspread. In breeding plumage both sexes have a black cap and nape, white forehead, grayish back and wings, snowy white underparts, orange legs, and a black-tipped orange-yellow bill. Immature birds have darker plumage, a dark bill, and dark eye stripes on their white heads.

There are no consistent morphological, behavioral, or vocal differences between the least tern (*Sterna antillarum antillarum*) and the California least tern (*S. a. browni*).

Behavior

Least terns live and breed in colonies. The nest is a simple unlined scrape, usually containing three brown-spotted, buffy eggs. Breeding colonies (terneries) usually consist of about 20 widely spaced nests. However, colonies of up to 75 nests have been reported on the Mississippi River. Egg-laying and incubation occur from late May to early August. Eggs are incubated for 20 days, and chicks fledge in another 20 days. Least terns capture small fish and minnows with a head-first dive into the water.

Habitat

Least terns inhabit both coastal areas and interior river systems. Only the interior populations, however, are listed as Endangered. Habitat requirements for interior least terns center around three ecological factors: presence of bare or nearly bare alluvial islands or sandbars, favorable water levels during the nesting season, and food availability.

Under natural river conditions, islands are created and destroyed by the river's erosion and deposition processes. Periodic inundation keeps some islands barren or sparsely vegetated. Although most nesting is in rivers, the least tern also nests on the barren flats of saline lakes and ponds such as the Salt Plains National Wildlife Refuge, Oklahoma.

Historic Range

The interior least tern historically bred along all the major inland river systems: the Colorado (in Texas), Red, Rio Grande, Arkansas, Missouri, Ohio, and Mississippi Rivers.

The wintering area for this population is unknown; however, least terns of undetermined populations winter along the Central American coast and the northern coast of South America from Venezuela to northeastern Brazil.

The least tern is not considered Endangered when found within 80 kilometers (50 mi) of the coast. The eastern least tern population breeds along the Atlantic coast from Maine to Florida and along the Gulf coast from Florida to Texas and probably winters in the Bahamas and Caribbean Islands.

Current Distribution

Formerly a common breeding bird throughout most of its current range, the interior least tern is now extremely limited in both numbers and distribution. Once found throughout the Mississippi and Red River valleys of Louisiana, it is now absent from that state. Today there are about 350 to 450 terns on the Mississippi River, concentrated at a few sites between Osceola, Arkansas, and Cairo, Illinois. In Arkansas, the least tern no longer breeds on the Ouachita and White Rivers and is nearly absent on the Arkansas River.

The least tern formerly bred along the Ohio River from its confluence with the Mississippi to the state of Ohio. In 1983 about ten terns frequented the lower Ohio River; none were present on the river between Indiana and Kentucky. It once bred on the Des Moines River and at many locations in central and eastern Iowa, but now occurs only in small numbers near the southern tip of Illinois.

The explorers Lewis and Clark frequently observed the tern and described the species in detail as a common breeder on the Missouri River and many of its tributaries. The tern is now entirely absent as a breeding bird on the Missouri River from St. Louis to north of Sioux City, Iowa, and there are only 100 to 200 birds between Ponca, Nebraska, and Yankton, South Dakota.

Because the remainder of the Missouri River in North and South Dakota is largely a reservoir where nesting habitat has almost completely disappeared since 1950, the tern is a rare breeder there. Along the remaining 145-kilometer (90-mi) natural segment of the Missouri River in North Dakota, from Garrison Dam to the headwaters of Lake Oahe, 90 to 120 terns breed on sandbars. The least tern was believed extirpated from the Missouri River in Montana, but in June 1987 a nesting pair was observed on a small island on Fort Peck Lake in the Charles M. Russell National Wildlife Range.

The Cheyenne River, a tributary of the Missouri River in South Dakota, harbors about 70 terns; about 100 occur on the Niobrara River, Nebraska. Least terns on the Platte River number 160 to 240. Their distribution on the Platte formerly included western Nebraska, but today the tern nests only in the Central and Lower Platte River regions.

In Kansas, recent research indicates low numbers (100 birds), low reproductive success, and continued threats to the tern's breeding habitat. It no longer breeds along the river systems in the northern part of the state and is currently only found on the Cimarron River in Cheyenne Bottoms Wildlife Management Area, and in the Quivira National Wildlife Refuge.

As many as 300 interior least terns breed on the Salt Plains National Wildlife Refuge, Oklahoma. Another 100 terns breed on the Cimarron River and Lake Optima. The tern is absent from several former breeding sites along the Red River between Texas and Oklahoma.

In the tern's western range it is extremely rare. In Texas, the Canadian and Red Rivers in the north and the Rio Grande in the south are visited by only about 140 birds. The Bitter Lake National Wildlife Refuge in New Mexico is a breeding site for about 20 terns. At the periphery of the bird's range in Colorado, breeding pairs are occasionally found on the Arkansas River in the southwestern part of the state.

In summary, the current breeding distribution of the interior least tern is a remnant of a much more widespread historic range. This change has taken place over a period of many decades, coinciding with man's modification of river systems.

Conservation and Recovery

Nesting habitat throughout the central and western U.S. has been altered by increased vegetation brought about by man-made changes in river flow. Maintenance of sandbar habitat will aid recovery, and although least terns prefer natural islands or sandbars, they will nest on man-made sites on river floodplains. Such sites, however, are usually connected to the shore and accessible to predators and human disturbance.

Among the many attempts to protect least terns, the Oklahoma Department of Wildlife Conservation and the U.S Fish and Wildlife Service have agreed on a recovery effort for least terns in Oklahoma. The joint project will focus on increasing public awareness of the least tern through television and newspaper coverage of the breeding season.

Bibliography

Downing, R. L. 1980. "Survey of Interior Least Tern Nesting Populations." *American Birds* 34(2):209-211.

Gochfeld, M. 1983. "Colony Site Selection by Least Terns: Physical Attributes of Sites." *Colonial Waterbirds* 6:205-213.

Schulenberg, J. H., and M. B. Ptacek. 1984. "Status of the Interior Least Tern in Kansas." *American Birds* 38(6):975-981.

Contact

Regional Office of Endangered Species
U.S. Fish and Wildlife Service
Federal Building, Fort Snelling
Twin Cities, Minnesota 55111

California Least Tern
Sterna antillarum browni

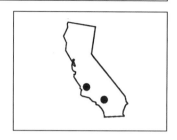

B. "Moose" Peterson

Status	Endangered
Listed	October 13, 1970
Family	Laridae; Subfamily Sterninae (Tern)
Description	Graceful gray and white seabird with black cap and nape.
Habitat	Open sandy areas along shores.
Food	Fish.
Reproduction	Clutch of 2 or 3 eggs.
Threats	Disruption of nesting sites, predation.
Region 1	California
Mexico	Baja California

Description

The California least tern is among the smallest members of the tern subfamily Sterninae, averaging 23 centimeters (9 in) in length and having a 40-centimeter (16-in) wingspread. It has a black cap and nape, gray wings with black wingtips, orange legs, and a black-tipped orange-yellow bill. Sexes appear similar. Immature birds have darker plumage and a dark bill; their white heads with dark eye stripes are distinctive.

This species has also been known by the scientific name *Sterna albifrons browni*.

Behavior

The California least tern is migratory, typically arriving in its breeding area during the last week of April and departing again in August. It has been recorded in the breeding range as early as mid-March and as late as mid-November. Some birds form pair bonds before arriving in the nesting areas. Others pair off within the colony almost immediately, and active courtship may be observed within the first few days after arrival.

Courtship follows a well-defined pattern, beginning with a "fish flight" in which a male carrying a fish is joined by one or two other terns in a high-flying aerial display. In later stages of courtship the male holds a small fish in his beak as he courts the female. During copulation, the female takes the fish from the male and eats it.

Nests are small depressions scooped out of the sand or dirt. If the soil is hard the bird will use a natural depression. After eggs are laid, nests are often lined with shell fragments and small pebbles.

Least tern eggs are buff-colored with brown and purple streaks and speckles; normal clutches consist of two or three eggs. Both parents participate in incubation, with the female taking the greater role. Newly hatched chicks are weak and helpless, but by the second day can make short walks from the nest. Nestlings can fly after about 20 days, but are not proficient feeders until after migration. The California least tern eats small fish, which it catches by diving head first into the water.

Habitat

The least tern usually chooses its nesting location in an open expanse of light-colored sand, dirt, or dried mud beside a lagoon or an estuary. Formerly, sandy ocean beaches were regularly used, but increased human activity has made most beaches uninhabitable. In recent years, terns have nested on mud and sand flats away from the ocean or on man-made landfills. Least terns live in colonies, which are less dense than those of most other terns.

The California least tern typically fishes in shallow estuaries and lagoons; colonies occasionally forage in the ocean. Fish known to be eaten, in order of importance, are northern anchovy, topsmelt, various surf-perch, killifish, and mosquitofish.

Historic Range

The historic breeding range of this subspecies extended along the Pacific Coast from Moss Landing (Monterey County), California, to San Jose del Cabo (southern Baja California), Mexico. Since 1970, nesting sites have been recorded from San Francisco Bay to Bathia de San Quintin, Baja California. The nesting range in California has apparently always been widely discontinuous, with the majority of birds nesting in southern Califor-

nia from Santa Barbara south through San Diego County. Between the city of Santa Barbara and Monterey Bay, a distance of over 320 kilometers (200 mi), the only certain breeding locations are the mouths of the Santa Ynez and Santa Maria rivers in Santa Barbara County.

Migration routes and winter distribution are largely unknown. No records confirm least terns on the Pacific Coast of South America, and only a few reports suggest the bird's presence along the Pacific Coast in Honduras, Guatemala, and Panama. Several subspecies of least terns gather seasonally in western Mexico, but since their winter plumage is almost identical, they cannot be distinguished visually.

No reliable estimates are available of original numbers of California least terns, but they once were considered abundant along the southern California coast. An observer in 1909 describes counting about 600 pairs along a single beach near San Diego.

Current Distribution

The California least tern breeding population averaged about 600 pairs between 1973 and 1975. In 1984 a state survey estimated the breeding population at 931 to 1001 pairs. The size of the Baja California population is unknown.

Conservation and Recovery

Human encroachment is largely responsible for the least tern's historic decline. The Pacific Coast Highway was constructed early this century along previously undisturbed beach, and summer cottages and beach homes were built in many areas. Increasing human use of the beaches disrupted nesting sites at the same time as feeding areas were being diminished by development or pollution.

Nesting and feeding habitat in the vicinity of most existing colonies can potentially be restored or expanded. Wildlife managers are focusing on recovering degraded coastal wetlands, creating nesting islands, and protecting nesting colonies from excessive human disturbance and predation. In addition, nesting sites are often protected by warning signs or fences.

Alternate nesting sites can be constructed in areas where currently used sites are highly vulnerable to disturbance or are jeopardized by habitat loss. In some wetland areas, improving tidal circulation is essential to restoring fish populations.

The California least tern is also threatened by predators, especially the red fox (*Vulpes vulpes*). During the 1988 breeding season, 75 percent of the terns nesting in three Orange County colonies were killed by foxes. Trapping efforts at the Seal Beach National Wildlife Refuge were overwhelmed by a large influx of foxes.

Bibliography

Anderson, W. 1970. "The California Least Tern Breeding in Alameda and San Mateo Counties." *California Fish & Game* 56(2):136-137.

Chandik, T., and A. Baldridge. 1967. "Nesting Season, Middle Pacific Coast Region." *Audubon Field Notes* 21(5):600-603.

U.S. Fish and Wildlife Service. 1980. "California Least Tern Recovery Plan." U.S. Fish and Wildlife Service, Portland.

Contact

Regional Office of Endangered Species
U.S. Fish and Wildlife Service
Lloyd 500 Building, Suite 1692
500 N.E. Multnomah Street
Portland, Oregon 97232

Roseate Tern
Sterna dougallii dougallii

Status . . . . . . Endangered in continental
U.S. (except Florida);
Threatened in Florida,
Puerto Rico, and the U.S.
Virgin Islands
Listed . . . . . . November 2, 1987
Family . . . . . . Laridae; Subfamily Ster-
ninae (Tern)
Description . . . Dove-sized shore bird, pale
gray above, white below,
black cap and nape.
Habitat . . . . . . Barrier islands.
Food . . . . Small fish.
Reproduction . . Clutch of 1 or 2 eggs.
Threats . . . . . . Competition with gulls,
predators.
Region 4 . . . . . Florida, Puerto Rico
Region 5 . . . . . Connecticut, Maine, Mass-
achusetts, New Hampshire,
New York

Frank J. Gallo

Description

The roseate tern is a dove-sized shore bird about 38 centimeters (15 in) long from the beak to the end of its long forked tail. It is pale gray above and white below, with a black cap and nape. In North America this species can be distinguished from its relatives by its over-all pale color, mostly black bill, and a slight rosy tint on its breast in summer. In winter, the black cap is largely replaced with a white forehead. The sexes look alike, but immature birds have a mottled brown cap and back.

Behavior

The roseate tern does not breed until it is three or four years old. It builds its nest directly on the ground, typically on a small island in the company of hundreds and sometimes thousands of other birds. Often more than one species will share the same nesting area. Terns are strong fliers that feed mainly on fish, captured by plunging head-first into the water.

Habitat

Almost every important colony of roseate terns nests along isolated beaches or on split-off islets of barrier islands. Roseate terns tend to conceal their nests under vegetation, boulders, and driftwood. Some roseate terns have attempted to nest in salt marshes with little success.

Historic Range

Historically, the roseate tern was found along the entire eastern coast of North America, including Canada, and throughout the islands of the Atlantic and Caribbean.

The nesting population in the northeastern U.S. was decimated in the late 19th century by hunting for the millinery trade. The Migratory Bird Treaty Act of 1916 and changing fashions eliminated that threat, and the population recovered to a high of about 8,500 pairs in the 1930s. It then declined to about 4,800 pairs by 1952 and may have reached a low of less than 2,500 pairs by 1977. Since then, the population has fluctuated between 2,500 and 3,300.

Although its nesting range in North America is often listed as extending from Nova Scotia to Virginia, North Carolina, or the southern tip of Florida, the roseate tern was always most common in the central portion—from Massachusetts to Long Island—and has all but disappeared from the edges of this range.

Current Distribution

The roseate tern is now found in scattered populations along the North Atlantic coast and on several islands in the Caribbean. There are also breeding colonies in northwestern Europe and at some locations along the south and east coasts of Africa. Some former breeding areas, such as Bermuda, have been abandoned.

The worldwide population of the species is somewhere between 20,000 and 44,000 birds. Population trends in the Caribbean islands are uncertain because of confusion there between the roseate and the common tern (*Sterna hirumdo*). There are an estimated 2,500 pairs in Puerto Rico and the U.S. Virgin Is-

lands, and between 1,000 and 2,000 pairs in small colonies in the Bahamas.

In Florida, a few dozen pairs nest every year among vast numbers of other terns on the Dry Tortugas, and about 40 pairs have nested on flat, gravelled rooftops in Key West. Roseate terns from the northeastern United States winter primarily in the waters off Trinidad and northern South America. Wintering grounds of the Caribbean populations are still unknown, but may be the same general areas used by terns from the northeastern U.S.

In 1986, outside of Florida, colonies nested only in the northeastern states of Connecticut, Maine, Massachusetts, and New York. In 1985, about 100 to 120 additional pairs nested in the province of Nova Scotia and two or three pairs on the Magdalen Islands in Quebec.

Conservation and Recovery

The major threat facing roseate terns is nesting competition with other seabirds such as herring gulls (*Larus argentatus*) and greater black-backed gulls (*Larus marinus*).

Many of the islands used by nesting terns were long-time sites of occupied lighthouses. The presence of humans usually discouraged gulls from nesting, but not terns. As lighthouses became automated and human operators moved away, gulls gradually took over the islands, forcing the terns out. A gull removal program at one Massachusetts lighthouse island has provided habitat for nearly 60 percent of all nesting roseate terns in North America, as well as for a large population of common terns. Other islands with formerly manned lighthouses or forts now support large tern colonies, but only because gulls have been prevented from nesting.

In the Caribbean, almost all known roseate tern breeding sites have been on very small islets, usually located off small islands. Although these islets are too small for development and have no gulls nesting, they are regularly visited by egg collectors who take the tern eggs for food.

Terns use these remote islands for nesting because predators, such as foxes, skunks and brown rats, are absent. If any of these animals does manage to invade the nests, terns eventually abandon the site, but sometimes only after consecutive years of reproductive failure. Predatory birds, particularly nocturnal feeders such as great-horned owls and black-crowned night herons, are a greater threat. Owls prey on adult terns or nearly grown young; night herons feed on eggs and recently hatched young.

The roseate tern is a state-protected species in Florida, New Hampshire, Massachusetts, Maine, New York, and Connecticut, but these listings have provided little practical protection. Most conservation work for the roseate tern has been by private conservation groups.

Bibliography

Buckley, P. A., and F. G. Buckley. 1981. "The Endangered Status of North American Roseate Terns." *Colonial Waterbirds* 4:166-173.

Cramp, S., ed., 1985. *The Birds of the Western Paleartic*, Vol. 4. Oxford University Press, London.

Contact

Regional Office of Endangered Species
U.S. Fish and Wildlife Service
One Gateway Center, Suite 700
Newton Corner, Massachusetts 02158

Regional Office of Endangered Species
U.S. Fish and Wildlife Service
Richard B. Russell Federal Building
75 Spring Street, S.W.
Atlanta, Georgia 30303

Laysan Finch
Telespyza cantans

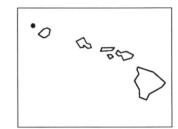

Robert J. Shallenberger

Status . . . . . . Endangered
Listed . . . . . . March 11, 1967
Family . . . . . . Fringillidae (Finch)
Description . . . Songbird; males yellow-
                  headed; females brownish
                  with faint greenish yellow
                  breast.
Habitat . . . . . . Tropical islands.
Food . . . . Seeds and other plant matter,
                  fly larvae.
Reproduction . . Clutch of 3 eggs.
Threats   Introduced plants and
                  animals, disease.
Region 1 . . . . . Hawaii

Description

The Laysan finch is a songbird about 14.5 centimeters (6 in) long, with a distinctive bluish gray, conical bill. Males have a conspicuous bright yellow head, throat and breast, with dark streaking on the upper back blending to gray on the lower back. Females are brown-streaked overall with a faint wash of greenish yellow, particularly on the breast. The Laysan finch was also known by the scientific name *Psittiorostra cantans*.

Behavior

The Laysan finch shows little fear of people and is easily caught. Because of its melodious song, it was considered a good cage bird by early explorers. It feeds on both plant and animal matter, including seeds, tender shoots of plants, flowers, and the eggs of other birds. It also forages on dead seabirds for fly larvae.

The Laysan finch builds its nest—a shallow cup of dead grass and rootlets—in clumps of bunchgrass or in holes in rocky areas. Females usually lay a clutch of three eggs between late April and early June. Incubation takes about 16 days, and the young fledge in another 15 days.

Habitat

Laysan Island is in the northwestern Hawaiian Islands, a chain extending from Nihoa Island, 400 kilometers (250 mi) northwest of Oahu, to Kure Atoll, over 1,600 kilometers (1,000 miles) to the northwest.

Laysan is a small coral island of about 5.1 square kilometers (2 sq mi), ringed with sand dunes. The maximum elevation is 17 meters (56 ft). A salt-water lagoon is located in the interior above an ancient volcanic crater.

The Laysan finch requires dense vegetation for nesting and foraging, typically shrubs and matting plants, such as the herb *Nama sandwichensis* and the shrub *Scaevola*. It favors bunchgrass (*Eragrostis variabilis*) for nesting.

Historic Range

Apparently this species of finch is adapted to Laysan Island and nearby reefs. Early explorers described the finch as "exceedingly common," and rough population estimates in the early 1900s ranged between 2,700 and 4,000 birds. Rabbits were introduced in 1903 and virtually denuded the island of vegetation, causing a rapid decline in finches. By 1923 estimates suggested that only about 100 finches remained. The Laysan finch was successfully introduced on East Island (Midway) in 1891 but disappeared after rats became established there in 1943.

Current Distribution

Today the Laysan finch is found in all the vegetated areas on the island. A separate population, established on Pearl and Hermes Reef, has spread from there to nearby small islands. The total Laysan finch population is about 15,600 birds.

Conservation and Recovery

After rabbits were removed from Laysan in 1923, vegetation reclaimed about half the island, stimulating recovery of the Laysan finch population. Other threats remain, however. The Laysan finch is highly susceptible to avian diseases, which are a constant threat to such a fragile island ecosystem. The Laysan finch population is currently monitored for signs of disease.

Any natural disaster, such as a severe hurricane or a tidal wave, could destroy a large part of the population, and probably has from time to time in the past. The introduction of finch populations to other islands has provided some measure of insurance against extinction from a natural disaster.

President Theodore Roosevelt established the Hawaiian Islands Reservation, which included Laysan Island, in 1909. In 1940 the area was made a wildlife refuge and has been designated as a Research Natural Area, under the jurisdiction of the Department of the Interior. Access to the island is prohibited except by special permit.

Bibliography

Scott, J. M., *et al.* 1988. "Conservation of Hawaii's Vanishing Avifauna." *Bioscience* 38(4):238-253.

U.S. Fish and Wildlife Service. 1984. "Recovery Plan for the Northwestern Hawaiian Islands Passerines." U.S. Fish and Wildlife Service, Portland.

Contact

Regional Office of Endangered Species
U.S. Fish and Wildlife Service
Lloyd 500 Building, Suite 1692
500 Multnomah Street
Portland, Oregon 97232

Office of Environmental Services
U.S. Fish and Wildlife Service
300 Ala Moana Boulevard
P.O. Box 50167
Honolulu, Hawaii 96850

Nihoa Finch
Telespyza ultima

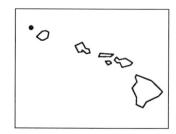

Robert J. Shallenberger

Status	Endangered
Listed	March 11, 1967
Family	Fringillidae (Finch)
Description	Songbird; males with yellow head and breast; females brownish.
Habitat	Tropical islands.
Food	Omnivorous.
Reproduction	Clutch of 3 eggs.
Threats	Hurricanes, tidal waves, introduced predators and diseases.
Region 1	Hawaii

Description

The Nihoa finch is a songbird about 13.5 centimeters (5.6 in) in length. Except for its smaller size, it closely resembles its near relative, the Laysan finch. Both species have a distinctive bluish gray conical bill. Male Nihoa finches have a bright yellow head, throat, and breast. There is dark streaking on the upper back, blending to gray on the lower back. Females are streaked with brown overall, are darker above, and have a faint wash of greenish yellow, particularly on the breast.

This finch was first described as a separate species, then as a subspecies of the Laysan finch. It is now considered a full species. It has also been known by the scientific name *Psittirostra ultima*.

Behavior

The Nihoa finch is omnivorous, eating a wide variety of plant seeds, flower heads, small invertebrates, and bird eggs. Nests are built in holes in rocky outcroppings. Females lay an average clutch of three eggs between late February and March. Little information is available on incubation and nesting, but one captive bird was observed to incubate eggs for about 15 days.

Habitat

Nihoa is an island about 400 kilometers (250 mi) northwest of Oahu, Hawaii, in the northwestern Hawaiian Island chain. Most of these islands are the remnants of once larger volcanic cones that have slowly eroded and subsided beneath the water. Nihoa has a 62-hectare (156-acre) land surface, consisting of steep slopes, rocky outcroppings, well-developed valleys, and precipitous cliffs on the west, north, and east. Its topography is notably rugged, and maximum elevation is 277 meters (910 ft).

Low shrubs cover the sides and much of the floors of the valleys. Bunchgrasses (*Eragrostis*) are more common on the ridges. Finches are widespread throughout the island but are more often seen near rocky outcroppings; the birds prefer a sparsely vegetated, open habitat.

Historic Range

The Nihoa finch is endemic to Nihoa. Before 1960, population estimates ranged between 500 and 1,200 birds. Estimates between 1964 and 1975 suggested a population of 3,000 to 5,000. Attempts to introduce the bird to other islands within the northwestern Hawaiian Islands (French Frigate Shoals, Tern Island, and East Island) have been unsuccessful.

Current Distribution

The Nihoa finch is now known only on Nihoa island. In 1986 the island supported a population of about 2,225 finches.

Conservation and Recovery

Island ecosystems, in general, are fragile and highly susceptible to the introduction of plants, animals, or microbes from the outside. Exotic plants can quickly out-compete island fauna; introduced predators can drastically alter the balance of wildlife; bird populations are highly susceptible to imported avian diseases. All of these factors

must be closely monitored and immediate steps taken to counter any introductions.

Because the Nihoa finch population is highly concentrated, a natural disaster, such as a severe hurricane or a tidal wave, could destroy a large part of it. Previous efforts to introduce the Nihoa finch to other islands have failed, leaving it especially vulnerable to natural disasters. The Fish and Wildlife Service Recovery Plan for the species suggests that a captive breeding program may be needed.

In 1909 President Theodore Roosevelt established the Hawaiian Islands Reservation, which included Nihoa Island. In 1940 the area was designated a wildlife refuge and has now been made a Research Natural Area under the jurisdiction of the Department of the Interior. Entry to the island is prohibited except by special permit.

Bibliography

Banks, R. C., and R. C. Laybourne. 1977. "Plumage Sequence and Taxonomy of Laysan and Nihoa Finches." *Condor* 79:343-348.

Berger, A. J. 1981. *Hawaiian Birdlife*. The University Press of Hawaii, Honolulu.

U.S. Fish and Wildlife Service. 1984. "Recovery Plan for the Northwestern Hawaiian Islands Passerines." U.S. Fish and Wildlife Service, Portland.

Contact

Regional Office of Endangered Species
U.S. Fish and Wildlife Service
Lloyd 500 Building, Suite 1692
500 N.E. Multnomah Street
Portland, Oregon 97232

Office of Environmental Services
U.S. Fish and Wildlife Service
300 Ala Moana Boulevard
P.O. Box 50167
Honolulu, Hawaii 96850

Attwater's Prairie Chicken

Tympanuchus cupido attwateri

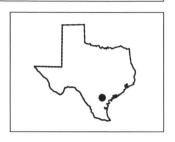

C. Allan Morgan

Status	Endangered
Listed	March 11, 1967
Family	Phasianidae (Grouse and Ptarmigans)
Description	Henlike bird, heavily barred with dark brown and buff; male has orange eye combs and neck skin.
Habitat	Coastal prairie.
Food	Plants, insects.
Reproduction	Average clutch of 12 eggs.
Threats	Agricultural and residential development.
Region 2	Texas

Description

Attwater's prairie chicken is a medium-sized grouse (about 43 cm or 17 in long), with a barred, brown and buff pattern. It has a short, rounded, dark tail (black in males, brownish in females). Males have orange combs over the eyes, and an area of orange skin on either side of the neck, which is inflated during courtship display.

Behavior

Prairie chickens feed on plants and insects. The bulk of their diet consists of the green foliage and seeds of wild plants. Insects are a seasonal part of their diet. In early spring in preparation for breeding, the male struts and erects his neck feathers to reveal an orange, inflated patch of skin. Breeding grounds are called "booming grounds" from the bird's low booming call. These grounds can be natural grassy flats or artificially maintained surfaces, such as roads, airport runways, or oil well pads. Nesting sites are usually located in tall grasses. Females lay an average clutch of 12 eggs during April; incubation is about 24 days. Young birds fledge in seven to ten days and are tended by the female.

Habitat

Attwater's prairie chicken inhabits coastal prairie. Most of the habitat is dominated by tall dropseed, little bluestem, sumpweed, broomweed, ragweed, and big bluestem. Prairie chickens use shorter grasses for courtship and feeding; tall grasses for nesting, loafing, and feeding.

Moderate cattle grazing can actually be beneficial to prairie chicken habitat. Grazing or, in its absence, prescribed burning maintains greater species diversity within grassland communities and helps prevent invasion of woody plants, such as Maccartney rose and eastern baccharis.

Historic Range

Attwater's prairie chicken once ranged in a narrow strip, 48 kilometers (30 mi) wide, that extended along the coast from the southern tip of Texas to mid-Louisiana. In the 1800s there were probably a million prairie chickens, but by 1940 the population had declined to about 8,700 individuals.

Current Distribution

At present, the prairie chicken is restricted to a very narrow band along the Texas coast, some offshore islands, and remnant inland populations. Over 40 percent of the present population lives in a contiguous area in Aransas, Goliad, and Refugio counties, Texas. A population has also been established at the Tatton Unit of the Aransas National Wildlife Refuge.

In Goliad County, the population peaked in 1974 at 486 birds, and by 1982 had declined to 62 birds. Land-use patterns have remained consistent during this period and the reason for this decline is unknown. The 1980 estimate for Refugio County was 726 chickens, but by 1982 was down to 438. Only 20 chickens were estimated for Aransas Country in 1982. Relatively large numbers also occur in Austin and Colorado counties, which had populations of 250 and 200, respectively, in 1982.

The population of Attwater's prairie chicken has continued to decline. A 1982 census counted 1,282 birds, but by 1988 the total population was estimated at only 926 birds.

Conservation and Recovery

In the 1960s, the World Wildlife Fund-U.S. purchased habitat for the prairie chicken in Colorado County, Texas. This step was closely followed by a private donation to the Fish and Wildlife Service (FWS) to provide chicken habitat adjoining Aransas National Wildlife Refuge. This land became the Attwater's Prairie Chicken National Wildlife Refuge when it was transferred to FWS control in 1972. Recent land acquisition has added several thousand acres to the refuge.

Even though refuge areas have been established, habitat loss continues, and the outlook for the Attwater's prairie chicken is not bright. If it is going to survive, larger blocks of native prairie must be preserved. In the near future, biologists predict that chicken populations in Galveston, Harris, and Brazoria counties will disappear because of continued urbanization. In 1988 biologists recommended establishing a captive propagation program to restock wild populations.

Bibliography

Jurries, R. 1979. "Attwater's Prairie Chicken." Report (Series F.S. No. 18), Project W-100-R. Texas Parks and Wildlife Department.

McCune, R. A. 1970. "Prairie Chicken Moving Days." Texas Parks and Wildlife Magazine 18:12-15.

U.S. Fish and Wildlife Service. 1983. "Attwater's Prairie Chicken Recovery Plan." U.S. Fish and Wildlife Service, Albuquerque.

Contact

Regional Office of Endangered Species
U.S. Fish and Wildlife Service
P.O. Box 1306
Albuquerque, New Mexico 87103

Bachman's Warbler
Vermivora bachmanii

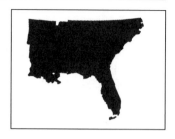

Status	Endangered (possibly extinct)
Listed	March 11, 1967
Family	Emberizidae (Warblers and Sparrows)
Description	Olive warbler with yellow face and underparts, black cap and bib.
Habitat	Palmetto and cypress swamps.
Food	Insects.
Reproduction	Clutch of 3 or 4 eggs.
Threats	Habitat loss.
Region 4	Alabama, Arkansas, Kentucky, Louisiana, South Carolina

J. H. Dick/VIREO

Description

The rarest native songbird of the U.S., Bachman's warbler is smaller than a sparrow and has a slender, somewhat downcurved bill. Males have an olive back, a yellow face and underparts, and a black cap and bib. Females are slightly duller, with gray cap and bib. This warbler was discovered in 1833 by John Bachman and described by John James Audubon.

Behavior

Bachman's warbler nests in dense, tangled vegetation close to the ground; it builds a cup-shaped nest of dried leaves, weed and grass stalks, and lines it with Spanish moss. Clutch size is thought to be three or four eggs, which are incubated by the female. The bird forages in dense foliage high in trees, deliberately gleaning insects from the vegetation. It winters in Cuba and the Isle of Pines and is an early emigrant to its breeding grounds, arriving in mid-March.

Habitat

This warbler needs dense, swampy woodlands for nesting. Current evidence suggests that the species is particularly adapted to swampy canebreaks or bamboo thickets and has declined as this specific habitat has become more rare.

Historic Range

At the turn of the century, Bachman's warbler was the seventh most common migrant of the Suwannee River in Florida, suggesting that it was moderately abundant in the Southeast. Although difficult to track, the species has been sighted in six states: Missouri, Arkansas, Kentucky, Alabama, South Carolina, and Louisiana. Feather hunters were known to take Bachman's warbler near Lake Pontchartrain in Louisiana.

Current Distribution

Bachman's warbler has not been seen recently and may already be extinct. In 1975 the American Ornithologists Union reported one sighting off the Louisiana coast and sporadic sightings in South Carolina swamplands. The last confirmed sighting was of a wintering female in Cuba in 1981.

Conservation and Recovery

Bachman's warbler was not numerous even when first discovered. It was decimated by feather hunters who indiscriminately killed any bird with colorful feathers for use in the millinery trade. Sometimes birds were stuffed and mounted whole on women's hats. One such specimen of a Bachman's warbler is now at the American Museum of Natural History in New York.

Its decline may be tied to the steady demise of canebrake habitat in the Southeast. Much of the bottomlands where the cane grows has been cleared for agriculture.

Because the bird is rare and difficult to locate, and because the reasons for its rarity are not completely understood, a recovery strategy has not been formulated.

Bibliography

Ehrlich, Paul R., David S. Dobkin, and Darryl Wheye, eds. 1988. "The Fate of Bachman's Warbler." In *The Birder's Handbook: A Field Guide to the Natural History of North American Birds*. Simon and Schuster, New York.

Hamel, P. B. 1986. *Bachman's Warbler: A Species in Peril*. Smithsonian Institution Press, Washington, D.C.

Remsen, J. V., Jr. 1986. "Was Bachman's Warbler a Bamboo Specialist." *Auk* 103:216-219.

Stevenson, H. M. 1972. "The Recent History of Bachman's Warbler." *Wilson Bulletin* 84:344-347.

Contact

Regional Office of Endangered Species
U.S. Fish and Wildlife Service
Richard B. Russell Federal Building
75 Spring Street, S.W.
Atlanta, Georgia 30303

Black-Capped Vireo
Vireo atricapillus

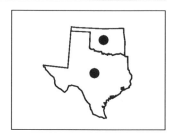

Steven Holt/VIREO

Status	Endangered
Listed	October 6, 1987
Family	Vireonidae (Vireo)
Description	Small olive-green songbird, with black cap and white "spectacles."
Habitat	Scattered trees and brush.
Food	Insects.
Reproduction	Clutch of 3 to 5 eggs.
Threats	Livestock grazing, cowbird brood parasitism.
Region 2	Oklahoma, Texas

Description

The black-capped vireo is a small songbird, about 12 centimeters (4.8 in) long. Adult males are olive-green above and white below, with faintly yellow-green flanks. The crown and upper half of the head is glossy black with white "spectacles" around the eyes. It has brownish eyes and a black bill. Adult females are duller with a slate gray crown, and the underparts are washed with greenish yellow. Females and immatures resemble the solitary vireo.

Behavior

Vireos are songbirds with a loud, emphatic warble. Cup-shaped nests are built in shrubs and small trees. Clutch size is from three to five tiny, white eggs. During the 14- to 17-day incubation period, the female incubates the eggs at night; males and females alternate during the day. Young fledge in 10 to 12 days, after which the female renests, occasionally with a different male. Black-capped vireos are shy and restless, flitting from twig to twig. Like other vireos, they are insectivorous.

Habitat

The species is found in areas with scattered trees and brush. Many vireo territories are located on steep ravine slopes in rugged terrain where woody vegetation grows in clumps. Thick ground foliage is important for nesting. Most nests are found 0.4 to 1.25

meters (18 to 49 in) above ground, screened from view by foliage. Black-capped vireo habitat is naturally maintained by wildfires and grazing animals, which keep vegetation in an early successional stage.

Historic Range

The black-capped vireo formerly bred from Kansas through Oklahoma and Texas to central Coahuila, Mexico, with an outlying, possibly temporary, colony in Nuevo Leon, Mexico. Winter residents ranged from Sonora to Oaxaca, Mexico, but occurred mostly in Sinaloa and Nayarit.

Current Distribution

By 1954 black-capped vireos had disappeared from Kansas; the northernmost breeding range was northern Oklahoma. The present range is from Blaine County in central Oklahoma south through Dallas, the Edwards Plateau, Big Bend National Park, Texas, to Sierra Madera in central Coahuila, Mexico.

A population count in 1986 found only 350 black-capped vireos: 44 to 51 adults at three sites in Oklahoma; slightly more than 280 adults at 33 sites in Texas; and 24 adults in Mexico.

Conservation and Recovery

The major threat to the black-capped vireo is loss of its nesting habitat. Suitable nesting areas have been altered by development, grazing by sheep and goats, and range improvements that remove broad-leaved, low, woody vegetation. The largest concentration of black-capped vireos is near Austin, Texas, in an area that is undergoing rapid development. Over 88 percent of the vireo population is immediately threatened by housing development and road construction. At the present rate, most of the bird's habitat will be lost within ten years.

Another important threat to the vireo is nest parasitism by brown-headed cowbirds. Deforestation and the expansion of cattle pasture over the past 150 years has favored the spread of the cowbird, which feeds near cattle. Cowbirds lay their eggs in vireo nests before the vireo clutch is complete. Cowbird eggs hatch two to four days before vireo eggs, and, by the time the vireos hatch, cowbird nestlings outweigh them tenfold. In all cases where a cowbird occupied the nest, no vireo chicks survived. When cowbird trapping was initiated in Texas and Oklahoma, nest parasitism dropped dramatically.

The black-capped vireo is especially attractive to ornithologists and amateur birders. Unfortunately, nests have failed or been abandoned due to excessive attention from these admirers. Some egg and nestling predation by snakes and scrub jays also occurs.

Probable conservation activities will include cowbird trapping in nesting areas and land management practices on government-owned land to maintain suitable habitat vegetation.

Bibliography

Graber, J. W. 1961. "Distribution, Habitat Requirements, and Life History of the Black-Capped Vireo (*Vireo atricapillus*)." *Ecological Monographs* 31:313-336.

Grzybowski, J. A. 1985. "Final Report: Population and Nesting Ecology of the Black-Capped Vireo." U.S. Fish and Wildlife Service, Albuquerque.

Contact

Regional Office of Endangered Species
U.S. Fish and Wildlife Service
P.O. Box 1306
Albuquerque, New Mexico 87103

Least Bell's Vireo
Vireo belli pusillus

B. "Moose" Peterson

Status	Endangered
Listed	May 2, 1986
Family	Vireonidae (Vireo)
Description	Small songbird, gray above, white below.
Habitat	Willow-dominated brush.
Food	Insects.
Reproduction	Clutch of 3 or 4 eggs.
Threats	Destruction of riparian woodlands, cowbird brood parasitism.
Region 1	California

Description

Least Bell's vireo, a subspecies of Bell's vireo, is a migratory songbird about 12 centimeters (4.8 in) long. It is gray above, white below and has inconspicuous white spectacles.

Three other subspecies of Bell's vireo are recognized by the American Ornithologists' Union: *Vireo bellii bellii* of the midwestern U.S., *V. b. medius* of Texas, and *V. b. arizonae* of the southwestern U.S. and northern Mexico. While all are similar in appearance, behavior, and life history, subspecies' breeding ranges are geographically distinct.

Behavior

Least Bell's vireo has a loud and persistent song. It builds cuplike nests 1 meter (39 in) off the ground between forking twigs, usually in dense brush along willow-dominated streambanks. It lays three or four spotted eggs that hatch in about 14 days. The young remain in the nest approximately 10 to 12 days. The diet consists of insects. Virtually all Bell's vireos winter in Mexico, arriving at the breeding ground mid-March to early April and departing in late August or September.

Habitat

The least Bell's vireo occupies a more restricted nesting habitat than other subspecies. It prefers dense, willow-dominated areas adjacent to streams and having lush understory vegetation. The range of other Bell's vireo subspecies extends into upland desert scrub.

The least Bell's vireo nests primarily in willows, but it will use other trees and shrubs. It forages along streambeds and in adjoining chaparral (scrub oak) habitat, usually staying within 275 meters (300 yds) of the nest.

Historic Range

Once widespread and abundant throughout California's Central Valley and other low-elevation riverine valleys, this vireo's historical breeding range extended from Red Bluff (Tehama County) in interior northern California to northwestern Baja California, Mexico.

Current Distribution

Over the last several decades, the least Bell's vireo has apparently been extirpated from the Sacramento and San Joaquin Valleys, once the center of its breeding range. By 1983, nesting was restricted to several localities in the Salinas River Valley (Monterey and San Benito counties); one locality along the Amargosa River (Inyo County); and numerous small populations in southern California south of the Tehachapi Mountains and in northwestern Baja California, Mexico.

Since 1977 several intensive surveys of virtually all potential vireo breeding habitat in California have been conducted. In total, 291 male least Bell's vireos have been reported from 46 of over 150 former localities. These surveys were based on singing (territorial) males, and the counts are an index to the population levels considered to be the maximum number present. It is estimated that several hundred breeding pairs are active in Baja California, Mexico.

Conservation and Recovery

No other passerine (perching songbird) species in California is known to have declined as dramatically as the least Bell's

vireo. Most current populations contain fewer than five breeding pairs.

Widespread loss of riparian habitats and brood parasitism by the brown-headed cowbird (*Molothrus ater*) are the main causes of the vireo's decline. The bird has been extirpated from an estimated 95 percent of its former range largely as a result of cowbird parasitism.

Before 1900, cowbirds were rare in California, but with the increase of irrigated agriculture and animal husbandry cowbird numbers expanded significantly. Destruction of riparian woodlands may have rendered the least Bell's vireo incapable of withstanding the spectacular increase of this nest parasite. Cowbirds do not build nests of their own but instead lay their eggs in the nests of other species, almost always to the detriment of the host birds' own eggs or young. Vireo nests appear to be among the easiest to locate by cowbirds and may be favored.

The narrow and limited nature of the vireo's habitat makes this subspecies more susceptible to major population loss than other Bell's vireo subspecies. Over 95 percent of historic habitat has been lost throughout the former breeding range in the Central Valley of California. Similar habitat losses have also occurred throughout its remaining range in southern California, and habitat is declining in Baja California as well.

These widespread losses have been caused by flood control and water development projects, agricultural development, livestock grazing, invasive exotic plants, off-road vehicles, and urban development. Human development has been accompanied by predators often attracted to the accessible vireo nest by the male's song, and feral cats have thus become a threat.

Historically, the Prado Basin and adjacent Santa Ana River supported a large number of wildlife species. Most of the Santa Ana River downstream from Prado Dam has been channelized and lined with concrete, greatly reducing wildlife habitat. The Prado Dam reservoir itself destroyed a large amount of riparian habitat when it was first flooded. Only two pairs of vireos are known to breed below Prado Dam on the Santa Ana River.

The riparian ecosystems required by the vireo are dynamic systems, and the scouring of vegetation during periodic floods is required to create the low-density vegetation favored by the bird. If flooding does not occur the willow habitat grows beyond the needs of the vireo.

In 1980 the least Bell's vireo was listed as Endangered by the state of California. A program to control cowbirds and a program to prevent habitat loss is credited with increasing vireo productivity.

There have, however, been setbacks in protecting vireo habitat. In 1986 a proposed flood control project on the San Luis Rey River in Oceanside (San Diego County) was identified as a threat to the least Bell's vireo. The same year, the Fish and Wildlife Service announced that an oil pipeline from Norwalk to San Diego, California, had caused extensive damage to wetlands in the San Elijo Lagoon, a breeding site of the vireo and two other endangered birds. Unauthorized landfills in San Diego County also were discovered that year to have destroyed a nesting site.

In 1986 a management plan was created to protect at least 8,065 hectares (20,000 acres) of least Bell's vireo habitat in 12 California locations. A 1988 census indicated that most of the larger vireo populations had increased significantly over the previous year. Smaller populations (those numbering less than ten) were hanging on precariously.

Bibliography

Garrett, K., and J. Dunn. 1981. *Birds of Southern California: Status and Distribution*. Los Angeles Audubon Society, Los Angeles.

Goldwasser, S. 1978. "Distribution, Reproductive Success and Impact of Nest Parasitism by Brown-Headed Cowbirds on Least Bell's Vireos." Pamphlet of the California Department of Fish and Game, Sacramento.

Goldwasser, S., D. Gaines, and S. Wilbur. 1980. "The Least Bell's Vireo in California: A De Facto Endangered Race." *American Birds* 34:742-745.

Wilbur, S. 1980. "The Least Bell's Vireo in Baja California, Mexico." *Western Birds* 11:129-133.

Contact

Regional Office of Endangered Species
U.S. Fish and Wildlife Service
Lloyd 500 Building, Suite 1692
500 N.E. Multnomah Street
Portland, Oregon 97232

REPTILES

Culebra Island
Giant Anole
Anolis roosevelti

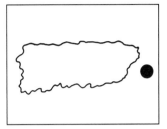

C. Kenneth Dodd, Jr.

Status	Endangered (possibly extinct)
Listed	July 21, 1977
Family	Iguanidae (Lizard)
Description	Brownish gray lizard with a prominent, deeply scalloped fin.
Habitat	Fig and gumbo-limbo forest.
Food	Figs, possibly insects and smaller lizards.
Reproduction	Unknown.
Threats	Loss of habitat.
Region 4	Puerto Rico

Description

The Culebra Island giant anole is a brownish gray lizard with a snout to vent (anal opening) length of about 16 centimeters (6.4 in). Two dark lines run down the lizard's side: one begins around the ear and extends to the groin; the other extends from the shoulder region into the groin. There is a distinct light spot on the temple. The eyelids are yellow; the throat is gray except for the lower rear quarter, which is light yellow. The underside is white, and the tail, with a deeply scalloped fin along most of its length, is yellowish brown.

Behavior

The reclusive giant anole is arboreal and is said to be most active when the fruits of trees are ripe. It has been observed feeding on figs but may also eat insects and other, smaller lizards. Little else about this lizard's behavior is known.

Habitat

Culebra Island is a small mountainous island located 40 kilometers (24 mi) east of the island of Puerto Rico. It is about 9 kilometers (6 mi) in length and 3 kilometers (1.9 mi) across at its widest point. If the giant anole still exists, it is thought to inhabit remaining tracts of fig and gumbo-limbo forest on Monte Resaca along the northern coast.

Historic Range

The giant anole has not been found outside of Culebra Island. It was first described by

Chapman Grant on the basis of two specimens collected in 1931 and 1932. The latter specimen, an adult male, was the last Culebra Island anole to be examined alive by herpetologists. There is reason to suspect, however, that unidentified anole specimens taken from Vieques and Beef Island in the British Virgin Islands are actually *Anolis roosevelti.*

Current Distribution

Because this lizard has not been collected since 1932, some biologists feel that it is extinct. Others give credence to local residents who claim to see the lizard on occasion. These sightings, together with possible occurrences in the British Virgins, have kept the question of this species' status open. It will not be declared extinct until adequate research has been done.

Conservation and Recovery

Much of Culebra Island has been deforested, including Flamenco Peninsula where the giant anole was first collected. Only a narrow band of suitable habitat remains along the steep northern slopes of the island. Loss of habitat has reduced the potential range for a species that was probably never very numerous. Other factors, such as predation, may have contributed to the species' decline, but research is lacking.

Critical Habitat was designated for the giant anole to include about 196 hectares (485 acres) on Monte Resaca. A large portion of this land falls within the boundaries of the Culebra Island National Wildlife Refuge, which was created in 1982. If the giant anole is not already extinct, this protected tract is considered large enough to ensure its survival.

Herpetologists are conducting periodic surveys of the habitat and examining popula-

tions of related anoles to develop a body of comparative data. The Fish and Wildlife Service expects ongoing ecological studies to provide guidance for management of the habitat.

Bibliography

Grant, C. 1931. "A New Species and Two New Sub-Species of the Genus *Anolis.*" *Journal of the Department of Agriculture of Puerto Rico* 15(3):219-222.

Honegger, R., ed. 1979. "Giant Anole, Culebra Giant Anole." In *IUCN Red Data Book*, Vol. 3. Morges, Switzerland.

U.S. Fish and Wildlife Service. 1982. "Giant Anole Recovery Plan." U.S. Fish and Wildlife Service, Atlanta.

Contact

Regional Office of Endangered Species
U.S. Fish and Wildlife Service
Richard B. Russell Federal Building
75 Spring Street, S.W.
Atlanta, Georgia 30303

Caribbean Field Office
U.S. Fish and Wildlife Service
P.O. Box 491
Boqueron, Puerto Rico 00622

Loggerhead Sea Turtle
Caretta caretta

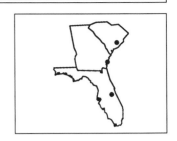

Status	Threatened
Listed	July 28, 1978
Family	Cheloniidae (Sea Turtle)
Description	Sea turtle with a reddish brown carapace, weighing up to 227 kg (500 lbs).
Habitat	Pelagic; undisturbed beaches for nesting.
Food	Mollusks, sponges, horseshoe crabs.
Reproduction	Average of 120 eggs per clutch.
Threats	Loss and disturbance of nesting habitat, incidental take by commercial fishermen.
Region 4	Florida, Georgia, North Carolina, South Carolina

USFWS

Description

The loggerhead is a large sea turtle, weighing as much as 227 kilograms (500 lbs) at maturity. The reddish brown carapace (shell) is oval, up to 114 centimeters (45 in) long, and divided into five or more shields that in juveniles sometimes overlap. The broad, scaly head is yellowish to olive-brown. Limbs are modified as flippers. In the Atlantic Ocean population, the front flippers possess two claws.

Behavior

Loggerheads are primarily carnivorous, feeding on a large variety of oceanic creatures, including mollusks, sponges, and horseshoe crabs. The turtle's powerful jaws are adapted for crushing hard-shelled mollusks. The life cycle consists of a brief terrestrial stage when eggs are deposited on beaches and hatch, and a pelagic stage that begins when hatchlings return to the ocean.

From May through August, adult females appear on the nesting beaches. There they lay an average of two clutches of eggs at 13-day intervals. Each clutch contains about 120 eggs. The eggs incubate for two months. Then hatchlings emerge as a group, usually during the night, and make their way to the water and eventually to the open ocean. When they reach sexual maturity—when the shell is longer than about 50 centimeters (20 in)—females return to shore to lay their eggs, often migrating long distances. Mature females return to the same "home" beaches at two- or three-year intervals.

Habitat

This ocean-dwelling turtle requires well-drained dunes, clean sand, and grassy vegetation for nesting. Nesting beaches should be relatively undisturbed by humans or by predators. Stable temperatures and moisture are required for at least 60 days so that eggs can develop properly. In the ocean, loggerheads migrate, following vegetation-laden ocean currents.

Historic Range

The loggerhead turtle is widely distributed throughout the world's temperate and subtropic oceans with Atlantic, Mediterranean, and Pacific populations. The largest population in the world nests on the beaches of the Sultanate of Oman and numbers about 30,000 individuals. The Fish and Wildlife Service (FWS) is primarily concerned with the stock that nests on the eastern seaboard of the U.S. and in the Greater Antilles.

Current Distribution

One of North America's largest nesting populations of loggerheads is found on the barrier island beaches of the southeastern U.S., from North Carolina to the Florida Keys. Ninety percent of turtle nesting occurs in Florida. A few loggerhead turtles have recently nested on barrier islands along the Texas coast.

Turtle populations are estimated by counting nesting females, an uncertain technique because individual nesting frequencies vary. The loggerhead nesting population of the U.S. is thought to number about 15,000 individuals each year. Surveys in the early 1980s in North Carolina and Georgia pointed to a 3 percent annual decline in numbers.

Conservation and Recovery

Like most other marine turtles, the loggerhead's historic nesting beaches have suffered degradation from residential and recreational coastal development, dune stabilization, beach sand mining, and erosion. The profusion of beachfront lighting tends to disorient hatchlings, causing them to move toward the lights rather than toward the sea. Predation of eggs by raccoons and dogs has been identified as a serious problem on some beaches.

Many organizations, universities, and wildlife agencies are working together to protect and rehabilitate nesting habitat. For example, the National Park Service, Merritt Island National Wildlife Refuge, and the Air Force are cooperating to protect 68 kilometers (42 mi) of nesting beaches at Cape Canaveral, Florida. Their predation control efforts have resulted in successful hatching of 60 percent of nearly 5,000 clutches deposited annually there. Previously, 95 percent of clutches failed to hatch.

The FWS, the Florida Department of Natural Resources, and Brevard County are cooperating to extend protection to a 35-kilometer (22-mi) stretch of beach between Melbourne Beach and Wabasso Beach. This crucial site accounts for up to 25 percent of all loggerhead and green turtle nesting in the U.S. In addition, Brevard County passed a pioneering ordinance to control beachfront lighting in 1985. Within one year, the problem of hatchling disorientation at county nesting sites was almost eliminated.

Efforts to protect habitat are underway at other sites, including Cape Lookout and Cape Hatteras national seashores (North Carolina), Cape Island (South Carolina), and Raccoon Key in the Ossahaw Sound (Georgia). Turtle nests are fenced to prevent predation or human disturbance. Clutches are relocated from eroding beaches. At some sites, beaches are tilled to loosen compacted sands that interfere with successful nesting.

At sea, the loggerhead turtle is often incidentally trapped in the trawling nets of commercial shrimp fishermen. The National Marine Fisheries Service (NMFS), which is responsible for marine turtle protection, estimates that over 11,000 air-breathing marine turtles drown in shrimp nets each year. Recently, the NMFS has developed regulations to require large shrimp boats to use turtle excluder devices (TEDs), which are fitted at the mouth of shrimp nets to divert turtles out of the nets. TEDs are considered the most important single recovery action that can be taken to immediately reduce turtle mortality.

Implementation of TED regulations has been fraught with controversy. Because early prototypes of these devices not only excluded turtles from nets but significantly reduced the size of the shrimp catch, many commercial fishermen—particularly in Texas and Louisiana—expressed opposition to using TEDs. In response, Congress repeatedly delayed implementation of TED requirements while the issue was further studied.

The NMFS and its parent agency the National Oceanic and Atmospheric Administration (NOAA) have worked with the National Academy of Sciences to improve TED design to minimize interference with the shrimp catch. The resulting TED—called a "Georgia Jumper"—has been shown in sea trials to reduce shrimp catch by only 2 to 5 percent. Observers feel that this rate can be reduced still further by training crews in the proper use of the device.

In July 1989, despite pressure from several Gulf state congressmen and a shrimpers' protest blockade of Galveston harbor, TED regulations for offshore shrimpers went into effect. The Coast Guard's enforcement of the regulations is certain to remain controversial.

Shrimpers along the Atlantic Coast have shown less resistance to employing TEDs. A recent spot check conducted by the Coast Guard revealed that 39 out of 40 shrimp trawlers had installed and were using TEDs even before the regulation was officially in effect. This cooperation bodes well for the loggerhead turtle, which nests mostly along the Atlantic Coast.

Bibliography

Carr, A. F., L. Ogren, and C. McVea. 1980. "Apparent Hibernation by the Atlantic Loggerhead Turtle *Caretta caretta* Off Cape Canaveral, Florida." *Biological Conservation* 19:7-14

Davis, G. E., and M. C. Whiting. 1977. "Loggerhead Sea Turtle Nesting in Everglades National Park, Florida, U.S.A." *Herpetologica* 33:18-28.

Talbert, D. R., *et al.* 1980. "Nesting Activity of the Loggerhead Turtle (*Caretta caretta*) in South Carolina." *Copeia* (4):709-718.

U.S. Fish and Wildlife Service. 1984. "Recovery Plan for Marine Turtles." U.S. Fish and Wildlife Service, Atlanta.

Contact

Office of Public Affairs
National Marine Fisheries Service
Department of Commerce
Washington, D.C. 20235

Regional Office of Endangered Species
U.S. Fish and Wildlife Service
Richard B. Russell Federal Building
75 Spring Street, S.W.
Atlanta, Georgia 30303

Green Sea Turtle
Chelonia mydas

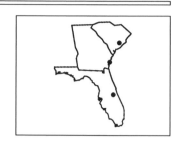

Status	. . . . . .	Endangered in Florida-Threatened elsewhere
Listed	. . . . . .	July 28, 1978
Family	. . . . .	Cheloniidae (Sea Turtle)
Description	. . .	Olive brown sea turtle, weighing up to 205 kg (450 lbs).
Habitat	. . . . . .	Pelagic; undisturbed beaches for nesting.
Food	. . . .	Mostly herbivorous; grasses and algae.
Reproduction	. .	Clutches of 100 to 200 eggs.
Threats	. . . .	Loss and disturbance of nesting habitat, incidental mortality caused by fishing nets, hunting.
Region 2	. . . . .	Texas coast (occasional)
Region 4	. . . . .	Florida, Georgia, North Carolina

C. Allan Morgan

Description

The long-lived green sea turtle achieves a shell (carapace) length of 122 centimeters (48 in) and a mature weight of 205 kilograms (450 lbs). The smooth, oval carapace lacks a central ridge. Adult shell coloring varies from light to dark olive-brown; hatchlings are black. In adults, the head appears small in comparison to body size. The front paddle-shaped flippers are strongly developed, each with a single claw.

Behavior

Adult green sea turtles spend most of their lives feeding on sea grasses and algae along the Continental Shelf. Adults migrate long distances and return to the same beaches periodically to nest. Turtles nest in Florida from June through August shortly after mating off the coast. Individual turtles mate at intervals of from two to four years.

When nesting, turtles crawl ashore at night, scoop out a deep depression in the beach sand, deposit eggs, and return to the sea, all in the space of an hour. Clutches may consist of 100 to over 200 eggs. Depending on temperatures, incubation requires from 48 to 70 days. Hatchlings swarm back to the water and are dispersed at sea.

Habitat

This ocean-dwelling turtle requires well-drained dunes, clean sand, and grassy vegetation for nesting. Nesting beaches should be relatively undisturbed by humans or by predators. Stable temperature and moisture are required for up to 70 days, so that eggs can properly develop. In the ocean, green sea turtles graze on offshore beds of sea grasses.

Historic Range

Nesting beaches are widely distributed along the tropical and subtropical coasts of the Atlantic Ocean, reaching from Cape Canaveral, Florida, in the north to as far south as French Guiana. The green sea turtle nests in the Gulf in Central America and Mexico and is occasionally seen in Texas. Mature turtles of the eastern stock appear to migrate within an area defined by the southeastern U.S. coast, Ascension Island, and northern Brazil. Young turtles are more widely dispersed, ranging as far north as Massachusetts.

Decline of the green sea turtle population was reported by Bermuda fishermen as early as 1620, when the first law was passed against harvesting sea turtles. In the late 1800s, a decline in numbers began to be noticed in Florida and elsewhere and continued unabated until recently. It is not clear that Florida ever had a large nesting population, although there is evidence that immature green sea turtles were once common there.

Current Distribution

Small numbers of green turtles have been reported during the last two decades along the Atlantic coast of Florida, with one nesting confirmed in Georgia and five in North Carolina. Up to 25 percent of the Atlantic breeding population nests on a narrow stretch of Flor- ida beach between Melbourne Beach and Wabasso Beach (Brevard County). The Florida population is increasing, and between 300 and 400 adult females nest there each year. Important nesting beaches in the Caribbean are found on Mona and Culebra Islands (Puerto Rico), on St. Thomas, St. John, and St. Croix, and on the Island of Vieques.

The largest green sea turtle colony in the world is found on Costa Rica's Tortugero Beach, where over 24,000 adult females nest each season. The Mexican population has declined steadily since the early 1960s, but its size and status are otherwise unknown.

Conservation and Recovery

Residential and recreational development of beachfront has eliminated or disturbed many historic nesting sites. The Fish and Wildlife Service (FWS), the Florida Department of Natural Resources, and many local agencies and universities are actively working to acquire and protect nesting habitat on the Florida coast. In 1987, the Florida State Legislature and the University Board of Regents established a Center for Sea Turtle Research at the University of Florida in Gainesville. The center's goals are to encourage and conduct research on all aspects of sea turtle biology, monitor population levels, and promote conservation through public education.

Green sea turtles have long been considered a source of meat in the Caribbean, Mexico, and South America and are actively hunted. Some nesting colonies—particularly in Mexico—have been decimated by commercial fishermen and egg poachers. In the U.S. the species is protected from hunting by the Endangered Species Act, state laws, and provisions of the Convention on International Trade in Endangered Species of Flora and Fauna (CITES). Other countries have protective laws, but enforcement is frequently ineffective.

Green sea turtles are taken incidentally by commercial fishermen trawling for shrimp. As many as 11,000 marine turtles become entangled in the nets and drown each year, including many green sea turtles. The National Marine Fisheries Service (NMFS) of the Department of Commerce, is responsible for marine turtle protection at sea. The FWS is responsible for protecting nesting habitat. Florida state regulations are particularly stringent and should provide effective protection for the state's nesting turtles.

Recently, the NMFS developed regulations to require larger shrimp boats to use turtle excluder devices (TEDs), which are fitted at the mouth of shrimp nets to keep sea turtles out. Widespread adoption of TEDs is considered the most important single recovery action that can be taken to immediately reduce sea turtle mortality.

Commercial fishermen—particularly in Texas and Louisiana—have protested TEDs, claiming that the devices substantially reduce the size of the shrimp catch. To address shrimpers' concerns, the NMFS redesigned TEDs to decrease interference with the shrimp catch. Tests show that improved designs reduce catch by only 2 to 5 percent, a rate that can be further reduced by training fishermen to use them correctly. The cost of acquiring and installing the device is minimal.

In July 1989, a first attempt was made to implement TED regulations, resulting in an outcry from several congressmen from Gulf states and a shrimpers' protest blockade of Galveston harbor. The Secretary of Commerce moved to delay enforcement but was overruled by court action. Enforcement of TED regulations is certain to remain controversial. The Atlantic Coast shrimp fleet has been more cooperative in adopting TEDs.

Bibliography

Bjorndal, K. A. 1980. "Demography of the Breeding Population of the Green Turtle, *Chelonia mydas*, at Tortuguero, Costa Rica." *Copeia* 1980(3):525-530.

Carr, A. F. 1975. "The Ascension Island Green Turtle Colony." *Copeia* 1975(3):547-555.

Dodd, C. K., Jr. 1982. "Nesting of the Green Turtle *Chelonia mydas* in Florida: Historic Review and Present Trends." *Brimleyana* 7:39-54.

U.S. Fish and Wildlife Service. 1984. "Recovery Plan for Marine Turtles." U.S. Fish and Wildlife Service, Atlanta.

Wood, J. R., and F. E. Wood. 1980. "Reproductive Biology of Captive Green Sea Turtles *Chelonia mydas*." *American Zoology* 20:499-505.

Contact

Office of Public Affairs
National Marine Fisheries Service
Department of Commerce
Washington, D.C. 20235

Regional Office of Endangered Species
U.S. Fish and Wildlife Service
Richard B. Russell Federal Building
75 Spring Street, S.W.
Atlanta, Georgia 30303

American Crocodile
Crocodylus acutus

P. Moler/USFWS

Status . . . . . . Endangered
Listed . . . . . December 18, 1979
Family . . . . . Crocodilidae (Crocodile)
Description . . . Large, dull gray reptile with a triangular head and long, pointed snout.
Habitat . . . . . . Tropical wetlands.
Food . . . . Carnivorous; fish, marine life.
Reproduction . . Clutch of about 40 eggs.
Threats . . . . . Habitat loss.
Region 4 . . . . . Florida

Description

The American crocodile grows to a mature length of 3.6 meters (12 ft) from the snout to the tip of the tail. Its hide is thick, scaly, and wart-covered. Adults are colored a dull gray; younger specimens are olive brown above and light yellow on the belly. This crocodile is similar to an alligator, except that its triangular head ends in a more pointed snout. The fourth tooth on either side of the lower jaw protrudes.

Behavior

This reptile lays a clutch of as many as 40 eggs, only a few of which survive to become adults. Crocodiles feed largely on fish, and in Florida are known to eat bass, tarpon, and mullet. Unlike the alligator, which is aggressive, the crocodile is shy of human activities.

Habitat

The American crocodile is found in mangrove-lined saltwater estuaries in extreme southern tropical Florida and nests along the banks of small streams. Crocodiles have also been found living and breeding in the cooling canals of a nuclear power plant in southern Florida.

Historic Range

This species is found in coastal wetlands along the Pacific Ocean from western Mexico south to Ecuador and along the Atlantic Ocean from Guatemala north to the extreme southern tip of Florida.

Current Distribution

The American crocodile is found in the U.S. in surviving tidal marshes in the Everglades along Florida Bay and in the Florida Keys (Monroe County). Increasing from a low of about two dozen nesting females in the 1970s, the population currently numbers more than 500 adults.

Conservation and Recovery

Never plentiful in the U.S., the crocodile has suffered habitat loss as a result of the explosive urban development throughout its south Florida habitat in Dade and Monroe counties. Crocodiles were also hunted extensively for their hides, which were used like alligator hides to make belts and handbags.

Provided early protection by the Endangered Species Act, the American crocodile has responded to recovery efforts. Surveys in 1987 and 1988, conducted by the Florida Game and Fresh Water Fish Commission, showed that the number of American crocodiles has increased significantly and the trend is strongly upward.

In 1980 with assistance from The Nature Conservancy, the Fish and Wildlife Service established the Crocodile Lake National Wildlife Refuge as part of the Florida Key Deer refuge in the northern Florida Keys. The refuge has recently expanded and now totals 2,830 hectares (7,000 acres). At Turkey Point, a nuclear power plant site in southern Florida, a group of crocodiles has taken up residence in the plant's cooling canals. The Florida Power and Light Company has sponsored crocodile research and has redesigned its facilities to accommodate the species' presence.

In 1967 the crocodile's freshwater relative, the American alligator, was federally listed as Endangered because of concern over unregulated exploitation by the hide industry. Once protected, the alligator made a dramatic recovery and is considered one of the major success stories of the Endangered Species Act. In 1987 the alligator was reclassified throughout its range as "Threatened Due to Similarity of Appearance," a designation that returns management responsibility to the states. Although the alligator is no longer considered in danger of extinction, this classification allows federal government to closely monitor the hide industry to ensure that Endangered American crocodiles are not hunted illegally.

Bibliography

Guggisberg, C. A. 1972. *Crocodiles: Their Natural History, Folklore and Conservation.* Stackpole Books, Harrisburg.

Webb, G. J., *et al.* 1987. *Wildlife Management: Crocodiles and Alligators.* Surrey Beatty and Sons, Australia.

Contact

Regional Office of Endangered Species
U.S. Fish and Wildlife Service
Richard B. Russell Federal Building
75 Spring Street, S.W.
Atlanta, Georgia 30303

New Mexican Ridgenose Rattlesnake

Crotalus willardi obscurus

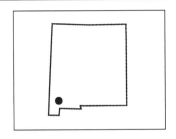

Status	Threatened
Listed	August 4, 1978
Family	Viperidae (Viper)
Description	Slender-bodied rattlesnake, grayish brown with irregular markings and a distinct ridge along its snout.
Habitat	Mountain canyons.
Food	Small mammals, birds, lizards.
Reproduction	Live-bearer.
Threats	Low numbers, limited distribution, collectors.
Region 2	New Mexico
Mexico	Chihuahua

Charles Painter

Description

The relatively short and slender-bodied ridgenose rattlesnake attains a maximum length of about 60 centimeters (24 in). It is grayish brown above with indistinct and irregular white cross bars edged with brown; it is buff and spotted beneath. This venomous snake's most distinctive characteristic is a prominent ridge on the snout. The New Mexican ridgenose rattlesnake is one of five subspecies of *Crotalus willardi*.

Behavior

The New Mexican ridgenose rattlesnake is most active in daylight hours from July through September. An active forager, it feeds on small mammals, birds, lizards, other snakes, and arthropods. The snake prefers to hide in leaf litter among cobbles and rocks along canyon floors. It frequently climbs into trees or shrubs and uses its perch to spot prey. It hibernates through the coolest part of the winter. The female rattlesnake is ovoviviparous, a live-bearer. She retains fertilized eggs within her body during hibernation and gives birth to live young when warm weather returns in April or May. The gestation period is about 13 months. Hatchlings disperse within a few days after birth.

Habitat

This snake is found in belts of pine woodland in narrow mountain canyons at elevations between 1,675 and 2,745 meters (5,500 and 9,000 ft). These woodland areas typically consist of scattered, open stands of pine and oak or pine and fir, with associated shrubs and grasses. Annual precipitation is about 51 centimeters (20 in).

Historic Range

Never common, this species is found very locally in the Animas Mountains of south-western New Mexico and adjacent portions of the Sierra de San Luis in northern Mexico. Other subspecies of ridgenose rattlesnake range through southern Arizona and New Mexico and as far south as Durango and Zacatecas in Mexico.

Current Distribution

The New Mexican ridgenose rattlesnake occurs in isolated enclaves in Hidalgo County in the extreme southwestern corner of the state. Habitat area is estimated to total no more than 5.2 square kilometers (2 sq mi). Populations have been found in the main stem and west fork of Indian Creek Canyon, in Bear Canyon, and in Spring Canyon. The U.S. population in the wild has not been surveyed but was estimated to consist of about 500 individuals in the 1960s. Collection may have reduced the population by one-fourth. The status of the Mexican population is unknown.

Conservation and Recovery

Because of its small size and distinctive characteristics, this snake was intensely exploited by collectors for the commercial market until 1974, when an agreement was reached with the landowner to restrict unauthorized access to the canyons. Although the state of New Mexico prohibits collecting without a permit, the snake's low reproductive rate has slowed its recovery.

Portions of the habitat, particularly along the canyon floors, were heavily grazed by cattle in the past, which denuded ground cover and disrupted leaf litter. The former landowner cooperated enthusiastically with the Fish and Wildlife Service to reduce the level of grazing in the canyons. In 1982, however, most of the property was sold to American Breco, a California-based corporation, and the conservation agreements have not been renewed. A resumption of heavy grazing would pose a serious threat to the snake's survival. While mining is also a potential threat, mineral exploration has so far been minimal. Tenneco retains mineral rights to much of the region.

Because of its limited range and numbers, the New Mexican ridgenose rattlesnake will probably always remain threatened. The goal of the Recovery Plan is to minimize habitat disturbance and discourage collection through negotiations with the current landowner. The highest elevations of the Animas Mountains are presently being managed as a wildlife preserve.

Researchers hope to arrange a joint research project with Mexican biologists to survey the status of the species in Mexico.

Bibliography

Dobrott, S. J. 1980. "A Management Plan for the Animas Mountains, Submitted to the Victorio Company." Hidalgo County, New Mexico.

Harris, H. S., and R. S. Simmons. 1975. "An Endangered Species, the New Mexican Ridgenose Rattlesnake." *Bulletin of the Maryland Herpetological Society* 11:1-7.

U.S. Fish and Wildlife Service. 1985. "New Mexico Ridgenose Rattlesnake Recovery Plan." U.S. Fish and Wildlife Service, Albuquerque.

Contact

Regional Office of Endangered Species
U.S. Fish and Wildlife Service
P.O. Box 1306
Albuquerque, New Mexico 87103

Mona Ground Iguana
Cyclura stegnegeri

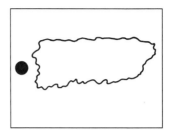

C. Kenneth Dodd, Jr.

Status	Threatened
Listed	February 3, 1978
Family	Iguanidae (Lizard)
Description	Large slow-moving, heavy-bodied lizard with a prominent crest along its back.
Habitat	Mona Island; escarpments and talus slopes.
Food	Omnivorous; fruit, leaves, insect larvae.
Reproduction	Clutch of 12 eggs.
Threats	Habitat disturbance by feral animals.
Region 4	Puerto Rico

Description

The Mona iguana is the largest Puerto Rican lizard, measuring up to 1.3 meters (4 ft) in total length. It has a heavy body, a large head, a loose jowl in the angle of the jaw, and a small horn on the snout. A prominent crest extends along its back from head to tail. The coloring is olive to olive-gray, sometimes marked with brown or blue lines.

Behavior

The omnivorous Mona ground iguana has been observed eating fruit, leaves, and insect larvae. It forages mostly on the ground, moving slowly and expending little energy. Except in mating season when it is more active, this iguana spends much of its day resting and sunning, always close to its burrow.

The breeding season begins in mid-June, when the male establishes and defends a territory that includes one or more female burrows. After mating, the female migrates to a favorable nesting ground to deposit a clutch of 12 eggs. She covers the nest, leaving an air space over the eggs. If the air space above the eggs collapses, the embryos will not develop. Eggs incubate for about three months and hatch in October and November. Hatchlings work together to dig their way out of the nest and then disperse.

Habitat

Mona Island is a rocky limestone island situated halfway between Puerto Rico and Hispaniola with a total surface area of about 5,500 hectares (2,226 acres). It is characterized by a flat central plateau (Mona Plateau) surrounded by steep cliffs. The plateau is covered by outcrops of limestone, interspersed with tracts of dry scrub, consisting of dwarfed trees and shrubs. Dominant plants include gumbo-limbo, wild fig, white cedar, and poison tree. Along the coasts, organ-pipe cacti form dense thickets. Mean annual rainfall is 80 centimeters (31 in).

The Mona ground iguana needs a deep, loose soil for nesting and commonly digs shelter burrows into escarpments or cliffside talus slopes.

Historic Range

This iguana is endemic to Mona Island and is found nowhere else.

Current Distribution

Mona ground iguanas are distributed throughout the island, but only about 5 percent of the island's soils are suitable for nesting. Nesting sites are located on Mona Plateau and on the narrow southwestern coastal plain. A 1984 estimate placed the size of the population at about 2,000 individuals.

Conservation and Recovery

The greatest threat to the Mona iguana are feral pigs, which were introduced to the island decades ago and are present in large numbers. Particularly in dry years, feral pigs root out iguana nests and eat the eggs. In wetter years when pigs can find other sources of food and moisture, the iguana has better reproductive success.

Much of the coastal plain that is most suitable for iguana nesting was planted with mahogany trees in the 1930s. These trees have matured to shade nesting sites; as a result the iguanas have abandoned these areas. Humans and animals have trampled nests in the past, compacting the ground, and causing egg loss. In recent years, several prime nesting sites have been fenced to exclude humans and pigs, which appears to have increased the survival rate for iguana hatchlings.

The Puerto Rican Department of Natural Resources manages Mona Island as a nature preserve and employs seven rangers and a biologist as year-round residents. Camping on the island has been restricted to designated sites to lessen the disturbance of wildlife, and visitors are encouraged to stay on the trails. The Fish and Wildlife Service (FWS) Recovery Plan's recommendation for a more aggressive campaign to control feral animals on the island will be phased in gradually. The FWS would consider the species recovered if the ground iguana population stabilizes or expands for ten consecutive years.

Bibliography

U.S. Fish and Wildlife Service. 1984. "Mona Iguana Recovery Plan." U.S. Fish and Wildlife Service, Atlanta.

Wiewandt, T. A. 1973. "Mona Amphibians, Reptiles, and Mammals." In *Mona and Monita Island: An Assessment of their Natural and Historical Resources*. Office of the Governor of Puerto Rico, Environmental Quality Board, San Juan.

Contact

Regional Office of Endangered Species
U.S. Fish and Wildlife Service
Richard B. Russell Federal Building
75 Spring Street, S.W.
Atlanta, Georgia 30303

Caribbean Field Office
U.S. Fish and Wildlife Service
P.O. Box 491
Boqueron, Puerto Rico 00622

Leatherback Sea Turtle
Dermochelys coriacea

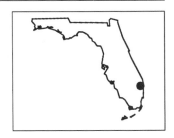

Status	. . . . . . Endangered
Listed	. . . . . . June 2, 1970
Family	. . . . . . Dermochelyidae
	(Leatherback Turtle)
Description	. . . Large leathery-backed sea turtle with an oval carapace, averaging 1.5 meters (61 in) long.
Habitat	. . . . . . Pelagic; nests on undisturbed beaches.
Food	. . . . Jellyfish, other soft-bodied sea animals.
Reproduction	. . Clutch of 30 to 40 eggs.
Threats	. . . . . . Beachfront development, plastic trash, incidental take by commercial fishermen.
Region 4	. . . . . Florida, St. Croix

P. C. H. Pritchard

Description

The leatherback is the largest sea turtle in the world. Carapace (upper shell) length averages about 1.5 meters (5 ft), although shells of nearly 2 meters (6.5 ft) have been recorded. The average weight is around 365 kilograms (800 lbs), and the maximum recorded weight is 590 kilograms (1,300 lbs). Limbs are modified as flippers and lack claws. The front flippers are very long and may span 2.7 meters (9 ft) in an adult. The leatherback can be distinguished from all other sea turtles by the rubbery texture of its shell. All other sea turtles have a bony-plated shell. The dominant color is black, with varying degrees of white spotting. The undersurface is pinkish white.

This sea turtle is so distinctive that it has been placed in a separate family, the Dermochelyidae. All other sea turtles belong to the family Cheloniidae. The leatherback has several anatomical features that are adaptations for ocean diving, including powerful front flippers and the capacity to eliminate waste gases through its skin, which allows it to stay under water for long periods.

Behavior

The leatherback is a powerful swimmer and spends most of its adult life in the open ocean, entering shallow bays and estuaries only at breeding time. It eats twice its body weight in jellyfish daily and supplements this staple with other soft-bodied sea creatures. It may feed on minnows but cannot digest larger fish, which become impacted in the digestive tract, often with fatal results.

Courtship and mating are consummated in offshore shallows shortly before females come ashore on the nesting beaches. In the northern hemisphere, nesting begins in March and continues into July. After being fertilized, the female leatherback comes ashore at night, excavates a nest, and lays about 35 whole eggs, plus 30 smaller yolkless eggs. She spends only about two hours ashore. The buried eggs incubate for about 60 days before hatching. Hatchlings dig out of the sand as a group and return to the sea.

Habitat

The leatherback turtle is a pelagic reptile, adapted to the open ocean. It ranges far from land for most of its life. For breeding, this turtle requires an expanse of undisturbed sandy beach, relatively free from animal and human predators.

Historic Range

The leatherback turtle is widely distributed in the world's oceans but was probably never numerous. It is known to migrate long distances, although few tagged individuals have ever been recovered. The few that have been recovered have only deepened the mystery of migration routes. For example, five females tagged in Surinam and French Guiana were rediscovered in widely separated places. Two turned up on the Atlantic coast, two along the Gulf coast in Texas and Mexico, and the fifth off the coast of Ghana, West Africa, over 6,800 kilometers (4,226 mi) from its starting point.

In West Africa, there are records of leatherbacks nesting from Senegal to Angola. In the Republic of South Africa, a 60-mile stretch of beach called the Tongaland Coast is the nesting site for about 200 to 400 female leatherbacks. A similar number nest on the coast of southern India and the island of Sri Lanka (Ceylon).

There are nesting areas on the Malay Peninsula, on the Island of Phuket, Thailand, and in the region of northern New Guinea and the Solomon Islands. From nesting grounds in New Guinea, turtles appear to migrate down the east coast of Australia.

Leatherbacks nest along the Pacific Coast from the states of Oacaca and Chiapas, Mexico, through Central America and down onto the coast of Ecuador. This 644 kilometer (400 mi) stretch of beach is the world's largest leatherback nesting site, used by as many as 50,000 females each year. Smaller nesting populations are found along the northern Atlantic coast of South America and in the Caribbean. The most studied population of nesting leatherbacks is found in French Guiana along a stretch of beach 24 kilometers (15 mi) long that is used by about 15,000 female leatherbacks each year.

The present world population of leatherback sea turtles is believed to number at least 100,000 sexually mature females, plus an undetermined number of males. The Fish and Wildlife Service, which is responsibile for turtle nesting habitat, is primarily concerned with the stock of leatherbacks that breeds in Florida and at St. Croix in the U.S. Virgin Islands. The pelagic range of these reptiles is difficult to define, since they are capable of migrating over a large expanse of the Atlantic Ocean.

Current Distribution

Only about 20 or 25 leatherback sea turtles are known to nest in the U.S. each year. These females come ashore on the Atlantic Coast of south central Florida and nest on the barrier islands that extend from Vero Beach (Indian River County) to Boca Raton (Palm Beach County), a distance of about 200 kilometers (120 mi). Beaches on St. Croix in the U.S. Virgin Islands are used by between 50 and 70 nesting leatherbacks each year.

Conservation and Recovery

All marine turtles are jeopardized to some extent by loss of nesting habitat. Development of coastal areas in many parts of the world has reduced the amount of available undisturbed beach. Nesting beaches have been degraded by recreational and residential development, by erosion, and by barriers constructed to combat erosion.

In addition, the leatherback faces problems worldwide. It is hunted in the Dominican Republic for food, exterminated in Ghana because it is a "worthless creature," and rendered for its oil in parts of Asia. Up to 95 percent of its eggs are collected for food in Malaysia each year. For the U.S. and Virgin Islands population, plastic trash is a particular threat. Because the leatherback feeds on jellyfish, it eats anything that looks like a jellyfish in the water. Consequently, leatherbacks have been killed by swallowing indigestible plastic bags.

At sea, the leatherback turtle is sometimes collected incidentally in the trawling nets of commercial fishermen. The National Marine Fisheries Service (NMFS), which is responsible for marine turtle protection, estimates that over 11,000 air-breathing marine turtles drown in shrimp nets each year, including an unknown number of leatherbacks. Recently, the NMFS developed regulations to require larger shrimp boats to use turtle excluder devices (TEDs), which are fitted at the mouth of shrimp nets to keep sea turtles out. In July 1989, the first steps were taken to enforce these controversial regulations in U.S. waters. TEDs are considered the most important single recovery action that can be taken to immediately reduce sea turtle mortality.

The St. Croix leatherback colony was only recently discovered by biologists. The most immediate threat to this population is the pending residential and commercial development of Sandy Point near Frederiksted, which will impinge on nesting sites. Negotiations are underway to secure this beach, either through acquisition or by negotiations with private landowners. Critical Habitat was designated for the leatherback to include Sandy Point and adjacent waters. A 1972 law, passed by the territorial government of the U.S. Virgin Islands, makes it illegal to kill or harm marine turtles during breeding season from May to September.

In addition to legal protection provided by the U.S. Endangered Species Act, the leatherback is listed by the Convention on International Trade in Endangered Species of Wild Fauna and Flora (CITES). The leatherback is protected by law in most of the countries where nesting occurs, but the level of enforcement varies.

Bibliography

Towle, E. L. 1978. "Report on Sea Turtle Nesting. . . (with Specific Reference to Leatherback Nests at Sandy Point, St. Croix)." Report. Island Resources Foundation, St. Thomas, U.S. Virgin Islands.

U.S. Fish and Wildlife Service. 1981. "Recovery Plan for the St. Croix Population of the Leatherback Turtle." U.S. Fish and Wildlife Service, Atlanta.

U.S. Fish and Wildlife Service. 1984. "Recovery Plan for Marine Turtles." U.S. Fish and Wildlife Service, Atlanta.

Contact

Office of Public Affairs
National Marine Fisheries Service
Department of Commerce
Washington, D.C. 20235

Regional Office of Endangered Species
U.S. Fish and Wildlife Service
Richard B. Russell Federal Building
75 Spring Street, S.W.
Atlanta, Georgia 30303

Eastern Indigo Snake

Drymarchon corais couperi

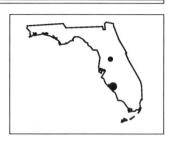

Ray E. Ashton, Jr.

Status	Threatened
Listed	January 31, 1978
Family	Colubridae (Snake)
Description . . .	Large, stout blue-black snake.
Habitat	Mature pine forests; gopher burrows.
Food	Small animals.
Reproduction . .	Unknown.
Threats	Loss of habitat, habitat degradation, killing, collection.
Region 4	Alabama, Florida, Georgia, Mississippi, South Carolina

Description

The eastern indigo is one of the largest and stoutest colubrid snakes of North America, attaining a maximum length of about 2.5 meters (8.5 ft). The head is barely distinct from the neck. Scales—arranged in 17 rows at midbody—are large, smooth, and shiny. The body color is a uniform lustrous blue-black. The chin, throat, and cheeks are tinged with red or cream. Smaller eastern indigo snakes may superficially resemble the common black racer (*Coluber constrictor*).

Behavior

The indigo snake feeds largely on other snakes, small tortoises, small mammals, and amphibians. The eastern indigo snake is highly dependent on burrows excavated by other animals, particularly the gopher tor-

toise (*Gopherus polyphemus*). These burrows are used as a refuge and for overwintering. The gopher tortoise, itself, is included on the federal list as a Threatened species.

Habitat

The indigo snake inhabits mature pine forests in central and northern Florida, and flatwoods, dry glades, tropical hammocks, and muckland fields in southern Florida. It is often found along canal banks, using crab holes for dens. In Georgia it inhabits ''sandhill'' regions, dominated by mature longleaf pines, turkey oaks, and wiregrass. This plant community is adapted to periodic fires. When fires are suppressed, laurel oaks and associated hardwoods succeed, making the habitat unsuitable for the eastern indigo snake. The gopher tortoise plays an integral

Historic Range

The species, *Drymarchon corais*, ranges from the coastal plain of the southeastern United States to northern Argentina. Of this broad group of snakes, only the eastern indigo and the Texas indigo subspecies are found within the U.S.

Historically, the eastern indigo snake ranged from South Carolina through Georgia and Florida to the Keys, and west to southern Alabama. Some evidence suggests that the snake also occurred in Mississippi.

Current Distribution

At present, the eastern indigo snake is found primarily in Georgia and Florida. It has been sighted recently in 50 Georgia counties and is particularly common in the southeastern quadrant of the state. It is considered locally abundant in Florida south of Sarasota. Populations are more fragmented north of Sarasota, and only a few small populations are known from the Panhandle. The species is now extremely rare, if it occurs at all, in Alabama, Mississippi, and South Carolina.

Conservation and Recovery

The decline of the eastern indigo snake mirrors the loss of mature longleaf pine forests in the South. In recent decades, agricultural and residential development have deforested millions of acres. Surviving stands of forest have been degraded by suppression of fire or by logging. Vast tracts of forest have been logged and replanted with fast-growing pines that can be more quickly harvested. These "young" forests cannot support the eastern indigo snake.

A steady loss of habitat has made this species more vulnerable to other human threats. Because it is large, conspicuous, and relatively slow, it often falls prey to people who "kill snakes on sight." On the other hand, commercial collectors value it for the pet trade because it is nonpoisonous, docile, and attractive. Mail order specimens can bring as much as $225. Therefore, the eastern indigo snake is in the unenviable position of being killed by some and collected by others.

To counter these threats, a public awareness program is needed to address snake phobia and discourage collecting. Existing state and federal laws prohibiting trade of the reptile should be more strictly enforced. The Fish and Wildlife Service has suggested a program to monitor sales in trade catalogs and to bring charges against dealers. But sales will not stop until informed reptile-lovers refuse to pay money for an Endangered species.

Ultimately, the survival of eastern indigo snake, the gopher tortoise, the red-cockaded woodpecker (*Picoides borealis*), and other endangered wildlife depends on the preservation of remaining tracts of mature, old-growth forests. This can be accomplished either through outright acquisition of land or by purchase of conservation easements. These efforts are hampered by the availability of funds.

Ideal indigo snake habitat is similar to that of the bobwhite and white-tailed deer, and management of national forests for these game animals will benefit the eastern indigo snake, as well. Beneficial management techniques include mechanical thinning and controlled burning to prevent overgrowth by hardwoods. Leases for logging on public lands that prohibit clear-cutting would preserve the snake's habitat.

This snake apparently reproduces well in captivity, and reintroduction into the wild can be attempted once its habitat has been protected.

In June 1989 the Interior Department created a new wildlife refuge for the Florida panther and other endangered species in south Florida. The 12,140-hectare (30,000-acre) Florida Panther National Wildlife Refuge is adjacent to the Big Cypress National Preserve and provides protected habitat for the Endangered wood stork (*Mycteria americana*), Everglade snail kite (*Rostrhamus sociabilis plumbeus*), bald eagle (*Haliaeetus leucocephalus*), red-cockaded woodpecker (*Picoides borealis*), peregrine falcon (*Falco peregrinus anatum*), and eastern indigo snake.

Bibliography

Behler, J., and W. King. 1979. *The Audubon Society Field Guide to North American Reptiles.* Alfred Knopf, New York.

Speake, D. W., *et al.* 1978. "Ecology and Management of the Eastern Indigo Snake in Georgia: A Progress Report." In R. Odon and L. Landers, eds., *Proceedings of the Rare and Endangered Wildlife Symposium.* Georgia Department of Natural Resources, Atlanta.

U.S. Fish and Wildlife Service. 1982. "Eastern Indigo Snake Recovery Plan." U.S. Fish and Wildlife Service, Atlanta.

Wharton, C. H. 1978. *The Natural Environments of Georgia.* Georgia Department of Natural Resources, Atlanta.

Contact

Regional Office of Endangered Species
U.S. Fish and Wildlife Service
Richard B. Russell Federal Building
75 Spring Street, S.W.
Atlanta, Georgia 30303

Puerto Rican Boa

Epicrates inornatus

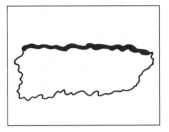

N. Snyder

Status	Endangered
Listed	October 13, 1970
Family	Boidae (Constrictor)
Description	Large, muscular snake; tan to dark brown with diffuse, irregular markings.
Habitat	Forests.
Food	Carnivorous; birds, mice, lizards, bats.
Reproduction	Live-bearer.
Threats	Deforestation.
Region 4	Puerto Rico

Description

The Puerto Rican boa is the largest snake found in Puerto Rico, measuring up to 2.2 meters (7.3 ft) in length. Color ranges from tan to dark brown. Patterning often consists of 70 to 80 irregular, diffuse markings along the back, but some snakes are uniformly dark. Underside scales are dark brown with pale edges. Juveniles are reddish brown with prominent markings; females are larger than males.

The Puerto Rican boa can be distinguished from its relative, the Mona boa (*Epicrates monensis*) of Mona and the Virgin Islands, by its larger size and darker coloration.

Behavior

The Puerto Rican boa is most active at night, during the day it basks in the sun or remains concealed in trees or caves. It feeds on birds, mice, rats, and lizards and is known to prey on bats. A boa will suspend itself from a branch near a cave entrance and seize bats as they emerge.

The Puerto Rican boa, like others of its family, is ovoviviparous. Eggs hatch within the mother's body, and the young are born alive. Evidence suggests that it mates between February and April and gives birth in September or October. Boas typically reach sexual maturity after six or seven years.

Habitat

The Puerto Rican boa is at home in a wide range of habitats. It is most common in northern Puerto Rico in a band that extends from Aguadilla on the western coast east to San Juan. This is a region of limestone karst topography, characterized by "haystack hills" and sinkholes. Hills support dry open forests, while sinkholes support a lush moist growth. These combined habitats produce a great variety of wildlife and an abundance of prey. Habitat elevation ranges from sea level to about 400 meters (1300 ft).

Historic Range

The Puerto Rican boa is a native of the island of Puerto Rico.

Current Distribution

The Puerto Rican boa appears to range throughout the island but is more common in the north. The snake's nocturnal habits have inhibited systematic research. But available data suggests that the population declined dramatically during the first half of this century, going from relative abundance to relative scarcity. This decline was blamed on widespread deforestation of the island. In the past ten years, however, many acres of former agricultural land have been abandoned, and the forests are returning. About 40 percent of the island is currently forested. As a result, the Puerto Rican boa population appears to be increasing.

Conservation and Recovery

Because exact population figures are not known, patterns of decline and recovery are difficult to measure. The Fish and Wildlife Service Puerto Rican Boa Recovery Plan establishes long-term research goals to answer questions about density and distribution, locate unknown populations, determine habitat preferences, and delineate limiting factors. The first phase of this research should be completed in the early 1990s after which quantifiable recovery goals can be set.

The Puerto Rican boa is protected from collecting and hunting by the commonwealth of Puerto Rico's Wildlife and Hunting Regulations of 1978. In 1985 the boa was listed as Endangered under Puerto Rico's Regulation to Govern the Management of Threatened and Endangered Species.

Bibliography

Reagan, D. P. and C. P Zucca. 1984. "Ecology of the Puerto Rican Boa in the Luquillo Mountains of Puerto Rico." *Caribbean Journal of Science* 20:3-4.

Rodriguez, G. A., and D. P. Reagan. 1984. "Bat Predation by the Puerto Rican Boa, *Epicrates inornatus.*" *Copeia* (1)219:220.

Tolson, P. K. 1984. "The Ecology of the Boid Genus *Epicrates* in the West Indies." In *5to. Simposio de Ecologia.* Universidad del Turabo, Caguas, Puerto Rico.

U.S. Fish and Wildlife Service. 1986. "Recovery Plan for the Puerto Rican Boa." U.S. Fish and Wildlife Service, Atlanta.

Contact

Regional Office of Endangered Species
U.S. Fish and Wildlife Service
Richard B. Russell Federal Building
75 Spring Street, S.W.
Atlanta, Georgia 30303

Caribbean Field Office
U.S. Fish and Wildlife Service
P.O. Box 491
Boqueron, Puerto Rico 00622

Mona Boa
Epicrates monensis monensis

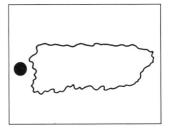

Felix Lopez

Status	Threatened
Listed	February 3, 1978
Family	Boidae (Boa)
Description . . .	Nonvenomous light-brown snake with dark brown markings.
Habitat	Mona Island; limestone outcroppings and scrub vegetation.
Food	Carnivorous; small mammals and reptiles.
Reproduction . .	Live-bearer; 8 to 30 young.
Threats	Limited distribution, low numbers.
Region 4	Puerto Rico

Description

The Mona boa is a nonvenomous snake about 1 meter (3.3 ft) in length when fully grown. Adults are light brown above with 44 dark brown markings. The underside is beige with a few scattered spots. Immature snakes are a yellow-brown with two rows of dark brown spots extending from the head to the end of the tail.

Behavior

The Mona boa is nocturnal and secretive, and Mona Island's rugged terrain and spiny plants provide an abundance of hiding places. Most captured specimens have been immature snakes, surprised in the open or taken from tree branches. The snake has not been studied in the wild. Scientists surmise that it stalks small mammals and reptiles and have observed it to capture rats, mice, and anoles. It is thought to prey upon bats, an important part of the diet of other boas. Members of the genus *Epicrates*, being ovoviviparous, bear their young alive, producing 8 to 30 at a time.

Habitat

Mona Island is a rocky limestone island situated halfway between Puerto Rico and Hispaniola. Its total surface area is about 5,500 hectares (2,226 acres). The island is characterized by a flat central plateau (Mona Plateau) surrounded by steep, sometimes sheer, cliffs. Much of the plateau is covered by outcrops of bedrock limestone, interspersed with tracts of dry scrub, consisting of dwarfed trees and shrubs. Dominant plants of this community are gumbo-limbo, wild fig, white cedar, and poison tree. Along the coasts, organ-pipe cacti become dominant, in places forming dense thickets. Mean annual rainfall is 80 centimeters (31 in).

Historic Range

The Mona boa is endemic to Mona Island and was probably once found throughout the island. The genus *Epicrates* is distributed throughout Central America, northern South America, and the Greater Antilles.

Current Distribution

The Mona boa has always been uncommon and was considered extinct until the 1970s when visitors to the island incidentally collected the snake. One specimen was kept as a pet until shown to a herpetologist, who recognized its importance. The size and status of the boa population on the island is largely unknown. Some scientists have suggested that the snake is more common than it seems because of its reclusive habits.

Conservation and Recovery

The decision to add the Mona Boa to the list of Endangered and Threatened Species was made as a precaution to protect this uncommon snake until further research is able to determine its relative abundance and evaluate potential threats. Predation by feral cats that were introduced to the island is considered a distinct possibility. A program to trap and remove feral cats was initiated in 1978 and continues. Other introduced animals, such as goats and pigs, have modified portions of the island's plant community. Scientists have also noted a decline in the island's bat population. All of these factors will be considered in the research strategy.

The Puerto Rico Department of Natural Resources took over management of Mona Island in 1973. In 1977, a special Ranger Corps was created to enforce conservation laws, monitor wildlife population levels, and educate visitors to the island. Seven rangers and a resident biologist now live on the island year-round and are charged with protecting the boa and other endemic fauna. The entire island has been designated as Critical Habitat for the Mona boa.

Bibliography

Campbell, H. W. 1978. "Observations of a Captive Mona Island Boa." *Bulletin of the Maryland Herpetological Society* 14(2):98-99.

Rivero, J. A. 1978. *Los Anfibios y Reptiles de Puerto Rico*. Editorial Universitaria, Universidad de Puerto Rico, San Juan.

Rivero, J. A., *et al.* 1982. "Cinco Nuevos Ejemplares del Culebron de la Mona *Epicrates monensis monensis*." *Caribbean Journal of Science* 17:1-4.

U.S. Fish and Wildlife Service. 1984. "Mona Boa Recovery Plan." U.S. Fish and Wildlife Service, Atlanta.

Contact

Regional Office of Endangered Species
U.S. Fish and Wildlife Service
Richard B. Russell Federal Building
75 Spring Street, S.W.
Atlanta, Georgia 30303

Caribbean Field Office
U.S. Fish and Wildlife Service
P.O. Box 491
Boqueron, Puerto Rico 00622

Hawksbill Sea Turtle

Eretmocheyls imbricata

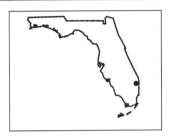

Douglas Faulkner/WWF

Status	Endangered
Listed	June 2, 1970
Family	Cheloniidae (Sea Turtle)
Description . . .	Brown-shelled sea turtle, weighing about 45 kg (100 lbs).
Habitat	Beaches for nesting; open ocean.
Food	Jellyfish, sponges, sessile organisms, algae.
Reproduction . .	Clutch of about 160 eggs.
Threats	Commercial trade.
Region 4	Florida, Puerto Rico, U.S. Virgin Islands

Description

The hawksbill turtle is one of the smaller sea turtles, having a carapace (upper shell) length at maturity of about 60 centimeters (2 ft) and weighing about 45 kilograms (100 lbs). The record weight is 126 kilograms (280 lbs). The carapace is brown and the undershell (plastron) is yellow. The name "hawksbill" refers to the turtle's prominent hooked beak.

Behavior

Primarily carnivorous, the hawksbill feeds near coral reefs on jellyfish, sponges, and other sessile organisms. Unlike the green turtle, the hawksbill does not migrate but occupies a relatively small home range. It breeds year-round in tropical waters, usually at two- or three-year intervals. The female comes ashore, scoops out a nest in the sand, and deposits about 160 eggs, which incubate for 50 days. Hatchlings emerge as a group and scurry perilously for the sea. While other sea turtles nest in colonies, the hawksbill prefers to nest alone, using the same nesting sites year after year.

Habitat

The hawksbill is pelagic, spending most of its life in the open ocean. It feeds in shallow reef areas in clear water. For nesting, the hawksbill requires isolated, undisturbed beaches.

Historic Range

The hawksbill turtle is found mainly in tropical seas throughout the world, separated into two distinct subspecies—Atlantic and Indo-Pacific. Pacific populations are concentrated around Madagascar and along the South American coast from Peru north to Mexico. Atlantic populations are found in the Gulf of Mexico and from southern Florida south to the southern coast of Brazil. This turtle is extremely difficult to census, and no population estimates are available.

Current Distribution

The hawksbill turtle rarely nests on the barrier islands of southern Florida and is only found occasionally on beaches in Puerto Rico and the U.S. Virgin Islands. Nesting sites are known on Culebra Island, the Island of Vieques, St. Thomas, St. John, and St. Croix. The National Marine Fisheries Service (NMFS) is charged with protecting turtles in U.S. and territorial waters. The Fish and Wildlife Service (FWS) has authority to protect nesting habitat.

Conservation and Recovery

The most serious threat to this species is commercial demand for its attractive shell, which is the source of natural tortoiseshell (carey). This material is used to make combs, brushes, fans, cigarette boxes, and many other ornamental items. Over 50,000 hawksbills have been killed for tortoiseshell each year since 1976. In the U.S. natural tortoiseshell has been largely replaced by plastics. Another threat to the species is a growing commercial trade in stuffed juvenile hawksbills, which are used as decoration.

All sea turtles are listed by the Convention on International Trade in Endangered Species (CITES), but member nations can exempt themselves from certain provisions of the CITES agreements. Japan registered an exemption for the hawksbill and remains the largest market for tortoiseshell products and stuffed juvenile turtles. Between 1981 and

1983, Japanese manufacturers imported 45,000 kilograms (99,000 lbs) of hawksbill shells from 21 different countries, paying as much as $225 per kilogram of shell. Main exporters of the products in 1988 were the Maldives, Jamaica, Cuba, Haiti, the Comoros Islands, Fiji, and the Solomons.

The recovery of this species will depend on greater international cooperation to reduce the lucrative trade in tortoiseshell and stuffed juvenile turtles. As long as it remains profitable for fishermen, stopping the trade on that end will be difficult. The Customs Service confiscates contraband tortoiseshell items at U.S. ports. Many overseas travelers are unaware that trade in these items violates international law, pointing to the need for greater public education.

Bibliography

Bjorndal, K., ed. 1981. *Biology and Conservation of Sea Turtles*. Smithsonian Institution Press, Washington, D.C.

Carr, A. F. and S. Stancyk. 1975. "Observations on the Ecology and Survival Outlook of the Hawksbill Turtle." *Biological Conservation* 8:161-172.

U.S. Fish and Wildlife Service. 1984. "Recovery Plan for Marine Turtles." U.S. Fish and Wildlife Service, Washington, D.C.

Witzell, W. N. 1983. "Synopsis of Biological Data on the Hawksbill Turtle." *FAO Fisheries Synopsis* 137:38.

Contact

Office of Public Affairs
National Marine Fisheries Service
Department of Commerce
Washington, D.C. 20235

Regional Office of Endangered Species
U.S. Fish and Wildlife Service
Richard B. Russell Federal Building
75 Spring Street, S.W.
Atlanta, Georgia 30303

Blue-Tailed Mole Skink
Eumeces egregius lividus

C. Kenneth Dodd, Jr.

Status . . . . . . Threatened
Listed . . . . . November 6, 1987
Family . . . . . Scincidae (Skink)
Description . . . Lizard with a long, narrow, cylindrical body; bluish tail in young.
Habitat . . . . . . Sand pine scrub.
Food . . . . Insects.
Reproduction . . Clutch 3 to 7 eggs.
Threats . . . . . . Agricultural and residential development.
Region 4 . . . . . Florida

Description

The blue-tailed mole skink has short, stubby legs and a thin, cylindrical body measuring from 9 to 13 centimeters (3.6 to 5.2 in). The tail—blue in juveniles and pinkish with age—is a little more than half the body length.

Behavior

Little is known of the biology of the blue-tailed mole skink, but it is presumed to be similar to the peninsular mole skink (*Eumeces egregius onocrepis*). The mole skink forages on the surface or digs into the soil to find insects, feeding mostly on cockroaches, spiders, and crickets. It mates during the winter, and females lay underground clutches of three to seven eggs in the spring. Skinks become sexually mature during the first year.

Habitat

The larger habitat of the blue-tailed mole skink is sand pine scrub communities. Dominant vegetation includes sand pine and rosemary, or longleaf pine and turkey oak associations. Within scrub areas, skinks occupy only localized pockets of sufficient leaf litter and moisture to provide abundant food and nesting sites. Moisture retained by litter is important for internal heat regulation in this species.

Unlike the Endangered sand skink (*Neoseps reynoldsi*), which forages underneath the sandy soil, the mole skink forages mostly on the surface. Therefore, the two skinks occupy different niches and do not compete for food, even though they are occasionally seen together.

Historic Range

The blue-tailed mole skink is endemic to central Florida and was probably fairly widespread before the large-scale conversion of its habitat for agriculture (particularly citrus groves). Over 14 species of birds and plants endemic to this region are listed as Endangered or Threatened as a result of agricultural expansion and residential development, including snakeroot (*Eryngium cuneifolium*) and Carter's mustard (*Warea carteri*).

Current Distribution

The blue-tailed mole skink is found in suitable habitat in Polk and Highlands counties. North of Polk County, the blue-tailed skink is replaced by the peninsula mole skink or by hybrids of the two subspecies. The Florida Natural Areas Inventory lists 20 population sites for the blue-tailed skink. In 1965, there were an estimated 20,234 hectares (50,000 acres) of available habitat. Within twenty years, roughly 65 percent of the skink's habitat has been lost.

Conservation and Recovery

Much of the blue-tailed skink's habitat is privately owned land that is being rapidly converted to citrus groves or rezoned for housing tracts. In remaining sand pine and long-leaf pine areas, naturally occurring fires have been suppressed. When sand pine scrub is unable to renew itself through fire, encroaching vegetation eventually replaces the scrub. Within protected areas, managed fires would be used to remove much of the

successional growth, benefiting the skink and other flora and fauna threatened by fire suppression.

The blue-tailed skink is found at a few protected sites such as Archbold Biological Station, Lake Kissimmee State Park, Lake Arbuckle, Saddle Blanket Lakes, and Tiger Creek. The State of Florida through the Florida Natural Areas Inventory has embarked on an aggressive campaign to acquire pine scrub habitat in the central portion of the state. A recent acquisition added over 405 hectares (1,000 acres) of wildlife refuge to the state system.

Bibliography

Christman, S. P. 1970. "Blue-Tailed Mole Skink." In Pritchard, P. C. H., ed., *Rare and Endangered Biota of Florida*, Vol. III. University Presses of Florida, Gainesville.

Mount, R. H. 1965. "Variation and Systematics of the Scincoid Lizard, *Eumeces egregius* Baird." *Bulletin of the Florida State Museum* 9(5):183-213.

Contact

Regional Office of Endangered Species
U.S. Fish and Wildlife Service
Richard B. Russell Federal Building
75 Spring Street, S.W.
Atlanta, Georgia 30303

Blunt-Nosed Leopard Lizard
Gambelia silus

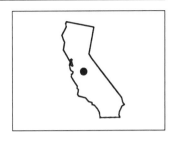

Susan Middleton

Status	Endangered
Listed	March 11, 1967
Family	Iguanidae (Lizard)
Description	Leopard lizard with short, broad skull and blunt snout; prominent markings.
Habitat	Sparsely vegetated plains and grasslands.
Food	Insectivorous.
Reproduction	Normally one clutch of 2 or 3 eggs per season.
Threats	Loss of habitat, fragmented distribution.
Region 1	California

Description

The blunt-nosed leopard lizard is a relatively long-lived reptile with a short, broad skull and blunt snout. Its rounded body and regenerative tail display a prominent pattern of dark spots and pale cross-bars. The male averages 9 to 12 centimeters (3.5 to 5 in) in length from snout to vent (anal opening). Females are slightly smaller. After breeding, females develop orange-red markings on the sides of the head and body, on the thighs and under the tail. Mating males develop a bright salmon color on the sides.

The scientific literature refers to the blunt-nosed leopard lizard variously as *Crotaphytus silus* or as *Crotaphytus wislizenii silus*, reflecting an ongoing debate on classification.

Behavior

The blunt-nosed leopard lizard emerges from hibernation in late March or early April and regulates its surface activity according to the air temperature. Through summer it is most active in the morning and late afternoon. When afternoon temperatures are excessive, it may delay foraging until early evening. The optimum air temperature for activity is near 30 degrees C (85 degrees F). This lizard is primarily insectivorous, feeding on cicadas, grasshoppers, flies, bees, and caterpillars. It supplements this diet with an occasional young lizard, including young of its own species.

The male lizard aggressively defends a territory against other males during breeding season, which runs from early May to mid-June. Several females may use portions of a single male's territory. Females normally breed once per season and occasionally twice. A clutch of two or three eggs is laid between early June and mid-July in a chamber excavated at the back of an abandoned rodent burrow. Eggs are large-yolked, about 3 centimeters (1.2 in) long. Hatchlings emerge in early August and reach sexual maturity in 9 to 21 months. During winter, adults and hatchlings remain inactive underground.

Adult lizards excavate shallow burrows for shelter but depend on the deeper burrows of rodents and other mammals for breeding and hibernation. Immature lizards use cover such as rock piles, trash piles, or brush.

Habitat

The blunt-nosed leopard lizard is adapted to the sparsely vegetated plains and grasslands of central California. It may be found on valley and canyon floors, on lower contiguous slopes, and in larger washes and arroyos. Soils vary from a gravelly hardpan to sandy loam. Associated vegetation is a valley/plain grassland community that includes goldenbush, Arabian grass, jackass clover, and San Joaquin tarweed. In places, the habitat overlaps with scrubland and Saueda flats.

The blunt-nosed leopard lizard cannot survive on lands that are under cultivation but is sometimes found along field edges or in roadside ditches. It will not repopulate an area until it has been left untilled for at least ten years.

Historic Range

The blunt-nosed leopard lizard was first collected in 1890 from near the city of Fresno, California. It originally ranged throughout the San Joaquin Valley and its adjacent foothills, including portions of Stanislaus, Merced, Madera, San Benito, Fresno, Tulare, Kings, San Luis Obispo, Kern, and Santa Barbara counties. The northern limit of distribution was the Sacramento-San Joaquin Delta. West of the San Joaquin Valley, the species occurred on the Kettleman and Carrizo plains, and in the Cuyama Valley. The southern limit to the range was the Techachapi Mountains and Sierra foothills.

Current Distribution

This species is still found throughout much of its historic range but in declining numbers and in increasingly isolated enclaves. Population densities are low and extremely variable, from about one to three per acre. The number of lizards surviving in the wild is uncertain.

Current population centers are in southern Merced County and western Kern counties, in the foothills of the Kettleman Hills, Antelope Hills, Panoche Hills, and Temblor Range. Remnant populations exist in the Cuyama Valley, Kettleman Plain, and Carrizo Plain.

Conservation and Recovery

The blunt-nosed leopard lizard has declined because of loss of habitat. The natural grasslands of the San Joaquin Valley consisted of as many as 3 million hectares (7.5 million acres) in the late 1800s, but habitat has diminished at a dramatic rate. By 1958, more than half of this acreage was under cultivation or supporting residential housing. But by 1979, under 7 percent of uncultivated grasslands remained, a staggering average loss of nearly 15,580 hectares (38,500 acres) per year. At the current rate, the entire San Joaquin Valley would be developed by 1996.

As the population shrinks, the effects of natural mortality factors, such as predation, disease, and accident, become more pronounced. Known predators include the spotted skunk, California ground squirrel, loggerhead shrike, San Joaquin shipsnake, and gopher snake. Road kills have increased. Lizards are often killed incidentally when rodent burrows are fumigated.

Past conservation efforts have included formal consultations under provisions of the Endangered Species Act between the Fish and Wildlife Service (FWS), the Bureau of Land Management, and the Department of Energy. These consultations have examined the impact of proposed oil and gas resource development and have resulted in closure of access roads, protective fencing, and provision of funding for research and habitat surveys. Unfortunately, these actions affect only a small portion of the remaining habitat, most of which is privately owned.

The Wildlife Conservation Board of the California Department of Fish and Game acquired tracts of habitat in the southern San Joaquin Valley in 1980 and again in 1984, totaling about 570 hectares (1,400 acres). Habitat acquisition is seen as the most viable strategy for recovering the blunt-nosed leopard lizard. The FWS Recovery Plan recommends the acquisition of at least 12,140 hectares (30,000 acres), but funds for land purchases have been limited.

The FWS and the California Department of Fish and Game are attempting to gain the cooperation of local governments in establishing protective zoning classifications in the San Joaquin Valley. In the absence of outright acquisition, local zoning restrictions are the most effective means for conserving remaining habitat.

Bibliography

Montanucci, R. R. 1965. "Observations on the San Joaquin Leopard Lizard, *Crotaphytus wislizenii silus* Stejneger." *Herpetologica* 21(4):270-283.

Montanucci, R. R., R. W. Axtell, and H. C. Dessauer. 1975. "Evolutionary Divergence among Collared Lizards (*Crotaphytus*), with Comments on the Status of *Gambelia*." *Herpetologica* 31(3):336-347.

U.S. Fish and Wildlife Service. 1985. "Blunt-Nosed Leopard Lizard Recovery Plan." U.S. Fish and Wildlife Service, Portland.

Contact

Regional Office of Endangered Species
U.S. Fish and Wildlife Service
Lloyd 500 Building, Suite 1692
500 N.E. Multnomah Street
Portland, Oregon 97232

Desert Tortoise
Gopherus agassizii

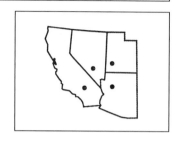

Susan Middleton

Status . . . . . . Endangered in California, Nevada, and Arizona above the Colorado River; Threatened in Utah.
Listed . . . . . . August 20, 1980
Family . . . . . Testudinidae (Tortoise)
Description . . . Land turtle with a dull-brown, six-sided carapace and elephantine limbs.
Habitat . . . . . . Desert and waste areas.
Food . . . . Low-growing plants, leaves.
Reproduction . . Clutch of 4 to 12 eggs.
Threats . . . . . Habitat disturbance, livestock grazing, collectors, vandalism, disease.
Region 1 . . . . California, Nevada

Description

The desert tortoise has a carapace (upper shell) length of 15 to 36 centimeters (6 to 14 in). Males are larger than females. Both carapace and plastron (undershell) are marked with growth rings. The six-sided carapace shields are dull brown or yellowish; the plastron is yellowish and unpatterned. The head is scaly; the limbs are elephantine with blunt nails and no webbing. Desert tortoise has also been described in the scientific literature as *Scaptochelys agassizii* and *Xerobates agassizii*. It is the official state reptile of both California and Nevada.

Behavior

This slow-moving tortoise is most active in the morning, except during extremely hot weather, when it emerges from its burrow only at night to avoid the heat. It builds dens by burrowing as far as 9 meters (30 ft) into an earthen bank and remains there, inactive, during the colder months. The desert tortoise is primarily herbivorous, browsing on low-growing plants and freshly fallen leaves.

During breeding the male hisses and butts the female in the flank. In a nest scooped out of the ground, the female lays 4 to 12 round, off-white eggs that can take up to four months to hatch. Shells of young turtles are soft during the first five years of life, slowly hardening as the animal matures. Sexual maturity is reached after 14 to 20 years. The desert tortoise can live as long as 100 years.

Habitat

The desert tortoise is found in semi-arid grasslands, gravelly desert washes, canyon bottoms, and on rocky hillsides at elevations up to 1,070 meters (3,530 ft).

Historic Range

Historically, this tortoise was found in the greater Mojave and Sonoran Basin deserts in southeastern California, the southern tip of Nevada, extreme southwest Utah, and western Arizona.

Current Distribution

The species still occurs throughout its range but in greatly decreased numbers. At one time, it was estimated that in some places there were as many as 1,000 tortoise per square mile. In a few areas in southern California, the population still reaches densities of 200 per square mile. The overall trend, however, reveals rapidly declining populations. Recent studies in California showed significant declines (up to 55 percent) at seven of eight tortoise study sites. The desert tortoise is considered Threatened in Utah where it occurs in low numbers on the Beaver Dam Slope in Washington County. Currently, an estimated 100,000 tortoises are thought to survive in the Mojave and Sonoran deserts.

Conservation and Recovery

The desert tortoise has suffered from loss of habitat, overcollecting, and vandalism. Though now illegal, collecting wild tortoises continues. They are killed by vehicles, shot for target practice, or deliberately tipped on their backs and left to die. Ravens, which have accompanied human development of desert habitats, are an increasing source of tortoise mortality.

In 1971 the Bureau of Land Management (BLM) established a 100-square kilometer (38-sq mi) sanctuary near California City,

California, as the Desert Tortoise Natural Area. This preserve is located in Kern County, north of Edwards Air Force Base. The area is closed to vehicles, livestock grazing, and mineral exploration.

Many conservationists have long urged the Bureau of Land Management (BLM), which administers 67 percent of all desert tortoise habitat, to reduce livestock grazing on those lands. Cattle and sheep trample tortoises directly, collapse their burrows, and compete for limited food supplies on overgrazed rangeland. Local ranchers, however, have insisted that BLM keep federal lands open to grazing.

In 1985 a petition to the Fish and Wildlife Service, filed jointly by the Defenders of Wildlife, the National Resources Defense Council, and the Environmental Defense Fund requested that the desert tortoise be listed as Endangered throughout its entire U.S. range. The petition expired, but was renewed again in 1989 by the same groups. As a result, the desert tortoise was reclassified as Endangered under the emergency provisions of the Endangered Species Act in August 1989. The revised status covers the Mojave Desert populations, encompassing all of California and Nevada, and Arizona above the Colorado River. The Sonoran Desert population was not included in the reclassification.

In October 1989, the BLM declared a special quarantine that closed 15,260 hectares (37,700 acres) of the Mojave Desert southwest of Ridgecrest, California, to human use for one year. This action was triggered by a severe epidemic of a respiratory infection that has spread through the tortoise population. The infection, which is common in domesticated turtles, clogs the tortoise's lungs and eventually causes death. It is thought to have been spread to the desert tortoise by released pets, and its effects have been worsened by recent drought conditions. This unprecedented

BLM action to protect an Endangered Species generated strong objections among developers, ranchers, and recreationalists in California and Nevada.

Bibliography

Berry, K. H., *et al..* 1986. *Changes in Desert Tortoise Populations at Four Study Sites in California.* Report. U.S. Bureau of Land Management, Riverside, California.

Campbell, F. T. 1988. "The Desert Tortoise." In W. J. Chandler, ed., *Audubon Wildlife Report 1988/1989.* Academic Press, San Diego.

Ferrara, J. 1984. "Digging In." *National Wildlife* 22(2)22-28.

Mathews, J. 1989. "Efforts to Save Tortoise Close Part of Mojave Desert." *Washington Post* October 2, 1989.

Contact

Regional Office of Endangered Species
U.S. Fish and Wildlife Service
Lloyd 500 Building, Suite 1692
500 N.E. Multnomah Street
Portland, Oregon 97232

Regional Office of Endangered Species
U.S. Fish and Wildlife Service
P.O. Box 25486
Denver Federal Center
Denver, Colorado 80225

Gopher Tortoise
Gopherus polyphemus

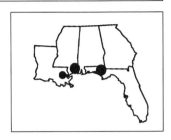

C. Kenneth Dodd, Jr.

Status	Threatened west of the Mobile and Tombigbee rivers
Listed	July 7, 1987
Family	Testudinidae (Tortoise)
Description . . .	Large dark brown land turtle with elephantine hind legs.
Habitat	Mature long-leaf pine forests.
Food	Herbivorous; grasses and forbs.
Reproduction . .	Clutch fewer than 6 eggs.
Threats	Loss of habitat, range fragmentation, hunting, road kills.
Region 4	Alabama, Florida, Louisiana, Mississippi

Description

The gopher tortoise is a large land turtle with a carapace (upper shell) length of between 15 and 37 centimeters (6 and 15 in). It is dark brown to grayish black with elephantine hind legs and shovel-shaped forelimbs. The neck projects through a yellowish, hingeless undershell (plastron).

Behavior

The gopher tortoise is long-lived. Females take 13 to 21 years to reach sexual maturity, and even then some do not nest every year. They lay on average fewer than six eggs per clutch. It is estimated that over 97 percent of young turtles are taken by predators before reaching their second year.

The gopher tortoise feeds on grasses and forbs and digs deep burrows for shelter and nesting. These burrows are used by many other wildlife species. Tortoises survive in drought years by migrating from marginal areas to adjacent areas that are better supplied with water. As gaps between habitat areas broaden, migration declines and eventually stops, and the marginal populations disappear.

Habitat

The primary habitat of the gopher tortoise is mature long-leaf pine forests. It is most often found on well-drained sandy soils in forest glades and transitional zones between forest and grassland. Wiregrass is often the dominant plant of the ground cover.

Historic Range

This species was found from Florida north through South Carolina and west through Louisiana.

Current Distribution

The gopher tortoise is still well distributed throughout its range except in those areas where it is considered Threatened—west of the Mobile and Tombigbee rivers in Alabama, Mississippi, and Louisiana.

Conservation and Recovery

Loss of mature forests to croplands, pasture, and expanding urban areas has steadily decreased the amount of habitat available to the gopher tortoise. Over 80 percent of mature pine forests have been cut since European settlement began. Remaining forests have been significantly degraded by widespread logging, clear-cutting, and replanting with fast-growing pines. These young forests do not support the diversity of plant life required by the gopher tortoise. Where suitable habitat still occurs, it is fragmented, and tortoise populations are isolated.

Land management practices have contributed to the decline. The pine forests are maintained and renewed by periodic wildfires. When fire is controlled, thick underbrush and ground cover develops. This drives the tortoise out to the forest edge and especially onto roadsides, where it is more vulnerable to traffic and collectors. Because of the late sexual maturity and low reproduction rate, replacement cannot keep pace with mortality and taking.

The tortoise receives no state protection in Louisiana but is on the Mississippi List of Endangered Species. It is considered a game animal in Alabama with no open season. Both actions provide some protection against taking but no habitat protection. Threatened status for the gopher tortoise will help in its protection as new management practices are adopted for national forests to preserve its habitat.

Bibliography

Auffenberg, W., and R. Franz. 1982. "The Status and Distribution of the Gopher Tortoise." In R. D. Bury, ed., *North American Tortoises: Conservation and Ecology*. U.S. Fish and Wildlife Service, Atlanta.

Ernst, C. H., and R. W. Barbour. 1972. *Turtles of the United States*. The University Press of Kentucky, Lexington.

Contact

Regional Office of Endangered Species
U.S. Fish and Wildlife Service
Richard B. Russell Federal Building
75 Spring Street, S.W.
Atlanta, Georgia 30303

Ringed Sawback Turtle

Graptemys oculifera

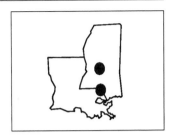

Roger W. Barbour

Status	Threatened
Listed	December 23, 1986
Family	Emydidae (Turtle)
Description . . .	Small, sawbacked turtle; dark olive brown with yellow-ringed shields.
Habitat	Undisturbed riverine habitat.
Food	Mollusks and crustaceans.
Reproduction . .	Clutch of 4 to 8 eggs.
Threats	Alteration of river habitat.
Region 4	Louisiana, Mississippi

Description

The ringed sawback turtle is a small, dark, olive brown turtle with a yellow ring on each shield of the upper shell (carapace). The carapace has a spiny, sawtooth ridge down the center. The undershell (plastron) is yellow. The head has two yellow stripes and a large yellow spot behind the eye. A yellow stripe covers the entire lower jaw. Females attain a shell length of 18 centimeters (7 in), and males average about 10 centimeters (4 in) in length.

Behavior

This species feeds primarily on snails and other small crustaceans found in and beside the river. It characteristically spends many hours on floating logs or other debris basking in the sun. The nesting season is from mid-May to early August. The female digs a nest in sand and deposits from four to eight eggs. Egg mortality is very high—nearly 90 percent.

Habitat

The ringed sawback turtle inhabits a riverine habitat where the river channel is narrow, and currents are moderate. Nesting habitat is on wide, flat sandy beaches or gravel bars. This turtle requires high water quality to support its main food sources.

Historic Range

The turtle is endemic and restricted to the main channels of the Pearl and Bogue Chitto rivers in Mississippi and Louisiana.

Current Distribution

This species is found in most reaches of the Pearl River from its mouth to Neshoba County in east-central Mississippi. It is found in the Bogue Chitto River from its mouth upstream to Franklinton in Washington Parish, Louisiana. While it is still relatively abundant at some localities, the population shows an overall decline in numbers along these rivers, and it has disappeared altogether from many historic sites. The highest densities in the Pearl River are above the Ross Barnett Reservoir and below the confluence with the Strong River in Simpson County. There is no current population estimate.

Conservation and Recovery

Much of the turtle's habitat along the Pearl River has been modified by construction of dams, dikes, and reservoirs. Currently, many remaining habitat sites are being threatened by proposed flood control projects and ongoing maintenance of river channels. Navigational and flood control maintenance requires the removal of debris from sand and gravel bars, and dredging of river channels, depriving the turtle of basking and nesting sites. These activities have increased the water turbidity and siltation, which has significantly decreased the numbers of aquatic snails and mollusks on which the turtle feeds. Water quality has been degraded throughout these river basins.

Projects planned or currently authorized by the Army Corps of Engineers would further impact nearly 30 percent of the remaining Pearl River habitat. These projects include a navigation channel in the East Pearl near Picayune, a navigation channel from Jackson to Carthage, a drainage channel from Carthage to Edinburg, and construction of the Shoccoe Dam. Channel modification and flood control studies are also planned for the Bogue Chitto River. The federal Soil Conservation Service has planned at least ten watershed projects within the Pearl River basin.

These federal agencies will be required to study the impact of proposed and ongoing projects on the ringed sawback turtle. Formal consultation with the Fish and Wildlife Service (FWS) will determine whether permits for the projects should be approved or denied.

The FWS Recovery Plan outlines three objectives for the recovery of the ringed sawback turtle: to protect 240 kilometers (150 mi) of river habitat in two stretches above and below the Ross Barnett Reservoir; to attain stable or increasing populations in both protected stretches; and to periodically monitor population trends and habitat quality.

Bibliography

Cagle, F. R. 1953. "The Status of the Turtle *Graptemys oculifera.*" *Zoologica* 83:137-144.

Cliburn, J. W. 1971. "The Ranges of Four Species of *Graptemys* in Mississippi." *Journal of the Mississippi Academy of Sciences* 16:16-19.

McCoy, C. J., and R. C. Vogt. 1980. "Distribution and Population Status of the Ringed Sawback in Mississippi and Louisiana." Report. U.S. Fish and Wildlife Service, Atlanta.

U.S. Fish and Wildlife Service. 1988. "Recovery Plan for the Ringed Sawback Turtle." U.S. Fish and Wildlife Service, Atlanta.

Contact

Regional Office of Endangered Species
U.S. Fish and Wildlife Service
Richard B. Russell Federal Building
75 Spring Street, S.W.
Atlanta, Georgia 30303

Kemp's Ridley Sea Turtle
Lepidochelys kempii

Stuart Porter

Status	Endangered
Listed	December 2, 1970
Family	Cheloniidae (Sea Turtle)
Description	Sea turtle, weighing up to 41 kg (90 lbs).
Habitat	Pelagic; undisturbed beaches for nesting.
Food	Blue crabs.
Reproduction	Clutch of 80 to 200 eggs.
Threats	Loss of nesting habitat, shrimp nets.
Region 2	Texas
Region 4	Florida, Georgia, Louisiana
Mexico	Tamaulipas

Description

The long-lived Kemp's ridley sea turtle reaches a mature carapace (upper shell) length of about 90 centimeters (36 in) and a weight of 41 kilograms (90 lbs). The oval shell is a dark, mottled green. Forelimbs are modified as flippers. Kemp's ridley is considered a small sea turtle, especially when compared to the leatherback, which often reaches weights of over 455 kilograms (1,000 lbs).

Behavior

The reclusive Kemp's ridley sea turtle follows a two-stage life cycle similar to that of other sea turtles. In the terrestrial stage, embryos develop from eggs buried in sandy beach nests. After about two months, hatchlings emerge as a group, dig out of the nest and return to the sea to begin a pelagic, or open ocean, stage. Hatchlings typically emerge at night and follow the reflections of moon and stars on the water to find the ocean. Juvenile turtles disperse so widely throughout the Gulf of Mexico and along the Atlantic Coast that scientists lose track of their wanderings and refer to this development phase as "the lost years." Eventually, mature female turtles return to nest on the beach where they were born. Individual females return to the nesting beaches every two to eight years between April and July, depositing from 80 to 200 eggs in nests scooped out of the sand.

Kemp's ridley is primarily carnivorous, its favorite food being the blue crab.

Habitat

Kemp's ridley sea turtle is an air-breathing reptile that is adapted to life in the open ocean. For nesting, this turtle requires a stable, sandy beach that is relatively undisturbed by human or animal predators. The nesting population is restricted primarily to a single wilderness beach on the coast of the Mexican state of Tamaulipas near the village of Rancho Nuevo. Nearly all reproduction occurs along an 8-kilometer (5-mi) stretch of beach north and south of a sandbar called Barra Coma.

Historic Range

The Kemp's ridley turtle ranges primarily throughout the Gulf of Mexico, but juveniles have been found all along the eastern coast of the U.S. from Florida to Cape Cod. Unlike other sea turtles that have numerous nesting beaches, this species is almost entirely restricted to the beach at Rancho Nuevo. In some years, a few turtles have nested on Padre Island off the coast of Texas, along other Mexican beaches, or even as far south as Colombia, but nesting at these sites is unusual and is thought to be caused by severe storms or strong currents. The Gulf population once numbered perhaps a hundred thousand. As many as 40,000 females came ashore on the Rancho Nuevo beach in 1947.

Current Distribution

Once fairly numerous, Kemp's ridley is now considered the most endangered of all sea turtles. In recent years, between 400 and 600 females have come ashore to nest at Rancho Nuevo. In spite of over 15 years of protection under federal and international law, numbers have not appreciably increased.

Conservation and Recovery

The Kemp's ridley sea turtle has declined because of many factors. Initially, predation on the nesting beaches took an incredible toll on eggs and hatchlings. Large numbers of coyotes voraciously devoured turtle eggs, and human poachers collected eggs for food. Together, these predators destroyed hundreds of thousands of eggs each year. Such high levels of predation were overcome only by the large annual numbers of nesting females. As numbers began to decline for other reasons, coyotes and poachers took a higher percentage of the overall reproductive effort, producing a spiraling decline in breeding numbers.

In November and December 1988, over 50 Kemp's ridley carcasses were found washed up along the Georgia coast. These are considered a small measure of the overall mortality caused by dangers of the open sea, such as boat propellers, pollution, and sharks. The main culprit in these deaths, however, was thought to be drowning caused by entanglement in shrimp nets.

The National Marine Fisheries Service (NMFS), which is responsible for marine turtle protection at sea, estimates that over 11,000 air-breathing marine turtles drown in shrimp nets each year, including large numbers of Kemp's ridleys. Recently, the NMFS developed regulations to require larger shrimp boats to use turtle excluder devices (TEDs), which are fitted at the mouth of shrimp nets to keep turtles out. In July 1989, the first steps were taken to enforce these regulations in U.S. waters. TEDs are considered the most important single action that can be taken to immediately reduce sea turtle mortality.

Implementation of the TED regulations is controversial. So far most Atlantic coast shrimpers have cooperated by installing and using TEDs, but the Gulf coast fleet based in Texas and Louisiana has been adamantly opposed, claiming that TEDs reduce the shrimp catch by as much as 50 percent. The NMFS counters that properly designed and used TEDs do not significantly interfere with the size of the shrimp catch and completely eliminate turtle mortality. Since the majority of mature Kemp's ridley turtles are found in the Gulf of Mexico, enforcement of TED regulations there will have a direct impact on the survival of the species.

Since 1978, the U.S. Fish and Wildlife Service (FWS) has cooperated with the Mexican government to protect the nesting beach at Rancho Nuevo. The beach is now patrolled by armed Mexican marines and airplanes during breeding season to prevent human disturbance of nests. The only human structure on the beach is the turtle conservation camp at Barra Coma. In recent years, biologists have systematically removed eggs to a coyote-proof hatchery to prevent predation. Up to 50,000 hatchlings are released each year, but the mortality rate among these tiny turtles is exceedingly high. It is estimated that only one female in a thousand survives to maturity to return to the nesting beaches. A small number of eggs are currently being transferred to Padre Island, Texas, each year in an attempt to establish a new breeding population there.

Bibliography

Center for Environmental Education. 1986. *Sea Turtles and Shrimp Trawlers*. Center for Environmental Education, Washington, D.C.

Hendrickson, J. R. 1980. "The Ecological Strategies of Sea Turtles." *American Zoologist* 20(3):597-608.

Marquez, M. R., *et al*. 1981. "The Population of the Kemp's Ridley Turtle in the Gulf of Mexico." In K. Bjorndal, ed., *Biology and Conservation of Sea Turtles: Proceedings of the World Conference on Sea Turtle Conservation*. Smithsonian Institution Press, Washington, D.C.

Pritchard, P. C. 1980. "Report on the United States/Mexico Conservation of Kemp's Ridley Sea Turtle at Rancho Nuevo, Tamaulipas, Mexico." Contract Report #14-16-002-80-216. U.S. Fish and Wildlife Service, Washington, D.C.

U.S. Fish and Wildlife Service. 1984. "Recovery Plan for Marine Turtles." U.S. Fish and Wildlife Service, Atlanta.

Contact

Office of Public Affairs
National Marine Fisheries Service
Department of Commerce
Washington, D.C. 20235

Regional Office of Endangered Species
U.S. Fish and Wildlife Service
P.O. Box 1306
Albuquerque, New Mexico 87103

Olive Ridley Sea Turtle
Lepidochelys olivacea

P. C. H. Pritchard

Status	Endangered in Mexico Threatened elsewhere
Listed	July 28, 1978
Family	Cheloniidae (Sea Turtle)
Description . . .	Oval-shelled, dark olive sea turtle.
Habitat	Pelagic.
Food	Crustaceans, mollusks.
Reproduction . .	Clutch of 80 to 200 eggs.
Threats	Commercial exploitation, poaching.
Range	Tropical coastal waters

Description

The long-lived olive ridley sea turtle reaches a mature carapace (upper shell) length of about 90 centimeters (36 in) and a weight of 41 kilograms (90 lbs). The oval shell is a mottled, olive green. Forelimbs are modified as flippers.

Behavior

The olive ridley sea turtle feeds on crabs, other crustaceans, and mollusks. It is strongly migratory, although migration routes have not been clearly delineated. The olive ridley is notable for its mass nesting behavior. Aggregations of tens of thousands, known as an "arribada," come ashore simultaneously to nest. Embryos develop from eggs buried in

sandy beach nests. After about 50 days, hatchlings emerge as a group, dig out of the nest, and return to the sea. Hatchlings usually emerge at night and follow the reflections of moon and stars on the water to find the ocean. Juvenile turtles disperse widely. After two to eight years, mature female sea turtles join an arribada and come ashore to nest, depositing from 80 to 200 eggs in nests scooped out of the sand. Typically over 75 percent of these eggs fail to hatch or else hatchlings die in the nest.

Historic Range

The olive ridley sea turtle is widely distributed in tropical coastal waters of the Pacific, Indian, and South Atlantic oceans.

Current Distribution

The olive ridley is thought to be the most abundant of all sea turtles. In the Americas it is known to nest in Argentina, Colombia, Ecuador, El Salvador, Guatemala, Nicaragua, Mexico, and Panama. Two of its major nesting beaches in Costa Rica—Playa Nancite and Playa Ostional—attract an estimated 500,000 females each season. Playa Nancite is located in Santa Rosa National Park in northwest Guanacaste Province; Playa Ostional is about 90 kilometers (56 mi) further south.

Conservation and Recovery

Although still numerous, the olive ridley has suffered a serious decline in recent years, primarily because of exploitation of its mass nesting behavior. Populations along the coasts of Mexico, Ecuador, and Orissa in India have been seriously depleted by commercial fishermen, who locate the arribadas and take large numbers in nets. Egg poaching at nearly all known nesting beaches is heavy and continuous. Of all the countries where the olive ridley nests, only Costa Rica provides legislated protection and sanctuary from commercial exploitation.

Until recently, the isolated Costa Rican beaches were thought to be secure because the population at Nancite appeared stable. Additional research, however, revealed that the Ostional population had declined by at least 30 percent over a ten-year period because of egg poaching and overharvesting in Ecuadorian waters, where Costa Rican sea turtles are known to migrate. Tagged Costa Rican ridleys have also been found in Mexican waters where harvesting continues unabated. These finds suggest that there is more mixing of coastal populations than was previously believed, putting all in jeopardy.

In 1980 a long-term tagging program was implemented under the sponsorship of the University of Costa Rica, the Costa Rican National Park Service, and the U.S. Fish and Wildlife Service. The goal of this research is to collect information on seasonal migrations, fidelity to nesting beaches, nesting strategies, and reproductive potential of the Costa Rican populations. During the dry season between December and June when nesting activity is at its peak, armed guards patrol the beaches to prevent poaching. Plans are being developed to establish a regional program to protect the olive ridley that would involve all countries where it nests.

Bibliography

Cornelius, S., and D. Robinson. 1983. "Abundance, Distribution, and Movements of Olive Ridley Sea Turtles in Costa Rica, III." U.S. Fish and Wildlife Service Endangered Species Special Report No. 13.

Limpus, C. J. 1973. "The Pacific Ridley and Other Sea Turtles in Northeastern Australia." *Herpetologica* 31:444-445.

Marquez, M., *et al.* 1981. "A Model for Diagnosis of Populations of Olive Ridleys and Green Turtles of West Pacific Tropical Coasts." In K. A. Bjorndal, ed., *Biology and Conservation of Sea Turtles: Proceedings of the World Conference on Sea Turtle Conservation.* Smithsonian Institution Press, Washington, D.C.

Contact

Office of Research and Development
U.S. Fish and Wildlife Service
Washington, D.C. 20240

Sand Skink
Neoseps reynoldsi

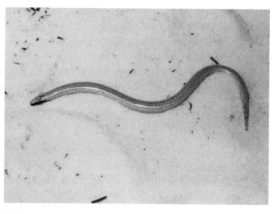

C. Kenneth Dodd, Jr.

Status . . . . . . Threatened
Listed . . . . . . November 6, 1987
Family . . . . . . Scincidae (Skink)
Description . . . Gray to tan skink with wedge-shaped head and retractable forelegs.
Habitat . . . . . . Lake Wales Ridge; loose, well-drained sands.
Food . . . . . . Insects and other invertebrates.
Reproduction . . Clutch of 2 eggs.
Threats . . . . . Agricultural and residential development.
Region 4 . . . . . Florida

Description

The sand skink is a small lizard, 10 to 13 centimeters (4 to 5 in) long from the snout to the tip of the tail. The tail makes up about half the length. Coloring is gray to tan. The tiny forelegs have one toe, the stouter hind legs two toes. This skink has a wedge-shaped head and body grooves into which the forelegs can be retracted. These features enable it to "swim" beneath the surface of loose sand by pushing with the rear legs. Its small eyes have transparent windows in the lower lids.

Behavior

The sand skink spends most of its time beneath the ground, burrowing up to 10 centimeters (4 in) into the sand. It feeds on a variety of small arthropods, principally beetle larvae, termites, and spiders. It is most active during the mating season from March to May. The female deposits two elongated eggs in early summer beneath logs or other cover. She remains with the eggs to protect or brood them.

Habitat

The sand skink requires well-drained sands in open glades free of rooted plants. Sand skinks are more abundant in early successional sand pine scrub, before the area is taken over by hardwoods. Sand pine renews itself through periodic fires at intervals of 20 years or more. Dominant vegetation within the habitat includes sand pine and rosemary, or long-leaf pine and turkey oak. Moisture is retained in the sand beneath the surface, typically by a covering of leaf-litter. This moisture is important for maintaining the skink's internal body temperature and provides the conditions necessary for egg incubation.

Historic Range

The sand skink was once found in localized populations throughout the Lake Wales Ridge region of central Florida. Over 14 plants and animals endemic to this region of Florida have been affected by encroaching agricultural expansion and residential development and are federally listed as Endangered or Threatened. The sand skink is found in association with the Endangered blue-tailed mole skink (*Eumeces egregius lividus*) over part of its range.

Current Distribution

The sand skink occurs in isolated populations in Marion, Orange, Lake, Polk, and Highlands counties where its habitat remains relatively undisturbed. The Florida Natural Areas Inventory has recorded 31 sand skink populations.

Conservation and Recovery

Sand pine scrub and sandhills are suitable for conversion to citrus groves, and nearly 65 percent of the original habitat of the sand skink has been converted for agriculture or residential subdivisions. Since the freezes of 1983 and 1984, citrus growers have been moving their operations southward into the skink's range.

Public lands offer some degree of protection. It is protected at the Ocala National Forest (Marion County), Lake Louisa State Park (Lake County), Bok Tower Nature Preserve, Tiger Creek Preserve, Saddle Blanket Lakes Preserve, and Lake Arbuckle State Park and Wildlife Management Area

(Polk County), Archbold Biological Station (Highlands County), and Wekiwa Springs State Park (Orange County). Controlled fires in pine scrub on public land are used to remove successional plants and renew the habitat.

The Nature Conservancy is actively involved in protecting pine scrub habitat along the Lake Wales Ridge. The State of Florida and the Florida Natural Areas Inventory are aggressively acquiring scrub habitat in central Florida and have recently added several large tracts to the state wildlife refuge system. These actions will go a long way toward stemming habitat loss in the region and may allow endemic species, such as the sand skink, to survive.

Bibliography

Christman, S. P. 1970. "The Possible Evolutionary History of Two Florida Skinks." *Quarterly Journal of the Florida Academy of Science* 33(4):291-293.

Cooper, B. W. 1953. "Notes on the Life History of the Lizard *Neoseps reynoldsi* Stejneger." *Quarterly Journal of the Florida Academy of Science* 16(4):235-238.

Myers, C.W., and S.R. Telford, Jr. 1965. "Food of *Neoseps*, the Florida Sand Skink." *Quarterly Journal of the Florida Academy of Science* 28(2):190-194.

Telford, S. R., Jr. 1959. "A Study of the Sand Skink, *Neoseps reynoldsi* Stejneger." *Copeia* 1959(2):100-119.

Contact

Regional Office of Endangered Species
U.S. Fish and Wildlife Service
Richard B. Russell Federal Building
75 Spring Street, S.W.
Atlanta, Georgia 30303

Atlantic Salt Marsh Snake
Nerodia fasciata taeniata

Robert S. Simmons/USFWS

Status	Threatened
Listed	November 29, 1977
Family	Colubridae (Water Snake)
Description . . .	Slender water snake; pale olive body with dark stripes and blotches.
Habitat	Tidal wetlands.
Food	Small fish.
Reproduction . .	2 to 14 young, born alive.
Threats	Loss of wetlands.
Region 4	Florida

Description

Also commonly known as the East Coast striped water snake, the Atlantic salt marsh snake has a pale olive body with a pattern of dark stripes on either side that fragment into blotches toward the tail. A single pale stripe extends down the center of the spine. The belly is black with a row of yellowish spots. This slender snake rarely exceeds 61 centimeters (2 ft) in length.

Behavior

The Atlantic salt marsh snake is most active at night during low tide, when it feeds on small fish that become entrapped in shallow tide pools. Its activities are strongly influenced by tidal rhythms. When disturbed it may seek shelter in fiddler crab burrows. Like its close relative, the Gulf salt marsh snake, the female bears two to fourteen young. Eggs hatch inside the mother's body, and young are born alive in mid-summer.

Habitat

Salt marsh snakes are the only group of North American snakes that are restricted to brackish and saline waters. The Atlantic salt marsh snake is found in salt marshes and tidal creeks, often associated with fiddler crab burrows and stands of glassworts, blackrush, or black mangrove.

Historic Range

This snake is thought to be a relict species derived from hybridization between two subspecies that disappeared from the Florida coast sometime in the Pleistocene.

Current Distribution

The Atlantic salt marsh snake is currently found in coastal salt marshes and mangrove swamps along the Atlantic coast of central Florida. Populations have been found at or near Daytona Beach, New Smyrna Beach, National Gardens, and the Tomoka River State Park (Volusia County); Merritt Island National Wildlife Refuge, Playalinda and Micco (Brevard County); and Gifford and Vero Beach (Indian River Country). It may also occur on federal lands at the Kennedy Space Center, Patrick Air Force Base, Cape Canaveral Air Force Station, and Pelican Island National Wildlife Refuge.

Conservation and Recovery

Progressive destruction of coastal marshes in central Florida has significantly decreased the range and available habitat of the Atlantic salt marsh snake. Coastal wetlands continue to be drained or filled to support waterfront construction. Disturbances caused by construction and recreational activities are also thought to be encouraging mixing and interbreeding between this snake and *Nerodia fasciata pictiventris*, a more common freshwater subspecies. Continued interbreeding would result in the loss of the Atlantic salt marsh snake as an identifiable subspecies. This species has also been targeted by snake collectors, but the number taken each year cannot be determined.

Because this snake has not been closely studied, recovery efforts will be based on the results of research being conducted by the Fish and Wildlife Service and state biologists. Prohibitions against collecting the snake on federal and state lands are being strictly enforced.

Bibliography

Dunson W. A. 1979. "Occurrence of Partially Striped Forms of the Mangrove Snake *Nerodia fasciata compressicauda* and Comments on the Status of *N. f. taeniata.*" *Florida Scientist* 42:102-112.

Hebrard, J. J., and R. C. Lee. 1981. "A Large Collection of Brackish Water Snakes from the Central Atlantic Coast of Florida." *Copeia* 1981:886-889.

McDiarmid, R. W., ed. 1978. *Rare and Endangered Biota of Florida*; Vol. 3, *Amphibians and Reptiles.* University Presses of Florida, Gainesville.

Woodard, D. W. 1980. "Selected Vertebrate Endangered Species of the Seacoast of the United States: The Atlantic Salt Marsh Snake." Coastal Ecosystems Project, Office of Biological Services, U.S. Fish and Wildlife Service, Atlanta.

Contact

Regional Office of Endangered Species
U.S. Fish and Wildlife Service
Richard B. Russell Federal Building
75 Spring Street, S.W.
Atlanta, Georgia 30303

Concho Water Snake
Nerodia harteri paucimaculata

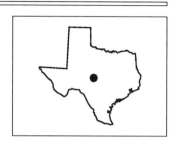

Robert and Linda Mitchell

Status	Threatened
Listed	September 3, 1986
Family	Colubridae (Water Snake)
Description	Water snake, grayish above with four rows of dark blotches.
Habitat	Colorado and Concho rivers; flowing streams.
Food	Minnows, amphibians, crustaceans.
Threats	Habitat loss and degradation, fragmented distribution.
Region 2	Texas

Description

The Concho water snake rarely achieves a length of more than 0.9 meter (3 ft). Its grayish upper surface is marked by four rows of irregular dark brown blotches arranged in alternate fashion along the top and sides. The Concho snake resembles its close relative, the Brazos water snake (*Nerodia harteri harteri*), except for details of coloration and patterning.

Behavior

This water snake feeds on minnows, frogs and toads, and small crustaceans.

Habitat

Adult snakes live in deep flowing water or in shallows where rocks and boulders pro-

vide secure hiding places. Woody vegetation along the stream banks is used for basking, while protected pools and rock piles provide suitable nesting sites. Immature snakes require stony-bottomed shallows and rocky banks.

Historic Range

Arising in the uplands near Big Spring, Texas, the Concho River flows southeast through San Angelo before joining the Colorado River near the town of Concho. The Colorado River arises in the region south of Lubbock and winds west and south, passing through Austin on its way to the Gulf of Mexico. The Concho water snake once occurred over about 450 kilometers (280 miles) of the Colorado and Concho rivers in west Texas.

Current Distribution

The Concho water snake's habitat has been fragmented by the construction of four large-scale dams and reservoirs along the main rivers, plus several smaller impoundments on tributaries. Completed in 1968, the Robert Lee Dam on the Colorado River eliminated a large population of Concho water snakes along with 45 kilometers (28 mi) of habitat. Currently under construction is the Stacy Reservoir and dam on the Colorado River, which will further segment the snake population.

This water snake now occurs in discontinuous localities along about 320 kilometers (200 mi) of the Colorado and Concho rivers in ten counties: Irion, Tom Green, Concho, Runnels, Coleman, McCulloch, Brown, Mills, San Saba, and Lampasas. There is no current population estimate, but numbers have declined significantly and are considered low.

Conservation and Recovery

The Concho water snake has declined because of the dams and diversion structures that have been constructed on the Colorado and Concho rivers. Dams inundate habitat upstream and alter water flow regimes downstream, leaving only isolated sections of river in a natural condition. Water snake populations are artificially separated and prevented from interbreeding, which further limits chances for survival.

Diversion of water, primarily for irrigation, has reduced water levels and flows in some stretches of river. Increased sedimentation also occurs when water flow is reduced. In addition, water pollution has increased, mainly because of fertilizer, herbicide, and pesticide runoffs.

The fate of the Concho water snake hinges on the politically divisive debate of habitat conservation versus access to water rights in a region where access to water often determines economic survival. Human population increases in the region demand the diversion of more water for residential and industrial use, which is causing a deterioration in the Concho water snake's habitat.

When the Concho water snake was first proposed for federal Threatened status, many local residents expressed the opinion that listing the snake was a ploy by opponents of the Stacy Reservoir to halt construction. The Fish and Wildlife Service determined that the snake qualified for listing, even without considering the impact of the reservoir. The Colorado River Municipal Water District, sponsors of the Stacy Dam project, have agreed to restore and maintain important stretches of river habitat in exchange for permits allowing construction to proceed.

Bibliography

Flury, J. W., and T. C. Maxwell. 1981. "Status and Distribution of *Nerodia harteri paucimaculata*." Endangered Species Office, Albuquerque.

Scott, N. J., Jr., and L. A. Fitzgerald. 1985. "Status Survey of *Nerodia harteri*, Brazos and Concho-Colorado Rivers, Texas." Denver Wildlife Research Center, U.S. Fish and Wildlife Service, Museum of Southwestern Biology, Albuquerque.

U.S. Fish and Wildlife Service. 1987. "Endangered and Threatened Species of Texas and Oklahoma (with 1988 Addendum)." U.S. Fish and Wildlife Service, Albuquerque.

Contact

Regional Office of Endangered Species
U.S. Fish and Wildlife Service
P.O. Box 1306
Albuquerque, New Mexico 87103

Alabama Red-Bellied Turtle

Pseudemys alabamensis

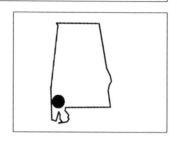

Robert Mount

Status	Endangered
Listed	June 16, 1987
Family	Emydidae (Turtle)
Description . . .	Brown to olive freshwater turtle with an elongated, arched carapace.
Habitat	Rivers, ponds, wetlands.
Food	Aquatic vegetation.
Reproduction . .	Clutch of 10 to 17 eggs.
Threats	Harassment, predation.
Region 4	Alabama

Description

The Alabama red-bellied turtle is a large, freshwater turtle with a carapace (upper shell) length of 20 to 25 centimeters (8 to 10 in). The elongated, arched carapace is brown to olive, with yellow, orange, or reddish streaks and mottling. The plastron (under-shell) grades from orange to red. The skin is olive to black with yellow to light orange facial stripes. There is a prominent notch at the tip of the upper jaw, bordered on either side by a toothlike cusp.

The Alabama red-bellied turtle has more head stripes than the Florida red-bellied turtle, and the arched shell and jaw notch and cusp distinguish it from the cooter (*Pseudemys floridana*) and the river cooter (*Pseudemys concinna*).

Behavior

Members of the genus *Pseudemys* breed in late spring and early summer. The female selects a nesting site in sandy soil usually within 90 meters (300 ft) of a pond and deposits 10 to 17 eggs. Incubation takes from 73 to 80 days at 25 degrees C (77 degrees F). The hatchlings are about 2.5 centimeters (1 in) long. Females may take up to 15 years to reach sexual maturity, although males mature more quickly. The Alabama red-bellied turtle is strictly herbivorous, feeding on aquatic vegetation.

Habitat

This turtle inhabits rivers, ponds, and freshwater wetlands. It is found most often in backwater bays with a water depth of 1 to 2 meters (3.3 to 6.6 ft), where there is extensive submerged and emergent vegetation, such as bulrushes. The turtle nests along the banks and uses the dense beds of aquatic vegetation for basking.

Historic Range

The Alabama red-bellied turtle was once found throughout the lower part of the flood plain of the Mobile River system in Baldwin and Mobile counties, Alabama, and as far north as the Little River State Park in southern Monroe County.

Current Distribution

This turtle is now found only in scattered areas in the lower Mobile River system below David Lake in Mobile County. It appears to be most abundant in a 21-kilometer (13-mi) stretch of the Tensaw River south of Hurricane Landing. One known nesting site survives on an island bank bordered on one side by a wooded swamp. The current size of the population is not known.

Conservation and Recovery

The last known nesting site is heavily used by campers during times when turtles are nesting. Camp lights, trampling, and noise disturb nesting turtles and have been observed to cause reproductive failure. Off-road vehicles have destroyed turtle nests and eggs.

Predation is a likely factor in turtle decline. The fish crow is probably the main predator of Alabama red-bellied turtle eggs. Egg-eating domestic pigs, which were released on the nesting island during the late 1960s constitute another menace.

The main nesting island is privately owned and divided into four different parcels. The owner of the largest parcel has agreed to cooperate with Fish and Wildlife Service efforts to protect the turtle.

Bibliography

Carr, A. F., Jr., and J. W. Crenshaw, Jr. 1957. "A Taxonomic Reappraisal of the Turtle *Pseudemys alabamensis* Baur." *Bulletin of the Florida State Museum* 2:25-42.

Ernst, C. H., and R. W. Barbour. 1972. *Turtles of the United States*. University Presses of Kentucky, Lexington.

Meany, D. B. 1979. "Nesting Habits of the Alabama Red-Bellied Turtle, *Pseudemys alabamensis*." *Journal of the Alabama Academy of Science* 50:113.

Pritchard, P. C. H. 1979. *Encyclopedia of Turtles*. T.F.H. Publications, Neptune, New Jersey.

Contact

Regional Office of Endangered Species
U.S. Fish and Wildlife Service
Richard B. Russell Federal Building
75 Spring Street, S.W.
Atlanta, Georgia 30303

Plymouth Red-Bellied Turtle

Pseudemys rubriventris bangsii

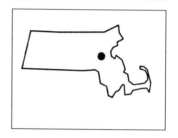

Jerry Graham

Status . . . . . . Endangered
Listed . . . . . April 2, 1980
Family . . . . . Emydidae (Turtle)
Description . . . Small aquatic turtle with mahogany-colored shell and reddish vertical bars.
Habitat . . . . . . Ponds and pond banks.
Food . . . . . . Aquatic plants and animals.
Reproduction . . Clutch of 10 to 17 eggs.
Threats . . . . . Limited range, loss of habitat, predation.
Region 5 . . . . . Massachusetts

Description

At maturity, the Plymouth red-bellied turtle achieves a carapace (upper shell) length of up to 31 centimeters (12 in). The carapace is typically black to deep mahogany with reddish vertical bars, but color and patterning vary widely. The male undershell (plastron) is pale pink, overlaid with a dark mottling. The female undershell is a brilliant coral red. The upper jaw is notched and displays distinct cusps.

Behavior

This turtle is primarily aquatic, preferring small ponds but is occasionally found on land near the water. It is most active from late March to October. In the winter it rests on the pond bottom beneath the ice in an inactive state similar to hibernation, known as brumation. It feeds on aquatic vegetation, crayfish, and other small pond fauna. In late spring and early summer, the female selects a nesting site in sandy soil close to the pond. After scooping a hole, she deposits 10 to 17 eggs, which incubate between 73 and 80 days. Hatchlings are only about 2.5 centimeters (1 in) long. Females reach sexual maturity in 8 to 15 years.

Habitat

The Plymouth red-bellied turtle prefers deep, permanent ponds with nearby sandy areas for nesting, and surrounding vegetation of pine barrens or mixed deciduous forest.

Historic Range

Archaeological evidence suggests that this species occurred in a fairly restricted area of eastern Massachusetts defined by Ipswich, Concord, and Martha's Vineyard. A closely related subspecies, the red-bellied turtle (*Pseudemys rubriventris rubriventris*), ranges from North Carolina to southern New Jersey.

Current Distribution

The Plymouth red-bellied turtle is thought to be limited to about twelve ponds in and near the towns of Plymouth and Carver (Plymouth County), Massachusetts. The size of the population was estimated at about 200 breeding individuals in 1985, but a captive breeding program has added about 100 young turtles to the population every year since 1987.

Conservation and Recovery

The greatest threat to this turtle is its limited distribution. Ten of twelve habitat ponds are within an area of only 607 hectares (1500 acres). In the early 1980s, Plymouth County experienced a development boom. Pondshore land, in particular, was considered prime for residential development. The Massachusetts Wetlands Protection Act provided some protection against alteration of turtle pond habitats. But even when ponds were left intact by construction, houses and roads eliminated nesting and basking sites.

To counter habitat loss, The Nature Conservancy included several turtle ponds in its land registry program in Massachusetts. Under this system, landowners voluntarily agreed to avoid activities on their lands that would harm the turtle. This voluntary program provided the nucleus for the establishment of a permanent federal wildlife refuge in 1986. The refuge includes all turtle ponds known to be inhabited and others that were once inhabited.

Predation by raccoons, skunks, and widemouth bass was identified as a further serious threat to the turtle population. Raccoons and skunks dig out nests and eat the eggs, while bass snatch turtle hatchlings from the water before the shells have a chance to harden. To counter this threat, researchers under the direction of the Massachusetts Natural Heritage and Endangered Species Program began locating turtle nests and fencing sites to exclude predators. At the time of fencing, several eggs are removed from each nest, then hatched and raised in a collaborative captive breeding program.

Hatchlings are held over the winter, during which time they develop at a rate five times faster than those remaining in the wild. By spring, these young turtles are able to resist predation and are released into the turtle ponds. Nearly 100 turtles were released in 1988, and more than 100 in spring of 1989. It is likely that most of these young turtles have survived.

Bibliography

Graham, T. E. 1984. "*Pseudemys rubriventris* Predation." *Herpetology Review* 15:19-20.

U.S. Fish and Wildlife Service. 1985. "Plymouth Red-Bellied Turtle Recovery Plan." U.S. Fish and Wildlife Service, Newton Corner, Massachusetts.

Contact

Regional Office of Endangered Species
U.S. Fish and Wildlife Service
One Gateway Center, Suite 700
Newton Corner, Massachusetts 02158

Monito Gecko
Sphaerodactylus micropithecus

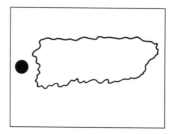

C. Kenneth Dodd, Jr.

Status	Endangered
Listed	October 15, 1982
Family	Gekkonidae (Gecko)
Description . . .	Small gray gecko with a contrasting tan or dark brown tail.
Habitat	Monito Island; rock crevices.
Food	Unknown.
Reproduction . .	Unknown.
Threats	Low numbers, limited distribution, predation.
Region 4	Puerto Rico

Description

The Monito gecko is a small lizard, only about 4 centimeters (1.5 in) long when fully grown. It is light to dark gray with a spotty patching of brown and tan. Occasionally individuals have white eye-shaped markings on the back. The tan or dark brown tail contrasts sharply with the body. Juveniles are consistently darker than adults. The tail, which is easily separated from the body, will regenerate. This gecko is similar in appearance and closely related to the Puerto Rican gecko (*Sphaerodactylus macrolepis*).

Behavior

Based on similar species and limited observations, Monito geckos are thought to breed between March and November. This species has not been closely studied, and little is known of diet, behavior, or habitat preference.

Habitat

Monito Island is an islet situated halfway between Puerto Rico and Hispaniola, 5 kilometers (3 mi) northwest of Mona Island. It consists of a limestone plateau with a total surface area of less than 15 hectares (38 acres), surrounded by nearly vertical cliffs. The highest elevation on the island is 66 meters (218 ft). Cliff bases have been eroded and undercut by wave action. Mean annual rainfall is 79 centimeters (31 in). The vegetation is a dry scrub, consisting mostly of shrubs, dwarfed trees, and cacti. Monito geckos have been observed sunning on rock piles and have scurried away to hide under rocks and plants.

Historic Range

This lizard has been found only on Monito Island.

Current Distribution

In 1982 personnel from the Fish and Wildlife Service (FWS) and the Puerto Rico Department of Natural Resources surveyed the entire island for the Monito gecko and observed 24 individuals. Because of the rugged topography, this count does not reflect the actual number of geckos on the island but is an indication of its relative rarity.

Conservation and Recovery

The Monito gecko is an extremely rare lizard with a range restricted by the small size of its island home. Never very numerous, it is further threatened by a large population of introduced black rats that are known to prey on young lizards and lizard eggs. After World War II, the island was used by the Air Force as a bombing range, which caused extensive damage to the habitat. Although the vegetation appears to have recovered somewhat, bomb damage is still very evident over much of the island.

Monito Island is owned by the Puerto Rican Commonwealth and is currently managed as a reserve for seabirds. To limit human disturbance of the habitat, unauthorized visitation of the island has been prohibited. The most pressing need is for some form of rodent control to diminish the rat infestation. In the absence of rats, it is likely that the gecko population would recover and stabilize.

In 1985, this species was listed as Endangered under Puerto Rico's Regulation to Govern the Management of Threatened and Endangered Species. The entire island has been designated as Critical Habitat for the Monito gecko.

Bibliography

Dodd, C. K., Jr., and P. R. Ortiz. 1983. "An Endemic Gecko in the Caribbean." *Oryx* 17(3):119-121.

Hammerson, G. A. 1984. "Monito Gecko Survey." Report. Department of Natural Resources, San Juan.

Ortiz, P. R. 1982. "Status Survey of the Monito Gecko." Report. Department of Natural Resources, San Juan.

Schwartz, A. 1977. "A New Species of *Sphaerodactylus* from Isla Monito, West Indies." *Proceedings of the Biological Society of Washington* 90(4):985-992.

U.S. Fish and Wildlife Service. 1986. "Monito Gecko Recovery Plan." U.S. Fish and Wildlife Service, Atlanta.

Contact

Regional Office of Endangered Species
U.S. Fish and Wildlife Service
Richard B. Russell Federal Building
75 Spring Street, S.W.
Atlanta, Georgia 30303

Caribbean Field Office
U.S. Fish and Wildlife Service
P.O. Box 491
Boqueron, Puerto Rico 00622

Flattened Musk Turtle
Sternotherus depressus

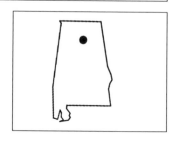

C. Kenneth Dodd, Jr.

Status	Threatened
Listed	June 11, 1987
Family	Kinosternidae (Musk Turtle)
Description . . .	Small, freshwater turtle with a dark brown to orange flattened carapace.
Habitat	Rivers, creeks, wetlands.
Food	Mollusks.
Reproduction . .	Clutch of 3 eggs.
Threats	Hybridization, habitat pollution.
Region 4	Alabama

Description

The flattened musk turtle is an aquatic turtle with a distinctly flattened carapace (upper shell), about 13 centimeters (5 in) long when fully grown. The carapace is dark brown to orange with dark bordered seams and a slightly serrated back edge. The undershell (plastron) is pink to yellowish. The head is greenish with narrow stripes on the top and neck. The chin has two sensors (called barbels), and all four feet are webbed. Males have thick, long, spine-tipped tails.

Behavior

This turtle feeds primarily on freshwater mollusks. Males mature in four to six years, females in six to eight. Females deposit one or two clutches of eggs each season with an average of three eggs per clutch.

Habitat

Although the flattened musk turtle is found in a variety of streams and in the headwaters of some dammed lakes, its optimum habitat appears to be free-flowing large creeks or small rivers with vegetated shallows, alternating with deeper, rock-bottomed pools.

Historic Range

The flattened musk turtle was once found in the upper Black Warrior River system of Alabama, upstream from Tuscaloosa, which is on the fall line between the Piedmont Plateau and the coastal plain. Since 1930 several dams have been built on the river and near the fall line. The resulting reservoirs were more favorable for another turtle, *Sternotherus minor peltifer*. Where the ranges of the two turtles overlapped, interbreeding occurred to the detriment of the flattened musk turtle population.

Current Distribution

Genetically pure populations of this turtle are now believed to exist only in the Black Warrior River system, upstream from Bankhead Dam in Blount, Cullman, Etowah, Jefferson, Lawrence, Marshall, Tuscaloosa, Walker, and Winston counties of north-central Alabama.

Conservation and Recovery

Collecting of the flattened musk turtle has reduced the overall population. Some dealers brazenly advertise the turtle for sale at high prices. The turtle's new status as an Endangered species should provide protection from collection and sale.

Clay siltation in the river system also may have had a great impact on the population size. Silting has been caused by a combination of forest clear-cuts, agricultural run-off, and mining operations. The upper Basin region is underlain by the Black Warrior and Plateau Coal Fields. New regulations have recently reduced the rate of new sediment being washed into the river system. Past deposits, however, continue to affect the quality of the habitat, and recovery will be slow.

Bibliography

Ernst, C. H., and R. W. Barbour. 1972. *Turtles of the United States.* University Press of Kentucky, Lexington.

Tinkle, D. W., and R. G. Webb. 1955. "A New Species of Sternotherus with a Discussion of the *Sternotherus carinatus* Complex." *Tulane Studies in Zoology* 3:52-67.

Contact

Regional Office of Endangered Species
U.S. Fish and Wildlife Service
Richard B. Russell Federal Building
75 Spring Street, S.W.
Atlanta, Georgia 30303

San Francisco Garter Snake
Thamnophis sirtalis tetrataenia

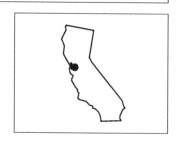

Susan Middleton

Status	Endangered
Listed	March 11, 1967
Family	Colubridae (Water Snake)
Description . . .	Red, black, and greenish striped garter snake.
Habitat	Wetlands, near standing water.
Food	Frogs, newts, toads, fish.
Reproduction . .	Ovoviviparous (young born alive).
Threats	Loss of wetlands, habitat fragmentation, collectors.
Region 1	California

Description

The San Francisco garter snake grows to a maximum length of 130 centimeters (51 in). Running down its back is a wide greenish yellow stripe edged in black and bordered on each side by a broad red stripe, which may be broken or divided. Parallel with this is a third black stripe. The belly is greenish blue, and the top of the head is red. The eyes are large.

Behavior

The harmless San Francisco garter snake is extremely wary and will flee into water or undergrowth if disturbed. It mates during the first few warm days in March. Ovulation occurs in spring, pregnancy in early summer, and birth sometime in July or August. The female plays a passive role, allowing several

males to court her. Males seek out the female by scent. Like most garter snakes, the San Francisco snake is ovoviviparous (eggs are hatched inside the body). Average litter sizes of closely related species are from 12 to 24.

This species is known to feed on red-legged frogs, Pacific tree frogs, immature California newts, western toads, threespine stickleback, and mosquito fish. Small mammals may occasionally be eaten as well.

Habitat

The San Francisco garter snake is seen most often near ponds, lakes, marshes, and sloughs. For cover it uses bankside vegetation, such as cattails, bulrushes, and spike rushes. It sometimes shelters in rodent burrows. Lower-lying marsh areas are used for foraging and breeding. The snake often basks on floating algae or rush mats or on grassy hillsides near drainages and ponds.

Recent research (1987), using implanted radio transmitters, has shown that the snake ranges much further from water than originally supposed. It has been found up to 180 meters (600 ft) away from water in rodent burrows on dry, grassy hillsides.

Historic Range

Historically, the San Francisco garter snake was found on the San Francisco Peninsula from the San Francisco County line south through San Mateo County to Ano Nuevo Point. It inhabited lowlands along both the western and eastern foothills of the Santa Cruz Mountains.

Current Distribution

The San Francisco garter snake survives at about 20 locations within its historic range. Significant populations are at Ano Nuevo State Reserve, Pescadero Marsh Natural Preserve, San Francisco State Fish and Game Refuge, Sharp Park Golf Course, Cascade Ranch, and Milbrae at San Francisco Airport.

Conservation and Recovery

Alteration and fragmentation of habitat are to blame for the decline of the San Francisco garter snake. Wetlands have been filled in or converted for recreation or residential sites. Streams have been diverted, streambank vegetation eliminated, and large areas brought into cultivation or developed for housing and industry. All this has driven the snake into diminishing pockets of habitat.

Because of the snakes' beautiful coloration, reptile dealers and fanciers pose a threat. Recently, Fish and Wildlife Service (FWS) agents arrested several dealers and collectors for possession of these snakes. Diligent enforcement of the laws protecting the species has helped reduce collecting.

Four areas managed for other species also offer incidental protection to populations of the garter snake. These are the Pescadero Marsh Natural Preserve, Ano Nuevo State Reserve, Laguna Salada at Sharp Park, and the San Francisco State Fish and Game Refuge.

The goal of the Recovery Plan is to expand protection to at least ten populations, each consisting of about 200 adult snakes. If this goal can be reached, and protected populations are shown to be stable for five consecutive years, then the FWS will consider reclassifying this species as Threatened.

Bibliography

Fitch, H. S. 1965. "An Ecological Study of the Garter Snake, *Thamnophis sirtalis*." *University of Kansas Publication of the Museum of Natural History* 15:493-564.

McGinnis, S. M. 1984. "The Current Distribution and Habitat Requirements of the San Francisco Garter Snake in Coastal San Mateo County." Report C-673. California Department of Fish and Game, Sacramento.

U.S. Fish and Wildlife Service. 1985. "Recovery Plan for the San Francisco Garter Snake." U.S. Fish and Wildlife Service, Portland.

Contact

Regional Office of Endangered Species
U.S. Fish and Wildlife Service
Lloyd 500 Building, Suite 1692
500 N.E. Multnomah Street
Portland, Oregon 97232

Coachella Valley
Fringe-Toed Lizard

Uma inornata

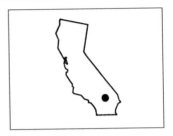

B. "Moose" Peterson

Status	Threatened
Listed	September 25, 1980
Family	Iguanidae (Lizard)
Description	Medium-sized, gray lizard with a wedge-shaped head and a fringe of scales on toes.
Habitat	Wind-blown sand dunes.
Food	Insects.
Reproduction	Breeds from April through mid-August.
Threats	Residential development, habitat degradation.
Region 1	California

Description

The Coachella Valley fringe-toed lizard has a wedge-shaped snout and a flattened body that can reach 24 centimeters (10 in) in length, including the long tail. This lizard is pale gray above and covered with a regular pattern of darker eye-shaped markings. The underside is white, sometimes with several black dots on each side of the abdomen and dusky lines on the throat. The body scales are smooth and overlap evenly, giving the skin a velvety texture. A sensor on the top of the head monitors solar radiation, stimulating the lizard to seek shelter if it gets too hot.

The lizard's most distinctive characteristic is a row of elongated scales on the edge of the toes. This fringe of scales, which helps the lizard maintain traction in loose sands, is the source of the common name for lizards in the genus *Uma*.

Behavior

The Coachella Valley fringe-toed lizard seeks shelter underground to avoid heat and predators, often using abandoned rodent burrows. It literally dives into the sand to escape predators. It retracts its front legs, closes flexible flaps to protect its ears, and uses its strong hind legs to push beneath the surface. The lizard can stay submerged for an indefinite time, breathing air trapped in the spaces between the grains of sand.

This lizard is active when the air temperature rises above 22 degrees C and stays below

39 degrees C (72 to 102 degrees F); it can bear much higher ground temperatures. Dormant in winter, lizards emerge in the spring and enter a prolonged breeding season, lasting from April to mid-August. Lizards reach sexual maturity in their second year.

The Coachella Valley fringe-toed lizard is an insectivore but occasionally rounds out its diet with plant matter. In years when rainfall is below normal, lizard reproduction is correspondingly low.

Habitat

The Coachella Valley fringe-toed lizard is superbly adapted to the harsh extremes of desert climate and to wind-blown sand dunes. Loose sands are essential for its burrowing nature. The sand that forms dunes in the Coachella Valley washes down from the mountains in storm run-off. The valley is located east of the resort city of Palm Springs and west of the Joshua Tree National Monument.

Historic Range

This lizard is endemic to the Coachella Valley (north central Riverside County), California, and occupied an original range of nearly 700 square kilometers (270 sq mi).

Current Distribution

By 1980 more than half of the original range had been lost to agricultural and residential development. The remaining dunes have been fragmented by roads and railroad cuts. Large tracts of dune have been stabilized by planted windbreaks. Once dunes are stabilized, the fringe-toed lizard is forced to seek out other sites.

Conservation and Recovery

Three Coachella Valley cities—Desert Hot Springs, Palm Desert, and Rancho Mirage—have experienced annual growth rates of between 13 and 19 percent. Construction of luxury homes and related commercial development continued at break-neck speed through the 1980s and threatened to engulf the entire valley.

Preservation groups, such as the Coachella Valley Fringe-Toed Lizard Advisory Committee and the Coachella Valley Ecological Reserve Foundation, formed as early as 1977 to prevent lizard habitat from disappearing. By 1983 with help from The Nature Conservancy, these foundations had acquired 172 hectares (425 acres) of lizard habitat to establish an ecological reserve—a good beginning, but not enough to ensure the lizard's survival.

In 1989 developers, conservationists, local, state, and federal agencies were able to forge a compromise agreement that will preserve a large part of remaining habitat, while allowing development in the rest of the valley to continue. The compromise plan will eventually set aside 5,260 hectares (13,000 acres) to be called the Coachella Valley Preserve. The goal is to maintain about 10 percent of the valley's area in its natural state. The preserve is designed to keep an open corridor for the wind-blown dunes, which will allow the habitat to replenish itself with new sand washing down from the mountains. Developers have agreed to pay a "lizard surcharge" for each acre that is developed, with funds going to support the preserve.

An amendment to the Endangered Species Act passed in 1982 allows a certain amount of "incidental taking" of a species in exchange for concessions that conserve the species as a whole. This has allowed conservationists a measure of flexibility in their negotiations with landowners and developers and is the basis for the Coachella Valley agreement. This plan has been described as a model for resolving many of the divisive issues that surround the preservation of endangered wildlife.

Bibliography

Adest, G. A. 1977. "Genetic Relationships in the Genus *Uma* (Iguanidae)." *Copeia* 1977:47-52.

Mayhew, W. W. 1964. "Taxonomic Status of California Populations of the Lizard Genus *Uma*." Herpetologica 20:170-183.

U.S. Fish and Wildlife Service. 1984. "Coachella Valley Fringe-Toed Lizard Recovery Plan." U.S. Fish and Wildlife Service, Portland.

Contact

Regional Office of Endangered Species
U.S. Fish and Wildlife Service
Lloyd 500 Building, Suite 1692
500 N.E. Multnomah Street
Portland, Oregon 97232

Island Night Lizard
Xantusia riversiana

U.S. Navy

Status	Threatened
Listed	August 11, 1977
Family	Xantusiidae (Lizard)
Description . . .	Medium-sized gray to brown, spotted lizard with sooty stripes.
Habitat	Thick low-lying vegetation on rocky soil.
Food	Omnivorous; small invertebrates, plant matter.
Reproduction . .	Ovoviviparous (young born alive).
Threats	Predation, habitat loss, low reproduction.
Region 1	California

Description

While the island night lizard is a medium-sized lizard, it is one of the largest members of its family. Adults range in length from 6.5 to 11 centimeters (2.5 to 4.5 in) from snout to vent (anal opening). Coloration is spotted gray to brown above with sooty stripes.

Its closest relatives on the California mainland are *Xantusia henshawi* and *X. vigilis*. It has been described in the literature by some herpetologists as *Klauberina riversiana*.

Behavior

The island night lizard is omnivorous and feeds on a wide variety of invertebrates and plant matter. In captivity this lizard has been known to eat other small lizards, and it is thought to cannibalize its young. The biology of the island night lizard is characterized by slow growth, a low reproductive rate, late maturation, and a long lifespan. It is ovoviviparous (young are born alive). This lizard does not attain sexual maturity until the third or fourth year, a long time for a lizard of its size. Mating begins in March, and most young are born in September.

This reclusive lizard seeks cover beneath rocks or in burrows as protection from predators and to regulate its body temperature. It limits its activity to times and places of optimal air temperature. This lizard cannot tolerate temperatures above 40 degrees C (90 degrees F) and retreats from extreme ground surface temperatures on hot days, usually to areas with dense ground cover.

Habitat

The preferred habitat for the night lizard appears to be areas of thick, low-lying vegetation growing on rocky soil. Where shafts of sunlight penetrate to the ground through the vegetation, a checkerboard of small areas with differing temperatures is created. Lizards move about to select a proper thermal environment and find food with minimal risk of exposing themselves to predators. Dominant plants in the habitat include thick patches of cacti, matted thickets of box thorn, and thickets of non-native Australian saltbush.

Historic Range

The island night lizard is thought to have diverged from its mainland ancestors during the Miocene epoch. It is endemic to the California Channel Islands, which lie in the Pacific Ocean south of Los Angeles and west of San Diego.

Current Distribution

This lizard is found in isolated portions of three of the Channel Islands—San Clemente, San Nicolas, and Santa Barbara. When this lizard was listed in 1987, it was estimated that the total lizard population on San Clemente Island was 800 to 1,300 individuals per hectare of prime habitat. The San Nicolas Island population was estimated at 14,800. The number of individuals on Santa Barbara Island was estimated to be from 550 to 700 individuals.

Conservation and Recovery

The lizard's low reproductive rate and late maturation magnify the effects of predation, which appears to be extensive. Many different mammals and birds prey on the night lizard, including the island fox, common raven, American kestrel, burrowing owl, San Clemente loggerhead shrike, and probably other raptor birds. Introduced predators are feral cats and possibly rats. Kestrels are thought to be the most successful predator.

Extensive habitat degradation has occurred on the rocky upland areas of the southern half of San Clemente Island. Because its habitat is widely dispersed on the island, and because the lizard occurs in small numbers in many isolated areas, the entire island of San Clemente has been designated as Critical Habitat for the species.

Removing feral cats will be an important step in this species' recovery. An ongoing program to remove feral animals has been highly successful on other Channel Islands, but many goats, pigs, and cats still remain on San Clemente Island.

Iceplant, a plant introduced from the mainland, may have had a negative impact on native vegetation on Santa Barbara Island and should probably be removed. Removal of other exotic vegetation from San Clemente has not been recommended, because it is thought that control of feral herbivores will allow natural vegetation to recover on its own.

Bibliography

Goldberg, S. R., and R. L. Bezy. 1974. "Reproduction in the Island Night Lizard, *Xantusia riversiana*." *Herpetologica* 30:350-360.

U.S. Fish and Wildlife Service. 1984. "Recovery Plan for the Endangered and Threatened Species of the California Channel Islands." U.S. Fish and Wildlife Service, Portland.

Contact

Regional Office of Endangered Species
U.S. Fish and Wildlife Service
Lloyd 500 Building, Suite 1692
500 N.E. Multnomah Street
Portland, Oregon 97232

AMPHIBIANS

Santa Cruz
Long-Toed Salamander
Ambystoma macrodactylum croceum

Ray E. Ashton, Jr.

Status	Endangered
Listed	March 11, 1967
Family	Ambystomidae (Salamander)
Description	Dark, stout-bodied salamander with a broad head, and blunt snout.
Habitat	Shallow, vegetated ponds.
Food	Omnivorous.
Reproduction	200 eggs laid singly.
Threats	Loss of habitat.
Region 1	California

Description

The Santa Cruz long-toed salamander, a subspecies of the long-toed salamander, has a snout-to-vent (anal opening) length of up to 8 centimeters (3.6 in). The body is stout, the head broad, and the snout blunt. Long, slender toes (four on the front and five on the rear feet) appear splayed. Color is a shiny dark brown to black with lighter spotting.

Behavior

To avoid the drying effects of direct sunlight, the Santa Cruz salamander spends most of its life underground in animal burrows or in chambers dug along the root sys-

tems of shrubs and woody plants. Adult salamanders are omnivorous, feeding on insects, eggs, larvae, plant matter, and sometimes smaller salamanders.

When the rainy season begins in September or October, salamanders leave their summer feeding grounds and migrate to habitual breeding ponds. Moving only on wet or foggy nights, individuals gradually make their way to these ponds, where they pair and breed. Mating reaches its peak during January and February when heavy rains have filled the ponds. The female lays her eggs on the submerged stalks of spike rush or similar aquatic plants. Each of about 200 eggs is laid singly and attached to the vegetation. Eggs hatch in about a week, and larvae begin to metamorphose, a process that takes from 90 to 140 days, depending on temperature and weather conditions.

In March, adult salamanders return to the summer feeding grounds, leaving the larvae to develop. When ponds begin to dry out toward the end of summer, juveniles seek shelter underground. During the next rainy season, these juveniles disperse and do not return to the breeding pond until sexually mature in three or four years.

Habitat

Summer habitat is typically moist soils in chapparal or more heavily forested upland areas along the coast. Shade and an abundance of soil humus are prime requirements. Breeding ponds are relatively shallow and support abundant submerged vegetation. They fill with rain water in winter and spring and dry by late summer. Ponds must hold water for at least 90 days, long enough for larvae to develop into juveniles.

Historic Range

The Santa Cruz long-toed salamander was discovered in 1954 at Valencia Lagoon in Santa Cruz County. A relict species, it was widely distributed throughout California over 10,000 years ago, during and immediately after the last glaciation. As the climate became warmer and drier, several populations were isolated in the region between Santa Cruz and Monterey and developed into a distinct subspecies.

Current Distribution

The Santa Cruz salamander is found only in Monterey and Santa Cruz counties in four distinct populations near the towns of Bennett, Ellicott, Seascape, and Valencia.

Conservation and Recovery

Because breeding ponds are used year after year, their destruction or alteration poses a grave threat to this salamander's survival. The breeding pond at Valencia—Valencia Lagoon—was half-filled during highway construction in 1955, and in 1969 the remaining wetlands were drained and an artificial pond built at the site. The salamander survived but did not flourish. In 1988 Fish and Wildlife Service personnel helped state agencies devise a management plan for the Valencia Lagoon. The plan includes a redesign of habitat ponds and provides piped-in water from a nearby well to maintain water levels in dry years.

Breeding ponds at Seascape and Bennett are threatened by agricultural and residential development. Ponds at Ellicott were purchased by the federal government and are now protected as a wildlife refuge. In addition to protecting the ponds, it is important to preserve upland woodlands, where the salamanders feed in the summer. The state of California owns the Santa Cruz Long-Toed Salamander Ecological Reserve and areas at Ellicott Station, which provide some protection for a portion of the salamander's habitat.

Bibliography

U.S. Fish and Wildlife Service. 1976. "Santa Cruz Long-Toed Salamander Recovery Plan." U.S. Fish and Wildlife Service, Portland.

Contact

Regional Office of Endangered Species
U.S. Fish and Wildlife Service
Lloyd 500 Building, Suite 1692
500 N.E. Multnomah Street
Portland, Oregon 97232

Desert Slender Salamander
Batrachoseps aridus

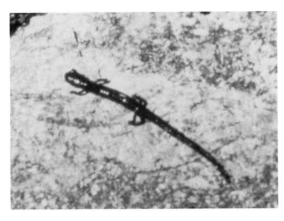

Virginia Maiorana

Status . . . . . . Endangered
Listed . . . . . . June 4, 1973
Family . . . . . Plethodontidae
(Lungless salamander)
Description . . . Reclusive, nocturnal sala-
mander.
Habitat . . . . . . Desert canyons; fractures in
limestone walls.
Food . . . . Insects.
Reproduction . . Eggs laid between November
and January.
Threats . . . . . . Low numbers, limited dis-
tribution.
Region 1 . . . . . California

Description

The desert slender salamander is an anatomically primitive member of its genus, measuring less than 10 centimeters (4 in) from the snout to the tip of the tail. It has four toes on each foot and a large rounded head. It is dark maroon to deep chocolate with numerous tiny silvery blue spots and scattered large patches of gold. The belly is dark maroon, and the tail a contrasting flesh color. This salamander was discovered and described as a new species in 1970.

Behavior

The reclusive desert slender salamander spends most of its life within porous-soil, bedrock fractures, or limestone sheeting, where groundwater seepage provides mois-ture. Occasionally found under loose rocks by day, the salamander is most active at night. When disturbed, it winds itself up into a watchspring-like coil.

This salamander stalks and eats small invertebrates, with flies and ants making up the bulk of its diet. The influence of season, temperature, moisture, food supply, predation, and breeding on the salamander's surface activity and population size are largely unknown. Little is known about the salamander's breeding habits. Females probably lay eggs between November and January soon after the first heavy rains of winter.

Habitat

This salamander lives in an arid region of low and erratic rainfall, high summer temperatures, and strong spring winds.

Seasonal watercourses between steep canyon walls of igneous and metamorphic rock are found above and below the limestone strata inhabited by the salamander. Exposed bedrock, talus, and coarse-grained sand form surface material on surrounding slopes. The sparse plant community, typical of a desert oasis, consists of fen palm, narrow-leaved willow, squaw-waterweed, stream orchid, maidenhair fern, and sugarbush.

Historic Range

Because it was so recently discovered, little information is available on the historical distribution of the desert slender salamander. It has been found only on the lower slopes of the Santa Rosa Mountains in Riverside County in southern California. Because of its isolation from other members of the genus and its primitive characteristics, scientists surmise that the slender desert salamander is a relict species that was more widespread during earlier, wetter geological epochs.

Current Distribution

The desert slender salamander is known from two locations—Hidden Palms Canyon and Guadalupe Canyon. Hidden Palms Canyon is at the box end of Deep Canyon, a large gorge that drains the surrounding slopes of the Santa Rosa Mountains. The inhabited area is less than an acre and supports fewer than 500 individuals. The Guadalupe Canyon population appears much smaller in range and numbers, consisting of perhaps 100 individuals, but this site has not been closely studied.

Conservation and Recovery

The major threat to the survival of this salamander is its extremely restricted dis-

tribution. This makes the species particularly vulnerable to any natural catastrophe. For example, unusually severe rainfall and flooding associated with a tropical storm in 1976 caused the erosion and collapse of a limestone wall that made up as much as one-third of the salamander's habitat at Hidden Palms. At the other extreme, an extended drought could dry up groundwater seepage, rendering the species extinct. Human activity in the area is slight.

Land surrounding both populations, comprising about 55 hectares (138 acres), was acquired by the state of California in 1973. The following year, this tract was established as the Hidden Palms Ecological Reserve, managed by the California Fish and Game Commission. After the flooding of 1976, the rock wall of the Hidden Palms habitat was reinforced to prevent any further collapse. Boulder barricades were constructed to restrict unauthorized access to both canyons. The management plan for the reserve will consider other steps as needed to stabilize the habitat or to discourage human disturbance.

Bibliography

Brame, A. H. 1970. "A New Species of *Batrachoseps* (Slender Salamander) from the Desert of Southern California." *Los Angeles County Museum Contributions to Science* No. 200.

U.S. Fish and Wildlife Service. 1982. "Desert Slender Salamander Recovery Plan." U.S. Fish and Wildlife Service, Portland.

Contact

Regional Office of Endangered Species
U.S. Fish and Wildlife Service
Lloyd 500 Building, Suite 1692
500 N.E. Multnomah Street
Portland, Oregon 97232

Wyoming Toad
Bufo hemiophrys baxteri

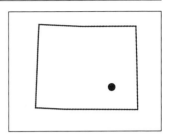

LuRay Parker/Wyoming Fish and Game Department

Status	. . . . . . Endangered
Listed	. . . . . . January 17, 1984
Family	. . . . . . Bufonidae (Toad)
Description	. . . Small, crested toad.
Habitat	. . . . . . Marshy areas adjacent to the Laramie River in Wyoming.
Food	. . . . Insects and larvae.
Reproduction	. . Lays egg masses in standing pools.
Threats	. . . . . . Herbicides, predation, irrigation practices.
Region 6	. . . . . Wyoming

Description

The Wyoming toad, the only toad in the Laramie Basin, is a small bufonid about 5 centimeters (2 in) long with crests on the head that form a humped ridge. Light brown with dark blotches, the body is covered with many warts.

The Canadian toad (*Bufo hemiophrys hemiophrys*), a closely related species, occurs in Manitoba, Alberta, Saskatchewan, Minnesota, Montana, and the Dakotas. Some scientists argue that the Wyoming toad is a full species, rather than a subspecies. Further research is needed to determine this toad's precise taxonomic classification.

Behavior

The tadpole of the Wyoming toad feeds primarily on plant matter, but the full-grown toad preys on insects, larvae, and any small organism that moves. Because of poor eyesight, the toad tends to miss motionless prey. The female discharges eggs in strips of jelly in standing pools. The male clings to her back and fertilizes the eggs as they reach the water. Tadpoles hatch between three and 20 days later, depending on the water temperature, and begin to metamorphose. The toad develops hind limbs first, then front limbs; as the lungs develop, its tail gets shorter and gradually disappears.

Habitat

This species is found in wetlands adjacent to the Laramie River in the Laramie Basin. It is strongly aquatic, spending most of its time in and around water.

Historic Range

The Wyoming toad was once common in the Laramie River basin in southeastern Wyoming and probably inhabited similar marshy habitats in other parts of the state. Fossils found throughout the region suggest that the species was abundant thousands of years ago. Researchers from the University of Wyoming have monitored breeding sites annually since 1945 and became alarmed when their 1978 and 1979 surveys found very few toads.

Current Distribution

In 1980 the University of Wyoming and the Fish and Wildlife Service (FWS) conducted an extensive survey of the Laramie Basin. A single population of the toad was located on private land in Albany County, where a number of males were heard calling, but no females, tadpoles, or eggs were found. The 16-hectare (40-acre) site was thought to support about 25 individuals. A survey of this site in 1983 revealed only two toads, and in the following year, none.

In 1987, a new population was discovered on private land in Albany County, which considerably brightens the Wyoming toad's chances for survival. The new site—about 16 kilometers (10 mi) west of Laramie—is home to about 200 toads, which scientists consider a fairly good breeding population.

Conservation and Recovery

The reasons for the toad's basin-wide disappearance are not understood, but the leopard frog (*Rana pipiens*), once fairly common, has also disappeared from the Laramie Basin. Scientists believe that the decline of both toads may be linked with herbicide application. Herbicides have been used by the Wyoming Department of Agriculture for weed control in roadside ponds and along field edges typically used by the Wyoming toad. Regional aerial application of Baytex (Fenthion) with diesel fuel began in 1975 to kill mosquitoes. The combination of Baytex and diesel fuel is highly toxic to toads and frogs.

Predation may also be a factor in the sudden decline of the Wyoming toad. The California gull has become more numerous in recent years. Local ranchers report that fields are sometimes "white with gulls" in early spring when toads are breeding. Other predators, such as raccoons, foxes, and skunks have all increased in number.

Because the only known population is on private land, the FWS recommended in 1988 that eggs be transplanted to a protected site to establish a new breeding colony. Eggs will most likely be transplanted to the Hutton Lake National Wildlife Refuge over the next few years. An agreement to protect the breeding population is currently being negotiated with the landowners.

Bibliography

Baxter, G. T., and M. Stone. 1980. "Amphibians and Reptiles of Wyoming." Wyoming Game and Fish Department Bulletin, Laramie.

Porter, K. P. 1968. "Evolutionary Status of a Relict Population of *Bufo hemiophrys* Cope." Evolution 22:583-594.

Contact

Regional Office of Endangered Species
U.S. Fish and Wildlife Service
P.O. Box 25486
Denver Federal Center
Denver, Colorado 80225

Houston Toad
Bufo houstonensis

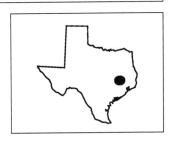

C. Allan Morgan

Status	Endangered
Listed	October 13, 1970
Family	Bufonidae (Toad)
Description . . .	Brown, dark-spotted toad with a distinctive call.
Habitat	Permanent or seasonal wetlands.
Food	Insects.
Reproduction . .	Egg masses of between 500 and 6,000 eggs.
Threats	Loss of wetlands, urbanization.
Region 2	Texas

Description

The Houston toad is brown (occasionally reddish) with dark brown or black spots. Its back is covered with single or multiple fused warts. Females reach up to 8 centimeters (3.2 in) in length; males average slightly smaller. The Houston toad is similar to the dwarf American toad (*Bufo americanus charlesmithi*) but displays larger crests behind the eye sockets. The toad's mating call is described as similar to the tinkling of a small bell.

Behavior

The Houston toad uses rain pools, flooded fields, and natural or man-made ponds for breeding, which occurs at sporadic intervals.

Females reach sexual maturity at about two years of age. Breeding begins in spring when the air temperature rises above 14 degrees C (57 degrees F). Masses of between 500 and 6,000 eggs are laid between mid-February and late June. For tadpoles to develop, pools must persist for at least 60 days. After breeding, the toad seeks refuge in leaf litter, under logs, or in burrows.

Habitat

Houston toads are found in seasonal or permanent ponds but are restricted to sandy loams that are suitable for burrowing. Surrounding vegetation varies from mixed deciduous forest to open coastal prairie grasslands. When spring rains are below normal, ponds dry up prematurely, killing tadpoles before they can metamorphose.

Historic Range

Historically, the Houston toad ranged across the central coastal region of Texas. Population sites have been documented from Austin, Bastrop, Burleson, Colorado, Fort Bend, Harris, and Liberty counties.

Current Distribution

The Houston toad is currently thought to survive near Austin in Bastrop County wetlands north of the Colorado River, in Burleson County south of Bryan (around Lake Woodrow), and in Harris County south of Hobby Airport. Several small, experimental populations were recently established in Colorado County.

The largest population is found in Bastrop County on state lands within Bastrop and Buescher state parks and an adjacent nature preserve. This population has increased in recent years and may number as many as 1,500 individuals. Low numbers of toads (probably under 50) still exist in Burleson County but often fail to breed because of insufficient water. The Houston toad has not been seen in Harris County since 1976 but may survive there. The toad's sporadic breeding pattern and secretive nature make it difficult to find new populations or even to relocate previously identified ones.

Conservation and Recovery

Drought in the 1950s sharply curtailed Houston toad numbers, and the subsequent expansion of the Austin and Houston metropolitan areas has permanently reduced the toad's habitat. Wetlands have been replaced with residential suburbs and related developments. In the mid-1960s, large tracts of forest in Bastrop County along the Colorado River were cleared for residential development and for recreational sites. Road construction and the laying of sewage lines significantly altered drainage patterns in the region, drying out many seasonal ponds.

The University of Texas Environmental Science Park (Buescher Division) was established in 1971, comprising 291 hectares (720 acres) adjacent to Buescher State Park in Bastrop County. Much of this area is now maintained as a nature preserve and is managed to enhance the habitat needs of the Houston toad. In 1979, 570 hectares (1,400 acres) were added to this preserve, including land previously designated as Critical Habitat for the toad.

In the early 1980s, biologists implemented a propagation program at the Houston Zoo and subsequently released captive-bred toads at the Bastrop County Preserve and at the Attwater Prairie Chicken National Wildlife Refuge in Colorado County. Egg masses were also moved from Bastrop County to ponds in Colorado County in an attempt to expand the toad's distribution.

Bibliography

Hillis, D. M., et al. 1984. "Reproductive Ecology and Hybridization of the Endangered Houston Toad." Journal of Herpetology 18:56-72.

U.S. Fish and Wildlife Service. 1984. "Houston Toad Recovery Plan." U.S. Fish and Wildlife Service, Albuquerque.

Contact

Regional Office of Endangered Species
U.S. Fish and Wildlife Service
P.O. Box 1306
Albuquerque, New Mexico 87103

Golden Coqui
Eleutherodactylus jasperi

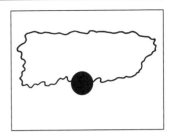

George Drewry

Status	Threatened
Listed	November 11, 1977
Family	Leptodactylidae (Frog)
Description	Gold-colored frog with a rounded snout.
Habitat	Mountaintops in dense bromeliad thickets.
Food	Insects.
Reproduction	Live-bearer.
Threats	Loss of habitat, limited distribution.
Region 4	Puerto Rico

Description

The golden coqui is a small frog, measuring up to 2.2 centimeters (1 in) from snout to vent (anal opening). Its small eyes protrude slightly from the sockets. The snout is rounded, rather than pointed as with its closest relatives. Coloration is a striking olive-gold or bright yellow-gold. The genus name—*Eleutherodactylus*—means "free-fingered," which describes an absence of webbing between the toes.

Behavior

The golden coqui lives in the water-filled leaf axils of large bromeliad plants. It hops out onto the leaves at night but retreats quickly to the shelter of the axils if disturbed. This is the only frog species in the New World family Leptodactylidae known to give birth to live young (ovoviviparous). Females produce two clutches of three to five young per year. The gestation period lasts about one month, during which time the froglets metamorphose internally. The coqui feeds on insects and is most active between midnight and dawn, when its vocalizations are most persistent.

Habitat

The golden coqui has been found in dense thickets of bromeliads, such as *Vriesia, Hohenbergia,* and *Guzmania*. These thickets grow on mountaintops between 700 and 850 meters (2,300 to 2,800 ft) elevation. These mountain tops receive heavy dew from a prevailing updraft, which is captured by the large leaves of the plants. Water droplets collect on the leaves and pool in the leaf axils, providing a secure, moist habitat for the golden coqui.

Historic Range

The golden coqui is endemic to Puerto Rico.

Current Distribution

The golden coqui is found in the mountainous region south of the city of Cayey and north of the village of Coqui on the southern coast of Puerto Rico. Populations are restricted to the summits of three mountains: Cerra Avispa, Monte el Gato, and Sierra de Cayey. The total area occupied by these three populations is not more than 24 hectares (10 acres). Field surveys conducted in 1973 and 1974 projected population figures as fewer than 10 individuals on Cerra Avispa, 500 to 1,000 on Monte El Gato, and 1,000 to 2,000 on Sierra de Cayey. Since these surveys, however, a large stand of bromeliad habitat was burned on Sierra de Cayey, causing undetermined coqui mortality.

Conservation and Recovery

Always relatively rare, the golden coqui has declined because of its total dependence upon bromeliads. The number and extent of bromeliad thickets has decreased steadily in Puerto Rico, primarily because the land has been cleared for agriculture. Surviving coqui populations are isolated from one another and unable to interbreed, weakening genetic diversity of the species. The golden coqui's low reproductive rate limits its ability to expand its range, even when sufficient habitat is present.

Because little research has been conducted, biologists working to recover the coqui are hampered by a lack of biological and ecological data. The Fish and Wildlife Service (FWS) Recovery Plan emphasizes the need for systematic study of the species. In the meantime, the population size will be monitored annually, and efforts are being made to prevent further modification of the mountaintops. Because most of this land is in private hands, FWS personnel are attempting to negotiate conservation agreements with landowners. Agreements will be supplemented by acquisition of essential habitat areas, through purchase or by land exchanges, or by purchase of easements.

The goal of the Recovery Plan is to establish three stable or expanding golden coqui populations, each of at least 1,000 individuals.

Bibliography

Drewry, G. E., and K. L. Jones. 1976. "A New Ovoviviparous Frog (*Eleutherodactylus jasperi*) from Puerto Rico." *Journal of Herpetology* 10:161-105.

Rivero, J. A. 1978. *The Amphibians and Reptiles of Puerto Rico*. Editorial Universitaria, University of Puerto Rico, San Juan.

U.S. Fish and Wildlife Service. 1984. "Golden Coqui Recovery Plan." U.S. Fish and Wildlife Service, Atlanta.

Wake, M. H. 1978. "The Reproductive Biology of *Eleutherodactylus jasperi* with Comments on the Evolution of Live-Bearing Systems." *Journal of Herpetology* 12:121-133.

Contact

Regional Office of Endangered Species
U.S. Fish and Wildlife Service
Richard B. Russell Federal Building
75 Spring Street, S.W.
Atlanta, Georgia 30303

Caribbean Field Office
U.S. Fish and Wildlife Service
P.O. Box 491
Boqueron, Puerto Rico 00622

San Marcos Salamander
Eurycea nana

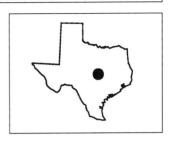

Robert and Linda Mitchell

Status	Threatened
Listed	July 14, 1980
Family	Plethodontidae (Salamander)
Description	Salamander with a long, narrow body; light brown above with a row of pale flecks.
Habitat	Lakes and rivers.
Food	Carnivorous.
Reproduction	Egg masses laid in standing pools.
Threats	Groundwater pumping.
Region 2	Texas

Description

The slender-bodied San Marcos salamander is about 6 centimeters (2.4 in) long and displays a prominent gill fringe behind the head. It is light brown above with a row of pale flecks on either side of the midline and yellowish white below. The large eyes have a dark ring around the lens. Limbs are short and slender with four toes on the forefeet and five on the hind feet. At first glance, it is similar to a lizard but lacks scales and claws. The specific name *nana* is from the Greek *nanos*, meaning "dwarf." This voiceless salamander is also earless.

Behavior

Salamanders lay jelly-covered eggs from which tiny fishlike larvae emerge and develop in the manner of tadpoles. The San Marcos salamander breeds and lays eggs in standing pools amid thick mats of aquatic vegetation. Eggs hatch in about 24 days. This species is carnivorous and feeds on amphipods, midge fly larvae, and aquatic snails. It remains stationary until prey pass closely and then abruptly snaps its head, taking the prey.

Habitat

The San Marcos salamander is found in shallow alkaline springs carved out of limestone with sand and gravel substrates. Pools and streambeds are often punctuated with large limestone boulders. Aquatic vegetation is profuse, and the pool surfaces are covered with moss (*Leptodictyium riparium*) and thick mats of coarse, blue-green algae.

Historic Range

This species appears to be endemic to the sources and upper portions of the San Marcos River in Hays County of Texas.

Current Distribution

The limited range of the San Marcos salamander comprises the San Marcos Springs, Spring Lake, and a few hundred feet of the San Marcos River. A second, smaller population was discovered in the Comal River, slightly to the west in Comal County. The total population was estimated between 17,000 and 21,000 individuals in 1984.

Conservation and Recovery

Although the population appears relatively stable for the moment, the salamander is threatened by potential degradation or modification of its very limited habitat. This region, which is halfway between San Antonio and Austin, has experienced an upsurge in residential and agricultural development. The rising demand for water for human use and irrigation may well cause the spring sources to dry up in a very few years. The Endangered Texas wild-rice (*Zizania texana*), found further downstream near the town of San Marcos, has suffered from generally lower water levels in recent years.

The owner of Spring Lake has taken care to safeguard the spring sources and has cooperated closely with biologists to ensure that wildlife populations are protected. The key to preserving the San Marcos salamander is controlling the amount of water that is pumped out of the ground—a divisive issue in semi-arid south-central Texas. Critical Habitat was designated for the salamander to include its entire known range in Hays County.

Bibliography

Bishop, S. C. 1943. *Handbook of Salamanders.* Comstock Publishing, Ithaca, New York.

Tupa, D. D., and W. K. Davis. 1976. "Population Dynamics of the San Marcos Salamander, *Eurycea Nana* Bishop." *Texas Journal of Science* 32:179-195.

U.S. Fish and Wildlife Service. 1984. "San Marcos River Recovery Plan." U.S. Fish and Wildlife Service, Albuquerque.

U.S. Fish and Wildlife Service. 1987. "Endangered and Threatened Species of Texas and Oklahoma (with 1988 Addendum)." U.S. Fish and Wildlife Service, Albuquerque.

Contact

Regional Office of Endangered Species
U.S. Fish and Wildlife Service
P.O. Box 1306
Albuquerque, New Mexico 87103

Puerto Rican Crested Toad
Peltophryne lemur

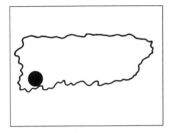

David M. Dennis

Status	. . . . . . Threatened
Listed	. . . . . . August 4, 1987
Family	. . . . . Bufonidae (Toad)
Description	. . . Medium-sized toad; yellow-olive to dark brown in color; distinctive long, upturned snout.
Habitat	. . . . . . Coastal plain on exposed limestone or porous soil.
Food	. . . . Insects.
Reproduction	. . Egg masses laid in fresh-water ponds.
Threats	. . . . . . Loss of habitat.
Region 4	. . . . . Puerto Rico

Description

The Puerto Rican crested toad ranges from 6.4 to 12 centimeters (2.5 to 4.5 in) in length from snout to vent (anal opening). Females are usually much larger than males. Color is yellowish olive to blackish brown, with prominent suborbital crests and a distinctive long, upturned snout. Females have more prominent crests.

Behavior

Adult Puerto Rican crested toads disperse widely when not breeding. They burrow extensively and feed on a wide variety of insects. Breeding, which is concentrated within a very short period, may be triggered by temperature and rainfall and occurs irregularly. This causes a large natural fluctuation in the size of the population. Females display a high fidelity to breeding sites that offer the right combination of elevation, topography, and water levels. Toadlets metamorphose and disperse within a few weeks.

Habitat

The Puerto Rican crested toad is found along the coastal plain below an elevation of 200 meters (660 ft). Exposed limestone outcroppings with many fissures and cavities or porous, well-drained soils support the largest populations. Seasonal ponds are required for breeding.

Historic Range

The toad is endemic to two islands on the Puerto Rican shelf—Puerto Rico and the is-

land of Virgin Gorda in the British Virgin
Islands. The known historic distribution on
Virgin Gorda was very limited, and as the
toad has not been observed there for at least
two decades, it is presumed to have disappeared from this island. Until 1966 it was
thought to be extinct in Puerto Rico, as well.
Many of its breeding sites were eliminated on
the north and south coasts of Puerto Rico.

Current Distribution

In 1975 a viable breeding population was
discovered in the Guánica Commonwealth
Forest on the southern coast. A 1984 census
estimated that the site supported about 1,000
toads. After this discovery, a captive breeding program was begun, which resulted in
the release of 850 toadlets in Cambalache
Commonwealth Forest on the northern coast.
It is still too early to determine how successful this reintroduction effort will be.

Conservation and Recovery

Lowland coastal wetlands of Puerto Rico
have been subject to residential development, conversion to cropland, and drainage
for mosquito control, all of which limit available habitat for this species. A range of
proposed developments, including road improvements and construction of a park
visitor center and a resort, threaten to over-
whelm the only known breeding area in the
Guánica Commonwealth Forest. Federal and
commonwealth agencies are working to find
alternatives to these developments to avoid
further destruction of habitat.

Recovery will hinge upon the success of the
ongoing captive breeding and reintroduction
program. Management plans for the commonwealth forests are being revised to consider the habitat requirements of the toad,
and additional tracts of protected habitat will

be sought. Fish and Wildlife Service personnel are considering reintroduction to Virgin
Gorda and neighboring islands.

Bibliography

Garcia Diaz, J. 1967. "Rediscovery of *Bufo lemur*
Cope and Additional Records of Reptiles
From Puerto Rico." *Stahlia* 10:1- 6.

Moreno, J. A. 1985. "Notes on *Peltophryne
lemur.*" Report. U.S. Fish and Wildlife Service,
Boqueron, Puerto Rico.

Pregill, G. 1981. "Cranial Morphology and the
Evolution of West Indian Toads: Resurrection
of the Genus *Peltophryne* Fitzinger." *Copeia*
1981:273-285.

Rivero, J. A., *et al.* 1980. "Sobre el *Bufo lemur*
Cope (Amphibia, Bufonidae)." *Caribbean
Journal of Science* 15:33-40.

Contact

Regional Office of Endangered Species
U.S. Fish and Wildlife Service
Richard B. Russell Federal Building
75 Spring Street, S.W.
Atlanta, Georgia 30303

U.S. Fish and Wildlife Service
Caribbean Field Office
P.O. Box 491
Boqueron, Puerto Rico 00622

Red Hills Salamander

Phaeognathus hubrichti

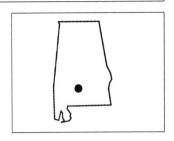

C. Kenneth Dodd, Jr.

Status	. . . . . . Threatened
Listed	. . . . . December 3, 1976
Family	. . . . . Plethodontidae (Salamander)
Description	. . . Salamander with short limbs and elongated body.
Habitat	. . . . . . Ravine slopes in mature hardwood forests.
Food	. . . . Insects.
Reproduction	. . Clutch size of 4 to 9 eggs.
Threats	. . . . . Highly restricted habitat, intensive logging.
Region 4	. . . . . Alabama

Description

A relatively large member of its family, the Red Hills salamander is 22.5 centimeters (9 in) long when fully grown. It has an elongated body, stubby limbs, and a prehensile tail. Coloration is a uniform dark gray to dark brown. It has a groove from nose to lip and lacks lungs. Adults lack gills.

Behavior

This highly specialized salamander is extremely sensitive to any alteration of its habitat. It burrows into the hillsides where soils are suitable. Based on observations of captive individuals, clutch size is probably four to nine eggs, which are deposited in cavities inside burrows. The overall reproductive rate of the species is low. It feeds almost exclusively on insects.

Habitat

Prime habitat for the Red Hills salamander is on moderately steep, forested ravines and bluffs with a northern exposure. The habitat is characterized by mature hardwoods in a loamy, friable topsoil. A layer of siltstone underlies many population sites, and salamander burrows almost invariably extend into cavities scooped out of this soft rock. Siltstone efficiently retains moisture, which is necessary for the salamander's survival. Individuals have been found nesting near groundwater seepages.

Historic Range

This species is endemic to the Red Hills region of the Gulf coastal plain of southern Alabama.

Current Distribution

The Red Hills salamander is restricted to a narrow band of the Red Hills, extending from the Alabama River in northern Monroe County, across Conecuh, Butler, and Covington counties, to the Conecuh River in southern Crenshaw County, a distance of about 115 kilometers (69 mi). Within this narrow band, the amount of suitable habitat has been estimated at 22,200 hectares (55,000 acres).

Conservation and Recovery

The most important limiting factors for this species are its specific habitat requirements and its low rate of reproduction. In optimal habitat, the salamander is found in uniform densities, suggesting that such factors as predation, food supply, insecticide contamination, or competition are not important threats.

Logging operations in the region have been detrimental to the species. A large tract of habitat—nearly 1,500 hectares (3,700 acres)—was clear-cut and mechanically bedded in 1976. Much of the tract was then planted with pine, creating conditions that do not support the salamander. It is estimated that another 1,250 hectares (3,090 acres) have been rendered marginally habitable by intensive select-cutting. On the other hand, long-rotation, limited select-cutting does not appear to harm the salamander.

Paper companies own up to 44 percent of the remaining habitat and are currently using a variety of timber management techniques. The International Paper Company, which owned about 13 percent of the habitat in 1983, publicly announced that it would adjust its management practices to benefit the salamander. Other paper companies have avoided intensive cutting on the steep slopes and bluffs that were likely to support the salamander.

The recommended recovery goal is to acquire or otherwise protect a refuge of at least 16,000 hectares (40,000 acres) within the current range. In 1983, only about 60 hectares (148 acre) were publicly owned.

Bibliography

Brandon, R. A. 1965. "Morphological Variation and Ecology of the Salamander *Phaeognathus hubrichti.*" *Copeia* 1965:67-71.

Highton, R. 1961. "A New Genus of Lungless Salamander from the Coastal Plain of Alabama." *Copeia* 1961:65-68.

Jordan, J. R., Jr. 1975. "The Status of the Red Hills Salamander." *Journal of Herpetology* 9:211-215.

U.S. Fish and Wildlife Service. 1983. "Red Hills Salamander Recovery Plan." U.S. Fish and Wildlife Service, Atlanta.

Contact

Regional Office of Endangered Species
U.S. Fish and Wildlife Service
Richard B. Russell Federal Building
75 Spring Street, S.W.
Atlanta, Georgia 30303

Texas Blind Salamander

Typhlomolge rathbuni

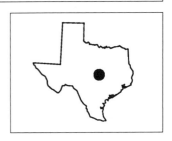

Robert and Linda Mitchell

Status	Endangered
Listed	March 11, 1967
Family	Plethodontidae (Salamander)
Description	Sightless, cave-dwelling amphibian; white or pinkish with a blood-red gill fringe.
Habitat	Underground water system.
Food	Insects, other invertebrates.
Reproduction	Unknown.
Threats	Ground water pumping, pollution.
Region 2	Texas

Description

The Texas blind salamander is a sightless, cave-dwelling salamander that reaches a mature length of about 13 centimeters (5 in). This slender, frail-legged amphibian is white or pinkish with a fringe of blood-red, external gills. The head and snout are flattened. Two small black eyespots mark the location of vestigial eyes.

Behavior

This totally aquatic species feeds on insects and other small invertebrate. Little else of its natural history is known.

Habitat

The Texas blind salamander lives in the underground water system of the limestone caverns of the Edwards Plateau. It spends its life in complete darkness. It is sensitive to changes of water quality and thus susceptible to groundwater pollutants.

Historic Range

This species is endemic to the caverns of the Edwards Plateau in Hays County, Texas.

Current Distribution

Biologists know of only one population of the Texas blind salamander, which occurs in the San Marcos Pool of the Edwards Fault Zone aquifer. The current population is apparently stable, although of limited numbers.

Conservation and Recovery

The Edwards Plateau is located in the vicinity of San Marcos, halfway between Austin and San Antonio. For many years, water has been pumped from the aquifer to supply irrigation ponds and ditches. More recently, growth of the city of San Marcos and suburban development associated with Austin and San Antonio have placed heavier demands on the aquifer. Water levels have dropped appreciably and will probably continue to fall in the foreseeable future. Increasing development of the region threatens to pollute groundwater with sediments and sewage run-off.

Survival of this salamander and other endemic cave-dwelling creatures depends upon the stability and continued purity of the Edwards aquifer. Local, state, and federal agencies are working to forge a compromise on the regulation of groundwater pumping. Any agreement is certain to be controversial, since economic growth in the region is tied directly to access to water.

Bibliography

Longley, G. 1978. "Status of the Texas Blind Salamander." Report No.2. U.S. Fish and Wildlife Service, Albuquerque.

U.S. Fish and Wildlife Service. 1987. "Endangered and Threatened Species of Texas and Oklahoma (with 1988 Addendum)." U.S. Fish and Wildlife Service, Albuquerque.

Contact

Regional Office of Endangered Species
U.S. Fish and Wildlife Service
P.O. Box 1306
Albuquerque, New Mexico 87103

FISH

Shortnose Sturgeon
Acipenser brevirostrum

Jim Couch

Status	Endangered
Listed	March 11, 1967
Family	Acipenseridae (Sturgeon)
Description	Sturgeon with short snout growing to about 90 centimeters (3 ft).
Habitat	Estuaries, freshwater rivers and streams.
Food	Crustaceans, insects, mollusks, plant matter, detritus.
Reproduction	Spawns between February and May.
Threats	River damming, pollution.
Region 4	Georgia, North Carolina, South Carolina
Region 5	Maine, New Jersey, New York
Canada	New Brunswick

Description

The shortnose sturgeon is often confused with a young Atlantic sturgeon (*Acipenser oxyrhynchus*), but it differs by having a wider mouth and shorter snout. Its underhanging mouth is preceded by four barbels, which function as sensory organs similar to the "whiskers" of a catfish. The yellowish brown body of the shortnose sturgeon is contrasted by its dark head and back. The undersurface is light yellow or white. The skeleton is largely cartilaginous, and scales are bony plates. Its maximum size is about 90 centimeters (3 ft), which is considerably smaller than a full-grown Atlantic sturgeon.

Behavior

Primarily nocturnal, the shortnose sturgeon feeds on crustaceans, insects, and small mollusks. It also ingests quantities of sediment, plant matter, and detritus. It is extremely long-lived, particularly in northern waters, sometimes reaching 50 years old.

It is a bay or estuary fish for most of its life but returns to freshwater streams and rivers to spawn. Very few individuals have ever been caught in the open ocean. Peak spawning occurs between February and May but may begin as early as January in the south. Females probably spawn only once every three years, depositing as many as 200,000 eggs, most of which do not survive. Juveniles mature in three to six years.

Habitat

The shortnose sturgeon prefers deep pools with soft substrates and vegetated bottoms and moves from shallow to deeper water in winter. It spawns in freshwater wetlands or stream areas with fast flow and a gravel-cobble bottom.

Historic Range

This shortnose sturgeon is found along the Atlantic coast from the Saint John River in Canada to the Indian River, Florida. It was common in the Hudson, Delaware, Potomac, Connecticut, and St. Johns rivers.

Current Distribution

The largest concentrations of the shortnose sturgeon are found in the Saint John River (New Brunswick), Kennebec River (Maine), Hudson River (New York), Delaware River (New Jersey), Winyah Bay, Pee Dee River, and Lake Marion (South Carolina), and the Altamaha River (Georgia). A population was recently discovered in the Cape Fear drainage in North Carolina. No population estimates are available.

Conservation and Recovery

In this century both the range and population size of the shortnose sturgeon have decreased. Part of this decline was caused by the countless dams that have been built along the Atlantic Coast, which cut off the sturgeon from many of its upriver spawning grounds. Water pollution has also been a significant factor in the decline of this species in the major rivers and estuaries. Late maturation,

slow growth, and periodic spawning make it difficult for the sturgeon to replenish its numbers.

Although it is occasionally taken by sport fishermen who do not recognize it as distinct from the Atlantic sturgeon, the shortnose sturgeon is thought to be adequately protected by existing game fish regulations. It is unlawful under provisions of the Endangered Species Act to possess (alive or dead) or harass a shortnose sturgeon. Recovery will first require further research to determine the extent of the spawning areas and to expand basic knowledge of the sturgeon's biology.

Bibliography

Dadswell, M. J., *et al.* 1984. "Synopsis of Biological Data on Shortnose Sturgeon, *Acipenser brevirostrum*." Report NMFS 14, National Marine Fisheries Service, Washington, D. C.

Ross, S. W., *et al.* 1988. *Endangered, Threatened, and Rare Fauna of North Carolina: A Re-evaluation of the Marine and Estuarine Fishes.* Occasional Papers of the North Carolina Biological Survey, Raleigh.

Vladykov, V. D., and J. R. Greeley. 1963. "Order Acipenseroidei in Fishes of the Western North Atlantic." *Memoir Sears Foundation for Marine Research* 1(3), 1963:24-60.

Contact

Regional Office of Endangered Species
U.S. Fish and Wildlife Service
One Gateway Center, Suite 700
Newton Corner, Massachusetts 02158

Office of Public Affairs
National Marine Fisheries Service
Department of Commerce
Washington, D.C. 20235

Ozark Cavefish
Amblyopsis rosae

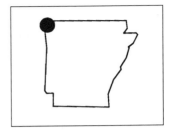

Russell Norton

Status	. . . . .	Threatened
Listed	. . . . .	November 1, 1984
Family	. . . . .	Amblyopsidae (Cavefish)
Description	. . .	Blind, albino cavefish.
Habitat	. . . . .	Cave streams.
Food	. . . . .	Plankton, small invertebrates.
Reproduction	. .	Undescribed.
Threats	. . . . .	Groundwater pollution.
Region 2	. . . .	Oklahoma
Region 3	. . . .	Missouri
Region 4	. . . .	Arkansas

Description

The Ozark cavefish is a true troglobitic (cave-dwelling) fish that grows to 5 centimeters (2 in). It has an elongate, flattened head, a body nearly devoid of pigment (albino), and a projecting lower jaw. The dorsal and anal fins are located far back on the body, the caudal fin is rounded, and the pelvic fins are absent. The Ozark cavefish has only vestigial eyes. It uses sensory papillae, which occur in two or three rows on its tail fin, to 'feel' its way through its environment.

The only other species in the genus *Amblyopsis* is the Northern cavefish (*Amblyopsis spelea*), found in southern Indiana and west central Kentucky.

Behavior

This species is rarely seen and little is known of its life history.

Habitat

The Ozark cavefish inhabits the caves that honeycomb the highly soluble Boone and Burlington limestone formations of the Ozark Mountains. Food supply in these stable, yet fragile, cave habitats is limited in diversity and quantity. Larger populations of the Ozark cavefish occur in caves used by the endangered gray bat (*Myotis grisescens*), where bat guano is the primary energy source.

Historic Range

The Ozark cavefish is the only cavefish within the Springfield Plateau of southwest Missouri, northwest Arkansas, and northeast Oklahoma. Early studies of the southern cavefish (*Typhlichthys subterraneus*) often confused it with the Ozark cavefish, and it is difficult to sort out actual sightings. Historic records place the Ozark cavefish in at least nine counties and possibly in an additional five. There are reports of the cavefish occurring in 52 caves; only 24 historic localities are confirmed, however.

Current Distribution

Recent surveys have confirmed cavefish populations in 14 caves in six counties in Arkansas, Missouri, and Oklahoma. Although these are spread across much of the historic range, the frequency of cavefish sightings is decreasing. In only eight of the 14 known populations could one expect to see any cavefish on a given visit, and in only two populations could one expect to see more than five cavefish.

At six historic sites in Greene County, Missouri, cavefish are no longer observed, and only two cavefish of the lone surviving population have been observed in the last 15 years. Nearly two-thirds of the entire population of Ozark cavefish is thought to inhabit a single Arkansas cave—Cave Springs Cave (Benton County).

Conservation and Recovery

The decline of the Ozark cavefish may be due to degradation of subsurface or groundwater. Northwest Arkansas is an area of heavy agricultural use where animal wastes from poultry and swine seep into the groundwater. Sinkholes in the soluble limestone bedrock increase the possibility of direct contamination of the groundwater. Researchers from the Arkansas Department of Pollution Control and Ecology have detected nitrate and ammonia levels in regional wells that are probably toxic to the cavefish. Industrial and residential development of Greene County, Missouri, have also caused water contamination. Toxic levels of nickel

from urban wastes have been found in at least one cave system.

A low reproduction rate and a confined habitat make the Ozark cavefish vulnerable to even casual collecting. There are several documented instances of scientific collectors taking large numbers of Ozark cavefish. A scientific collection in the 1930s from one Arkansas cave may be responsible for reducing that population to a very low level. Pet stores often display blind cavefish (possibly Ozarks) for sale to aquarists. Another threat to the cavefish is disturbance caused by groups of amateur spelunkers. Protection of cavefish requires that human disturbance be kept to a minimum.

Arkansas' Cave Springs Cave is now owned by the state, providing some protection for the largest known cavefish population. Missouri recently purchased Turnback Creek Cave which, although it contains only a small Ozark cavefish population, has considerable cavefish habitat and may support a reintroduction effort.

Bibliography

Poulson, T. L. 1963. "Cave Adaptation in Amblyopsid Fishes."*American Midland Naturalist* 70(2):257-290.

Willis, L. D. and A. V. Brown. 1985. "Distribution and Habitat Requirements of the Ozark Cavefish, *Amblyopsis rosae*." *American Midland Naturalist* 114(2):311-317.

U.S. Fish and Wildlife Service. 1980. "Recovery Plan for the Ozark Cavefish, *Amblyopsis rosae*." U.S. Fish and Wildlife Service. Atlanta.

Contact

Regional Office of Endangered Species
U.S. Fish and Wildlife Service
Richard B. Russell Federal Building
75 Spring Street, S.W.
Atlanta, Georgia 30303

Modoc Sucker

Catostomus microps

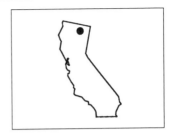

P. Moyle

Status	. . . . . . Endangered
Listed	. . . . . . June 11, 1985
Family	. . . . . Catostomidae (Sucker)
Description	. . . Dwarf, olive-gray sucker.
Habitat	. . . . . . Small streams, shallow pools with cover.
Food	. . . . Aquatic invertebrates, algae, detritus.
Reproduction	. . Spawns in spring.
Threats	. . . . . . Siltation, hybridization.
Region 1	. . . . . California

Description

The Modoc sucker is a dwarf species of the family Catostomidae. Individuals begin to mature at 7 to 8.5 centimeters (2.75 to 3.3 in) with few adults exceeding 18 centimeters (4.2 in) in length. The Modoc sucker is green-brown to deep gray-olive above and lighter on the sides with some yellow pigment beneath. It is cream-colored to white ventrally, and with caudal, pelvic and pectoral fins that are a light yellowish orange. A bright orange band appears on the sides during spawning season.

Behavior

The Modoc sucker feeds on bottom-dwelling invertebrates, algae, and detritus. During spring spawning runs, it ascends creeks or tributaries that may be dry during summer months.

Habitat

The Modoc sucker prefers small streams that have soft sediments, clear water, and large shallow pools with overhanging trees or cliffs.

Historic Range

The Modoc sucker has been found in small tributary streams of the Pit River in Modoc and Lassen counties, California. A 1978 California Department of Fish and Game survey reported the species from eight creeks: Washington, Hulbert, Turner, Willow, Ash, Dutch Flat, Johnson, and Rush. At one time, the species inhabited additional streams, but because it is restricted to small, often intermittent streams it was probably never common.

Current Distribution

Presently, the species is restricted to portions of Turner and Rush Creeks, two small drainage systems in Modoc County. The federal government manages about half of the land and the rest is privately owned. Recent information indicates that genetically pure Modoc suckers are restricted to Turner Creek and its tributaries, Washington, Hulbert, and Johnson creeks, and to smaller unnamed feeder streams. About 1,300 individuals are estimated to inhabit this creek system.

Conservation and Recovery

The recent decline of the Modoc sucker can largely be attributed to habitat degradation and to hybridization with the more common Sacramento sucker (*Catostomus occidentalis*). Severe erosion, caused by overgrazing by livestock, has increased the amount of silt carried by streams, dramatically degrading water quality. Even before the federal listing of this species, the Bureau of Lands Management voluntarily removed many riparian areas from grazing, which has improved water quality in the watershed to some degree.

Waterfalls, steep gradients, and rocky rapids always separated the Modoc sucker from the Sacramento sucker, which ranges downstream in the larger creeks and reservoirs of the Pit River system. When the Sacramento sucker moved upstream to spawn, these natural barriers prevented its encroachment into Modoc sucker habitat. Artificial channeling of these streams removed many natural barriers, and now the two species are interbreeding. Ongoing hybridization could eliminate the Modoc sucker as

a separate and distinct species from many streams. Redirection of stream flow has also allowed predator fish access to the Modoc sucker's habitat.

Critical Habitat was designated in Modoc County to include 42 kilometers (26 mi) of stream bed and a buffer zone along the banks of Turner, Washington, Hulbert, and Johnson creeks. Through cooperation of Fish and Wildlife Service, the Forest Service, and the California Department of Fish and Game, the Modoc sucker has been reintroduced into Turner Creek, and plans have been developed to rehabilitate Rush Creek and reintroduce the Modoc sucker there.

Bibliography

California Department of Fish and Game. 1980. *At the Crossroads: A Report on the Status of California's Endangered and Rare Fish and Wildlife.* State of California Resources Agency, Sacramento.

Martin, M. 1972. "Morphology and Variation of the Modoc Sucker, *Catostomus microps* Rutter, with Notes on Feeding Adaptations." *California Fish and Game* 58:277-284.

Mills, T. J. 1980. "Life History, Status, and Management of the Modoc Sucker, *Catostomus microps* (Rutter) in California, with a Recommendation for Endangered Classification." Endangered Species Program Special Publication 80-6. California Department of Fish and Game, Inland Fish.

Moyle, P. B. and A. Marciochi. 1975. "Biology of the Modoc Sucker, *Catostomus microps*, in Northern California." *Copeia* 1975:556-560.

Contact

Regional Office of Endangered Species
U.S. Fish and Wildlife Service
Lloyd 500 Building, Suite 1692
500 N.E. Multnomah Street
Portland, Oregon 97232

Warner Sucker
Catostomus warnerensis

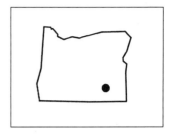

Mark Stern

Status . . . . . Threatened
Listed . . . . . September 27, 1985
Family . . . . . Catostomidae (Sucker)
Description . . . Sucker, up to 51 cm (20 in) in length; bright orange stripe when spawning.
Habitat . . . . . Lakes and associated wetlands.
Food . . . . . . Bottom feeder.
Reproduction . . Spawns in spring.
Threats . . . . . Introduced predators, dams and diversion structures.
Region 1 . . . . . Oregon

Description

The Warner sucker is a moderate-sized sucker, reaching a maximum length of about 51 centimeters (20 in). It matures at three to four years of age at a length of 13 to 16 cm (3 to 4 in). A bright orange lateral stripe is present on adults during spawning runs. The Warner Sucker is a species that was isolated in the remaining waters of a Pleistocene lake that previously covered much of the Warner Basin floor. When glaciers retreated and the climate became drier, the lake gradually disappeared.

Behavior

Although primarily lacustrine (lake-dwelling), in spring this species spawns in the headwaters of streams that feed the lakes. It requires a silt-free, gravel stream bed for spawning.

Habitat

The habitat of the Warner sucker encompasses large natural lakes and associated marshes. Early residents in the area recalled when suckers were very abundant and ascended the creeks in masses to spawn.

Historic Range

The Warner sucker is endemic to the streams and lakes of the Warner Basin in south-central Oregon.

Current Distribution

The Warner sucker now inhabits portions of Crump and Hart Lakes, the spillway canal north of Hart Lake, and portions of Snyder, Honey, Twentymile, and Twelvemile Creeks—all in Lake County, Oregon. Portions of Crump and Hart Lakes are included within the Hart Mountain National Wildlife Refuge. Much of the stream habitat is held by the Bureau of Land Management. Land on the valley floor is for the most part privately owned.

Conservation and Recovery

Dams and diversion structures, some in place since before the turn of the century, have prevented this sucker from reaching its spawning and rearing grounds in the stream headwaters. Water pollution and siltation at the few remaining spawning sites also threaten the survival of eggs and hatchlings.

Hart Lake and a portion of Crump Lake dried up in the early 1930s and again in the early 1960s, but periodic fluctuations in lake levels seem to be a natural feature of the Warner Valley. The Warner sucker survives these droughts by seeking refuge in streams that feed the lakes, but at a high cost in population mortality. Increased irrigation demands during such periods aggravate and prolong natural drought conditions, keeping both the water table and sucker population levels low.

To assist Warner sucker recovery, existing dams and diversion structures could be modified to allow movement of the species. For example, fish screens could keep adult and juvenile suckers from washing into irrigation ditches. Fish ladders or other passage structures could give the fish access to upstream spawning areas. Implementation of these recommendations is dependent on the availability of federal and state funds.

Critical Habitat has been designated for the Warner sucker to include streams in Lake County: Twelvemile, Twentymile, Snyder, and Honey creeks, and the spillway canal north of Hart Lake. In addition to the streams themselves, the designation includes a buffer zone along both banks to preserve vegetation and prevent siltation and runoff of other pollutants. The shade from small trees and shrubs helps maintain suitable water temperature and dissolved oxygen levels in the streams.

Bibliography

Bond. C. E. 1973. "Keys to Oregon Freshwater Fishes." Technical Bulletin 58. Oregon State University, Agricultural Experiment Station.

Bond, C. E. 1974. "Endangered Plants and Animals of Oregon, I. Fishes." Special Report 205. Oregon State University, Agricultural Experiment Station.

Coombs, C. I., C. E. Bond, and S. F. Drohan. 1979. "Spawning and Early Life History of the Warner Sucker (*Catostomus warnerensis*)." Report to U.S. Fish and Wildlife Service, Sacramento.

Contact

Regional Office of Endangered Species
U.S. Fish and Wildlife Service
Lloyd 500 Building, Suite 1692
500 N.E. Multnomah Street
Portland, Oregon 97232

Shortnose Sucker

Chasmistes brevirostris

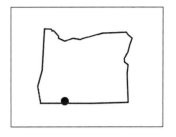

California Department of Fish and Game

Status . . . . . . Endangered
Listed . . . . . . July 18, 1988
Family . . . . . . Catostomidae (Sucker)
Description . . . Sucker with a terminal obli-
que mouth and vestigial
papillae on the lips.
Habitat . . . . . . Lakes; streams for spawning.
Food . . . . Bottom feeder.
Reproduction . . Spawns in spring.
Threats . . . . . . Dam construction, hybrid-
ization.
Region 1 . . . . . California, Oregon

Description

The shortnose sucker can grow as long as 64 centimeters (25 in) at maturity. It is distinguished from other members of the genus *Chasmistes* by its terminal, oblique mouth, which has no (or only vestigal) papillae on the lips.

Behavior

In the spring, the shortnose sucker moves from its lake habitat to stream headwaters to spawn. Suckers are adapted to feed by suction, siphoning and filtering food from lake bottoms. The species is long-lived; several fish have been netted that were over 40 years old. The shortnose sucker was a food fish for the Klamath Indians for thousands of years.

Habitat

The shortnose sucker is lake-dwelling and prefers the freshwater reservoirs of moun-

tainous, southeastern Oregon. It requires free-flowing streams for spawning.

Historic Range

The shortnose sucker was once found throughout the Klamath Basin of south-central Oregon and north-central California. A shortnose sucker population in Lake of the Woods, Oregon, was lost during a program to eradicate carp and perch in 1952. A population in the Clear Lake Reservoir shows distinct evidence of interbreeding with the Klamath largescale sucker, creating a genetically impure hybrid. Specimens collected from Copco Reservoir in 1962, 1978, and 1979 were found to have hybridized with the Klamath smallscale sucker.

Current Distribution

Upper Klamath Lake and its tributaries are now the primary refuge for the shortnose sucker. A substantial population also survives in Copco Reservoir on the Klamath River but recent declines have been drastic. Remnant populations exist in the Clear Lake Reservoir on Lost River (California) and along the Klamath River in Iron Gate Reservoir (California) and J.C. Boyle Reservoir (Oregon).

A 1984 survey estimated the number of spawning shortnose suckers swimming out of Upper Klamath Lake at 2,650 individuals. Surveys in 1985 and 1986 found significantly fewer fish. The catch of shortnose suckers declined 34 percent between the 1984 and 1985 spawning runs. In 1986, the spawning run declined 74 percent compared to 1985.

Conservation and Recovery

The shortnose sucker was considered a sport fish until 1987, when, because of drastically declining numbers, the Oregon Fish and Wildlife Commission placed it on the state's list of protected species.

The primary cause of this decline is the overall reshaping of the Klamath Basin through dams, water diversion, dredging, and the elimination of marshes. Although reservoirs provide suitable habitat for the shortnose sucker, the dams block the fish's spawning runs. Surviving suckers are almost all older fish. There has been no significant addition of young to the population since the Sprague River Dam was constructed at Chiloquin, Oregon, in 1970, cutting off 85 percent of the spawning range. The shortnose sucker has not spawned successfully in 19 years.

Fish ladders, installed at the Sprague River Dam, have been little or no help. Although the shortnose sucker is a strong swimmer, it cannot leap the rungs of the ladders. Damming has also facilitated hybridization with other sucker species in the dam's tailwaters.

Non-native fishes have also contributed to shortnose sucker decline through hybridization and competition.

The Klamath Indian Tribe and local biologists alerted the Oregon Fish and Wildlife Commission to the critical situation of both the shortnose sucker and the federally Endangered Lost River sucker (*Deltistes luxatus*). Recovery of the species will require the cooperation of these groups and the Fish and Wildlife Service to reopen a breeding range for these fish. Otherwise, the shortnose sucker is doomed to die off.

Bibliography

Coots, M. 1965. "Occurrences of the Lost River Sucker, *Deltistes luxatus* (Cope), and Shortnose Sucker, *Chamistes brevirostris* (Cope) in Northern California." *California Fish and Game* 51:68- 73.

Miller, R. R., and G. R. Smith. 1981. "Distribution and Evolution of *Chamistes* (Pisces: Catostomidae) in Western North America." *Occasional Papers of the Museum of Zoology*, University of Michigan 696:1-46.

Moyle, P. B. 1978. *Inland Fishes of California*. University of California Press, Berkeley.

Contact

Regional Office of Endangered Species
U.S. Fish and Wildlife Service
Lloyd 500 Building, Suite 1692
500 N.E. Multnomah Street
Portland, Oregon 97232

Cui-ui
Chasmistes cujus

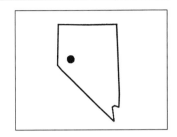

Utah Division of Wildlife Resources

Status . . . . . . Endangered
Listed . . . . . . March 11, 1967
Family . . . . . Catostomidae (Sucker)
Description . . . Olive to blackish-brown sucker.
Habitat . . . . . . Lakes; headwaters for spawning.
Food . . . . Bottom feeder.
Reproduction . . Spawns in spring.
Threats . . . . . . Dam construction, degraded water quality.
Region 1 . . . . . Nevada

Description

The cui-ui is a sucker, which attains a maximum length of about 64 centimeters (25 in) and a maximum weight of about 3.2 kilograms (7 lbs). It has a plump, robust body, and coarse scales. The head is large and blunt with small eyes. The mouth, atypical for a sucker, is oblique, rather than rounded, with thin lips and weak or nearly absent papillae. The cui-ui is pale olive to blackish-brown above, and white below. Breeding males have reddish sides.

Behavior

Little is known of the life history of this bottom-feeding sucker.

Habitat

The cui-ui spends its adult life in lakes and rivers and swims upstream in the spring to spawn.

Historic Range

The cui-ui was once plentiful throughout Truckee River and Pyramid Lake (Nevada); Klamath Lake and its tributaries (Oregon and California); and Utah Lake (Utah).

Current Distribution

This species is now extremely rare or absent throughout its historic range. Although no population figures are available, the most viable remaining population of cui-ui appears to be in the Truckee River, Nevada.

Conservation and Recovery

The natural habitat of the cui-ui has been drastically altered since the turn of the century by the construction of dams and water diversion channels. Water quality has steadily declined as flows decreased and the influx of silt and pollutants increased. Non-native fish species have preyed on cui-ui young, significantly reducing the population.

The Fish and Wildlife Service Recovery Plan for this species calls for restoring a portion of the Truckee River and Pyramid Lake to a natural and balanced condition. If a significant portion of this essential habitat can be reclaimed, the cui-ui stands a good chance of surviving. A captive breeding program is underway with the goal of restocking cui-ui in Pyramid Lake.

Until April 1987, Nevada's Truckee River population was cut off from its spawning grounds at the river's headwaters. Then the Marble Bluff Fish Facility, designed to pass spawning fish of all types upstream past the Truckee River Dam, was opened. Almost immediately biologists observed a run of the endangered Lahontan cutthroat trout (*Salmo clarki henshawi*) through the facility, soon followed by over 4,000 cui-ui.

Bibliography

U.S. Fish and Wildlife Service. 1983. "Cui-ui Recovery Plan: Revision." U.S. Fish and Wildlife Service, Portland.

Contact

Regional Office of Endangered Species
U.S. Fish and Wildlife Service
Lloyd 500 Building, Suite 1692
500 N.E. Multnomah Street
Portland, Oregon 97232

June Sucker
Chasmistes liorus

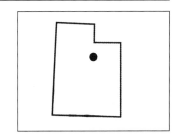

Status . . . . . . Endangered
Listed . . . . . . March 31, 1986
Family . . . . . . Catostomidae (Sucker)
Description . . . Small sucker with an under-
hanging mouth.
Habitat . . . . . . Shallow, saline waters.
Food . . . . Bottom feeder.
Reproduction . . Spawns in June.
Threats . . . . . . Predation, water diversion.
Region 6 . . . . . Utah

Description

Named for its peak spawning time, the June sucker is a small fish, attaining a mature length of only about 3 centimeters (1.25 in). It has often been confused with the Utah sucker but can be readily distinguished by its under-hanging mouth, relatively smooth, divided lips, a broad skull, and greater numbers of gill rakers.

The species as it exists today differs slightly from specimens collected in the 1800s. It is hypothesized that the June and Utah suckers interbred during a prolonged drought in the 1930s when their populations were seriously stressed. The name *Chasmistes liorus liorus* was assigned to specimens collected in the 1800s, and *C. l. mictus* to those collected after 1939. To avoid confusion, the June sucker is now being classified as a full species—*C. liorus*. It has retained its distinct character-istics and is not actively interbreeding with any other species today.

Behavior

In spite of its former abundance, biological data for this bottom-feeding species is mostly wanting. The adult June sucker ascends the Provo River during the second or third week of June and completes spawning within five to eight days.

Habitat

The June sucker thrives in the shallow, saline waters of Utah Lake, Utah, a 38,000-hectare (94,000-acre) remnant of ancient Lake Bonneville. The lake's average depth is three meters (10 ft) and maximum depth only about four meters (14 ft). Its turbid waters are slightly saline. The June sucker spawns in the Provo River, the largest tributary of the lake, with limited activity in the Spanish Fork River.

Historic Range

Millions of June suckers were reported in Utah Lake in the late 1800s and composed an important part of the commercial fish harvest. During the early 1930s, hundreds of tons of suckers were lost when the lake was nearly drained because the water was needed for irrigation. In 1951 the June sucker was considered the second most abundant species in Utah Lake; by 1959 it was considered fourth in abundance; by 1970 it ranked seventh.

Current Distribution

The June sucker is restricted to Utah Lake and the lower portion of the Provo River (Utah County). Spawning is restricted because the fish can travel only about 8 kilometers (5 mi) upstream to where a diversion barrier blocks further movement. It is suspected that fewer than 1,000 adult June suckers currently survive, and all appear to be over 15 years of age. Possibly, the entire surviving population is very old, with little or no replacement occurring.

Conservation and Recovery

In the past 100 years over 20 non-native fishes have been introduced into Utah Lake, including largemouth bass, black bullhead, channel catfish, and carp. The decline of the sucker population to its present low level corresponds closely with the introduction of white bass and walleye to the lake in the mid-1950s. The June sucker suffers from competition with and predation by these non-native fishes.

The Central Utah Water Conservancy District, the Provo River Water Users Association, and several other groups questioned the efficacy of listing the June sucker as Endangered. These groups feared that listing would interfere with the Central Utah Project, an ongoing, federally funded, construction project designed to supply more water for irrigation and human use. The Governor of Utah supported the listing. Subsequently, the Fish and Wildlife Service (FWS) determined that existing plans to dike Goshen and Provo bays and to create further upstream reservoirs would result in habitat losses. Because federal funds are involved, these proposals are subject to formal consultation with the FWS and are currently being revised to maintain suitable spawning habitat for the June sucker.

The state of Utah is currently implementing sections of a June Sucker Management Plan to ensure the survival of the species and attempt to overcome the impacts of predation. The Bonneville Chapter of the American Fisheries Society has been involved in the recovery effort.

Bibliography

Bureau of Reclamation. 1979. "Central Utah Project, Bonneville Unit, Municipal and Industrial System, Final Environmental Statement, Volume I." Bureau of Reclamation, Salt Lake City.

Radant, R. D. 1983. "Fisheries Impact Analysis of Utah Lake Diking Plan, Irrigation and Drainage System, Bonneville Unit, Central Utah Project." Utah Division of Wildlife Resources with the Bureau of Reclamation, Salt Lake City.

Radant, R. D., and T. J. Hickman. 1984. "Status of the June Sucker." In *Proceedings of the Desert Fishes Council 15th Annual Symposium*. Bishop, California.

Contact

Regional Office of Endangered Species
U.S. Fish and Wildlife Service
P.O. Box 25486
Denver Federal Center
Denver, Colorado 80225

White River Springfish
Crenichthys baileyi baileyi
Hiko White River Springfish
Crenichthys baileyi grandis

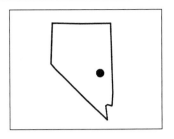

White River springfish   John N. Rinne

Status . . . . . . Endangered
Listed . . . . . September 27, 1985
Family . . . . . Cyprinodontidae (Killifish)
Description . . . Small killifish; greenish above and silvery below with a dark lateral stripe.
Habitat . . . . . . Springs.
Food . . . . . . Unknown.
Reproduction . . Undescribed.
Threats . . . . . . Low numbers, restricted range, predation.
Region 1 . . . . . Nevada

Description

Crenichthys baileyi is one of two species within the genus *Crenichthys*. Distinctive characteristics of the genus include a lack of pelvic fins, a long, coiled intestine, and restricted range. Fishes in this genus have been of particular scientific interest because of their adaptation to extremely high temperatures and low dissolved oxygen.

The White River springfish and Hiko White River springfish were described in 1981 as two of five subspecies of *C. baileyi*. These two subspecies are visually similar. Greenish above and silvery below, both have a dark lateral stripe that runs from behind the gills to the tail fin.

Behavior

Because of small populations and restricted ranges, little is known of the life history of either the White River or Hiko White River springfish.

Habitat

Both subspecies are known from single populations in springs in the Pahranagat Valley in Lincoln County, Nevada.

Historic Range

The species is endemic to the remnant waters of the White River system in eastern Nevada; these two subspecies are restricted to the Pahranagat Valley. During pluvial times, 10,000 to 40,000 years ago, a far larger White River flowed into the Colorado River by way of the Virgin River. When the White River dried up, the springfishes were restricted to the remaining permanent springs and outflows.

Current Distribution

The White River springfish is presently found only in Ash Springs, which is used for public swimming and is principally inhabited by non-native fishes. Recent surveys indicate a severe reduction in numbers. The Hiko White River springfish was extirpated from Hiko Spring when game fishes were introduced in 1967, and it now survives as a single population of less than 100 individuals in Crystal Springs. The springs and most of the surrounding lands are privately owned, but a small portion is managed by the Bureau of Land Management.

Conservation and Recovery

The desert springs inhabited by these springfishes are extremely localized and vulnerable to alteration by diversion of water or introduction of non-native fishes. Efforts to restock the Hiko White River springfish in Hiko Spring have been made in recent years but the long-term viability of this restocking effort is questionable. Most of the restocked springfish have fallen prey to the numerous exotic fishes that inhabit the spring, such as the convict cichlid and mosquitofish.

Critical Habitat was designated for both subspecies to include Ash Springs for the White River springfish, and Crystal and Hiko Springs for the Hiko White River springfish. The Desert Fishes Council opposed designation of Critical Habitat because it feared that the action would attract undue animosity from local landowners.

Bibliography

Deacon, J. E., C. Hubbs, and B. J. Zahuranec. 1964. "Some Effects of Introduced Fishes on the Native Fish Fauna of Southern Nevada." *Southwestern Naturalist* 12:31-44.

Williams, J. E., and G. R. Wilde. 1981. "Taxonomic Status and Morphology of Isolated Populations of the White River Springfish, *Crenichthys baileyi* (Cyprinodontidae)." *Southwestern Naturalist* 25:485-503.

Contact

Regional Office of Endangered Species
U.S. Fish and Wildlife Service
Lloyd 500 Building, Suite 1692
500 N.E. Multnomah Street
Portland, Oregon 97232

Railroad Valley Springfish
Crenichthys nevadae

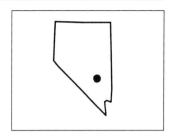

Thomas M. Baugh

Status	Threatened
Listed	March 31, 1986
Family	Cyprinodontidae (Killifish)
Description . . .	Robust killifish, lacking pelvic fins.
Habitat	Thermal springs.
Food	Insects and plant matter.
Reproduction . .	Spawns year round.
Threats	Predation, water diversion.
Region 1	Nevada

Description

The robust-bodied Railroad Valley spring-fish is a member of the order Cyprinodontiformes, which lack spines in the fins. This springfish, like its relative *Crenichthys baileyi*, has no pelvic fins and is adapted to thermal waters. It is about 7 centimeters (3 in) long, greenish above and silvery beneath.

Behavior

Springfishes live out their short lives within a narrowly defined, geographic area, feeding on insects and plant matter. Breeding occurs year round.

Habitat

The Railroad Valley springfish is found in warm spring pools, outflow streams, and adjacent marshes.

Historic Range

This species is restricted to springs within the Railroad Valley (Nye County) in Nevada.

Current Distribution

The Railroad Valley springfish is native to four thermal springs—Big, North, Hay Corral, and Reynolds—near Locke's Ranch and two thermal springs on the Duckwater Shoshone Indian Reservation—Big Warm and Little Warm. Additionally, the species has been introduced into Chimney Springs, about 10 kilometers (6 mi) south of Locke's Ranch. This is a seepage area which forms small thermal ponds at Sodaville in Mineral County, Nevada. The springfish has also been introduced into springs at the source of Hot Creek, 64 kilometers (40 mi) west of Locke's Ranch.

Conservation and Recovery

All of the springs inhabited by the Railroad Valley springfish have been physically altered, primarily to serve as watering holes for grazing livestock, and the species has declined in numbers as a result. Spring pools have been diked, waters diverted, and outflows channeled, reducing the amount of suitable habitat. Vegetation around some of the springs (particularly, North Spring) have also been trampled by the cattle. Habitats are further threatened by groundwater pumping, which causes a decrease in spring discharges. In 1981 the introduced springfish population at Chimney Springs was lost after spring discharge ceased altogether. Springfish were reintroduced into Chimney Springs when flows resumed. Several other springs in the region have also failed.

Non-native fishes, which have been introduced into the limited habitat, also threaten this springfish. Guppies have become established in Big Warm Spring and have nearly eliminated springfish from the main pool. Development of one outflow channel of Big Warm Spring as a fish farm resulted in escape of catfish into the spring system.

Critical Habitat has been designated for the springfish in Nye County to include six springs and associated streams and marshes within the historic range of the springfish. The designated area does not include habitat in the outflow creek of Big Warm Spring. Introduced populations near Sodaville, in Chimney Springs, and Hot Creek are not included in the designation.

Federal listing of the Railroad Valley springfish is expected to have some impact on the leasing of Bureau of Land Management lands for livestock grazing and mineral exploration.

Bibliography

Deacon, J. E., C. Hubbs, and B. J. Zahuranec. 1964. "Some Effects of Introduced Fishes on the Native Fish Fauna of Southern Nevada." *Southwestern Naturalist* 12:31-44.

Deacon, J. E., and J. E. Williams. 1984. "Annotated List of the Fishes of Nevada." *Proceedings of the Biological Society of Washington* 97(1):103-118.

Hubbs, C., and J. E. Deacon. 1964. "Additional Introduction of Tropical Fishes into Southern Nevada." *Southwestern Naturalist* 9:249-251.

Minckley, W. L. 1973. "Fishes of Arizona." Report to the Arizona Game and Fish Department, Phoenix.

Contact

Regional Office of Endangered Species
U.S. Fish and Wildlife Service
Lloyd 500 Building, Suite 1692
500 N.E. Multnomah Street
Portland, Oregon 97232

Leon Springs Pupfish
Cyprinodon bovinus

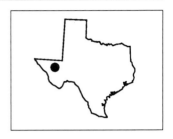

Status . . . . . . Endangered
Listed . . . . . . August 15, 1980
Family . . . . . . Cyprinodontidae (Killifish)
Description . . . Dusky gray to iridescent blue pupfish.
Habitat . . . . . . Shallow, open streams.
Food . . . . Vegetation-consuming invertebrates, detritus, diatoms, vascular plants.
Threats . . . . . . Oil pollution, groundwater pumping, hybridization.
Region 2 . . . . . Texas

James E. Johnson

Description

Leon Springs pupfish is a small, robust-bodied fish, about 4 centimeters (1.5 in) long at maturity. Its color varies from dusky gray to iridescent blue.

Behavior

Pupfish do much of their feeding from the muddy bottom. Their diet consists of tiny invertebrates, detritus, diatoms, and vascular plants. Male pupfish guard small spawning areas in shallow water, where the females deposit eggs. Breeding occurs throughout the year.

Habitat

The Leon Springs pupfish inhabits shallow saline springs, pools, and outflow streams. The pupfish has an extended breeding season, wide salinity and temperature tolerances, and broad food habits, and appears to thrive in a simple community with few competing species.

Historic Range

This pupfish was discovered in 1851 at Leon Springs, 13 kilometers (8 mi) west of Fort Stockton in southwestern Texas. Sometime before 1938, the pupfish disappeared from the spring and was thought to be extinct. In 1958, Leon Springs dried up because of excessive groundwater pumping. In 1965 the species was rediscovered at Diamond Y Spring in Pecos County, 14.5 kilometers (9 mi) north of Fort Stockton.

Current Distribution

The Leon Springs pupfish probably survives only in Diamond Y Spring and Leon

Creek, its outflow stream. Recently, this small population has been stable with summer densities reaching three or more fish per square meter.

Conservation and Recovery

Much of the original habitat of this pupfish was destroyed by diversion of water for irrigation and excessive groundwater pumping. In recent years, the Diamond Y Spring has experienced diminishing flow and will probably dry up if pumping continues at the present rate. In addition, the springs area is in the midst of an active oil and gas field. A refinery is located upstream from the main spring head for the pupfish's habitat. The oil companies have acted to minimize leakage into Diamond Y Spring and Leon Creek, but past oil spills have caused considerable fish mortality, and the potential for further accidents still exists.

In 1974 the common sheepshead minnow was released into Leon Creek. Interbreeding between it and the Leon Springs pupfish resulted in extensive hybridization, threatening the genetic purity of the species. A carefully supervised fish poisoning program and intensive selective seining efforts successfully removed all sheepshead minnows and hybrids by August 1978. Although the present Leon Springs pupfish population seems to be genetically pure, the habitat remains accessible and still vulnerable to the release of harmful exotic fishes.

The entire known range of this species from the head of Diamond Y Spring downstream to above the State Highway 18 crossing has been designated as Critical Habitat.

Bibliography

Echelle, A. A., and C. Hubbs. 1978. "Haven for Endangered Pupfish." *Texas Parks and Wildlife Magazine* 36:9-12.

Kennedy, S. E. 1978. "Life History of the Leon Springs Pupfish, *Cyprinodon bovinus.*" *Copeia* 1977:93-103.

U.S. Fish and Wildlife Service. 1985. "Leon Springs Pupfish Recovery Plan." U.S. Fish and Wildlife Service, Albuquerque.

Contact

Regional Office of Endangered Species
U.S. Fish and Wildlife Service
P.O. Box 1306
Albuquerque, New Mexico 87103

Devil's Hole Pupfish

Cyprinodon diabolis

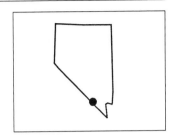

Thomas M. Baugh

Status	Endangered
Listed	March 11, 1967
Family	Cyprinodontidae (Killifish)
Description . . .	Tiny pupfish, lacking pelvic fins.
Habitat	Limestone cavern.
Food	Algae.
Reproduction . .	Breeds year round.
Threats	Groundwater depletion, siltation.
Region 1	Nevada

Description

The Devil's Hole pupfish is the most distinctive member of its genus, characterized by its extremely small size, which rarely exceeds two centimeters (0.8 in) in length, its absence of pelvic fins, and the lack of vertical crossbars in mature males. It has a long tail, and a large head and eyes.

Behavior

Little is known of Devil's Hole pupfish behavior. Its food supply is thought to consist entirely of algae. Algae growth, in turn, depends on the amount of sunlight that strikes the surface of the shelf pool within Devil's Hole. During the summer, the shelf receives about four hours of sunlight a day; no direct sunlight reaches the water surface during winter. Any decline in water level directly affects the amount of sunlight reaching the water, and thus food availability for the pupfish.

Pupfish are believed to live about one year. They are thought to spawn throughout the year, with most activity in the spring.

Habitat

The spring pool of Devil's Hole (Nevada) is located some 15 meters (60 ft) below the land surface, where there is a shallow rock shelf approximately 2 by 4 meters (8 by 16 ft). Just beyond the shelf, the spring descends to an unknown depth into a myriad of chasms, mostly unexplored. Most of the pupfish's reproductive and feeding activity takes place on the shallow shelf.

Historic Range

This pupfish has probably been isolated within its current habitat for many thousands of years.

Current Distribution

The Devil's Hole pupfish occurs naturally only at Devil's Hole, a deep, water-filled limestone cavern located in Ash Meadows (Nye County), Nevada. Probable population is from 300 to 900 individuals.

Conservation and Recovery

Throughout the 1960s, pumping groundwater for irrigation lowered the water level within Devil's Hole. The reduction was so serious that in 1972 twenty-seven Devil's Hole pupfish were moved to the Hoover Dam Refugium (Clark County), Nevada, to establish a captive breeding population. This captive population is reproducing, and numbers have fluctuated from 48 to 69 pupfish in recent years.

The primary threat to the pupfish's survival in the wild continues to be reduction of water levels needed to maintain the habitat. Other potential threats include surface runoff, which carries sand and silt into the underground caverns. Devil's Hole is part of the Ash Meadows National Wildlife Refuge, which has acquired water rights in the region.

The first goal of recovery is to stabilize the Devil's Hole habitat, but the species will probably remain threatened, even if pristine conditions are reestablished. For this reason, it is important to maintain the captive population. Scientists are concerned that the Hoover Dam population is not genetically pure, since these pupfish are larger in body size than the Devil's Hole population.

Bibliography

Miller, R. R. 1961. "Man and the Changing Fish Fauna of the American Southwest." *Papers of the Michigan Academy of Science, Arts and Letters* 46:365-404.

Minckley, C. O., and J. E. Deacon. 1975. "Foods of the Devil's Hole Pupfish." Southwestern Naturalist 20(1):105-111.

Williams, J. E. 1977. "Observations on the Status of the Devil's Hole Pupfish in the Hoover Dam Refugium." Report REC-ERC-77-11. U.S. Fish and Wildlife Service, Albuquerque.

U.S. Fish and Wildlife Service. 1980. "Devil's Hole Pupfish Recovery Plan." U.S. Fish and Wildlife Service, Albuquerque.

Contact

Regional Office of Endangered Species
U.S. Fish and Wildlife Service
Lloyd 500 Building, Suite 1692
500 N.E. Multnomah Street
Portland, Oregon 97232

Comanche Springs Pupfish
Cyprinodon elegans

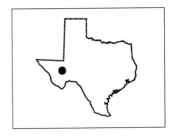

James E. Johnson

Status	Endangered
Listed	March 11, 1967
Family	Cyprinodontidae (Killifish)
Description	Silvery brown pupfish.
Habitat	Springs and outflows.
Food	Plant matter, insects.
Reproduction	Spawns in springs and pools.
Threats	Water diversion, competition.
Region 2	Texas

Description

Fish in the genus *Cyprinodon* average about 7 centimeters (2.8 in) in length. The Comanche Springs pupfish is one of the most distinctive species of pupfish. Both sexes are silvery brown and lack vertical bars; males exhibit a "speckled" color pattern.

Behavior

This pupfish has not been extensively studied and little is known of its behavior. It spawns in spring outflows and in small pools of standing water. It feeds on insects and plant material in all areas of its habitat.

Habitat

The Comanche Springs pupfish is known from freshwater and prefers shallow runs with slow current. Since most other pupfishes occupy more saline waters, long isolation from other species of the genus is probable.

Historic Range

The Comanche Springs pupfish was known to inhabit two isolated spring systems, 190 kilometers (114 mi) apart, in the Pecos River drainage of southwestern Texas. The first included Comanche Springs and the headwaters (now dry) of a group of streams that presently fall within the city limits of Fort Stockton (Pecos County). Comanche Springs dried up during the 1950s, completely destroying that pupfish population. The second spring system was found near Balmorhea in Reeves County, Texas. These springs and associated marshes have been extensively modified to support an irrigation network.

Current Distribution

At present, the species occurs only in Reeves County in Giffin and San Solomon Springs, an irrigation network fed by Phantom Lake, and Toyah Creek. The water from Phantom Lake Spring is diverted by a system of earthen dams into concrete irrigation ditches. Water is directed down a canal to merge with flows from San Solomon Spring and then enters two major channels for diversion into agricultural fields. The pupfish population is locally numerous but generally sparse throughout most of the network. Fish are seen sporadically near the mouth of a concrete irrigation canal entering Lake Balmorhea. No current population estimates have been made.

Conservation and Recovery

Other pupfish have been introduced into the same water system and threaten the Comanche Springs pupfish in two ways: by direct competition for limited food supplies; and by possible interbreeding and hybridization. The main threat to the Comanche pupfish, however, remains the artificial conditions of water flow within its habitat. Seasonal drying can strand and kill large numbers of fish, and recovery efforts have focused on methods to moderate the extreme pattern of drying and flooding of the stream and irrigation network.

To support the long-term survival of the species, some means must be found to stabilize the water table in the area. Increased pumping of groundwater for agriculture and human use has lowered water levels and reduced spring flows. Large artesian springs near Balmorhea are diminishing in flow, and Phantom Lake Spring is expected to dry up within 50 years. In fact, most large springs of West Texas have measurably diminished.

The Texas Parks and Wildlife Department has constructed a refuge at Balmorhea State Recreation area to provide stable flowing water for several thousand Comanche Springs pupfish. The Dexter National Fish Hatchery in New Mexico maintains a genetic stock of the pupfish, which will be used for reintroduction if the wild population is eliminated by drought or other cause.

Bibliography

Davis, J. R. 1979. "Die-Offs of an Endangered Pupfish, *Cyprinodon elegans* (Cyprinodontidae)." *Southwestern Naturalist* 24:534-536.

Hubbs, C. 1957. "Distributional Patterns of Texas Fresh-Water Fishes." *Southwestern Naturalist* 2:89-104.

U.S. Fish and Wildlife Service. 1980. "Comanche Springs Pupfish (*Cyprinodon elegans*) Recovery Plan." U.S. Fish and Wildlife Service, Albuquerque.

Contact

Regional Office of Endangered Species
U.S. Fish and Wildlife Service
P.O. Box 1306
Albuquerque, New Mexico 87103

Desert Pupfish
Cyprinodon macularius

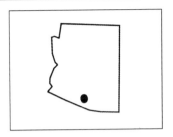

Status	Endangered
Listed	March 31, 1986
Family	Cyprinodontidae (Pupfish)
Description	Small, laterally compressed pupfish; males are marked with blue and yellow when breeding.
Habitat	Desert streams and rivers.
Food	Plant matter and insects.
Reproduction	Spawns in spring and summer.
Threats	Dam construction, predation.
Region 1	California
Region 2	Arizona
Mexico	Sonora

B. "Moose" Peterson

Description

The desert pupfish is a small, laterally compressed fish with a smoothly rounded body. The larger male rarely grows longer than 7.5 centimeters (3 in). During the reproductive season males turn bright blue on the head and sides and yellow on the caudal fin and tail. Females and juveniles usually have tan to olive backs and silvery sides. Adults have narrow, vertical, dark bars on the side, which are often interrupted to give the impression of a disjunct, lateral band.

Behavior

The Desert pupfish matures rapidly and may produce up to three generations per year. Spawning occurs throughout the spring and summer months. Females lay eggs on submerged plants in shallow water. Males defend the eggs, which hatch within about three days. After a few hours, the young begin to feed on small plants and insects. Individuals survive for about a year.

Habitat

This species is adapted to a harsh desert environment and is capable of surviving extreme conditions, sometimes living in water with temperatures in excess of 43 degrees C (110 F). It is capable of withstanding oxygen levels as low as 0.1 parts per million, and salinities nearly twice that of seawater.

Historic Range

The desert pupfish was described in 1853 from specimens collected in the San Pedro River of Arizona. It was once common in the desert springs, marshes, and tributary streams of the lower Gila and Colorado River drainages in Arizona, California, and Mexico. It was also found in the slow-moving reaches of some large rivers, including the Colorado, Gila, San Pedro, and Santa Cruz.

Current Distribution

The desert pupfish is now found in several Salton Sea tributaries in California—San Felipe Creek and San Sebastian Marsh (Imperial County), and Salt Creek (Riverside County). It is also found in shoreline pools and irrigation drains in the region. Surveys of Salt Creek and related irrigation ditches indicate that the populations there may no longer be viable.

In Arizona the desert pupfish inhabits Quitobaquito Spring within the Organ Pipe Cactus National Monument (Pima County). The pupfish is also thought to survive in low numbers in the Colorado River, the Rio Sonoyta drainage, and Santa Clara Slough in Sonora, Mexico. The status of the Mexican population is unknown.

Conservation and Recovery

The construction of dams on the Gila, Colorado, and Salt Rivers for irrigation and flood control dewatered the lower Gila and Salt Rivers and eliminated many of the marshy pools in which the Colorado River desert pupfish bred. The desert pupfish was then forced into mainstream channels where it was preyed upon by larger fishes. Although it is extremely hardy in many respects, the desert pupfish cannot tolerate competition and is readily displaced by introduced fishes, such as tilapia, shortfin mollies, mosquitofish, and largemouth bass.

Breeding populations of desert pupfish have been established in Arizona at Bog Hole and Research Ranch, Arizona-Sonora Desert Museum, Boyce Thompson Arboretum, and Arizona State University. In California, captive populations were established at Salton Sea State Park, the Living Desert Reserve, and Anza-Borrego State Park. Most of these small populations are maintained in artificial refugia.

Desert pupfish are also being held at Dexter National Fish Hatchery in Dexter, New Mexico. These fish, obtained from Santa Clara Slough, are being used to stock reintroduction efforts in Arizona. Populations were recently introduced into three springs on Bureau of Land Management land in Arizona at Peoples Canyon in the Bill Williams River (Yavapai County), Howard Well in the Gila River (Graham County), and Mesquite Spring (Pinal County). It will be several years before it is known whether these introductions produce self-sustaining populations.

Bibliography

Black, G. F. 1980. "Status of the Desert Pupfish, *Cyprinodon macularius*, in California." Special Publication 80-1. State of California, Department of Fish and Game, Sacramento.

Kynard, B. E. 1981. "Study of Quitobaquito Pupfish: Systematics and Preservation." Final Report. National Park Service.

McMahon, T. E., and R. R. Miller. 1985. "Status of the Fishes of the Rio Sonoyta Basin, Arizona and Sonora, Mexico." *Proceedings of the Desert Fishes Council*, Vol. 14. Bishop, California.

Contact

Regional Office of Endangered Species
U.S. Fish and Wildlife Service
Lloyd 500 Building, Suite 1692
500 N.E. Multnomah Street
Portland, Oregon 97232

Regional Office of Endangered Species
U.S. Fish and Wildlife Service
P.O. Box 1306
Albuquerque, New Mexico 87103

Ash Meadows Amargosa Pupfish
Cyprinodon nevadensis mionectes

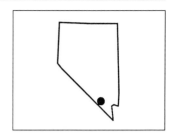

Peter Sanchez

Status . . . . . Endangered
Listed . . . . . May 10, 1982 (Emergency listing)
Reclassified . . . September 2, 1983
Family . . . . . Cyprinodontidae (Killifish)
Description . . . Small, iridescent, silver-blue minnow.
Habitat . . . . . Ash Meadows; thermal springs.
Food . . . . . . Insects, aquatic invertebrates.
Reproduction . . Spawns year round.
Threats . . . . . Water diversion, competition with introduced fishes.
Region 1 . . . . . Nevada

Description

The Ash Meadows Amargosa pupfish is a small minnow, rarely exceeding 7 centimeters (2.75 in) in length. Normally silver gray and darker across the back, breeding males turn an iridescent silver-blue.

Behavior

This pupfish breeds throughout the year with peak periods in spring and early summer. Like other pupfish, it feeds on insects and small, aquatic invertebrates.

Habitat

This pupfish inhabits pools and outflows of warm springs. Habitat springs are at elevations ranging from 655 to 700 meters (2,150 to 2,300 ft). Water temperatures of the springs are consistently 24 to 29 degrees Centigrade (75 to 85 F).

Historic Range

The Amargosa pupfish is endemic to the Ash Meadows region, an unusual desert wetland east of the Amargosa River in western California and eastern Nevada. These wetlands are maintained by springs and seeps fed by an extensive groundwater system.

Current Distribution

The Ash Meadows Amargosa pupfish is restricted to the large springs and outflows at Ash Meadows and are found in Fairbanks, Rogers, Longstreet, Jack Rabbit, Big, and point of Rocks springs, Crystal Pool, and two springs of the Bradford Springs group.

Conservation and Recovery

Early homesteaders attempted to farm Ash Meadows, using the free-flowing water from the springs for irrigation. These efforts failed because the salty, clay soils were not suitable for crops. Commercial farming ventures in the late 1960s and early 1970s resulted in large tracts of land being plowed and the installation of ground water pumps and diversion ditches to support a cattle-feed operation. As a result, many populations of plants and animals and their wetland habitats were destroyed by soil disturbance and the lowering of the water table.

In 1977 the owners of the agricultural interests sold about 60 square kilometers (23 sq mi) of land at Ash Meadows to a real estate developer. The developer hoped to build a residential community at Ash Meadows for 55,000 people, and initial construction resulted in extensive recontouring of the land and large-scale water diversions. In 1984, after attempts by the FWS to negotiate adequate conservation agreements failed, the developer sold about 4,450 hectares (11,000 acres) to The Nature Conservancy. The property was later purchased by the federal government to establish the Ash Meadows National Wildlife Refuge.

Numerous non-native species have been introduced into the springs, including the largemouth bass, Mexican mollie, mosquitofish, crayfish, and bullfrogs, all of which prey on the Ash Meadows pupfish. These exotic fishes have replaced the pupfish and other endemics as the dominant species in the affected springs. Large snails have also become established in several springs, where they compete with native fishes for food.

Critical Habitat for the Ash Meadows Amargosa pupfish has been designated in the following springs and their outflows in Nye County, Nevada: Fairbanks, Rogers, Longstreet, Crystal Pool, Bradford, Jack Rabbit, Big, Point of Rocks, and three unnamed springs. The Critical Habitat designation also includes a buffer zone immediately sur-

rounding these springs. The buffer zone is essential to the conservation of the fish because it provides vegetative cover that contributes to providing the uniform water and feeding conditions preferred by the pupfish.

Bibliography

Miller, R.R. 1948. "The Cyprinodont Fishes of the Death Valley System of Eastern California and Southwestern Nevada." *Miscellaneous Publications of the Museum of Zoology, University of Michigan* 68:1-155.

Soltz, D. L., and R. J. Naiman, eds. 1978. "The Natural History of Native Fishes in the Death Valley System." *Natural History Museum of Los Angeles County, Science Series* 30:17.

Contact

Regional Office of Endangered Species
U.S. Fish and Wildlife Service
Lloyd 500 Building, Suite 1692
500 N.E. Multnomah Street
Portland, Oregon 97232

Warm Springs Pupfish

Cyprinodon nevadensis pectoralis

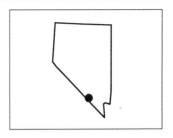

Nevada Department of Wildlife

Status	Endangered
Listed	October 13, 1970
Family	Cyprinodontidae (Killifish)
Description	Silvery sided pupfish; males bright blue.
Habitat	Thermal springs.
Food	Omnivorous.
Reproduction	Spawns year round.
Threats	Groundwater pumping.
Region 1	Nevada

Description

The warm springs pupfish, the smallest of the four extant subspecies of the Nevada pupfish, ranges from 4 to 6.5 centimeters (1.5 to 2.5 in) long. Females and juveniles are silvery; males are bright blue.

Behavior

Because of its rarity, little is known of the life history of this pupfish. The spawning season runs for most of the year, with a peak from April through June. Like other pupfish, the warm springs subspecies is probably omnivorous, feeding on insects and plant matter.

Habitat

Although these pupfish reside in the outlet streams of all of their habitat springs, they do not reproduce there. Essential habitat for the warm spring pupfish is the springs' physically stable source pools or headwaters.

Historic Range

The warm springs pupfish has only been found in the Ash Meadows region of Nevada. The species was never very widespread.

Current Distribution

The warm springs pupfish is found in Lovell's Spring, sometimes referred to as School's Spring, a kilometer northwest of Devil's Hole at Ash Meadows (Nye County), Nevada. It is also found in five additional spring flows, all within 1 kilometer (0.6 mi) of Lovell's Spring. The Fish and Wildlife Service estimates that the total warm springs pupfish population is less than 500 fish, with almost half living in School Spring.

Conservation and Recovery

The warm springs pupfish is especially threatened by groundwater pumping that is lowering the water table throughout the region. Because the springs are quite small, they dry quickly when the water level falls. Competition with the introduced mosquitofish could become a problem if they penetrate any further into spring pools. Some predation on the warm springs pupfish is occurring, especially by birds such as the belted kingfisher.

Essential for the continued existence of the warm springs pupfish is protection of its very limited habitat, especially spring water levels. This will involve procuring and enforcing water rights so that spring water levels can be maintained, the control of emergent vegetation around the springs, and the addition of supplemental water whenever necessary.

In 1977 agricultural interests sold about 60 square kilometers (23 sq mi) of land at Ash Meadows to a real estate developer. Attempts by the developer to construct a residential community at Ash Meadows for 55,000 people resulted in widespread land disturbance and water diversions. In May 1982 the Fish and Wildlife Service (FWS) used emergency provisions of the Endangered Species Act to invoke protection of several fishes at Ash Meadows. In 1984, after attempts by the FWS to negotiate adequate conservation agreements failed, the developer sold about 4,450 hectares (11,000 acres) to The Nature Conservancy. The property was later purchased by the federal government to establish the Ash Meadows National Wildlife Refuge.

Bibliography

Miller, R. R., and J. E. Deacon. 1973. "New Localities of the Rare Warm Springs Pupfish, *Cyprinodon nevadensis pectoralis*, from Ash Meadows, Nevada." *Copeia* 1973:137-140.

Soitz, D. L. 1974. "Variation in Life History and Social Organization of Some Populations of Nevada Pupfish, *Cyprinodon nevadensis.*"

Ph.D. Dissertation. University of California, Los Angeles.

U.S. Fish and Wildlife Service. 1976. "Warm Springs Pupfish Recovery Plan." U.S. Fish and Wildlife Service, Albuquerque.

Contact

Regional Office of Endangered Species
U.S. Fish and Wildlife Service
Lloyd 500 Building, Suite 1692
500 N.Ed. Multnomah Street
Portland, Oregon 97232

Owens Pupfish
Cyprinodon radiosus

B. "Moose" Peterson

Status . . . . . . Endangered
Listed . . . . . . March 11, 1967
Family . . . . . . Cyprinodontidae (Killifish)
Description . . . Short, thick pupfish; fe-
males silvery with dark ver-
tical bars; males olive
above and slate gray
beneath.
Habitat . . . . . . Springs and small streams.
Reproduction . . Spawns in spring.
Threats . . . . . . Water diversion, ground-
water pumping, introduced
predators.
Region 1 . . . . . California

Description

The Owens pupfish is a small (6.8 cm; 2.5 in) deep-bodied fish with a laterally compressed shape. The sexes display differing size and color patterns. The larger males are olive above and slate gray beneath, with an overall bluish cast. Their lateral bars are deep purplish with posterior bars having some gold. The lower head is silver and blue, and the dorsal and anal fins are blue with an orange-amber border. The smaller females are deep olive with brown lateral blotches and purplish vertical bars.

Behavior

Pupfish are omnivorous and feed on algae, aquatic insects, crustaceans, and plankton. The spawning season begins in April when water temperatures reach 20 degrees C (68 F).

When spawning, males turn bright blue and become territorial, defending their spawning area from male pupfish and from other fish species. Females can deposit 50 to 200 eggs during the season but rarely lay more than one or two eggs at a time. Eggs hatch in seven to ten days, depending on water temperature. Newly hatched pupfish larvae begin feeding the day they hatch. Pupfish fry, which live along the shoreline where warmer water supports abundant food, mature in three to four months.

Habitat

Basic habitat requirements for the Owens pupfish consists of good quality water, aquatic vegetation, and a silt- or sand-covered bottom. It is normally found near the margins of bulrush marshes, in wide, well-vegetated shallow sloughs, or in spring pools.

Historic Range

The Owens pupfish has been found in east-central California in the Owens River and adjacent springs as far south as the springs around Owens Lake in Inyo County. In 1915 the species was plentiful along the Big Bend areas of the Owens River northeast of Bishop, but had mostly disappeared by 1934. During the 1940s the Owens pupfish was considered extinct. In 1956, however, a small population was discovered in Fish Slough. This population has been the source for all Owens pupfish populations that have been reestablished and exist today.

Current Distribution

The Owens pupfish is now confined to four springs in the Fish Slough area north of Bishop (Mono County), California. The protected area includes the Owens Valley Native Fish Sanctuary and a Bureau of Land Management spring refuge. There are no current population estimates.

Conservation and Recovery

Most Owens pupfish habitat was destroyed when dams and upstream diversions on the Owens River prevented seasonal flooding of shallow marshy areas. Groundwater pumping for irrigation continues to threaten aquifers supplying water to the remaining spring habitats, and vandals have destroyed structures built to help maintain the habitats.

The sanctuary at Fish Slough was created in the late 1960s to provide protected habitat for the speckled dace, the Owens sucker and the federally listed Owens tui chub (*Gila bicolor snyderi*) as well as the pupfish. Fish Slough, a unique wetland in an arid environment, contains a number of rare species besides the Owens pupfish, including the Fish Slough milkvetch and an undescribed species of mollusk.

Recently, recovery efforts at the sanctuary received a set-back, when it was discovered that the predatory largemouth bass had penetrated the Owens pupfish refuge at Fish Slough. In a single year, the bass managed to invade all four habitat springs. California Fish and Game personnel suspect that the bass were purposely introduced above fish barriers to threaten the survival of the pupfish. Repeated efforts to eradicate the bass have been only partially successful.

Because much of the habitat within the historic range can never be restored, FWS personnel hope to transplant the fish to the adjacent Adobe Valley, where good habitat still exists.

Bibliography

Brown, J. H. 1971. "The Desert Pupfish." *Scientific American* 225:104-110.

Soltz, D. L., and R. J. Naiman. 1978. "The Natural History of Native Fishes in the Death Valley System." *Natural History Museum of Los Angeles County Science Series* 30:1-76.

U.S. Fish and Wildlife Service. 1984. "Recovery Plan for the Owens Pupfish, *Cyprinodon radiosus*." U.S. Fish and Wildlife Service, Portland.

Contact

Regional Office of Endangered Species
U.S. Fish and Wildlife Service
Lloyd 500 Building, Suite 1692
500 N.E. Multnomah Street
Portland, Oregon 97232

Lost River Sucker

Deltistes luxatus

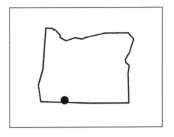

California Department of Fish and Game

Status	Endangered
Listed	July 16, 1988
Family	Catostomidae (Sucker)
Description . . .	Large sucker with a maximum weight of about 4.5 kg (10 lbs).
Habitat	Lakes; flowing streams for spawning.
Food	Bottom feeder; plant matter and detritus.
Reproduction . .	Spawns in spring.
Threats	Dam construction.
Region 1	California, Oregon

Description

The Lost River sucker, known locally as mullet, is one of the larger members of the sucker family, growing to 60 centimeters (25 in) in length and weighing as much as 4.5 kilograms (10 lbs). It has a short, terminal mouth, a hump on its snout, and triangular gill rakers, which are bony appendages that direct food into the gullet. Once classified in the genus *Chasmistes*, the species was moved into a separate genus, *Deltistes*, in 1896 based on the shape of its gill rakers.

Behavior

The Lost River sucker leaves its lake habitat in the spring and swims into smaller mountain streams to spawn. Maximum life span is about 45 years. It is a bottom feeding species, adapted to siphoning sediments for plant matter and detritus.

Habitat

This lake-dwelling species spawns in the headwaters of small, flowing streams in spring.

Historic Range

The Lost River sucker ranged in the lakes that fed the Lost and Klamath rivers in the Klamath Basin of south-central Oregon and north-central California. Before the region was heavily farmed, beginning in the late 19th century, large numbers of spawning suckers were taken from Sheepy Creek, a tributary of Sheepy Lake. The Sheepy, Lower Klamath, and Tule lakes were drained temporarily in 1924, eliminating Lost River suckers from these waters.

Current Distribution

Upper Klamath Lake and its tributaries in Klamath County, Oregon, provide the primary refuge for surviving Lost River suckers. A 1984 survey estimated the number of spawning suckers moving out of Upper Klamath Lake to be 23,120. By 1985 the number had declined to 11,860. A few suckers have been collected over the last several years from J.C. Boyle Reservoir in the Klamath River between Upper Klamath Lake and Copco Reservoir. The species has been almost eliminated from the river's Copco Reservoir in Siskiyou County, California. Despite an intensive search, only one specimen was collected there in 1987.

The Clear Lake Reservoir in Modoc County, California, supports a remnant population, the last known in the Lost River system. This population is small and suffers from competition with large numbers of non-native fishes and closure of its spawning area.

Conservation and Recovery

Early surveys of the Klamath Basin found Lost River suckers in sufficient abundance to constitute a major food source for the Klamath Indians and early settlers. In the late 1890s a cannery was operated near Olene, Oregon, to commercially harvest the fish.

The entire Klamath River basin, however, has been transformed by dam construction, water diversion, and dredging. Although the large artificial reservoirs technically provide new habitat for lake-dwelling fish, the dams block the fishes' spawning runs. The most significant event in the decline of the Lost River sucker was construction of the Sprague River Dam at Chiloquin, Oregon, in 1970,

which cut off the species from more than 95 percent of its historical spawning habitat. Since this dam was built, significant numbers of young have not been added to the population. Most living fish are at least 19 years old.

In 1988, thousands of Lost River suckers in Upper Klamath Lake were killed because of blue-green algal blooms. These toxic algal blooms occur in particularly hot and dry years. Pollution of the lake and decreased summer inflows aggravate this problem.

Fish ladders, constructed to assist fishes over the dams, have not aided the Lost River sucker, a fish that does not leap. Unless some way is found to lift this fish over the dams and into spawning waters, the species is doomed. The Oregon Fish and Wildlife Commission placed the Lost River sucker on the state's list of protected species in 1987, and California law recognizes it as Endangered.

Bibliography

Coots, M. 1965. "Occurrences of the Lost River Sucker, *Deltistes luxatus* (Cope), and Shortnose Sucker, *Chamistes brevirostris* (Cope) in Northern California." *California Fish and Game* 51:68-73.

Moyle, P. B. 1978. *Inland Fishes of California*. University of California Press, Berkeley.

Contact

Field Office
U.S. Fish and Wildlife Service
Lloyd 500 Building, Suite 1692
500 NE Multnomah Street
Portland, Oregon 97232

Pahrump Killifish

Empetrichthys latos latos

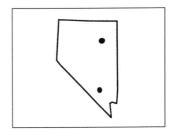

Doug Selby

Status . . . . . . Endangered
Listed . . . . . . March 11, 1967
Family . . . . . . Cyprinodontidae (Killifish)
Description . . . Slender fish; greenish above and silvery green below.
Habitat . . . . . . Alkaline mineral springs.
Food . . . . Insects and plant matter.
Reproduction . . Peak spawning in spring.
Threats . . . . . . Decreased spring discharge.
Region 1 . . . . . Nevada

Description

The Pahrump killifish is a slender fish, reaching a length of 8 centimeters (3 in). It has a broad mouth, a short and slender head, and no pelvic fins. Both sexes are greenish above and silvery green below. During spawning season males appear lightly washed with blue. The Pahrump killifish is one of two surviving species in the genus *Empetrichthys*. The Ash Meadows killifish (*E. merriami*), became extinct in the late 1940s.

Behavior

Young Pahrump killifish are more active during daylight while adults are more active at night. Peak spawning occurs in the spring, although different groups will spawn throughout the year. During her breeding cycle, the female seeks seclusion for egg-laying in remote corners of the springs. The fry remain near the bottom or in areas that offer protection from predation. This fish is omnivorous and eats a wide variety of insects, plant matter, and detritus.

Habitat

The Pahrump killifish is adapted to alkaline mineral springs and outflow streams. Adults prefer deeper pools; juveniles are found near the surface in shallower areas of the springs, where there is aquatic vegetation. The ancestral spring of this species maintained a constant, year-round temperature of 24.4 degrees C (76 F).

Historic Range

The Pahrump killifish and two subspecies inhabited separate springs in the Pahrump Valley in Nevada. Both of the other subspecies (*E. l. concavus* and *E. l. pahrump*) are now extinct. Originally, this killifish was known only from Manse Spring on the Manse Ranch in Nye County. It was eliminated from this spring in 1975 when the water dried up. An early transplant site at Latos Pools near Boulder City was lost to a flood in 1975.

Current Distribution

Two transplanted populations of the Pahrump killifish survive—in Corn-Creek Springs Pond on the Desert National Wildlife Range northwest of Las Vegas in Clark County, and in the Shoshone Pond southeast of Ely in White Pine County. No more than several hundred of these fish are thought to survive.

Conservation and Recovery

The Manse Spring dried up because of excessive groundwater pumping for irrigation. The drying of the spring had been predicted by biologists, who moved the fish to other localities. The Corn-Creeks Springs population may eventually be threatened by increased groundwater pumping related to the growth of the Las Vegas metropolitan area. Because habitat in Shoshone Pond is considered less than optimal, Fish and Wildlife Service (FWS) biologists consider the site as a temporary holding pool.

Low numbers and restricted distribution make the Pahrump killifish greatly vulnerable to extinction. The major recovery strategy will be to protect the two existing populations until further transplant sites can be located. The FWS hopes to establish at least three protected populations, each of 500 or more adults. Success in this effort would warrant delisting the species. An attempt is currently being made to rehabilitate Manse Spring, the Pahrump killifish's ancestral pool.

Bibliography

La Rivers, Ira. 1962. *Fishes and Fisheries of Nevada*. Nevada State Fish and Game Commission, Reno.

U.S. Fish and Wildlife Service. 1980. "Pahrump Killifish Recovery Plan." U.S. Fish and Wildlife Service, Portland.

Contact

Regional Office of Endangered Species
U.S. Fish and Wildlife Service
Lloyd 500 Building, Suite 1692
500 N.E. Multnomah Street
Portland, Oregon 97232

Desert Dace
Eremichthys acros

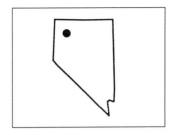

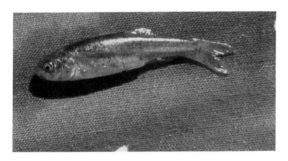

Gary Vinyard

Status	Threatened
Listed	December 10, 1985
Family	Cyprinidae (Minnow)
Description . . .	Olive-green minnow with horny sheaths on its jaws.
Habitat	Thermal springs and outflow streams.
Food	Algae, diatoms, snails, insects.
Reproduction . .	Spawns year round.
Threats	Channelization of outflows, predation, geothermal exploration.
Region 1	Nevada

Description

The desert dace, the only member of the genus *Eremichthys*, is an olive-green minnow about 7 centimeters (2.5 in) long. Under optimal conditions, individuals may occasionally reach a length of 25 centimeters (10 in). An unusual aspect of this fish's anatomy is the presence of prominent horny sheaths on the jaws, which probably allow the fish to scrape algae from rocks. No other cyprinid possesses such a feeding adaptation.

Behavior

The desert dace feeds on algae, diatoms, and sometimes snails and insects. It is notable for its tolerance for high temperatures, often surviving in waters as hot as 38 degrees C (100 F). Little life history information is available. It breeds year round.

Habitat

The desert dace inhabits thermal springs where waters are warmer than 19 degrees C (67 F). Water temperature appears to be a major factor controlling the distribution of desert dace within a spring system. In very hot springs, the dace finds its temperature range in the cooler outflow streams.

Historic Range

The desert dace is endemic to a group of thermal springs in the Soldier Meadows area of Humboldt County, Nevada.

Current Distribution

The species survives in eight of 20 or more springs in Soldier Meadows.

Conservation and Recovery

Most of the desert dace's habitat is privately owned. At many of the Soldier Meadows springs, water has been diverted from natural channels into concrete-lined ditches, primarily to water livestock. Channelization changes the temperature gradient of the outflows and interferes with the dace's need to locate optimal water temperatures. Additionally, artificial channels do not readily support the abundance of tiny life forms, which supply the bulk of the desert dace's diet. Two reservoirs, located 5 kilometers (3 mi) from the habitat springs, contain many non-native fishes, such as channel catfish and smallmouth bass. There is danger that these fishes will escape into the springs and prey upon the dace.

Because Soldier Meadows is recognized for having significant geothermal resources, there is some threat of regional exploration and development of this alternative energy source. Such activities would severely disturb the thermal aquifer that feeds the local springs. Tentative geothermal wells were drilled several years ago but were eventually abandoned.

Critical Habitat has been designated for the desert dace to include all thermal springs and outflows within Soldier Meadows, an area of about 21 square kilometers (8 sq mi).

Bibliography

Hubbs, C. L. and R. R. Miller. 1948. "Two New, Relict Genera of Cyprinid Fishes from Nevada." *Occasional Papers of the Museum of Zoology*, University of Michigan, Vol. 507.

Ono, R. D., J. D. Williams, and A. Wagner. 1983. *Vanishing Fishes of North America*. Stonewall Press, Washington, D.C.

Contact

Regional Office of Endangered Species
U.S. Fish and Wildlife Service
Lloyd 500 Building, Suite 1692
500 N.E. Multnomah Street
Portland, Oregon 97232

Slackwater Darter
Etheostoma boschungi

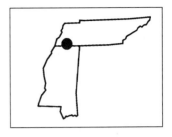

Richard Biggins

Status . . . . . . Threatened
Listed . . . . . . September 9, 1977
Family . . . . . . Percidae (Perch)
Description . . . Darter with a blue-black bar under the eye and prominent dorsal saddles.
Habitat . . . . . . Streams with adjacent seepage areas.
Food . . . . Insects, small crustaceans.
Reproduction . . Spawns in March.
Threats . . . . . . Loss of breeding habitat, degraded water quality.
Region 4 . . . . . Alabama, Tennessee

Description

The slackwater darter was recently placed in a new subgenus, *Ozarka*. This group of medium-sized darters range from 4 to 7 centimeters (1.6 to 3 in) in length. The slackwater darter is distinguished from members of its group by a bold blue-black bar under the eyes and three prominent dark dorsal saddles.

Behavior

The slackwater darter feeds on insects and small crustaceans. Its life span is probably no more than three years. Spawning usually begins in early March but may vary from year to year depending on temperature and rainfall. Water temperature must be warmer than 14 degrees C (57 degrees F), and rainfall must be heavy enough to "lift" adults into their spawning grounds. Females attach eggs to *Juncus* and *Eleocharis* plants. Males aggressively defend egg-laden clumps of plants. Fry develop in late March and April and return to streams in late April or early May.

Habitat

The slackwater darter has distinct breeding and non-breeding habitats. It normally inhabits small to moderate, slow-flowing, upland streams, no more than 12 meters (40 ft) in width and shallower than 2 meters (6.6 ft). In wider streams, darters tend to gather in sluggish water beneath overhanging banks. It avoids riffles and rapids.

Ready-to-spawn darters are lifted by heavy spring rains into seepage areas in open fields, pastures, and woods, where they spawn. Water in these seepages is typically no more than 8 centimeters (3 in) deep.

Historic Range

The remaining populations of the slackwater darter are probably remnants of a more widespread and continuous distribution throughout the smaller streams of the Tennessee River basin.

Current Distribution

Slackwater darter populations are currently found in five tributaries of the south bend of the Tennessee River: Buffalo River and Shoal Creek in Lawrence County, Tennessee; and Flint River (Madison County), Swan Creek (Limestone County) and Cypress Creek (Lauderdale County), Alabama. In 1984 the population was estimated at 3,600 in Cypress Creek, where the heaviest concentration of slackwater darters is found. Other streams may support only a few hundred of the fish. Biologists consider the population dangerously low.

Conservation and Recovery

The slackwater darter's breeding habitats have been in slow but steady decline for the past 200 years. Heavy use of groundwater for agriculture and human consumption has caused water tables to fall throughout the region, drying up many seepage areas that were historically used for spawning. Numerous spawning seepages have been diked to form agricultural ponds. More recently herbicides, pesticides, industrial wastes, and sewage have entered the groundwater system, degrading water quality.

The slackwater darter's specialized breeding habitats for the Buffalo and Flint rivers, and Shoal and Swan creeks, have not been fully mapped. This was the first task established by the Fish and Wildlife Service (FWS) Recovery Plan. The FWS hopes to purchase breeding sites or obtain management easements from private owners to protect breeding areas on at least three of currently inhabited streams. Without protection, it is feared that most seepage areas will disappear completely in the next twenty years.

Bibliography

Page, Lawrence M. 1983. *Handbook of Darters.* T.H.F. Publishers, Neptune City, New Jersey.

U.S. Fish and Wildlife Service. 1984. "Slackwater Darter Recovery Plan." U.S. Fish and Wildlife Service, Atlanta.

Wall, B. R., and J. D. Williams. 1974. "*Etheostoma boschungi*, a New Percid Fish from the Tennessee River Drainage in Northern Alabama and Western Tennessee." *Tulane Studies in Zoology and Botany* 18(4):172-182.

Williams, J. D., and H. W. Robison. 1980. "*Ozarka*: A New Subgenus of *Etheostoma.*" *Brimleyiana* 4:149-156.

Contact

Regional Office of Endangered Species
U.S. Fish and Wildlife Service
Richard B. Russell Federal Building
75 Spring Street, S.W.
Atlanta, Georgia 30303

Fountain Darter
Etheostoma fonticola

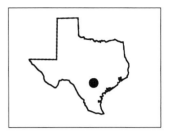

Roger W. Barbour

Status	Endangered
Listed	October 13, 1970
Family	Percidae (Perch)
Description	Tiny, reddish brown darter with dark horizontal lines on sides.
Habitat	Clear, quiet waters.
Food	Insect larvae, small crustaceans.
Reproduction	Spawns year round.
Threats	Aquifer depletion, dam construction, recreational use of habitat.
Region 2	Texas

Description

The fountain darter is a reddish brown darter with an average length of 2.5 centimeters (1 in). It displays a series of dark, horizontal, stitch-like lines along its sides and three dark spots at the base of the tail. Dark bars appear below, behind, and in front of the eyes. Breeding males develop black, red, and clear stripes along the dorsal fin.

Behavior

The fountain darter feeds primarily in daylight on aquatic insect larvae and small crustaceans. It is a selective feeder and prefers moving prey, remaining stationary until prey passes within striking distance. The fountain darter spawns year round, with peaks in early spring and August. After attaching eggs to mosses and algae, the female abandons the sight, providing no care to eggs or fry.

Habitat

The fountain darter prefers clear, quiet backwaters with a profuse bottom growth of aquatic plants and matted algae. It is found in the San Marcos and Comal rivers, which arise from two groups of springs located along the same fault line. These springs discharge a constant flow of high quality water from their source, the Edwards Aquifer. The San Marcos Springs and River ecosystem supports a greater diversity of aquatic organisms than any other ecosystem in the region. The San Marcos River provides habitat for three other federally listed species—San Marcos gambusia (*Gambusia georgei*), the San Marcos salamander (*Eurycea nana*), and Texas wildrice (*Zizania texana*).

Although typically drying in summer, over the course of the year Comal Springs discharge more water than any springs in the southwestern U.S. The San Marcos Springs are active year round.

Historic Range

The historic range of the fountain darter included the sources, headwaters, and sections of the San Marcos and Comal rivers in south-central Texas.

Current Distribution

The fountain darter is found in Spring Lake (Hays County) at the headwaters of the San Marcos River, in the main channel of the river to the confluence of the Blanco River, and in Comal River. Estimates for the number of fountain darters in the San Marcos River vary from about 1,000 to over 10,000. No population estimates have been made for Spring Lake or the Comal River. The Comal River population of fountain darters was completely eliminated when its habitat was reduced to isolated pools by excessive water removal, but it has since been reintroduced into the upper portion of the river in limited numbers.

Conservation and Recovery

Actions that threaten the fountain darter include the destruction of aquatic vegetation in Spring Lake and the San Marcos River, recreational use of the San Marcos River, and long-term water depletion from the Edwards aquifer. Swimmers and divers disturb the algae mats used by the darter for spawning, and the aquifer, which is part of a vast underground water system, supplies the water needs of over a million people throughout the region, including the city of San Antonio.

A dam on the lower portion of the San Marcos River apparently eliminated fountain darter habitat in that section of the river.

The Texas Department of Water Resources forecasts that groundwater pumping for human uses will continue to increase well into the 21st century. At the current rate of increase, scientists predict that the Edwards Aquifer will be so depleted that flow from the San Marcos Springs will cease around the year 2000 and flow from the Comal Springs will be severely reduced. Without the cooperation of state and local agencies to reduce the amount of groundwater extracted from the aquifer, recovery of the fountain darter is considered unlikely.

Bibliography

Schenck, J.R., and B.G. Whiteside. 1976. "Distribution, Habitat Preference and Population Size Estimate of *Etheostoma fonticola*." *Copeia* 1976:697-703.

U.S. Fish and Wildlife Service. 1984. "San Marcos River Recovery Plan." U.S. Fish and Wildlife Service, Albuquerque.

Contact

Regional Office of Endangered Species
U.S. Fish and Wildlife Service
P.O. Box 1306
Albuquerque, New Mexico 87103

Niangua Darter
Etheostoma nianguae

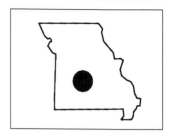

William Roston

Status . . . . . . Threatened
Listed . . . . . . June 12, 1985
Family . . . . . Percidae (Perch)
Description . . . Slender darter with 8 dark cross-bars on back, and spots at base of caudal fin.
Habitat . . . . . . Shallow pools with silt-free bottoms.
Food . . . . Aquatic insects.
Reproduction . . Spawns in spring.
Threats . . . . . . Reservoir construction, stream channelization.
Region 3 . . . . . Missouri

Description

The slender Niangua darter is 7.5 to 10 centimeters (3 to 4 in) long, has eight dark cross-bars on its back, and is readily distinguished from other Missouri darters by the presence of two small jet-black spots at the base of the caudal fin. The only near-relative of the Niangua darter is the arrow darter (*Etheostoma sagitta*), which occurs in eastern Kentucky and northern Tennessee.

Behavior

The Niangua darter feeds on aquatic insects and spawns in spring in swift currents over gravel bottoms.

Habitat

The species inhabits clear, medium-sized streams that run off hilly areas underlain by chert and dolomite. It is usually found in the margins of shallow pools with silt-free, gravel or rocky bottoms.

Historic Range

The Niangua darter is part of a diverse fish fauna, encompassing 107 species in the Osage basin. It is known only from a few tributaries of the Osage River in Missouri, where eight populations along 205 kilometers (128 mi) of the river basin were reported in the early 1970s. These populations were in the Maries River and Lower Maries Creek (Osage County); Big Tavern Creek and upper Little Tavern Creek, Barren Fork, and Brushy Fork (Miller County); Niangua River and Greasy Creek (Dallas County); Little Niangua River, Starks Creek, Thomas Creek, and Cahoochie Creek (Camden, Hickory, and Dallas counties); Little Pomme de Terre River (Benton County); Pomme de

Terre River (Green and Webster counties); Brush Creek (Cedar and St. Clair counties); and the North Dry Sac River (Polk County).

Current Distribution

The Niangua darter population is believed to have declined at most Missouri sites in recent years. An intensive on-site habitat analysis concluded that the species is rare, localized in occurrence, and vulnerable to extinction.

Conservation and Recovery

Construction of the Truman Reservoir formed a barrier to the Niangua darter's movement between tributary streams, fragmenting its range. Migration between these tributary streams is considered important to the long-term survival of the species.

Highway and bridge construction projects frequently straighten and widen stream channels, and landowners channel streams to control local flooding. These practices have led to pervasive sedimentation and silt pollution throughout this darter's range. In addition to stream channelization, the practice of removing woody vegetation from stream banks causes increased erosion, changes in the character of the stream substrate, elimination of pools, and the alteration of stream flow, all of which seriously disrupt the stream ecosystem.

Spotted bass and rock bass were introduced into the Osage Basin before 1940 and are now widely distributed. Diffusion of these predatory fishes from reservoirs into tributary streams inhabited by the Niangua darter could further reduce the population.

Habitat considered critical for the darter's survival has been designated for portions of Camden, Cedar, Dallas, Greene, Hickory, Miller, and St. Clair counties, Missouri. It

encompasses some 145 kilometers (90 mi) of inhabited stream and a 15-meter (50-ft) streambank buffer zone.

Bibliography

Missouri Department of Conservation. 1974. "Rare and Endangered Species of Missouri." Pamphlet. Missouri Department of Conservation, Jefferson City.

Pflieger, W. L. 1971. "A Distributional Study of Missouri Fishes." *Museum of Natural History, University of Kansas Publications* 20(3):229-570.

Pflieger, W. L. 1975. "The Fishes of Missouri." Missouri Department of Conservation, Jefferson City.

Pflieger, W. L. 1978. "Distribution, Status, and Life History of the Niangua Darter, *Etheostoma nianguae.*" Aquatic Series No. 16. Missouri Department of Conservation, Jefferson City.

Contact

Regional Office of Endangered Species
U.S. Fish and Wildlife Service
Federal Building, Fort Snelling
Twin Cities, Minnesota 55111

Watercress Darter

Etheostoma nuchale

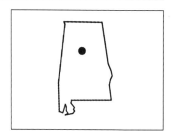

Roger W. Barbour

Status . . . . . . Endangered
Listed . . . . . . October 13, 1970
Family . . . . . . Percidae (Perch)
Description . . . Small darter; breeding males blue, with red-orange belly.
Habitat . . . . . . Deep, slow-moving back-waters of springs.
Food . . . . Insects, crustaceans, and snails.
Reproduction . . Undescribed.
Threats . . . . . . Limited distribution, ur-banization, water pollution.
Region 4 . . . . . Alabama

Description

The watercress darter is a small, robust fish growing to a maximum length of 5 centimeters (2 in). Breeding males are blue above, red-orange below, and have blue and red-orange fins.

Behavior

This darter feeds on aquatic insects, crustaceans, and snails. Its reproductive behavior has not been described.

Habitat

The watercress darter inhabits deep, slow-moving backwaters of spring outflows. These areas support dense aquatic vegetation and particularly watercress (*Nasturtium of-*

ficinale), which attracts a large community of aquatic insects, the darter's principal food.

Historic Range

The species was discovered in 1964 at Glenn Springs near Bessemer, Alabama. Because of its recent discovery, the historic range of the watercress darter is unknown.

Current Distribution

The watercress darter has been found in three springs in Jefferson County, Alabama: Glenn Springs and Thomas' Spring in Bessemer, and Roebuck Springs in Birmingham. No population estimates have been made, but researchers believe that populations at Glenn Springs and Thomas' Spring are declining, while the population at Roebuck Springs is increasing.

Conservation and Recovery

The greatest threats to this species appear to be habitat alteration and pollution. The growth of the Birmingham-Bessemer metropolitan area has resulted in extensive residential construction and the paving of large areas for streets and parking lots. The springs supporting the watercress darter depend on rainfall for recharging, much of which has now been diverted into drains and gutters. As a result, water levels in the springs tend to fluctuate widely.

Roebuck Spring, which had been a source for local drinking water, was condemned in the 1970s because of a level of bacteria too numerous to count. This contamination was possibly caused by seepage from nearby residential septic tanks. Darters in the spring suffer from "gas bubble disease," which is caused by high levels of sewage-derived nitrogen in the water. Nitrogen gas builds up in the body of the fish, eventually killing it. The watercress darter may not survive in this spring.

Grass carp were introduced into Thomas' Spring and by 1977 had removed all vegetation up to the shoreline and eliminated the natural darter population. In 1980 the Fish and Wildlife Service purchased Thomas' Spring and 2.8 hectares (7 acres) of surrounding land for the Watercress Darter National Wildlife Refuge, which is administered as part of the Wheeler National Wildlife Refuge. The grass carp were removed, the spring revegetated, and the watercress darter reintroduced from the Glen Springs population. An additional pond has been built at the refuge and three small dams at Glenn Springs should restore the darter's habitat there. The owner of Glenn Springs has signed an agreement, allowing habitat management and conservation.

Bibliography

Howell, W. M., and R. D. Caldwell. 1965. "*Etheostoma (Oligocephalus) nuchale*, a New Darter from a Limestone Spring in Alabama." *Tulane Studies in Zoology* 12(4):101-108.

U.S. Fish and Wildlife Service. 1984. "Recovery Plan for the Watercress Darter (*Etheostoma nuchale*)." U.S. Fish and Wildlife Service, Atlanta.

Contact

Regional Office of Endangered Species
U.S. Fish and Wildlife Service
Richard B. Russell Federal Building
75 Spring Street, S.W.
Atlanta, Georgia 30303

Okaloosa Darter

Etheostoma okaloosae

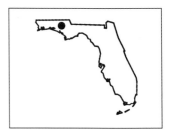

Roger W. Barbour

Status	Endangered
Listed	June 4, 1973
Family	Percidae (Perch)
Description	Light brown darter with dark olive stripes.
Habitat	Shallow streams of swift current.
Food	Insects and plant matter.
Reproduction	Undescribed.
Threats	Road and dam construction, siltation, competition.
Region 4	Florida

Description

The Okaloosa darter ranges from 7.5 to 10 centimeters (3 to 4 in) long. It is light brown with dark olive striping along the sides. Fins are large and transparent, occasionally tinged with red.

Behavior

The Okaloosa darter feeds on aquatic insects and plant matter. Its breeding behavior has not been described but is presumed to be similar to other darters.

Habitat

The Okaloosa darter is an opportunistic species, in that it inhabits a variety of habitats within streams from sluggish, heavily vegetated areas to swift-flowing stretches over sandy bottom. It seems to be most numerous in portions of the streams where currents are moderately swift and the depth of water is no more than 1.5 meters (5 ft). Water temperatures range between 7 and 24 degrees C (45 and 75 F). Much of the watershed drains pine and scrub oak, "sand-hill" habitat.

Historic Range

The Okaloosa darter was first described in the 1940s from specimens taken from Little Rocky Creek in Okaloosa County. It is considered endemic to six Choctawhatchee Bay tributaries in Okaloosa and Walton counties in the Florida Panhandle. This watershed comprises nearly 43,730 hectares (113,000 acres), most of which falls within Eglin Air Force Base. Only about 4,860 hectares (12,000 acres) are privately owned.

Current Distribution

This darter is found along about 305 kilometers (190 mi) of stream habitat in Tom's, Turkey, Mill, Swift, and Rocky creeks, primarily within Eglin Air Force Base.

Conservation and Recovery

The Okaloosa darter population has declined because of deterioration and loss of habitat, caused by road and dam construction, and siltation from land clearing. In addition, this species has suffered in competition with the more common brown darter, which has moved into headwaters formerly occupied exclusively by the Okaloosa darter.

Personnel from Eglin Air Force Base, the Florida Game and Freshwater Fish Commission, the Alabama Biological Survey, the Florida State University, and the U.S. Fish and Wildlife Service collaborated on production of a Recovery Plan for the Okaloosa darter. The plan lays out four primary goals: to determine biological characteristics; protect extant populations and habitats; increase population sizes; and reestablish the species throughout its former range. A management plan has been developed for Eglin Air Force Base and outlines ways to improve habitat, reduce competitors, and periodically sample and monitor the population.

Bibliography

Crews, R. C. 1976. "Aquatic Baseline Survey on Selected Test Areas on Eglin Air Force Base Reservation, Florida." Report No. AFATL-TR-76-4. Eglin Air Force Base.

U.S. Fish and Wildlife Service. 1981. "Okaloosa Darter Recovery Plan." U.S. Fish and Wildlife Service, Atlanta.

Contact

Regional Office of Endangered Species
U.S. Fish and Wildlife Service
Richard B. Russell Federal Building
75 Spring Street, S.W.
Atlanta, Georgia 30303

Bayou Darter

Etheostoma rubrum

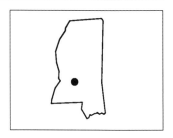

Tom Thornhill

Status	Threatened
Listed	September 25, 1975
Family	Percidae (Perch)
Description . . .	Brownish yellow darter with russet markings.
Habitat	Gravel bottoms in shallow flowing water.
Food	Insects (mayfly larvae) and plant matter.
Reproduction . .	Spawns in spring.
Threats	Limited range and habitat.
Region 4	Mississippi

Description

Only about 5 centimeters (1.9 in) long at maturity, the bayou darter displays russet markings on a field of dusky yellow. The back is a darker brownish yellow. Both males and females have a prominent double spot on the tail fin and a dark bar under the eyes. Males are decidedly larger than females.

The bayou darter is the second smallest species in the subgenus *Nothonotus*, the smallest being the Tippecanoe darter (*Etheostoma tippecanoe*) found in the Ohio River system. The bayou darter is closely related to the yellow cheek darter (*E. moorei*) found in the Devil's Fork and Little Red River of Arkansas' White River system.

Behavior

The bayou darter spawns in mid-summer when it is about two years old, and probably lives three years. Darter fry hatch at the same time that mayfly larvae emerge in the same riffle habitat, and darter minnows are thought to feed almost exclusively on mayfly larvae. Adults feed on insects and plant matter.

Habitat

The watershed, where this darter is found, arises in coastal hills with elevations around 137 meters (450 ft). From their sources, the creeks fall in steps to the coastal plain, where water flow has eroded through deposits of gravel, interspersed with sand. This has resulted in numerous gravel or sandstone riffles of moderate to swift current, which seem to be preferred by the bayou darter. The water in these riffles is typically only about 15 centimeters (6 in) deep.

Historic Range

The bayou darter was first described in 1966 from specimens collected at Mississippi Highway 18 Bayou Pierre crossing. This species is probably endemic to the Bayou Pierre and its five major tributaries, a watershed that drains about 2,500 square kilometers (965 sq mi) of western Mississippi. The source of Bayou Pierre is a small seep near Brookhaven in Lincoln County.

Current Distribution

The bayou darter has been found in Bayou Pierre and three of its tributaries (White Oak Creek, Foster Creek, and Turkey Creek). Range of the bayou darter seems to be limited upstream by waterfalls and downstream by the gradual loss of suitable riffle habitat. The largest concentration of bayou darters is in sections of Bayou Pierre and Foster Creek north of state highway 548 in Copiah County. Researchers consider the population to be limited but also report that they have not observed any significant decline in numbers in recent years.

Conservation and Recovery

The major limitation on bayou darter numbers is its dependence on its specialized habitat—sand and gravel riffles. Some sand and gravel mining already occurs in the area, directly threatening the bayou darter's habitat. Agriculture is widespread in the region, particularly along portions of Turkey Creek and lower Bayou Pierre. In some places, streambank vegetation has been cleared, causing severe erosion and siltation. Nearby petroleum exploration may also pose some threat to water quality.

In the 1970s the Soil Conservation Service conceived the Bayou Pierre Watershed Project to dredge and straighten stream beds, build flood walls and dikes, and construct 24 dams to provide recreational pools. The project would have eliminated most of the bayou's habitat from the affected streams.

After consultation with the Fish and Wildlife Service (FWS), the project's sponsors eliminated the dredging, channel work, and dams, and agreed to evaluate the effects of flood wall construction on downstream water quality. An agreement between the FWS and the Soil Conservation Service allowed construction of one dam on Turkey Creek above the Turkey Creek Falls.

The State of Mississippi has listed the darter as Endangered, providing it some protection from collection. It has been noted that clearcutting along the stream banks could contribute to erosion and alter the water temperature. Timber companies operating in the area have been careful to provide buffer zones along streams, such as Bayou Pierre, as part of their stated policy of conserving riparian habitat.

Bibliography

Deacon, J. E., *et al*. 1979. "Fishes of North America: Endangered, Threatened, or of Special Concern." *Fisheries* 42:29-44.

U.S. Fish and Wildlife Service. 1983. "Bayou Darter Recovery Plan." U.S. Fish and Wildlife Service, Atlanta.

Contact

Regional Office of Endangered Species
U.S. Fish and Wildlife Service
Richard B. Russell Federal Building
75 Spring Street, S.W.
Atlanta, Georgia 30303

Maryland Darter

Etheostoma sellare

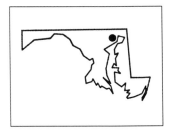

Roger W. Barbour

Status	Endangered
Listed	March 11, 1967
Family	Percidae (Perch)
Description	Silvery darter with dark saddles across its back.
Habitat	Riffle areas in slow-moving streams.
Food	Insects, snails, some plant matter.
Reproduction	Spawns in April or May.
Threats	Dam construction, degradation of water quality.
Region 5	Maryland

Description

The silvery Maryland darter reaches a maximum length of about 7 centimeters (2.8 in). It can be distinguished from closely related darters by four dark saddles across its back and a small dark spot behind the lower rear margin of its eye. The saddles may be poorly developed in juveniles and appear as a series of X-shaped blotches on the sides.

Behavior

The Maryland darter is believed to spawn in late April or early May. Reproduction is probably similar to other members of its genus, which prefer riffle areas over a gravel substrate for spawning. The darter feeds on snails, insect larvae, aquatic insects, and some plant matter.

Habitat

Most specimens have been found in shallow riffle areas over a gravel or silt bottom in a single drainage system in Maryland. Normal flow velocities for streams in this basin are slight, scarcely maintaining a flow under drought conditions. Rooted aquatic plants are riverweed and water moss.

Historic Range

The Maryland darter was originally described in 1913 from specimens collected in Swan Creek adjacent to Gasheys Run near Aberdeen, Maryland. It is believed to have once been more abundant in the lower Susquehanna River drainage.

Current Distribution

The Maryland darter has been found only in the lower Susquehanna River basin near Aberdeen and Havre de Grace, Maryland, in Deer Creek, Swan Creek, and Gasheys Run. Biologists believe that the Deer Creek population may currently be the only viable population. Very few recent sightings of this species have been made. Field surveys at various locations in the early 1980s found only from one to ten individuals at any location.

Conservation and Recovery

The Maryland darter's range was reduced when the Susquehanna River was dammed earlier in the century, causing extensive silting of darter habitat. It is probable that the lack of suitable habitat prevents the darter from breeding in Gasheys Run and that darters found there are stragglers from the Deer Creek population.

The Fish and Wildlife Service has designated Critical Habitat for the Maryland darter to include: the Deer Creek main channel from Elbow Branch to the Susquehanna River; and Gasheys Run main channel from the Penn Central Railroad crossing south to Swan Creek. The most immediate threats to the Maryland darter are runoff into Deer Creek containing excessive nutrients or wastes and the possible construction of other dams and impoundments that would increase water turbidity.

Bibliography

Collette, B. B., and L. W. Knapp. 1966. "Catalog of Type Specimens of the Darters (Pisces, Percidae, Etheostomatini)." *Proceedings of the U.S. Natural History Museum* 119(3550):1-88.

Knapp, L. 1976. "Redescription, Relationships and Status of the Endangered Maryland Darter, *Etheostoma sellare* (Radcliffe and Welsh)." *Proceedings of the Biological Society of Washington* 89(6):99-117.

U.S. Fish and Wildlife Service. 1985. "Revised Maryland Darter Recovery Plan." U.S. Fish and Wildlife Service, Newton Corner, Massachusetts.

Contact

Regional Office of Endangered Species
U.S. Fish and Wildlife Service
One Gateway Center, Suite 700
Newton Corner, Massachusetts 02158

Boulder Darter

Etheostoma sp.

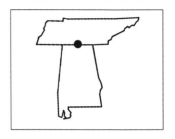

Richard Biggins

Status	Endangered
Listed	September 1, 1988
Family	Percidae (Perch)
Description . . .	Olive to gray darter with dark patches below and behind the eye.
Habitat	Deep, fast-moving water over boulder substrate.
Food	Unknown.
Reproduction . .	Undescribed.
Threats	Dam construction.
Region 4	Alabama, Tennessee

Description

The boulder darter, also known as the Elk River darter, is an olive to gray fish, reaching a maximum length of 7.6 centimeters (3 in). Females are generally lighter, but both sexes have dark patches below and behind the eye. The boulder darter lacks the red spots characteristic of closely related species. The species has also been classified in the genus *Nothonotus*. The abbreviation "sp." in the current scientific name simply means that the formal name of the species has not yet been determined.

Behavior

Less than 50 specimens of the boulder darter have ever been collected. Because of this rarity, nothing is known of its life history or breeding biology.

Habitat

The preferred habitat of the boulder darter is deep, fast-moving water over boulder and slab rock bottoms.

Historic Range

This darter has been found in the Elk River from Fayetteville (Lincoln County, Tennessee) downstream through Giles County into Limestone County, Alabama. Specimens have also been collected from three Elk River tributaries: Indian and Richland creeks (Giles County, Tennessee) and Shoal Creek (Lauderdale County, Alabama). Biologists believe that the species once inhabited the southern bend of the Tennessee River, near its confluence with the Elk River.

Current Distribution

The boulder darter is now restricted to about 43 kilometers (23 mi) of the Elk River (Giles County, Tennessee, and Limestone County, Alabama) and 3 kilometers (2 mi) of Indian and Richland creeks (Giles County, Tennessee). Within this restricted range, the darter is further limited by its specific habitat requirements.

Conservation and Recovery

Decline of the boulder darter is the result of habitat alteration associated with dam construction. Extirpation of the boulder darter from the upper Elk River in Tennessee was likely due to cold water releases from Tims Ford Reservoir. The loss of the Shoal Creek population and any Tennessee River populations resulted from water impoundments behind Wheeler and Wilson Dams.

Although no new dams are currently planned for the watershed, other factors, such as increased siltation, improper pesticide use, toxic chemical spills, and phosphate mining could further threaten the species in the limited habitat it now occupies.

Bibliography

O'Bara, C. J., and D. A. Etnier. 1987. "Status Survey of the Boulder Darter." U.S. Fish and Wildlife Service, Asheville.

Contact

Regional Office of Endangered Species
U.S. Fish and Wildlife Service
Richard B. Russell Federal Building
75 Spring Street, S.W.
Atlanta, Georgia 30303

Big Bend Gambusia
Gambusia gaigai

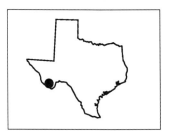

James E. Johnson

Status	Endangered
Listed	March 11, 1967
Family	Poeciliidae (Livebearer)
Description	Small, yellowish gambusia with dark bars under eyes and chin, and a faint lateral stripe.
Habitat	Clear, shallow spring-fed water.
Food	Unknown.
Reproduction	Bears live young.
Threats	Limited habitat, introduced competitors.
Region 2	Texas

Description

The Big Bend gambusia grows to a length of about 3 centimeters (1.2 in). It is yellowish overall, with dark bars beneath the eye and chin and a faint lateral stripe. The male's anal fin is adapted as a sex organ for transferring sperm to the female.

Behavior

The gambusia is a livebearer. Eggs hatch inside the mother's body and are born alive. It is thought that females store sperm for several months after being impregnated. Big Bend gambusia's feeding habits are unknown.

Habitat

The Big Bend gambusia's natural habitat is clear, shallow streams and marshes fed by warm springs. This fish is most abundant amid shoreline vegetation, where there are overhanging trees.

Historic Range

The Big Bend gambusia is known only from springs in Big Bend National Park in Texas. Biologists surmise that at least two separate populations originally existed—at Boquillas Spring, and at Spring 4, east of the present Rio Grande Village campground. It probably existed in other springs in the vicinity of Rio Grande Village. The Boquillas Spring population and the original Spring 4 population have been extirpated.

Current Distribution

Currently, the Big Bend gambusia is restricted to the outflow stream of a single spring near Rio Grande Village in the Big

Bend National Park (Brewster County), Texas. Descendants of the original Spring 4 population are being maintained in a natural holding pool nearby.

Conservation and Recovery

Surface runoff and flooding of the Rio Grande River continually threaten the Big Bend gambusia's survival. Periods of high rainfall increase the amount of silt carried by surface runoff, increasing stream turbidity and bottom deposition. Floods provide an avenue for mosquitofish (*Gambusia affinis*) and other competitors to invade the Big Bend gambusia's pools. Over the years, federally sponsored projects, designed to enhance the "oasis image" of the Rio Grande Village area, have diverted spring outflows into artificial ditches and ponds. Groundwater levels have been lowered, decreasing the flow from the gambusia's springs.

The Park Service's current management goals for recovery of the species include supplementing spring flows from wells in the dry season, and rehabilitating sections of two spring outflows to approximate pre-development conditions. Plans also call for eradication of mosquitofish from springs and streams in the campground area and the eventual establishment of this gambusia in other suitable locations.

Past conservation efforts led to the establishment of a captive population of Big Bend gambusia at the Dexter National Fish Hatchery in New Mexico. The hatchery stock allows replacement if the Texas population suffers high mortality.

Bibliography

Brune, G. 1981. *Springs of Texas*. Branch-Smith, Fort Worth.

Hubbs, C., and J. G. Williams. 1979. "A Review of Circumstances Affecting the Abundance of *Gambusia gaigei*, an Endangered Fish Endemic to Big Bend National Park." In R. Linn, ed., *Proceedings of the First Conference on Scientific Research in the National Parks.*

Minckley, W. L. 1962. "Two New Species of Fishes of the Genus *Gambusia* (Poeciliidae) from Northeastern Mexico." *Copeia* 1962: 391-396.

U.S. Fish and Wildlife Service. 1984. "Big Bend Gambusia Recovery Plan." U.S. Fish and Wildlife Service, Albuquerque.

Contact

Regional Office of Endangered Species
U.S. Fish and Wildlife Service
P.O. Box 1306
Albuquerque, New Mexico 87103

San Marcos Gambusia
Gambusia georgei

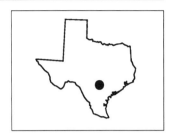

Robert J. Edwards

Status . . . . . . Endangered
Listed . . . . . . July 14, 1980
Family . . . . . Poeciliidae (Livebearer)
Description . . . Small, faintly striped gambusia with lemon-yellow fins.
Habitat . . . . . . Quiet, shallow waters of constant temperature.
Food . . . . Invertebrates.
Reproduction . . Bears live young.
Threats . . . . . . Aquifer depletion, degradation of water quality.
Region 2 . . . . . Texas

Description

The San Marcos gambusia ranges in length from 2.5 to 4 centimeters (1 to 1.6 in). It has lemon-yellow median fins and a diffuse mid-lateral stripe along the length of its body. The dark body displays a bluish sheen, and scales tend to be strongly cross-hatched.

Behavior

The San Marcos gambusia is a livebearer, which means eggs hatch inside the female's body and emerge alive. The female is capable of bearing up to 60 young in a single brood. This gambusia feeds on insect larvae and other invertebrates in slow-moving waters that are shaded by overhanging trees or bridges.

Habitat

The San Marcos River begins at a group of springs found along a fault line within the city limits of San Marcos. These springs discharge a constant flow of high quality water from their source, the Edwards Aquifer. The San Marcos Springs and River ecosystem supports a greater diversity of aquatic organisms than any other ecosystem in the region. The San Marcos River provides habitat for three other federally listed species—the fountain darter (*Etheostoma fonticola*), the San Marcos salamander (*Eurycea nana*), and Texas wildrice (*Zizania texana*).

The San Marcos gambusia prefers quiet backwaters, adjacent to the main thrust of the river current. Its primary habitat requirements appear to be clean and clear water of a constant temperature. Temperatures in the river vary by only a few degrees throughout the year, averaging about 23 degrees C (73 F). The bottom is muddy but generally unsilted.

Historic Range

The gambusia's entire known range is restricted to the San Marcos River near the city of San Marcos (Hays County) in south-central Texas.

Current Distribution

The San Marcos gambusia is currently restricted to a 1-kilometer (0.6-mi) section of the San Marcos River. Most specimens have been found between the Interstate Highway 35 crossing and Thompson's Island. This gambusia is extremely rare as determined by surveys conducted in 1978 and 1979 in the San Marcos River. Biologists netted more than 20,000 *Gambusia* specimens but counted only 18 San Marcos gambusia among them.

Conservation and Recovery

The San Marcos gambusia's very restricted distribution in the river and its absence from the headwaters at Spring Lake indicate very specific habitat requirements. It is extremely sensitive to any alteration of its habitat. Changes in water turbidity caused by runoff from land clearing and construction, an increase in water temperatures caused by lowered water flows, and excessive pumping of groundwater from the Edwards Aquifer, which supplies water to the city of San Antonio, could easily eliminate the species. The entire known range has been designated as habitat critical to the survival of the San Marcos gambusia.

The Texas Department of Water Resources forecast that groundwater pumping for human uses in the region will continue to increase well into the 21st century. At the current rate of increase, scientists predict that the Edwards Aquifer will be so depleted that flow from the San Marcos Springs will cease around the year 2000. Without the cooperation of all state and local agencies that manage use of the aquifer, recovery of the San Marcos gambusia and other endemic wildlife is considered a remote possibility.

Bibliography

Brune, G. 1981. *Springs of Texas*. Branch-Smith, Fort Worth.

Hubbs, C., and A. E. Peden. 1969. "*Gambusia georgei* from San Marcos, Texas." *Copeia* 1969(2)357-364.

U.S. Fish and Wildlife Service. 1984. "San Marcos River Recovery Plan." U.S. Fish and Wildlife Service, Albuquerque.

Contact

Regional Office of Endangered Species
U.S. Fish and Wildlife Service
P.O. Box 1306
Albuquerque, New Mexico 87103

Clear Creek Gambusia
Gambusia heterochir

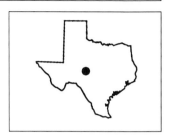

Glen Mills

Status . . . . . . Endangered
Listed . . . . . . March 11, 1967
Family . . . . . Poeciliidae (Livebearer)
Description . . . Small, stocky fish with a metallic sheen.
Habitat . . . . . . Limestone springs.
Food . . . . Aquatic invertebrates.
Reproduction . . Bears live young.
Threats . . . . . Limited distribution, hybridization.
Region 2 . . . . . Texas

Description

The Clear Creek gambusia is a stocky gambusia with a pronounced metallic sheen and distinctive, dark concentric markings on the back and sides. Females have a pronounced anal spot. Males are distinguished from other livebearers by a deep notch in the dorsal margin of the pectoral fin (behind the gills).

Behavior

The female Clear Creek gambusia may store sperm for several months after being inseminated and is fertile for seven months of the year from March through September. During this time, she is capable of producing about 50 young every 42 days. Eggs hatch inside the mother's body, and young emerge alive.

Habitat

This gambusia is restricted to springs and outflow streams with clear, clean water, low pH (acid), and nearly constant, year-round temperatures. It prefers areas of profuse aquatic vegetation. Upper Clear Creek arises from the Wilkinson Springs, a group of limestone springs that discharges water from the Edwards Aquifer.

Historic Range

The Clear Creek gambusia is endemic to the source pools and headwaters of Clear Creek, a small tributary of the San Saba River in Menard County, central Texas.

Current Distribution

The population is restricted to the main pools of the Wilkinson Springs at the headwaters of Upper Clear Creek on the Clear Creek Ranch, situated 16 kilometers (10 mi) west of Menard near Ft. McKavett. The headspring pool covers an area of about 1 hectare (2.2 acres). The natural course of Upper Clear Creek has been modified extensively to provide water for livestock, irrigation, and humans. About 75 meters (250 ft) downstream from the headsprings, a series of four dams impounds the creek into pools.

Conservation and Recovery

The main threat to this species is simply its extremely limited distribution and dependence on a single group of springs. Should the water table fall because of groundwater pumping or water flows be diverted to support more intensive human uses, the population would be eliminated. The Clear Creek gambusia is also threatened by its ready ability to interbreed with other more common gambusia species, which are found in Clear Creek below the dams.

Of particular concern is the predatory mosquitofish (*Gambusia affinis*), which in the 1970s found its way into some of the dam pools through a deteriorated section of an aging, earthen-concrete dam. This dam was extensively repaired in 1979 by Fish and Wildlife Service (FWS) personnel, and mosquitofish were removed. Although the site is privately owned, the FWS has reached a conservation agreement with the landowner to manage the habitat pools. Since the repairs to the dam were completed the primary goal of recovery has been "to maintain the status quo." Should the habitat be further jeopardized, for example, by sale of the ranch to resort developers, the FWS anticipates a more aggressive intervention.

Bibliography

Hubbs, Clark. 1957. "*G. heterochir*, a New Poeciliid fish from Texas with an Account of Its Hybridization with *G. affinis*." *Tulane Studies in Zoology* 5:1-16.

Minckley, W. L. 1962. "Two New Species of Fishes of the Genus *Gambusia* (Poeciliidae) from Northeastern Mexico." *Copeia* 1962:391-396.

Rosen, D. E., and R. M. Bailey. 1963. "The Poeciliid Fishes (Cyprinodontiformes): Their Structure, Zoogeography, and Systematics." *Bulletin of the American Museum of Natural History* 126:1-176.

U.S. Fish and Wildlife Service. 1980. "Recovery Plan for Clear Creek Gambusia *Gambusia heterochir*." U.S. Fish and Wildlife Service, Albuquerque.

Contact

Regional Office of Endangered Species
U.S. Fish and Wildlife Service
P.O. Box 1306
Albuquerque, New Mexico 87103

Pecos Gambusia
Gambusia nobilis

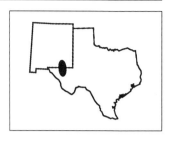

James E. Johnson

Status	Endangered
Listed	October 13, 1970
Family	Poeciliidae (Livebearer)
Description	Robust, silvery yellow fish with arched back.
Habitat	Springs and outflow streams.
Food	Insects, other invertebrates.
Reproduction	Bears live young.
Threats	Fragmentation of habitat, drying of springs.
Region 2	New Mexico, Texas

Description

The Pecos gambusia, also known as the Texas gambusia, is closely related to the common mosquitofish (*Gambusia affinis*). It is a small, robust silvery yellow fish, and in profile, shows an arched back. Females have a black area on the abdomen that surrounds the anal fin. The anal fin of the male is modified as an organ to transfer milt during copulation.

Behavior

The Pecos gambusia gives birth to live young. It feeds on the surface, taking a wide variety of insects and small invertebrates. It shelters from predators in beds of aquatic vegetation.

Habitat

The Pecos gambusia is found in springs and outflow streams over a large geographic range in the Pecos River Basin—from an elevation of 1,180 meters (3,870 ft) in the uplands of New Mexico to about 820 meters (2,690 ft) in Texas. It is found in springheads, limestone sinks, spring-fed creeks, and sedge-covered marshes. Common factors among these habitats are: clear, clean water, stable flows, and fairly constant temperatures. The Pecos gambusia is intolerant of water temperatures above about 38 degrees C (100 F).

Historic Range

The Pecos gambusia is endemic to the Pecos River Basin in southeastern New Mexico and western Texas, occurring from Fort Sumner in De Baca County, New Mexico, as far south as Fort Stockton in Pecos County, Texas. New Mexican populations, known from the Pecos River south of Fort Sumner and the North Spring River near Roswell, have been extirpated. Texas populations in Leon and Comanche springs were eliminated when the springs dried up.

Current Distribution

In New Mexico, populations occur in Ink Pot within the Salt Creek Wilderness Area, in a group of springs, sinkholes, and outflows at Bitter Lake National Wildlife Refuge (Chaves County), at Living Desert State Park, and in Blue Spring and its outflows (Eddy County). In Texas, populations are found near Balmorhea in East Sandia, Phantom Lake, and Giffin springs (Reeves County), and near Fort Stockton in Leon Creek and Diamond-Y Spring outflows (Pecos County).

In 1980, the total population of the Pecos gambusia was estimated at about two million fish, divided fairly equally among sites in New Mexico and Texas. The largest concentrations occurred in Pecos County, Texas. In spite of the seemingly large numbers, all populations are considered vulnerable because of alterations to the Pecos River.

Conservation and Recovery

Water diversion from the Pecos River for irrigation intensified after five major and three lesser dams were constructed along the main river channel. A new dam (Brantley Dam) to replace the existing McMillan Dam was recently proposed for construction.

Although the mainstream never provided preferred habitat for the Pecos gambusia, it enabled fish to migrate from dry springs to habitable ones during drought years. Dam construction and water diversion have reduced natural stream flows, increased salinity and turbidity, and altered water temperatures, prohibiting migration. The isolated gambusia populations now depend on uninterrupted spring discharges for survival. Introduction of non-native gambusia

into the river system has been an additional factor in limiting the Pecos gambusia's range. Although it is better adapted to springs and outflows, its competitors are better suited to existing downstream conditions.

During the 1970s Fish and Wildlife Service personnel attempted to transplant the Pecos gambusia to more than 20 springs and sinkholes within the Bitter Lake National Wildlife Refuge in an effort to expand its range and improve its chances of survival. Most of these attempts were unsuccessful, but small populations were established at Bitter Creek, Sago, and two smaller springs. In 1987 Bitter Creek and Sago Spring supported a population of about 500 gambusia.

In the past, the Dexter National Fish Hatchery in New Mexico successfully raised a captive population of the Pecos gambusia. Although this population was eventually released, the hatchery's success demonstrates that a captive stock could be used to replenish drought-depleted populations.

Bibliography

Bednarz, J. C. 1979. "Ecology and Status of the Pecos Gambusia, *Gambusia nobilis* (Poeciliidae), in New Mexico." *Southwest Naturalist* 24:311-322.

U.S. Fish and Wildlife Service. 1983. "Pecos Gambusia Recovery Plan." U.S. Fish and Wildlife Service, Albuquerque.

Contact

Regional Office of Endangered Species
U.S. Fish and Wildlife Service
P.O. Box 1306
Albuquerque, New Mexico 87103

Unarmored Threespine Stickleback

Gasterosteus aculeatus williamsoni

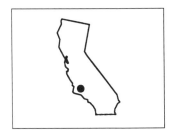

B. "Moose" Peterson

Status . . . . . . Endangered
Listed . . . . . . October 13, 1970
Family . . . . . . Gasterosteidae (Stick-
leback)
Description . . . Small, olive-brown fish with
prominent dorsal spines.
Habitat . . . . . . Vegetated, slow-flowing,
shallow streams.
Food . . . . Insects and snails.
Reproduction . . Spawns year round.
Threats . . . . . Urbanization, hybridization,
predation.
Region 1 . . . . . California

Description

One of three subspecies of threespine stickleback in North America, the unarmored threespine stickleback grows to a length of about 6 centimeters (2.4 in). Its streamlined body is olive-brown to dark green above and light yellow, white, or silvery below. The head, and sometimes the back, of breeding males turns bright red. Most sticklebacks are heavily plated on the sides, but this subspecies is "zero plated" or unarmored. It is called "threespine" because two spiny projections replace the first dorsal fin, and a third spine protrudes in front of the rear back fin.

Behavior

The unarmored threespine stickleback is an opportunistic feeder, subsisting mostly on insects and snails. It reproduces throughout the year with a peak of activity in March. The male establishes a territory and constructs a nest from aquatic vegetation on the river bottom. After the female lays eggs in the nest, the male fans the eggs to aerate them and aggressively drives away predators. After hatching, fry remain in the nest until large enough to fend for themselves. Individuals live for one year.

Habitat

Optimum stickleback habitat consists of clean, clear-flowing streams in deeper pools where there is a slow, steady current. In stronger currents, adults shelter behind obstructions. Juveniles congregate in backwaters, hidden among aquatic plants. This fish is not found in waters that are even slightly turbid.

Historic Range

Threespine sticklebacks are common throughout much of North America. The unarmored threespine stickleback, however, was found only in southern California. At one time, its range included the portions of the Los Angeles, San Gabriel, and Santa Ana rivers, which now pass directly through metropolitan Los Angeles (Los Angeles County). It also occurred in the headwaters of the Santa Clara River (northern Los Angeles County), and the Santa Maria River and San Antonio Creek (Santa Barbara County).

Current Distribution

At present, the unarmored threespine stickleback survives in the headwaters of the Santa Clara River near the towns of Acton and Saugus, and in San Antonio Creek near Lompoc. A transplanted population is thought to survive in Honda Creek on the Vandenburg Air Force Base Reservation. A remnant population of the fish may have been located in Shay Creek (San Bernardino County).

Conservation and Recovery

This stickleback has been extirpated from the Los Angeles Basin by urbanization. Groundwater pumping, water diversion, stream channelization, and degraded water quality have combined to permanently eliminate most of its historic habitat. Where it survives in San Antonio Creek, the unarmored threespine stickleback has interbred with another subspecies (*Gasterosteus aculeatus microcephalus*), which was accidentally introduced into the river system. If interbreeding continues, the unarmored threespine stickleback will lose its unique characteristics.

Populations in the upper Santa Clara River have survived because the mountainous region is largely undeveloped, and natural barriers have prevented hybridization. In these headwaters, however, sticklebacks have been forced to compete for food and breeding sites with the introduced mosquitofish. Sometime in the 1970s, the African clawed frog (*Xenopus laevis*), which was a popular pet until prohibited, became established in a Santa Clara River tributary. This carnivorous frog is regarded as a threat to all native fishes. The Fish and Wildlife Service (FWS) has undertaken a project to eliminate the frog from streams in the region.

The FWS continues its research into the biology and ecology of the unarmored threespine stickleback and will attempt to re-establish additional populations within the historic range. Because several habitat streams are in danger of being dried up by groundwater pumping, the FWS has implemented a strategy to supply emergency water to these streams or to salvage fish populations if necessary. A major goal of the FWS Recovery Plan is to control the many non-native fishes and pests that abound in the watershed. Without some effort to remove these exotics, the native unarmored threespine stickleback will be unable to return to formerly inhabited streams.

Bibliography

Irwin, J. F., and D. L. Soltz. 1982. "The Distribution and Natural History of the Unarmored Threespine Stickeback in San Antonio Creek, California". Report. U.S. Fish and Wildlife Service, Sacramento.

U.S. Fish and Wildlife Service. 1985. "Revised Unarmored Threespine Stickleback Recovery Plan." U.S. Fish and Wildlife Service, Portland.

Contact

Regional Office of Endangered Species
U.S. Fish and Wildlife Service
Lloyd 500 Building, Suite 1692
500 N.E. Multnomah Street
Portland, Oregon 97232

Mohave Tui Chub

Gila bicolor mohavensis

L. Fisk

Status	Endangered
Listed	October 13, 1970
Family	Cyprinidae (Minnow)
Description	Olive to brown chub with a chunky body, large head, and short snout.
Habitat	Deep pools fed by alkaline mineral springs.
Food	Plankton, insect larvae, detritus.
Reproduction	Spawns in spring.
Threats	Hybridization, habitat degradation.
Region 1	California

Description

The Mohave tui chub is a moderate to large subspecies of the tui chub, 5 to 9.2 centimeters (2 to 3.7 in) long. It has a thick, chunky body with a large head and short snout, an oblique mouth, and short, rounded fins. In older fish, a distinct hump sometimes develops behind the head. This chub is bright brassy-brown to dusky-olive on the sides and bluish-white to silver on the belly. The fins are olive to rich brown.

The Mohave tui chub is similar in appearance to the Endangered Owens tui chub (*Gila bicolor snyderi*) and the Lahontan tui chub (*G. b. obesa*).

Behavior

The Mohave tui chub is adapted for feeding on plankton and also consumes insect larvae and detritus. It spawns in March or April when water warms to 18 degrees C (65 F) and may spawn again in the fall. Females affix fertilized eggs to aquatic plants, primarily the ditchgrass. Fry form schools in the shallows, but mature fish are solitary. The life span is probably no more than two years.

Habitat

The Mohave tui chub occurs in mineralized, alkaline waters in deep pools or more shallow outflow streams. It was once found in the mainstream of the Mohave River but prefers lakes and mineral spring pools. Dominant plants in the habitat include ditchgrass, bulrush, cattail, rush, saltgrass. Because it does not withstand flooding well, it is dependent on populations in lakes and pools to replenish fish that are washed downstream and out of the river.

Historic Range

The Mohave tui chub is the only fish known to be endemic to the Mohave River basin in southwestern California. During the Pleistocene, the river was fed by three large lakes—Mohave, Little Mohave, and Manix—which supplied ideal habitat for this chub. When the climate grew more arid and the lakes dried, the Mohave tui chub became restricted to the Mohave River downstream from Victorville, and to a series of springs between Victorville and the river sources.

Current Distribution

The Mohave tui chub is currently found in three extensively modified pools at Soda Springs, situated near the southeastern edge of the dry bed of Soda Lake in San Bernardino County. The springs were an important water stop for travelers on the Mohave Road, which was a supply road from Los Angeles to Ft. Mohave on the Colorado River. In 1940 Lake Tuendae, the largest pool, was excavated and channeled for a health spa which operated until 1974. Groundwater pumping has decreased the size of the other pools.

In the 1970s Mohave tui chubs were transplanted to Lark Seep Lagoon on the China Lake Naval Weapons Center. This is now the largest existing population, consisting of several thousand individuals. The Desert Research Station Pond near Hinkley, about 16 kilometers (10 mi) northwest of Barstow, supports a transplanted population of 1,500 to 2,000.

Conservation and Recovery

When the Arroyo chub (*Gila orcutti*) was introduced as a baitfish into the Mohave River during the 1930s, the Mohave tui chub entered a precipitous decline. The two fish interbred so extensively that the Mohave tui chub was almost eliminated as a unique subspecies by 1967. In addition, construction of dams and reservoirs at the headwaters altered water flow in the mainstream and provided better habitat for many non-native fishes, which compete more aggressively for food.

After a string of failures, the success of recent relocation efforts has generated cautious optimism for the recovery of the Mohave tui chub. The Fish and Wildlife Service plans to establish three more protected populations of at least 500 fish each. Likely transplant sites are along the Mohave River at Camp Cady Wildlife Area, Afton Canyon Campground, and Mohave Narrows Regional Park. Once these transplants are deemed successful, biologists will consider removing this chub from the federal list. Biologists are currently assessing the feasibility of removing the Arroyo chub from the Mohave River and restocking the river with the indigenous Mohave tui chub.

Bibliography

Hoover, F., and J. A. St. Amant. 1983. "Results of Mohave Tui Chub, *Gila bicolor mohavensis*, Relocations in California and Nevada." *California Fish and Game* 69:54-56.

U.S. Fish and Wildlife Service. 1984. "Recovery Plan for the Mohave Tui Chub, *Gila bicolor mohavensis*." U.S. Fish and Wildlife Service, Portland.

Contact

Regional Office of Endangered Species
U.S. Fish and Wildlife Service
Lloyd 500 Building, Suite 1692
500 N.E. Multnomah Street
Portland, Oregon 97232

Owens Tui Chub

Gila bicolor snyderi

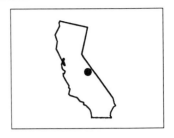

California Department of Fish and Game

Status	Endangered
Listed	August 5, 1985
Family	Cyprinidae (Minnow)
Description	Olive and white chub with lateral blue and gold reflections.
Habitat	Streams, rivers, irrigation ditches.
Food	Insects.
Reproduction	Undescribed.
Threats	Water diversion, non-native fishes, hybridization.
Region 1	California

Description

The Owens tui chub is a moderate to large subspecies of *Gila bicolor,* with males reaching 10 centimeters (4 in) and females slightly over 13 centimeters (5 in) in length. It is olive above and whitish below, with lateral blue and gold reflections. The side of the head is noticeably gold. The Owens tui chub has been known since the late 1800s, but was not described as a new subspecies until 1973.

Habitat

Based on past collections, the Owens tui chub occupied various habitats ranging from thermal spring pools, supporting only a few hundred individuals, to the mainstream of the Owens River, where the population numbered in the tens or hundreds of thousands. Primary habitat requirements appear to be clear, clean water, adequate cover in the form of rocks, undercut banks, or aquatic vegetation, and sufficient insect food.

Historic Range

The Owens tui chub has been recorded in Owens Lake, Owens River, tributary streams, and irrigation ditches throughout the Owens River basin (Inyo and Mono counties), California.

Current Distribution

Because of extensive hybridization throughout the basin, genetically pure populations of the Owens tui chub are now known from only two locations in Mono County—in the source springs of Hot Creek, and a 13-kilometer (8-mi) stretch of the Owens River below Long Valley Dam. Both sites are within the Inyo National Forest but are owned by the City of Los Angeles. The present distribution represents less than 1 percent of its historic range.

Conservation and Recovery

Demand for water from the Owens River basin for irrigation and human consumption is high. The river has been dammed at several places and much of its water diverted through aqueducts to Los Angeles, over 415 kilometers (260 mi) to the south. The resulting reduction of stream flow has degraded water quality and greatly restricted available habitat for this chub.

The surviving Owens tui chub populations are also threatened by predators, such as the introduced brown trout, and by interbreeding with the Lahontan tui chub (*Gila bicolor obesa*). This non-native chub was introduced illegally into the Owens River as a baitfish.

The California Department of Fish and Game, Bureau of Land Management, and Fish and Wildlife Service (FWS) have repeatedly tried to reintroduce the Owens tui chub to Fish Slough in Mono County. To date, however, transplanted chubs have not survived. Further reintroduction efforts will be based on the results of ongoing research into the chub's habitat preferences.

In 1986 the FWS and the state Department of Fish and Game reached an agreement to maintain the chub's habitat at Hot Creek Springs.

Bibliography

Miller, R. R. 1973. "Two New Fishes, *Gila bicolor snyderi* and *Catostomus fumeiventris*, from the Owens River Basin, California." *Occasional Papers of the Museum of Zoology, University of Michigan* 667:1-19.

Pister, E. P. 1981. "The Conservation of Desert Fishes." In R. J. Naiman and D. L. Solts, eds., *Fishes in North American Deserts*. John Wiley and Sons, New York.

Contact

Regional Office of Endangered Species
U.S. Fish and Wildlife Service
Lloyd 500 Building, Suite 1692
500 N.E. Multnomah Street
Portland, Oregon 97232

Hutton Spring Tui Chub
Gila bicolor ssp.

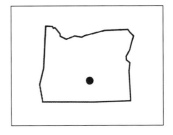

Oregon Nature Conservency

Status . . . . . . Threatened
Listed . . . . . March 28, 1985
Family . . . . . . Cyprinidae (Minnow)
Description . . . Silvery sided chub with a
dusky olive back.
Habitat . . . . . . Springs and outflows.
Food . . . . Snails, insects, and am-
phipods.
Reproduction . . Spawns between April and
June.
Threats . . . . . . Limited numbers, ground-
water pumping, con-
taminants.
Region 1 . . . . . Oregon

Description

The silvery sided Hutton tui chub ranges from 12 to 15 centimeters (4.7 to 6 in) in length. It has a dusky olive back and white belly. Its head is longer, the dorsal fin smaller, and the eyes larger than closely related chubs. Tui chubs in general have only one row of teeth on the pharyngeal bone, and the teeth of this tui chub are exceptionally robust. The Hutton Spring tui chub has been proposed for classification as *Gila bicolor oregonensis,* but this is not official.

Behavior

The omnivorous Hutton tui chub feeds on a wide range of snails, terrestrial and aquatic insects, amphipods, and perhaps algae. It prefers deeper pools and spawns in shallower water over beds of aquatic vegetation.

Females deposit eggs between April and June, which hatch after about nine days.

Habitat

The Hutton tui chub is confined to two freshwater springs and associated outflow streams. It requires clean water of constant temperature. Hutton Spring was widened and diked in the 1970s to create a pool about 12 meters (39 ft) in diameter. Dredging removed most aquatic vegetation, except for a dense stand of rushes in the center of the pool. The Hutton Spring tui chub is currently the only fish inhabiting the spring.

Historic Range

Populations of the Hutton Spring tui chub have been found in two spring pools and related outflow streams and marshes in Lake

County, Oregon. The springs are situated at the northwestern edge of the dry Alkali Lake.

Current Distribution

The Hutton Spring tui chub is known only from Hutton Spring and Three Eighths Spring—a smaller spring located slightly southeast of Hutton Spring. The chub population in Hutton Spring is thought to number about 300 individuals, and Three Eighths Spring supports an additional 150 chubs.

Conservation and Recovery

Surviving populations of the Hutton Spring tui chub are threatened by groundwater pumping for irrigation, which has caused spring discharges and water levels in the region to fall. The property owner has generally been protective of Hutton Spring and has fenced the area to exclude livestock. Three Eighths Spring remains unfenced and has been slightly disturbed by cattle. Both springs are vulnerable to habitat modification, either by dredging or diversion of water into artificial channels. Although it has not yet occurred, the introduction of nonnative fishes into the springs would have a disastrous effect on the Hutton tui chub because of the narrow confines of the pools.

A nearby dump is a repository for an estimated 25,000 55-gallon drums of highly toxic chemicals. Residues from these improperly disposed wastes have leached into the surface and groundwater of the Alkali Lake area. It is possible that the springs inhabited by the Hutton Spring tui chub will become contaminated within the foreseeable future if the corroded storage drums continue to leak. The Bureau of Land Management, the Environmental Protection Agency, and the Oregon Department of Environmental Quality are examining ways to reclaim the toxic waste disposal site.

Bibliography

Bills, F. 1977. "Taxonomic Status of Isolated Populations of Tui Chub Referred to as *Gila bicolor oregonensis* [Snyder]." M.A. Thesis. Oregon State University, Corvallis, Oregon.

Bond. C. E. 1973. "Keys to Oregon Freshwater Fishes." Technical Bulletin No. 58. Agricultural Experiment Station, Oregon State University.

Bond, C. E. 1974. "Endangered Plants and Animals of Oregon; Fishes." Special Report No. 205. Agricultural Experiment Station, Oregon State University.

Contact

Regional Office of Endangered Species
U.S. Fish and Wildlife Service
Lloyd 500 Building, Suite 1692
500 N.E. Multnomah Street
Portland, Oregon 97232

Borax Lake Chub
Gila boraxobius

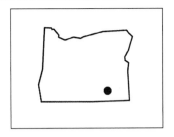

Jack Williams

Status	Endangered
Listed	October 5, 1982
Family	Cyprinidae (Minnow)
Description	Dwarf chub with olive green back and silvery sides with purplish sides.
Habitat	Mineralized lake fed by thermal spring.
Food	Diatoms, aquatic invertebrates, terrestrial insects.
Reproduction	Spawns year round.
Threats	Water diversion, geothermal exploration.
Region 1	Oregon

Description

The Borax Lake chub is a dwarf chub, ranging from 3.3 to 6 centimeters (1.3 to 2.4 in) in length. It has an olive green back with a dark mid-line, and silvery sides with black flecking, and a purplish iridescence. The eyes are large and protuberant. The jaw is elongated.

Behavior

This chub is an opportunistic omnivore, feeding on diatoms, tiny crustaceans, insects and larvae, and detritus. It spawns throughout the year with peaks in spring and fall. Young are prominent in the shallow coves around the lake margin in May and June. Individuals live from one to three years.

Habitat

Borax Lake is a 4.1-hectare (10.2-acre), highly mineralized natural lake, characterized by shallow waters (1 m; 3.3 ft), sparse aquatic vegetation, and a constant inflow from thermal springs. Outflow from the lake maintains a small pond and, in the past, extensive marshes between the lake and the pond. Over time, precipitation of salts from the spring water has raised the perimeter of the lake approximately 9 meters (30 ft) above the valley floor, isolating the chub from the surrounding watershed.

From 1898 to 1907 the extensive salt deposits of the area were mined for borax. The lake is the site of the original Twenty Mule Team Borax Works, which shipped borax in wagons hauled by 20-mule teams to the railroad at Winnemucca, Nevada.

Historic Range

It is thought that this species evolved within the last 10,000 years in Harney County, Oregon. Alford Lake, a large pluvial lake, once covered this area. About 10,000 years ago the lake began to dry, and native fishes were restricted to remaining springs, lakes, and creeks. An ancestral stock became isolated in the springs of Borax Lake and adapted to the extreme conditions of the habitat, evolving into the form now recognized as the Borax Lake chub.

Current Distribution

The Borax Lake chub is found only in Borax Lake, its outflow, and Lower Borax Lake, situated in the Alvord Basin of south-central Oregon (Harney County). Population estimates for Borax Lake made in 1986 and 1987 ranged between 6,000 and 14,000. There are thought to be an additional 8,000 to 10,000 chubs in Lower Borax Lake. The Borax Lake chub apparently experiences large swings in population caused by hot weather die-offs. Renewed spawning activity in the fall signals a rebound to pre-summer levels.

Conservation and Recovery

Borax Lake is a fragile aquatic ecosystem, which is particularly sensitive to alteration. In 1980 a modification of the lake perimeter to divert water lowered the water level by about 0.3 meter (1 ft). This decreased the total area of chub habitat and increased the average water temperature of the lake. Much of the adjacent marsh dried up as a result of this diversion. Marshes around the lower lake retain water from permanent seepage.

The entire Alvord Basin is geothermally active, and the Bureau of Land Management (BLM) has leased geothermal exploration rights to private companies. Biologists fear that exploratory drilling in the area will disrupt interconnecting channels within the aquifer, lower water pressure, and cause the lake, which is above the valley floor, to go dry. The BLM is currently reassessing its permit granting procedure for the region.

Within an area defined as habitat critical to the survival of the Borax Lake chub, the BLM owns 130 hectares (320 acres). Another 130 hectares is privately owned, including the lake itself. In 1983 the Nature Conservancy secured a ten-year lease to the lake and—with the assistance of the Oregon Department of Fish and Wildlife and the BLM—has undertaken a program to rehabilitate the marshes by returning lake outflows to previous levels.

Bibliography

Ono, R. D., J. Williams, and A. Wagner. 1983. *Vanishing Fishes of North America.* Stonewall Press, Washington, D.C.

Williams, J. E., and C. E. Bond. 1980. "*Gila boraxobius,* a New Species of Cyprinid Fish from Southeastern Oregon with a Comparison to *Gila alvordensis* Hubbs and Miller." *Proceedings of the Biological Society of Washington* 92(2):291-298.

U.S. Fish and Wildlife Service. 1987. "Recovery Plan for the Borax Lake Chub, *Gila boraxobius.*" U.S. Fish and Wildlife Service. Portland.

Contact

Regional Office of Endangered Species
U.S. Fish and Wildlife Service
Lloyd 500 Building, Suite 1692
500 N.E. Multnomah Street
Portland, Oregon 97232

▲ Masked Bobwhite *(p. 594)*

Attwater's Prairie Chicken *(p. 710)* ▼

▲ American Peregrine Falcon *(p. 607)*

Hawaiian Hawk *(p. 584)* ▼

Audubon's Crested Caracara *(p. 675)* ▼

▲ Hawaiian Stilts *(p. 634)*

Hawaiian Common Moorhen *(p. 613)* ▼

▲ Mississippi Sandhill Cranes *(p. 618)*

Hawaiian Coot *(p. 610)* ▼

▲ Nihoa Finch *(p. 708)*

Least Bell's Vireo *(p. 716)* ▼

▲ Florida Scrub Jay *(p. 579)*

Whooping Cranes *(p. 615)* ▼

▲   Desert Tortoise *(p. 750)*

▲   Green Sea Turtle *(p. 724)*

Ringed Sawback Turtle *(p. 755)*   ▼

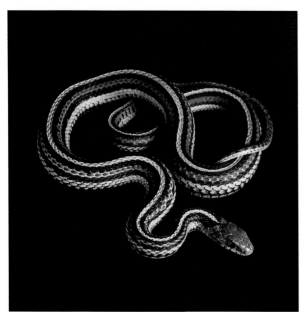

▲ Eastern Indigo Snake *(p. 736)*

▲ San Francisco Garter Snake *(p. 776)*

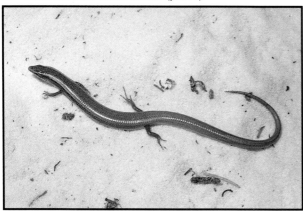

▲ Blue -Tailed Mole Skink *(p. 745)*

▲ Concho Water Snake *(p. 766)*

Atlantic Salt Marsh Snake *(p. 764)* ▼

▲   Mona Ground Iguana *(p. 731)*

Blunt-Nosed Leopard Lizard *(p. 747)*   ▼

Golden Coqui *(p. 791)*   ▼

▼   Puerto Rican Crested Toad *(p. 795)*

▲ Houston Toad *(p. 789)*

Santa Cruz Long-Toed Salamander *(p. 783)* ▲

▼ San Marcos Salamander *(p. 793)*

▲ Wyoming Toad *(p. 787)*

Maryland Darter *(p. 851)* ▼

▲ Gila Trout *(p. 948)*

◄ Shortnose Sturgeon *(p. 801)*

▼ Little Kern Golden Trout *(p. 940)*

Devil's Hole Pupfish *(p. 821)* ▲

Unarmoured Threespine Stickleback *(p. 863)* ▼

▲   Okaloosa Darter *(p. 847)*

Snail Darter *(p. 921)*   ▼

Watercress Darter *(p. 845)*   ▼

Oahu Tree snail *(p. 1041)* ▲

▼ Oahu Tree Snail *(p. 1041)*

Oahu Tree snail *(p. 1041)* ▲

▼ Flat-Spired Three -Toothed Snail *(p. 1058)*

▼ Endangered Freshwater Mussels

1	*Quadrula sparsa*
2	*Quadrula intermedia*
3	*Fusconaia maculata maculata* *
4	*Fusconaia maculata lesueuriana* *
5	*Fusconaia cuneolus*
6	*Fusconaia edgariana*
7	*Lexingtonia dolabelloides* *
8	*Plethobasus cicatricosus*
9	*Plethobasus cooperianus*
10	*Pleurobema clava* *
11	*Pleurobema plenum*
12	*Cyrtonaias tampicoensis tecomatensis*
13	*Cyprogenia alberti* *
14	*Dromus dromas*
15	*Potamilus capax*
16	*Toxolasma cylindrellus*
17	*Conradilla caelata*
18	*Villosa trabalis*
19	*Lampsilis higginsi*
20	*Lampsilis orbiculata*
21	*Lampsilis virescens*
22	*Epioblasma torulosa torulosa*
23	*Lampsilis satura* *
24	*Lampsilis streckeri*
25	*Epioblasma sulcata delicata*
26	*Epioblasma turgidula*
27	*Epioblasma florentina florentina*
28	*Epioblasma walkeri*
29	*Epioblasma rangiana* *
30	*Epioblasma torulosa gubernaculum*
31	*Epioblasma florentina curtisi*

*Protected by International Treaty

▲ Kentucky Cave Shrimp *(p. 1033)*

California Freshwater Shrimp *(p. 1037)* ▼

▲ Oahu Tree Snails *(p. 1041)*

▲ Elderberry Longhorn Beetle *(p. 1067)*

Tooth Cave Ground Beetle *(p. 1095)* ▼

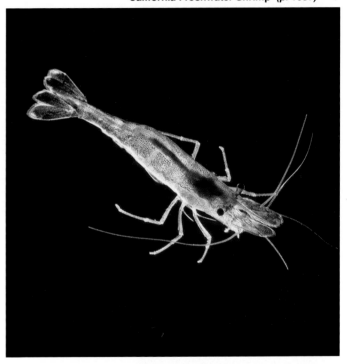

Delta Green Ground Beetle *(p. 1069)* ▼

Bay Checkerspot Butterfly *(p. 1075)* ▼

▲   Pawnee Montane Skipper *(p. 1083)*

▲   San Bruno Elfin Butterfly *(p. 1065)*

▲   Lange's Metalmark Butterfly *(p. 1063)*

Schaus Swallowtail Butterfly *(p. 1081)*   ▲

▼   Palos Verdes Blue Butterfly *(p. 1079)*

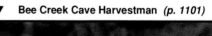

Tooth Cave Spider *(p. 1087)*   ▲

▼   Bee Creek Cave Harvestman *(p. 1101)*

Humpback Chub
Gila cypha

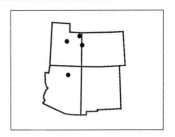

Bill Miller

Status	. . . . . . Endangered
Listed	. . . . . . March 11, 1967
Family	. . . . . . Cyprinidae (Minnow)
Description	. . . Large olive or brown chub with a hump behind the head.
Habitat	. . . . . . Swift currents and deep channels.
Food	. . . . Bottom-feeder.
Reproduction	. . Spawns in May or June.
Threats	. . . . . . Dam construction, competition with non-native fishes.
Region 2	. . . . . Arizona
Region 6	. . . . . Colorado, Utah, Wyoming

Description

The humpback chub is a large chub, between 30 and 38 centimeters (12 and 15 in) in length, with a prominent hump behind the head. It has a flat, fleshy snout, and small eyes. It is olive or brown on the back and silvery on the sides and belly.

Behavior

Little research has been done on the humpback chub. Spawning probably occurs in May or June when water temperatures reach 18 degrees C (64 F). The chub's underhanging mouth suggests bottom feeding, but food preferences are unknown.

Habitat

The humpback is adapted to the Colorado River system, one of the most severe swift-water fish habitats in North America. Its specific habitat requirements are not known, but it has generally been associated with fast currents and deep channels. Juveniles prefer a slower current, a silt substrate, and a depth of less than 1 meter (3.3 ft).

Historic Range

The humpback chub was probably found throughout much of the Colorado River basin. It has been documented from the Colorado River from its headwaters in Colorado to its lower reaches along the Arizona-California border; the Green River from its

Wyoming headwaters to confluence with the Colorado River in Utah; the lower Yampa River, a Colorado tributary of the Green River; and the White River in Utah.

Current Distribution

When Flaming Gorge Dam was completed in Daggett County, Utah, in 1962, the humpback chub was eliminated from long stretches of the Green River above and below the dam. The cold tailwaters of Glen Canyon Dam (built in Coconino County, Arizona) have caused reductions in both the distribution and abundance of humpback chubs in Marble and Grand canyons. The fish is sporadically found in the Green River in Desolation and Gray canyons (Uintah and Grand counties, Utah), and in the Yampa River at Dinosaur National Monument (Moffat County, Colorado).

Conservation and Recovery

The humpback chub has declined significantly since the Flaming Gorge and Glen Canyon dams were completed, but populations were probably lost in the 1930s when the Hoover Dam was built. When the dam reservoirs were filled, cold tailwaters forced out the humpback chub, which prefers warmer waters. Below the dams, water flows were significantly decreased. The Fish and Wildlife Service (FWS) has determined that any additional diversion of water from the Colorado River would jeopardize the survival of the humpback chub, the bonytail chub (*Gila elegans*), and the Colorado squawfish (*Ptychocheilus lucius*).

When these fishes were granted protection under the Endangered Species Act, the western states threatened a protracted confrontation with the federal government over water rights. In 1984 the FWS convened the Upper Colorado River Basin Coordinating Committee. Members included representatives of the FWS, the Bureau of Reclamation, the states of Colorado, Utah, and Wyoming, and private water development interests.

In 1988 all parties agreed on a recovery program for the Colorado River basin and established a committee to oversee implementation. The unprecedented agreement calls for maintaining an adequate stream flow throughout the system. On the Colorado and Green rivers prescribed releases from federal reservoirs will provide the needed water. On the Yampa and White Rivers, the FWS will purchase water rights to assure an adequate flow. The agreement also contains provisions for habitat rehabilitation, restocking of native fishes, and continued monitoring of wildlife populations.

A captive propagation program has been established to stock reclaimed portions of the Colorado River with native fishes. Fish hatcheries in the region, such as Rifle Falls State Fish Hatchery and the Hotchkiss National Fish Hatchery, will probably be expanded to include facilities for the humpback chub. In 1989 in a multi-agency cooperative effort, 1,800 humpbacks were captured in the Little Colorado; 450 were tagged with radio transponders to enable biologists to track the fish's movements in the river.

Bibliography

U.S. Fish and Wildlife Service. 1979. "Humpback Chub Recovery Plan." U.S. Fish and Wildlife Service, Albuquerque.

Contact

Regional Office of Endangered Species
U.S. Fish and Wildlife Service
P.O. Box 1306
Albuquerque, New Mexico 87103

Sonora Chub
Gila ditaenia

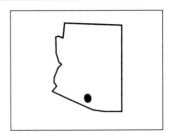

James E. Johnson

Status	Threatened
Listed	April 30, 1986
Family	Cyprinidae (Minnow)
Description	Medium-sized chub with 2 dark bands on the sides.
Habitat	Intermittent streams and perennial pools.
Food	Small invetebrates, insects, plant matter.
Reproduction	Undescribed.
Threats	Low numbers, limited distribution.
Region 2	Arizona
Mexico	Sonora

Description

Sonora chub is generally less than 12 centimeters (5 in) long. It has a dark back, two prominent dark bands on its sides, and a dark spot at the base of the tail. A breeding male's lower fins turn red and his belly turns orange.

Behavior

This chub has not been adequately studied but apparently feeds on small invetebrates, insects, and plant matter. Its reproduction has not been described.

Habitat

This chub has been found in clear, shallow, intermittently flowing streams, about 1.5 meters (5 ft) wide, with fairly swift currents over a sand, gravel, or bedrock bed. The principal associated vegetation is watercress in stream backwaters. During part of the year, stream flows dry up, leaving only isolated pools of varying depths, wherein the chubs seek refuge. Some pools are fed by underground flow. During years of heavier-than-normal rainfall, water flows are more stable, and the Sonora chub is able to expand its population somewhat.

Sycamore Canyon supports several rare and unique plant and animal species in addition to the Sonora chub. One of these, the Tarahumara frog, which is a candidate for federal listing, experienced a catastrophic die-off in Sycamore Canyon in 1974 and has not been found there since. The factors causing its disappearance are not known.

Historic Range

The Sonora chub was first collected in 1893 from Sycamore Canyon in Arizona. In 1940 it was found in the Rio Magdalena near La Casita in Sonora, Mexico.

Current Distribution

The Sonora chub is found in a few streams and pools in extreme southern Arizona—Sycamore Creek, Penasco Creek, an unnamed tributary, and Yank's Spring. These waters are within the Coronado National Forest, situated northwest of Nogales (Santa Cruz County). The Mexican border is 8 kilometers (5 mi) downstream from Yank's Spring.

Sycamore Creek is the main watercourse of the Sycamore Canyon basin. Penasco Creek drains a large portion of the east side of the watershed, but has only intermittent flow. The unnamed tributary supports three perennial bedrock pools just above its confluence with Sycamore Creek; the lower two pools support the largest concentration of Sonora chubs. Yank's Spring is a perennial spring that has been impounded in a concrete tank for many years.

Conservation and Recovery

The Sonora chub's low numbers and limited distribution make it susceptible to any habitat disturbance, especially during dry years. Sycamore Canyon, itself, is largely unaltered and undisturbed, and the Forest Service has pledged to keep it that way. Portions of the inhabited creeks are contained in the Pajarito Wilderness Area and Goodding Research Natural Area. Although some nearby land is allotted to livestock grazing, there has been little direct effect on the habitat .

Although currently no companies are mining anywhere within the Sycamore Creek watershed, there are active operations in California Gulch, just one watershed to the west. Uranium explorations in 1981 on the upper eastern slopes of the Sycamore drainage discovered enough ore so that companies have maintained claims in the area.

The designation of Critical Habitat for this species includes all inhabited waters and a riparian buffer zone to protect water quality. A special rule allows for the taking of Sonora chub without a federal permit if a state collecting permit is obtained and all other state wildlife conservation laws and regulations are satisfied. The special rule acknowledges the fact that incidental netting by state-licensed recreational fishermen is not a significant threat to this species.

Little is known about the long-term viability of the several known Sonora chub populations in Mexico. In 1981 a habitat stream near Cienega La Atascosa was surveyed and found in good condition. It supported a healthy population of Sonora chubs. There is no official protection for either habitat or chub in Mexico.

Bibliography

Arizona Game and Fish Commission. 1982. *Threatened Native Wildlife in Arizona.* Arizona Game and Fish Department Publication, Phoenix.

Miller, L. 1949. "Field Notes on the Minnow, *Gila ditaenia* in Southern Arizona." *Copeia* 1949:148-150.

Contact

Regional Office of Endangered Species
U.S. Fish and Wildlife Service
P.O. Box 1306
Albuquerque, New Mexico 87103

Bonytail Chub
Gila elegans

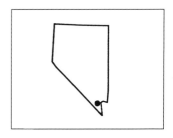

John N. Rinne

Status	Endangered
Listed	April 23, 1980
Family	Cyprinidae (Minnow)
Description . . .	Large, silver chub with greenish back.
Habitat	Turbid, swift-flowing rivers.
Food	Insects and algae.
Reproduction . .	Spawns in spring.
Threats	Dam construction, water diversion, competition with non-native fishes.
Region 1	California, Nevada

Description

The bonytail chub is a relatively large chub, averaging 30 centimeters (12 in) in length. Its chunky body is silver with a greenish tinge along the back. The head is flattened, the back slightly humped, the eyes very small and of little use. The narrow tail terminates in a V-shaped caudal fin. The breeding male's belly turns bright orange-red. The bonytail chub was once considered a subspecies of the roundtail chub (*Gila robusta*) but has since been accorded full species status.

Behavior

The bonytail chub is omnivorous, feeding mainly on terrestrial insects, larvae, algae, and detritus. In spring it spawns in schools over rocky shoals of smaller tributaries.

Habitat

This species is found in larger rivers and displays a high tolerance for turbidity. It is most frequently associated with eddies just outside the main river current. The bonytail chub is susceptible to changes in water temperature and flow, and low levels of chemical pollution.

Historic Range

The bonytail chub was once abundant throughout the Colorado River and its larger tributaries. It has been collected from the Green River in Wyoming and Utah, Yampa and Gunnison Rivers in Colorado, the Colorado River in Arizona, Nevada and California, and the Gila and Salt Rivers in Arizona.

Current Distribution

In the 1960s a dramatic decline in bonytails was recorded in the Green River after the Flaming Gorge Dam was completed. The Bureau of Reclamation has since adjusted water flows from the dam to improve downstream habitat, but no corresponding recovery of the bonytail has been noted. Recent surveys indicate that the bonytail chub may survive only in Lake Mohave along the Arizona-Nevada border. The surviving wild population appears to consist of older fish that are not reproducing.

Conservation and Recovery

Massive reservoir impoundment and hydroelectric dams have changed the character of the Colorado River basin. Many stretches of river—for example, the Dolores River below the McPhee Dam—are dry through portions of the year. Massive amounts of water are diverted each year for irrigation and human consumption. The Fish and Wildlife Service (FWS) has determined that any additional diversion of water from the Colorado River would jeopardize the survival of the bonytail chub, humpback chub (*Gila cypha*), and the Colorado squawfish (*Ptychocheilus lucius*).

Introduction of exotic fishes into the river basin has also contributed to the bonytail chub's decline. Predation on larval chubs by red and redside shiners may account for the absence of bonytail fry. Non-native fishes now outnumber native fishes in the Colorado River basin.

In 1984 the FWS convened the Upper Colorado River Basin Coordinating Committee to defuse controversy over the federal listing of several Endangered fishes. The committee—a forum for discussion and negotiation—consisted of representatives of the FWS, the Bureau of Reclamation, the states of Colorado, Utah, and Wyoming, and private water development interests. In 1988 the committee forged an unprecedented regional agreement to improve water flow and quality in the Colorado River basin.

In 1986, the Fish and Wildlife Service (FWS) and the Division of Refuge Management initiated a cooperative effort to hold Endangered Colorado River fish in refuges along the lower Colorado River. Use of these refuges—typically riverside ponds with controlled river access—permits fish fry to be reared to subadult size before being released into the river, improving survival chances. The bonytail chub was the first fish to be transplanted to a pond at Imperial National Wildlife Refuge in Arizona, using stock from the Dexter National Fish Hatchery.

Bonytail fry have also been stocked in ponds at the Havasu, Cibola, and Buenos Aires national wildlife refuges and subsequently returned to the river with promising results, but the bonytail chub is still a long way from recovery. The Colorado River Fishes Recovery Team recommended in 1987 that all bonytails netted in the wild be transported to the Dexter facility for use in the captive propagation effort.

Bibliography

Ono, R. D., J. D. Williams, and A. Wagner. 1983. *Vanishing Fishes of North America.* Stonewall Press, Washington, D.C.

Sigler, W. F., and R. R. Miller. 1963. *Fishes of Utah.* Utah State Department of Fish and Game, Salt Lake City.

Contact

Regional Office of Endangered Species
U.S. Fish and Wildlife Service
P.O. Box 1306
Albuquerque, New Mexico 87103

Chihuahua Chub
Gila nigrescens

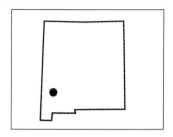

James E. Johnson

Status . . . . . . Threatened
Listed . . . . . . October 11, 1983
Family . . . . . Cyprinidae (Minnow)
Description . . . Medium-sized, dusky brown chub.
Habitat . . . . . Deep pools in small streams.
Food . . . . . . Insects, aquatic invertebrates, plant matter.
Reproduction . Spawns in April or May.
Threats . . . . . Water diversion, dam construction, pollution.
Region 2 . . . . New Mexico
Mexico . . . . . Chihuahua

Description

The Chihuahua chub is a medium-sized minnow, ranging from 8 to 15 centimeters (3 to 6 in) long. It is a dusky brown above and whitish beneath. During the breeding season an orange-red color develops around the mouth and lower fins.

In the past, this species has also been variously classified as *Gila pulchella* and *Tigoma nigrescens*. To add to the confusion, the name *Gila nigrescens* has been applied by some authors to a different chub found in the Rio Grande and Pecos rivers.

Behavior

The Chihuahua chub, like a trout, takes insects from the surface of the water. It feeds also on small, aquatic invertebrates, fish fry, and some plant matter. Chubs spawn in April and May over beds of aquatic vegetation in deeper, quiet pools. The habitat is subject to extreme drying in summer and violent flash floods in the rainy season. Seven centuries ago when the watershed was more stable, the Mimbres Indians took large numbers of these chubs for food and used the fish as a design element on their pottery.

Habitat

This species inhabits smaller streams in canyonlands. Average water depth is only about 1 meter (3 ft), but the shallow stream beds are often interspersed with deeper pools. This chub prefers overhanging vegetation, undercut banks, or submerged trees for cover. Associated with the Chihuahua chub in some of the same streams is the Endangered beautiful shiner (*Notropis formosus*)

Historic Range

The Chihuahua chub once ranged throughout the Guzman basin, which includes the Mimbres River of southwestern New Mexico and the Rio Casas Grandes, Rio Santa Maria, and Laguna Bustillos rivers of Chihuahua, Mexico.

Current Distribution

When surveys for the Chihuahua chub were conducted in 1979, one small, relict population of about 100 fish was found in the Mimbres River in Grant County, New Mexico. In 1981 and 1982 the New Mexico Department of Game and Fish discovered a second small population in the mainstream of the river. The presence of all age grades suggests that successful reproduction has continued despite severe flooding of previous years.

Conservation and Recovery

The Mimbres River of New Mexico has been significantly modified by agricultural and flood control developments. Chihuahua chub populations have declined because of the diversion of water for irrigation, dam and levee construction, and artificial stream channelization. The excessive pumping of groundwater has caused many springs in the region to dry up. These conditions have restricted the Chihuahua chub to one small section of the river. Continuing flood reclamation work, irrigation diversions, and channelization will undoutedly contribute to further decline.

Delisting of this fish could only be considered when conservation easements are in place along the springfed headwaters of the river and two additional populations have been reestablished within its former range. The Chihuahua chub is currently being propagated at the Dexter National Fish Hatchery at Dexter, New Mexico. This captive population will be used as reintroduction stock.

Water pollution has been responsible for eliminating the chub from most of its range in Mexico. Development of hydroelectric facilities, diversion of surface waters for irrigation, and excessive pumping from the underground aquifers have completely dried up many streams and springs in the region.

Bibliography

Hatch, M. D. 1980. "Management Plan for the Chihuahua Chub, *Gila Nigrescens* (Girard, 1856), in New Mexico." New Mexico Department of Game and Fish, Santa Fe.

Hubbard, J. P., *et al.* 1978. *Handbook of Species Endangered in New Mexico.* New Mexico Department of Game and Fish, Santa Fe.

U.S. Fish and Wildlife Service. 1986. "Chihuahua Chub Recovery Plan." U.S. Fish and Wildlife Service, Albuquerque.

Contact

Regional Office of Endangered Species
U.S. Fish and Wildlife Service
P.O. Box 1306
Albuquerque, New Mexico 87103

Yaqui Chub
Gila purpurea

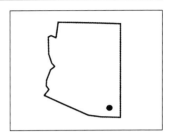

James E. Johnson

Status	Endangered
Listed	August 31, 1984
Family	Cyprinidae (Minnow)
Description . . .	Medium-sized silvery minnow with darker stripe and tail spot.
Habitat	Flowing streams and pools.
Food	Insects and plant matter.
Reproduction . .	Undescribed.
Threats	Water diversion, groundwater depletion, predation and competition.
Region 2	Arizona
Mexico	Chihuahua, Sonora

Description

A medium-sized silvery minnow, the Yaqui chub ranges in size from 12.5 to 15 centimeters (5 to 6 in). Its streamlined shape terminates in a narrow tail and V-shaped caudal (tail) fin. It displays a single dark band on its side, and a dark spot at the base of the tail. Fins are enlarged and nearly fan-shaped. When breeding, the male's belly turns reddish.

Behavior

This chub feeds on insects, plant matter, and detritus. It uses backwaters of streams and springs beneath undercut and overgrown banks for feeding and shelter. Breeding behavior has not been described, but the fish probably spawns in deep pools, where there is aquatic vegetation.

Habitat

The Yaqui chub requires clean, narrow, permanent streams and spring pools, free of introduced fishes. Streams typically consist of deep pools separated by riffles and flowing stretches of moderate current.

Historic Range

This species is endemic to the Rio Yaqui basin of southeastern Arizona, northwestern Sonora, and portions of eastern Chihuahua, Mexico. This chub has also been recorded from the Rio Sonora and Rio Matape on the Pacific slope of Mexico. It was first collected from San Bernardino Creek, just south of the Arizona-Sonora border. The Yaqui chub survived in San Bernardino Creek in Arizona until spring flows diminished and the creek dried up. Remaining habitat was severely trampled by drinking livestock, making it uninhabitable.

Current Distribution

Surviving Arizona populations are known from a few springs on the San Bernardino National Wildlife Refuge and Leslie Creek in Cochise County. Contract biologists from the Arizona State University and the University of Michigan surveyed the Rio Yaqui basin in 1979 and found only a single chub, signaling a serious decline in numbers. The current size of the surviving population has not been estimated. The status of the Mexican populations is largely unknown beyond the fact that a severe decline in numbers has occurred.

Conservation and Recovery

The range of the Yaqui chub decreased significantly because of habitat modifications, such as arroyo cutting, water diversion, dam construction, and excessive pumping of groundwater from the aquifer. The American Fisheries Society proposed protection for the Yaqui chub as early as 1979, and in 1983 the Desert Fishes Council petitioned the Fish and Wildlife Service (FWS) to list the chub on the basis of its disappearance from San Bernardino Creek.

The Bureau of Land Management (BLM) has issued leases for geothermal resources on lands adjacent to the San Bernardino National Wildlife Refuge. Biologists fear that exploration and development of these leases could cause further depletion of the underground aquifers or create channels for pollution of groundwater. The BLM will examine these threats in consultation with the FWS.

Introduced predatory fishes, such as largemouth bass, bluegill, black bullhead, channel catfish, and green sunfish are present in some portions of the Rio Yaqui basin and probably feed on the Yaqui chub.

Other springs and outflow streams within the San Bernardino National Wildlife may provide suitable habitat for the Yaqui chub. The FWS is currently surveying sites there in preparation for a translocation effort.

Many rivers in Mexico, formerly inhabited by the Yaqui chub, have been highly modified into an artificially channeled canal system to support irrigation agriculture. Water quality has declined drastically due to chemical and sewage contamination. The Yaqui chub receives no legal protection from the Mexican government.

Bibliography

Hendrickson, D. A., *et al.* 1980. "Fishes of the Rio Yaqui Basin, Mexico and United States." *Journal of the Arizona-Nevada Academy of Science* 15(3):65-106.

Silvey, W. 1975. "Statewide Fisheries Investigations: Fishes of Leslie Creek, Cochise County, Arizona." Statewide Survey of Aquatic Resources, Federal Aid Project F-7-R-17. Arizona Fish and Game Department, Phoenix.

U.S. Fish and Wildlife Service. 1979. "Environmental Assessment of the Proposed Land Acquisition of San Bernardino Ranch, Cochise County, Arizona." U.S. Fish and Wildlife Service, Albuquerque.

Contact

Regional Office of Endangered Species
U.S. Fish and Wildlife Service
P.O. Box 1306
Albuquerque, New Mexico 87103

Pahranagat Roundtail Chub

Gila robusta jordani

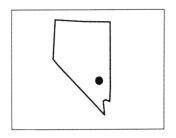

John N. Rinne

Status . . . . . . Endangered
Listed . . . . . . October 13, 1970
Family . . . . . . Cyprinidae (Minnow)
Description . . . Medium to large, greenish chub with black blotches.
Habitat . . . . . . Thermal waters with mud or sand substrate.
Food . . . . Mostly plant matter, detritus, insects.
Reproduction . . Spawns in spring.
Threats . . . . . . Habitat destruction, competition with exotic species.
Region 1 . . . . . Nevada

Description

The Pahranagat roundtail chub, also known as the Pahranagat bonytail chub, is a medium-sized fish, growing to about 25 centimeters (10 in). It has an elongated body with a narrow tail and a deeply cleft caudal fin. Its coloring is greenish with black blotches.

The Pahranagat roundtail chub is most similar in appearance to the common roundtail chub (*Gila robusta robusta*), which is found in the Colorado River and its larger tributaries.

Behavior

Unlike other roundtail chubs, adults of the Pahranagat subspecies are primarily herbivorous, feeding on a wide range of plant matter and detritus. Insects make up a large part of the diet of juveniles. The fish uses different parts of its spring and stream system according to the seasons. From late April through January the adult population is restricted to a single pool about 10 meters (33 ft) in length. During spring the chubs migrate downstream to an unidentified spawning area.

Habitat

This species lives in pools where water temperatures range from 27 to 30 degrees C (81 to 86 F). Aquatic vegetation includes algae, *Chara zeylania*, *Compsopogon coeruleus*, *Najas marina*, and a variety of diatoms. It inhabits water with bottoms ranging from mud to firm sand.

Historic Range

The Pahranagat roundtail chub is endemic to the Pahranagat Valley in Lincoln County, Nevada. Precise limits of the historic range are not known because the valley waters were extensively altered before the fish was discovered. However, it is known to have occurred in Crystal, Hiko, and Ash Springs, and in the Pahranagat River.

Two other Endangered fishes are found in the Pahranagat Valley—White River springfish (*Crenichthys baileyi baileyi*) and Hiko White River springfish (*C. b. grandis*). These fishes were historically the most abundant species found in Crystal, Hiko and Ash Springs.

Current Distribution

The Pahranagat roundtail chub is considered one of the rarest fish in North America. Less than 75 adult chubs and, perhaps, 200 yearlings are thought to survive in approximately 2,300 meters (7,590 ft) of an unmodified portion of the Pahranagat River downstream from Ash Springs on Burns Ranch. Fry and juveniles are sometimes found in irrigation ditches, where they usually do not survive.

Conservation and Recovery

Habitat modification and the introduction of non-native fishes to the watershed are primarily responsible for the decline of the Pahranagat chub. Streams in the Pahranagat Valley have been extensively altered to accommodate irrigation. The present restricted habitat of the Pahranagat chub is one of the few stream reaches that has not been lined with concrete. Non-native fishes competing with the chub include the convict cichlid, carp, mosquitofish, and the shortfin molly.

Twenty chubs relocated to the Endangered Fish Facility at Shoshone Ponds in Nevada failed to reproduce, but in 1985 the Fish and Wildlife Service successfully established a captive population of the Pahranagat roundtail chub at the Dexter National Fish Hatchery. Alerted to severe drying of an inhabited irrigation ditch, personnel from the Nevada Department of Wildlife and the Great Basin Complex netted about 50 juveniles, held them overnight in a live trap in a stream, and transferred them the next day in plastic sacks filled with stream water to the airport at Las Vegas. From there the fish were flown to Roswell, New Mexico, and handed over to hatchery personnel. The facility is located south of Roswell near Dexter in Chaves County. Previous attempts to translocate the chub to the hatchery had failed.

It is hoped that this captive stock can be used as the basis for a reintroduction effort when suitable habitat can be located or significant stretches of the Pahranagat River rehabilitated.

Bibliography

Courtenay, W. R., Jr., *et al.* 1985. "Comparative Status of Fishes along the Course of the Pluvial White River, Nevada." *Southwestern Naturalist* 30:503-524.

Deacon, J., C. Hubbs, and B. Zahuranec. 1964. "Some Effects of Introduced Fishes on the Native Fish Fauna of Southern Nevada." *Copeia* 2:384-388.

U.S. Fish and Wildlife Service. 1985. "Recovery Plan for the Pahranagat Roundtail Chub, *Gila robusta jordani*." U.S. Fish and Wildlife Service. Portland.

Contact

Regional Office of Endangered Species
U.S. Fish and Wildlife Service
Lloyd 500 Building, Suite 1692
500 N.E. Multnomah Street
Portland, Oregon 97232

Slender Chub

Hybopsis cahni

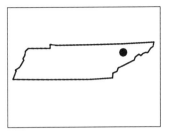

John Harris

Status	Threatened
Listed	September 9, 1977
Family	Cyprinidae (Minnow)
Description	Small, elongated, olive minnow.
Habitat	Warm springs with shoals.
Food	Insects, mollusks.
Reproduction	Spawns from mid-April to early June.
Threats	Dam construction, siltation, pollution.
Region 4	Tennessee
Region 5	Virginia

Description

The slender chub has a moderately elongated body and reaches a maximum length of about 7.7 centimeters (3 in). It has a long snout, large eyes, and a slightly underhanging mouth. Olive to brown above, it has silvery sides, a whitish underside, and a dark lateral stripe.

Behavior

Little is known of the slender chub's reproductive behavior. Spawning probably begins in mid to late April and extends into early June. Young mature in three to four years and die shortly after. It feeds primarily on insects and mollusks.

Habitat

From April to September the slender chub inhabits large warm streams, 30 to 125 meters (100 to 413 ft) wide, which have wide shoals of clean gravel. The fish's winter habitat is unknown.

Historic Range

The slender chub is endemic to the upper Tennessee River basin and has been recorded from the Clinch, Powell, and Holston rivers. It was collected from the Holston River only one time, in 1941, and has not been seen there since.

Current Distribution

The slender chub has one of the smallest ranges of any eastern North American minnow. Today, it is found in nine population centers on the Powell and Clinch Rivers in Tennessee and Virginia. It occurs in sections of the main channel of the Powell River from Lee County, Virginia, downstream to Norris Lake, Tennessee. In the Clinch River it is found in localized populations from Scott County, Virginia, downstream to Norris Lake.

Conservation and Recovery

The Holston River population was lost when the Cherokee Reservoir was completed by the Tennessee Valley Authority (TVA) in the 1940s. The river above the reservoir is now silted and polluted by industrial discharges from Kingsport, Tennessee. Habitat below the reservoir is affected by cold water releases. Clinch River populations have also suffered from reservoir development and from chemical spills and discharges in the 1960s and 1970s.

The Powell River headwaters arise in the heart of coal mining country, and the affects of runoff from the mines are evident in the river and its tributaries. Coal silt has been measured as deep as one meter in pools and backwaters at McDowell Ford. These conditions are only expected to worsen in the near future. Gravel shoals in the Clinch and Powell rivers have been dredged, further disturbing slender chub habitat.

The recovery of the slender chub and other aquatic life in the Powell River hinges entirely on the cooperation of mining companies in decreasing coal silt runoff into the streams. The TVA, the Tennessee Wildlife Resources Agency, the Tennessee Heritage Program, and the Virginia Commission of Game and Inland Fisheries have consulted to determine the adequacy of existing legislation for lessening contamination in the Upper Tennessee watershed.

Bibliography

Burkhead, N. M., and R. E. Jenkins. 1982. "Five-year Status Review of the Slender Chub, *Hybopsis cahni*, a Threatened Cyprinid Fish of the Upper Tennessee Drainage." U.S. Fish and Wildlife Service Report. Newton Corner, Massachusetts.

U.S. Fish and Wildlife Service. 1983. "Slender Chub Recovery Plan." U.S. Fish and Wildlife Service, Atlanta.

Contact

Regional Office of Endangered Species
U.S. Fish and Wildlife Service
Richard B. Russell Federal Building
75 Spring Street, S.W.
Atlanta, Georgia 30303

Spotfin Chub
Hybopsis monacha

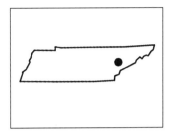

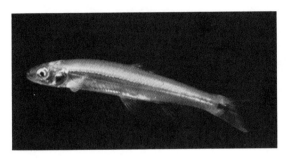

William Roston

Status	Threatened
Listed	September 9, 1977
Family	Cyprinidae (Minnow)
Description	Small, dusky green chub.
Habitat	Flowing water over clean substrate.
Food	Insects.
Threats	Habitat degradation, pollution.
Region 4	Tennessee

Description

The spotfin chub measures about 2 centimeters (0.8 in) in the first year and grows to about 8.5 centimeters (3.4 in) by the third. It has a slightly compressed, elongated body, which is dusky green above and silver below. Gold and green stripes radiate from a distinct lateral line. Breeding males turn a metallic blue above the lateral line, and the fins develop white margins.

Behavior

Although biologists believe the spotfin chub spawns from mid-May to late August, little detail is known of its reproductive behavior. Its diet consists almost entirely of insects.

Habitat

The spotfin forages in shallow rivers of slow to swift current where there is little siltation. It is found in water with sandy or rocky bottoms.

Historic Range

The spotfin chub's range once included twelve tributaries in the Tennessee River drainage in Alabama, Georgia, North Carolina, Tennessee, and Virginia. These were the French Broad, Little Tennessee, Clinch, Powell, North and South forks of the Holston, Emory, and Duck rivers and Chickamauga, Whites, Shoal, and Little Bear creeks.

Current Distribution

Presently the spotfin survives in four isolated tributary systems: the Duck, Little Tennessee, Emory, and the North Fork of the Holston. In 1988 a population was introduced into Abrams Creek, Tennessee, within the Great Smoky Mountains National Park.

Conservation and Recovery

The spotfin is threatened by habitat degradation, including siltation, coal sedimentation, pollution, and inundation by reservoir developments. Additionally, it is not a strongly competitive species; it is unaggressive and apparently cannot alter its feeding habits to adapt to habitat changes.

Recovery of this species is tied to the larger effort to reduce pollution and slow the decline of river systems throughout the region.

In 1988, the Fish and Wildlife Service (FWS), in cooperation with the North Carolina Wildlife Resources Commission, introduced 250 spotfin chubs into Abrams Creek, Tennessee, within the Smoky Mountains National Park. The fish were collected from the Little Tennessee River in North Carolina. Current FWS plans call for annual restocking over the next four years.

Bibliography

Feeman, J. C. 1980. "A Quantitative Survey of Fish and Macroinvertebrates of the Holston River Basin: August-September 1973." Report WR(70)-40-4-80.1. Tennessee Valley Authority, Division of Water Resources.

Jenkins, R. E., and N. M. Burkhead. 1982. "Description, Biology and Distribution of the Spotfin Chub, a Threatened Cyprinid Fish of the Tennessee River Drainage." Report. U.S. Fish and Wildlife Service, Atlanta.

U.S. Fish and Wildlife Service. 1983. "Recovery Plan for the Spotfin Chub." U.S. Fish and Wildlife Service, Atlanta.

Contact

Regional Office of Endangered Species
U.S. Fish and Wildlife Service
Richard B. Russell Federal Building
75 Spring Street, S.W.
Atlanta, Georgia 30303

Yaqui Catfish
Ictalurus pricei

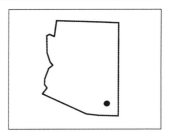

John N. Rinne

Status	Threatened (Extirpated from the U.S.)
Listed	August 31, 1984
Family	Ictaluridae (Catfish)
Description . . .	Catfish with mottled brown back, silvery sides, and reddish coloration on head, fins, and tail.
Habitat	Large streams in slow to moderate current.
Food	Bottom feeder.
Reproduction . .	Spawns in late spring.
Threats	Water diversion, groundwater depletion, hybridization.
Region 2	Arizona
Mexico	Sonora, Chihuahua

Description

The Yaqui catfish is a medium-sized catfish, ranging in length from 15 to 20 centimeters (6 to 8 in). The back is a lightly mottled brown. Sides are silvery. A reddish coloration is prominent beneath the head, and on the fins and tail.

Behavior

Similar to the channel catfish, the Yaqui catfish spawns in late spring. Eggs are laid in a nest, constructed on the bottom and guarded by the male. He incubates the eggs by fanning away silt. Hatchlings collect in small schools that are protected by the male. This catfish feeds opportunistically on insects and larvae, crustaceans, plant matter, and detritus—almost anything that is found on the bottom of the stream.

Habitat

The Yaqui catfish inhabits large streams in areas of slow to moderate current. It feeds over mud or sandy gravel bottoms in pools and backwaters. Aquatic habitats in the region are subject to severe drying in summer and sudden flooding in the rainy season. Streams flow intermittently during the dry season, and the catfish seeks refuge in permanent, often springfed, pools.

Historic Range

This species is endemic to the Rio Yaqui basin of southeastern Arizona, northwestern

Sonora, and portions of eastern Chihuahua, Mexico. It was first collected from San Bernardino Creek in extreme southeastern Arizona. The Yaqui catfish survived in San Bernardino Creek until spring flows diminished because of groundwater pumping and the creek dried up. Remaining habitat there was severely trampled by drinking livestock, making it uninhabitable. This species is now considered extirpated from the U.S..

Current Distribution

Contract biologists from the Arizona State University and the University of Michigan surveyed the Rio Yaqui basin in 1979 and found populations of the Yaqui catfish seriously depleted in the Mexican portion of its historic range and absent from Arizona.

Conservation and Recovery

The range and numbers of the Yaqui catfish have decreased significantly because of habitat modifications, such as arroyo cutting, water diversion, dam construction, and excessive pumping of groundwater from the aquifers. Many rivers in Mexico, formerly inhabited by the Yaqui catfish, have been modified into an artificially channeled canal system to support irrigation agriculture. Water quality has declined due to chemical and sewage contamination. The Yaqui catfish receives no legal protection from the Mexican government.

The Yaqui catfish appears to be interbreeding with two non-native catfish, the channel catfish (*Ictalurus punctatus*) and blue catfish (*I. furcatus*), which have become established in the Rio Yaqui system. If hybridization continues, the distinctive characteristics of this species could be lost.

If sufficient habitat can be secured and maintained in the San Bernardino National Wildlife Refuge (Cochise County, Arizona), the catfish could be reintroduced there, using Mexican stock. Habitat at the wildlife refuge, however, is considered in jeopardy because of generally lowered water tables in the region. The Bureau of Land Management (BLM) has issued leases for geothermal resources on lands adjacent to the San Bernardino National Wildlife Refuge. Biologists fear that exploration and development of these leases could cause further depletion of the underground aquifers or create channels for pollution of groundwater. The BLM will examine these threats in consultation with the Fish and Wildlife Service.

Bibliography

Hendrickson, D. A., *et al.* 1980. ''Fishes of the Rio Yaqui Basin, Mexico and United States.'' *Journal of the Arizona-Nevada Academy of Science* 15(3):65-106.

Miller, R. R. 1977. ''Composition of the Native Fish Fauna of the Chihuahuan Desert Region.'' In Wauer and Riskind, eds., *Transactions of the Symposium on the Biological Resources of the Chihuahuan Desert Region.* Transactions of Proceedings Series No. 3. U.S. Department of the Interior, Washington, D.C.

Contact

Regional Office of Endangered Species
U.S. Fish and Wildlife Service
P.O. Box 1306
Albuquerque, New Mexico 87103

White River Spinedace

Lepidomeda albivallis

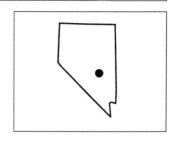

John N. Rinne

Status	. . Endangered
Listed	. . September 12, 1985
Family	. . Cyprinidae (Minnow)
Description . . .	. Bright green to olive fish, red coloration on head.
Habitat	. . Swiftly flowing desert streams.
Food	. . Small insects and other invertebrates.
Reproduction . .	. Undescribed.
Threats	. Stream channelization, water diversion, introduced competitors.
Region 1	. Nevada

Description

The White River spinedace is one of the larger species of *Lepidomeda*, sometimes growing to a length of 13 centimeters (5 in). Its distinctive body coloration is bright green (or olive) above, bright silver with brass overtones on the sides, and silvery-white below. The sides of the head are coppery-red to red with gilt reflections on the cheeks. The mouth is oblique.

The White River spinedace, first collected in 1934, is one of six species belonging to the Plagopterini, a unique tribe of cyprinid fishes noted for their adaptation to small, swiftly flowing desert streams. Members of the Plagopterini are restricted to the lower Colorado River system.

Behavior

There has been little research on the natural history of the White River spinedace. It feeds on insects and other invertebrates.

Habitat

This spinedace is adapted to cool, swiftly flowing springs and outflows. Surrounding vegetation is needed for shade to maintain a consistent water temperature and as habitat for the insects the spinedace feeds upon.

Historic Range

The White River spinedace inhabits the upper White River system in southern White

Pine County and extreme northeastern Nye County, Nevada. During pluvial times (10,000 to 40,000 years ago), the White River was a tributary of the Colorado River by way of the Virgin River. As the pluvial waters declined, the White River spinedace became isolated within springs and sections of the White River that held water throughout the year. Currently, the White River is dry over much of its course.

In the mid-1900s, the White River spinedace was known from Preston Big Spring, Nicholas, Arnoldson, Cold, Lund, and Flag springs, as well as from the White River near its confluence with Ellison Creek.

Current Distribution

Today, viable populations of the White River spinedace are found only in Lund Spring and Flag Springs. Flag Springs is included within a state wildlife management area. Lund Spring is privately owned.

Conservation and Recovery

Primary threats to the White River spinedace are water channelization, diversion of the springs, and the introduction of non-native fishes, such as guppies, mosquitofish, and goldfish. These fishes prey on the spinedace and its eggs, or compete for the limited food supply.

Habitat critical to the survival of the White River spinedace has been designated and includes three areas in Nevada: Preston Big Spring and Lund Spring in White Pine County; and Flag Springs in northeastern Nye County. While there is currently no White River spinedace population in Preston Big Spring, it is within the fish's historic range. Re-establishing a viable spinedace population at this spring is considered essential for maintaining genetic viability in the species and is a goal of conservation efforts.

Bibliography

Deacon, J. E., C. Hubbs, and B. J. Zahuranec. 1964. "Some Effects of Introduced Fishes on the Native Fish Fauna of Southern Nevada." *Copeia* 1964:384-388.

Hardy, T. 1980. "The Inter-Basin Area Report-1979." *Proceedings of the Desert Fishes Council* 11:5-21.

Hubbs, C. L., R. R. Miller, and L. C. Hubbs. 1974. "Hydrographic History and Relict Fishes of the North-Central Great Basin." *Memoirs California Academy of Science* 7:1-259.

Miller, R. R. and C. L. Hubbs. 1960. "The Spiny-Rayed Cyprinid Fishes (Plagopterini) of the Colorado River System." *Miscellaneous Publication of the Museum of Zoology, University of Michigan* 115:1-39.

Contact

Regional Office of Endangered Species
U.S. Fish and Wildlife Service
Lloyd 500 Building, Suite 1692
500 N.E. Multnomah Street
Portland, Oregon 97232

Big Spring Spinedace

Lepidomeda mollispinis pratensis

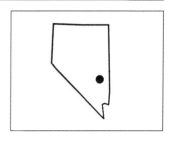

Nevada Department of Wildlife

Status . . . . . . Threatened
Listed . . . . . . March 28, 1985
Family . . . . . . Cyprinidae (Minnow)
Description . . . Small, silver minnow with two spiny rays in the dorsal fin.
Habitat . . . . . . Clear, clean, shallow stream.
Food . . . . Undescribed.
Reproduction . . Undescribed.
Threats . . . . . . Limited distribution.
Region 2 . . . . . Nevada

Description

A small, minnow-like fish, characterized by two weak, spiny rays in the dorsal fin. Bright silver in color, it ranges from 5 to 7.6 centimeters (2 to 3 in) in total length. This sub-species is one of seven taxa belonging to the Plagopterini, a unique tribe of fishes that is restricted to the lower Colorado River system.

Behavior

This species has been little studied. Its behavior and breeding biology are largely undescribed.

Habitat

The Big Spring spinedace inhabits a clear, clean, shallow stream fed by perennial springs. When first discovered, it appeared restricted to a spring-fed marsh that has since dried up.

Historic Range

The ancestors of this species became isolated in remote, spring-fed meadows of southern Nevada at the end of pluvial times, when the climate became warmer and drier. The region where the spinedace is found—Meadow Valley Wash—once contained Lake Carpenter and Carpenter River, which flowed into the Colorado River more than 10,000 years ago. The Big Spring spinedace was first discovered in a large marsh adjacent to Big Spring near the town of Panacea (Lincoln County), Nevada. Subsequently, diversion of water from the spring for irrigation caused the marsh to dry up, and the Big Spring dace was thought to be extinct.

Current Distribution

In 1978 personnel from the Nevada Department of Wildlife discovered a small population of the Big Spring spinedace in Condor Canyon, just northeast of Panacea. Condor

Canyon comprises about 6.5 kilometers (4 mi) of Meadow Valley Wash with perennially flowing water. In 1980 state biologists transplanted spinedace above a barrier falls to establish the fish in all portions of the available habitat.

Conservation and Recovery

The Big Spring spinedace is threatened by its very limited distribution, which prevents any expansion of the population. In some places the stream in Condor Canyon is only a few feet wide and could be disrupted by water diversion, use by livestock, or prolonged drought. The Bureau of Land Management administers about 75 percent of the canyon and includes most of the land in a grazing allotment. The allotment has been inactive for some time, however, and is not expected to be renewed. The Nature Conservancy owns about 16 hectares (40 acres) of land at the upper end of Condor Canyon and has agreed to cooperate with the Fish and Wildlife Service (FWS) to recover this species.

On the basis of ongoing research, state and federal biologists will determine a suitable transplant location within the fish's historic range and attempt to establish a new population. In the meantime, every effort will be made to prevent accidental or purposeful introduction of the mosquitofish—a non-native pest found in many regional waters—into Condor Canyon. Based on previous experience, the mosquitofish could eliminate the spinedace population in short order.

Bibliography

Deacon, J. E., C. Hubbs, and B. Zahuranec. 1964. "Some Effects of Introduced Fishes on the Native Fish of Southern Nevada." *Copeia* 1964:384-388.

Hardy, T. 1980. "Interbasin Report to the Desert Fishes Council." *Proceedings of the Desert Fishes Council* 10:5-21; 11:68-70.

Miller, R. R., and C. Hubbs. 1960. "The Spiny-Rayed Cyprinid Fishes of the Colorado River System." *Miscellaneous Publications of the Museum of Zoology, University of Michigan* 115:1-39.

Contact

Regional Office of Endangered Species
U.S. Fish and Wildlife Service
Lloyd 500 Building, Suite 1692
500 N.E. Multnomah Street
Portland, Oregon 97232

Little Colorado Spinedace

Lepidomeda vittata

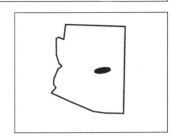

James E. Johnson

Status	Threatened
Listed	September 16, 1987
Family	Cyprinidae (Minnow)
Description	Small, olive and silver minnow.
Habitat	Streams with gravel or mud-silt bottoms.
Food	Insects, detritus.
Reproduction	Spawns in early summer.
Threats	Dams, groundwater pumping, competition with introduced fish.
Region 2	Arizona

Description

The Little Colorado spinedace is a small minnow, about 10 centimeters (4 in) long. It is olive above and silvery below, with a lateral band. The back is olive or bluish to lead gray. It has a small head and relatively large eyes.

Behavior

This spinedace spawns primarily in early summer, continuing at a reduced rate until early fall. In courtship behavior, males pursue females, nibbling them about the vent. Like other minnows, the Little Colorado spinedace feeds on small insects and detritus.

Habitat

This spinedace inhabits pools in narrow to moderately sized streams where the water flows over a fine gravel or silt-mud bottom.

During drought, it retreats to springs and intermittent stream bed pools. During flooding it spreads out again throughout the stream.

Historic Range

The Little Colorado spinedace occurred throughout the upper portions of the Little Colorado River drainage in Arizona. It was first described in 1874 from specimens taken from the river between the mouth of the Zuni River and Sierra Blanca in Arizona.

Current Distribution

It is now found only in portions of the Little Colorado River and East Clear, Chevelon, Silver, and Nutrioso creeks in Coconino, Navajo, and Apache counties, Arizona.

Conservation and Recovery

The decline of the Little Colorado spinedace is the result of habitat alteration associated with human settlement. Dam building, water pumping, stream channeling, and road building have radically altered the water system within the spinedace's habitat. Introduced fish species also prey upon and compete with the spinedace.

Proposed water projects would further reduce this fish's viable habitat. For example, Wilkin's Dam at the confluence of Clear and East Clear creeks is proposed as part of the Bureau of Reclamation's larger Mogollon Mesa project. Wilkin's Dam would inundate about eight miles of stream, significantly decreasing downstream flows. The project is currently inactive and is not expected to be reactivated in the near future.

The spinedace's best protection at the moment is federal ownership of much of its habitat. The East Clear Creek population is located within the Coconino and Apache-Sitgreaves National Forests, as are portions of the Little Colorado River, Silver and Nutrioso creeks populations.

The Fish and Wildlife Service has declared portions of East Clear Creek, Chevelon Creek, and Nutrioso Creek as habitat critical to the continued existence of the Little Colorado spinedace.

Bibliography

Miller, R. R. 1983. "Distribution, Variation and Ecology of *Lepidomeda vittata*, a Rare Cyprinid Fish Endemic to Eastern Arizona." *Copeia* 1963:1-5.

Minckley, W. L. 1973. *Fishes of Arizona*. Sims Printing, Phoenix.

Contact

Regional Office of Endangered Species
U.S. Fish and Wildlife Service
P.O. Box 1306
Albuquerque, New Mexico 87103

Spikedace
Meda fulgida

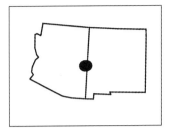

John N. Rinne

Status	Threatened
Listed	July 1, 1986
Family	Cyprinodon (Minnow)
Description	Slender, silvery fish with sharp spines in dorsal and pelvic fins.
Habitat	Stream pools and riffles in flowing water.
Food	Insects, larvae, plant matter.
Reproduction	Spawns in spring.
Threats	Dam construction, channelization, water diversion, and groundwater pumping.
Region 2	Arizona, New Mexico

Description

The only species in the genus *Meda*, the spikedace is a small, slender fish, less than 7.5 centimeters (3 in) in length. It is characterized by silvery sides and sharp spines in the dorsal and pelvic fins. During the breeding season, males develop a brassy golden color.

Behavior

The highly mobile spikedace has a high reproductive potential but periodically experiences large fluctuations in population size. It spawns in spring and feeds on a range of insects, larvae, and plant matter.

Habitat

The spikedace is found in stream pools and shallow riffles with gravel or rubble sub-strates and moderate to swift currents. It is tolerant of periodic flooding, which gives it a competitive edge over other native fishes in the watershed.

Historic Range

The spikedace is endemic to the Gila River basin upstream (east) of the city of Phoenix, Arizona. It was once common in the Verde, Aqua Fria, Salt, San Pedro, San Francisco, and Gila rivers. The historic range may have included the upper San Pedro River in Sonora, Mexico, where habitat no longer exists.

Current Distribution

In Arizona this species is found in Aravaipa Creek in Graham and Pinal counties, Eagle Creek in Greenlee County, and a portion of the upper Verde River in Yavapai County. It also occurs in a section of the Gila River upstream from the town of Red Rock in Grant and Catron counties in southwestern New Mexico. The current distribution represents only about 6 percent of the historic range.

Conservation and Recovery

The distribution and numbers of the spikedace have been greatly reduced by dam construction, artificial channeling of stream beds, water diversion, and groundwater pumping. The San Pedro River in Mexico has been almost totally dewatered by diversion of water to support irrigation agriculture. The species is also threatened by the spread of non-native predators and competitors, such as rainbow trout, smallmouth bass, channel catfish, and red shiner.

The federal Bureau of Reclamation, as part of the Central Arizona Project/Upper Gila River Supply Study, is currently considering construction of a major new dam on the mainstream Gila River to control flooding and supply water for irrigation and municipal development. Among several possibilities are a high dam and reservoir at the Conner site near the lower end of Middle Box Canyon, a smaller dam at the Hooker site just downstream from Turkey Creek, or an off-stream storage reservoir at Mangas Creek. It is thought that a dam constructed at either the Hooker or Conner site would affect large portions of the spikedace's habitat. The effects of an off-stream facility on the spikedace are unknown.

Federal listing of the spikedace aroused opposition from the Southwest New Mexico Industrial Development Corporation, the Hooker Dam Association, the Arizona Cattle Growers Association, the Arizona Mining Association, the Town of Silver City, New Mexico, and the Soil Conservation Service of New Mexico, among others. Many opponents expressed the opinion that the listing

of the spikedace was premature or was being used as a pretext to stop dam construction, flood control efforts, and municipal development. The Fish and Wildlife Service, however, replied that the listing was based on sound biological evidence.

The Bureau of Land Management owns portions of spikedace habitat on Aravaipa Creek and the Gila River and will assess the effects of its land use strategies—in particular, livestock grazing—on the species. Most spikedace habitat on the Verde River falls within the Prescott National Forest, administered by the Forest Service. The spikedace is offered some protection in New Mexico by its occurrence within the Gila National Forest, Gila Wilderness, and Gila River Research Natural Area.

Bibliography

Barrett, P. J., *et al.* 1985. "Draft Upper Verde River Aquatic Study." U.S. Fish and Wildlife Service, Arizona Game and Fish Department, and U.S. Bureau of Reclamation.

LaBounty, J. F., and W. L. Minckley. 1972. "Native Fishes of the Upper Gila River System, Mew Mexico." In *Symposium on Rare and Endangered Wildlife of the Southwestern United States.* New Mexico Department of Game and Fish, Santa Fe.

Propst, D. 1986. "Distribution Status and Biology of the Spikedace in the Gila River Basin, New Mexico." New Mexico Department of Game and Fish, Santa Fe.

Contact

Regional Office of Endangered Species
U.S. Fish and Wildlife Service
P.O. Box 1306
Albuquerque, New Mexico 87103

Waccamaw Silverside

Menidia extensa

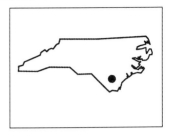

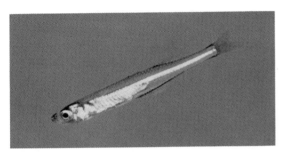

J. F. Parnell

Status	. . . . . . Threatened
Listed	. . . . . . April 8, 1987
Family	. . . . . . Atherinidae (Silverside)
Description	. . . Small, slender, almost transparent fish.
Habitat	. . . . . . Shallow, open water over dark bottoms.
Food	. . . . Plankton.
Reproduction	. . Spawns from April through June.
Threats	. . . . . . Water pollution.
Region 4	. . . . . North Carolina

Description

The Waccamaw silverside, also known as the skipjack or glass minnow, is a long, slender, almost transparent fish with a silvery stripe along each side. Adults reach about six centimeters (2.5 in) in length. Its eyes are large, and the jaw angles sharply upward.

Behavior

The Waccamaw silverside is a lake dweller, where it forms schools near the surface over shallow, dark-bottomed shoals. It reaches sexual maturity at one year of age and spawns from April through June. Most silversides die shortly after spawning, but a few may survive a second winter. The adults feed on plankton. Silversides are an important food source for larger fishes in Lake Waccamaw.

Habitat

This silverside's habitat, Lake Waccamaw, is rich in its diversity of aquatic fauna and flora. The Waccamaw basin supports more unique non-marine mollusks than any other locale in North Carolina. About 50 fish species, including many popular game fish, are found in the lake and its drainages. Many endemic species are of special interest to biologists.

The lake has a surface area of 3,640 hectares (9,000 acres) and an average depth of only 2.3 meters (7.5 ft). Although fed by acidic swamp streams, it has a virtually neutral pH. This neutral condition of the water, unusual among North Carolina's coastal plain lakes, is believed to be caused by the buffering effect of the calcareous Waccamaw Limestone formation, which underlies the lake and is exposed on the north shore. Lake Waccamaw is a registered North Carolina

Natural Heritage Area and has been proposed as a National Natural Landmark.

Historic Range

The Waccamaw silverside is endemic to North Carolina's Waccamaw basin. The Lake Waccamaw's 220-square kilometer (85-sq mi) watershed is predominantly rural, dominated by small farms and forested tracts owned by large timber companies.

Current Distribution

This species inhabits Lake Waccamaw (Columbus County) and its feeder stream, Big Creek, upstream to the County Road 1947 crossing. It is found downstream only during periods of high water when individuals are washed over Lake Waccamaw Dam into the river, where they do not appear to survive. The state of North Carolina administers the lake and Lake Waccamaw State Park, a relatively undeveloped 110-hectare (273-acre) tract. With the exception of the state park, the remainder of the lake shoreline is privately owned.

Conservation and Recovery

Studies of Lake Waccamaw and its fish and mussel fauna, conducted between 1979 and 1981 and funded through the North Carolina Wildlife Resources Commission, indicated that increasing amounts of organic matter and agricultural chemicals are being washed into the lake. Silt from upstream logging activities has also increased. This slow but steady deterioration in water quality could threaten much of Lake Waccamaw's fauna and, particularly, the silverside, which uses the clean, sandy bottom of the lake for spawning.

In 1987 the Fish and Wildlife Service (FWS) initiated a program of water-quality monitoring to compile baseline data for the lake, so that serious problems can be discovered at an early stage. All federally funded activities, which might affect the fish's habitat, currently require a consultation with the FWS to limit harm to the silverside. For example, the Department of Transportation has been asked to consider alternatives to a proposal to widen U.S. Highway 74 across Friar Swamp. In addition, an emergency plan is being developed to minimize damage from potential hazardous chemical spills along the highway.

Bibliography

Cooper, .J. E., ed. 1977. *Endangered and Threatened Plants and Animals of North Carolina.* North Carolina Museum of Natural History, Raleigh.

Davis, J. R., and D. E. Louder. 1969. "Life History of *Menidia* extensa." *Transactions of the American Fisheries Society* 98(3):466-472.

Fuller, S. L. H. 1977. "Freshwater and Terrestrial Mollusks." In J. E. Cooper, ed., *Endangered and Threatened Biota of North Carolina.* North Carolina Museum of Natural History, Raleigh.

Lindquist, D. G. 1981. "Endemic Fishes of Lake Waccamaw." *Kin'Lin* 2(5):38-41.

Contact

Regional Office of Endangered Species
U.S. Fish and Wildlife Service
Richard B. Russell Federal Building
75 Spring Street, S.W.
Atlanta, Georgia 30303

Moapa Dace
Moapa coriacea

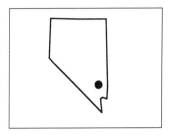

John N. Rinne

Status	. Endangered
Listed	. March 11, 1967
Family	. Cyprinidae (Minnow)
Description . .	. Gold or bronze minnow with a dark mid-dorsal stripe.
Habitat	. Thermal springs and pools.
Food	. Insects and plants.
Reproduction . .	. Spawns year round.
Threats	. Habitat reduction, introduced competitors.
Region 1	. Nevada

Description

The Moapa dace measures 7.6 centimeters (3 in) in standard length. The back and sides are an iridescent gold or bronze, marked by a dark mid-dorsal stripe. There is a distinctive black spot at the base of the caudal fin. It is similar in profile to both the roundtail chub (*Gila robusta*) and the Moapa speckled dace (*Rhinichthys osculus moapae*) but can be easily distinguished by its markings. The specific name, *coriacea*, refers to its decidedly "leathery" appearance.

Behavior

The Moapa dace feeds primarily on insects but also eats plant matter. Like other desert fishes that inhabit thermal springs, it spawns

year round with a peak in late spring or early summer.

Habitat

The Moapa dace inhabits clear, warm, slow-flowing waters, fed by thermal springs. Spring pools and outflow streams may have sand, gravel, pebble, or mud bottoms. Algae in these waters is abundant, and overhanging vegetation includes mesquite, tamarist, and the only palm tree native to Nevada (*Washingtonia filifera*).

Historic Range

This species has probably always been restricted to the sources and headwaters of Nevada's Muddy (Moapa) River system. Before 1933, it was considered common in 25 springs and up to 16 kilometers (10 mi) of outflow streams and river channel.

Current Distribution

The Moapa dace is now found in low numbers in only three springs and along less than 3.2 kilometers (2 mi) of outflow streams and river in the Warm Springs, Nevada area. Reproduction is known to occur in only a single, 100-yard length of spring outflow which is on private property. This short length of stream is the only place where juvenile Moapa dace have been found in recent years.

Conservation and Recovery

During the 1950s and 1960s, most of the springs on the Desert Oasis Warm Springs Resort and the former 7-12 Resort were cemented, graveled, channeled, chlorinated, and otherwise cleared of vegetation, actions severely restricting Moapa dace habitat. In addition, studies indicate a strong correlation between the decline of the Moapa dace and the introduction of the predatory shortfin molly sometime around 1963.

In 1972, an unsuccessful attempt was made to transplant 20 Moapa dace to Shoshone Ponds near Ely, Nevada, a Bureau of Land Management facility for conserving endangered fishes. In 1979 the Fish and Wildlife Service purchased the 7-12 Resort and established the Moapa National Wildlife Reserve to protect the dace. In 1988 the National Fisheries Research Center in Seattle completed a three-year study on the life history and habitat requirements for the Moapa dace so that suitable habitat can be provided at the refuge.

Bibliography

Cross, J. N. 1976. "Status of the Native Fish Fauna of the Moapa River, Clark County, Nevada." *Transactions of the American Fisheries Society* 105(4):503-508.

La Rivers, I. 1962. *Fishes and Fisheries of Nevada.* Nevada State Fish and Game Commission, Reno.

U.S. Fish and Wildlife Service. 1983. "The Moapa Dace Recovery Plan." U.S. Fish and Wildlife Service, Portland, Oregon.

Contact

Regional Office of Endangered Species
U.S. Fish and Wildlife Service
Lloyd 500 Building, Suite 1692
500 N.E. Multnomah Street
Portland, Oregon 97232

Beautiful Shiner

Notropis formosus

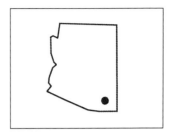

John N. Rinne

Status	Threatened (Extirpated from the U.S.)
Listed	August 31, 1984
Family	Cyprinidae (Minnow)
Description . . .	Small, silvery minnow with a metallic iridescence and red-orange coloration.
Habitat	Riffles in smaller streams.
Food	Terrestrial and aquatic insects, algae.
Reproduction . .	Probably spawns in late spring.
Threats	Water diversion, groundwater depletion, hybridization.
Region 2	Arizona, New Mexico
Mexico	Sonora, Chihuahua

Description

The beautiful shiner is a small, silvery minnow with a metallic iridescence. It ranges from 7.6 to 15.2 centimeters (3 to 6 in) in length. The belly, fins, and tail are diffused with an attractive red-orange coloration.

Behavior

The male scoops a nest out of gravel in shallow, fast-flowing water, where the female deposits her eggs, probably in late spring. The beautiful shiner feeds mostly on terrestrial and aquatic insects, augmented with algae and other plant matter.

Habitat

The beautiful shiner occurs in a variety of stream habitats, but the largest concentrations are found in the riffles of smaller streams. Aquatic habitats in the region are subject to severe drying in summer and sudden flooding in the rainy season. Streams flow intermittently during the dry season, and the shiner seeks refuge in permanent, spring-fed pools.

Historic Range

This species is endemic to the Rio Yaqui basin of southeastern Arizona, northwestern

Sonora, and portions of eastern Chihuahua, Mexico. It was also found in the various closed drainages of the Guzman basin, including Rio Mimbres in New Mexico and the Casa Grandes, Santa Maria, and Del Carment, just east of the Rio Yaqui. It was first collected from San Bernardino Creek in extreme southeastern Arizona. The beautiful shiner survived in San Bernardino Creek until spring flows diminished because of groundwater pumping, and the creek dried up. Remaining habitat there was severely trampled by drinking livestock, making it uninhabitable. The water flow of the Mimbres River has been depleted by diversion and groundwater pumping. This species is now considered extirpated from the U.S.

Current Distribution

Contract biologists from the Arizona State University and the University of Michigan surveyed the Rio Yaqui basin in 1979 and found populations of the beautiful shiner seriously depleted in the Mexican portion of its historic range. It was found to be absent from Arizona and New Mexico.

Conservation and Recovery

The range and numbers of the beautiful shiner have decreased significantly because of habitat modifications, such as arroyo cutting, water diversion, dam construction, and excessive pumping of groundwater from the aquifers. Many rivers in the lowlands of Mexico, formerly inhabited by the beautiful shiner, have been modified into an artificially channeled canal system to support irrigation agriculture. This has destroyed many of the pools used by fishes to survive a drought. Water quality has declined due to chemical and sewage contamination. The beautiful shiner currently receives no legal protection from the Mexican government.

Of particular danger to the beautiful shiner is the indiscriminate release into the watershed of the closely related red shiner (*Notropis lutrensis*), a fish used as bait for sport fishing. The expanding population of the red shiner appears to be reducing the beautiful shiner by competition and interbreeding.

If sufficient habitat can be secured and maintained in the San Bernardino National Wildlife Refuge (Cochise County, Arizona) or reclaimed in the Mimbres River (Luna County, New Mexico), the catfish could be reintroduced at either place, using Mexican stock. The aquatic habitats of the wildlife refuge are considered in jeopardy because of generally lowered water tables in the region. The Bureau of Land Management (BLM) has issued leases for geothermal resources on lands adjacent to the San Bernardino National Wildlife Refuge. Biologists fear that exploration and development of these leases could cause further depletion of the underground aquifers or create channels for pollution of groundwater. The BLM will examine these threats in consultation with the Fish and Wildlife Service.

Bibliography

Hendrickson, D. A., *et al.* 1980. "Fishes of the Rio Yaqui Basin, Mexico and United States." *Journal of the Arizona-Nevada Academy of Science* 15(3):65-106.

Miller, R. R. 1977. "Composition of the Native Fish Fauna of the Chihuahuan Desert Region." In Wauer and Riskind, eds., *Transactions of the Symposium on the Biological Resources of the Chihuahuan Desert Region.* Transactions of Proceedings Series No. 3. U.S. Department of the Interior, Washington, D.C.

Contact

Regional Office of Endangered Species
U.S. Fish and Wildlife Service
P.O. Box 1306
Albuquerque, New Mexico 87103

Cape Fear Shiner
Notropis mekistocholas

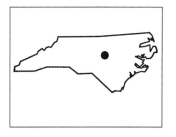

Richard Biggins

Status . . . . . . Endangered
Listed . . . . . . September 25, 1987
Family . . . . . . Cyprinidae (Minnow)
Description . . . Small, silvery yellow minnow with a dark lateral stripe.
Habitat . . . . . . Pools, slow riffles, and runs.
Food . . . . Plant matter.
Reproduction . . Undescribed.
Threats . . . . . . Dam construction.
Region 4 . . . . . North Carolina

Description

The Cape Fear shiner is a pale metallic yellow minnow that rarely exceeds 5 centimeters (2 in) in length. A black lateral stripe runs the length of the side. The fins are yellow and pointed, the upper lip is black, and the lower lip bears a thin black bar along its margin.

Behavior

This shiner, unlike most other members of the large genus *Notropis*, feeds extensively on plant matter, and its digestive tract has a long, convoluted intestine. Nothing is known of its breeding biology.

Habitat

The Cape Fear shiner is usually found in pools, riffles, and runs over gravel, cobble, or boulder bottoms. It is usually associated with schools of related species but is never the most numerous. Juveniles are often found in slack water, among mid-stream rock outcrops, and in side channels and pools.

Historic Range

The Cape Fear shiner has been documented from nine rivers and streams in central North Carolina: Bear and Robeson creeks, and Rocky River (Chatham County); Fork Creek (Randolph County); Deep River (Moore, Randolph, Chatham, and Lee counties); and Cape Fear River, Kenneth, Neals, and Parkers creeks (Hartnett County).

Current Distribution

This shiner is now restricted to only four North Carolina populations. The largest and most stable population is located near the confluence of the Rocky Deep rivers in Chatham and Lee counties. A second population center is found in Chatham County above the Rocky River hydroelectric dam, and a third inhabits the Deep River system in Randolph and Moore counties above the Highfalls Hydroelectric Reservoir. In 1987, a viable population was discovered in Neals Creek in Harnett County.

Conservation and Recovery

The Cape Fear shiner may always have been rare, but there is no doubt that the population has suffered a sharp decline. Construction of dams along the Cape Fear River system has inundated portions of the shiner's riverine habitat and fragmented the population.

Potential future threats could come from road construction, channel modification, additional damming, and waste water discharges. A proposed dam project, the Randleman Dam, would consist of a reservoir in the Deep River in Randolph County, above shiner habitat. Another proposed project, the Howards Mill Reservoir would be on the Deep River in Moore and Randolph counties and would flood shiner habitat.

Bibliography

Pottern, G. B., and M. T. Hulsh. 1985, 1986, 1987. "Status Surveys of the Cape Fear Shiner (*Notropis mekistocholas*)." U.S. Fish and Wildlife Service, Atlanta.

Snelson, F. F. 1971. "*Notropis mekistocholas*, a New Cyprinid Fish Endemic to the Cape Fear River Basin, North Carolina." *Copeia* 1971:449-462.

U.S. Fish and Wildlife Service. 1988. "Cape Fear Shiner Recovery Plan." U.S. Fish and Wildlife Service, Atlanta.

Contact

Regional Office of Endangered Species
U.S. Fish and Wildlife Service
Richard B. Russell Federal Building
75 Spring Street, S.W.
Atlanta, Georgia 30303

Pecos Bluntnose Shiner
Notropis simus pecosensis

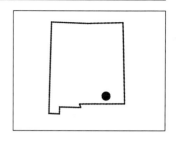

Michael Hatch

Status	Threatened
Listed	February 20, 1987
Family	Cyprinidae (Minnow)
Description	Small, silvery minnow with a bluntly rounded snout.
Habitat	Shallow, flowing water over sandy bottom.
Food	Probably insects, algae, plant matter.
Reproduction	Undescribed.
Threats	Dam construction, water diversion.
Region 2	New Mexico, Texas

Description

The Pecos bluntnose shiner is a small minnow, reaching an adult length of up to 9 centimeters (3.5 in). It has a slender, silvery body, and a large mouth overhung by a bluntly rounded snout. This shiner was first thought to be part of a single species (*Notropis simus*), whose range extended throughout the Rio Grande River basin. In 1982 biologists determined that the species was made up of two subspecies—the Rio Grande (*N. s. simus*), and the Pecos (*N. s. pecosensis*). The Rio Grande subspecies, once commonly used as a baitfish, has not been collected since 1964 and is believed extinct.

Behavior

Little information on the life history of this species is available. It is thought to feed mostly on terrestrial and aquatic insects, augmented with algae and plant matter.

Habitat

The Pecos bluntnose shiner inhabits the main channel of the Pecos River, a slow-flowing, shallow (41 cm, 16 in) river with a sandy bottom. Younger fish have been found in backwaters, riffles, and pools. Natural springs, such as those in the Santa Rosa and Lake McMillan areas, also support small populations.

Historic Range

This subspecies was first collected in 1874 from the Rio Grande near San Ildefonso, New Mexico. It was subsequently found in the Pecos River between Santa Rosa and Carlsbad.

Current Distribution

The Pecos bluntnose shiner occurs in the Pecos River from Fort Sumner downstream to Artesia (De Baca, Chaves, and Eddy counties), New Mexico. A 1982 survey netted only 76 specimens, compared with 818 in 1941, and 1,482 in 1939. The waters of the Pecos River are administered by the states of New Mexico and Texas through the Pecos River Compact. The Bureau of Reclamation and the Army Corps of Engineers operate dams on the river in accordance with the compact. Land along the Pecos River is mostly privately owned. Federal land includes a few small parcels between Fort Sumner and Roswell, administered by the Bureau of Land Management. A short section of the river flows through the Bitter Lakes National Wildlife Refuge.

Conservation and Recovery

The Fish and Wildlife Service (FWS) has expressed concern over the status of this shiner since 1978, when it was determined that the water flows in the Rio Grande and Pecos rivers had been greatly reduced by dam construction and diversion of water for irrigation. The FWS believed for a time that the Pecos bluntnose shiner was already extinct. Efforts to list the fish as Endangered were stalled until specimens were rediscovered in New Mexico.

The FWS has designated two sections of the Pecos River in New Mexico as critical for the survival of the Pecos bluntnose shiner: 102 kilometers (64 mi) from Fort Sumner downstream into Chaves County, and 59 kilometers (37 mi) between Hagerman and Artesia. Both areas support relatively abundant, reproducing populations of the shiner. But flow in the river below Fort Sumner could be radically reduced by further dam construction.

The New Mexico Parks and Recreation Commission was recently granted a permit to establish a permanent recreation pool in Santa Rosa Reservoir, which would reduce flows below Alamogordo Reservoir. Construction on the Brantley Dam in that area commenced in 1983. The Pecos River is already highly managed, with dams and diversion structures along most of its course. Most structures on the river have been built by the Army Corps of Engineers, which has stated that future flood control measures can be managed to preserve the Pecos bluntnose shiner.

The state of New Mexico has provided some legal protection for this species through the New Mexico Wildlife Conservation Act, which prohibits taking of any listed species without a scientific collecting permit. The state also has a limited ability to protect the habitat through the Habitat Protection Act, water-pollution legislation, and tangentially through a legal provision that protects areas used by game fish.

Bibliography

Chernoff, B., R. R. Miller, and C. R. Gilbert. 1982. "Notropis orca and Notropis simus, Cyprinid Fishes from the American Southwest." Occasional Papers of the Museum of Zoology, University of Michigan 698:1-49.

New Mexico Department of Game and Fish. 1982. "The Status of Notropis simus pecosensis in the Pecos River of New Mexico." Office of Endangered Species, Albuquerque.

Contact

Regional Office of Endangered Species
U.S. Fish and Wildlife Service
P.O. Box 1306
Albuquerque, New Mexico 87103

Smoky Madtom
Noturus baileyi

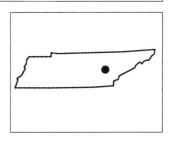

Richard Biggins

Status . . . . . . Endangered
Listed . . . . . . October 26, 1984
Family . . . . . . Ictaluridae (Catfish)
Description . . . Small, light brown catfish.
Habitat . . . . . . Mountain streams in riffles and pools.
Food . . . . Aquatic insects.
Reproduction . . Spawns during the spring and summer.
Threats . . . . . Limited distribution, mineral exploration.
Region 4 . . . . . Tennessee

Description

The smoky madtom is a small, light brown catfish with a somewhat elongated, bow-shaped body, small eyes and a rounded caudal fin. The largest known specimen was 7 centimeters (2.9 in) long.

Behavior

The smoky madtom has been found in various stages of breeding condition during the spring and summer, and nests containing an average of 35 eggs have been located during July under large slab rocks in pool areas. This fish is probably nocturnal and is thought to feed on aquatic insects.

Habitat

From May to November this small catfish is generally found beneath slab rocks at either the crest or base of riffles. It utilizes silt-free riffles during other times of the year.

Historic Range

The smoky madtom was both discovered and nearly extirpated at the same time. In 1957 a Fish and Wildlife Service crew was treating Abrams Creek in the Great Smoky Mountains National Park (Blount County, Tennessee) with a fish toxicant. The purpose of the operation was to remove non-native fishes from the watershed before closure of the Chilhowee Dam. Five dead smoky madtom specimens were taken from the creek and provided the basis for its scientific description. The species was thought to be extinct until it was rediscovered in Citico Creek in the Cherokee National Forest in 1980.

Current Distribution

The only known population of the smoky madtom is the rediscovered population inhabiting a 10.4-kilometer (6.5-mi) stretch of Citico Creek in Monroe County, Tennessee. The habitat is administered by the Forest Service. No population estimates have been made.

Conservation and Recovery

The smoky madtom's limited range is threatened by logging activities, road and bridge construction, and mineral exploration within the Citico Creek watershed, where formations of anakeesta shale have been found. On contact with water, this type of shale forms poisonous sulfuric acid. The acidic water also leaches metals—particularly aluminum—from the soil, which are extremely toxic to aquatic species. Any activities that expose the shale may result in acid contamination of Citico Creek.

When shale was exposed during construction of the Tellico-Robbinsville highway in the 1970s, acidic runoff increased the concentration of sulfates, heavy metals, and acidity in Grassy Branch, a tributary of the South Fork Citico Creek. Later surveys of Grassy Branch revealed no fish life.

Several species of madtoms have been eliminated from portions of their range for unknown reasons. Biologists think that, in addition to more obvious habitat degradation, they are unable to cope with even trace amounts of complex organic chemicals that may have been added to their habitat. Organic pollution is minimal in the Citico Creek system, but any increase could jeopardize this small, isolated population.

Bibliography

Bauer, B. H., G. R. Dinkins, and C. A. Etnier. 1983. "Discovery of *Noturus baileyi* and *N. flavipinnis* in Citico Creek, Little Tennessee River System." *Copeia* 1983:558-560.

Dinkins, G. R. 1982. "Status Survey of the Smoky Madtom (*Noturus baileyi*)." U.S. Fish and Wildlife Service, Asheville, North Carolina.

U.S. Fish and Wildlife Service. 1985. "Smoky Madtom Recovery Plan." U.S. Fish and Wildlife Service, Atlanta.

Contact

Regional Office of Endangered Species
U.S. Fish and Wildlife Service
Richard B. Russell Federal Building
75 Spring Street, S.W.
Atlanta, Georgia 30303

Yellowfin Madtom

Noturus flavipinnis

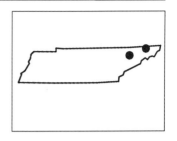

J. R. Shute

Status . . . . . . Threatened
Listed . . . . . . September 9, 1977
Family . . . . . Ictaluridae (Catfish)
Description . . . Small catfish, tinged with yellow.
Habitat . . . . . Moderately flowing, warm streams.
Food . . . . . . Aquatic insects.
Reproduction . . Spawns in the spring.
Threats . . . . . Water diversion, pollution, siltation.
Region 4 . . . . Georgia, Tennessee
Region 5 . . . . Virginia

Description

The yellowfin madtom is a small, elongated catfish that grows to a maximum length of about 9 centimeters (3.6 in). It has large eyes, a rounded caudal fin, and a dark spot on the upper sides just in front of the tail fin. The body, especially the fins, are tinged with yellow.

Behavior

Very little is known of the yellowfin madtom's reproductive behavior since few specimens have been collected during spawning. However, it is thought they spawn in the late spring, and like other madtoms, deposit their eggs on the underside of stones upstream from the usual habitat. The yellowfin madtom feeds on a variety of aquatic insects, and is most active at night.

Habitat

This small catfish inhabits moderately-flowing streams with clean, warm water, adequate plant cover, and little siltation. At night the nocturnal yellowfin madtom is likely to be found on the streambed away from the banks and riffle areas.

Historic Range

The yellowfin madtom was probably once widely distributed throughout many of the lower streams of the Tennessee River basin above Chattanooga, Tennessee. It has been collected from six streams—Chickamauga Creek, Hines Creek, the North Fork of the Holston River, Cooper Creek, Powell River, and Citico Creek.

Current Distribution

Only three known populations remain in Citico Creek (Monroe County) and Powell River (Hancock County) in Tennessee, and Copper Creek (Scott and Russell counties) in Virginia. An experimental population has been established on the Holston River in Tennessee and Virginia. There are no current population estimates.

Conservation and Recovery

Three of the six historical populations have been lost because of water impoundment and pollution. At present, the Powell River site is threatened by coal siltation. Even if all coal mining stopped now, previously deposited siltation would continue to threaten yellowfin madtom habitat. The Citico Creek locality in the Cherokee National Forest is probably the most secure, but faces some danger of acid contamination because of the nature of shale strata in the region.

The Fish and Wildlife Service (FWS) has finalized plans to establish a "non-essential experimental" population on the North Fork of the Holston River in Washington County, Tennessee. A non-essential experimental population is one whose survival is not considered essential to the survival of the species. This designation allows scientists more management flexibility. Authority over the experiment is assigned to the state of Virginia.

For the last several years FWS has been working with the National Park Service to reintroduce the yellowfin madtom in Abrams Creek within the Great Smoky Mountains National Park (Blount County, Tennessee). When this population is established, FWS will turn its efforts to the Holston River reintroduction.

Bibliography

Bauer, B. H., G. L. Denkins, and D. A. Etnier. 1983. "Discovery of *Noturus baileyi* and *N. flavipinnis* in Citico Creek, Little Tennessee River System." *Copeia* 1983:2-3.

Taylor, W. R., R. E. Jenkins, and E. A. Lachner. 1971. "Rediscovery and Description of the Ictalurid Catfish, *Noturus flavipinnis*." *Proceedings of the Biological Society of Washington* 83:469-476.

U.S. Fish and Wildlife Service. 1983. "Yellowfin Madtom Recovery Plan." U.S. Fish and Wildlife Service, Atlanta.

Contact

Regional Office of Endangered Species
U.S. Fish and Wildlife Service
Richard B. Russell Federal Building
75 Spring Street, S.W.
Atlanta, Georgia 30303

Scioto Madtom
Noturus trautmani

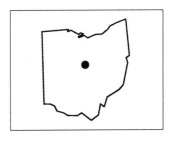

Status . . . . . . Endangered (possibly extinct)
Listed . . . . . . September 25, 1975
Family . . . . . . Ictaluridae (Catfish)
Description . . . Small dusky olive or dark brown catfish.
Habitat . . . . . . Stream riffles of moderate flow over gravel bottom.
Food . . . . Bottom browsing; plant matter and detritus.
Reproduction . . Probably spawns in summer.
Threats . . . . . . Critically low numbers.
Region 3 . . . . . Ohio

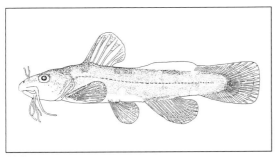

M. Troutman

Description

The Scioto madtom is a small catfish that ranges from 3.6 to 6 centimeters (1.4 to 2.3 in) in length. It is a dusky olive or dark brown, mottled with gray. It has four distinct, dark saddle markings across the back. The belly is unspotted and milky white. The caudal (tail) fin is marked by a dark bar or crescent.

Behavior

It is assumed that the Scioto madtom is a bottom browser and, like most of its relatives, feeds on plant and animal detritus. Although breeding sites have not been located, this species is thought to spawn in summer and migrate downstream in the fall.

Habitat

From the limited information available, it would appear that the Scioto madtom prefers stream riffles of moderate flow over a substrate of gravel. Water is of generally high quality with little suspended sediment.

Historic Range

This species was first collected in 1943 from Big Darby Creek (Pickaway County), a tributary of the Scioto River basin. It is thought to be endemic to this central Ohio watershed. Only 18 specimens have ever been netted, most in a single stretch of creek near the village of Fox.

Current Distribution

Few rare fish have been sought as avidly as the Scioto madtom, but it has not been collected since 1957, and many biologists have declared it extinct.

Conservation and Recovery

Because no population centers have ever been located, it is difficult to determine what, if any, environmental factors have contributed to the Scioto madtom's decline. If this madtom still exists, it survives in very low numbers.

Although this fish may be extinct, the Fish and Wildlife Service has deemed it prudent to maintain its Endangered status. If a population is rediscovered, it will be afforded immediate protection under the provisions of the Endangered Species Act. If it is removed from the list and then rediscovered, the entire listing process would have to be reinitiated.

Bibliography

Trautman, M. B. 1981. *The Fishes of Ohio*. The Ohio State University Press, Columbus.

Contact

Regional Office of Endangered Species
U.S. Fish and Wildlife Service
Federal Building, Fort Snelling
Twin Cities, Minnesota 55111

Amber Darter
Percina antesella

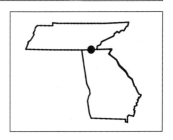

Roger W. Barbour

Status . . . . . . Endangered
Listed . . . . . . August 5, 1985
Family . . . . . . Percidae (Perch)
Description . . . Small, golden brown darter.
Habitat . . . . . . Riffle areas over sand or gravel bottoms.
Food . . . . Aquatic insects.
Reproduction . . Spawns in late winter or early spring.
Threats . . . . . . Dam construction, stream channelization.
Region 4 . . . . . Georgia, Tennessee

Description

The amber darter is a short, slender-bodied fish generally less than 6 centimeters (2.5 in) long. The upper body is golden brown with dark saddle markings; its belly is yellow-to-cream in color, and the throat of a breeding male is blue.

Behavior

In late winter or early spring, the amber darter swims up small streams to spawn in shallow marshy areas. It feeds primarily on snails and insects.

Habitat

The amber darter only inhabits areas of gentle riffles over sand and gravel bottoms. The species has not been observed in slack current in areas with debris or a mud bottom.

As summer progresses, the amber darter uses the profuse vegetation that grows in the riffles for feeding and cover.

Historic Range

A study completed in October 1983 concluded that the amber darter was restricted to the upper Conasauga River basin (a tributary of the Coosa River) in Georgia and Tennessee, with the exception of a small population in the Etowah River in Cherokee County, Georgia.

The amber darter's preference for gentle riffles may explain why the species has not been found above the U.S. Highway 411 crossing in Polk County, Tennessee, where the Conasauga River's gradient steepens. Downstream, the amber darter's range is probably limited by heavy siltation.

As recently as 1982 and 1983, biologists could not find the amber darter in the Etowah

River. If there is still a population in this river, it is very small. The only other collection record for the amber darter was from Shoal Creek, a tributary to the Etowah River (Cherokee County), Georgia, where the fish is no longer found. The Shoal Creek amber darter population was probably destroyed in the 1950s when Allatoona Reservoir inundated the lower portion of Shoal Creek.

Current Distribution

The amber darter is now found along 53 kilometers (33 mi) of the Conasauga River from the U.S. 411 bridge near the town of Conasauga, Tennessee, downstream to the Tibbs Bridge in Murray County, Georgia. This stretch of the Conasauga River passes along the southern edge of Polk and Bradley counties, Tennessee, and curves south through Murray and Whitfield counties, Georgia. There is no current population estimate.

Conservation and Recovery

The upper Conasauga River flows through the Chattahoochee and Cherokee national forests, and this undisturbed flow provides partial protection for the amber darter's downstream habitat. However, the amber darter is threatened by runoff from agricultural and urban development in portions of the watershed. Because of its limited distribution, the amber darter could be jeopardized by a single catastrophic event. Heavy truck traffic across river bridges poses the threat of a toxic chemical spill that could eliminate a large percentage of the population.

Increased tree farming activities, road and bridge construction, stream channel modifications, impoundments, changes in land use, and other projects in the watershed could have adverse impacts. Further water control projects in the drainage would re-

quire consultation with the Fish and Wildlife Service under provisions of the Endangered Species Act.

Bibliography

Etnier, D. A., B. H. Bauer, and A. G. Haines. 1981. "Fishes of the Gulf Coastal Drainage of North Georgia." Unpublished Report. U.S. Fish and Wildlife Service, Atlanta.

Freeman, B. J. 1983. "Final Report on the Status of the Trispot Darter and the Amber Darter in the Upper Coosa River System in Alabama, Georgia, and Tennessee." Report, Contract No. 14-16-0004-48. U.S. Fish and Wildlife Service, Atlanta.

Starnes, W. C., and D. A. Etnier. 1980. "Fishes." In D. C. Eagar and R. M. Hatcher, eds., *Tennessee's Rare Wildlife;* Vol. 1, *The Vertebrates.* Tennessee Heritage Program, Knoxville.

U.S. Fish and Wildlife Service. 1986. "Conasauga Logperch and Amber Darter Recovery Plan." U.S. Fish and Wildlife Service, Atlanta.

Contact

Regional Office of Endangered Species
U.S. Fish and Wildlife Service
Richard B. Russell Federal Building
75 Spring Street, S.W.
Atlanta, Georgia 30303

Conasauga Logperch
Percina jenkinsi

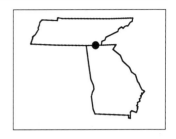

Bruce Thompson

Status . . . . . Endangered
Listed . . . . . . August 5, 1985
Family . . . . . . Percidae (Perch)
Description . . . Large darter with dark tiger stripes over a yellow body.
Habitat . . . . . . Swift-flowing streams.
Food . . . . Aquatic invertebrates.
Reproduction . . Probably spawns in the spring.
Threats . . . . . . Limited range, siltation, water pollution.
Region 4 . . . . . Georgia, Tennessee

Description

The Conasauga logperch, also known as the reticulate logperch, is a large, slender darter, sometimes exceeding 15 centimeters (6 in) in length. It is characterized by "tiger-like" vertical dark stripes over a yellow upper body.

Behavior

Little is known of the behavior of this logperch. Collected specimens suggest that it spawns in the spring, most likely in fast-flowing riffles over gravel bottoms. It has been observed to feed on aquatic invertebrates by flipping over stones with its pig-like snout.

Habitat

The Conasauga logperch requires clean, unpolluted water. It inhabits flowing pools and riffles over clean rubble, sand, and gravel bottoms. Siltation, which often results when lands are cleared for agriculture or other uses, is a major threat to the quality of these stream habitats.

Historic Range

This logperch has only been known from a single stretch of the Conasauga River in extreme southeastern Tennessee and north Georgia. Part of its range overlaps with that of the Endangered amber darter (*Percina antesella*).

Current Distribution

The Conasauga logperch is restricted to about 18 kilometers (11 mi) of the upper Conasauga River. It has been found from just above the junction of Minnewauga Creek (Polk County), Tennessee, downstream through Bradley County, Tennessee, to the State Highway 2 bridge (Murray County), Georgia. The species has never been found outside this short stretch of river.

Conservation and Recovery

The upper Conasauga River flows through the Chattahoochee and Cherokee national forests, providing some protection for the downstream habitat where the logperch is found. However, agricultural and urban runoff from developed areas continue to jeopardize the habitat. Because of its limited range and clean water requirements, the Conasauga logperch could be jeopardized by a single catastrophic event, such as a toxic chemical spill.

A proposed reservoir project on the lower Conasauga River could also affect the fishes upstream. Fishes common to reservoirs, such as carp (*Cyprinus carpio*), dramatically increase in number after dam construction and could migrate upstream into the logperch's range. In 1982 an island in the Conasauga River in Murray County, Georgia, was removed for flood control purposes. Before this channel work was done, Conasauga logperch were present but now cannot be located at the site.

The Fish and Wildlife Service (FWS) has designated habitat critical to the survival of the Conasauga logperch to encompass its entire current range in Polk and Bradley Counties, Tennessee, and Murray County, Georgia. The water quality of this river section remains high; siltation and runoff are slight. FWS and state personnel are periodically monitoring the logperch population and are tracking developments that may potentially degrade the river. Pending the results of ongoing research, the FWS may attempt to introduce the logperch into another stream in the region to reduce the chances of accidental or catastrophic loss.

Bibliography

Ramsey, J. S. 1976. "Freshwater Fishes," In H. Boschung, ed., *Endangered and Threatened Plants and Animals of Alabama*. Bulletin of the Alabama Museum of Natural History. No. 2.

Thompson, B. A. 1985. "*Percina jenkinsi*, a New Species of Logperch (Pisces: Percidae) from the Conasauga River, Tennessee and Georgia." *Occasional Papers of the Museum Zoology Louisiana State University*, No. 62.

U.S. Fish and Wildlife Service. 1986. "Conasauga Logperch and Amber Darter Recovery Plan." U.S. Fish and Wildlife Service, Atlanta.

Contact

Regional Office of Endangered Species
U.S. Fish and Wildlife Service
Richard B. Russell Federal Building
75 Spring Street, S.W.
Atlanta, Georgia 30303

Leopard Darter
Percina pantherina

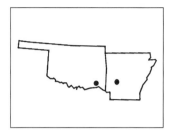

Roger W. Barbour

Status . . . . . Threatened
Listed . . . . . January 27, 1978
Family . . . . . Percidae (Perch)
Description . . . Small, olive-colored darter.
Habitat . . . . . Streams with rubble, boulder, or bedrock bottoms.
Food . . . . . . Algae, invertebrates.
Reproduction . . Spawns in spring.
Threats . . . . . Low numbers, stream impoundment.
Region 2 . . . . Oklahoma
Region 4 . . . . Arkansas

Description

The leopard darter is a small fish (8 cm, 3 in), light olive above and white below. It has dark eyes and dark spots and saddles over the sides. Closely related to the blackside darter (*Percina maculata*), it can be distinguished by its smaller scales and other scientific criteria.

Behavior

Early literature described the leopard darter as a riffle-dwelling species; more recent studies, however, found that moderately shallow pools are the preferred habitat of adult leopard darters. Although little is known, biologists believe that the fish feeds on algae and small invertebrates and spawns in riffles during the spring.

Habitat

Adult leopard darters typically are found in streams with relatively steep gradients that drain mountainous or hilly terrain and have rubble, boulder, and bedrock bottoms. They do not appear to inhabit the smaller headwater tributaries.

Historic Range

The leopard darter has been collected only from the Little River basin in southeastern Oklahoma and southwestern Arkansas.

Current Distribution

Before 1977, 64 separate collecting efforts from 30 different locations resulted in a count of only 165 leopard darters. The largest population center was in Glover Creek in

Oklahoma. Since 1977, the leopard darter has been studied extensively in the Glover Creek drainage, and it appears to be the second most abundant darter species there. There are no current estimates for the size of this apparently stable population.

Conservation and Recovery

A number of dams and reservoirs have been constructed on the Little River system: Pine Creek Reservoir, Broken Bow Lake, DeQueen Reservoir, Gillham Reservoir, and Dierks Reservoir. Only three leopard darters have ever been collected below these reservoirs. Further damming might well be fatal to the species because of its low numbers and restricted distribution. Also, the incidence of fish kills in the Little River is increasing. In one incident, creosote, flushed from a lumber treatment waste pond into the Cossatot River, poisoned 16 kilometers (10 mi) of stream.

The Fish and Wildlife Service has designated habitat critical to the survival of this species to include the main channel of the Little River in both Oklahoma and Arkansas, reaches of Black Fork Creek, the main channel of Glover Creek, including portions of the east and west forks, and the main channel of the Mountain Fork Creek. Research into the biology and population dynamics of this species is ongoing.

Bibliography

Bailey, R. M., H. E. Winn, and C. L. Smith. 1954. "Fishes from the Escambia River, Alabama and Florida, with Ecologic and Taxonomic Notes." *Proceedings of the Academy of Natural Science, Philadelphia* 106:109-164.

Eleyy, R. L., J. C. Randolph, and R. J. Miller. 1975. "Current Status of the Leopard Darter, *Percina pantherina.*" *Southwest Naturalist* 20(3):343:354.

Miller, R. J., and H. W. Robison. 1973. *The Fishes of Oklahoma.* The Oklahoma State University Press, Stillwater.

U.S. Fish and Wildlife Service. 1984. "Recovery Plan for the Leopard Darter (*Percina pantherina* Moore and Reeves)." U.S. Fish and Wildlife Service, Albuquerque.

Contact

Regional Office of Endangered Species
U.S. Fish and Wildlife Service
Box 1306
Albuquerque, New Mexico 87103

Regional Office of Endangered Species
U.S. Fish and Wildlife Service
Richard B. Russell Federal Building
75 Spring Street, S.W.
Atlanta, Georgia 30303

Snail Darter
Percina tanasi

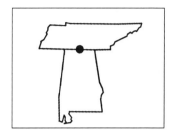

Roger W. Barbour

Status	Threatened
Listed	October 9, 1975 (Endangered)
Reclassified	July 5, 1984
Family	Percidae (Perch)
Description	Small brown darter with dark brown saddle marks.
Habitat	Vegetated streams with sandy bottoms.
Food	Invertebrates.
Reproduction	Spawns between January and mid-March.
Threats	Dam construction, water pollution.
Region 4	Alabama, Georgia, Tennessee

Description

The snail darter is a small, robust fish, rarely exceeding 9 centimeters (3.4 in) in length. Brown, with a faint trace of green above and white below, it has four dark brown, saddle-like patches across the back. The upper portion of its head is dark brown, the cheeks are mottled brown and yellow.

Behavior

Between January and mid-March, adult snail darters spawn on river shoals. Eggs deposited in gravel or on rocks hatch in 15 to 20 days. Newly hatched darters drift downstream and later return to the shoal areas. Snail darters are relatively short-lived, reaching a maximum age of five or six years.

Aquatic snails make up about 60 percent of the darter's food, although its diet tends to vary seasonally.

Habitat

Most snail darters prefer moderately flowing, vegetated streams with sandy bottoms and wide shoals for spawning.

Historic Range

The snail darter was first collected in 1973 in the lower reaches of the Little Tennessee River in Loudon County, Tennessee, an area that was eventually inundated by completion of the Tellico Dam, a project of the Tennessee Valley Authority (TVA). According to the Fish and Wildlife Service (FWS), it is difficult to determine the range of the snail darter before construction of the dam. Snail darters were probably confined to the upper portions of the Tennessee River upstream from north-central Alabama, and the lower portions of the Hiwassee, Clinch, Little Tennessee, French Broad and Holston rivers.

Current Distribution

The snail darter is now found in the main channel of the Tennessee River and in six of its tributaries. Darters have been found in small numbers in three Tennessee reservoirs—Watts Bar (Loudon County), Nickajack (Hamilton County), and Guntersville (Marion County). Only adult darters have been found and researchers think these fish migrated from tributary spawning grounds. No reproduction has been documented in these reservoirs.

In 1975 and 1976 snail darters were successfully transplanted to the Hiwassee River (Polk County). Surveys have indicated the population is thriving.

Additional snail darter populations have been located since the fish was initially described. In 1980 the first new naturally occurring population of snail darters was discovered in South Chickamauga Creek, which straddles the Tennessee-Georgia border (Hamilton County, Tennessee, and Catoosa County, Georgia). In 1981 small snail darter populations were discovered in the Sequatchee River (Marion County) and Sewee Creek (Meigs County) in Tennessee. An additional population was found in September 1981 in the Paint Rock River (Jackson and Madison counties) in Alabama.

Conservation and Recovery

Unknown to anyone before 1973, the snail darter became the focus of a major political controversy during the late 1970s when its existence halted the completion of the TVA's Tellico Dam on the Little Tennessee River. It was listed as an Endangered Species in 1975 with the Little Tennessee River designated as habitat critical to its survival. At the time of listing the only known population was threatened by the flooding of its habitat by the Tellico Dam.

In 1977 a federal appeals court ruled (*TVA v. Hill*) that the dam could not be completed since it would likely eliminate the snail darter. The following year, the U.S. Supreme Court upheld that decision, maintaining that the Endangered Species Act of 1973 was clear on the matter and that exceptions to the law must be made by the U.S. Congress, not the court.

In response to the Supreme Court's decision, Congress amended the Endangered Species Act in 1978, creating an Endangered Species Committee. The committee was given the responsibility for considering exemptions to the Act for resource development projects which had an unresolvable conflict with the Act. Since the committee was given the power to approve projects that would likely cause the extinction of a species, it soon became known as the "God Committee."

In 1979, however, contrary to many expectations, the committee voted unanimously *not* to exempt the Tellico Dam from compliance with the Endangered Species Act. Congress responded by passing legislation, which was signed into law, exempting Tellico Dam from the Act and mandating its completion. This act went on record as the first official U.S. government decision to extirpate a species.

Prior to the climax of the political controversy in 1979, the FWS attempted a number of transplants of the snail darter into other Tennessee waters. Only one transplant has proven successful. In 1975 and 1976, 710 snail darters were introduced into the Hiwassee

River in Polk County. Regular surveys have confirmed reproduction, and the darter appears to be thriving there.

In 1980, following the exemption awarded the Tellico Dam by Congress, a new snail darter population was discovered in South Chickamauga Creek, in Tennessee and Georgia. Other small populations were subsequently discovered in Tennessee and Alabama.

In light of the discovery of additional snail darter populations, the FWS "downlisted" the snail darter from Endangered to Threatened in 1984. If substantial new snail darter populations are discovered or if current populations remain stable or increase over a ten-year monitoring period, the FWS Recovery Plan states the agency will consider removing the snail darter from the federal Endangered Species list.

Bibliography

Etnier, D.A. 1976. "*Percina tanasi,* a New Percid Fish from the Little Tennessee River, Tennessee." *Proceeds of the Biological Society* 88(44):469-645.

U.S. Fish and Wildlife Service. 1983. "Snail Darter Recovery Plan." U.S. Fish and Wildlife Service, Atlanta.

U.S. Fish and Wildlife Service. 1983. "Snail Darter Survey (July, August, and October 1983)." U.S. Fish and Wildlife Service, Asheville.

Contact

Regional Office of Endangered Species
U.S. Fish and Wildlife Service
Richard B. Russell Federal Building
75 Spring Street, S.W.
Atlanta, Georgia 30303

Blackside Dace
Phoxinus cumberlandensis

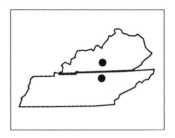

John MacGregor

Status . . . . . Threatened
Listed . . . . . . June 12, 1987
Family . . . . . Cyprinidae (Minnow)
Description . . . Small, green-gold fish with a black lateral stripe.
Habitat . . . . . . Streams with undercut banks.
Food . . . . Algae, detritus, insects.
Reproduction . . Spawns in May and June.
Threats . . . . . Stream siltation, competition.
Region 4 . . . . . Kentucky, Tennessee

Description

The blackside dace is a small fish less than 8 centimeters (3 in) long with a single black lateral stripe, a green-gold back with black specks, and a pale or sometimes brilliant scarlet belly. The fins are often bright yellow with metallic silver surrounding the base of the pelvic and pectoral fins.

Behavior

The life history of this species has not been well documented. It spawns in May and June and is thought to feed on algae, detritus, and sometimes insects.

Habitat

This fish has been found in streams with large rocks and undercut banks. Larger concentrations are found where the banks are lined with lush vegetation. Plantlife helps to maintain cool water temperatures and minimize siltation. The stream current must be swift enough to sweep away silt.

Historic Range

Because this fish was only recently discovered, its historic range is not known. However, it may have been extirpated from as many as 52 streams within Kentucky and Tennessee before it was discovered and described.

Current Distribution

The blackside dace is found in small streams in the upper Cumberland River basin, primarily above Cumberland Falls, in Pulaski, Laurel, McCreary, Whitley, Knox, Bell, Harlan, and Letcher counties in Kentucky; and Scott, Campbell, and Claiborne counties in Tennessee. In spite of its seeming widespread distribution, it now occupies little more than 23 kilometers (14 mi) of about 30 streams.

Conservation and Recovery

Siltation caused by coal mining, agriculture, and road-construction runoff are responsible for the decline of this fish. Many of the streams, which continue to support blackside dace, remain threatened by these activities. The blackside dace also faces competition from an introduced dace—the southern redbelly dace (Phoxinus *erythrogaster*)—which may have displaced it in warmer waters within its range.

The states of Kentucky and Tennessee prohibit taking this fish for any purpose. However, there are no regulations covering mining or farming practices that might degrade streams within the habitat.

Bibliography

O'Bara, C. J. 1985. "Status Survey of the Blackside Dace (*Phoxinus cumberlandensis*)." U.S. Fish and Wildlife Service, Asheville, North Carolina.

Starnes, W. C., and D. A. Etnier. 1980. "Fishes." In Enger and Hatcher, eds., *Tennessee's Rare Wildlife*; Vol. 1, *The Vertebrates*. Tennessee Wildlife Resources Agency and Tennessee Conservation Department, Knoxville.

Starnes, W. C., and L. B. Starnes. 1978. "A New Cyprinid of the Genus *Phoxinus* Endemic to the Upper Cumberland River Drainage." *Copeia* 1978:508-516.

Contact

Regional Office of Endangered Species
U.S. Fish and Wildlife Service
Richard B. Russell Federal Building
75 Spring Street, S.W.
Atlanta, Georgia 30303

Woundfin

Plagopterus argentissimus

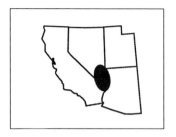

John N. Rinne

Status . . . . . . Endangered
Listed . . . . . . October 13, 1970
Family . . . . . . Cyprinidae (Minnow)
Description . . . Silvery minnow with a flat head and sharp, dorsal spine.
Habitat . . . . . . Shallow water near riffles.
Food . . . . Omnivorous.
Reproduction . . Spawns in May.
Threats . . . . . Dam construction, water diversion.
Region 1 . . . . . Nevada
Region 2 . . . . . Arizona

Description

The silvery blue woundfin, which grows to a length of about 7.5 centimeters (3 in), has a flattened head, giving it a torpedo shape. Its sharp dorsal spine is responsible for its name. It is scaleless, except for small plates of bone in the leathery skin, and has barbels (sensors) on its lips like a catfish.

The woundfin is a member of the unique tribe, Plagopterini, which is endemic to the lower basin of the Colorado River and its ancestral tributary, the White River. This tribe has only three genera, two of which consist of a single species.

Behavior

The woundfin's reproductive cycle is probably triggered by increasing temperature, lengthening daylight, and declining spring runoff in late May. Spawning females leave pools to join groups of males in swifter

flowing water over cobble or gravel beds. After spawning, the females return to pools.

Woundfins are omnivorous and eat algae, detritus, seeds, insects, and larvae.

Habitat

Woundfins prefer runs and quiet waters adjacent to shallow riffles with a depth of less than 0.5 meter (20 in) and sand or gravel bottoms. Spawning areas have a swifter flow and sand or mud substrates.

Historic Range

The original range of the woundfin included the Colorado and Gila river basins in Arizona, Nevada, and Utah. It was found on the Colorado from Yuma upstream into the Virgin River in Nevada and Utah. It was also found in the Gila River from Yuma upstream to the confluence of the Salt River.

Current Distribution

The woundfin now ranges from LaVerkin Springs (Washington County), Utah, on the mainstream of the Virgin River downstream through Mohave County, Arizona, to Lake Mead (Clark County), Nevada. No population estimates have been made.

Conservation and Recovery

The woundfin declined when the flow of the Virgin River was altered by dams, reservoirs, canals, and other diversion structures. Many spawning streams have been depleted by the diversion of water for irrigation and municipal uses.

Remaining populations are threatened by an introduced fish, the red shiner (*Notropis lutrensis*), which has completely replaced the woundfin in some areas. In 1988 Fish and Wildlife Service regional personnel, in cooperation with the Utah Division of Wildlife Resources and the Washington County Water Conservancy District, eliminated red shiners from a 34-kilometer (21-mi) portion of the upper Virgin River.

During the 1970s the state of Arizona attempted to transplant the woundfin to a number of rivers and creeks. These initial transplants, however, appear to have been unsuccessful. The Endangered Species Act allows "experimental populations" to be established through transplantation, and plans for reintroducing the woundfin into its original range and other suitable habitat are now being developed.

Bibliography

Deacon, J. E., and W. L. Minckley. 1973. "A Review of Information on the Woundfin, *Plagopterus argentissimus* Cope (Pisces: Cyprinidae): Progress Report on Population Dispersion and Community Structure of Fishes of the Virgin River System." U.S. Fish and Wildlife Service, Salt Lake City.

U.S. Fish and Wildlife Service. 1985. "Recovery Plan for Woundfin, *Plagopterus argentissimus* Cope." U.S. Fish and Wildlife Service, Albuquerque.

Contact

Regional Office of Endangered Species
U.S. Fish and Wildlife Service
P.O. Box 1306
Albuquerque, New Mexico 87103

Regional Office of Endangered Species
U.S. Fish and Wildlife Service
P.O. Box 25486
Denver Federal Center
Denver, Colorado 80225

Gila Topminnow
Poeciliopsis occidentalis occidentalis
Yaqui Topminnow
Poeciliopsis occidentalis sonoriensis

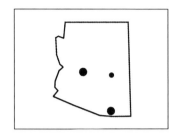

Gila Topminnow   James E. Johnson

Status	Endangered
Listed	March 11, 1967
Family	Poeciliidae (Livebearer)
Description . . .	Small guppy-like tan to olive fishes.
Habitat	Varied; usually shallow, quiet waters.
Food	Plant and animal material, detritus.
Reproduction . .	Bears live young.
Threats	Water projects, competition.
Region 2	Arizona

Description

The Gila topminnow is a guppy-like livebearer that averages 3 to 4 centimeters (1.2 to 1.6 in) in length; it is tan to olive above and white below. Breeding males darken to jet black and develop bright yellow fins and golden tints along the midline.

The Gila topminnow species consists of two subspecies—the Gila topminnow (*Poeciliopsis occidentalis occidentalis*) and the Yaqui topminnow (*P. o. sonoriensis*). Although the two subspecies are visually very similar, the Yaqui topminnow has a longer snout and its mouth is positioned higher on its head. Both subspecies are federally listed as Endangered.

Behavior

Topminnow lifespan appears to be about one year. Onset of breeding is affected by water temperature, daylight, and food availability. Gestation varies from 24 to 28 days for the Gila topminnow and 12 to 14 days for the Yaqui subspecies. Young are born alive from the mother.

Topminnows feed on a wide variety of plant and animal material and bottom detritus.

Habitat

Topminnows can live in a broad range of habitats. They prefer shallow, warm, fairly quiet waters, but can also be found in moderate currents and depths up to 1 meter (3.3 ft). They inhabit permanent and intermittent streams, marshes, and may be found close to the banks of larger rivers. Preferred habitat contains dense mats of algae and debris, usually along stream margins or below riffles, with sandy substrates sometimes covered with mud and debris.

Historic Range

The Gila topminnow was historically abundant throughout the Gila River system in Arizona, New Mexico, and northern Mexico. The species was first described in 1853 from a specimen collected from the Santa Cruz River near Tucson. The Yaqui subspecies was formerly abundant throughout the Rio Yaqui drainage in southeastern Arizona and in Sonora and Chihuahua, Mexico.

Current Distribution

Each subspecies now occupies only a remnant of its historic U.S. range. Populations of this once abundant species are so small and suitable habitat so fragmented that there is a definite concern for the survival of the species in the U.S.

The Gila topminnow is now found in natural populations at only eight isolated locations in the Santa Cruz River system in southeastern Arizona: Monkey, Cottonwood, Sheehy, and Sharp springs; Cienega and Sonoita creeks; Redrock Canyon; and the Santa Cruz River. It is also found at Salt Creek on the San Carlos Indian Reservation. In addition to the natural populations, a number of successful introductions of the Gila topminnow have been made on tributaries of the Salt, Gila, and Aqua Fria rivers. Extensive groundwater pumping and diversion of water for irrigation agriculture in Mexico are believed to have extirpated the Gila topminnow from that country.

The Yaqui topminnow is found at only eight locations within the Yaqui River headwaters. Seven of these populations occur in springs and creeks on the San Bernardino National Wildlife Refuge. The remaining population is in Leslie Creek and was introduced in the 1970s. Although Endangered in its U.S. range, the Yaqui topminnow is more abundant throughout its Mexican range.

Conservation and Recovery

Water projects have transformed all free-flowing southwestern rivers into intermittent, deeply cut streams or broad, sandy washes subject to flooding. As a result the Gila and Yaqui topminnows have been reduced to a fraction of their pre-1860s range.

Beginning in the late 1800s, exotic fish species were introduced into the habitat. The aggressive and predatory mosquitofish (*Gambusia affinis*), introduced in 1926, has been the cause of much of the topminnow decline. The mosquitofish harasses adult topminnows and eats juveniles. Only when the habitat is sufficiently large and complex, can the two species coexist.

Topminnow populations on the San Bernardino National Wildlife Refuge are well protected. The land for the refuge was purchased by The Nature Conservancy and donated to the Fish and Wildlife Service. The topminnow has been successfully reared at the Dexter National Fish Hatchery in New Mexico, and this stock will be used for reintroduction into the wild.

Bibliography

Minckley, W. L. 1969. "Native Arizona Fishes: Livebearers." *Wildlife Views* 16:6-8.

Naiman, R. J., and D. L. Soltz. 1981. *Fishes in North American Deserts.* John Wiley and Sons, New York.

U.S. Fish and Wildlife Service. 1984. "Sonoran Topminnow (Gila and Yaqui) Recovery Plan." U.S. Fish and Wildlife Service, Albuquerque.

Contact

Regional Office of Endangered Species
U.S. Fish and Wildlife Service
P.O. Box 1306
Albuquerque, New Mexico 87103

Colorado Squawfish
Ptychocheilus lucius

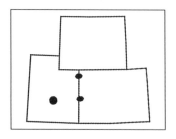

Harold M. Tyus

Status . . . . . Endangered
Listed . . . . . March 11, 1967
Family . . . . . Cyprinidae (Minnow)
Description . . . Largest of the minnow family; dark olive above with a pointed snout and large mouth.
Habitat . . . . . River eddies and pools.
Food . . . . . . Aquatic invertebrates, insect larvae, fish.
Reproduction . . Upstream migration to spawn in late spring.
Threats . . . . . River-flow reduction, competition.
Region 6 . . . . . Colorado, Utah

Description

The Colorado squawfish is the largest of the large Cyprinidae (minnow) family, sometimes attaining a length of 1.5 meters (5 ft) and a weight of 36 kilograms (80 lbs). It is long and slender, with a pointed snout, flattened head, and large mouth. Adults are dark olive above, whiter below.

Behavior

Squawfish are predatory feeders. Newly hatched young feed on zooplankton and insect larvae. On reaching 10 centimeters (4 in), they begin to prey on other fish. Squawfish migrate upstream for spawning in late spring, and eggs hatch in less than four days at water temperatures of about 21 degrees C (70 degrees F).

Habitat

This species has adapted to a watershed known for its variable flow, high silt loads, and turbulence. Adults spend most of their time in eddies, pools, and protected pockets just outside of the main current. Young fish are found in quieter water, usually over silt or sand bottoms.

Historic Range

The squawfish was once found in the Colorado River basin throughout the mainstream and major tributaries from Arizona to Wyoming. By states, its range included: the Gila River Basin in Arizona; the Colorado River from the Mexican border to the Nevada state line in California; the Colorado River and lower reaches of the

Gunnison, White, Yampa, Dolores, San Juan, Uncompahgre and Animas rivers in Colorado; the San Juan and Animas rivers in New Mexico; the Colorado River mainstream in Nevada; the entire reach of the Colorado and Green rivers, the San Juan, White, and Dolores rivers in Utah; and the Green River in Wyoming.

Current Distribution

Remaining Colorado squawfish occur for the most part in the Green River in Utah, and in the Yampa and Colorado rivers in Colorado and portions of Utah. The fish is absent from the lower Colorado River and rare throughout the remainder of the range. It is probably extirpated from the Gila River basin in Arizona, but reintroduction of the species is planned.

Conservation and Recovery

The Colorado River was once one of the world's most turbulent rivers. Fish thriving in its turbid and highly mineralized waters were specially adapted to these extreme conditions, and the squawfish was plentiful. Many early settlers preferred the "white, flaky, and sweet" flesh of the squawfish over any of the native trout.

Since the construction of Hoover Dam in the 1930s and subsequent massive water control projects on the Colorado, water flow has been greatly reduced, radically altering the riverine environment. The decline in squawfish has been especially pronounced in areas below reservoirs, which are characterized by extreme water temperature fluctuations, altered flow patterns, lower turbidity, higher salinity, and the presence of introduced fishes, such as the red shiner, redside shiner, and green sunfish.

As a part of the effort to recover the Colorado squawfish, the Fish and Wildlife

Service (FWS) and the Arizona Game and Fish Department have begun a collaborative project to establish experimental populations in Arizona's Salt and Verde rivers. In 1985 over 175,000 fingerlings from the Dexter National Fish Hatchery in New Mexico were introduced into those rivers. In 1987, 100,000 more were released.

Also in 1987, the FWS proposed that a third experimental population be established in the main Colorado channel between Imperial Dam and Parker Dam. Under this plan, 100,000 fingerlings would be released the first year, followed by annual restockings over the next ten years. The FWS hopes to establish a sport fishery for the squawfish in the lower Colorado River. A special FWS regulation will allow anglers to take squawfish in this stretch of the river, as long as they comply with all other state regulations.

Bibliography

Stalnaker, C. B., and P. B. Holden. 1973. "Changes in Native Fish Distribution in the Green River System, Utah-Colorado." *Utah Academy Proceedings* 50(1):25-32.

U.S. Fish and Wildlife Service. 1978. "Colorado Squawfish Recovery Plan." U.S. Fish and Wildlife Service, Denver.

Vanicek, C.D., and R.H. Kramer. 1969. "Life History of the Colorado Squawfish and the Colorado Chub in the Green River in Dinosaur National Monument." *Transactions of the American Fish Society* 98(2):193-208.

Contact

Regional Office of Endangered Species
U.S. Fish and Wildlife Service
P.O. Box 25486
Denver Federal Center
Denver, Colorado 80225

Ash Meadows Speckled Dace

Rhinichthys osculus nevadensis

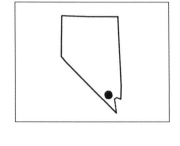

Donald W. Sada

Status	Endangered
Listed	May 10, 1982 (Emergency)
Reclassified . . .	September 2, 1983
Family	Cyprinidae (Minnow)
Description . . .	Small, plain minnow with poorly defined markings.
Habitat	Warm springs and outflows.
Food	Aquatic fauna.
Reproduction . .	Spawns in early spring and late summer.
Threats	Groundwater pumping, predation by introduced fish species.
Region 1	Nevada

Description

The Ash Meadows speckled dace is a small silvery minnow about 8 centimeters (3 in) long. It is plain except poorly defined blotches and speckles on the sides. All fish in the genus have a double row of teeth in the pharynx. This fish was first described in 1893 as a full species, *Rhinichthys nevadensis*. However, in 1948, it was determined to be a subspecies of *Rhinichthys osculus*.

Behavior

The Ash Meadows speckled dace spawns once in early spring and again in late summer. It feeds on a variety of small aquatic animals that inhabit the thermal springs.

Habitat

This speckled dace is found only in the warm springs and outflows at Ash Meadows in Nye County, Nevada. Ash Meadows is a unique desert wetland comprising several dozen springs scattered throughout an inter-mountain valley about 120 kilometers (75 mi) northwest of Las Vegas. These thermal springs support the highest concentration of endemic plant and animal species in the U.S. Besides the speckled dace, three other Endangered fishes inhabit springs at Ash Meadows—Devil's Hole pupfish (*Cyprinodon diabolis*), Warm Springs pupfish (*C. nevadensis pectoralis*), and Ash Meadows Amargosa pupfish (*C. n. mionectes*). Seven plants protected by the Endangered Species Act, including the Ash Meadows gumplant

(*Grindelia fraxinopratensis*) and the Amargosa niterwort (*Nitrophilia mohaveensis*), are found there.

The ecosystem also supports rare insect species, including the threatened Ash Meadows naucorid (*Ambrysus amargosus*) and a great variety of freshwater snails and mollusks, many of which have not been scientifically described.

Unfortunately a number of exotic fish species, such as the mosquitofish and black molly have been introduced to Ash Meadows where they compete with and prey on native fishes. The Ash Meadows killifish (*Empetrichthys merriami*), now extinct, was eliminated by predation from introduced species.

Historic Range

The Ash Meadows speckled dace has not been found outside of Ash Meadows. It formerly inhabited much of the interconnected surface warm springs and outflows.

Current Distribution

Dace populations and suitable habitat have been severely reduced by agricultural and residential development and groundwater pumping. The fish is now restricted to Jack Rabbit Spring, Big Spring, and the two westernmost springs of the Bradford Springs group, as well as their outflows.

Conservation and Recovery

Early homesteaders attempted to farm Ash Meadows using the free-flowing water from the springs for irrigation. These efforts failed because the salty, clay soils were poorly suited for crops. During the late 1960s and early 1970s Ash Meadows again came under the pressure of agricultural development, resulting in the plowing of large tracts of land and the installation of groundwater pumps

and diversion ditches. As a consequence many populations of plants and animals were destroyed.

In 1977 the agricultural interests sold about 60 square kilometers (23 sq mi) of land at Ash Meadows to a real estate developer. Attempts by the developer to construct a residential community at Ash Meadows for 55,000 people resulted in widespread land disturbance and water diversions. In May 1982 the Fish and Wildlife Service (FWS) used emergency provisions of the Endangered Species Act to invoke protection for the speckled dace and the Amargosa pupfish.

In 1984, after attempts by the FWS to negotiate adequate conservation agreements failed, the developer sold about 4,450 hectares (11,000 acres) to The Nature Conservancy. The property was later purchased by the federal government to establish the Ash Meadows National Wildlife Refuge.

Bibliography

Beatley, J. C. 1977. "Ash Meadows: Nevada's Unique Oasis in the Mojave Desert." *Mentzelia* 3:20-24.

Gilbert, C. H. 1983. "Report on the Fishes of the Death Valley Expedition Collected in Southern California and Nevada in 1891 with Descriptions of New Species." *North American Fauna* 7:220- 234.

Soltz, D. L., and R. J. Naiman, eds. 1978. "The Natural History of Native Fishes in the Death Valley System" *Natural History Museum of Los Angeles County, Science Series* 30:17.

Contact

Regional Office of Endangered Species
U.S. Fish and Wildlife Service
Lloyd 500 Building, Suite 1692
500 N.E. Multnomah Street
Portland, Oregon 97232

Foskett Speckled Dace
Rhinichthys osculus ssp.

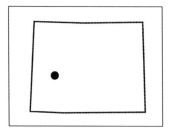

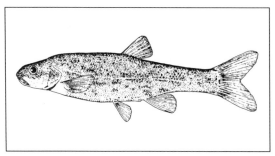

Speckled dace

Status . . . . . . Threatened
Listed . . . . . . March 28, 1985
Family . . . . . . Cyprinidae (Minnow)
Description . . . A silvery dace with dark blotches.
Habitat . . . . . . Freshwater springs and outflows
Food . . . . Detritus, fish eggs.
Reproduction . . Spawns in June and July.
Threats . . . . . Limited distribution, habitat disturbance, pollution.
Region 1 . . . . . Oregon

Description

The silvery Foskett speckled dace ranges from 4.5 to 8 centimeters (1.8 to 3.1 in) in length. It is often marked with dark blotches on its rear half. The belly may turn orange or red during breeding season.

Behavior

This dace collects in small schools and is rarely found singly. It is a bottom browser, feeding on insects, detritus, and other fishes' eggs. It spawns in June and July.

Habitat

This species is restricted to a single spring system and requires clean, fresh water of fairly constant temperature.

Historic Range

The Foskett speckled dace is endemic to a small spring system in the Coleman Basin on the west side of Warner Valley (Lake County) in arid south-central Oregon.

Current Distribution

Foskett speckled dace still occurs in portions of the Foskett Spring system. In 1982, an attempt was made to transplant the fish to other ponds in the region with indifferent success. When this species was federally listed in 1985, less than 1,500 individuals survived, and the number has not appreciably increased.

Conservation and Recovery

This species is threatened by actual or potential modification of its springs habitat.

Ground water levels in the area have been lowered by pumping to support irrigation agriculture and may eventually decrease the flow of the Foskett Spring, which is already considered minimal. Ditching or otherwise tampering with the pools and outflows would probably destroy the entire spring system. Trampling by livestock that come to drink at the spring is a particular problem.

Because the springs are located on private land, the options for recovery are limited. The Fish and Wildlife Service hopes to negotiate a conservation agreement with the landowner to allow fencing of the springs and general habitat maintenance. Attempts to transplant the fish into nearby protected springs will continue.

Bibliography

Bond. C. E. 1973. "Keys to Oregon Freshwater Fishes." Technical Bulletin 58. Oregon State University, Agricultural Experiment Station.

Bond, C. E. 1974. "Endangered Plants and Animals of Oregon; Fishes." Special Report 205. Oregon State University, Agricultural Experiment Station.

Contact

Regional Office of Endangered Species
U.S. Fish and Wildlife Service
Lloyd 500 Building, Suite 1692
500 N.E. Multnomah Street
Portland, Oregon 97232

Kendall Warm
Springs Dace
Rhinichthys osculus thermalis

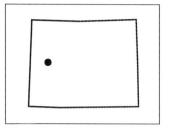

William R. Gould

Status . . . . . . Endangered
Listed . . . . . . October 13, 1970
Family . . . . . . Cyprinidae (Minnow)
Description . . . Small minnow; male is
purple, female is olive
green.
Habitat . . . . . . Warm springs and seeps.
Food . . . . Aquatic insects.
Reproduction . . Spawns several times a
year.
Threats . . . . . Water pollution, habitat
destruction.
Region 6 . . . . . Wyoming

Description

The Kendall Warm Springs dace is a small minnow about 5.4 centimeters (2 in) long. Breeding males are often a bright purple color; females are typically dull olive green.

This dace was first given the name *Apocope osculus thermalis*. The 1970 revision of Wyoming Fishes considered the Kendall Warm Springs dace and the Green River dace (*Rhinichthys osculus yarrowi*) to make up a single species. However, further comparison showed that the Kendall dace differed by having fewer scales and fin rays, a larger head and fins, and a smaller body. Its taxonomic status remains unclear.

Behavior

Although the Kendall Warm Springs dace has not been closely studied, spawning probably occurs several times a year, if not year round. Dace usually gather in small schools, due either to space limitations or to an inborn behavioral preference. A skittering flight to the nearest clump of plants is a typical reaction to danger, although some flee to the deeper, turbulent areas in the main current of its spring habitat.

Habitat

Kendall Warm Springs in Wyoming consists of numerous seeps and springs scattered along the north face of a limestone ridge at an elevation of 2,390 meters (7,840 ft) in the Bridger-Teton National Forest. The spring outflow flows southwest for 300 meters (984 ft) before cascading into the Green River over an embankment formed by the water's mineral deposits. Water from the springs has a constant temperature of 29 degrees C (85 F). It is slightly alkaline, mineralized, and high in dissolved solids.

Vegetation near the spring complex is limited to various grasses, forbs, and low-growing shrubs and trees, such as willow and sagebrush. Monkeyflower and moss are the dominant aquatic plants in the upper pool; below that area, sage pondweed, moss, and stonewart predominate.

Historic Range

The Kendall Warm Springs dace has probably always been restricted to the Kendall Warm Springs near the Green River drainage in Sublette County, Wyoming.

Current Distribution

Because of the fish's small size and the inefficiency of survey techniques, population figures are uncertain. In 1934, biologists estimated the total population as between 200,000 and 500,000 individuals. Recent observations suggest that even the lower figure may have been exaggerated.

Conservation and Recovery

Over the course of many years, human activities have altered the Kendall Warm Springs dace's habitat. A road built across the creek built before 1934 is still the main access route to the upper Green River and the northern Bridger Wilderness. A culvert divides the upper half of the dace population from the lower.

Several rock dams have been built over the years to provide small bathing and soaking pools, and people have washed clothes in the warm water. To preserve water quality, the Forest Service closed the springs to bathing and prohibited the use of soaps, detergents, and bleaches.

For many years, fishermen used Kendall dace as fish bait until prohibited by the Wyoming Game and Fish Department in the early 1960s.

Sixty-four hectares (160 acres) have been designated by the Forest Service as the Kendall Warm Springs Biological Management Unit. The boundaries include most of the small watershed and surrounding land. Because of this designation, mineral exploration, seining, and trapping are prohibited. The immediate area around the springs has been fenced and interpretive signs posted. To control traffic along the creek, vehicle access has been blocked.

The thermal spring and surrounding land may qualify as a research natural area. If so, a formal designation could provide more complete habitat protection.

Bibliography

Baxter, G. T., and J. R. Simon. 1970. "Wyoming Fishes." Bulletin 4. Game and Fish Department, Cheyenne.

Binns, N. A. 1978. "Habitat Structure of Kendall Warm Springs, with Reference to the Endangered Kendall Warm Springs Dace." Fisheries Technical Bulletin No. 3, Wyoming Game and Fish Department, Cheyenne.

U.S. Fish and Wildlife Service. 1982. "Kendall Warm Springs Dace Recovery Plan." U.S. Fish and Wildlife Service, Denver.

Contact

Regional Office of Endangered Species
U.S. Fish and Wildlife Service
P.O. Box 25486
Denver Federal Center
Denver, Colorado 80225

Apache Trout
Salmo apache

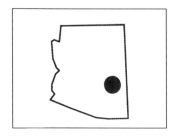

Bob Hines

Status . . . . . . Threatened
Listed . . . . . . July 16, 1975
Family . . . . . . Salmonidae (Trout)
Description . . . Medium-sized, yellowish trout with dark brown spots.
Habitat . . . . . . Stream headwaters.
Food . . . . Insects.
Reproduction . . Spawns from March to mid-June.
Threats . . . . . Competition.
Region 2 . . . . . Arizona

Description

Also known as the Arizona trout, the Apache trout has a deep, compressed body with a large dorsal fin. It grows to a mature length of between 18 and 23 centimeters (7 and 9 in). The yellowish or yellow olive back and sides are covered with uniformly spaced dark brown spots.

Behavior

The Apache trout feeds primarily on terrestrial and aquatic insects, taking them from the surface. After reaching three years of age, females spawn from March through mid-June.

Habitat

The Apache trout inhabits cool, fast-flowing mountain streams. The severe winters typically deplete trout populations, which must recover sufficiently the following summer.

Historic Range

This species was known historically from the headwaters of the Little Colorado, Salt, San Francisco, White and Black river systems in the White Mountains of eastern Arizona (Greenlee County) and western New Mexico (Catron County).

Current Distribution

Currently, the headwaters of the White and Black river systems on the Fort Apache Indian Reservation support the greatest concentrations of the Apache trout. Streams in the Gila and Apache-Sitgreaves national forests have been rehabilitated to support reintroduced populations. Several thousand of the fish have been counted in Bonita Creek on the East Fork White River. Before reintroductions began, the range of the Apache trout was reduced to about 48 kilometers (30 mi) of stream, less than 5 percent of the historic range.

Conservation and Recovery

Competition with introduced, non-native fishes has been the major factor in the decline of the Apache trout. Brook, rainbow, and brown trouts were introduced into many streams in the region as game fishes and expanded their populations to the detriment of the Apache trout. The Apache trout also has the ability to interbreed with the brown trout, and hybrids were spreading into many streams. Continuing hybridization would mean the extinction of the Apache trout as an identifiable species.

In the late 1970s the Fish and Wildlife Service (FWS) began a project to rehabilitate streams on the Fort Apache Indian Reservation. Ord Creek was treated repeatedly to remove introduced trout, and Apache trout from Bonita Creek were relocated there. But in spite of precautions, the brook trout reappeared in the stream the following year. Biologists have erected artificial barriers in several streams to separate the species. The Bureau of Indian Affairs and the White Mountain Apache Tribe have cooperated extensively in these reintroduction efforts.

In 1984 Dry Creek in the Gila National Forest was rehabilitated to accept a transplanted population of Apache trout. The stream was sampled and found to still contain trout hybrids that would dilute the genetic purity of transplanted Apaches. The project was delayed until hybrids could be removed.

In 1986 the Williams Creek National Fish Hatchery succeeded for the first time in raising the Apache trout in captivity. Personnel at the facility designed an innovative feeding system that simulates natural stream conditions and automatically dispenses brine shrimp for the fry. The Hatchery hopes to raise 50,000 Apache trout fingerlings each year for restocking streams on the Fort Apache Reservation and Apache-Sitgreaves National Forest Service. The success of this hatchery program and continuing reintroduction efforts virtually ensure the long-term survival of the Apache trout.

Bibliography

U.S. Fish and Wildlife Service. 1979. "Recovery Plan for the Arizona Trout, *Salmo apache*." U.S. Fish and Wildlife Service, Albuquerque.

Contact

Regional Office of Endangered Species
U.S. Fish and Wildlife Service
P.O. Box 1306
Albuquerque, New Mexico 87103

Little Kern Golden Trout

Salmo aquabonita whitei

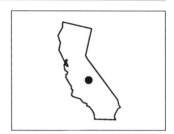

Susan Middleton

Status	Threatened
Listed	April 13, 1978
Family	Salmonidae (Trout)
Description . . .	Olive-backed trout with red cheeks and belly and golden underside.
Habitat	Clear, cool flowing water.
Food	Insects.
Reproduction . .	Spawns in late June.
Threats	Competition and hybridization with rainbow trout, pollution.
Region 1	California

Description

The Little Kern golden trout, a subspecies of the golden trout, reaches an adult size of 20 to 31 centimeters (8 to 12 in) and weighs up to 0.45 kilogram (1 lb). It is olive above a broad reddish lateral line, golden yellow below, and has red cheeks and belly.

Behavior

The golden trout usually spawns in late June in gravel riffle areas. Males reach sexual maturity in about two years, females in three. The trout's diet consists primarily of aquatic insects.

Habitat

This trout inhabits clear, cool, swift-flowing streams.

Historic Range

The Little Kern golden trout has been found only in the Little Kern River (Tulare County), California.

Current Distribution

Genetically pure populations of Little Kern golden trout now survive only in headwater streams that were not stocked with rainbow trout or that have falls preventing upstream migration of rainbow trout. There are no current population figures.

Conservation and Recovery

In the 1930s rainbow trout were introduced into the Little Kern River system and hybridization with the golden trout resulted. Additional threats to the Little Kern golden trout are the possibility of water quality degradation from off-road vehicle use in the area, improper road construction, careless logging, pollution from mining operations, and overgrazing in the drainage basin.

The staff of the Sequoia National Forest has consulted informally with the Fish and Wildlife Service (FWS) to determine the best way to harvest timber in the forest without disturbing the golden trout's habitat.

The main channel and tributary streams of the Little Kern river above the barrier falls have been designated by the FWS as habitat critical for the survival of the Little Kern golden trout. The state Department of Fish and Game has established the Golden Trout Wilderness Area, encompassing the FWS-designated area in the Sequoia National Forest, and has developed a management plan for the species.

Bibliography

Behnke, R. J. 1980. *Monograph of the Native Trouts of the Genus* Salmo *of Western North America.* U.S. Fish and Wildlife Service, Denver.

Moyle, Peter. 1976. *Inland Fishes of California.* University of California Press, Berkeley.

Contact

Regional Office of Endangered Species
U.S. Fish and Wildlife Service
Lloyd 500 Building, Suite 1692
500 N.E. Multnomah Street
Portland, Oregon 97232

Lahontan Cutthroat Trout

Salmo clarki henshawi

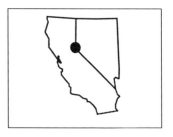

Lloyd Skinner

Status	. . . . . .	Threatened
Listed	. . . . .	October 13, 1970
Family	. . . . . .	Salmonidae (Trout)
Description	. . .	Green to greenish blue trout with a bright red cutthroat mark.
Habitat	. . . . . .	Cool, well-oxygenated water.
Food	. . . .	Aquatic insects.
Reproduction	. .	Spawns in April and May.
Threats	. . . . .	Dam construction, degradation of water quality, competition with other trouts.
Region 1	. . . . .	California, Nevada

Description

The Lahontan cutthroat trout, a subspecies of the cutthroat trout, can be distinguished by its larger relative size. This trout ranges from 25 to 38 centimeters (10 to 15 in) in length and usually has a bright red stripe, or "cutthroat" mark, under each side of the lower jaw. The body is elongated and compressed with a relatively long head. The back is greenish to greenish blue. The head, fins, and sides may be yellowish, and the belly is silvery. Some biologists consider the Lahontan a separate subspecies only because of its geographic isolation from other cutthroat trouts.

Behavior

The life history of the Lahontan cutthroat is similar to that of other cutthroat trouts, which feed on aquatic insects and spawn from the middle of April to late May. The eggs hatch in six to eight weeks.

Habitat

This species requires cool, well-oxygenated water during all its life stages and must have access to flowing water with clean gravel substrates for spawning. The Lahontan subspecies is adapted to the highly mineralized waters found in many of the region's lakes.

Historic Range

The Lahontan cutthroat trout is endemic to the enclosed Lahontan basin of west-central Nevada and adjacent portions of California. It once inhabited Winnemucca Lake, which is now dry, and was eliminated from Lake Tahoe by competing species.

Current Distribution

In Nevada, the Lahontan cutthroat trout inhabits Pyramid Lake and the Truckee River (Washoe County), both forks of the Walker River and Walker Lake (Mineral County), Summit Lake, and Carson River and its tributaries (Douglas and Lyon counties). It is found in the headwaters of the Walker River (Mono County), and Catnip and Heenan reservoirs in California. No current population estimates have been made.

A captive population of the Lahontan trout, used to replenish stocks in Pyramid Lake, is maintained at the Verdi Hatchery, Nevada. The California Department of Fish and Game has established a captive population at its Kernville Hatchery.

Conservation and Recovery

The Lahontan cutthroat trout declined throughout its range because of damage to its spawning beds caused by timber harvesting, forest fires, and grazing livestock. Streams have been dammed and water diverted for irrigation or municipal uses. Construction of the Marble Bluff Dam closed off spawning grounds in the headwaters of the Truckee River until recent construction of a fish ladder there. Water pollution, particularly downstream from Reno and Carson City, has also been a limiting factor.

In 1986 Fish and Wildlife Service (FWS) personnel assisted more than 1,400 Lahontan cutthroat trout over the Marble Bluff Dam, the largest trout run in the fish facility's history. These spawning trout were expected to contribute to the recovering natural population in the Truckee River.

In 1987 FWS personnel conducted an emergency operation to salvage some 200 Lahontan cutthroats from drought-depleted sections of By-Day Creek in Mono County, California. These fish were transferred to a headwater stream in the East Walker River basin, then used to restock Slinkard Creek the following year.

With planned recovery activities nearly 50 percent complete, the FWS accelerated its stream rehabilitation efforts in 1989, spurred by recent successes in artificial propagation at the Kernville Hatchery. Under the current schedule, the species could be proposed for delisting as early as 1992.

Bibliography

Behnke, R. J. 1980. *Monograph of the Native Trouts of the Genus* Salmo *of Western North America*. U.S. Fish and Wildlife Service, Denver.

Moyle, P. B. 1976. *Inland Fishes of California*. University of California Press, Berkeley.

Contact

Regional Office of Endangered Species
U.S. Fish and Wildlife Service
Lloyd 500 Building, Suite 1692
500 N.E. Multnomah Street
Portland, Oregon 97232

Paiute Cutthroat Trout
Salmo clarki seleniris

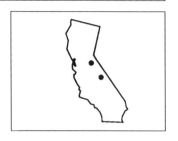

Robert H. Smith

Status	Threatened
Listed	March 11, 1967
Family	Salmonidae (Trout)
Description . . .	Purplish pink trout with few or no body spots and a cutthroat mark under jaw.
Habitat	Cool, well-oxygenated streams.
Food	Insects.
Reproduction . .	Spawns in early summer.
Threats	Limited distribution, hybridization.
Region 1	California

Description

The Paiute cutthroat trout is a subspecies of the cutthroat trout, growing to 25 to 30 cm (10 to 12 in). Its body is elongated and compressed, its head is relatively long, and it has a bright red stripe, or "cutthroat" mark, under each side of the lower jaw. Distinguishing characteristics of the Paiute cutthroat are its purplish pink color and the absence (or near absence) of body spots. Before being reduced to subspecies status in 1947, it was classified as a full species (*Salmo seleniris*).

Behavior

The Paiute cutthroat trout matures sexually at two years and spawns during the early summer in flowing waters above a clean gravel stream bed. Eggs hatch in six to eight weeks. Fingerlings often move into tributary streams until large enough to survive in the main streams. The largest fish vigorously defend stream pools, driving smaller ones into runs and riffles in available unoccupied habitat.

Habitat

The Paiute cutthroat trout requires cool, well-oxygenated water during all its life stages and prefers streams with moderate current in meadow areas. It can survive in lakes but must have access to flowing water for spawning.

Historic Range

This subspecies was first collected above Llewellyn Falls in Alpine County, California, and has an extremely limited range. Historically, it was found only in Silver King Creek in the East Fort Carson River watershed in the Toiyabe National Forest. Silver King Creek is a headwater tributary of the enclosed Lahontan basin of Nevada.

Current Distribution

The Paiute cutthroat trout was eliminated from much of its range in the early 20th century because of interbreeding with the introduced rainbow trout. Several small populations had previously been transplanted into the upper reaches of Silver King Creek above Llewellyn Falls, an impassable barrier for other trouts. Some of these fish were transplanted into other California lakes and streams, and at least two populations survive outside the native drainage—Cottonwood Creek (Mono County), and Stairway Creek (Modero County). Recent estimates placed the number of Paiute cutthroat trout at about 2,550. Except for one small inholding in the Silver King basin, the major habitat streams are within the Toiyabe National Forest.

Conservation and Recovery

Probably the greatest threat to this subspecies, besides its limited distribution, is competition and interbreeding with other non-native trouts. Where other trout have invaded its habitat, the Paiute cutthroat trout has been displaced or hybridized out of existence. Waters managed for the Paiute cutthroat trout must be protected from the natural or accidental introduction of other trouts.

The extremely limited native range—approximately 15 kilometers (9 mi) in three streams—has complicated recovery efforts. Recovery activities have focused on protecting existing habitat, rehabilitating new sections of streams by removing non-native fishes, and reintroducing the Paiute. State and federal personnel have cooperated to reduce sedimentation and promote the regrowth of native streambank vegetation in the watershed.

In 1988 the Fish and Wildlife Service (FWS), in cooperation with the Forest Service, completed the first phase of planned recovery activities for Paiute cutthroat trout populations in the Toiyabe National Forest. Several low, instream dams were constructed to improve spawning habitat; a barrier was built to prevent competing trouts from intermingling with the Paiute on Fourmile Creek; sections of river bank were recontoured to decrease erosion and promote regrowth of natural vegetation; work was completed on the banks of a tributary to reduce sedimentation in Silver King Creek; and solar-powered electric fences were installed to exclude cattle and protect the growth of willow trees along streams. Volunteers donated more than 1100 hours of labor to these projects.

Bibliography

Behnke, R. J. 1980. *Monograph of the Native Trouts of the Genus* Salmo *of Western North America.* U.S. Fish and Wildlife Service, Denver.

Diana, J. S., and E. D. Lane. 1978. "The Movement and Distribution of Paiute Cutthroat Trout in Cottonwood Creek, California." *Transactions of the American Fisheries Society* 107:444-448.

U.S. Fish and Wildlife Service. 1985. "Paiute Cutthroat Trout Recovery Plan." U.S. Fish and Wildlife Service, Portland.

Contact

Regional Office of Endangered Species
U.S. Fish and Wildlife Service
Lloyd 500 Building, Suite 1692
500 N.E. Multnomah Street
Portland, Oregon 97232

Greenback Cutthroat Trout

Salmo clarki stomias

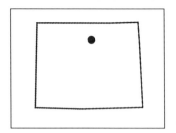

Bob Benke/USFWS

Status	Threatened
Listed	March 11, 1967 (Endangered)
Reclassified . . .	April 18, 1978
Family	Salmonidae (Trout)
Description . . .	Heavily spotted trout; males often with blood-red belly.
Habitat	Flowing mountain streams.
Food	Aquatic insects.
Reproduction . .	Spawns in spring.
Threats	Competition with non-native trout, mining and logging, water diversion.
Region 6	Colorado

Description

The cutthroat trout typically ranges from 25 to 38 centimeters (10 to 15 in) in length. The body and head are elongated. Of all cutthroat trout subspecies, the greenback generally has the largest spots and the most numerous scales. It displays a dark "cutthroat" mark under each side of the jaw. The belly of the mature male is often a vivid, blood-red color.

Behavior

The greenback cutthroat trout feeds on aquatic insects and spawns in the spring. In head-to-head competition with the brook trout, the greenback cutthroat is invariably the loser. Although adults rarely interact, brook trout juveniles are more aggressive and drive greenback juveniles out of shallow,

protective streams into larger creeks and rivers, where they are devoured by predators.

Habitat

This trout requires clear, swift-flowing mountain streams where there is cover, such as overhanging banks and vegetation. Riffle areas are used for spawning. Juveniles tend to shelter in shallow backwaters until large enough to fend for themselves in the mainstream.

Historic Range

The greenback cutthroat trout is the only trout endemic to the Rocky Mountain sources of the South Platte and Arkansas River systems of north-central and central Colorado.

Its range extended from the headwaters of both rivers to the foothills along the Front Range.

Current Distribution

The greenback cutthroat trout is found in the headwaters of the South Platte River, including the east slope drainage of the Rocky Mountain National Park (Cow, Hidden Valley, Pear Reservoir, West and Fern creeks, Fern, Bear, Caddis and Odessa lakes, and the Big Thompson River). It is known from Como Creek in the North Boulder Creek watershed (Boulder County), South Boxelder Creek (Douglas County), and the South Fork of Cache la Poudre River in Roosevelt National Forest and Black Hollow Creek (Larimer County). The headwaters of the Arkansas River, including South Huerfano and Cascade creeks in San Isabel National Forest, and Hourglass Creek, also support populations of the greenback cutthroat trout.

There are no recent estimates, but the greenback population has increased because of successful reintroduction efforts.

Conservation and Recovery

Diversion of water for irrigation, water pollution and sedimentation caused by mining and logging, and introduction of non-native trout into the greenback's native watersheds—all contributed to the fish's decline throughout its historic range.

Efforts to conserve the greenback began as early as 1959 when fingerlings from the Forest Canyon headwaters of the Big Thompson River were stocked in Fay Lake after non-native trout were removed. Unable to survive in Fay Lake, the trout managed to establish a self-sustaining population in Caddis Lake, immediately downstream. In 1967 a brook trout population was eliminated from Black Hollow Creek, and the greenback

cutthroat was reintroduced, using stock from Como Creek. A barrier was constructed to prevent the return of brook trout, and the stream was designated a sanctuary for greenback cutthroat trout.

After brook trout were eliminated from Hidden Valley Creek in 1973, the greenback population in the stream recovered. In 1975 state and federal biologists successfully transplanted greenbacks to Bear Lake after removing brook trout. Because of these successes, the greenback cutthroat trout was "downlisted" from Endangered to Threatened in 1978. Recovery efforts continue under the direction of the Fish and Wildlife Service and the Park Service with cooperation of researchers at Colorado State University.

Bibliography

Gagnon, J. G. 1973. "The Greenback." *Trout: Quarterly Publication of Trout Unlimited* 144:12, 13-28, 30.

U.S. Fish and Wildlife Service. 1977. "Greenback Cutthroat Trout Recovery Plan." U.S. Fish and Wildlife Service, Denver.

Contact

Regional Office of Endangered Species
U.S. Fish and Wildlife Service
P.O. Box 25486
Denver Federal Center
Denver, Colorado 80225

Gila Trout

Salmo gilae

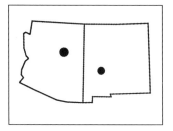

John N. Rinne

Status	Endangered
Listed	March 11, 1967
Family	Salmonidae (Trout)
Description . . .	Iridescent, golden trout with prominent, irregular spotting.
Habitat	Headwater streams with cover and riffle areas.
Food	Aquatic invertebrates.
Reproduction . .	Spawns in spring.
Threats	Restricted range, hybridization.
Region 2	Arizona, New Mexico

Description

The Gila trout grows 25 to 34 centimeters (10 to 14 in) in length and is readily identified by its iridescent golden sides, which grade to a dark copper on the gill covers. Irregular spotting is prominent on the back and sides. Dorsal, pelvic, and anal fins have white to yellowish tips. During spawning season the normally white belly may be streaked with yellow or orange.

Behavior

Spawning occurs in April and May when mid-day water temperatures reach 8 to 12 degrees C (46 to 54 F). Gila trout are opportunistic predators, feeding on insects and aquatic invertebrates.

Habitat

The Gila trout inhabits clear, cool headwater streams with moderate current and sufficient depth and cover to provide refuge during severe droughts. Gila trout usually congregate in deeper pools and in shallow water only where there is protective debris or plant beds.

Historic Range

The Gila trout is native to the Mogollon Plateau of New Mexico and Arizona. It was once common in the Gila and San Francisco rivers and tributary streams, in southwestern New Mexico, and in the Verde and Agua Fria drainages in Arizona. By the 1960s, it was eliminated from the Verde and Agua Fria drainages.

Current Distribution

When the Recovery Plan was completed in 1978, native populations of the Gila trout were confined to five streams in New Mexico—Diamond, South Diamond, Mc-Kenna, Spruce, and Upper Iron creeks. In addition, two other streams in Mexico and Arizona harbored introduced populations—McKnight and Sheep Corral creeks. Less than 10,000 individuals survived, and many were stunted because of crowding or insufficient food sources. Fortunately, healthy breeding populations survived on protected land in the Gila Wilderness Area, providing a strong base for reintroduction efforts.

Conservation and Recovery

The Gila trout declined in its native waters because of degraded water quality, heavy fishing, and hybridization with non-native trouts, which were introduced as game fish into the watersheds. Dam building, water pumping, stream channeling, road building, and logging have radically altered the water system within the Gila trout's range.

Recovery efforts have focused on removing non-native trouts from selected sections of higher quality streams, erecting barriers to prevent their return, and then restocking the waters with populations of the Gila trout. This strategy essentially creates refuges within the streams, where the Gila trout is the preferred and dominant trout species. The Fish and Wildlife Service (FWS), the Forest Service, New Mexico Department of Game and Fish, and New Mexico State University have collaborated on recovery.

By the end of 1987, biologists had restored seven populations in designated wilderness areas—six within the Gila National Forest in New Mexico, and one in Prescott National Forest in Arizona. Restoration has been so successful that the FWS has proposed to "downlist" the Gila trout from Endangered to Threatened.

The recovery team has attracted the support of local residents and sport fishermen by emphasizing the Gila trout's potential as a game fish. The proposed reclassification contains a special rule that would enable the state to set up a regulated sport fishery for the trout. Because many of the habitat streams are at or near their carrying capacity, sport fishing is not expected to interfere with the recovery of the Gila trout. If unforeseen problems developed, the sport season could be terminated.

FWS biologists recently implemented a captive propagation program by transferring 36 adult fish and 1,800 eggs to Mescalero National Fish Hatchery in New Mexico. Captive-raised fingerlings will be used to build a brood stock and restock new streams. Future efforts will concentrate on rehabilitating and restocking larger streams to expand the Gila trout's range.

Bibliography

Behnke, R. J., and M. Zarn. 1976. *Biology and Management of Threatened and Endangered Western Trouts.* U.S.D.A. Forest Service General Technical Report RM-23 Rocky Mountain Forest and Range Experiment Station, Fort Collins.

Minckley, W. L. 1973. *Fishes of Arizona.* Arizona Game and Fish Department, Phoenix.

U.S. Fish and Wildlife Service. 1979. "Gila Trout Recovery Plan." U.S. Fish and Wildlife Service, Albuquerque.

Contact

Regional Office of Endangered Species
U.S. Fish and Wildlife Service
P.O. Box 1306
Albuquerque, New Mexico 87103

Alabama Cavefish

Speoplatyrhinus poulsoni

Thomas C. Barr

Status	Endangered
Listed	September 9, 1977 (Threatened)
Reclassified . . .	September 28, 1988
Family	Amblyopsidae (Cavefish)
Description . . .	Small, eyeless, albino cavefish.
Habitat	Underground pools and streams.
Food	Aquatic invertebrates, smaller cavefish.
Reproduction . .	Undescribed.
Threats	Groundwater degradation, low numbers.
Region 4	Alabama

Description

The Alabama cavefish is about 8 centimeters (3 in) long and has no discernible pigmentation, appearing pinkish-white. It is eyeless and has transparent fins and skin. It has a large head, which makes up over a third of its length.

The Alabama cavefish is the rarest American cavefish and one of the rarest freshwater fishes in North America.

Behavior

Although little is known about the Alabama cavefish, it probably incubates eggs within a chamber underneath the gills. It feeds on small aquatic invertebrates and smaller cavefish and has a life span of five to ten years.

Habitat

The cavefish's only known habitat is Key Cave in Alabama. The cave has cool, year-round temperatures and receives no direct light. It is located within the Warsaw limestone formation, which is a large, stable aquifer and an excellent conveyer of groundwater. The Warsaw limestone rests on underlying rock strata that are honeycombed with channels to allow passage of groundwater.

Flooding is generally responsible for washing organic matter into the pools and streams within the caves, providing food for cave fauna, which in turn provides food for higher lifeforms. In Key Cave, the guano of the gray bat is probably the major source of the organic matter at the bottom of the food chain.

The aquatic community in this cave includes fairly large populations of two cave-adapted crayfish, as well as numerous isopods and amphipods.

Historic Range

The Alabama cavefish is known from a single location, which is reflected in its current distribution.

Current Distribution

The Alabama cavefish has been found only in Key Cave in Lauderdale County, Alabama. Only nine specimens have ever been collected. Because the underground water system in the area is so widespread, it was hoped that the cavefish had been dispersed to other sites. However, studies of 120 other caves in the area, conducted since 1977, have failed to locate any other cavefish populations. The number of individuals in the Key Cave population is estimated to be less than 100.

In 1988 the Alabama cavefish was reclassified from Threatened to Endangered.

Conservation and Recovery

The quality of the groundwater directly affects the fragile ecology of the cave. When water is degraded by fertilizers, pesticides, or sewage run-off, the food supply for the cavefish diminishes, which in turn reduces its longevity and reproductive capabilities. The Fish and Wildlife Service (FWS) is working with the Environmental Protection Agency to control sources of groundwater pollution in the area.

The population level of the gray bat within the cave also affects the Alabama cavefish. In recent years, bat numbers have declined, reducing guano, and lessening habitat viability. FWS personnel are currently exploring management techniques for stabilizing the population of the Endangered gray bat (*Myotis grisescens*). As the Gray Bat Recovery Plan is implemented, it will also benefit the cavefish.

Further research is needed to plan the recovery of the Alabama cavefish. The little that is currently known, however, is not encouraging. Captive breeding of cave-dwelling species has invariably failed in the past, and it is not considered a viable recovery strategy for the Alabama cavefish. Transplanting the fish to other sites is not considered feasible, and biologists' options are limited.

Bibliography

Cooper, J. E., and R.A. Kuehne. 1974. "*Speolplatyrhinus poulsoni*, a New Genus and Species of Subterranean Fish from Alabama." *Copeia* 2:486-493.

Poulson, T. L. 1963. "Cave Adaptation in Amblyopsid Fishes." *American Midland Naturalist* 70(2):257-290.

U.S. Fish and Wildlife Service. 1982. "Alabama Cavefish Recovery Plan." U.S. Fish and Wildlife Service, Atlanta.

U.S. Fish and Wildlife Service. 1982. "Gray Bat Recovery Plan." U.S. Fish and Wildlife Service, Atlanta.

Contact

Regional Office of Endangered Species
U.S. Fish and Wildlife Service
Richard B. Russell Federal Building
75 Spring Street, S.W.
Atlanta, Georgia 30303

Loach Minnow
Tiaroga cobitis

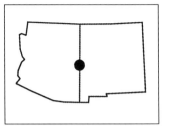

John N. Rinne

Status . . . . . . Threatened
Listed . . . . . . October 28, 1986
Family . . . . . . Cyprinidae (Minnow)
Description . . . Slender, olive-colored min-
now with an oblique mouth
and upturned eyes.
Habitat . . . . . . Swift-flowing, perennial
streams and rivers.
Food . . . . Insects and plant matter.
Reproduction . . Undescribed.
Threats . . . . . Habitat destruction,
degradation of water
quality, competition with in-
troduced fishes.
Region 2 . . . . . Arizona, New Mexico

Description

The slender, olive-colored loach minnow is the only species in its genus. It is typically less than 8 centimeters (3.1 in) in standard length. It is characterized by a highly oblique terminal mouth, eyes that point markedly upward, and a group of dirty white spots at the base of the dorsal and tail fins. Breeding males develop vivid red-orange markings, particularly on the belly.

Behavior

The loach minnow has been poorly studied. It probably feeds on insects and plant matter, which it takes by browsing along the bottom.

Habitat

The loach minnow inhabits streams with perennial flow and is concentrated in shal-

low, turbulent riffles over a cobble substrate. Recurrent flooding keeps the substrate free of silt and sediments and, because it is better adapted to strong currents, allows the loach minnow to maintain its population against encroaching non-native fishes.

Historic Range

This species was once locally common throughout much of the Verde, Salt, San Pedro, San Francisco, and Gila river systems. It inhabited mainstreams and tributaries up to about 2,200 meters (7,200 ft) in elevation. It is thought that the fish once inhabited about 2,800 kilometers (1,750 mi) of stream habitat.

Current Distribution

The loach minnow now inhabits a greatly reduced range. In Arizona it is found in

Aravaipa Creek (Graham and Pinal counties), the Blue River (Greenlee County), and the White River near the confluence of the mainstream and the East Fork (Navajo County). In New Mexico it survives in the headwaters of the Gila River (Gila, Grant, and Catron counties), and portions of the San Francisco and Tularosa rivers and Whitewater Creek (Catron County). The current range totals about 580 kilometers (363 mi) of stream habitat, a reduction in range of nearly 80 percent.

This species occurred historically in the San Pedro River in Sonora, Mexico, but habitat there has been largely destroyed by diversion of water for irrigation.

Conservation and Recovery

The native fishes of the Gila Rivers system, including the loach minnow, have been seriously harmed by human alteration of the ecosystem. Stream impoundments, water diversion, and groundwater pumping have greatly changed the conditions of these once free-flowing streams. Introduced non-native fishes have added the further stresses of predation and competition. It is estimated that 35 percent of the basin's endemic fishes are currently classified as Endangered or Threatened under federal law, and an additional 35 percent are considered in jeopardy by state wildlife offices.

Large sections of the remaining inhabited streams occur on public lands. Seventy-five percent of Aravaipa Creek is protected by its designation as the Aravaipa Canyon Wilderness. Defenders of Wildlife administers portions of the headwaters as the George Whittell Wildlife Preserve. The Blue River is contained within the Apache-Sitgreaves National Forest. The Gila River flows through the Gila National Forest, which includes the Gila Wilderness, the Lower Gila River Bird Habitat Management Area, and the Gila

River Research Natural Area—all managed by the Forest Service. The Forest Service also administers major portions of the San Francisco and Tularosa rivers and Whitewater Creek. The White River population occurs on the Fort Apache Indian Reservation and has been the focus of recovery efforts conducted by the tribal council and with the Bureau of Indian Affairs.

The Middle Box Canyon on the Gila River (Grant County, New Mexico) has been proposed as the site for construction of the Conner Dam and Reservoir. The Southwest New Mexico Industrial Development Corporation, the Hooker Dam Association, the Arizona Cattle Growers Association, the Arizona Mining Association, the Town of Silver City, New Mexico, and the Soil Conservation Service of New Mexico, among others, opposed federal listing of the loach minnow because it might stop or slow construction of the dam. This continuing conflict over water rights in the region promises to propel the loach minnow and other Gila River fishes into the limelight of controversy in the 1990s.

Bibliography

Propst, D. L. 1986. "Distribution, Status, and Biology of the Loach Minnow in the Gila River Basin." New Mexico Department of Game and Fish, Santa Fe.

U. S. Forest Service. 1985. "Proposed Gila National Forest Plan." USFS Southwestern Region, Albuquerque, New Mexico.

Contact

Regional Office of Endangered Species
U.S. Fish and Wildlife Service
P.O. Box 1306
Albuquerque, New Mexico 87103

MUSSELS

Birdwing Pearly Mussel

Conradilla caelata

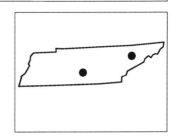

A. E. Spreitzer/OSU Museum of Zoology

Status	. . . . . Endangered
Listed	. . . . . June 14, 1976
Family	. . . . . Unionidae
	(Freshwater Mussel)
Description	. . . Small mussel, olive or dark green shell with irregular growth lines.
Habitat	. . . . . Silt-free substrates in fast-flowing streams and rivers.
Threats	. . . . . Impoundments, siltation, pollution.
Region 4	. . . . . Tennessee
Region 5	. . . . . Virginia

Description

The birdwing pearly mussel is a relatively small Cumberlandian mussel, seldom over 5 centimeters (2 in) in width. The valves are solid, slightly inflated (especially in females), and triangular or egg-shaped. The surface of the shell is marked by strong, irregular growth lines, and the outer coloring is olive green or dark green. Inside coloring of the shell is always white. Fish hosts for this mussel are thought to be a shiner (*Notropis galacturus*) and at least one darter. This species is sometimes referred to as *Lemiox rimosus*, as described in 1834 from the Cumberland River.

Life Cycle of Freshwater Mussels

Freshwater mussels are bivalve mollusks and are often simply called "clams." The life cycle of mussels is complex, and reproductive success depends upon a stable habitat—unaltered stream conditions, clean water, and an undisturbed stream bottom. The cycle also depends upon the abundance of suitable fish hosts to complete the mussel's larval development.

To reproduce, males discharge sperm, which are dispersed by stream currents. In the process of feeding, females nearby or downstream take in sperm, which fertilizes eggs stored in the female's gills. The gills are modified as brood pouches (marsupia) where the glochidia (larvae) hatch and begin to develop. After a time, these glochidia are released into the stream. A few mussels actually have inner parts that resemble a tiny minnow and can be manipulated to lure host fish. When a fish gets close to the shell, the mussel expels its glochidia.

Glochidia have tiny bean- or spoon-shaped valves that attach to the gill filaments of host fishes. Glochidia can only progress to the juvenile stage while attached to a fish's gills. Those that do not fortuitously encounter a host fish do not survive when released by the female. They sink to the bottom and die.

When the juvenile has developed a shell and is large enough to survive on its own, it detaches from the host fish and falls to the stream bottom, beginning a long association with a single stretch of stream. Maturing mussels bury themselves in riffles and shoals with only the shell margins and feeding siphons exposed to the water and feed by siphoning phytoplankton and other plant matter from the water. Undigestible particles are expelled from the shell by reverse siphoning. Silt in the water can kill mussels by clogging their feeding siphons. Some mussels live 50 years or more.

The family Unionidae, which includes nearly all of the freshwater mussels in the U.S., is separated into two groups based on the length of time the glochidia remain in the female's marsupia. The eggs of short-term (tachytictic) breeders are fertilized in spring and glochidia are released by late summer of the same year. Long-term (bradytictic) breeders hold developing glochidia in the brood pouch over winter and release them in spring.

Habitat

Cumberlandian freshwater mussels are found in clean, fast-flowing streams and rivers in riffles and shoals where the bottom consists of firm rubble, gravel, or sand.

Historic Range

The birdwing pearly mussel once was widely dispersed in small numbers within the Tennessee River and its major tributary streams. Collectors have always considered it a rare shell. Although a few records have located the birdwing pearly mussel in other watersheds, these records are now considered in error.

Current Distribution

The birdwing pearly mussel is presently found only in larger tributaries of the Tennessee River—the Duck, Elk, Clinch, and Powell rivers. The mussel is abundant in Duck River but limited to a 64-kilometer (40-mi) reach between Lillard Mill Dam and the older Columbia Dam. The population there has been estimated at between 20,000 and 30,000 individuals. This section of river is scheduled for inundation by the Columbia Dam project of the Tennessee Valley Authority (TVA).

Conservation and Recovery

Major water control projects flood upstream valleys, reduce downstream flows, alter temperature gradients, cause extreme water level fluctuations, increase turbidity and silting, and create seasonal oxygen deficits. These factors can eliminate mussels that are fixed to a single locality. The Columbia Dam on the Duck River is expected to extirpate the entire Duck River population.

In order to fill the reservoir behind the Columbia Dam, TVA is striving to establish other viable populations of this mussel in suitable habitat. In 1982, the TVA transplanted 1,000 birdwing pearly mussels from the Lillard Mill Dam site to the Duck River (Bedford County), the Buffalo River (Wayne County), Nolichucky River (Greene County), and North Fork Holston River (Hawkins County), Tennessee. If these transplants prove successful, the dam project may be allowed to continue.

The Fish and Wildlife Service Recovery Plan for the birdwing pearly mussel stresses the need to seek agreements with landowners along the rivers to preserve streambank habitat and the need to develop a public education program to discuss the uniqueness of this river system and the rarity of the resources at risk. As suitable sites are identified within the historic range, reintroduction of the species will be attempted.

The TVA is currently working on a comprehensive water management plan, which would guarantee constant minimum flows in all rivers in the Tennessee and Cumberland basins by timing water discharges from its dams. Such an effort might mollify many of the negative effects of dams and reservoirs on remaining stretches of mussel habitat.

Bibliography

Bates, J. M., and S. D. Dennis. 1978. "The Mussel Fauna of the Clinch River, Tennessee and Virginia." *Sterkiana* 69/70:3-23.

Pardue, J. W. 1981. "A Survey of the Mussels (Unionidae) of the Upper Tennessee River, 1978." *Sterkiana* 71:41-51.

U.S. Fish and Wildlife Service. 1983. "Birdwing Pearly Mussel Recovery Plan." U.S. Fish and Wildlife Service, Atlanta.

Contact

Regional Office of Endangered Species
U.S. Fish and Wildlife Service
Richard B. Russell Federal Building
75 Spring Street, S.W.
Atlanta, Georgia 30303

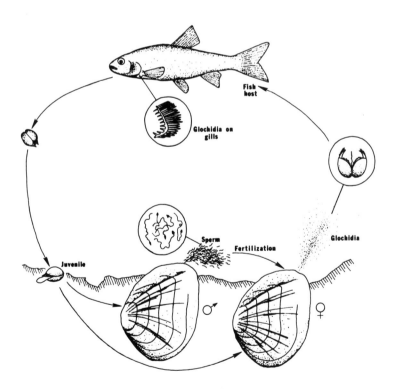

Life Cycle of Freshwater Mussels

Dromedary Pearly Mussel
Dromus dromas

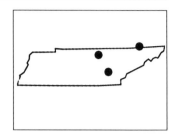

A. E. Spreitzer/OSU Museum of Zoology

Status	Endangered
Listed	June 14, 1976
Family	Unionidae (Freshwater Mussel)
Description . . .	Medium-sized triangular to elliptical shell, yellow-green with green rays.
Habitat	Shallow riffle and shoal areas.
Threats	Impoundments, pollution.
Region 4	Tennessee
Region 5	Virginia

Description

The dromedary pearly mussel is a medium-sized species, round to triangular or elliptical in outline. Valves are generally solid and inflated. The outer surface of the shell has a hump with a curved row of smaller knobs near the middle of the shell. The outer covering is yellow-green with broken green rays covering the shell. The inner shell color is generally white or pinkish in the big river mussels (*Dromus dromas*), while the nacre of the headwaters mussels (*D. d. caperatus*) is whitish pink, salmon, or reddish. *D. dromas* was first described from the Harpeth and Cumberland rivers in Tennessee. *D. d. caperatus* was first described from the Clinch River in Virginia and Tennessee.

For a general discussion of the life cycle of freshwater mussels see the species account of the birdwing pearly mussel (*Conradilla caelata*).

Habitat

These mussels bury themselves in the substrate in shallow riffle and shoal areas, in relatively firm rubble, gravel, and sand swept free of silt by clean fast-flowing water.

Historic Range

Cumberlandian mussels are endemic to the southern Appalachian Mountains and the Cumberland Plateau region. The dromedary pearly mussel was once widely distributed in the upper Tennessee and Cumberland River basins, from the headwaters of the Tennessee River as far south as Muscle Shoals, Alabama. It was also reported from the Caney Fork of the Cumberland River system, where it may have been more abundant than in the Tennessee River.

Current Distribution

Both forms of this mussel are now found only in portions of the Tennessee, Cumberland, Clinch, and Powell Rivers. Since 1918 only three live specimens have been reported from the Tennessee River. In 1981 five live specimens were reported from the Cumberland River, 16 from the Clinch River, and six from the Powell River. These figures provide a measure of relative abundance but do not reflect the actual population size.

Conservation and Recovery

The reasons for the decline of these mussels are not well understood, but stream damming and channeling, siltation, and pollution are thought to be major factors. Dams and reservoirs flood some habitats, reduce water flows in others, alter water temperatures, and increase siltation—all of which have a negative impact on mussels. The effects of pollution are intensified for filter feeders, because large quantities of water are drawn through the mussel's feeding system to extract food.

Transplantation of mussels from larger, more viable populations to smaller populations will be attempted. Since the largest concentrations of dromedary pearly mussels are in the Clinch and Powell rivers, the identification, survey, and protection of these populations will be the first priority for recovery. As abundance increases, the Fish and Wildlife Service will attempt to reestablish mussel populations in at least three additional streams.

Sections of the Clinch and Powell Rivers are probably eligible for Scenic River status under the National Wild and Scenic Rivers Act. If so designated, the law would provide additional protection for these mussels and their habitat. The state of Tennessee has designated portions of the Tennessee and Cumberland Rivers and the Clinch and Powell rivers as mussel sanctuaries, but the headwaters for each of these streams originate in Kentucky and Virginia, where no protection is yet offered.

Bibliography

Bates, J. M., and S. D. Dennis. 1978. "The Mussel Fauna of the Clinch River, Tennessee and Virginia." *Sterkiana* 69/70:3-23.

Dennis, S. D. 1981. "Mussel Fauna of the Powell River, Tennessee and Virginia." *Sterkiana* 71:1-7.

Jenkinson, J. J. 1981. "The Tennessee Valley Authority Cumberlandian Mollusk Conservation Program." *Bulletin of the American Malacological Union* 1980:62-63.

U.S. Fish and Wildlife Service. 1983. "Dromedary Pearly Mussel Recovery Plan." U.S. Fish and Wildlife Service, Atlanta.

Contact

Regional Office of Endangered Species
U.S. Fish and Wildlife Service
Richard B. Russell Federal Building
75 Spring Street, S.W.
Atlanta, Georgia 30303

Tar River Spinymussel

Elliptio steinstansana

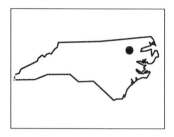

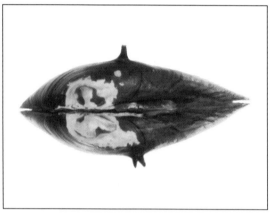

A. E. Spreitzer/OSU Museum of Zoology

Status	Endangered
Listed	June 27, 1985
Family	Unionidae (Freshwater Mussel)
Description . . .	Medium-sized, rhomboidal shell with fine concentric rings and several short spines.
Habitat	Soft mud or sand bottoms of streams.
Threats	Low numbers.
Region 4	North Carolina

Description

The Tar River spinymussel reaches a mature length of 6 centimeters (2.4 in), and the rhomboidal shell is distinguished by having several short spines. The shell surface is smooth and shiny, marked with fine concentric rings. The inequilateral valves are regularly rounded, becoming slightly wider at the hinges and ending in a blunt point. The inner shell nacre is yellowish or pinkish, and young specimens have an orange-brown outer scale with greenish rays.

Aside from the Tar River spinymussel, only two other freshwater spiny mussels are known to exist: a small-shelled and short-spined species (*Fusconaia collina*) found only in the James River in Virginia and considered Endangered, and a large-shelled and long-spined species (*Elliptio spinosa*) collected from the Altamaha River system in Georgia. The shell size and spine length of the Tar River mussel is intermediate between these two. It has been alternatively classified as *Canthyria steinstansana*.

For a general discussion of the life cycle of freshwater mussels see the species account of the birdwing pearly mussel (*Conradilla caelata*).

Habitat

This spinymussel has been collected on sand and mud substrates. The mussel's spines help it maintain an upright position as it works its way through the soft streambed.

Historic Range

The Tar River spinymussel was first discovered in the Tar River (Edgecombe County), North Carolina, in 1966. Records suggest that the species inhabited the mainstream Tar River from Nash County downstream through Edgecombe County to Pitt County near the town of Falkland, North Carolina.

Current Distribution

The only surviving population, estimated at between 100 and 500 individuals, is restricted to about 19 kilometers (12 mi) of the Tar River in Edgecombe County.

Conservation and Recovery

The Tar River spinymussel may have always been rare, but its recent reduction in range and small population size make it vulnerable to extinction from a single catastrophic event, such as a tank-truck accident involving a toxic chemical spill—a real possibility, since an Interstate highway bridge passes directly over its habitat. Water quality is also a problem. The North Carolina Department of Natural Resources and Community Development reports that levels of nutrients and pesticides are above average in the river.

As a further threat, the Tar River has become infested by the Asiatic clam, considered a pest. The Asiatic clam feeds in densities estimated at 1,000 individuals per square meter in some places, reducing the availability of phytoplankton needed as a food source for the Tar River spiny mussel.

Because this species has only recently been described and its approximate range located, notoriety for such a unique and rare mussel could increase collection pressure from shell dealers and collectors. And because the population is small, the unlawful removal of any individuals could seriously affect the species' survival. North Carolina State law prohibits collecting wildlife without a state permit.

State law does not protect the species' habitat from the potential impact of large-scale construction projects. Federal listing protects the Tar River spiny mussel by requiring federal agencies to consult with the Fish and Wildlife Service when projects they fund, authorize, or carry out may affect the species. Three specific projects have been identified that could affect the spiny mussel—a hydroelectric project on the Tar River at Rocky Mount, a navigation and flood control project on the Tar River, and a stream obstruction removal project on Tar River tributaries. These projects may have to be redesigned to protect this mussel.

Bibliography

Johnson, R. I., and A. H. Clarke. 1983. "A New Spiny Mussel, *Elliptio* (Canthyria) *steinstansana* (Bivalvia: Unionidae), from the Tar River, North Carolina." *Occasional Papers on Mollusks* 4(6):289-298.

Shelley, R. M. 1972. "In Defense of Mollusks." *Wildlife in North Carolina* 36:4-8, 26-27.

U.S. Fish and Wildlife Service. 1987. "Recovery Plan for Tar River Spiny Mussel." U.S. Fish and Wildlife Service, Atlanta.

Contact

Regional Office of Endangered Species
U.S. Fish and Wildlife Service
Richard B. Russell Federal Building
75 Spring Street, S.W.
Atlanta, Georgia 30303

Curtis' Pearly Mussel

Epioblasma florentina curtisi

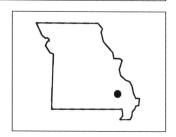

A. E. Spreitzer/OSU Museum of Zoology

Status . . . . . . Endangered
Listed . . . . . . June 14, 1976
Family . . . . . . Unionidae
(Freshwater Mussel)
Description . . . Small mussel, yellow-brown
shell with fine, evenly spaced
rays.
Habitat . . . . . . Sand and gravel substrates in
shallow water.
Threats . . . . . Impoundments, siltation, pol-
lution.
Region 3 . . . . . Missouri

Description

The oval shell of Curtis' pearly mussel is usually less than four centimeters (1.5 in) in length—with males being slightly larger than females. The valve-end of the shell is bluntly pointed and biangular, the front smoothly rounded. In both sexes, the shell color is yellow-brown to light brown, sometimes with fine, evenly spaced rays over most of its length. The interior shell surface (nacre) is white to whitish blue.

Curtis' pearly mussel is bradytictic—eggs are fertilized in the fall and glochidia (larvae) are released in the spring. For a general discussion of the life cycle of freshwater mussels see the species account of the birdwing pearly mussel (*Conradilla caelata*).

First described as Truncilla curtisi in 1915 from White River specimens, this species has also been classified as *Dysnomia florentina cur-*

tisi. Seven other species of genus *Epioblasma* have been federally listed as Endangered. These are yellow-blossom pearly mussel (*E. florentina florentina*), penitent mussel (*E. penita*), white cat's paw pearly mussel (*E. sulcata delicata*), green-blossom pearly mussel (*E. torulosa gubernaculum*), tubercled-blossom pearly mussel (*E. torulosa torulosa*), turgid-blossom pearly mussel (*E. turgidula*), and tan riffle shell (*E. walkeri*).

Habitat

This pearly mussel is found in transitional zones between swift-flowing stream headwaters and the more leisurely currents of lowland meanders. It buries itself in stable substrates of sand and gravel, or among cobbles or boulders, particularly in shallow water at depths of up to 76 centimeters (30 in). Populations require clear, unsilted water.

Historic Range

Curtis' pearly mussel was identified from scattered locations in the White and St. Francis River basins in southern Missouri and northern Arkansas. A record from 1916 indicates that Curtis' pearly mussel also occurred in the South Fork of the Spring River, a tributary of the Black River in Arkansas.

Current Distribution

Since the mid-1970s, Curtis' pearly mussel has been found in southeastern Missouri, in the Castor River, Cane Creek (a Black River tributary), and Little Black River. Only about 10 kilometers (6-mi) of the upper Little Black River and 11.2 kilometers (7 mi) of the Castor River upstream from the Headwater Diversion Channel still support minimal numbers. From 1981 to 1983 over 140 probable locations on 26 streams were sampled, but this mussel was found at only six sites. In spite of over 13 years on the federal list of Endangered Species, it is still extremely uncommon and is thought to remain near extinction.

Conservation and Recovery

Much of Curtis' pearly mussel historic range has been inundated by reservoir construction. Lake Taneycomo, completed in 1913, flooded a long stretch of its habitat. The White River has been dammed repeatedly—in 1952 to create Bull Shoals Reservoir, in 1959 to fill Table Rock Lake, and again in 1966 to create Beaver Reservoir. These impoundments drastically reduced water flows on the river, resulting in stagnant bottom waters and accumulations of silt. Stream channelization and gravel dredging have reduced substrate stability, and poor land management practices have further exacerbated problems of siltation and chemical runoff.

The Missouri Department of Conservation has conducted low intensity research into the biology of this species, but there are still many unanswered questions. The immediate goal of recovery is to stave off extinction by preventing further loss or damage to the habitat. When the state of research permits, biologists will attempt to transfer mussels from viable reproducing populations to depleted areas to stimulate reproduction. An effort will be made to produce juveniles by artificial culture to assist restocking of suitable habitat within the historic range.

Bibliography

Hudson, R. G., and B. G. Isom. 1984. "Rearing Juveniles of the Freshwater Mussels (Unionidae) in a Laboratory Setting." *Nautilus* 98(4):129-135.

Johnson, R. I. 1978. "Systematics and Zoogeography of *Plagiola* (=*Sysnomia*, =*Epioblasma*), an Almost Extinct Genus of Freshwater Mussels (Bivalvia: Unionidae) from Middle North America." *Bulletin of the Museum of Comparative Zoology* 148(6):239-321.

U.S. Fish and Wildlife Service. 1986. "Curtis' Pearly Mussel Recovery Plan." U.S. Fish and Wildlife Service, Twin Cities.

Contact

Regional Office of Endangered Species
U.S. Fish and Wildlife Service
Federal Building, Fort Snelling
Twin Cities, Minnesota 55111

Yellow-Blossom Pearly Mussel

Epioblasma florentina florentina

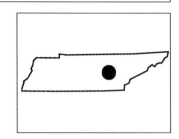

A. E. Spreitzer/OSU Museum of Zoology

Status	Endangered (possibly extinct)
Listed	June 14, 1976
Family	Unionidae (Freshwater Mussel)
Description . . .	Medium-sized elliptical shell, honey yellow with numerous green rays.
Habitat	Sand or gravel substrate in clear, flowing water.
Threats	Impoundments, siltation, pollution.
Region 4	Alabama, Tennessee

Description

The yellow-blossom pearly mussel is a Cumberlandian species with an elliptical shell seldom exceeding 6 centimeters (2.4 in) in length. The slightly inflated valves are of unequal length, and the shell surface is marked by uneven growth lines. The shell is a shiny honey yellow or tan with numerous green rays uniformly distributed over the surface. The inner shell surface is bluish white.

Epioblasma florentina florentina represents the big-river form of this species, which may grade into the smaller, headwaters form *E. f. walkeri*. This species has also been classified as *Dysnomia florentina florentina*.

For a discussion of the life cycle of freshwater mussels see the account of the birdwing pearly mussel (*Conradilla caelata*).

Habitat

The yellow-blossom pearly mussel's natural habitat is in the sand and gravel substrates of shallow, fast-flowing streams and rivers.

Historic Range

Cumberlandian mussels are endemic to the southern Appalachian Mountains and the Cumberland Plateau region. Historically, the yellow-blossom mussel was widespread in the drainages of the Cumberland and Tennessee rivers. It has been documented from the Flint, Elk, Duck, Holston, Clinch, and Little Tennessee rivers, and from other Tennessee River tributaries, including Hurricane, Limestone, Bear, and Cypress creeks in northern Alabama and the Citico Creek in Tennessee.

Current Distribution

Because this subspecies has not been reliably documented in over a half century, noted malacologist D. H. Stansbery considers it extinct. A report from the General Accounting Office, issued in December 1988, also considered the mussel "probably extinct." Specimens that may represent yellow-blossom pearly mussel, however, were collected from Citico Creek in 1957 and from the Little Tennessee River in the mid-1960s. Therefore, the Fish and Wildlife Service (FWS) agreed to maintain the current status of Endangered until further research can settle the question.

Conservation and Recovery

The single greatest factor in the decline or extinction of this species has been the construction of large dams on its habitat rivers. Since the 1930s, the Tennessee Valley Authority (TVA), the Aluminum Company of America, and the Army Corps of Engineers have constructed 51 dams on the Tennessee and Cumberland rivers for flood control, generation of hydroelectric power, and recreation. Many segments of the rivers that once supported large populations of mussels have been permanently flooded. In addition, altered downstream flows have changed water temperatures, and increased turbidity. Strip mining, coal washing, farming, and logging have all added loads of silt and pollutants to the streams and rivers of the region. Turbid water clogs the feeding apparatus of mussels, and siltation smothers mussel beds.

Fish species of all kinds, including those that play host to mussel glochidia (larvae), have declined, making mussel reproduction problematic. When glochidia are released into the streams by female mussels, they must fortuitously encounter a suitable fish host in order to develop to maturity. When a fish host is not encountered, the glochidia sink to the bottom and die.

At the beginning of the century, nearly 80 species of freshwater mussels were documented from these waters, but by 1964 the count had declined to only 59. Many of these surviving species are now rare or threatened with extinction.

Recovery strategies for this subspecies cannot be developed until a viable breeding population is discovered. The Tennessee Wildlife Resources Agency, the Tennessee Heritage Program, and the TVA continue to support research into the status of this and other freshwater mussels in the state. Mussel research in Alabama is promoted by the Alabama Department of Conservation and Natural Resources.

Bibliography

Bogan, A., and P. Parmalee. 1983. "Tennessee's Rare Mollusks." In *Tennessee's Rare Wildlife, Final Report*. Tennessee Department of Conservation and Tennessee Heritage Program, University of Tennessee, Knoxville.

General Accounting Office. 1988. "Endangered Species: Management Improvements Could Enhance Recovery Program." GAO/RCED-89-5. U.S. General Accounting Office, Washington, D.C.

U.S. Fish and Wildlife Service. 1985. "Recovery Plan for the Tubercled-Blossom Pearly Mussel, Turgid-Blossom Pearly Mussel, and Yellow-Blossom Pearly Mussel." U.S. Fish and Wildlife Service, Atlanta.

Contact

Regional Office of Endangered Species
U.S. Fish and Wildlife Service
Richard B. Russell Federal Building
75 Spring Street, S.W.
Atlanta, Georgia 30303

Penitent Mussel
Epioblasma penita

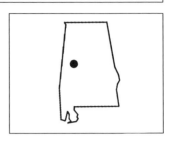

A. E. Spreitzer/OSU Museum of Zoology

Status	Endangered
Listed	April 7, 1987
Family	Unionidae
	(Freshwater Mussel)
Description . . .	Yellowish rhomboid shell with irregular growth lines.
Habitat	Sandy gravel river bottoms.
Threats	Dams, dredging, siltation.
Region 4	Alabama, Georgia, Mississippi

Description

The penitent mussel is a bivalve mollusk about 5.5 centimeters (2.1 in) long. The rhomboid shell is yellowish, greenish yellow, or tawny, sometimes with dark spots. The surface is characterized by irregular growth lines and a radially sculptured posterior. The inner shell surface (nacre) is white or straw-colored. Females have a large, grooved swelling at the rear of the shell. First described as *Unio penitus* in 1834, this species has been variously classified since then, most commonly as *Dysnomia penita*.

For a general discussion of the life cycle of freshwater mussels see the species account of the birdwing pearly mussel (*Conradilla caelata*).

Habitat

The penitent mussel is found in the shallow reaches of larger streams and rivers where there is a moderately strong current. It prefers riffle runs or shoals with a stable substrate composed of sandy gravel or cobbles. Specimens have rarely been found in waters deeper than 70 centimeters (2.3 ft).

Historic Range

The species was known from the Tombigbee, Alabama, Buttahatchie, Cahaba, and Coosa rivers in Alabama, Georgia, and Mississippi. In the Tombigbee River it was found from the confluence of Bull Mountain Creek above Amory, Mississippi, downstream to

Epes, Alabama. The Alabama River supported populations at Claiborne and Selma. A population was known from the stretch of the Cahaba River below Centreville, Alabama.

The penitent mussel has not been collected from the Alabama and Cahaba Rivers since the 1800s. It was last collected from the mainstream Tombigbee River in 1972. It disappeared from the Coosa River after 1974, when a new dam inundated its habitat there.

Current Distribution

The penitent mussel survives in the Gainesville Bendway of the Tombigbee River (Sumter County, Alabama). This cut-off section of the river provides only marginal habitat, which is subject to siltation, reduced water flows, and degraded water quality. It also survives in sections of the Buttahatchie River and the East Fork Tombigbee River.

Conservation and Recovery

The penitent mussel has declined because of loss of habitat. The once free-flowing Tombigbee River has been modified into a series of locks and channels to form a barge canal. Physical destruction of mollusks during dredging and construction and the resulting increase of siltation, reduction of water flow, and disturbance of host fish movements have all but eliminated the mollusk from this river. Further siltation in the Gainesville Bendway would probably eliminate the penitent mussel there.

Bull Mountain Creek contributes nearly half of the flow of the East Fork of the Tombigbee River. During canal construction, the creek was diverted and its cool waters redirected into the warm canal, resulting in warmer water temperatures in the East Fork. Warmer waters stress the mussels and diminish their food supply. Changes in cur-

rent and river flow interfere with reproduction, since this species depends on currents to carry mature gametes downstream to other mussels for fertilization. Mussel beds also suffer from degraded water quality from the runoff of fertilizers and pesticides, resulting in algal blooms and vegetation excesses that kill off native fauna.

Both Mississippi and Alabama require permits to take freshwater mussels. It is difficult to detect and apprehend violators, however, and regulations do not prevent habitat degradation. Recovery of the penitent mussel will require developing some means to ensure adequate water flow in remaining, unmodified sections of the river. Flood control projects and canal maintenance activities will need to consider the presence of mussel beds.

The range of the penitent mussel is currently threatened by two proposed channel improvement projects. If implemented these projects would dredge and straighten 95 kilometers (59 mi) of the Buttahatchie, and 85 kilometers (53 mi) of the East Fork.

Bibliography

Clench, W. J. and R. D. Turner. 1956. "Freshwater Mollusks of Alabama, Georgia, and Florida From the Escambia to the Suwannee River." *Bulletin of the Florida State Museum (Biological Sciences)* 1:97-239.

Johnson, R. I. 1978. "Systematics and Zoogeography of *Plagiola*, an Almost Extinct Genus of Freshwater Mussels." *Bulletin of the Museum of Comparative Zoology* 148:239-320.

Stansbery, D. H. 1976. "Naiade Mollusks." In H. Boschung, ed., *Bulletin of the Alabama Museum of Natural History* No. 2.

Contact

Regional Office of Endangered Species
U.S. Fish and Wildlife Service
Richard B. Russell Federal Building
75 Spring Street, S.W.
Atlanta, Georgia 30303

White Cat's Paw
Pearly Mussel
Epioblasma sulcata delicata

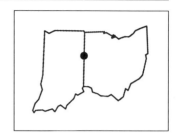

A. E. Spreitzer/OSU Museum of Zoology

Status . . . . . . Endangered
Listed . . . . . . June 14, 1976
Family . . . . . . Unionidae
(Freshwater Mussel)
Description . . . Greenish yellow shell with
numerous green rays;
females with tiny teeth along
shell margin.
Habitat . . . . . . Shoals and riffles of streams
and rivers.
Threats . . . . . Siltation, pollution.
Region 3 . . . . . Indiana, Ohio

Description

The white cat's paw pearly mussel rarely exceeds 4.5 centimeters (1.7 in) in shell length. The outer surface of the shell is greenish yellow with numerous light green rays that radiate from posterior to anterior. The species is sexually dimorphic, meaning that males and females differ in structure and appearance. The larger female is more pointed at the valve end and bears little teeth along the shell margin. The teeth give the appearance of tiny claws, hence the name "cat's paw."

For a general discussion of the life cycle of freshwater mussels see the species account of the birdwing pearly mussel (*Conradilla caelata*).

Habitat

This mussel inhabits freshwater streams and rivers and favors stable, sandy gravel bottoms. It prefers reaches where the water is fairly shallow and the current strong enough to keep silt scoured from the bottom.

Historic Range

The white cat's paw pearly mussel was carried into its current range during the warming period after the last glaciation. As the Wisconsin Glacier melted, fish carried mussel eggs north into the Maumee River and its tributaries, such as the St. Joseph and Auglaize rivers, which drain into Lake Erie. There is evidence to suggest that a population was established at the edge of Lake Erie in the vicinity of Toledo, Ohio. Other populations were found in the Wabash River, which arises close to the Maumee River but drains instead to the southwest, eventually emptying into the Ohio River west of Evansville. Populations in this drainage were probably centered near the confluence of the Eel River in Cass County, Indiana.

Current Distribution

The current distribution of the white cat's paw pearly mussel is extremely limited relative to its historic range. Since 1985 surveys have located the white cat's paw pearly mussel in the St. Joseph River that joins the St. Marys River at Fort Wayne, Indiana, to form the Maumee. Mussels were found in both Indiana and Ohio portions of the river. Scattered individuals were also found in Fish Creek in Indiana. The cat's paw survives in a few viable beds in fairly low numbers.

Conservation and Recovery

The great forests that once stretched across most of Ohio and Indiana have largely been cleared to support intensive agriculture. Poor agricultural practices in many cases have clouded the rivers with topsoil runoff, raising turbidity levels and smothering once favorable stretches of mussel habitat with silt. This is probably the primary cause of the overall decline of the white cat's paw pearly mussel.

Pesticide and fertilizer contamination probably played a role in degrading habitat. Filter feeders like mussels must siphon many gallons of water to extract food, concentrating poisonous residues in their tissues. Because surviving populations are very localized, a single catastrophic event, such as a toxic chemical spill, would extirpate a large percentage of the species.

The Fish and Wildlife Service will encourage local landowners to follow more ecologically sound agricultural practices to reduce the amount of suspended solids in habitat waters. Known populations are being monitored at least every two years to determine trends, and potential habitat in the basin is being surveyed to locate additional populations and to identify possible sites for reintroduction.

Bibliography

Johnson, R. I. 1980. "Zoogeography of North American Unioniacea (Mollusca: Bivalvia) North of the Maximum Pleistocene Glaciation." *Bulletin of the Museum of Comparative Zoology* 149(2):77-189.

Stansbery, D. H. 1971. "Rare and Endangered Freshwater Mollusks in Eastern North America." In S. Jorgensen and R. Sharp, eds., *Rare and Endangered Mollusks (Naiads) of the U.S.* Fish and Wildlife Service, Twin Cities.

Contact

Regional Office of Endangered Species
U.S. Fish and Wildlife Service
Federal Building, Fort Snelling
Twin Cities, Minnesota 55111

Green-Blossom
Pearly Mussel
Epioblasma torulosa gubernaculum

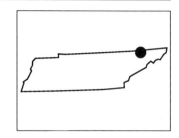

A. E. Spreitzer/OSU Museum of Zoology

Status . . . . . . Endangered
Listed . . . . . . June 14, 1976
Family . . . . . . Unionidae
(Freshwater Mussel)
Description . . . Medium-sized tawny or
straw-colored shell, irregular-
ly elliptical.
Habitat . . . . . . Clear, fast-flowing streams
with sand or gravel sub-
strates.
Threats . . . . . Dams, siltation, pollution.
Region 4 . . . . . Tennessee
Region 5 . . . . . Virginia

Description

The green-blossom pearly mussel is a medium-sized Cumberlandian mussel with an irregularly elliptical shell, which is smooth and shiny, tawny or straw-colored, and patterned with numerous fine green rays. The shell surface is marked with distinct growth lines. The nacre (inner shell) color varies from white to salmon-red. The species is sexually dimorphic—the anatomies of males and females differ noticeably. The female's shell is generally larger than the male's and the posterior margin is more broadly rounded. The female possesses a large, flattened marsupial swelling, usually green in color and marked with radial furrows.

The green-blossom pearly mussel (previously classified as *Dysnomia torulosa gubernaculum*) is smaller, has a more compressed shell, and less developed knobs than its downstream relative, the tubercled-blossom pearly mussel (*Epioblasma torulosa torulosa*). Also federally listed as Endangered, the tubercled-blossom may well be extinct.

For a general discussion of the life cycle of freshwater mussels see the species account of the birdwing pearly mussel (*Conradilla caelata*).

Habitat

This mussel is found in clean, fast-flowing streams that contain firm rubble, gravel, and sand substrates, swept free of silt by the current. Mussels bury themselves in shallow riffles and shoals.

Historic Distribution

Cumberlandian mussels are endemic to the southern Appalachian Mountains and the

Cumberland Plateau region. Of 90 species of freshwater mussels found in the Tennessee River, 37 are considered Cumberlandian. Twenty-seven of 78 species found in the Cumberland River are Cumberlandian. Records indicate that the green-blossom pearly mussel has always been restricted to the headwaters of the Tennessee River above Knoxville, Tennessee.

Current Distribution

The green-blossom pearly mussel is now found only in the free-flowing reaches of the upper Clinch River above Norris Reservoir. One of the larger tributaries of the Tennessee River, the Clinch River arises in Tazewell County, Virginia, and flows southwest through the Cumberland Gap region into Tennessee. Biologists from the Tennessee Valley Authority (TVA) have conducted extensive surveys along the Clinch River from Cedar Bluff, Virginia, to the Norris Reservoir. A single live specimen was found in 1982, the first green-blossom collected since 1965.

Conservation and Recovery

The green-blossom pearly mussel has always been rare but is now on the verge of extinction. The genus *Epioblasma* has generally suffered because its members are typically found only in shallow portions of major rivers with rapid currents. Water control projects have greatly diminished this type of habitat. Although the green-blossom is found in a river, which supports the most abundant and diverse freshwater mussel community in the U.S., it is being eliminated by factors that are not yet affecting other mussels. Dam construction, siltation, and pollution are likely causes.

The TVA has built nine major dams on the main channel of the Tennessee River and 27 smaller dams on tributary streams. The Nor-

ris Dam created one of the largest reservoirs in the state and probably flooded a crucial portion of the green-blossom's historic range. Silt runoff from strip mining and agriculture has buried many of the gravel and sand bottoms in which the pearly mussel lives. It is estimated that over 67 percent of coal production in the Appalachian region is extracted by strip mining. Because mussels siphon gallons of water each day while feeding, the effects of water pollutants, such as herbicides and pesticides, are intensified. Silt clogs the mussles' feeding siphons.

Sections of the Clinch River appear eligible for Scenic River status under the National Wild and Scenic Rivers Act. Such a designation would provide additional protection for this and other freshwater mussels. The state of Tennessee has designated all of the Clinch River in Tennessee as a mussel sanctuary, but the headwaters for the Clinch originate in Virginia, where coal mining is extensive.

Bibliography

Bates, J. M., and S. D. Dennis. 1978. "The Mussel Fauna of the Clinch River, Tennessee and Virginia." *Sterkiana* 69/70:3-23.

Neel, J. K., and W. Allen. 1964. "The Mussel Fauna of the Upper Cumberland Basin Before Its Impoundment." *Malacologia* 1(3):427- 459.

U.S. Fish and Wildlife Service. 1983. "Green-Blossom Pearly Mussel Recovery Plan." U.S. Fish and Wildlife Service, Atlanta.

Contact

Regional Office of Endangered Species
U.S. Fish and Wildlife Service
Richard B. Russell Federal Building
75 Spring Street, S.W.
Atlanta, Georgia 30303

Tubercled-Blossom Pearly Mussel

Epioblasma torulosa torulosa

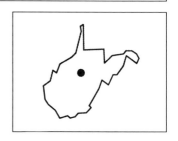

A. E. Spreitzer/OSU Museum of Zoology

Status	Endangered (possibly extinct)
Listed	June 14, 1976
Family	Unionidae (Freshwater Mussel)
Description . . .	Medium-sized egg-shaped or elliptical shell, yellow or greenish in color with numerous green rays.
Habitat	Sand or gravel shoals in larger rivers.
Threats	Habitat loss, pollution, siltation.
Region 4	Kentucky, Tennessee
Region 5	West Virginia

Description

The tubercled-blossom pearly mussel is a medium-sized freshwater mussel, reaching about 9 centimeters (3.6 in) in shell length. The shell is irregularly egg-shaped or elliptical, slightly sculptured and corrugated with distinct growth lines. The outer surface is smooth and shiny, tawny, yellowish green, or straw-colored, usually with numerous green rays. The inner shell surface is white to salmon-red. Females are generally larger than males and display a large, rounded marsupial swelling, which is often a darker green than the rest of the shell.

The tubercled-blossom is a more inflated, big-river form of the federally Endangered green blossom pearly mussel (*Epioblasma torulosa gubernaculum*), a subspecies found in the headwater tributaries of the Tennessee River above Knoxville. The tubercled-blossom pearly mussel was first described from the Ohio and Kentucky rivers as *Amblema torulosa* and later as *Dysnomia torulosa torulosa*.

For a general discussion of the life cycle of freshwater mussels see the species account of the birdwing pearly mussel (*Conradilla caelata*).

Habitat

The tubercled-blossom pearly mussel inhabited the larger rivers within its range, preferring to bury itself into sand and gravel shoals.

Historic Range

This mussel was once fairly abundant and widespread throughout all the major rivers of the eastern U.S. and southern Ontario, Canada. These rivers included in particular the Tennessee, Cumberland, Ohio and St. Lawrence.

Current Distribution

One specimen, thought to be freshly dead, was collected in 1969 from the Kanawha River below Kanawha Falls in West Virginia, but no other recent collections have been made, and this subspecies may well be extinct. A General Accounting Office report released in December 1988 included this mussel among those species "believed to be extinct but not yet officially declared so."

Conservation and Recovery

Studies of the Kanawha River in 1982 and 1983 found no further evidence of the tubercled-blossom pearly mussel. A detailed scuba search below the Kanawha Falls turned up nothing, and scientists concluded that the species no longer occurred in the drainage.

Mussels have declined steadily in the major rivers because of increased turbidity and siltation triggered by deforestation and the spread of intensive agriculture throughout the East. The decline of the genus *Epioblasma* may have begun in earnest when settlers crossed the Appalachians to farm the rich Ohio and Tennessee river valleys.

More recently, major rivers have suffered from extensive chemical pollution, caused by both agricultural and industrial runoff. Because mussels filter many gallons of water to extract food, pollutants build up in their tissues, eventually killing off the beds. The health of mussel populations in major rivers can be used as a general indicator of the health of the ecosystem.

Understandably, this mussel has been accorded a low priority in the allocation of research funds. If a viable population can be located, then further recovery strategies will be designed and implemented.

Bibliography

Bogan, A., and P. Parmalee. 1983. "Tennessee's Rare Mollusks." In *Tennessee's Rare Wildlife, Final Report.* Tennessee Department of Conservation and Tennessee Heritage Program, University of Tennessee, Knoxville.

General Accounting Office. 1988. "Endangered Species: Management Improvements Could Enhance Recovery Program." GAO/RCED-89-5. General Accounting Office, Washington, D.C.

Jenkinson, J. J. 1981. "Endangered or Threatened Aquatic Mollusks of the Tennessee River System." *Bulletin of the American Malacological Union* 1980:43-45.

U.S. Fish and Wildlife Service. 1985. "Recovery Plan for the Tubercled-Blossom Pearly Mussel, Turgid-Blossom Pearly Mussel, and Yellow-Blossom Pearly Mussel." U.S. Fish and Wildlife Service, Atlanta.

Contact

Regional Office of Endangered Species
U.S. Fish and Wildlife Service
Richard B. Russell Federal Building
75 Spring Street, S.W.
Atlanta, Georgia 30303

Turgid-Blossom Pearly Mussel

Epioblasma turgidula

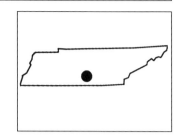

mm
in

A. E. Spreitzer/OSU Museum of Zoology

Status . . . . . . Endangered (possibly extinct)
Listed . . . . . . June 14, 1976
Family . . . . . Unionidae (Freshwater Mussel)
Description . . . Elliptical, egg-shaped, or
round shell, shiny yellow-
green in color with irregular
growth lines.
Habitat . . . . . . Sand and gravel substrates in
flowing water.
Threats . . . . . Habitat loss, pollution, siltation.
Region 4 . . . . . Alabama, Tennessee

Description

The turgid-blossom pearly mussel is a small Cumberlandian species, seldom exceeding 4 centimeters (1.6 in) in shell length. The species is strongly dimorphic—males and females differ in shape and structure. Shells of the male tend to be more elliptical or oval, while females tend to be more rounded. Valves are inequilateral, solid, and slightly inflated. The outer shell is shiny yellowish green with numerous fine green rays over the entire surface. The shell surface is marked by irregular growth lines, that are especially strong on females. The inner shell surface is bluish white.

Male and female specimens were originally described as two separate species. The turgid-blossom mussel was previously classified as *Dysnomia turgidula*.

For a general discussion of the life cycle of freshwater mussels see the species account of the birdwing pearly mussel (*Conradilla caelata*).

Habitat

The turgid-blossom pearly mussel buries itself in sand and gravel substrates of shallow, fast-flowing streams. Clear, unpolluted water is required for healthy freshwater mussel populations.

Historic Range

Cumberlandian mussels are endemic to the southern Appalachian Mountains and the Cumberland Plateau. This species was relatively widespread within this region and was also found in the Ozarks. It is documented from the Tennessee River and its tributaries, including Elk, Duck, Holston, Clinch, and Emory rivers in Tennessee, and Shoals and Bear creeks in Alabama. Large numbers were found in the Cumberland River and its tributaries. In the Ozark Mountains it occurred in Spring Creek, Black River, and White River in Arkansas and Missouri.

Current Distribution

The turgid-blossom pearly mussel was last reported in the mid-1960s from the Duck River near Normandy, Tennessee. D. H. Stansbery and J. J. Jenkinson, the experts on Cumberlandian mussels, consider this species extinct. A General Accounting Office report released in December 1988, included this mussel among those species "believed to be extinct but not yet officially declared so."

Conservation and Recovery

The construction of dams and reservoirs by the Tennessee Valley Authority (TVA), the Aluminum Company of America, and the Army Corps of Engineers, completely and abruptly changed the character of the Tennessee and Cumberland rivers, endangering many freshwater mussels in the process. Since the 1930s, 51 dams have been constructed on the Tennessee and Cumberland rivers for flood control, generation of hydroelectric power, and recreation.

Segments of these rivers that once supported healthy populations of mussels have been permanently inundated. In addition, altered water flows and random water releases have changed water temperatures, increased turbidity, and contributed to problems of siltation. Strip mining, coal washing, farming, and logging have all added silt and pollutants to the streams of the region. Turbid

water and siltation clog the feeding apparatus of mussels and smother mussel beds.

Many fish species, including those that play host to mussel glochidia (larvae), have declined in numbers, making mussel reproduction problematic. When glochidia are released into the streams by female mussels, they must chance upon a suitable fish host in order to develop to maturity. When a fish host is not encountered, the glochidia sink to the bottom and die.

Recovery strategies for this subspecies cannot be developed until a viable breeding population is discovered. The Tennessee Wildlife Resources Agency, the Tennessee Heritage Program, and the TVA continue to support research into the status of mussels in the state. Mussel research in Alabama is promoted by the State Department of Conservation and Natural Resources.

Bibliography

General Accounting Office. 1988. "Endangered Species: Management Improvements Could Enhance Recovery Program." GAO/RCED-89-5. General Accounting Office, Washington, D.C.

Stansbery, D. H. 1971. "Rare and Endangered Mollusks in Eastern United States." In S. E. Jorgenson and R. E. Sharp, eds., Proceedings of a Symposium on Rare and Endangered Mollusks (Naiades). U.S. Fish and Wildlife Service, Twin Cities.

U.S. Fish and Wildlife Service. 1985. "Recovery Plan for the Tubercled-Blossom Pearly Mussel, Turgid-Blossom Pearly Mussel, and Yellow-Blossom Pearly Mussel." U.S. Fish and Wildlife Service, Atlanta.

Contact

Regional Office of Endangered Species
U.S. Fish and Wildlife Service
Richard B. Russell Federal Building
75 Spring Street, S.W.
Atlanta, Georgia 30303

Tan Riffle Shell
Epioblasma walkeri

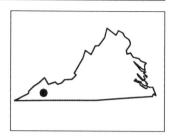

A. E. Spreitzer/OSU Museum of Zoology

Status . . . . . . Endangered
Listed . . . . . . August 23, 1977
Family . . . . . . Unionidae
　　　　　　　　(Freshwater Mussel)
Description . . . Dull brownish green or yel-
　　　　　　　　lowish green shell with
　　　　　　　　numerous faint green rays.
Habitat . . . . . . Mid-sized streams and rivers
　　　　　　　　in sand or gravel shoals.
Threats . . . . . Restricted range, siltation,
　　　　　　　　degraded water quality.
Region 4 . . . . . Kentucky, Tennessee
Region 5 . . . . . Virginia

Description

The tan riffle shell is a medium-sized freshwater mussel (7 cm; 2.8 in) characterized by
a dull brownish green or yellowish green
shell surface with numerous, evenly distributed, faint green rays. The subinflated
valves are of unequal length and are marked
with uneven growth rings. The inner shell
surface is bluish white. The thin, posterior
swelling of the female has one or more con-
strictions which give the shell a lobed appearance.

For a general discussion of the life cycle of
freshwater mussels see the species account of
the birdwing pearly mussel (*Conradilla
caelata*).

Habitat

This mussel inhabits shallow riffles and
shoals of mid-sized tributaries and the
mainstream of larger rivers. It buries itself in
a sand or gravel bottom.

Historic Range

This mussel was first collected in the East
Fork Stones River in Rutherford County,
Tennessee, but appears to have disappeared
from this locality. It was found in the headwaters of the Cumberland River downstream
to Neeley's Ford in Cumberland County,
Kentucky. In the 1970s it was found in the
lower Red River (a Cumberland River

tributary) in Montgomery County, Tennessee, and in the Duck and Buffalo rivers.

In the upper Tennessee River drainage, this mussel was documented from the Middle Fork Holston River (Smyth County, Virginia), the South Fork Holston River (Washington County, Virginia, and Sullivan County, Tennessee), and the main stem of the Holston River (Grainger and Knox counties, Tennessee). It was also noted from the Flint River and Limestone Creek in northern Alabama.

Current Distribution

The tan riffle shell has not been relocated in the Duck or Red rivers, and probably survives only in the Middle Fork Holston River in Virginia. It has been collected recently from near Chilhowie (Smyth County) and further downstream at Craig Bridge (Washington County).

Conservation and Recovery

The drastic decline in range of the tan riffle shell is probably in response to the extensive alteration of the Cumberland and Tennessee river basins by the construction of more than 50 dams and reservoirs. The South Fork Holston River was impounded by the Ruthton Dam to create the South Holston Lake, inundating miles of former mussel habitat along the river. The cold tailwaters of the reservoir have proven inimical to endemic mussels and many species of fishes that serve as hosts for mussel larvae.

The general effects of impoundments on mussel habitat have been widely documented. In addition, water quality in most watersheds within the tan riffle shell's historic range has deteriorated because of heavy siltation caused by logging, strip-mining, dredging, and poor agricultural practices.

The Tennessee Valley Authority is currently developing a comprehensive water management plan for the region that would establish minimum, year-round flows in all rivers in the Tennessee and Cumberland basins by carefully timing water discharges from its many dams. The recovery of the tan riffle shell will depend on the success of this and other regional efforts to improve water quality and rehabilitate freshwater mussel habitat.

Bibliography

Tennessee Valley Authority. 1978. "Water Quality Progress in the Holston River Basin." Report No. TVA/EP-78/08. Tennessee Valley Authority, Knoxville.

U.S. Fish and Wildlife Service. 1984. "Tan Riffle Shell Mussel Recovery Plan." U.S. Fish and Wildlife Service, Atlanta.

Virginia State Water Control Board. 1982. "Water Quality Inventory: Report to EPA and Congress." Bulletin No.546. Virginia State Water Control Board, Richmond, Virginia.

Contact

Regional Office of Endangered Species
U.S. Fish and Wildlife Service
Richard B. Russell Federal Building
75 Spring Street, S.W.
Atlanta, Georgia 30303

Fine-Rayed Pigtoe
Pearly Mussel
Fusconaia cuneolus

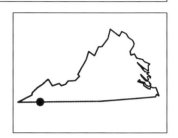

A. E. Spreitzer/OSU Museum of Zoology

Status . . . . . . Endangered
Listed . . . . . . June 14, 1976
Family . . . . . Unionidae
                (Freshwater Mussel)
Description . . . Medium-sized shell, yellow-
                green to light brown with
                numerous fine, green rays.
Habitat . . . . . . Sand and gravel shoals of
                streams and rivers.
Threats . . . . . Dams, siltation, pollution.
Region 4 . . . . . Alabama, Tennessee
Region 5 . . . . . Virginia

Description

The fine-rayed pigtoe pearly mussel is of medium size, up to 6 centimeters (2.5 in) in length. This Cumberlandian species is distinguished by the many fine green rays that radiate over the yellowish green to light brown background of its ovoid shell. The hinged-end of the shell is rounded, while the front margin is straight. The shell surface has a smooth, satiny appearance and is indistinctly patterned with growth lines. The inner shell surface is white. It is a short-term breeder, reproducing in the spring (tachytictic).

For a general discussion of the life cycle of freshwater mussels see the species account of the birdwing pearly mussel (*Conradilla caelata*).

Habitat

The fine-rayed pigtoe occupies shallow riffles and shoals of freshwater streams and rivers. It buries itself in the stream bottom in gravel or compacted sand but is rarely found in pools. It displays a higher tolerance for muddy bottoms than most other freshwater mussels.

Historic Range

Endemic to the southern Appalachian Mountains, the fine-rayed pigtoe pearly mussel was first described in 1840 from the Holston River, where it occurred in the river's North Fork in Washington County, Virginia, downstream to Grainger County, Tennessee. It was subsequently documented from Big Moccasin Creek (Scott County, Virginia). The fine-rayed pigtoe was reported in the Powell River from Lee County, Virginia, downstream to Union County, Tennessee. The mussel was collected from Clinch Creek, Emory River, and Popular Creek from Clinchport, Virginia, downstream to Roane County, Tennessee, and was found in the Clinch River from Tazewell County, Virginia, downstream to the Norris Reservoir (Claiborne County, Tennessee).

In the early 20th century it was discovered in the Tennessee River and its smaller tributaries at and below Knoxville, Tennessee. It is believed that the mussel has been extirpated from former locations in the Little and Sequatchie rivers.

Current Distribution

Although this species was thought to have disappeared from its original collection site in the Holston River, four freshly dead specimens were collected along the river in 1982 at Cloud Ford, Tennessee. Industrial and chemical pollution from upstream at Saltville, Virginia, has severely degraded the water quality there. Live specimens have yet to be found but may indeed exist. Recent surveys in other upper Tennessee River tributaries, such as Nolichucky, French Broad, Flint, Buffalo rivers, failed to locate specimens.

From 1975 to 1981 surveys of the Powell River located populations at Buchanan Ford and McDowell Shoal in Tennessee, and at Fletcher Ford in Virginia. Water quality in this river has also deteriorated significantly due to strip mining and coal-washing runoff and discharge of municipal wastes.

More recently, this mussel has been found at nearly 30 sites in the Clinch River and its smaller tributaries between Cedar Bluff, Virginia, and Kelly Branch, Tennessee. Since 1970, the fine-rayed pigtoe has been collected

from the Elk and Paint Rock rivers, tributaries of the Tennessee River above Muscle Shoals, Alabama. The mussel's former range and habitat suggests that additional populations may be located on other tributary streams of the Tennessee River in Tennessee and Alabama.

Conservation and Recovery

Construction of dams and multi-purpose reservoirs across the former range of the fine-rayed pigtoe have altered the free-flowing character of these rivers. Such impoundments produce siltation, fluctuating water temperatures, changes in water acidity, and lowered oxygen content. Impoundments also fragment the range of the species into isolated populations, which are then unable to interbreed.

Increased stream turbidity, caused by soil erosion and industrial runoff, reduces light penetration, which affects the growth of aquatic vegetation and decreases the population of fish hosts. Suspended solids can be fatal to mussels. Dead and dying mussels are often found with silt clogging their gills. Mussels are very susceptible to agricultural and industrial pollutants, particularly heavy metals, which become concentrated in their tissues.

The fairly widespread distribution of the fine-rayed pigtoe affords it some protection against early extinction, if federal, state, and local agencies act now to reduce habitat degradation. The Fish and Wildlife Service Recovery Plan for this species recommends further systematic surveys to locate new populations and a program to reestablish populations in areas of suitable habitat. Additionally, better enforcement of state and federal environmental regulations is needed to prevent further degradation of water quality. Creation of mussel sanctuaries in the Virginia headwaters, similar to those on the

Clinch and Powell rivers in Tennessee, would be highly beneficial.

Bibliography

Bogan, A. E., and P. W. Parmalee. 1983. *Tennessee's Rare Wildlife: the Mollusks.* Tennessee Wildlife Resources Agency, Tennessee Department of Conservation, and Tennessee Natural Heritage Program, University of Tennessee Press, Knoxville.

Carter, L. J. 1977. "Chemical Plants Leave Unexpected Legacy in Two Virginia Rivers." *Science* 198:1015-1020.

Dennis, S. D. 1981. "Mussel Fauna of the Powell River, Tennessee and Virginia." *Sterkiana* 71:1-7.

Imlay, M. J. 1982. "Use of Shells of Freshwater Mussels in Monitoring Heavy Metals and Environmental Stresses: A Review." *Malacology Review* 15:1-14.

U. S. Fish and Wildlife Service. 1984. "Fine-Rayed Pigtoe Pearly Mussel Recovery Plan," U.S. Fish and Wildlife Service, Atlanta.

Contact

U.S. Fish and Wildlife Service
Richard B. Russell Federal Building
75 Spring Street, S.W.
Atlanta, GA 30303

Regional Office of Endangered Species
U.S. Fish and Wildlife Service
One Gateway Center, Suite 700
Newton Corner, Massachusetts 02158

Shiny Pigtoe
Pearly Mussel
Fusconaia edgariana

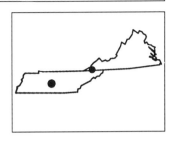

A. E. Spreitzer/OSU Museum of Zoology

Status	Endangered
Listed	July 1976
Family	Unionidae (Freshwater Mussel)
Description . . .	Smooth, shiny, dull brown shell with dark green or black rays.
Habitat	Shoals in streams and rivers.
Threats	Loss of habitat, siltation, pollution.
Region 4	Alabama, Tennessee
Region 5	Virginia

Description

The shiny pigtoe pearly mussel is about 6.4 centimeters (2.5 in) long with a very smooth and shiny outer covering (periostracum). The shell displays prominent dark green to black rays on a yellow to brown background. Young specimens generally have bold black or green ray patterns; older mussels are dull brown with indistinct rays fading toward the valve margins. Valves are triangular with concentric growth marks. The inner shell surface is white.

The shiny pigtoe is a short term breeder, breeding in spring and releasing glochidia by mid- to late summer of the same year. The glochidia of the shiny pigtoe are horseshoe shaped and parasitic on the gills of fish. Some of the fish hosts are the whitetail shiner, com-

mon shiner, the warpaint shiner, and the telescope shiner.

For a general discussion of the life cycle of freshwater mussels see the species account of the birdwing pearly mussel (*Conradilla caelata*).

Habitat

The shiny pigtoe is found along fords and in shoals of clear, moderate- to fast-flowing streams and rivers with stable substrates. It is not found in deeper pools or reservoirs.

Historic Range

The shiny pigtoe was once found in Alabama in the Elk, Flint, and Paint Rock rivers, and in the Clinch River from Russell

County, Virginia, downstream to Anderson County, Tennessee. It was found in the Powell River from Lytton Mill (Lee County, Virginia) downstream to Claiborne County, Tennessee. It was also found in the Holston River (Washington County, Virginia) downstream to Hawkins County, Tennessee, and in the Tennessee River from Knoxville downstream for 32 kilometers (20 mi).

Current Distribution

The shiny pigtoe is now found in the North Fork Holston River in Virginia from Broadford to Saltville. In the Clinch River, it is found in scattered locations from Nash Ford in Virginia to Kyles Ford, Tennessee, with smaller populations in the Copper Creek tributary. In the Powell River it occurs sporadically from Flanary's Ford, Virginia, downstream to Combs, Tennessee. In the Elk River it inhabits scattered localities near Fayetteville, Tennessee. A few populations occur in the Paint Rock River near Princeton, Alabama. No recent population figures are available.

Conservation and Recovery

Like other freshwater mussels the shiny pigtoe has suffered from the industrialization of its range and the massive Tennessee Valley Authority (TVA) projects that have dammed and redirected all of the major rivers and streams within its historic range. In addition, runoff from strip mining and coal washing, herbicides, pesticides, and industrial pollutants—particularly heavy metals—has severely degraded water quality throughout the mussel's range.

It is unlikely that any major portion of the shiny pigtoe's historic habitat will ever be restored. Therefore, recovery strategies are focused on preserving habitat in the areas where the mussel can still be found. Some

portions of the range, including the Paint Rock River, may be eligible for Scenic River status under the National Wild and Scenic Rivers Act, a designation that would provide additional protection for the species.

Bibliography

Bogan, A. E., and P. W. Parmalee. 1983. *Tennessee's Rare Wildlife: The Mollusks*. Tennessee Wildlife Resources Agency, University of Tennessee Press, Knoxville.

Burch, J. B. 1975. *Freshwater Unionacean Clams* (Mollusca: Pelecypoda) *of North America*. Malacological Publications, Hamburg, Michigan.

U.S. Fish and Wildlife Service. 1983. "Recovery Plan: Shiny Pigtoe Pearly Mussel, *Fusconaia edgariana*." U.S. Fish and Wildlife Service, Atlanta.

Contact

Regional Office of Endangered Species
U.S. Fish and Wildlife Service
Richard B. Russell Federal Building
75 Spring Street, S.W.
Atlanta, Georgia 30303

Higgins' Eye Pearly Mussel
Lampsilis higginsi

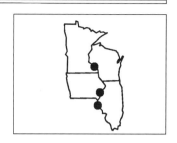

A. E. Spreitzer/OSU Museum of Zoology

Status . . . . . . Endangered
Listed . . . . . . June 14, 1976
Family . . . . . . Unionidae (Freshwater Mussel)
Description . . . Tan or brown shell with fine
                black rays.
Habitat . . . . . . Major rivers and tributaries.
Threats . . . . . . Dam construction, dredging,
                siltation, pollution.
Region 3 . . . . . Illinois, Iowa, Minnesota, Mis-
                souri, Wisconsin

Description

The Higgins' eye pearly mussel averages 6 centimeters (2.4 in) in length with females slightly smaller than males. Fine black rays are present along the growth lines against a background shell of tan to brown. The Higgins' eye is a long-term breeder, holding fertilized glochidia (larvae) over winter and releasing them in spring. The larval host fish is thought to be the sauger or freshwater drum. Females reach sexual maturity by their third year.

For a general discussion of the life cycle of freshwater mussels see the species account of the birdwing pearly mussel (*Conradilla caelata*).

Habitat

This species inhabits major rivers and tributaries in depths of up to 4.6 meters (15 ft). It has been found on mud-gravel bottoms in areas of swift current.

Historic Range

The Higgins' eye pearly mussel is endemic to the Mississippi River and its major tributaries. It was found in the mainstream of the Mississippi River from north of St. Louis, Missouri, to the Twin Cities, Minnesota. Population centers have been documented near Prescott, Minnesota, La Crosse, and Prairie du Chien, Wisconsin, and Muscatine and Davenport, Iowa.

Populations were found in the Illinois River from Mason County to the confluence of the Mississippi, in the Sangamon River near Chandlerville, Illinois, in the St. Croix River, near Hudson, Wisconsin, the Wapsipinicon River near Dixon, Iowa, in the Cedar River near Cedar Bluff, Iowa, and in the Iowa River near Gladwin, Iowa.

Current Distribution

Although widely distributed, this mussel occurred in discrete localities and was never considered numerous. In the late 1970s and early 1980s the Mississippi River was heavily surveyed for occurrences of the Higgins' eye pearly mussel. Scattered populations were found to survive in sections of river near La Crosse, Wisconsin, from the Minnesota state line south to Prairie du Chien, Wisconsin, from Clayton downstream to Dubuque, Iowa, and from Clinton south to West Burlington, Iowa. Except for a remnant population near the confluence of the Missouri River, population centers south of West Burlington in the mainstream appear to have been largely extirpated. The St. Croix River still supports several populations upstream from Hudson (St. Croix County), Wisconsin.

Biologists estimate that the Higgins' eye pearly mussel has been eliminated from nearly 55 percent of its historic range.

Conservation and Recovery

Construction of major dams for flood control and electricity generation have created conditions along portions of the upper Mississippi River that are no longer conducive to the survival of the Higgins' eye pearly mussel. River impoundments have inundated habitat upstream and contributed to erratic water flows, altered water temperatures, and increased siltation downstream. Degradation of water quality caused by municipal, industrial, and agricultural effluents has also contributed to this mussel's decline.

Seven sites have been designated as habitat essential to the survival of the Higgins' eye pearly mussel. These are the St. Croix River above Hudson, Wisconsin, and the Mississippi River at Whiskey Rock, Prairie du Chien, and McMillan Island, Wisconsin, Harpers Slough, Iowa, and Cordova and Arsenal Island, Illinois.

Relocation of mussels to existing mussel beds not currently populated with Higgins' eye is recommended in the Fish and Wildlife Service Recovery Plan for this species. Research is ongoing to determine practical methods of propagation and reintroduction.

Bibliography

Ecological Analysts. 1981. "Relocation of Freshwater Mussels in Sylvan Slough of the Mississippi River Near Moline, Illinois." Report. Shappert Engineers, Belvidere, Illinois, and Ecological Analysts, Northbrook, Illinois.

Ecological Analysts. 1981. "Survey of Freshwater Mussels at Selected Sites in Pools 11 through 24 of the Mississippi River." Ecological Analysts, Northbrook, Illinois.

Havlik, M. E. 1981. "The Historic and Present Distribution of the Endangered Mollusk *Lampsilis higginsi* (Lea, 1857)." *Bulletin of the American Malacological Union* 1980:19-22.

U.S. Fish and Wildlife Service. 1982. "Recovery Plan for the Higgins' Eye Pearly Mussel." U.S. Fish and Wildlife Service, Twin Cities.

Contact

Regional Office of Endangered Species
U.S. Fish and Wildlife Service
Federal Building, Fort Snelling
Twin Cities, Minnesota 55111

Pink Mucket Pearly Mussel

Lampsilis orbiculata

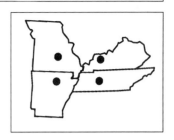

A. E. Spreitzer/OSU Museum of Zoology

Status	Endangered
Listed	June 14, 1976
Family	Unionidae (Freshwater Mussel)
Description	Large yellow to brown elliptical shell with wide greenish rays.
Habitat	Major rivers and tributaries.
Threats	Habitat decline, siltation.
Region 3	Ohio, Missouri
Region 4	Alabama, Arkansas, Kentucky, Tennessee
Region 5	West Virginia

Description

The pink mucket pearly mussel's elliptical to quadrangular shell attains a length of 10 centimeters (4 in) long, a width of 6 centimeters (2.4 in), and a thickness of 8 centimeters (3 in). The yellow to brown surface of the shell is smooth except for relatively dark, concentric growth marks and wide greenish rays, which are more prominent in juveniles. The shell is glossy in younger specimens and dull in older individuals. The valves are thick, heavy, and unsculptured.

The pink mucket is a long-term breeder (bradytictic). Males release sperm into the water in late summer or autumn. Females take in sperm but brood fertilized larvae (glochidia) over winter in gill pouches and release them in the following spring. For a general discussion of the life cycle of fresh-

water mussels see the species account of the birdwing pearly mussel (*Conradilla caelata*).

Habitat

The pink mucket pearly mussel inhabits shallow riffles and shoals of major rivers and tributaries. It is found in rubble, gravel, or sand substrates, which have been swept free from silt by the current.

Historic Range

This pearly mussel is considered endemic to the Interior Basin and was found primarily in the Tennessee, Cumberland, and Ohio river drainages, although specimens have been collected from the Missouri, Black, and Mississippi rivers. This mussel has been documented from 25 rivers and tributaries in

11 states—West Virginia, Pennsylvania, Ohio, Illinois, Indiana, Kentucky, Tennessee, Alabama, Arkansas, Missouri, and Iowa. Populations appear to have been extirpated from the northern portion of the range (Ohio, Indiana, and Illinois).

Current Distribution

The pink mucket pearly mussel is presently known from 16 rivers and tributaries, with the greatest concentrations in the Tennessee, Cumberland, Osage, and Meramec rivers. Although it is found over a wide geographic area, this mussel was never collected in large numbers and has always been considered uncommon.

Populations occur in the Tennessee River below Pickwick, Wilson, Guntersville, and Watts Bar dams (Tennessee and Alabama), above New Hope on Paint Rock River (Alabama), in the Clinch River below Melton Hill Dam (Tennessee), in the Cumberland River at Bartletts Bar, Cotton Bar, Rome Island, and Carters Island (Kentucky and Tennessee), in the Green River (Butler County, Kentucky), and on the Kanawha River below Kanawha Falls (West Virginia). West of the Mississippi River populations are found in the Osage River below Bagnell Dam, in the Meramec River, Big River, Black and Little Black, and Gasconde rivers (Missouri), and in Current and Spring rivers (Arkansas).

Conservation and Recovery

Possibly the greatest single factor in the decline of the pink mucket pearly mussel has been the construction of dams and reservoirs on the major rivers for flood control, navigation, hydroelectric power production, and recreation. Impounding the natural river flow eliminates those mussels and fishes that are unable to adapt to reduced and sporadic flows, altered water temperatures, and seasonal oxygen deficiencies. Although a few dams have actually created downstream habitat for the pink mucket, in most cases, this has been at the expense of inundating large stretches of upstream habitat.

Heavy loads of silt have been introduced into most watersheds from strip mining and coal washing, dredging, and intensive logging. Deforestation and poor agricultural practices are probably responsible for the loss of many native mussel populations, particularly in the midwestern states. Siltation smothers mussel beds or decreases the abundance of fish hosts, which are necessary to complete the mussel's life cycle.

The states of Tennessee and Alabama have designated portions of the Tennessee and Cumberland Rivers as mussel sanctuaries. Because of these protections the pink mucket pearly mussel is again reproducing well in localized areas. Recently, live specimens were discovered in the upper Ohio River, where this species has not been collected for 75 years. Scientists have taken this occurrence as evidence that water quality in this region has improved in recent years.

Bibliography

Fuller, S. 1974. "Clams and Mussels." In Hart and Fuller, eds., *Pollution Ecology of Freshwater Invertebrates*. Academic Press, New York.

Isom, B. G. 1969. "The Mussel Resources of the Tennessee River." *Malacologia* 7(2-3):397-425.

U.S. Fish and Wildlife Service. 1985. "Recovery Plan for the Pink Mucket Pearly Mussel." U.S. Fish and Wildlife Service, Atlanta.

Contact

Regional Office of Endangered Species
U.S. Fish and Wildlife Service
Richard B. Russell Federal Building
75 Spring Street, S.W.
Atlanta, Georgia 30303

Speckled Pocketbook Mussel

Lampsilis streckeri

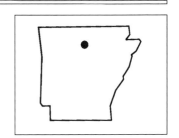

A. E. Spreitzer/OSU Museum of Zoology

Status . . . . . . Endangered
Listed . . . . . . July 25, 1989
Family . . . . . Unionidae (Freshwater Mussel)
Description . . . Dark yellow or brown, elongated, elliptical shell with
chevron spots and chain-like
rays.
Habitat . . . . . . Coarse to muddy sand in constantly flowing water.
Threats . . . . . . Stream impoundment,
dredging, degraded water
quality.
Region 4 . . . . . Arkansas

Description

The speckled pocketbook mussel has an
elongated, elliptical shell up to 8 centimeters
(3.1 in) long. Shells are dark yellow or brown
with chevron-like spots and chain-like rays.
Female shells are broader than male shells
and more evenly rounded at the base.

For a general discussion of the life cycle of
freshwater mussels see the species account of
the birdwing pearly mussel (*Conradilla
caelata*).

Habitat

This species buries itself in coarse to muddy
sand where there is a constant flow of water
no more than 0.4 meters (1.3 ft) deep. It cannot survive in slow currents, pools, or
stretches of river with erratic flow.

Historic Range

This mussel appears to be endemic to the
Little Red River basin (Searcy, Stone, Van
Buren, and Claiborne counties) in north
central Arkansas. It occurred in the Little Red
River, South Fork, Middle Fork, and Archey
Fork.

Current Distribution

The speckled pocketbook is currently
found in about 10 kilometers (6 mi) of the
Middle Fork of the Little Red River in Stone
and Van Buren counties, Arkansas. All land
abutting this stretch of river between
Meadow Creek upstream and Tick Creek
downstream is privately owned. From Tick
Creek to the Greers Ferry Reservoir, habitat
in the Middle Fork appears suitable for the

speckled pocketbook, but no live specimens have been found there.

Conservation and Recovery

The speckled pocketbook has declined in range and numbers because of reservoir construction, channel dredging and modification, and water quality degradation. Completion of Greers Ferry Reservoir inundated a large portion of the historic habitat in Van Buren and Claiborne counties. Cold water discharges from the dam have made downstream portions of the river uninhabitable. The speckled pocketbook was eliminated from the South and Archey forks by increased water velocities and scouring, caused by upstream channel modifications.

Federal listing of this species requires that all activities funded or administered by federal agencies be reviewed to ensure that these actions do not jeopardize the survival of the speckled pocketbook. The Army Corps of Engineers currently conducts channel maintenance for flood control on the Archey and South Forks and will consult with the Fish and Wildlife Service to lessen any risk to the mussel or potential habitat that would support reintroduction. The Environmental Protection Agency has been involved with regional efforts to prevent water quality degradation from pesticides.

One of the first goals of recovery is to establish the speckled pocketbook in the stretch of the Middle Fork from Tick Creek downstream to Greers Ferry Reservoir. Eventually, it is hoped that habitat in the South and Archey forks can be rehabilitated and restocked with the speckled pocketbook.

Bibliography

Clarke, A. E. 1987. "Status Survey of *Lampsilis streckeri* and *Arcidens wheeleri*." Report. U.S. Fish and Wildlife Service, Atlanta.

Johnson, R. I. 1980. "Zoogeography of North American Unionacea North of the Maximum Pleistocene Glaciation." *Bulletin of the Museum of Comparative Zoology* 149(2):77-189.

Contact

Regional Office of Endangered Species
U.S. Fish and Wildlife Service
Richard B. Russell Federal Building
75 Spring Street, S.W.
Atlanta, Georgia 30303

Alabama Lamp Pearly Mussel

Lampsilis virescens

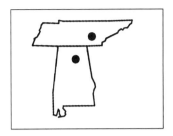

A. E. Spreitzer/OSU Museum of Zoology

Status . . . . . . Endangered
Listed . . . . . . June 14, 1976
Family . . . . . . Unionidae (Freshwater Mussel)
Description . . . Yellowish to greenish brown, elliptical shell, sometimes with faint rays.
Habitat . . . . . . Sand and gravel substrates in small to medium-sized streams.
Threats . . . . . . Dams, reservoirs, siltation, pollution.
Region 4 . . . . . Alabama, Tennessee

Description

The Alabama lamp pearly mussel has an elliptical shell, typically about 6 centimeters (2.5 in) long. The smooth, shiny surface of the shell ranges in color from yellowish brown to greenish brown and is sometimes faintly rayed. Shell beaks are full and sculptured with many delicate ridges. Males are more bluntly pointed at the hinge, while females are rounder and slightly more inflated.

For a general discussion of the life cycle of freshwater mussels see the species account of the birdwing pearly mussel (*Conradilla caelata*).

Habitat

The Alabama lamp buries in sand or gravel substrates in small to medium-sized streams.

It requires clear, cool water with little sediment and moderate current.

Historic Range

The Alabama lamp pearly mussel is a Cumberlandian mussel—native to the southern Appalachians and the Cumberland Plateau. It was apparently restricted to the lesser tributaries of the Tennessee River from above the confluence of the Clinch River downstream to Tuscumbia, Alabama. Within this broadly defined range, this species was found in extremely localized beds in relatively low numbers.

Populations were documented in the Emory River (Roane and Morgan counties), and Coal Creek (Anderson County), Tennessee, and in Paint Rock River (Jackson County), Beech and Brown creeks (Marshall

County), Spring Creek (Colbert County), and Bear and Little Bear creeks (Franklin County), Alabama.

Current Distribution

Currently, the only populations of the Alabama lamp pearly mussel known to survive occur in the Paint Rock River and its tributaries—Hurricane Creek, Estill Fork, and Larkin Fork (Franklin and Jackson counties, Alabama). Some evidence has been collected to suggest that the species may still survive in the Little Emory River (Roane County), Tennessee.

Conservation and Recovery

The natural, unimpeded flow of the Tennessee River and its tributaries has been irrevocably altered by the construction of a series of major flood control, navigation, and hydroelectric dams on the main channel. Poor agricultural practices, strip mining, logging, and road construction have contributed heavy loads of silt to the basin's rivers and streams, in many cases smothering mussel beds or potential habitat. In particular, all of the mussel beds in Coal Creek, Tennessee, have been smothered by coal wastes and runoff. Gravel dredging within the range of the Alabama lamp pearly mussel has disturbed substrates and made stretches of river uninhabitable for mussels and host fishes.

Chemical and heavy metal contaminants from industries located along the river have also degraded general water quality. Because mussels filter many gallons of water each day to feed, contaminants become concentrated in the soft tissues, weakening or killing the mussel.

The Fish and Wildlife Service and state biologists have cooperated to redistribute the Paint Rock River population so that a single accident, such as a toxic chemical spill, would not result in loss of the total population. Pending the results of ongoing research into the ecology of this species, populations will be reintroduced to habitable streams within its historic range.

An innovative technique, being developed by the Virginia Cooperative Fishery Research Unit, would enable reintroduction of mussels by stocking a stream with host fishes, which have been inoculated with mussel glochidia (larvae). This method provides a promising alternative to transplanting adult mussels, which are typically of limited number.

Bibliography

Ahlstedt, S. A. 1983. "The Molluscan Fauna of the Elk River in Tennessee and Alabama." *American Malacological Bulletin* 1:43-50.

Isom, B. G. 1968. "The Naiad Fauna of Indian Creek, Madison County, Alabama." *American Midland Naturalist* 79(2):514-516.

Isom, B. G. 1969. "The Mussel Resources of the Tennessee River." *Malacologia* 7(2/3):397-425.

Isom, B. G., and P. Yokley, Jr. 1968. "Mussels of Bear Creek Watershed, Alabama and Mississippi, with a discussion of the Area Geology." *American Midland Naturalist* 79(1):189-196.

Contact

Regional Office of Endangered Species
U.S. Fish and Wildlife Service
Richard B. Russell Federal Building
75 Spring Street, S.W.
Atlanta, Georgia 30303

Louisiana Pearlshell

Margaritifera hembeli

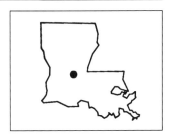

A. E. Spreitzer/OSU Museum of Zoology

Status . . . . . . Endangered
Listed . . . . . . February 5, 1988
Family . . . . . . Margaritiferidae (Freshwater Mussel)
Description . . . Dark brown to black, elliptical shell with white nacre.
Habitat . . . . . . Shallow, flowing streams with sand or gravel substrate.
Threats . . . . . . Stream diversion, reservoir construction, pollution.
Region 4 . . . . . Louisiana

Description

Louisiana pearlshell is a freshwater mussel with a generally elliptical shell, about 10 centimeters (4 in) long, 5 centimeters (2 in) high, and 3 centimeters (1.2 in) wide. The outer shell surface (periostracum) is dark brown to black, and the inner shell surface (nacre) is white.

Like members of the family Unionidae, the pearlshell is a filter feeder and takes nourishment by siphoning water. The female also takes in male sperm during the siphoning process. Freshwater mussels produce larvae that attach themselves to the gills of fish hosts during early development stages. The fish host for the pearlshell is not known. For a general discussion of the life cycle of freshwater mussels see the species account of the birdwing pearly mussel (*Conradilla caelata*).

Habitat

Louisiana pearlshells can be found in very shallow, clear-flowing streams with gravel and sand substrate. Water depths range from 30 to 60 centimeters (12 to 20 in). Vegetation in the surrounding watershed is mostly mixed hardwood-loblolly pine forest.

Historic Range

This species is thought to have ranged throughout most of the headwater streams of Bayou Boeuf in Rapides Parish, Louisiana.

Current Distribution

In 1983 biologists from the Louisiana Natural Heritage Program, after an extensive search, found the pearlshell in 11 streams.

The total population was estimated at 10,000 individuals, about 90 percent of which inhabited four streams—Long Branch, Bayou Clear, Loving Creek, and Little Loving Creek. Most of pearlshell's range is within the Kisatchie National Forest, administered by the Forest Service. Other parcels are owned by the Air Force. Only a small portion of the watershed is privately owned.

Conservation and Recovery

The pearlshell's range has been reduced by dam construction, stream diversion, and generally degraded water quality. Logging operations in Rapides Parish have included clear-cutting up to stream banks, which has increased erosion and runoff. Freshwater mussels are especially vulnerable to siltation because their feeding siphons are easily clogged. A large population was lost in the early 1980s to natural processes, when beavers constructed a dam that flooded a section of stream habitat.

The Louisiana pearlshell, one of the rarest members of its family, has been avidly sought by both amateur and scientific collectors. As this mussel is already very limited in numbers, any collection can have an adverse affect.

Because this mussel occurs within a national forest and on land administered by the Air Force, the Forest Service and the Air Force are required to formally consult with the Fish and Wildlife Service concerning any proposed actions that would potentially harm the pearlshell or its habitat.

Bibliography

Athearn, H. D. 1970. "Discussion of Dr. Heard's Paper (Eastern Freshwater Mollusks, the South Atlantic and Gulf Drainages)." *Malacologia* 20(1):1-56.

Johnson, R. E. 1983. "*Margaritifera marrianae*, A New Species of Unionacea (Bivalvia: Margaritiferidae) From Mobile-Alabama-Coosa and Escambia River Systems, Alabama." *Occasional Papers on Molusks, Museum of Comparative Zoology, Harvard University* 4(62):299-304.

Contact

Regional Office of Endangered Species
U.S. Fish and Wildlife Service
Richard B. Russell Federal Building
75 Spring Street, S.W.
Atlanta, Georgia 30303

Little-Wing Pearly Mussel
Pegias fabula

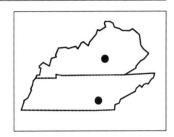

A. E. Spreitzer/OSU Museum of Zoology

Status . . . . . Endangered
Listed . . . . . November 14, 1988
Family . . . . . Unionidae (Freshwater Mussel)
Description . . . Light green or dark yellowish brown shell with dark rays and a chalky, eroded patina.
Habitat . . . . . Cool, swift-flowing streams; transitional zones between riffles and pools.
Threats . . . . . Degradation of water quality, siltation, coal exploration.
Region 4 . . . . Kentucky, Tennessee
Region 5 . . . . Virginia

Description

The little-wing pearly mussel does not exceed 3.8 centimeters (1.5 in) in length and 1.3 centimeters (0.5 in) in width. The shell is light green or dark yellowish brown with variable dark rays along the anterior portion. The shell surface often has an eroded chalky or ashy white patina.

For a general discussion of the life cycle of freshwater mussels see the species account of the birdwing pearly mussel (*Conradilla caelata*).

Habitat

This species is restricted to cool, high-to-moderate gradient streams, and is usually found only in the narrow zone where riffle flow deepens into pools. The species is highly sensitive to alterations of current.

Historic Range

At one time, this Cumberlandian mussel was widely distributed in at least 27 of the smaller, cool-water tributaries of the Tennessee and Cumberland Rivers. The species apparently has been extirpated from Alabama and North Carolina. Three populations in Kentucky, nine in Tennessee, and six in Virginia are believed to have died out.

Current Distribution

This species is currently found in Kentucky, Tennessee, and Virginia. A 1986 survey of 55 potential and historic habitats located only 17 live specimens. Four of six known populations are threatened by activities associated with exploration for coal.

After an exhaustive search of 16 kilometers (10 mi) of Horse Lick Creek (Jackson and Rockcastle counties), Kentucky, only seven live little-wing pearly mussels were found, and this is considered the healthiest surviving population. A recent study reported a small population from a 3.2-kilometer (2-mi) stretch of the Big South Fork Cumberland River (McCreary County), Kentucky. Three live and 126 recently dead specimens were found in 16 kilometers (10 mi) of the Little South Fork Cumberland River (McCreary and Wayne counties), Kentucky. This locality has experienced a recent deterioration of water quality.

Four live specimens were taken from Cane Creek above Great Falls Lake (Van Buren County), Tennessee, where suitable habitat is limited by downstream siltation. Three live mussels were found in the North Fork Holston River (Smyth County), Virginia— one near Saltville, the others at Nebo.

Conservation and Recovery

Always relatively uncommon because of its more specialized habitat requirements, the little-wing pearly mussel has declined throughout its range because of degradation of water quality. Wastes from coal mining and industrial sites have made many former population sites uninhabitable. Runoff from strip mining, coal washing, and agriculture has clouded waters that were once crystal clear and smothered mussel beds beneath layers of sediment. Toxic chemical releases were apparently responsible for the demise of several mussel populations.

Part of the mussel's Kentucky watershed lies within the Daniel Boone National Forest, and Horse Lick Creek has been identified as one of Kentucky's Outstanding Resource Waters. State and federal biologists are cooperating to rejuvenate populations at these protected sites. Ongoing exploration for new coal reserves in the region threatens to degrade the water quality of the remaining habitat.

State laws in Kentucky, Tennessee, and Virginia prohibit the collection of freshwater mussels without a permit.

Bibliography

Ahlstedt, S. A. 1986. "A Status Survey of the Little-Wing Pearly Mussel." Report, Contract No. 14-16-0004-84-927. U.S. Fish and Wildlife Service, Atlanta.

Biggins, R. G. 1989. "Technical/Agency Draft Recovery Plan for Little-Wing Pearly Mussell." U.S. Fish and Wildlife Service, Asheville, North Carolina.

Soulé, M. E. 1980. "Thresholds for Survival: Maintaining Fitness and Evolutionary Potential." In M. E. Soulé and B. A. Wilcox, eds., *Conservation Biology*. Sinauer Associates, Sunderland, Massachusetts.

Stansbery, D. H. 1976. "Status of Endangered Fluviatile Mollusks in Central North America: *Pegias fabula*." Report, Contract No. 14-166-0008-755. U.S. Fish and Wildlife Service, Asheville.

Contact

Regional Office of Endangered Species
U.S. Fish and Wildlife Service
Richard B. Russell Federal Building
75 Spring Street, S.W.
Atlanta, Georgia 30303

White Wartyback Pearly Mussel

Plethobasus cicatricosus

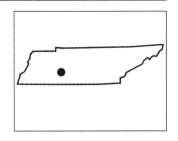

A. E. Spreitzer/OSU Museum of Zoology

Status . . . . . Endangered (possibly extinct)
Listed . . . . . . June 14, 1976
Family . . . . . . Unionidae (Freshwater Mussel)
Description . . . Thick, egg-shaped, greenish yellow or yellow brown shell.
Habitat . . . . . . Sand or gravel substrate in flowing water.
Threats . . . . . . Habitat loss, pollution, siltation.
Region 4 . . . . . Alabama, Tennessee

Description

The shell of the white wartyback pearly mussel is somewhat egg-shaped, thick, solid, and inflated. The greenish yellow or yellow-brown shell surface is marked by uneven, concentric growth lines and a row of knobs (tubercles) in the middle portion of the shell. The iridescent inner shell surface is white. Individuals can live as long as 50 years. The white wartyback has sometimes been confused with a closely related species, *Plethobasus cyphyus.*

For a general discussion of the life cycle of freshwater mussels see the species account of the birdwing pearly mussel (*Conradilla caelata*).

Habitat

The white wartyback mussel buries itself in sand and gravel substrates in shallow stretches of larger rivers where currents are slow to moderate.

Historic Range

This mussel was first collected in 1829 from the Wabash River in Indiana, and is thought to have enjoyed a widespread distribution in the Ohioan or Interior Basin. It was documented from the Kanawha River (West Virginia), the Ohio River (Ohio and Indiana), the Cumberland and Holston rivers (Tennessee), and the Tennessee River below Wilson Dam (Alabama).

Current Distribution

Since the mid-1960s only two Tennessee River specimens have been discovered, both near Savannah, Tennessee, below the Pickwick Dam. The species may be extinct or near extinction in the Tennessee River. No live specimens have been taken from the Cumberland River since 1885. In spite of extensive surveys, there is no recent evidence of this species in the Ohio, Wabash, or Kanawha rivers.

Conservation and Recovery

The white wartyback pearly mussel was historically found only in large rivers and was never very common. Possibly the single greatest factor in this mussel's decline has been the alteration of the Tennessee and Cumberland river basins by the construction of major dams for flood control, hydroelectric power production, and navigation. Dam reservoirs have inundated large stretches of river that once supported mussel populations, while sections of former habitat below the dams have been rendered uninhabitable by erratic water levels, altered water temperatures, and seasonal oxygen deficits.

In addition to numerous locks and dams, the historic conditions of the Wabash and Ohio Rivers have been significantly altered by deforestation and poor agricultural practices that have increased water turbidity and siltation. Water quality has been further degraded by chemical runoff, industrial effluents, and sewage.

Unless a viable reproducing population is found, little in the way of recovery can be considered. The white wartyback pearly mussel may benefit from more general efforts aimed at improving the environmental

quality of the Interior Basin's major rivers. The Tennessee Valley Authority is currently working on a comprehensive water management plan, which would guarantee constant minimum flows in all rivers in the Tennessee and Cumberland basins by timing water discharges from its dams. Such an effort might mollify many of the negative effects of dams and reservoirs on remaining stretches of mussel habitat.

Although unfortunate from the standpoint of local residents, economic slowdown—the closing of steel mills and other major industrial polluters in the region of the Ohio River's headwaters—has resulted in almost immediate improvement in water quality in the upper river. Recently, freshwater mussels have been rediscovered in stretches of the river where they have been absent for more than 70 years.

Bibliography

Bogan, A., and P. Parmalee. 1983. *"Tennessee's Rare Mollusks."* In *Tennessee's Rare Wildlife, Final Report.* Tennessee Heritage Program of the Department of Conservation and the University of Tennessee, Knoxville.

Isom, B. G. 1969. "The Mussel Resources of the Tennessee River." *Malacologia* 7(2-3):397-425.

Jenkinson, J.J. 1981. "The Tennessee Valley Authority Cumberlandian Mollusk Conservation Program." *Bulletin of the American Malacological Union* 1980:662-63.

U.S. Fish and Wildlife Service. 1984. "Recovery Plan for the White Wartyback Pearly Mussel (*Plethobasus cicatricosus*)." U.S. Fish and Wildlife Service, Atlanta.

Contact

Regional Office of Endangered Species
U.S. Fish and Wildlife Service
Richard B. Russell Federal Building
75 Spring Street, S.W.
Atlanta, Georgia 30303

Orange-Footed Pearly Mussel
Plethobasus cooperianus

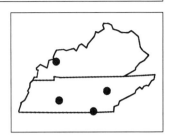

A. E. Spreitzer/OSU Museum of Zoology

Status	Endangered
Listed	June 14, 1976
Family	Unionidae (Freshwater Mussel)
Description . . .	Large, nearly circular, yellowish to chestnut brown shell.
Habitat	Medium to large rivers in gravel and rubble substrates.
Threats	Dam construction, siltation, pollution.
Region 3	Illinois
Region 4	Alabama, Kentucky, Tennessee

Description

Also known as the pimple-back pearly mussel, the orange-footed pearly mussel is nearly circular, attains a mature shell length of up to 9.5 centimeters (3.7 in), and a thickness of 4.6 centimeters (18 in). Valves are solid and moderately swollen. The shell surface is yellowish brown to chestnut brown and is marked by dark, concentric, irregular growth lines. The posterior two-thirds of the shell is covered with numerous raised knobs (turbercles). Greenish rays are found only in younger specimens. The inner shell surface (nacre) varies in color from white to pink.

The orange-footed pearly mussel is probably a "tachytictic bivalve," or short term breeder, which breeds in spring and releases glochidia by late summer. Individuals can live as long as 50 years. For a general discus-sion of the life cycle of freshwater mussels see the species account of the birdwing pearly mussel (*Conradilla caelata*).

Habitat

The orange-footed pearly mussel is found in medium to large rivers in depths of 3.6 to 8.8 meters (12 to 29 ft). It buries itself into sand and gravel with only the margin of the shell and feeding siphons exposed to the water.

Historic Range

The orange-footed pearly mussel is an Interior Basin species with distribution in the Ohio, Cumberland, and Tennessee River drainages. This species was locally abundant in the Ohio River between St. Marys (West Virginia) and Marietta (Ohio) and around the confluence of the Wabash River (Indiana). In the lower Ohio River, it was found between the Cumberland and Tennessee rivers and the Mississippi River (Illinois). It was locally abundant in the Wabash River (Indiana) and common to rare in the mainstream of the Cumberland River (Tennessee). It has been documented in the Rough River (Kentucky), the Duck, French Broad, Holston, and Clinch rivers (Tennessee), and the Kanawha River (West Virginia).

Current Distribution

The orange-footed pearly mussel has been extirpated from the Kanawha, upper Ohio, and Wabash rivers, and its range elsewhere has been greatly reduced.

In the Tennessee River, orange-footed pearly mussels have been found below the Fort Loudoun Dam (Loudon County, Tennessee), Guntersville Dam (Marshall County, Alabama), and several clustered sites below Pickwick Dam (Hardin County, Tennessee).

The mussel survives in the Cumberland River only below Cordell Hull Dam (Smith County, Tennessee). Other populations survive in the lower Ohio River between Metropolis and Mound City (Massac and Pulaski counties, Illinois).

Conservation and Recovery

Because it occurred in small numbers in localized beds, the orange-footed pearly mussel has always been somewhat rare. Possibly the single greatest factor in this mussel's decline has been the alteration of the Tennessee and Cumberland river basins by the construction of dams for flood control, hydroelectric power production, navigation, and recreation. Dam reservoirs have inundated stretches of river that once supported mussel populations, while sections of former

habitat below the dams have been rendered uninhabitable by erratic water levels.

In addition to numerous locks and dams, the historic conditions of the Wabash and Ohio Rivers have been altered by deforestation and poor agricultural practices, which increased water turbidity and siltation. Water quality has been further degraded by chemical runoff, industrial effluents, and sewage.

The recovery of this species will depend upon the success of larger efforts to reclaim river habitat throughout the Interior Basin. The Tennessee Valley Authority is currently working on a comprehensive water management plan, which would guarantee constant minimum flows in all rivers in the Tennessee and Cumberland basins by timing water discharges from its dams. Such an effort might mollify many of the negative effects of dams and reservoirs on remaining mussel habitat. In recent years, the water quality of the upper Ohio River has improved. If this improvement continues the orange-footed pearly mussel may be reintroduced to its historic range above Marietta, Ohio.

Bibliography

Clark, C. F. 1976. "The Freshwater Naiads of the Lower End of the Wabash River, Mt. Carmal, Illinois, to the South." *Sterkiana* 61:1-14.

U.S. Fish and Wildlife Service. 1984. "Recovery Plan for the Orange-Footed Pearly Mussel." U.S. Fish and Wildlife Service, Asheville, North Carolina.

Contact

Regional Office of Endangered Species
U.S. Fish and Wildlife Service
Richard B. Russell Federal Building
75 Spring Street, S.W.
Atlanta, Georgia 30303

James River Spinymussel

Pleurobema collina

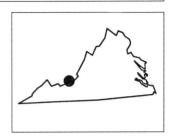

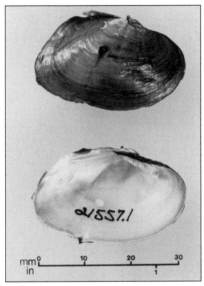

A. E. Spreitzer/OSU Museum of Zoology

Status . . . . . . Endangered
Listed . . . . . . July 22, 1988
Family . . . . . Unionidae (Freshwater Mussel)
Description . . . Medium-sized spinymussel;
1 to 3 prominent spines on
each valve of juveniles.
Habitat . . . . . . Slow-flowing stretches of
headwater streams.
Threats . . . . . . Habitat modification, com-
petition with the Asiatic clam.
Region 5 . . . . . Virginia, West Virginia

Description

Also known as the Virginia spinymussel or James spinymussel, the James River spinymussel is described as having an intermediate shell size (5 to 9 cm; 2 to 3.5 in) and spine length. Shells of juvenile mussels usually bear one to three short but prominent spines on each valve. Adult shells typically lack the spines. The foot and mantle of the adult are strongly orange; the mantle is darkened in a narrow band around edges of the branchial and anal openings. Scientists have variously classified this species as *Fusconaia collina*, *Elliptio collina*, and *Cantheria collina*.

Only two other freshwater spinymussels are known—*Elliptio spinosa* from the Altamaha River in Georgia, and the Tar River spinymussel (*Elliptio steinstansana*) from the

Tar River in North Carolina. The Tar River spinymussel was listed as Endangered in 1985.

For a general discussion of the life cycle of freshwater mussels see the species account of the birdwing pearly mussel (*Conradilla caelata*).

Habitat

The James River spinymussel requires freshwater streams with high water quality and a fairly high mineral content. It has been collected from sand and gravel substrates, generally in slow-moving water.

Historic Range

The James River spinymussel was first discovered in the Calfpasture River (Rockbridge

County), Virginia, in 1836. It was once widely distributed in the James River drainage, which includes the Rivanna River, Mill Creek, the Calfpasture River, Johns Creek, and numerous headwater creeks. The range of this species has been reduced to less than 10 percent of its historic size.

Current Distribution

Currently, the James River spinymussel survives in a few headwater streams of the James River—Craig, Catawba, and Johns creeks (Craig and Botetourt counties, Virginia), and Potts Creek (Monroe County, West Virginia).

Conservation and Recovery

Habitat modification has been a major factor in the decline of this spinymussel. The few drainages that still support the species are threatened by harmful agricultural runoff of silt, fertilizers, and herbicides. It is hoped that federal control over issuance of permits for mineral exploration, timber sales, recreational development, stream channelization, and bridge construction and maintenance can be used to prevent further disturbance of the watershed.

The Asiatic clam (*Corbicula fluminea*) has invaded many formerly inhabited streams. This clam establishes very dense populations which filter most of the phytoplankton from the water—in essence, starving the spiny and other native mussels. Survival of the James River spinymussel will probably require a program to control Asiatic clam populations.

Bibliography

Burch, J. B. 1975. *Freshwater Unionacean Clams of North America*. Malacological Publications, Hamburg, Michigan.

Diaz, R. J. 1974. "Asiatic Clam *Corbicula manilensis* in the Tidal James River, Virginia." *Chesapeake Science* 15(2):118-120.

Zeto, M. A., and J. E. Schmidt. 1984. "Freshwater Mussels of Monroe County, West Virginia." *Nautilus* 96(4):147-151.

Contact

Regional Office of Endangered Species
U.S. Fish and Wildlife Service
One Gateway Center, Suite 700
Newton Corner, Massachusetts 02158

Curtus' Mussel

Pleurobema curtum

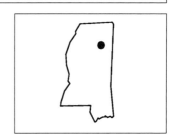

A. E. Spreitzer/OSU Museum of Zoology

Status	Endangered
Listed	April 7, 1987
Family	Unionidae (Freshwater Mussel)
Description . . .	Greenish brown, subtriangular shell.
Habitat	Sand and gravel substrate in flowing rivers.
Threats	Low numbers, restricted range, dredging, siltation.
Region 4	Alabama, Mississippi

Description

The shell of Curtus' mussel is about 5 centimeters (2 in) long and varies in color from light green in young mussels to a dark greenish brown in older ones. The shell is subtriangular and inflated in front. The thin inner shell surface is an iridescent bluish white. This species was first classified as *Unio curtus*.

The identity of species within the genus *Pleurobema* is currently the focus of debate among malacologists. The Fish and Wildlife Service (FWS) has adopted the majority view but acknowledges that further research may warrant reclassification of Curtus' and other mussels of the genus.

For a general discussion of the life cycle of freshwater mussels see the species account of the birdwing pearly mussel (*Conradilla caelata*).

Habitat

Curtus' mussel is found in clean, swift-flowing rivers where the bottom is formed of firm rubble, gravel, or sand. This mussel prefers shallow riffles and shoals, where the current is strong enough to keep the bottom scoured of silt.

Historic Range

Curtus' mussel has been found in the East Fork and mainstream of the Tombigbee River, and has been collected from only five locations. Reports of this species from the Big

Black River in Mississippi are probably erroneous.

Current Distribution

Curtus' mussel is thought to survive in an unmodified segment of the East Fork Tombigbee River (Itawamba and Monroe counties), Mississippi. Only two living specimens have been found since 1974. An extensive survey of the river conducted in 1987 failed to turn up any living or recently dead specimens. The FWS believes that Curtus' mussel survives, but its population is critically low.

Conservation and Recovery

When the Tennessee-Tombigbee Waterway was constructed to allow barge traffic between the Tennessee and Tombigbee rivers, most of the East Fork Tombigbee River was modified into a series of channels, locks, and impounds. The dams and locks inundated mussel shoals and slowed the flow of water, increasing siltation, which smothers mussel beds. Dredging to create a navigable channel physically destroyed many mussel beds, and periodic maintenance dredging continues to disturb the river bottom. Bull Mountain Creek, which provided nearly half the water supply of the East Fork, was diverted to feed the waterway. The creek's cooler waters are warmed when routed through the canal, making this part of the river inimical to both mussels and host fishes.

The last free-flowing stretch of the East Fork Tombigbee River is threatened by plans to dredge 85 kilometers (53 mi) to improve navigability. Siltation in this portion of the river has become more severe in the last few years and may already be smothering the surviving mussel beds.

Under provisions of the Endangered Species Act, federal agencies are required to consult with the FWS to ensure that any actions they authorize or fund do not jeopardize an Endangered species. This rule affects current and proposed flood control and navigation projects sponsored by the Army Corps of Engineers and watershed projects proposed by the Soil Conservation Service of the Department of Agriculture. In the past, similar consultations have resulted in the redesign of projects to preserve significant portions of habitat.

Recovery of Curtus' mussel would require construction of sediment basins and selective dredging to limit siltation.

Bibliography

Schultz, C. A. 1981. ''North Mississippi Fisheries Investigation: Tombigbee Basin Preimpoundment Studies.'' Report No. 18. Mississippi Department of Wildlife Conservation, Bureau of Fisheries and Wildlife, Jackson.

Stansbery, D. H. 1976. ''Naiade Mollusks.'' In H. Boschung, ed., ''Endangered and Threatened Plants and Animals in Alabama.'' *Bulletin of the Alabama Museum of Natural History*, No. 2.

Stansbery, D. H. 1983. ''The Status of *Pleurobema curtum*.'' Unpublished Report. U.S. Fish and Wildlife Service, Atlanta.

Contact

Regional Office of Endangered Species
U.S. Fish and Wildlife Service
Richard B. Russell Federal Building
75 Spring Street, S.W.
Atlanta, Georgia 30303

Marshall's Mussel

Pleurobema marshalli

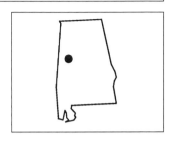

A. E. Spreitzer/OSU Museum of Zoology

Status	. . . . . . Endangered
Listed	. . . . . . April 7, 1987
Family	. . . . . . Unionidae (Freshwater Mussel)
Description	. . . Oval or elliptical, dark brown shell with a shallow cavity.
Habitat	. . . . . . Gravel and sand substrate in flowing water.
Threats	. . . . . . Restricted distribution, dam construction, siltation.
Region 4	. . . . . Alabama, Mississippi

Description

The oval or obliquely elliptical shell of Marshall's mussel is about 6 centimeters (2.4 in) long, 5 centimeters (2 in) high, and 3 centimeters (1.2 in) thick. It has a shallow cavity and very low pustules or welts on the post-ventral surface. Older shells are a dark brown with irregular concentric black growth lines. The thin, inner shell surface (nacre) is bluish white.

The identity of species within the genus *Pleurobema* is currently the focus of debate among malacologists. The Fish and Wildlife Service (FWS) has adopted the majority view but acknowledges that further research may warrant reclassification of Marshall's and other mussels of the genus.

For a general discussion of the life cycle of freshwater mussels see the species account of the birdwing pearly mussel (Conradilla caelata).

Habitat

Marshall's mussel is found in clean, fast-flowing water in relatively shallow stretches where the bottom is composed of firm rubble, gravel, or sand, swept free of silt.

Historic Range

This mussel was known from the mainstream of the Tombigbee River from Tibbee Creek near Columbus (Lowndes County), Mississippi, downstream to Epes (Sumter County), Alabama, above the confluence of Noxubee River. The absence of specimens from anywhere except the Tombigbee River suggests that this species was historically restricted to this single stretch of river.

Current Distribution

This mussel was collected alive in Sumter and Pickens counties, Alabama, in 1972. The Pickens County site and former sites in Mississippi have suffered from heavy sedimentation since that time and are no longer considered viable habitat. The only remaining viable habitat for this species in the Tombigbee River is a gravel bar in the Gainesville Bendway in Sumter County, Alabama. The bendway is a remnant of the old river bed that was bypassed when a navigable channel was constructed.

Conservation and Recovery

Low numbers and very restricted occurrence make Marshall's mussel one of the most immediately endangered of the freshwater mussels. Completion of the Gainesville Dam and other structures of the Tennessee-Tombigbee Waterway effectively eliminated much of the historic habitat of Marshall's mussel except for the gravel bars in the Gainesville Bendway. A 1987 survey conducted in the bendway documented extensive siltation and found only a few common mussel species. Few of the more uncommon varieties were found. A recently completed dam on Bull Mountain Creek, the source of most of the water for the East Fork Tombigbee River, slowed currents and reduced water flow throughout the system, causing the sedimentation. Current conditions of the river have caused a decline of common fish hosts.

Freshwater mussels in the Tombigbee Basin have also suffered from runoff of fertilizers and pesticides, resulting in algal blooms and excesses of aquatic vegetation that are fatal to mussels and fish hosts.

Addition of this mussel to the federal list, provides the FWS with influence over the design and implementation of future projects on the waterway. Under provisions of the Endangered Species Act, federal agencies are required to consult with the FWS to ensure that any actions they authorize or fund do not jeopardize federally listed species. This rule will affect projects sponsored by the Army Corps of Engineers and the Soil Conservation Service of the Department of Agriculture. In the past, similar consultations have resulted in the redesign of projects to preserve significant portions of habitat.

Because the condition of the Gainesville Bendway has deteriorated so abruptly, the FWS may be forced to attempt an emergency relocation of mussel populations, if other suitable habitat can be found. There is some question whether enough of the mussels survive to justify such a drastic measure or whether the relocation attempt would, in itself, result in extinction for Marshall's mussel.

Bibliography

U.S. Army Corps of Engineers. 1981. "Water Resources Development in Alabama." Report. Mobile District Office, Mobile, Alabama.

U.S. Department of Agriculture. 1983. "Soil Conservation Service Watershed Progress Report—Mississippi." U.S. Department of Agriculture, Washington, D.C.

Stansbery, D. H. 1983. "The Status of *Pleurobema marshalli*." Unpublished Report. U.S. Fish and Wildlife Service, Atlanta.

Contact

Regional Office of Endangered Species
U.S. Fish and Wildlife Service
Richard B. Russell Federal Building .
75 Spring Street, S.W.
Atlanta, Georgia 30303

Rough Pigtoe Pearly Mussel

Pleurobema plenum

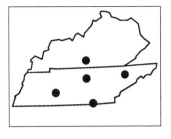

A. E. Spreitzer/OSU Museum of Zoology

Status	Endangered
Listed	June 14, 1976
Family	Unionidae (Freshwater Mussel)
Description	Triangular, yellowish to reddish brown shell with heavy, inflated valves.
Habitat	River shoals.
Threats	Habitat reduction, siltation, pollution.
Region 4	Alabama, Kentucky, Tennessee

Description

The shell of the rough pigtoe pearly mussel is somewhat triangular in outline with mature dimensions of 6.5 centimeters (2.6 in) long, 7.1 (2.8 in) centimeters high, and 4.3 centimeters (1.7 in) wide. The inflated valves are solid and heavy. The shell surface is marked by irregular, concentric growth marks and has a cloth-like texture. It is a slightly glossy, yellowish to reddish brown. The inner shell surface (nacre) varies in color from white to pinkish, reddish, or orange.

The family Unionidae is separated into two groups based on the length of time glochidia (larvae) remain in the female. The rough pigtoe pearly mussel is probably "tachytictic," a short-term breeder, which breeds in spring and releases glochidia by late summer of the same year. Long-term breeders hold developing glochidia in a brood pouch over winter and release them in spring. The fish hosts for this species are thought to include the rosefin shiner and possibly the bluegill.

For a general discussion of the life cycle of freshwater mussels see the species account of the birdwing pearly mussel (*Conradilla caelata*).

Habitat

The rough pigtoe is a big-river shoal species, which is found in deeper waters in streams 20 meters (66 ft) wide or wider. It buries itself in the gravel or sandy bottom with only the posterior margin of the shell and siphons exposed to the water.

Historic Range

First discovered in the Ohio River near Cincinnati in 1840, this mussel was subsequently documented from four major regions—the Cumberland and Tennessee River basins (Virginia, Tennessee, Alabama, and Kentucky), the Ohio River drainage (Ohio, Indiana, and Illinois), the Ozarks (Kansas, Missouri, and Arkansas), and the mainstream Mississippi River (Arkansas).

Current Distribution

The rough pigtoe is currently known from near the confluence of the Green and Barren rivers (Warren County, Kentucky), a river system that empties into the Ohio River near Evansville, Indiana. It survives in the Clinch River near Kyles Ford (Hancock County), Tennessee, and in the Tennessee River below Guntersville Dam (Marshall County, Alabama), Wilson Dam (Lauderdale County, Alabama), and Pickwick Dam (Hardin County, Tennessee). There are no current population estimates.

Conservation and Recovery

The reasons for the decline of the rough pigtoe are not fully understood, but the longevity of most mussel species—up to 50 years—and their sedentary nature make them especially vulnerable to habitat alterations caused by dam construction, dredging, siltation, and pollution. Since the early 1930s and 1940s, the Tennessee Valley Authority, the Army Corps of Engineers, Aluminum Company of America, and other water authorities have constructed more than 50 dams in the Tennessee and Cumberland watersheds alone. The Ohio River has been extensively modified by a series of dams and locks along its length. Heavy siltation, caused by poor agricultural practices, has rendered large portions of this mussel's historic habitat unsuitable. Agricultural chemicals and industrial wastes have generally degraded the water quality of major rivers, such as the Ohio, Missouri, and Mississippi.

The states of Tennessee and Alabama have designated portions of the Tennessee and Cumberland Rivers as freshwater mussel sanctuaries; however, the headwaters originate in Virginia, where pollutants introduced by strip mining and coal washing have affected these rivers throughout the drainage. The recovery of this species will depend upon the success of regional efforts to improve water quality. The Tennessee Valley Authority (TVA), which administers the operation of dams on the Tennessee and Cumberland rivers, is currently developing a comprehensive water management plan. This plan would guarantee constant minimum flows in all rivers in the region by timing water discharges from TVA dams. Such an effort might mollify many of the negative effects of dams and reservoirs on remaining stretches of mussel habitat.

Bibliography

Bates, J. M., and S. D. Dennis. 1978. "The Mussel Fauna of the Clinch River, Tennessee and Virginia." *Sterkiana* 69-70:3-23.

Isom, B. G. 1974. "Mussels of the Green River, Kentucky." *Proceedings of the Kentucky Academy of Science* 35(1-2):55-57.

U.S. Fish and Wildlife Service. 1984. "Rough Pigtoe Pearly Mussel Recovery Plan." U.S. Fish and Wildlife Service, Atlanta.

Contact

Regional Office of Endangered Species
U.S. Fish and Wildlife Service
Richard B. Russell Federal Building
75 Spring Street, S.W.
Atlanta, Georgia 30303

Judge Tait's Mussel

Pleurobema taitianum

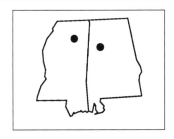

A. E. Spreitzer/OSU Museum of Zoology

Status	Endangered
Listed	April 7, 1987
Family	Unionidae (Freshwater Mussel)
Description	Brownish black triangular shell with narrow, pointed beaks.
Habitat	River shoals.
Threats	Navigation and flood control projects, siltation, water diversion.
Region 4	Alabama, Mississippi

Description

Judge Tait's mussel is a bivalve mollusk about 5 centimeters (2 in) long, 4.5 centimeters (1.8 in) high, and 3 centimeters (1.2 in) wide. The obliquely triangular shell is brown to brownish black. The shell beaks are narrowly pointed forward with shallow cavities. The inner shell surface (nacre) is pinkish white.

The identity of species within the genus *Pleurobema* is currently the focus of debate among malacologists. The Fish and Wildlife Service (FWS) has adopted the majority view but acknowledges that further research may warrant reclassification of Curtus' and other mussels of the genus. For a general discussion of the life cycle of freshwater mussels see the species account of the birdwing pearly mussel (*Conradilla caelata*).

Habitat

This mussel prefers clear, fast-flowing water in shallow reaches where the bottom is composed of relatively firm rubble, gravel, or sand. The current must be strong enough to scour the bottom of silt. Free-flowing, shallow riffles and shoals are increasingly rare due to extensive modification of the river channels.

Historic Range

Judge Tait's mussel has been found in the Tombigbee River from the mouth of Tibbee Creek near Columbus, Mississippi, downstream to Demopolis, Alabama. Other populations were found far downstream in the Alabama River at Claiborne and Selma, in the lower Cahaba River, and possibly the

Coosa River. In the early 1980s, several shells were found at one site on the Buttahatchie River, a Mississippi tributary of the Tombigbee River. This species has also been reported from the East Fork Tombigbee and Sipsey rivers in Alabama.

Current Distribution

Only four portions of suitable habitat remain for the Judge Tait's mussel: the Gainesville Bendway of the Tombigbee River (Sumter County, Alabama); the Sipsey River (Pickens and Greene counties, Alabama); and the East Fork Tombigbee and Buttahatchie rivers (Mississippi). A 1987 survey of the Gainesville Bendway documented extensive siltation caused by decreased water flows. No specimens of Judge Tait's were found during this survey. This mussel was last collected from the East Fork Tombigbee River in 1972, but much of the habitat along the Tombigbee River has since been altered by the construction of the Tennessee-Tombigbee Waterway, a navigable canal built to connect the Tennessee and Tombigbee rivers.

Conservation and Recovery

Habitat for Judge Tait's mussel on segments of the Buttahatchie and the Sipsey rivers is considered marginal, and remaining mussels must cope with the siltation, reduced water flows, water quality degradation, and decline of fish hosts needed for larval development. These habitat alterations were induced by large-scale flood control and navigation projects.

Several current and proposed water control projects threaten to eliminate this mussel's habitat altogether—a 95-kilometer (59-mi) channel improvement project in the Buttahatchie, an 85-kilometer (53-mi) clearing and snagging project in the East Fork Tom-

bigbee, and a 136-kilometer (84-mi) channel improvement project in the Sipsey River. These projects are directed by the Army Corps of Engineers or by the Soil Conservation Service of the Department of Agriculture.

The Endangered status of Judge Tait's mussel provides the Fish and Wildlife Service (FWS) with some control over these and other proposed projects that would damage or destroy remaining habitat. Under provisions of the Endangered Species Act, federal agencies are required to consult with the FWS to ensure that any actions they authorize or fund do not jeopardize federally protected wildlife. In the past, similar consultations have resulted in the redesign of projects to preserve significant portions of habitat.

Bibliography

Fuller, S. L. H. 1974. "Clams and Mussels (Mollusca: Bivalvia)." In C. Hart, Jr., and S. Fuller, eds., *Pollution Ecology of Freshwater Invertebrates*. Academic Press, New York.

Stansbery, D. H. 1983. "Status of *Pleurobema taitianum*." Unpublished Report. U.S. Fish and Wildlife Service, Atlanta.

Contact

Regional Office of Endangered Species
U.S. Fish and Wildlife Service
Richard B. Russell Federal Building
75 Spring Street, S.W.
Atlanta, Georgia 30303

Fat Pocketbook Pearly Mussel

Potamilus capax

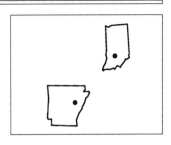

A. E. Spreitzer/OSU Museum of Zoology

Status . . . . . . Endangered
Listed . . . . . . June 14, 1976
Family . . . . . . Unionidae (Freshwater Mussel)
Description . . . Shiny yellow to brown shell with a strong S-curved hinge line.
Habitat . . . . . . Flowing water in sand, mud, and gravel substrates.
Threats . . . . . . Dams, siltation, pollution.
Region 3 . . . . . Indiana
Region 4 . . . . . Arkansas

Description

The fat pocketbook pearly mussel has a smooth, shiny yellow to brown shell that lacks rays or other distinctive markings. The nearly spherical shell averages 10 centimeters (4 in) in length. The strong S-curve of its hinge differentiates fat pocketbook from similar bivalves. The beautifully iridescent inner shell surface (nacre) is bluish white. This species has also been classified as *Proptera capax*.

For a general discussion of the life cycle of freshwater mussels see the species account of the birdwing pearly mussel (*Conradilla caelata*).

Habitat

The fat pocketbook has been found in the sand, mud, or gravel bottoms of flowing streams and rivers in stretches less than 2.5 meters (8 ft) deep.

Historic Range

This species has been documented in the Wabash River (Indiana) and the Ohio River (Illinois). It was reported from the upper and lower Illinois River (Illinois), and from discrete populations in the mainstream of the Mississippi River between Wabasha, Minnesota, and Grafton, Illinois. The fat pocketbook appears to have been eliminated from most of its historic range by dam construction, artificial channeling, dredging, siltation, and agricultural chemical contamination.

The fat pocketbook was subsequently discovered in a Mississippi River tributary in Arkansas. Although geographically widespread, the fat pocketbook never occurred in large concentrations.

Current Distribution

Surveys of the St. Francis River, conducted in 1979 and 1980, discovered a population of the fat pocketbook near the town of Madison (St. Francis County), Arkansas. The stretch above Madison, which consists of a series of shoals and islands, is the only section of the St. Francis River that has not been dredged. A 1986 survey confirmed that the fat pocketbook was the most common mussel in the St. Francis River, numbering over 11,000 postjuveniles.

In 1975 several specimens were found near New Harmony (Posey County), Indiana, in the Wabash River. In 1976 one live and three dead specimens were found in the White River (a tributary of the Wabash) near Bowman (Pike County), Indiana. It is uncertain whether the fat pocketbook survives in this watershed as a viable, reproducing population.

Conservation and Recovery

Major rivers within the fat pocketbook's historic range have been dammed, artificially channeled, and repeatedly dredged for flood control and navigation. Sediment loosened by dredging and topsoil runoff from poor agricultural practices smother mussel beds. Agricultural pesticides, herbicides, and fertilizers are carried into streams in rain runoff, generally degrading water quality.

Seasonal flooding is an acknowledged problem along the St. Francis River, and there is heavy public pressure for continued dredging. The Fish and Wildlife Service Recovery Plan for this species recommends that dredging be prohibited in the stretch of river above Madison, and biologists hope to establish at least two other populations in suitable habitat within the St. Francis watershed. The Army Corps of Engineers has recommended that transplant attempts be made on the White River in Indiana, at two sites on the upper Mississippi River, or in the Hatchie River in Tennessee. Although the Hatchie River is not part of the historic range of this mussel, it supports similar species and is currently protected under the Wild and Scenic Rivers Act. Transplantation outside the fat pocketbook's historic range would require special dispensation under the Endangered Species Act, but it is considered a possible recovery strategy.

Bibliography

Bates, J. M., and S. D. Dennis. 1983. "Mussel (Naiad) Survey—St. Francis, White, and Cache Rivers, Arkansas and Missouri." Report No. DACW66-78-C-0147. U.S. Army Corps of Engineers, Memphis.

Clark, A. H. 1984. "Draft Report Mussel (Naiad) Study; St. Francis and White Rivers; Cross, St. Francis, and Monroe Counties, Arkansas." Report No. 84M 1666R. U.S. Army Corps of Engineers, Memphis.

U.S. Fish and Wildlife Service. 1985. "Fat Pocketbook Pearly Mussel Recovery Plan," U.S. Fish and Wildlife Service, Atlanta.

Contact

Regional Office of Endangered Species
U.S. Fish and Wildlife Service
Richard B. Russell Federal Building
75 Spring Street, S.W.
Atlanta, Georgia 30303

Cumberland Monkeyface Pearly Mussel

Quadrula intermedia

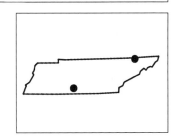

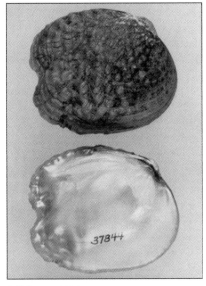

A. E. Spreitzer/OSU Museum of Zoology

Status . . . . . . Endangered
Listed . . . . . . June 14, 1976
Family . . . . . . Unionidae (Freshwater Mussel)
Description . . . Medium-sized, triangular to quadrangular, greenish yellow shell with numerous markings.
Habitat . . . . . . Shallow, fast-flowing water with substrate.
Threats . . . . . . Impoundments, siltation, pollution.
Region 4 . . . . . Alabama, Tennessee
Region 5 . . . . . Virginia

Description

The shell of the Cumberland monkeyface pearly mussel is medium-sized (7 cm; 2.8 in), triangular to quadrangular in outline, and marked with numerous tubercles or knobs. The valves are flat and display a deep beak cavity. The outer shell surface is greenish yellow with green spots, chevrons, or zig-zags, and sometimes broken green rays. The inner shell surface is white, straw-colored, or salmon.

A short-term breeder, this mussel produces glochidia (larvae) in the spring and releases them by mid- to late summer of the same year. The fish hosts for this pearly mussel are unknown.

For a discussion of the life cycle of freshwater mussels see the species account of the birdwing pearly mussel (*Conradilla caelata*).

Habitat

This mussel is typically found in shallow, fast-flowing water with a stable, clean substrate of sand or coarse gravel. It requires highly oxygenated water and, therefore, does not survive in still pools.

Historic Range

The monkeyface pearly mussel was historically restricted to the headwaters of the Tennessee River and probably the upper Cumberland River. It is a Cumberlandian species—endemic to the southern Appalachian Mountains and the Cumberland Plateau. Of the 90 species of freshwater mussels found in the Tennessee River, 37 are Cumberlandian; of 78 species found in the Cumberland River, 27 are considered Cumberlandian. Together, these mussels represent the largest number of freshwater mussel species found in any of the world's rivers.

Current Distribution

The Cumberland monkeyface currently survives in three tributaries of the Tennessee River—the Duck, Elk, and Powell rivers.

The Duck River arises in south-central Tennessee and flows northwest to join the Tennessee River near the town of Waverly. The Cumberland Monkeyface has been collected in a 56-kilometer (35-mi) section of the river east of the city of Columbia in Marshall and Maury counties. Surveys continue to locate live mussels in the shoals downstream from Milltown, including the discovery of one live female in 1988. Although the population in this river is small, it is probably reproducing. This section of river is directly upstream from the proposed site for the new Columbia Dam and would probably be inundated if the dam were completed.

The Elk River arises from the Tims Ford Reservoir south of the sources of the Duck River and flows southwest to join the Tennessee River near the town of Coxey, Alabama. The Cumberland monkeyface has been collected from about 77 kilometers (48 mi) of the Elk River in Lincoln County, Tennessee, near Fayetteville.

The sources of the Powell River are in the Appalachians of southwestern Virginia. The river flows southwest to join the Clinch River at the Norris Reservoir, Tennessee. The Cumberland monkeyface has been collected from a 74-kilometer (46-mi) stretch of the upper Powell in Lee County, Virginia, and Hancock County, Tennessee, and is probably more plentiful in this river than anywhere else within its range.

Conservation and Recovery

This pearly mussel was apparently never abundant, and the reasons for its decline are not fully understood. Impoundments, siltation, and pollution are presumed to be the major causes of decline. The Tennessee Valley Authority (TVA) has constructed 36 dams in the Tennessee River basin. These dams and reservoirs have inundated mussel shoals upstream, disrupted stream flow, and altered downstream habitat with sporadic cold-water discharges. Siltation caused by strip mining and poor agricultural practices often covers the substrates of gravel and sand and smothers mussel beds. Because mussels must siphon gallons of water each day to feed, the effects of water pollutants, such as herbicides and pesticides, are intensified.

Surveys conducted by the TVA in 1988 and 1989 reveal that mussel populations in the Duck River have stabilized. The status of mussel populations in the Elk and Powell rivers has not yet been determined. Sections of the Powell River appear eligible for Scenic River status under the National Wild and Scenic Rivers Act. Such a designation would provide additional protection for the Cumberland monkeyface and its habitat.

If the Columbia Dam is completed, most of the Cumberland monkeyface's habitat in the Duck River would be lost. The dam project is currently stalled by controversy. Whenever the TVA has expressed an opinion that the Columbia Dam should be abandoned, powerful local interests have continued to push for its completion. The TVA is currently working on a comprehensive water management plan, which would time water discharges from its dams so as to guarantee constant minimum flows in the Tennessee and Cumberland basins. Such an effort might mollify many of the negative effects of dams and reservoirs on remaining stretches of mussel habitat.

Bibliography

Dennis, S.D. 1981. "Mussel Fauna of the Powell River, Tennessee and Virginia." *Sterkiana* 71:1-7.

Isom, B. G. and P. Yokley, Jr. 1968. "The Mussel Fauna of Duck River in Tennessee, 1965." *American Midland Naturalist* 80(1):34-42.

U.S. Fish and Wildlife Service. 1982. "Cumberland Monkeyface Pearly Mussel Recovery Plan." U.S. Fish and Wildlife Service, Atlanta.

Contact

Regional Office of Endangered Species
U.S. Fish and Wildlife Service
Richard B. Russell Federal Building
75 Spring Street, S.W.
Atlanta, Georgia 30303

Appalachian Monkeyface Pearly Mussel

Quadrula sparsa

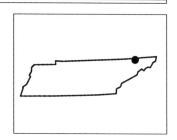

A. E. Spreitzer/OSU Museum of Zoology

Status . . . . . Endangered
Listed . . . . . June 14, 1976
Family . . . . . Unionidae (Freshwater Mussel)
Description . . . Medium-sized quadrangular shell; yellow-green or brown with distinctive markings.
Habitat . . . . . Fast-flowing water in shallow shoals.
Threats . . . . . Impoundments, siltation, pollution.
Region 4 . . . . . Tennessee
Region 5 . . . . . Virginia

Description

The yellow-green or brown shell of the Appalachian monkeyface pearly mussel is medium-sized (7 cm; 2.8 in) and nearly quadrangular in shape. The shell surface is marked with small green zig-zags, triangles, or chevrons and strong, concentric growth rings. This mussel is thought to breed from May to July. Its fish hosts are unknown.

For a general discussion of the life cycle of freshwater mussels see the species account of the birdwing pearly mussel (*Conradilla caelata*).

Habitat

This freshwater Cumberlandian mussel is found most often in clean, shallow river stretches where the bottom is composed of relatively firm rubble, gravel, and sand. Swift currents in these shoals typically sweep the bottom free of silt.

Historic Range

This species was first collected in 1841 from the Holston River in eastern Tennessee and is thought to have been widespread in tributaries of the upper Tennessee and Cumberland river systems.

Current Distribution

The Appalachian monkeyface survives in free-flowing reaches of the Powell and Clinch rivers, two of the larger tributaries of the Tennessee River. It is thought to have been extirpated from the Holston River.

The Powell River arises in the Appalachians of southwestern Virginia and flows southwest to join the Clinch River at the Norris Reservoir in Tennessee. The Appalachian monkeyface has been collected from a 64-kilometer (40-mi) stretch of the upper Powell River in Lee County, Virginia, and Hancock and Claiborne counties, Tennessee. In 1981 freshwater mussel samplings found six live specimens at McDowell Ford and one freshly dead specimen at Fletcher Cliff, both in the Powell River.

The Clinch River also arises in southwestern Virginia and flows generally parallel to the Powell River southwest into the Norris Reservoir. Mussels have been collected recently from only one locality on the river, near Ft. Blackmore (Scott County), Virginia.

Conservation and Recovery

The Appalachian monkeyface was apparently never abundant, and the reasons for its decline are not fully understood, but impoundments, siltation, and pollution are presumed to be the major causes. The Norris Dam, in particular, probably inundated this mussel's habitat shoals in both the Powell and Clinch rivers. The cold tailwaters have made long upstream portions of the rivers uninhabitable for both mussels and host fishes.

Siltation caused by strip mining, coal washing, and poor agricultural practices have buried gravel and sand shoals and smothered mussel beds. Because mussels must siphon gallons of water each day to feed, the effects of water pollutants, such as herbicides and pesticides, are intensified.

Surveys conducted by the Tennessee Valley Authority (TVA) in 1988 and 1989 suggest that mussel populations in the Clinch River continue to decline. The status of populations in the Powell River has not yet been determined. Recovery for this mussel will require rehabilitation of at least part of its historic habitat to allow populations to be reestablished.

The TVA, which administers the operation of dams on the Tennessee and Cumberland rivers, is currently developing a comprehensive water management plan. This plan would guarantee constant minimum flows in all rivers in the region by timing water discharges from TVA dams. Such an effort might mollify many of the negative effects of dams and reservoirs on remaining stretches of mussel habitat.

Bibliography

Bogan, A., and P. Parmalee. 1983. "Tennessee's Rare Mollusks." In *Tennessee's Rare Wildlife, Final Report*. Department of Conservation and Tennessee Heritage Project, University of Tennessee, Knoxville.

Branson, B. A. 1974. "Stripping the Appalachians." *Natural History* 83(9):53-60.

Fuller, S. 1974. "Clams and Mussels (Mollusca: Bivalvia)." In Hart and Fuller, eds., *Pollution Ecology of Freshwater Invertebrates*. Academic Press, New York.

Neel, J. K., and W. R. Allen. 1964. "The Mussel Fauna of the Upper Cumberland Basin before Its Impoundment." *Malacologia* 1(3):427-459.

Pardue, J. W. 1981. "A Survey of the Mussels (Unionidae) of the Upper Tennessee River, 1978." *Sterkiana* 71:41-51.

U.S. Fish and Wildlife Service. 1983. "Appalachian Monkeyface Pearly Mussel Recovery Plan." U.S. Fish and Wildlife Service, Atlanta.

Contact

Regional Office of Endangered Species
U.S. Fish and Wildlife Service
Richard B. Russell Federal Building
75 Spring Street, S.W.
Atlanta, Georgia 30303

Stirrup Shell
Quadrula stapes

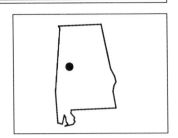

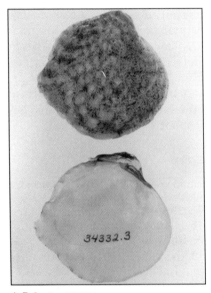

A. E. Spreitzer/OSU Museum of Zoology

Status . . . . . Endangered
Listed . . . . . April 7, 1987
Family . . . . . Unionidae (Freshwater Mussel)
Description . . . Quadrangular, yellowish green shell with zig-zag markings.
Habitat . . . . . Sand and gravel substrates in flowing water.
Threats . . . . . Loss of habitat, sedimentation, dredging.
Region 4 . . . . . Alabama, Mississippi

Description

The stirrup shell is a bivalve mollusk, 5.5 centimeters (2.2 in) long, with a quadrangular shell. The yellowish green shell is marked with zig-zag lines, which are light green on young shells and dark brown on older shells. Its truncated posterior has a sharp ridge and tubercles. The inner shell surface is silvery white.

For a general discussion of the life cycle of freshwater mussels see the species account of the birdwing pearly mussel (*Conradilla caelata*).

Habitat

This mussel is found in the shoals and riffles of fast-flowing rivers, buried in relatively firm, silt-free rubble, gravel, and sand substrates.

Historic Range

The stirrup shell was found historically in the Tombigbee River from near Columbus, Mississippi, downstream to Epes, Alabama; in the Black Warrior, Sipsey, Alabama rivers.

Current Distribution

The stirrup shell has not been found in the Alabama or Black Warrior rivers for several decades. It is presently known from only two sites in Alabama—the Sipsey River (Pickens and Green counties), and the Gainesville Bendway (Pickens County), a meander of the East Fork Tombigbee River that was cut off by construction of the Tennessee-Tombigbee Waterway.

Conservation and Recovery

When the Tennessee-Tombigbee Waterway was completed to allow barge traffic between the Tennessee and Tombigbee rivers, most of the East Fork Tombigbee River was modified into a series of channels, locks, and impoundments. The dams and locks inundated mussel shoals and slowed the flow of water, increasing siltation, which smothers mussel beds. Dredging to create a navigable channel physically destroyed many mussel beds, and periodic maintenance dredging continues to disturb the river bottom. Bull Mountain Creek, which provided nearly half the water supply of the East Fork, was diverted to feed the waterway. The creek's cooler waters are warmed when routed through the canal, making this part of the river inimical to both mussels and host fishes.

Mussels native to the Tombigbee and Sipsey rivers are threatened by continued flood control and navigation improvement projects. Such activities add silt to waters and increases turbidity, clogging the mussel's feeding apparatus and smothering mussel beds. A currently proposed 136-kilometer (84-mi) channel improvement project would degrade or destroy mussel habitat on the Sipsey River.

The last free-flowing stretch of the East Fork Tombigbee River is threatened by plans to dredge 85 kilometers (53 mi) to improve navigability. Siltation in the Bendway has become more severe in the last few years and may already be smothering surviving mussel beds.

Under provisions of the Endangered Species Act, federal agencies are required to consult with the Fish and Wildlife Service (FWS) to ensure that any actions they authorize or fund do not jeopardize Threatened or Endangered species. This rule affects all watershed projects proposed by the Army Corps of Engineers and the Soil Conservation Service of the Department of Agriculture. In the past, similar consultations have resulted in the redesign of projects to preserve significant portions of habitat.

Bibliography

Fuller, S. L. H. 1974. "Clams and Mussels (Mollusca: Bivalvia)." In Hart and Fuller, eds., *Pollution Ecology of Freshwater Invertebrates.* Academic Press, New York.

Stansbery, D. H. 1976. "Naiad Mollusks." In H. Boschung, ed., "Endangered and Threatened Plants and Animals in Alabama." *Bulletin of the Alabama Museum of Natural History* 2:42-55.

Contact

Regional Office of Endangered Species
U.S. Fish and Wildlife Service
Richard B. Russell Federal Building
75 Spring Street, S.W.
Atlanta, Georgia 30303

Pale Lilliput Pearly Mussel
Toxolasma cylindrellus

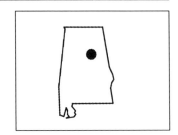

A. E. Spreitzer/OSU Museum of Zoology

Status	Endangered
Listed	June 14, 1976
Family	Unionidae (Freshwater Mussel)
Description	Yellowish green, nearly cylindrical shell.
Habitat	Gravel and rubble substrates.
Threats	Loss of habitat, pollution.
Region 4	Alabama, Tennessee

Description

The shell of the pale lilliput pearly mussel measures 4.4 centimeters (1.8 in) long, 2.5 centimeters (1 in) high, and 1.6 centimeters (0.64 in) wide. The valves are solid, elongated, and appear nearly cylindrical. The smooth shell surface is yellowish green. The inner shell surface (nacre) varies from white to light yellow with metallic tints of blue and purple. This Cumberlandian species was formerly classified as *Carunculina cylindrellus*.

For a general discussion of the life cycle of freshwater mussels see the species account of the birdwing pearly mussel (*Conradilla caelata*).

Habitat

This mussel inhabits narrow streams and prefers clean, shallow, fast-flowing water with a firm, silt-free rubble, gravel, or sandy bottom.

Historic Range

The pale lilliput pearly mussel probably ranged in the narrower tributaries of the Tennessee River in Tennessee and Alabama. It was documented from the Flint and Elk rivers in the 1920s, from the Sequatchie and Little Sequatchie rivers in the 1950s, from the Buffalo River in 1973, and from the Duck River as recently as 1976. Of its reported occurrences, it continues to survive only in the Paint Rock River watershed in northern Alabama.

Current Distribution

This pearly mussel is known only from a 16-kilometer (10-mi) section of the Paint Rock

River and its tributary streams, Hurricane Creek and Estill Fork, in Jackson County, Alabama. Specimens have not been collected in recent years from the Duck and Buffalo rivers. The pale lilliput is considered extremely rare.

Conservation and Recovery

The pale lilliput pearly mussel has been rare at least since its discovery but has disappeared from much of its former range because of dam construction, stream siltation, and pollution. Siltation caused by strip mining, coal washing, dredging, clear-cutting, and poor agricultural practices have buried gravel and sand shoals and smothered mussel beds in many watersheds. Because mussels must siphon gallons of water each day to feed, the effects of water pollutants, such as herbicides and pesticides, are intensified. All these factors have resulted in the reduction in range and numbers of most Cumberlandian pearly mussels, including the pale lilliput.

Recovery of this species will depend on the larger effort of rehabilitating pearly mussel habitat in the Tennessee Valley.

The Tennessee Valley Authority is currently developing a comprehensive water management plan for the region that would establish minimum, year-round flows in all rivers by carefully timing water discharges from its many dams. In addition, the Paint Rock River may be eligible for Scenic River status under the National Wild and Scenic Rivers Act, a designation that would provide additional protection for this species and its remaining habitat. Pending the results of ongoing research, the Fish and Wildlife Service may attempt to reintroduce the pale lilliput to suitable stretches of habitat within its historic range.

Bibliography

Bogan, A., and P. Parmalee. 1983. "Tennessee's Rare Mollusks." In *Tennessee's Rare Wildlife, Final Report*. Tennessee Heritage Program, Department of Conservation, University of Tennessee Press, Knoxville.

Isom, B. G. 1969. "The Mussel Resources of the Tennessee River." *Malacologia* 7:(2-4):397-425.

U.S. Fish and Wildlife Service. 1984. "Pale Lilliput Pearly Mussel Recovery Plan." U.S. Fish and Wildlife Service, Atlanta.

Contact

Regional Office of Endangered Species
U.S. Fish and Wildlife Service
Richard B. Russell Federal Building
75 Spring Street, S.W.
Atlanta, Georgia 30303

Cumberland Bean Pearly Mussel

Villosa trabalis

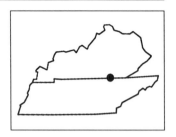

A. E. Spreitzer/OSU Museum of Zoology

Status	Endangered
Listed	June 14, 1976
Family	Unionidae (Freshwater Mussel)
Description . . .	Small to medium-sized elongated shell.
Habitat	Fast-flowing water in sandy substrate.
Threats	Impoundments, siltation, pollution.
Region 4	Kentucky, Tennessee

Description

The Cumberland bean pearly mussel is a small to medium-sized Cumberlandian freshwater species with solid, elongated oval valves. The shell is unsculptured except for concentric growth marks and ridges on the beak. The surface is somewhat glossy, olive-green, yellowish brown, or blackish, and covered with many narrow, wavy, dark-green or blackish rays. The inner shell surface is white except for an iridescent blue-green posterior. This species was formerly classified as *Micromya trabalis*.

For a general discussion of the life cycle of freshwater mussels see the species account of the birdwing pearly mussel (*Conradilla caelata*).

Habitat

The Cumberland bean pearly mussel is found in clean, fast-flowing water in gravel and sand shoals that have been swept free of silt by the action of the current.

Historic Range

This species was widely distributed in many of the larger tributary streams of upper Cumberland River and was considered rare in the Tennessee River drainage. In the 1920s it was reported in the Tennessee River and its tributaries—South Chicamauga Creek (northern Georgia), Paint Rock and Flint rivers (northern Alabama), the Hiwasee and Clinch rivers (Tennessee). It has been reported more recently from the Cumberland River and its tributaries—Buck and Beaver creeks, and the Obey and Rockcastle rivers (Kentucky).

Current Distribution

The largest concentration of Cumberland bean pearly mussels is presently found in a 32-kilometer (20-mi) stretch of the Little South Fork Cumberland River (McCreary County, Kentucky). It has been found at Station Camp Creek in the Tennessee headwaters of the Big South Fork. Several healthy populations still survive in the Rockcastle River and its tributaries—Roundstone and Horse Lick creeks, and Middle Fork (Laurel County, Kentucky)—and in Buck Creek (Pulaski County, Kentucky).

Conservation and Recovery

The Cumberland bean pearly mussel was probably eradicated from the Tennessee River watershed by the construction of major dams on the river for flood control and hydroelectric power production. Since the 1930s the Tennessee Valley Authority (TVA) has erected 36 dams in the Tennessee River basin. Five major dams have been located on the Cumberland River and six others on its tributaries. The cold tailwaters from these dams have made long upstream portions of these rivers uninhabitable for both mussels and host fishes. Siltation caused by strip mining, coal washing, logging, and poor agricultural practices within the watersheds have buried gravel and sand shoals and smothered mussel beds. Because mussels must siphon gallons of water each day to feed, the effects of water pollutants, such as herbicides and pesticides, are intensified.

Buck Creek and the Little South Fork Cumberland River both appear eligible for Scenic River status under the National Wild and Scenic Rivers Act. Such a designation would provide additional protection for the species and its habitat. The Tennessee Valley Authority is currently developing a comprehensive water management plan for the region that would establish minimum, year-round flows in all rivers by carefully timing water discharges from its dams.

Bibliography

Branson, B. A. 1974. "Stripping the Appalachians." *Natural History* 38(9):53-60.

Jenkinson, J. J. 1981. "The Tennessee Valley Authority Cumberlandian Molusk Conservation Program." *Bulletin of the American Malacological Union* 1980:62-63.

U.S. Fish and Wildlife Service. 1984. "Cumberland Bean Pearly Mussel Recovery Plan." U.S. Fish and Wildlife Service, Atlanta.

Contact

Regional Office of Endangered Species
U.S. Fish and Wildlife Service
Richard B. Russell Federal Building
75 Spring Street, S.W.
Atlanta, Georgia 30303

CRUSTACEANS

Madison Cave Isopod
Antrolana lira

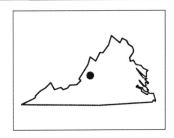

Russell Norton

Status . . . . . Threatened
Listed . . . . . . October 4, 1982
Family . . . . . Cirolanidae (Cave Isopod)
Description . . . White, blind, shrimp-like crustacean.
Habitat . . . . . Subterranean freshwater pools.
Food . . . . Detritus.
Threats . . . . . Habitat disturbance, pollution.
Region 5 . . . . . Virginia

Description

The only member of the genus *Antrolana*, the Madison Cave isopod is a white, shrimp-like crustacean lacking eyes. This cave-adapted (troglobitic) isopod grows up to 12 millimeters (0.4 in) in length.

Behavior

The Madison Cave isopod consumes organic matter, such as leaf litter or dead insects, that is washed into its aquatic habitat by surface runoff. Females carrying eggs have never been found, but juveniles have been located, showing that reproduction is occurring. It is believed that females may hide in the leaf litter in the bottom of the fissures or in the inaccessible channels, which feed the pools.

Habitat

The Madison Cave isopod inhabits three freshwater, subterranean pools, which are fed primarily by an aquifer. Biologists have observed a slow seepage of water from the pools into the nearby South River, a tributary of the South Fork Shenandoah River. Water levels in the cave vary somewhat with the river flow. Two pools are found in Madison Cave—one about 11 meters (35 ft) deep, the other 23 meters (75 ft) deep. The third pool in Stegers Fissure is the deepest at 30.4 meters (100 ft).

Madison Cave was the first cave ever mapped in the U.S., and the mapper was none other than Thomas Jefferson. George Washington also visited the cave and left his signature on the cave wall.

Historic Range

The Madison Cave isopod is endemic to Madison Cave and the nearby Stegers Fissure (Augusta County), Virginia. This isopod is the only member of the Cirolanidae family in the Eastern United States. Other members are found in Texas, Mexico, and the Caribbean.

Current Distribution

Only a few of these isopods have ever been collected, and the size of the population is unknown. It is believed to inhabit not only the cave pools but also the fissures and channels that connect the pools with the aquifer and the South River.

Conservation and Recovery

As early as 1812 deposits of bat guano in Madison Cave were mined for saltpeter (potassium nitrate) for use in the manufacture of gunpowder. Over the years visitors and spelunkers have left behind an accumulation of trash and contributed to siltation of the pools by trampling the steep clay talus banks. The entrance to the cave has now been secured against unauthorized entry, and the cave's private owner has developed a conservation plan, which is designed to satisfy parties interested in the cave's history, as well as those interested in the welfare of the Madison Cave isopod.

The aquatic resources of Madison Cave and Stegers Fissure face the serious threat of mercury contamination. High levels of mercury have been measured in the South River, discharged by the now-defunct E. I. du Pont de Nemours and Company factory upstream at Waynesboro. Although no mercury has yet been found in the cave pools, it is feared that the groundwater could be contaminated during prolonged periods of high water. Even low levels of contamination would jeopardize the surviving population of the Madison Cave isopod.

Bibliography

Bowman, T. E. 1964. "*Antrolana lira*, A New Genus and Species of Troglobitic Cirolanid Isopod from Madison Cave, Virginia." *International Journal of Speleology* 1(1-2):229-236.

Holsinger, J. R. 1979. "Freshwater and Terrestrial Isopod Crustaceans (Order Isopoda)." *Proceedings of the Endangered and Threatened Plants and Animals of Virginia Conference 1978.* Virginia Department of Fish and Game, Richmond.

Contact

Regional Office of Endangered Species
U.S. Fish and Wildlife Service
One Gateway Center, Suite 700
Newton Corner, Massachusetts 02158

Cave Crayfish
Cambarus zophonastes

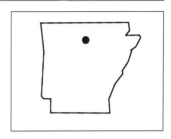

Ken Smith

Description

The cave crayfish is a cave-adapted species that lacks pigment in the body and eyes. Its beaklike snout bears several spines. The overall body length reaches about 6.4 centimeters (2.5 in) at maturity. The carapace is translucent.

Behavior

This slow-moving crayfish feeds on organic matter and detritus gleaned from the bottom and appears lethargic because of a low metabolic rate. It reproduces very slowly; females deposit eggs perhaps only once in five years.

Habitat

The cave crayfish is adapted to a constant, cool temperature and total absence of light.

Status	Endangered
Listed	April 7, 1987
Family	Cambaridae (Crayfish)
Description	Translucent, cave-dwelling crayfish.
Habitat	Underground pools and streams.
Food	Organic matter and detritus.
Reproduction	Breeds at intervals of five years.
Threats	Restricted distribution, groundwater pollution.
Region 4	Arkansas

For food, deep cave organisms depend for the most part on organic matter imported in the groundwater. One of the primary sources of organic matter in caves is bat guano deposited by colonies of gray bats (*Myotis grisescens*), a federally Endangered mammal. When bat populations decline, the entire cave ecosystem suffers from the loss of guano as an energy source.

The cave crayfish is found in an Ozark Mountain cave system that has been carved out of the Plattin Limestone formation.

Historic Range

The historic range of this species has not been clarified, but it could not have enjoyed a widespread distribution. Over 170 caves in north-central Arkansas and over 430 caves in Missouri have been surveyed for this crayfish without success.

Current Distribution

The only known population of the cave crayfish is found in Hell Creek Cave in Stone County, Arkansas. Scuba divers located only 15 individuals in deep cave pools in 1983. In 1984 the total population was estimated at less than 50.

Conservation and Recovery

Probably the most significant cause of crayfish decline has been the decline of the gray bat population. In the past a colony of over 16,000 gray bats used Hell Creek Cave, but few bats have been seen there is recent years. A return of the bat would certainly benefit the cave crayfish.

Over the last decade, the quality of groundwater has deteriorated as runoff from agricultural chemicals has increased. The possibility that the area immediately surrounding the cave will be developed for housing raises the threat of sewage contamination.

The Arkansas Natural Heritage Commission owns a 65-hectare (160-acre) tract that includes the entrance of Hell Creek Cave. The agency regulates access to the cave to prevent human disturbance, but much of the watershed surrounding the cave is privately owned. Protection of the habitat can only be assured by controlling the introduction of foreign substances into the groundwater. Monitoring of water quality and population levels will be conducted periodically.

Bibliography

Aley, T., and C. Aley. 1985. "Water Quality Protection Studies at Hell Creek Cave, Arkansas." Report. Arkansas Natural Heritage Commission and the Arkansas Nature Conservancy, Little Rock.

Harvey, M. J., *et al.* 1981. "Endangered Bats of Arkansas: Distribution, Status, Ecology, and Management." Report. Arkansas Game and Fish Commission, U.S. Forest Service, and National Park Service, Little Rock.

Smith, K. L. 1984. "The Status of *Cambarus zophonastes*, an Endemic Cave Crayfish from Arkansas." Report. U.S. Fish and Wildlife Service, Atlanta.

U.S. Fish and Wildlife Service. 1988. "A Recovery Plan for the Cave Crayfish, *Cambarus zophonastes*." U.S. Fish and Wildlife Service, Atlanta.

Contact

Regional Office of Endangered Species
U.S. Fish and Wildlife Service
Richard B. Russell Federal Building
75 Spring Street, S.W.
Atlanta, Georgia 30303

Nashville Crayfish

Orconectes shoupi

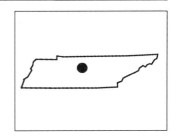

Dick Biggins

Status	. . . . . . Endangered
Listed	. . . . . . September 26, 1986
Family	. . . . . . Cambaridae (Crayfish)
Description	. . . Freshwater, decapod crustacean.
Habitat	. . . . . . Pools and flowing water.
Food	. . . . Animal and vegetable matter.
Threats	. . . . . . Urbanization, degradation of water quality.
Region 4	. . . . . Tennessee

Description

The Nashville crayfish is a decapod crustacean that grows as large as 15 centimeters (6 in). Crayfish have four pairs of walking legs and two large claws in front, which are used to capture prey.

Behavior

Very little is known about the biology of this species. It is an efficient bottom scavenger and feeds on plant and animal detritus, small invertebrates, and fish eggs. It breeds in the winter months, and females carrying eggs have been observed in the spring.

Habitat

The Nashville crayfish has been found in a wide range of aquatic habitats in Tennessee, including swift-flowing cobble runs and deep, still pools with mud bottoms. It often hides along the stream banks under limestone slabs. Crayfish require very high quality water and have a low tolerance for pollution and siltation.

Historic Range

The Nashville crayfish has been collected from four Tennessee localities—Mill Creek watershed (Davidson and Williamson counties), Big Creek in the Elk River system (Giles County), South Harpeth River (Davidson County), and Richland Creek, a Cumberland River tributary (Davidson County). Surveys conducted in 1985 suggest that the Nashville crayfish has been eliminated from all but the Mill Creek watershed.

Current Distribution

The Nashville crayfish is currently found only in the Mill Creek basin in Davidson and Williamson counties, Tennessee. There are no current population estimates.

Conservation and Recovery

The Nashville crayfish has been eliminated from much of its former range by residential and urban development, which has contributed to a steep decline in water quality. Contaminants carried by rainwater runoff, silt from land clearing and residential construction, and diversion of groundwater have degraded many former portions of the crayfish's habitat. The lower Mill Creek basin lies within the Nashville metropolitan area, and it is estimated that over 40 percent of the watershed has already been developed. Construction of a proposed wastewater management facility and a reservoir would seriously jeopardize the survival of this species. The upper Mill Creek basin has been degraded by silt and chemicals from agricultural runoff.

Crayfish are frequently used for bait by sports fishermen, and this rare species is often taken along with the more common crayfish. To counter this threat, personnel from the Tennessee Department of Conservation, Tennessee Wildlife Resources Agency, Army Corps of Engineers, and Fish and Wildlife Service (FWS) collaborated to develop a public awareness program to enable sports fishermen to identify the Nashville crayfish.

The FWS Nashville Crayfish Recovery Plan recommends that a second self-sustaining population be established outside of the immediate Mill Creek basin to guard against any accidental catastrophic event, such as a toxic chemical spill. If the Mill Creek population stabilizes and a second population proves stable for at least ten years, the FWS would consider reclassifying this species as Threatened. Because of its low numbers and limited range, it is doubtful whether the Nashville crayfish could ever be completely removed from the protection of the Endangered Species Act.

Bibliography

Bouchard, R. W. 1984. "Distribution and Status of the Endangered Crayfish *Orconectes shoupi* (Decapoda: Cambaridae)." Tennessee Technical University, Cookeville.

Hobbs, H. H., Jr. 1948. "On the Crayfishes of the Limosus Section of the Genus *Orconectes* (Decapoda, Astycidae)." *Journal of the Washington Academy of Science* 38(1):14-21.

O'Bara, C. J. 1985. "Status Survey of the Nashville Crayfish (*Orconectes shoupi*)." Report. U.S. Fish and Wildlife Service, Asheville, North Carolina.

U.S. Fish and Wildlife Service. 1987. "The Nashville Crayfish Recovery Plan." U.S. Fish and Wildlife Service, Atlanta.

Contact

Regional Office of Endangered Species
U.S. Fish and Wildlife Service
Richard B. Russell Federal Building
75 Spring Street, S.W.
Atlanta, Georgia 30303

Shasta Crayfish
Pacifastacus fortis

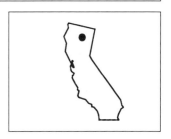

Darlene McGriff

Status	. . . . . Endangered
Listed	. . . . . September 30, 1988
Family	. . . . . Cambaridae (Crayfish)
Description	. . . Decapod crustacean with a dark green or dark brown back and bright orange beneath.
Habitat	. . . . . Spring-fed lakes, cool rivers and streams.
Threats	. . . . . Competition with non-native crayfishes, degradation of water quality, stream diversion, groundwater pumping.
Region 1	. . . . . California

Description

Also known as the placid crayfish, the Shasta crayfish is a small, decapod crustacean with a carapace length of 25 to 50 millimeters (1 to 2 in). Its color varies from dark green to greenish brown above, and the underside is bright orange or red. The often mottled coloration of the back provides excellent camouflage against stream and pool bottoms of volcanic rubble. Occasional individuals in isolated populations may be blue-green or blue on the top with a salmon-colored underside.

Adult Shasta crayfish are sexually dimorphic—males have narrower abdomens and larger pincers than females, and their first two pairs of swimming legs (swimmerets) are modified to transfer sperm to the female during mating.

Behavior

This species primarily feeds upon encrusting organisms, aquatic invertebrates, detritus, and dead fish. It is active mainly after dark, unlike other related crayfish species. The Shasta crayfish is a solitary creature, except during mating season. As it grows it undergoes several molts, during which it sheds its carapace. It mates in late September and October after the last molt of the year. Females lay an average of 40 eggs in the fall, which hatch the following spring. Crayfish reach sexual maturity after five years.

Habitat

The Shasta crayfish prefers clear, spring-fed lakes, streams, and rivers, and usually congregates near spring flows where the water remains cool throughout the summer. Most colonies are found in still or slow currents over a base composed of cobbles and pebbles or of clean sand.

Historic Range

This species is endemic to a portion of the Pit River basin in extreme northern California. The Pit River arises in the mountains above the town of Alturus and flows south and west to empty into Shasta Lake. A population recorded from Sucker Spring Creek was extirpated before 1970. Populations documented from Lake Britton, Burney, Clark, Kosk, Goose, Lost, and Rock creeks disappeared some time before a 1974 census. Since 1978 the crayfish has disappeared from Baum Lake and Spring Creek.

Current Distribution

The Shasta crayfish is currently found in the Pit River and in the watersheds of two of its tributaries—Hat Creek and Fall River (Modoc, Lassen, and Shasta counties), California. The largest concentrations of crayfish are found in the Fall River feeders— Big Lake and Bitt Tule River, Mallard, Squaw, and Lava creeks, and Crystal, Thousands, and Rainbow springs. Lesser densities occur in the Hat Creek feeders—Rising River Lake and Lost Creek. In 1980 the total population was estimated at under 6,000 individuals, but by 1988 it probably amounted to no more than 3,000.

Conservation and Recovery

Because the Shasta crayfish is slow to reach sexual maturity and has a low rate of reproduction, it is being displaced by two faster-breeding species of introduced crayfishes

(*Pacifastacus leniusculus* and *Orconectes virilis*). These crayfishes reach sexual maturity within two years, and each female lays up to 150 eggs. Since 1978 more than half of the Shasta's historic range has been taken over by these aggressive species.

Human activities have also played a role in the Shasta crayfish's decline. Streams and springs have been impounded and diverted into artificial channels to support irrigation agriculture. Agricultural chemicals have washed into streams, degrading water quality, and excessive pumping of groundwater has lowered the water table.

Although much of the Pit River basin falls within the boundaries of the Modoc, Lassen, and Shasta national forests, most of crayfish's streams and spring pools are privately owned, making it difficult to implement a unified recovery effort. The Fish and Wildlife Service has recommended trapping the nonnative crayfishes and eliminating them from the Pit River basin.

Bibliography

Daniels, R. A. 1980. "Distribution and Status of Crayfishes in the Pit River Drainage, California." *Crustaceana* 38:131-138.

Eng, L. L., and R. A. Daniels. 1982. "Life History, Distribution, and Status of *Pacifastacus fortis.*" *California Fish and Game* 68:197-212.

Schwartz, F. J., R. Rubelmann, and J. Allison. 1963. "Ecological Population Expansion of the Introduced Crayfish *Orconectes virilis.*" *Ohio Journal of Science* 63:266-273.

Contact

Regional Office of Endangered Species
U.S. Fish and Wildlife Service
Lloyd 500 Building, Suite 1692
500 N.E. Multnomah Street
Portland, Oregon 97232

Alabama Cave Shrimp
Palaemonias alabamae

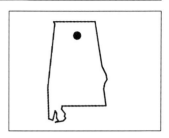

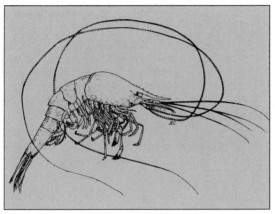

John E. Cooper

Status . . . . . . Endangered
Listed . . . . . . September 7, 1988
Family . . . . . . Atyidae (Freshwater Shrimp)
Description . . . Small decapod crustacean with a transparent shell.
Habitat . . . . . . Cave pools.
Food . . . . Detritus and plant matter.
Threats . . . . . . Contamination of groundwater, collectors.
Region 4 . . . . . Alabama

Description

The Alabama cave shrimp is a small (20 mm; 0.8 in) decapod crustacean. It is similar in outward form to a common ocean shrimp, but its carapace (outer shell) is colorless and largely transparent. It differs from the only other species of the genus, the Endangered Kentucky cave shrimp (*Palaemonias ganteri*), by having a shorter rostrum and fewer dorsal spines.

Behavior

The Alabama cave shrimp feeds on detritus and plant matter that is washed into the caves. It is thought to have a low reproductive potential—bearing one-half to one-third fewer eggs than its closest relative, the Kentucky cave shrimp.

Habitat

This albino shrimp is adapted to underground pools and streams eroded into the Warsaw Limestone formation of the Interior Low Plateau. Water levels in the inhabited caves—Shelta and Bobcat caves—fluctuate seasonally; some portions of the caves dry out completely during the summer. Shelta Cave consists of three large chambers with several smaller alcoves. Presently, the water quality within the caves is very high, but related cave systems have been contaminated by surface runoff, which has entered through limestone sinkholes.

Historic Range

A search of over 200 caves in northern Alabama has failed to locate the Alabama cave shrimp anywhere but two localities in Madison County, Alabama.

Current Distribution

The Alabama cave shrimp is known to inhabit Shelta and Bobcat caves in the Huntsville Spring Branch and Indian Creek drainages. The entrances to Shelta Cave are owned by the National Speleological Society, which has erected gates to control unauthorized access to the caves. The small population of shrimp in this cave has declined appreciably in recent years, and many researchers fear that it may already have been eliminated from Shelta Cave. Bobcat Cave is found on the Redstone Arsenal, administered by the Army. The size of the shrimp population has not been estimated, but numbers are considered very low because of the limited size of the cave habitats. Any disturbance of the habitat would place the cave shrimp in jeopardy of extinction.

Conservation and Recovery

The expanding urban environs of Huntsville have intruded into the vicinity of the caves. Residential and commercial development are expected to disrupt the ecological balance of the underground water supply, either by introducing contaminants in rainwater runoff or by diverting water from the aquifer. Increased groundwater pumping could reduce the water table, causing the caves to dry.

The Fish and Wildlife Service (FWS) and the Army are cooperating to develop a habitat management plan to protect Bobcat Cave against potentially damaging groundwater contamination. The FWS is also working closely with the National Speleological Society to develop regulation for recreational spelunkers who use Shelta Cave. In the past there was evidence that spelunkers collected the cave shrimp, and, because of its low rate of reproduction, collection may have caused the shrimp's decline.

Bibliography

Bouchard, R. W. 1976. "Crayfishes and Shrimps." In H. Boschung, ed., *Endangered and Treatened Plants and Animals of Alabama.* Bulletin No. 2. Alabama Museum of Natural History, Birmingham.

Environmental Protection Agency. 1986. "Report on the Remedial Action to Isolate DDT from People and the Environment in the Huntsville spring Branch-Indian Creek System Wheeler Reservoir, Alabama." Environmental Protection Agency, Atlanta.

Smalley, A. E. 1961. "A New Cave Shrimp from Southeastern United States." *Crustaceana* 3(2):127-130.

Contact

Regional Office of Endangered Species
U.S. Fish and Wildlife Service
Richard B. Russell Federal Building
75 Spring Street, S.W.
Atlanta, Georgia 30303

Kentucky Cave Shrimp

Palaemonias ganteri

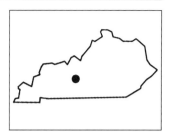

Chip Clark

Status	Endangered
Listed	October 12, 1983
Family	Atyidae (Freshwater Shrimp)
Description	Nearly transparent, decapod crustacean with only rudimentary eyestalks.
Habitat	Cave streams and pools.
Food	Protozoans, insects, fungi, algae.
Reproduction	Brood of 16 to 24 eggs.
Threats	Groundwater contamination.
Region 4	Kentucky

Description

The Kentucky cave shrimp is a small, nearly transparent decapod crustacean, characterized by rudimentary eyestalks, and bristlelike hairs on its unequally sized pincers. It is superficially similar to a common ocean shrimp, but the presence of reduced eyes and a lack of pigmentation indicate that this crustacean has survived underground for perhaps thousands of years.

Behavior

The cave shrimp is a non-selective grazer, feeding on sediments and detritus. Tiny protozoans and insects, fungi, and algae appear to make up the bulk of the diet. This species breeds year round. Females produce from 16 to 24 eggs.

Habitat

The Kentucky cave shrimp inhabits the lowest passages of the Flint-Mammoth Cave System, the most extensive cave system ever discovered. In the absence of light, food sources must enter the cave in groundwater. The cave drainage comprises a complex network of still pools and flowing streams. These free-swimming shrimp are concentrated in deeper pools where currents are minimal.

Historic Range

The Kentucky cave shrimp is endemic to the Flint-Mammoth Cave System, extending beneath Edmonson, Barren, and Hart counties, Kentucky. This broad system of passages and pools includes the Mystic, Echo, Styx and Colossal rivers, Lake Lethe, and the

Golden Triangle. In 1983 two crustaceans resembling the Kentucky cave shrimp were sighted in Blue Spring (Hart County), Kentucky. If confirmed, this sighting would extend the known range of the species outside of the caves proper.

Current Distribution

Surveys in the early 1980s examined 95 sites in 37 caves, and produced a population estimate for the Kentucky cave shrimp of only 500 individuals.

Conservation and Recovery

The Flint-Mammoth Cave region has been extensively developed for tourism, and, although this shrimp has weathered many individual events, the cumulative effects of development on the quality of the groundwater may now be materializing. Recent surveys have shown that the Mammoth Cave fauna have significantly declined over the last ten years due to pervasive groundwater pollution. The shrimp's small population makes it particularly vulnerable to extinction.

Because groundwater contamination recognizes no convenient boundaries, protecting the aquatic habitat of the caves is considered a regional problem. Several communities adjacent to the national park are known to have inadequate sewage treatment facilities or lack facilities altogether. Untreated sewage could enter the cave system at numerous points and contribute to oxygen deficiencies or nutrient toxicity. Additionally, contaminants from traffic accidents or roadside businesses have been introduced into the drainage. In 1980 a truck carrying toxic cyanide salts overturned on Interstate Highway 64 south of the park, and the result-

ing contamination killed thousands of aquatic cave organisms.

The Fish and Wildlife Service (FWS) and the Park Service hope to work closely with county and municipal governments to improve regional standards of sewage treatment and disposal. Additionally, a plan has been proposed to reroute vehicles carrying toxic chemicals, solvents, and fuels, to provide a measure of security for the watershed of the Mammoth Cave National Park.

A section of habitat considered critical for the survival of this species has been designated to include 1.6 kilometers (1 mi) of the Roaring River passage of Mammoth Cave. The FWS has stated that it may expand the size of Critical Habitat in the future, if groundwater contamination worsens.

Bibliography

Environmental Protection Agency. 1981. "Final Environmental Impact Statement, Mammoth Cave Area, Kentucky: Wastewater Facilities." Report No. EPA 904/9-81-076. Environmental Protection Agency, Atlanta.

Holsinger, J. R. and A. T. Leitheuser. 1983. "Ecological Analysis of the Kentucky Cave Shrimp, *Palaemonias ganteri* Hay, Mammoth Cave National Park (Phase III)." Report. National Park Service, Atlanta.

Leitheuser, A. T. , and J. R. Holsinger. 1983. "Ecological Analysis of the Kentucky Cave Shrimp at Mammoth Cave National Park." *Central Kentucky Cave Survey Bulletin* 1:72-80.

Contact

Regional Office of Endangered Species
U.S. Fish and Wildlife Service
Richard B. Russell Federal Building
75 Spring Street, S.W.
Atlanta, Georgia 30303

Hay's Spring Amphipod
Stygobromus hayi

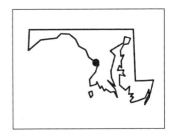

C. Kenneth Dodd, Jr.

Status . . . . . . Endangered
Listed . . . . . . February 5, 1982
Family . . . . . . Crangonyctidae
Description . . . White aquatic crustacean, 12
mm (0.4 in) long.
Habitat . . . . . . Springs.
Food . . . . Organic matter.
Threats . . . . . . Flooding, construction, collection.
Region 5 . . . . . District of Columbia

Description

The Hay's Spring amphipod is a white, eyeless, shrimplike crustacean only about 12 millimeters (0.4 in) in length.

Behavior

Hay's Spring amphipod feeds on organic matter, such as leaf litter and dead insects. Individuals may live five to ten years. Females carry eggs attached to their belly until they hatch.

Habitat

Hay's Spring is a small spring with a pool area of about 1.5 square meters (5 sq ft). Water emerges from the rocky western wall of Rock Creek Valley and flows about 10.6 meters (35 ft) into Rock Creek.

Historic Range

This crustacean is endemic to Hay's Spring, a small outflow located within Rock Creek National Park in the District of Columbia.

Current Distribution

Hay's Spring amphipod is only known from Hay's Spring, on the grounds of the National Zoological Park in Washington, D.C. Although there are other springs within Rock Creek National Park, this species has not been found elsewhere since its discovery in 1940. No more than 10 individuals have ever been seen at the site at any one time.

From what is known about similar species, such as *Stygobromos tenuis*, this amphipod probably evolved as a cave-adapted inhabitant of underground cracks and crevices. A second amphipod found in Rock Creek National Park is the undescribed *Stygobromos* sp., also a candidate for federal Endangered status.

Conservation and Recovery

Flood waters from Rock Creek occasionally reach the level of the spring habitat, degrading water quality and disturbing the leaves and bottom sediments that form the amphipod's microhabitat. The site of the spring has been fenced, although protection is minimal, and no signs have been posted. Because the zoo attracts so many visitors, administrators fear that calling further attention to the small spring would cause greater harm than good. The Smithsonian Institution's National Zoological Park has developed a Memorandum of Understanding with the Fish and Wildlife Service to protect the amphipod and the area adjacent to the spring.

Bibliography

Holsinger, J. R. 1977. "A Review of the Systematics of the Holarctic Amphipod Family Crangonyctidae." *Proceedings of the 3rd International Colloquium on* Gammarus *and* Niphargus, *Schlitz, West Germany*: *Crustaceans* 4:244-281.

Holsinger, J. R. 1978. "Systematics of the Subterranean Amphipod Genus *Stygobromus* (Crangonyctidae), Part II: Species of the Eastern United States." *Smithsonian Contributions to Zoology* No. 266.

Contact

Regional Office of Endangered Species
U.S. Fish and Wildlife Service
One Gateway Center, Suite 700
Newton Corner, Massachusetts 02158

California
Freshwater Shrimp

Syncaris pacifica

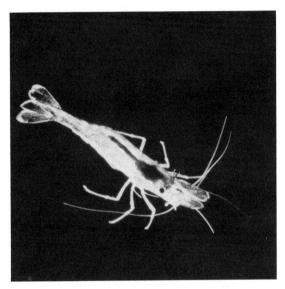

Susan Middleton

Status . . . . . . Endangered
Listed . . . . October 31, 1988
Family . . . . . . Atyidae (Freshwater Shrimp)
Description . . . Decapod crustacean; translucent when submerged; greenish gray with pale blue tail fins out of water.
Habitat . . . . . . Freshwater streams with low gradients, slow currents and overhanging vegetation.
Threats . . . . . . Agricultural and residential development, gravel dams.
Region 1 . . . . . California

Description

The California freshwater shrimp is a decapod crustacean similar in outward form to common ocean shrimp. Adult shrimps may reach 5 centimeters (2.5 in) in length and are nearly transparent when submerged. Out of the water, adults look greenish-gray or almost black with pale blue tail fins.

Behavior

Being almost invisible in the water and very quick to escape from any disturbance, this shrimp is rarely seen by the inexperienced observer. Females are slow to reach sexual maturity and lay relatively few eggs—between 50 and 120. The female carries eggs on her body for eight or nine months as they develop over the winter. Typically, only

about half of these eggs survive to produce viable embryos. Shrimp larvae develop rapidly during the summer and reach full size after about two years.

Habitat

This species is found in lower elevation streams (below 91 m; 300 ft) where gradients are gentle and currents slow to moderate. It prefers quiet stretches of tree-lined streams that support moderate underwater vegetation. It does not tolerate salt or brackish water.

Historic Range

The California freshwater shrimp is endemic to a three-county region in California directly north of San Francisco Bay in the

Russian River, and related coastal drainages. Out of 53 habitat streams surveyed in 1985 and 1986, only 12 continued to support the shrimp.

Current Distribution

Recent surveys have located the California shrimp in the Napa River near Calistoga (Napa County), and in Big Austin, East Austin, Blucher, Green Valley, Huichica, Jonive, Lagunitas, Salmon, Walker, and Yulupa creeks (Marin and Sonoma counties).

Conservation and Recovery

The freshwater stream habitat of this shrimp has suffered serious decline in recent years, mostly from rapid agricultural and residential development in the watershed. Water has been diverted for consumption or irrigation, lowering water levels. Runoff from fields and construction sites has led to silting and a general decline in water quality.

In some streams, particularly the Austin Creek drainage, it has been common practice to construct temporary gravel dams in the summer to retain water for irrigation. This practice is particularly destructive to species habitat because it alters stream flow, increases the turbidity of the water, and adds tons of gravel each year to the stream bottoms, when these dams wash out from high winter water levels.

The Army Corps of Engineers, which must issue permits for the construction of temporary dams, will now be required to ascertain the impact of these dams on the habitat of the freshwater shrimp. Although not all types of temporary dams are destructive, the Army Corps is expected to discourage or disallow gravel dams after 1990.

This species was listed as endangered by the State of California in 1980, and the California Department of Fish and Game has sponsored a significant amount of research on the ecology and the distribution of the freshwater shrimp. The Soil Conservation Service and the Coastal Conservancy are working with landowners along Salmon and Blucher creeks to develop conservation measures for the shrimp.

Bibliography

Eng, L. L. 1981. "Distribution, Life History, and Status of the California Freshwater Shrimp, *Syncaris pacifica*." Endangered Species Special Publication 18-1, Sacramento.

Hedgpeth, J. W. 1975. "California Fresh and Brackish Water Shrimps, with Special Emphasis to the Present Status of *Syncaris pacifica*." Report. U.S. Fish and Wildlife Service, Portland.

Contact

Regional Office of Endangered Species
U.S. Fish and Wildlife Service
Lloyd 500 Building, Suite 1692
500 N.E. Multnomah Street
Portland, Oregon 97232

Socorro Isopod

Thermosphaeroma thermophilum

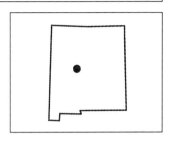

USFWS

Status . . . . . Endangered
Listed . . . . . March 27, 1978
Family . . . . . Sphaeromatidae (Isopod)
Description . . . Tiny crustacean with a flattened, oblong to egg- shaped body.
Habitat . . . . . Warm springs, algae-covered pools.
Food . . . . Algae, detritus.
Reproduction . . Brood size 3 to 57.
Threats . . . . . Restricted habitat.
Region 2 . . . . . New Mexico

Description

The Socorro isopod is a tiny aquatic crustacean with an average length of 8 millimeters (0.32 in). It has a flattened oblong to egg-shaped body with as many as eight mid-region (thoracic) segments. The abdomen is formed of two distinct segments. It has seven pairs of legs, antennae on the head and oar-like extensions (uropods) on the last segment. The body is smooth and colored grayish brown with small black spots and lines forming a band through each of the thoracic segments. Exposed edges of the body are tinged with bright orange. Various species of isopods are called pill bugs, sow bugs, or wood lice. The Socorro isopod was previously classified as *Exosphaeroma thermophilum*.

Behavior

Females produce broods every two months with April being the peak reproductive period. Brood sizes range from 3 to 57 eggs, and gestation is about 30 days. Isopods feed on algae, detritus, dragonfly larvae, and are occasionally cannibalistic.

Habitat

The Socorro isopod habitat consists of two small pools and two runs with relatively stable physical characteristics. Water temperatures range between 31 and 32 degrees C (88 and 90 F). Algae covers most of the pool surfaces.

Historic Range

The Socorro isopod is found naturally only in Socorro County, New Mexico, in three inter-connected warm springs.

Current Distribution

The surviving population is confined to the water system of an abandoned bathhouse known as the "Evergreen" about three kilometers (1.8 mi) west of the city of Socorro. This water system is supplied by thermal outflows from Cedillo Springs and consists of an animal watering tank, a smaller pool, and about 40 meters (132 ft) of irrigation pipe. Captive populations have been established at the University of New Mexico in Albuquerque and at the Dexter National Fish Hatchery in Dexter, New Mexico. The wild population is relatively stable at about 2,500.

Conservation and Recovery

The Socorro isopod is threatened by the limited size of its existing habitat. Its native warm springs were long ago capped and the water diverted to the city of Socorro's municipal water supply. The amount of water in the isopod's present pool is so small that any interruption of flow jeopardizes its survival. In 1987 the plumbing broke down, the water system dried up, and the isopod ceased to exist in the wild. Captive isopod populations at the University of New Mexico and the Dexter Fish Hatchery were used to restock the repaired pool, and population levels have nearly returned to normal.

In 1988 the state of New Mexico received a grant from the federal government to construct a larger, more natural, and more stable habitat for the Socorro isopod. This habitat will consist of a series of connected pools supplied by a natural water flow. Coopera-

tion among the state, the city of Socorro (which owns the water rights), the private landowner, and the Fish and Wildlife Service on behalf of the isopod has been exceptional. In fact, this little crustacean has attracted such favorable local attention that a nearby school's soccer team has been named the "Socorro Isopods."

Bibliography

Cole, G. A. and C. A. Bane. 1978. "*Thermosphaeroma subequalum* (Crustacea: Isopoda) from Big Bend National Park, Texas." *Hydrobiologia* 59(3):23-28.

U.S. Fish and Wildlife Service. 1982. "Socorro Isopod (*Thermosphaeroma thermophilum*) Recovery Plan." U.S. Fish and Wildlife Service, Albuquerque.

Contact

Regional Office of Endangered Species
U.S. Fish and Wildlife Service
P.O. Box 1306
Albuquerque, New Mexico 87103

SNAILS

Oahu Tree Snails

Achatinella sp.

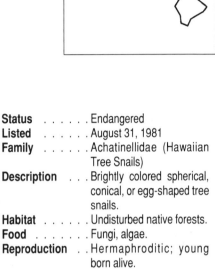

William P. Mull

Status	Endangered
Listed	August 31, 1981
Family	Achatinellidae (Hawaiian Tree Snails)
Description	Brightly colored spherical, conical, or egg-shaped tree snails.
Habitat	Undisturbed native forests.
Food	Fungi, algae.
Reproduction	Hermaphroditic; young born alive.
Threats	Deforestation, collectors, predation.
Region 1	Hawaii

Description

The *Achatinellae* are divided into three subgenera according to shell shape, which is either spherical, conical, or egg-shaped. Adult shell length is one-half to slightly over 2.5 centimeters (1 in), depending on the species. The number of whorls varies between five and seven. All species are brightly colored and distinctively patterned. Most species have glossy shells, but some have a sculptured surface.

Some species of *Achatinella,* such as A. *juncea,* A. *buddii,* and A. *papyracea,* were rare as long ago as the 1930s. Other extremely rare species, such as *A. lehuiensis, A. thaanumi,* and *A. spaldingi,* became extinct soon after being discovered. It is believed that only 19 of 41 documented species of the snail still exist. All surviving species are federally listed as Endangered.

Those species still living but in danger of extinction are *A. apexfulva, A. bellula, A. bulimoides, A. byronii, A. concavospira, A. curta, A. decipiens, A. fulgens, A. fuscobasis, A. leucorraphe, A. lila, A. lorata, A. mustelina, A. pulcherrima, A. pupukanioe, A. sowerbyana, A. swiftii, A. taeniolata,* and *A. turgida.*

Behavior

Oahu tree snails live singly or in small clusters in the crevices of tree bark, on the undersides of branches and foliage, or in deep leaf litter around the base of the trunk. Most species are nocturnal, feeding on fungi and algae. Individual snails are sedentary and may spend their entire life on a single tree.

As a group, the *Achatinellae* are hermaphroditic (with both male and female reproductive organs) but not self-fertilizing. They breed year round and usually bear one live young, born complete with shell. Studied species were found to grow at a rate of about 2 millimeters in length per year and to reach sexual maturity in six or seven years.

Habitat

The island of Oahu encompasses some 1,433 square kilometers (607 sq mi). Over 35 percent of this land area is devoted to urban areas or agricultural crops, 45 percent to grazing land, and less than 20 percent to forest lands, mostly at high elevations. Only a small portion of this forest (2 to 3 percent) is still in relatively pristine condition.

Oahu tree snails are dependent upon the remnants of undisturbed forests and upon native trees. A single species of snail is often associated with a specific tree species. Rarely do any of these species cross over to trees that have been introduced from outside the island.

Historic Range

Much of the island of Oahu, Hawaii, was once heavily forested, and tree snails were dispersed throughout. It is estimated that the original extent of forested land has been reduced by about 85 percent by agriculture and human settlement. Native trees have declined in numbers, losing ground to introduced, non-native trees.

Current Distribution

Tree snails survive in scattered enclaves throughout portions of the historic range, typically at higher elevations along the crests of ridges where the forests are least disturbed. Only two such areas on Oahu remain—the Waianae Range, and the Koolau Range. Current population levels are low for all of the tree snails, perhaps only five to ten percent of 1960 levels.

A biologist, who extensively surveyed the snails' forest habitat in the early 1980s, has suggested that the most abundant of these endangered species are *A. mustelina* and *A. sowerbyana,* numbering perhaps 400 individuals each. Estimated at about 200 individuals or less were the species *A. curta, A. decipiens,* and *A. lila.*

The species *A. fuscobasis* and *A. pupukanioe* numbered perhaps 100 individuals each. Achatinella concavospira and *A. pulcherrima* numbered 50 or less individuals each. *Achatinella bellula, A. bulimoides, A. byronii, A. fulgens, A. leucorraphe, A. lorata, A. swiftii, A taeniolata,* and *A. turgida,* all numbered less than 20 individuals. There is no current population estimate for the species *A. apexfulva.*

Conservation and Recovery

The most obvious reason for the precipitous decline of tree snail populations is the loss of native forests on the island. Oahu's lower elevation forests were long ago converted to agriculture, pasture, or for residences. Much of the remaining forests have been degraded by the intermingling of non-native trees and plants, changing the composition of plants; this in turn affects the abundance and dispersal of the snails' chief food sources—the algae and fungi.

Hikers along forest trails often collect the brightly colored snails. But because of late sexual maturity and a slow growth rate (natural replacement of a reproducing adult takes at least six years) tree snail populations can be quickly depleted by even casual collecting. Several of these tree snails have come to the attention of more serious collectors, who seem willing to finance the depletion of these rare snails by purchasing specimens.

Another immediate threat for these tree snails is an exotic, carnivorous snail (*Euglandina rosea*), that was introduced from Florida to control another snail pest, the giant African snail (*Achatina fulica*). This carnivorous snail had little impact on the African snail, but in areas where it has become established, Oahu tree snails are now entirely absent.

Recovery for these tree snails will depend ultimately upon saving the remaining acreage of native forests on Oahu, stopping collectors, and ridding the habitat of predators. The Fish and Wildlife Service, the state of Hawaii, and The Nature Conservancy of Hawaii have begun to cooperate in a more aggressive campaign to acquire and protect forestland. The results of these efforts are slow to materialize, and it remains an open question whether many of these tree snails will survive.

Bibliography

Hart, A. D. 1975. "Living Jewels Imperiled." *Defenders* 50:482- 486.

Hart, A. D. 1978. "The Onslaught Against Hawaii's Tree Snails." *Natural History* 87:46-57.

Van der Schalie, H. 1969. "Man Meddles with Nature—Hawaiian Style." *The Biologist* 51:136-146.

Whitten, H. 1980. "Endangered Hawaiian Tree Snail." Article. *Honolulu Star Bulletin* July 14, 1980.

Young, G. 1979. "Which Way Oahu?" *National Geographic Magazine* 156(5):652-679.

Contact

Regional Office of Endangered Species
U.S. Fish and Wildlife Service
Lloyd 500 Building, Suite 1692
500 N.E. Multnomah Street
Portland, Oregon 97232

Office of Environmental Services
U.S. Fish and Wildlife Service
300 Ala Moana Boulevard
P.O. Box 50167
Honolulu, Hawaii 96850

Painted Snake Coiled Forest Snail

Anguispira picta

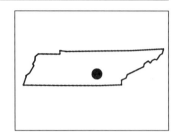

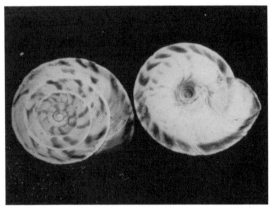

R. W. Van Devender

Status	Threatened
Listed	July 3, 1978
Family	Discidae (Forest Snail)
Description . . .	Dome-shaped snail with six whorls; off-white with brown blotches.
Habitat	Limestone outcrops.
Food	Lichens.
Reproduction . .	Undescribed.
Threats	Logging, grazing, quarrying.
Region 4	Tennessee

Description

The painted snake coiled forest snail is a dome-shaped snail with a sharp, smooth keel-shaped ridge along the shell called a carina. Mature shells measure up to 2.1 centimeters (0.8 in) long and 1 centimeter (0.4 in) high. Shells have six whorls and indistinct ribbing, particularly on the body whorl. The adult shell is an opaque, off-white color with chocolate brown blotches on the upper surface. The lower surface has one row of large dark blotches and a second row of narrow, flame-like markings, extending into the hole at the base of body whorl. Juvenile shells are translucent.

This snail is similar in appearance to *Anguispira cumberlandiana* found on the Cumberland Plateau.

Behavior

This snail's biology is almost completely unknown. It is thought to feed on lichens. Related snails deposit eggs with a calcareous shell in the soil.

Habitat

The coiled forest snail has been found only on damp limestone outcrops, typically in crevices or under overhanging ledges. Slopes are very steep, often terminating in sheer cliffs that drop to the creek bed below. The habitat is thickly forested and has a profuse ground cover. The forest community is composed of American beech, sugar maple, shagbark hickory, tulip poplar, white oak, and chinkapin oak. Ground cover is dominated by ironwood, dogwood, witch hazel, sycamore, and many herbaceous plants, such as walking fern, alumroot, and wild ginger. The snail does not occur in adjacent tracts that have been heavily logged or clear-cut.

Historic Range

The historic range of this species is unknown, but it is probably endemic to the valleys and coves that are characteristic of the southwestern rim of the Cumberland Plateau in southern Tennessee west of Chattanooga.

Current Distribution

The painted snake coiled forest snail is found at Buck Creek Cove, southwest of Sherwood in Franklin County. Buck Creek Cove is an enclosed stream valley about one mile long and half a mile wide. Snails are found on both sides of the stream but are more common toward the southern end of the cove. Initial research indicated that the population was stable at about 2,000 individuals. Subsequent studies suggest that as many as 20,000 snails may inhabit the privately owned cove.

Conservation and Recovery

The painted snake coiled forest snail is endangered by the restricted size of its range. Any substantial disturbance of the habitat could precipitate a sudden population decline. Logging, livestock grazing, and limestone quarrying are important sources of income to the residents of the Franklin County. So far, the landowners of the cove have refused to sell timber or mineral rights to commercial interests and have cooperated with the Fish and Wildlife Service (FWS) to protect the habitat.

The FWS Recovery Plan for this species outlines a systematic research program that includes periodic monitoring of the population. Protection of the cove by land acquisition or by purchase of conservation easements is anticipated as funds become available. The Nature Conservancy and the Tennessee Wildlife Resources Agency have been active in securing the cooperation of local landowners.

Bibliography

Elwell, A. S., and M. Ulmer. 1971. "Notes on the Biology of *Anguispira alternata.*" *Malacologia* 11(1):199-215.

Pilsbry, H. A. 1948. *Land Mollusca of North America (North of Mexico).* Academy of Natural Sciences, Philadelphia.

Smith, T. 1980. "Potential Preserve Site Summary." Report. The Nature Conservancy, Tennessee Field Office.

U.S. Fish and Wildlife Service. 1982. "Painted Snake Coiled Forest Snail Recovery Plan." U.S. Fish and Wildlife Service, Atlanta.

Contact

Regional Office of Endangered Species
U.S. Fish and Wildlife Service
Richard B. Russell Federal Building
75 Spring Street, S.W.
Atlanta, Georgia 30303

Iowa Pleistocene Snail
Discus macclintocki

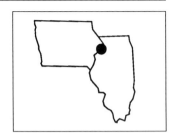

Terry Frest

Status	Endangered
Listed	July 3, 1978
Family	Discidae (Forest Snail)
Description . . .	Six-whorled, tightly coiled, dome-shaped snail; brown or greenish white.
Habitat	Talus slopes under logs or in leaf litter.
Food	Leaves of birch and maple trees.
Reproduction . .	Hermaphroditic; 2 to 6 eggs per clutch.
Threats	Restrictive habitat, low numbers.
Region 3	Iowa

Description

The Iowa Pleistocene snail is an average-sized member of its genus with an adult width of 8 millimeters (0.5 in). The dome-shaped shell is tightly coiled, typically with six whorls. Shell color may be brown or off-white with a greenish cast. Ribs are relatively fine and confined to the upper half of each whorl.

Behavior

This snail feeds on the leaves of white and yellow birch, hard maple, or occasionally dogwood and willow. It is active from spring through summer but becomes lethargic in August when the habitat dries. It remains near the soil surface until the first hard freeze, then burrows into the soil to hibernate.

Like most North American land snails, the Iowa snail is hermaphroditic (with both male and female reproductive organs) but not self-fertilizing. Adults can apparently lay eggs as well as fertilize the eggs of other snails. Breeding occurs from late March to August. Eggs are laid under logs and bark, in protected moist rock crevices, and in the soil. Clutch sizes vary from two to six eggs with an incubation time of 28 days. Life span is about five years.

Habitat

The Iowa Pleistocene snail is found in pockets of a very specialized microhabitat known as an "algific talus slope." These cool, moist areas develop around the entrances to fissures and caves where circulating air and infiltrating water create a condition of nearly permanent underground ice. The Iowa snail lives on the surface in deep, moist leaf litter that is cooled throughout the summer by this icy substrate. The snail prefers deciduous leaf litter and typically avoids mossy ground cover or coniferous litter. Most algific talus slopes are steep and north-facing, composed of fragments of a porous carbonate rock. This cool, moist habitat reproduces conditions that were more common during previous glacial epochs. This snail is often associated with northern wild monkshood (*Aconitum noveboracense*), a federally Endangered plant.

Historic Range

The geologic record of the Iowa Pleistocene snail goes back over 300,000 years, when it was fairly widespread throughout the Midwest. Its maximum range during cooler glacial periods included Iowa, Nebraska, Missouri, Illinois, Indiana, and Ohio. The center of distribution apparently was once Illinois.

Current Distribution

The snail survives at 18 known locations in a region known as the Driftless Area, which encompasses portions of Clayton and Dubuque counties, Iowa, and Jo Davies County, Illinois. These populations are estimated to number no more than 60,000 snails.

Conservation and Recovery

The major long-term cause of decline is cyclic climatic change. The species has survived several such cycles in the past and, with a return of glacial conditions, would certainly replenish itself over a large range.

The most immediate threat to its survival is human disturbance. An estimated 75 percent of its specialized habitat has been destroyed in the last 150 years by agriculture, road construction, quarrying, and other human intrusions.

In 1986, The Nature Conservancy, the Iowa Conservation Commission, and the Fish and Wildlife Service implemented the Driftless Area Project in northeast Iowa to protect remaining pockets of algific talus slope habitat. Over two-thirds of all landowners that were contacted agreed to register a commitment to conserve habitat on their properties. Registration is voluntary and is considered an interim solution, until land can be acquired and protected permanently. Public support for habitat conservation in the region is very high.

Bibliography

Baker, F. C. 1928. "Description of New Varieties of Land and Fresh Water Mollusks from Pleistocene Deposits in Illinois." *Nautilus* 41:132-137.

Ferst, T. J. 1981. "Final Report, Project SE-1-2, Iowa Pleistocene Snail." Iowa State Conservation Commission, Des Moines.

Hulbricht, L. 1955. "*Discus macclintocki* (F.C. Baker)." *Nautilus* 69:34.

U.S. Fish and Wildlife Service. 1984. "Recovery Plan for the Iowa Pleistocene Snail (*Discus macclintocki*)." U.S. Fish and Wildlife Service, Twin Cities.

Contact

Regional Office of Endangered Species
U.S. Fish and Wildlife Service
Federal Building, Fort Snelling
Twin Cities, Minnesota 55111

Noonday Snail

Mesodon clarki nantahala

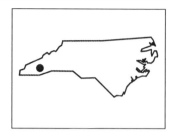

C. Kenneth Dodd, Jr.

Status	Threatened
Listed	July 3, 1978
Family	Polygyridae (Land Snail)
Description	Land snail with a rounded, glossy red shell of 5 1/2 whorls.
Habitat	Profuse vegetation along rocky cliffs.
Food	Probably fungi.
Reproduction	Undescribed.
Threats	Limited distribution.
Region 4	North Carolina

Description

The noonday snail has a rounded shell with five and one-half whorls and a depressed spire. It measures about 18 millimeters (0.72 in) in width and 11 millimeters (0.44 in) in height. The glossy red shell is sculptured by coarse bands.

Behavior

This snail is most active during wet weather and is presumed to feed on fungi. It is found in thick tangles of vegetation, beneath rocks, or in deep, moist leaf litter. Reproductive behavior and other aspects of its life history have not been adequately studied.

Habitat

The noonday snail is found in a damp oak-hickory woodland with a profuse, herbaceous undergrowth. It is particularly common along cliffs with a northern exposure. This area of rock outcroppings and rich, humus-laden soils supports a complex plant community. The habitat is kept moist year round by an abundance of springs, seepages, streams, and waterfalls. The elevation rises steeply from 580 to 945 meters (1,900 to 3,100 ft).

Dominant trees include oak, hickory, American beech, American elm, basswood, birch, and tulip poplar. Rhododendrons and many species of ferns are prominent components of the undergrowth. In recent years, non-native plants such as kudzu and honeysuckle have invaded the habitat.

Historic Range

Woodland snails of the genus *Mesodon* are common throughout the eastern U.S., displaying the greatest diversity in the southern Appalachians. The noonday snail was historically confined to an area of southeastern Tennessee, extreme western North Carolina, and northern Georgia.

Current Distribution

The noonday snail is found in the Nantahala Gorge in North Carolina, along the high cliffs that line the southern banks of the Nantahala River. The portion of the gorge inhabited by the snail extends for several miles along the river near Blowing Springs from Wesser to Hewitt (Swain County). Most of the habitat falls within the boundaries of the Nantahala National Forest. No estimate of the size of the population has been attempted because of the ruggedness of the terrain.

Conservation and Recovery

The noonday snail is restricted to a narrow section of the Nantahala Gorge and is adapted to very specialized conditions of moisture and temperature. Any degradation of the habitat would result in the decline of this species. In recent years, the gorge has become a popular site for canoeing, kayaking, hiking, climbing, and camping. Several camping areas are located close to the habitat. This recreational traffic increased the risks of trampling, forest fires, or other disturbance.

Because the noonday snail is found on public land, protecting its habitat has been relatively straightforward. The Forest Service and the state of North Carolina devised a cooperative habitat management agreement and are conducting further research into the snail's biology. Recreational access to critical portions of the habitat is now closely regulated. Over the next few years, similar habitats along the Nantahala River will be surveyed to determine if other populations of the snail exist.

Bibliography

Roe, C., and J. Moore. 1983. "Recommendations to the U.S. Forest Service Regarding the Designation of the Noonday Snail's Primary Habitat as a Protected Natural Area." Report. North Carolina Department of Natural Resources and Community Development, Raleigh.

U.S. Fish and Wildlife Service. 1984. "Recovery Plan for the Noonday Snail (*Mesodon clarki nantahala*)." U.S. Fish and Wildlife Service, Atlanta.

Contact

Regional Office of Endangered Species
U.S. Fish and Wildlife Service
Richard B. Russell Federal Building
75 Spring Street, S.W.
Atlanta, Georgia 30303

Magazine Mountain Shagreen

Mesodon magazinensis

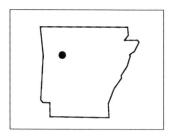

Ron Caldwell

Status . . . . . . Threatened
Listed . . . . . . July 5, 1989
Family . . . . . Polygyridae (Land Snail)
Description . . . Medium-sized, dusky brown, or buff colored shell.
Habitat . . . . . . Rock slide rubble; cool, moist, rocky crevices.
Threats . . . . . Limited distribution, recreational development, military exercises.
Region 4 . . . . . Arkansas

Description

Also known as the Magazine Mountain middle-toothed snail, the Magazine Mountain shagreen is a dusky brown or buff-colored medium-sized land snail, 13 millimeters (0.5) wide and 7 millimeters (0.3 in) high. The shell surface is roughened by half-moon shaped scales. The outer lip of the aperture has a small triangular tooth, while the inner side has a single blade-like tooth. It is similar in appearance to the more common *Mesodon infectus.*

Habitat

This snail has been collected from rock slide rubble at the base of a north-facing rocky escarpment. It prefers cool, moist conditions and burrows far back into crevices in the cliffs, during the hottest part of summer. Habitat elevation ranges from 600 to 790 meters (2,000 to 2,600 ft).

Historic Range

This species is known only from a single location on Magazine Mountain in Logan County, Arkansas. Magazine Mountain is relatively separate from other mountains in the region and is considered an "island" ecosystem—one that supports a diversity of endemic species within a narrowly defined range.

Current Distribution

The shagreen's known range is included within the Ozark National Forest and is classified as a Special Interest Area. Magazine

Mountain was recently proposed as a candidate for designation as a Research Natural Area.

Conservation and Recovery

Because of this snail's extremely limited range, it would be vulnerable to any land use change or other activity that might disrupt the habitat's fragile ecological balance. In 1989 the Arkansas Department of Parks and Tourism applied for a Special Use permit from the Forest Service to develop a state park on Magazine Mountain. The Fish and Wildlife Service (FWS) has expressed the opinion that construction of access roads, buildings, pipelines, and trails would adversely affect the snail if these activities disrupted rock slide rubble on the north slope. The FWS, the Forest Service, and the state are currently negotiating to determine the feasibility of the proposed state park.

The Army has petitioned to use the vicinity of Magazine Mountain for training exercises, and the FWS has expressed the same reservations. Military exercises could only be permitted if troop, vehicle, and artillery movements did not disturb the north slope of the mountain. Under provisions of the Endangered Species Act, the Army is required to consult with the FWS before any exercises are undertaken. Such a consultation might allow exercises to be held, so long as conditions to protect the snail's habitat are met.

The Forest Service will consider the welfare of the shagreen in the next draft of its management plan for the Ozark National Forest.

Bibliography

Caldwell, R. S. 1986. "Status of *Mesodon magazinensis*, the Magazine Mountain Middle-Toothed Snail." Report for Grant No. 84-

1. Arkanasas Nongame Species Preservation Program, Little Rock.

Hubricht, L. 1972. "The Land Snails of Arkansas." *Sterkiana* 46:15-16.

Contact

Regional Office of Endangered Species
U.S. Fish and Wildlife Service
Richard B. Russell Federal Building
75 Spring Street, S.W.
Atlanta, Georgia 30303

Stock Island Snail
Orthalicus reses reses

Sterling ♦'mmitt

Status . . . . . Threatened
Listed . . . . . July 3, 1978
Family . . . . . Bulimulidae (Tree Snail)
Description . . . Large conical snail, up to 5.5 cm (2.2 in) long, white or buff shell with narrow, flamelike purple stripes.
Habitat . . . . . Tropical hardwood forests.
Threats . . . . Limited distribution, residential and recreational development.
Region 4 . . . . . Florida

Description

The Stock Island snail is a large, conical tree snail, which attains a mature shell length of 5.5 centimeters (2.2 in). The translucent shell is thin and lightweight compared to most other snails of this genus. The color is white to buff with three poorly developed bands and narrow flamelike purple stripes. The shell spirals into two or three whorls.

Behavior

The Stock Island snail lives exclusively in trees, hiding in holes, bark crevices, and leaf clusters. It feeds on lichen, fungi, and algae, and is most active between June and December after a rainfall. This snail is hermaphroditic (with both male and female reproductive organs), although it is not self-fertilizing. It needs a mate to reproduce. During dry weather, the snail enters a dormant state, known as aestivation.

Habitat

The Stock Island snail inhabits a wide range of tropical hardwood trees and has adapted to several types of exotic ornamentals. It has been found on such native trees as sweet acacia, saffron plum, gumbo-limbo, icaco-coco plum, and mahogany. Non-native trees include Jamaica caper, lead tree, and tamarind.

Historic Range

The historic range encompassed Stock Island and Key West in Monroe County,

Florida. The snail has since disappeared from Key West.

Current Distribution

When the snail was placed on the federal list in 1978, the population was estimated between 200 and 800 individuals, found at two sites on Stock Island. In 1986, a survey conducted by The Nature Conservancy determined that a major portion of the habitat had been lost to residential development and golf course expansion. Fewer than 100 of the snails were thought to survive on about 2 hectares (5 acres) on Stock Island adjacent to the Key West Municipal Golf Course. In 1987, Fish and Wildlife Service (FWS) biologists visited the site and determined that the snail population was confined to about 20 trees and probably numbered less than 50.

Conservation and Recovery

The snail's remaining range is so restricted that almost any natural or man-made disaster could render the species extinct. Much of the ground area near inhabited trees has been paved to accommodate a county parking lot. County workers, in a misguided effort to protect snail-inhabited trees, surrounded the bases of the trees with gravel. This gravel deprived the snail of access to leaf litter and humus in which to lay its eggs. In 1988, the FWS successfully negotiated with the county to remove the gravel and replace the natural soil and organic litter.

The precipitous decline of the snail population has forced FWS personnel to consider translocating snails and eggs to a more protected location. The population has declined to such a low level, however, that translocation might actually exterminate the snail. A second problem with translocation is that no suitable habitat appears to remain in the Florida Keys. Biologists have little material to work with and no room for error. The FWS and Florida chapters of the Audubon Society and The Nature Conservancy have unsuccessfully surveyed the region for other populations of the snail.

Bibliography

U.S. Fish and Wildlife Service. 1982. "Stock Island Tree Snail Recovery Plan." U.S. Fish and Wildlife Service, Atlanta.

Contact

Regional Office of Endangered Species
U.S. Fish and Wildlife Service
Richard B. Russell Federal Building
75 Spring Street, S.W.
Atlanta, Georgia 30303

Virginia Fringed
Mountain Snail
Polygyriscus virginianus

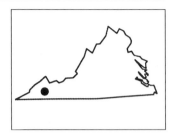

Robert E. Batie

Status . . . . . Endangered
Listed . . . . . July 3, 1978
Family . . . . . Helicodiscidae (Mountain Snail)
Description . . . Flat, spiral-shelled snail, greenish brown with white opening.
Habitat . . . . . Damp clay soils.
Food . . . . . . Unknown.
Reproduction . . Clutch of 2 eggs per season.
Threats . . . . . Restricted range.
Region 5 . . . . Virginia

Description

The tiny shell of the Virginia fringed mountain snail measures only 4.5 millimeters (0.18 in) in diameter. The shell has four to five whorls, increasing in thickness toward the rim. The shell is pale greenish brown with a white aperture. Eight to ten spiral, comb-like fringes occur inside the low spiral grooves of the shell surface. The living animal inside the shell is white with unpigmented eyestalks and is probably blind.

The fringed mountain snail is the only species in it genus. It was originally described in 1947 from weathered shells found in the soil and was not known as a living species until 1971, when Leslie Hubricht found 14 living adults and seven immature specimens. This snail has been studied very little because of its rarity, limited distribution, and secretive habits. It is considered one of the rarest land snails in North America.

Behavior

Little is known about the biology of this snail. It is a burrower and almost never comes to the surface except during extremely wet weather. Its reproduction may be similar to that of *Helicodiscus parallelus*, which lays two eggs per season.

Habitat

This species has a very restricted habitat. It occurs along a steep river bank beneath the surface of permanently damp clay soils, loosened with limestone chips. The surface of the ground is relatively free of leaf litter. The site is dominated by pine and oak scrub and honeysuckle.

Historic Range

The Virginia fringed mountain snail is presumed to be endemic to Pulaski County, Virginia.

Current Distribution

The Virginia fringed mountain snail has been found only at a single site on the north bank of the New River opposite the town of Radford in Pulaski County. Only about 30 of these snails have ever been found alive. The entire known range consists of a strip of bluff, embankment, and talus slope, 2.5 kilometers (1.5 miles) long, along the river. The size of the population remains unknown because excavating to census the buried snails would severely disturb the habitat. It is considered very rare.

Conservation and Recovery

Any organism as rare as the Virginia snail can be seriously endangered by events and circumstances that would have little impact on a more plentiful species. Possible threats include the application of herbicides along nearby roadsides, road construction and maintenance, and reactivation of an old quarry adjacent to the habitat. None of these activities is currently anticipated.

On the positive side, the habitat appears stable; if left strictly alone, the snail would probably continue to survive in small numbers as it has for centuries. The Fish and Wildlife Service (FWS) Recovery Plan stresses the need for additional research to aid the recovery effort. Suitable habitat within a ten-mile radius will be surveyed in the hope of locating additional populations. The FWS has negotiated temporary conservation agreements with private landowners to protect the river bank. Eventually, the land could be acquired and managed as a snail preserve.

Bibliography

Grimm, F. W. 1981. "Distribution, Habitat Requirements and Recovery Needs of the Endangered Land Snail, *Polygyriscus virginianus*." Contract Report. U.S. Fish and Wildlife Service, Newton Corner, Massachusettes.

Hubricht, L. 1972. "Endangered Land Snails of the Eastern United States." *Sterkiana* 45:33.

Solem, A. 1975. "*Polygyriscus virginianus*: A Helicodiscid Land Snail." *Nautilus* 89(3):80-86.

U.S. Fish and Wildlife Service. 1983. "Virginia Fringed Mountain Snail Recovery Plan." U.S. Fish and Wildlife Service, Atlanta.

Contact

Regional Office of Endangered Species
U.S. Fish and Wildlife Service
One Gateway Center, Suite 700
Newton Corner, Massachusetts 02158

Chittenango Ovate Amber Snail

Succinea chittenangoensis

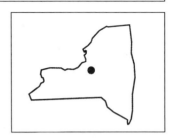

Peter Nye

Status	Threatened
Listed	July 3, 1978
Family	Succineida (Land Snail)
Description . . .	Land snail with a slender, egg-shaped, spiral shell; pale yellow to off-white marked with growth wrinkles and lines.
Habitat	Vegetation in waterfall spray zone.
Food	Microscopic plants.
Reproduction . .	Clutch of up to 15 eggs.
Threats	Extremely limited range.
Region 5	New York

Description

The translucent shell of the Chittenango ovate amber snail is a slender egg-shape, about 2 centimeters (0.8 in) long, spiraling into three and one-half whorls. The color is a pale yellow to off-white. The shell surface is glossy and marked with growth wrinkles and lines. The color of the living animal is a pale, translucent yellow. The mantle (the outer covering of the soft parts) is pale yellow, tinted with olive, and often marked with black streaks and blotches.

This snail was first described as a subspecies of the more widespread ovate amber snail (*Succinea ovalis*) and is referred to in many publications as *S. o. chittenangoensis*.

Behavior

The Chittenango ovate amber snail is a terrestrial species that prefers cool, sunlit areas of lush plant growth within the spray zone of waterfalls. The snail apparently feeds on microscopic plants and in some way ingests high levels of calcium carbonate for its shell development.

Sexually mature snails deposit up to 15 transparent, jelly-like eggs at the base of plants or in loose wet soil. The young snails hatch in two to three weeks and grow to maturity during the following spring. After two years, snails reach their full size. They then die, completing their life span in about two and one-half years.

Habitat

The ovate amber snail is found among the vegetation that covers slopes adjacent to a single waterfall. It is prominent among patches of watercress at the very edges of the stream. Most of the fall's spray zone is covered with patches of mosses and liverworts. Skunk cabbages and angelica grow in the drier areas. Temperatures are mild and relatively constant, regulated by the waterfall mist. Humidity in the habitat is high.

Historic Range

This species may have been widely distributed during the Pleistocene epoch throughout portions of Arkansas, Illinois, Iowa, Michigan, Missouri, Nebraska, and Ontario, as well as in New York. It was first discovered at Chittenango Falls in central New York in 1905.

Current Distribution

One colony of this snail is known to survive at Chittenango Falls State Park (Madison County), New York. The population is divided into two groups living on either side of the falls. The total population was estimated in 1982 at less than 500 snails.

Conservation and Recovery

The primary reason for listing this species as threatened is its extremely limited range and its apparent decline since its discovery. Since it has been studied so little, actual causes for the decline are unknown.

Although the water quality of the stream is relatively high, these snails may be intolerant of trace amounts of chemical runoff. Most of the watershed of Chittenango Creek is used for agriculture, and fertilizers, herbicides, and pesticides enter the drainage. Winter road salt increases the salinity of the water. Recovery of this species will require strict protection of its habitat and reduction of pollutants entering the stream.

Over 100,000 visitors come to the state park each year for recreation. Although the immediate falls area is fairly inaccessible, some trampling and dislodging of rocks has been observed. These disturbances can have a severe effect on the success of snail reproduction. State park personnel have developed a management plan to redirect visitors away from the habitat area and to restrict visitor access to the immediate vicinity of the falls.

Further recovery actions will depend on the results of ongoing research into the snail's biology and habitat requirements. Biologists feel that there is a good chance that other populations of the snail may yet be found in central New York state.

Bibliography

Grimm, F. W. 1981. "A Review of the Chittenango Ovate Amber Snail, *Succinea chittenangoensis*." Report. New York State Department of Environmental Conservation, Albany.

Hubricht, L. 1972. "Endangered Land Snails of the Eastern United States." *Sterkiana* 45:33-34.

Solem, A. 1976. "Status of *Succinea ovalis chittenangoensis* Pilsbry, 1908." *Nautilus* 90(3): 107-114.

U.S. Fish and Wildlife Service. 1983. "Chittenango Ovate Amber Snail Recovery Plan." U.S. Fish and Wildlife Service, Newton Corner, Massachusetts.

Contact

Regional Office of Endangered Species
U.S. Fish and Wildlife Service
One Gateway Center, Suite 700
Newton Corner, Massachusetts 02158

Flat-Spired
Three-Toothed Snail

Triodopsis platysayoides

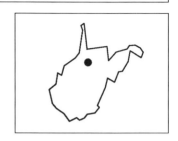

Craig W. Stihler

Status	Threatened
Listed	July 3, 1978
Family	Polygyridae (Land Snail)
Description . . .	Land snail with a light or red-dish brown five-whorled shell.
Habitat	Deciduous and mixed-pine deciduous forest.
Food	Lichens.
Reproduction . .	Undescribed.
Threats	Restricted distribution, habitat disturbance.
Region 5	West Virginia

Description

The flat-spired three-toothed snail has a thin, flattened, five-whorled shell, 3 centimeters (1.2 in) in diameter and up to 1.1 centimeters (0.4 in) thick. The shell is light brown to light reddish brown with oblique banding. The aperture is oblique with a narrow white lip. A thick, white conical tooth is present on the inner wall of the shell. This species was first classified as *Polygra platysayoides*.

Behavior

This snail feeds mainly on lichens on rock surfaces and in leaf litter and will occasionally feed on other snails. Densities must be sustained at less than four snails per square foot to prevent cannibalism. These snails breed in captivity in temperatures between 5

degrees and 15 degrees C (41 and 59 F). In damp, cool weather, snails venture out into the deep, shaded litter at the base of cobbles and boulders. In dry, hot weather they retreat into the crevices of exposed sandstone boulders. Predators are thought to be shrews and beetles.

Habitat

These snails live mostly in a deep, moist layer of leaf litter among sandstone boulders in a mixed pine and deciduous forest. Habitat elevation ranges between 540 and 600 meters (1,800 and 2,000 ft).

Historic Range

This species is extremely rare and probably never ranged much outside of Monongalia County, West Virginia. The genus Triodopsis is relatively widespread in the eastern U.S. where 28 species are known. Closely related species are *T. complanata* in Kentucky and *T. tennesseensis* in Kentucky, Tennessee, West Virginia, Virginia, and North Carolina.

Current Distribution

The flat-spired three-toothed snail inhabits an area below the summit of Cooper's Rock adjacent to Cheat River Canyon in Monongalia County. Most of the habitat falls within the Cooper's Rock Recreational Area which is part of Cooper's Rock State Forest. Research in the early 1970s placed the population at between 300 to 500 individuals. More recent studies suggest that the population may number closer to 1,000.

Conservation and Recovery

Cooper's Rock Recreational Area and State Forest attracts over 450,000 visitors annually. Facilities and concessions on top of Cooper's Rock draw heavy traffic to the summit. Many visitors do not keep to the trails and seriously disturb the leaf litter in which the snail forages.

Because so little is known about this species, the recovery strategy will depend on the results of ongoing research to determine distribution, reproduction, and habitat requirements. In the meantime, state park personnel have limited access to the population site by fencing and rerouting hiking trails. If disturbance can be minimized, the snail population will probably stabilize.

Bibliography

Brooks, S. T. 1933. "*Polygra platysayoides*, a New Species from West Virginia." *Nautilus* 46:54

Hubricht, L. 1972. "Endangered Land Snails of the Eastern United States." *Sterkiana* 45:33.

MacMillan, G. K. 1949. "Land Snails of West Virginia." *Annals of the Carnegie Museum* 31:89-239

U.S. Fish and Wildlife Service. 1983. "The Flat-Spired, Three-Toothed Snail Recovery Plan." U.S. Fish and Wildlife Service, Newton Corner, Massachusetts.

Contact

Regional Office of Endangered Species
U.S. Fish and Wildlife Service
One Gateway Center, Suite 700
Newton Corner, Massachusetts 02158

INSECTS
ARACHNIDS

Ash Meadows Naucorid

Ambrysus amargosus

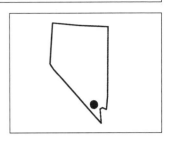

Status	Threatened
Listed	May 20, 1985
Family	Naucoridae (Naucorid)
Description	Small aquatic insect.
Habitat	Ash Meadows; spring out-flows.
Food	Plant matter, detritus.
Threats	Limited range, stream channelization and water diversion.
Region 1	Nevada

Dan A. Polhemus

Description

The Ash Meadows naucorid is a small aquatic insect of the family Naucoridae, order Hemiptera; it is 6 millimeters (0.2 in) in length and superficially resembles a common brown waterbug.

Behavior

This species lives its complete life cycle in an aquatic habitat. It feeds on plant matter. All life stages feed on small aquatic insect larvae and other benthic arthropods.

Habitat

The Ash Meadows naucorid has been found only in a single warm spring and associated outflow streams with rock and gravel substrates.

Ash Meadows is a unique desert wetland east of the Amargosa River in California and Nevada, maintained by springs and seeps from an underground aquifer. The habitat supports an extraordinary diversity of freshwater mollusk species. Of special interest are the numerous varieties of snails found within Ash Meadows, giving this area the highest concentration of endemic species of any region of comparable size within the United States.

Historic Range

There is no evidence that this species ever occured in other springs or streams of the Ash Meadows region in Nevada. Most Ash

Meadows springs are cold, while this species requires thermal waters. Channelization of spring flows for irrigation and other purposes has restricted the original habitat.

Current Distribution

This naucorid is found only at Point of Rocks Springs and its outflow streams in east-central Ash Meadows. In the late 1970s a developer dammed the Point of Rocks Springs outflow to supply a planned residential and resort community of 55,000. Although this project was eventually abandoned, the natural streams inhabited by the naucorid were lost, and the species is now restricted to several narrow artificial channels less than 10 meters (33 ft) long. There is no current population estimate.

Conservation and Recovery

One threat to the naucorid's survival is potential groundwater depletion, which would decrease spring flows. In 1982, it was found that users were certified to consume more water per year than the Ash Meadows aquifer actually discharged. If users drew the maximum amount of water allowed, the habitats supporting the Ash Meadows flora and fauna would be destroyed. Subsequently, the courts acted to limit the amount of groundwater that could be pumped from the aquifer.

In 1984 The Nature Conservancy purchased land and water rights to nearly 4,533 hectares (11,200 acres) to establish the Ash Meadows Wildlife Refuge in a bid to ensure that the habitat remained undeveloped. In 1985, after funds were appropriated, the Fish and Wildlife Service acquired the refuge and made it part of the national refuge system. This is an important step in the recovery of Ash Meadows naucorid and other endangered species in the area.

Remaining habitat of the Ash Meadows naucorid falls within the refuge. About 4 hectares (10 acres) has been designated as Critical Habitat for the species, including Point of Rocks Springs and its immediate outflows. The federally listed Ash Meadows Amargosa pupfish (*Cyprinodon nevadensis mionectes*) shares the same spring outflow area with the naucorid.

Bibliography

La Rivers, I. 1953. "New Gelastocorid and Naucorid Records and Miscellaneous Notes with a Description of the New Species, Ambrysus amargosus (Hemiptera: Naucoridae)." *The Wasmann Journal of Biology* 11:83-96.

Contact

Office of Endangered Species
U.S. Fish and Wildlife Service
Lloyd 500 Building, Suite 1692
500 N.E. Multnomah Street
Portland, Oregon 97232

Lange's Metalmark Butterfly

Apodemia mormo langei

Richard A. Arnold

Status	Endangered
Listed	June 1, 1976
Family	Lycaenidae (Gossamer-Winged Butterfly)
Description	Orange, brightly patterned butterfly with white and black markings.
Habitat	Sand dunes.
Host Plant	Buckwheat.
Threats	Competition with introduced plants, land-clearing.
Region 1	California

Description

Lange's metalmark butterfly is a bright reddish orange butterfly, brightly patterned above with four black-bordered, pearl-white squares on the front wings. Back wings have large white squares and polygons. The wingspan is from 2 to 3.2 centimeters (0.8 to 1.25 in).

Behavior

The swift-flying Lange's metalmark is seen between early August and mid-September. Adult females can fly long distances—as far as 400 meters (1,300 ft)—before perching head-up or head-down to feed on flower nectar. It lays grayish eggs singly or in small clusters on the lower half of the larval host plant. The eggs remain dormant until the rainy season, when the larvae hatch and crawl to the base of the plant where they overwinter. Larvae are nocturnal and feed on new plant growth in late fall and early winter. This species produces one brood in a season.

Habitat

This butterfly inhabits stabilized sand dunes along the San Joaquin River. Its primary host plant is a subspecies of naked buckwheat (*Eriogonum nudum* var. *auriculatum*). It depends on host plants for breeding but feeds on the nectar of other wildflowers, if buckwheat is not available. Neither sex strays far from buckwheat stands, but females tend to fly more frequently between clumps than do the less mobile males.

Historic Range

Lange's metalmark is endemic to the Antioch Dunes, which are situated at the confluence of the San Joaquin and Sacramento rivers east of the City of Antioch in Contra Costa County, California.

Current Distribution

The present range of this subspecies has been reduced to about 6 hectares (15 acres). Annual surveys during peak breeding season produced counts of 150 butterflies in 1986; 140 in 1987; and 500 in 1988. The total population is extrapolated from these counts and is thought to average about 400.

The Fish and Wildlife Service (FWS) acquired approximately 28 hectares (70 acres) of the Antioch Dunes, including a portion of the Lange's metalmark's range, adding it as a satellite to the San Francisco Bay National Wildlife Refuge Complex.

Conservation and Recovery

The size of the population is limited by the abundance of the butterfly's host buckwheat, which has been crowded out of much of the Antioch Dunes by invading non-native plants. Other stands of buckwheat were destroyed by maintenance activities along a powerline right-of-way in the late 1970s. Portions of the dunes have been mined for sand. These cleared areas eventually recover, and private groups have helped reseed disturbed areas.

In the 1980s Antioch Dunes began to feel the negative effects of increased recreational use. Visitors severely trampled and littered the fragile dunes habitat. The *coup de grace* was applied by the unexpected visit of

"Humphrey the Humpback Whale." When this whale—ironically an endangered species, itself—was stranded for a time in the Sacramento River, the highly publicized rescue attempt brought large crowds to the refuge, causing severe damage to plantlife. As a result, the FWS closed the Antioch Dunes National Wildlife Refuge to unescorted groups in 1988 and 1989.

Captive breeding of this butterfly and cultivation of its host plant—along with the removal of introduced plants—may be necessary for its recovery. FWS personnel have discussed importing sand to restore the dunes area. A local utility operating a right-of-way adjacent to the refuge funded buckwheat planting and habitat restoration both on its land and within the refuge.

A public awareness program to provide informational brochures and place interpretive signs has been implemented to alert visitors to the fragility of the dunes habitat.

Bibliography

Arnold, R. A. 1978. "Status of Six Endangered California Butterflies." Report. California Department of Fish and Game, Sacramento.

Arnold, R. A. 1983. "Ecological Studies on Six Endangered Butterflies (Lepidoptera: Lycaenidae): Island Biogeography, Patch Dynamics, and the Design of Habitat Preserves. "University of *California Publications in Entomology*" 99:1-161.

U.S. Fish and Wildlife Service. 1984. "Revised Recovery Plan for Three Endangered Species Endemic to Antioch Dunes, California." U.S. Fish and Wildlife Service, Portland.

Contact

Regional Office of Endangered Species
U.S. Fish and Wildlife Service
Lloyd 500 Building, Suite 1692
500 N.E. Multnomah Street
Portland, Oregon 97232

San Bruno Elfin Butterfly

Callophrys mossii bayensis

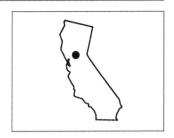

Richard A. Arnold

Status	Endangered
Listed	June 1, 1976
Family	Lycaenidae (Gossamer-Winged Butterfly)
Description	Small, brown-winged butterfly with gray undersides.
Habitat	Grasslands and coastal scrub.
Host Plant	Liveforever, stonecrop.
Threats	Urbanization.
Region 1	California

Description

The San Bruno elfin is a diminutive butterfly with brown upperside front wings, and undersides that are patterned with gray or dark brown. Hind wings are without tails.

Behavior

The San Bruno elfin produces one brood per year. Adults emerge from pupae late February to mid-April, with a peak in late March. Eggs are laid primarily on the foliage of the larval host plant. The larvae hatch in five to seven days. By the time the host plant blooms, third instar (stage) larvae crawl up the flowering stalks and feed on the flower-heads. Third and fourth instar larvae are tended by ants. The larvae secrete a honeydew substance, which the ants take in exchange for protecting the larvae from predators. Pupation occurs around the base of the host plant and lasts from June until the following March.

Habitat

San Bruno elfin butterflies are found in a mountainous area with a grassy ground cover. The mountain side supports scattered patches of coastal scrub and woodlands and is crossed by several intermittent streams. The San Bruno elfin butterfly's larval host plants are liveforever (*Sedum spathulifolium*) and stonecrop.

Historic Range

The historic range of this butterfly probably encompassed hilltops and ridges from northern San Mateo County, California, to the San Francisco Peninsula and northward into Marin County.

Current Distribution

San Bruno Mountain, the major population site for the San Bruno elfin butterfly, is immediately south of the city of San Francisco in San Mateo County and is the northernmost extension of the Santa Cruz Mountains. The habitat is bordered by South San Francisco on the south, Brisbane on the east, Colma on the southwest, and Daly City on the north. The mountain encompasses about 1,465 hectares (3620 acres)—about half of which is owned by the San Mateo County Parks and Recreation Department. Smaller parcels are owned by the California State Parks Foundation and by Visitacion Associates, a development company.

Additional, small populations of San Bruno elfin butterfly occur at Milagra Ridge, southwest of San Bruno Mountain adjacent to the city of Pacifica, and further south at Montara Mountain, Whiting Ridge, and Peak Mountain, adjacent to the city of Montara. No recent population figures are available, although quarrying recently wiped out a major population.

Conservation and Recovery

Continuing urbanization in the San Francisco Bay area threatens to reduce the San Bruno elfin butterfly's aleady limited habitat. A major portion of its remaining habitat has been under private ownership since the late 1800s. The habitat has been disturbed by road and utility-line construction, rock and sand quarrying, livestock grazing, invasion of exotic species, and water diversion.

Grazing and frequent grassfires have encouraged the growth of many introduced plants in the grasslands and reduced the coastal scrub. The permit for the exisiting rock quarry expires in the mid-1990s and it will close at that time subject to renewal. A reclamation plan emphasizing revegetation of the area is currently being reviewed.

In the early 1980s a Habitat Conservation Plan was developed to allow private and public development on the mountain while minimizing the adverse effects on endangered species. The plan's goal is the long-term preservation of all rare species within the area. In the meantime, the Fish and Wildlife Service Recovery Plan recommends a program to minimize the use of herbicides and other toxic substances, to remove non-native plants, and to reestablish native plants, especially the host plant of the San Bruno elfin butterfly.

Bibliography

Arnold, R. A. 1983. "Ecological Studies o Six Endangered Butterfliew (Lepidoptera: Lycaenidae): Island Biogeography, Patch Dynamics, and the Design of Habitat Preserves." *University of California Publications in Entomology* 99:1-161.

San Bruno Mountain Habitat Conservation Plan Steering Committee. 1982. "San Bruno Mountain Area Habitat Conservation Plan." San Mateo County Planning Division, Redwood City, California.

U.S. Fish and Wildlife Service. 1984. "Recovery Plan for the San Bruno Elfin and Mission Blue Butterflies." U.S. Fish and Wildlife Service, Portland.

Contact

Regional Office of Endangered Species
U.S. Fish and Wildlife Service
Lloyd 500 Building, Suite 1692
500 N.W. Multnomah Street
Portland, Oregon 97232

Valley Elderberry Longhorn Beetle

Desmocerus californicus dimorphus

Richard A. Arnold

Status	Threatened
Listed	August 8, 1980
Family	Cerambycidae (Longhorn Beetle)
Description	Brightly colored beetle with elongated cylindrical body.
Habitat	Elderberry thickets in moist riparian woodlands.
Host Plant	Elderberry.
Threats	Agricultural development, levee construction, maintenance activities.
Region 1	California

Description

The valley elderberry longhorn beetle is a member of the family Cerambycidae (subfamily Lepturinae), distinguished by a cylindrical body as long as 5 centimeters (2 in). Males of the species exhibit several patterns of coloration: dark metallic green above with a bright reddish orange border; four oblong metallic green spots on the outer wings (elytra); or gradations. Males possess longer, more robust antennae than females. Females are larger than males. This beetle is similar in appearance to the California elderberry longhorn beetle (*Desmocerus californicus californicus*).

Behavior

About 400 species of longhorn beetles are found in California; all are herbivorous and frequently associated with a particular plant host. The valley elderberry longhorn beetle is associated with three species of elderberry (*Sambucus*). It deposits eggs in cracks and crevices of the bark of living elderberry bushes, which hatch soon afterward. The larvae bore into the pith of larger stems and roots and, when ready to pupate, open holes through the bark. The life cycle probably encompasses two years. Adults emerge about the same time the elderberry blooms—as early as mid-March—and may live until mid-June.

Habitat

The valley elderberry longhorn beetle inhabits elderberry thickets in moist oak woodlands along the banks of streams and rivers. The host plant sometimes suffers from fungus attack at the emergence holes bored by the beetle, weakening or killing the plant.

Historic Range

This beetle is endemic to the banks of the Sacramento, American, and San Joaquin rivers and their tributaries in the Central Valley of California. The beetle's major population center is along the American River.

Current Distribution

Remnant populations of this longhorn beetle are found in the few stands of natural riverside (riparian) woodlands that remain in the Central Valley. As of 1988, the beetle was known from ten localities in five counties: Merced, Sacramento, San Joaquin, Stanislaus, and Yolo. Sacramento County supports the largest concentrations of the beetle.

Populations are found along the American River bordering the American River Parkway; the Merced River in the McConnell State Recreation Area; Putah Creek in Solano Creek Park; and the Stanislaus River. A 1987 survey found beetle emergence holes in elderberry bushes along the Feather, Cosumnes, and upper Sacramento rivers.

Conservation and Recovery

The primary threat to the valley elderberry longhorn beetle is continued loss of habitat. Riparian woodlands have largely diminished due to agricultural conversion, levee construction, and stream channelization. Elderberry bushes were destroyed during maintenance on the American River Flood Control Project in 1985, but the California Department of Water Resources agreed to replant bushes and prevent future disturbance. In 1987, however, personnel from the state reclamation district mowed the habitat along the east levee of the American River, claiming that all wild growth—without exception—must be removed. This decision has been contested by the Fish and Wildlife Service (FWS).

In 1986, 174 hectares (430 acres) were purchased by Sacramento County along the American River Parkway. The county plans to maintain this land as a habitat for the beetle and to reclaim portions that were previously used for other purposes.

As part of a mitigation agreement, FWS and state botanists have transplanted elderberry bushes infested with beetle larvae to new locations. At one transplant site near Sacramento, beetles were seen to emerge from transplanted trees in April 1988. A second site near Sacramento's main landfill was destroyed by leaking contaminants. Remnants of riparian woodlands within the historic range of the valley elderberry longhorn beetle are being surveyed to identify other potential transplant sites.

Bibliography

Eng, L. L. 1983. "Rare, Threatened, and Endangered Invertebrates in Californian Riparian Systems." California Riparian Systems Conference, Sacramento.

Sands, A. 1982. "The Value of Riparian Habitat." *Fremontia* 10:3-7.

U.S. Fish and Wildlife Service. 1984. "Valley Elderberry Longhorn Beetle Recovery Plan." U.S. Fish and Wildlife Service, Portland.

Contact

Regional Office of Endangered Species
U.S. Fish and Wildlife Service
Lloyd 500 Building, Suite 1692
500 N.E. Multnomah Street
Portland, Oregon 97232

Delta Green
Ground Beetle
Elaphrus viridis

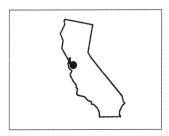

Fred Andrews

Status . . . . . . Threatened
Listed . . . . . . August 8, 1980
Family . . . . . . Carabidae (Ground Beetle)
Description . . . Predatory beetle; dull golden above, metallic green beneath.
Habitat . . . . . . Edges of vernal pools.
Food . . . . Springtails.
Threats . . . . . . Loss of seasonal wetlands.
Region 1 . . . . . California

Description

The delta green ground beetle is about 6 millimeters (0.25 in) long when mature. It is golden or bronze above and metallic green beneath. This beetle resembles a tiger beetle with its relatively large abdomen, smaller but distinct thorax and head, and long slender legs. It is smaller than the tiger beetle and has spotlike depressions on its leathery outer wings. Its antennae are short and blunt.

Behavior

In general, the genus *Elaphrus* is associated with temperate wetland habitats. Many specific details of the life history of the delta ground beetle are unknown. The primary food source is thought to be springtails (flea-like insects of the order Collembola). The delta green ground beetle is active during the warmest and sunniest part of the day early February to mid-May. The nocturnal larvae are found in greater concentrations and inhabit damper areas than adults. This species produces one generation per year.

Habitat

Adult beetles inhabit the grassy edges of vernal pools that are filled by winter rains but dry up by late summer. Typically, pools are small depressions within generally level terrain. Water inundates the area long enough to inhibit development of typical grassland vegetation. The climate is Mediterranean, with cool rainy winters and warm, dry summers.

Historic Range

Although this beetle was first described in 1878, its range remained a mystery until 1974 when a student from the University of California discovered a population at the Jepson Prairie in Solano County. The species was originally widespread in the once numerous vernal pools of central California.

Current Distribution

The delta green ground beetle is known to inhabit two sites in Solano County, California, south of Dixon at Olcott Lake. A portion of the habitat falls within the Jepson Prairie Preserve, which is owned and managed jointly by The Nature Conservancy and the University of California (Davis). Between 1974 and 1985, only 75 individuals were observed at the preserve.

Conservation and Recovery

Many vernal pools have disappeared from the California landscape because of the increased human control of natural water flows. Rivers have been dammed and channeled for irrigation, and wetlands have been drained or filled for cropland. Only a few seasonal pools remain intact. Plowing and water pumping have already caused remaining pools to shrink or dry up earlier in the summer, a change in timing that has a critical impact on the life cycle of dependent insects. In 1980 plowing and grading damaged one inhabited pool, and further disturbance would probably eliminate the beetle from this site.

The Jepson Prairie Preserve already provides some protection for the delta green ground beetle, and Critical Habitat was designated to include both known population sites. Recovery will focus on limiting further habitat disturbance and translocating the beetle to other suitable sites within its range. A portion of Olcott Lake outside the preserve has been identified as a potential reintroduction site.

Bibliography

Holland, R. F. and F. T. Griggs. 1976. "A Unique Habitat—California's Vernal Pools." *Fremontia* 4:3-6.

U.S. Fish and Wildlife Service. 1985. "Delta Green Ground Beetle and Solano Grass Recovery Plan." U.S. Fish and Wildlife Service, Portland.

Contact

Regional Office of Endangered Species
U.S. Fish and Wildlife Service
Lloyd 500 Building, Suite 1692
500 N.E. Multnomah Street
Portland, Oregon 97232

El Segundo Blue Butterfly

Euphilotes battoides allyni

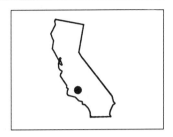

Richard A. Arnold

Status	. . . . . Endangered
Listed	. . . . . June 1, 1976
Family	. . . . . Lycaenidae (Gossamer-Winged Butterfly)
Description	. . . Small bright blue butterfly with black margins on under-wings.
Habitat	. . . . . Coastal sand dunes.
Host Plant	. . . . Wild buckwheat.
Threats	. . . . . Urbanization.
Region 1	. . . . . California

Description

The El Segundo blue butterfly is 20 to 25 millimeters (0.8 to 1 in) long. Males are bright blue above with black margins on their hindwings; females are dark brown above. Both sexes are light grayish below with black squares or spots and an orange band, bordered on both sides by a row of black dots. Formerly classified as *Shijimiaeoides battoides allyni*, this species is difficult to distinguish from other members of its genus.

Behavior

The butterfly lays its eggs on flower buds of the wild buckwheat plant (*Eriogonum parvifolium*). The caterpillar, which is the same color as the buckwheat blossoms, pupates in litter at the base of the host plant or in flower heads. One brood is produced each year, simultaneous with buckwheat flowering. Adults live about one month.

Habitat

The El Segundo blue is found on coastal sand dunes. Urbanization has destroyed or degraded nearly 99 percent of the sand dune habitat.

Historic Range

Historically, this butterfly ranged throughout the El Segundo sand hills in Los Angeles County, California.

Current Distribution

The El Segundo blue is now found only on remnants of the dune ecosystem, limited to a few acres of an oil refinery near El Segundo and to a larger area at the west end of the Los Angeles International Airport.

Conservation and Recovery

The decline of the El Segundo blue can be directly attributed to urbanization. Much of its shorefront habitat has been destroyed by the expansion of the Los Angeles metropolitan area, and further development of remaining habitat would almost certainly cause the butterfly's extinction. The Los Angeles Airport has agreed to manage its dunes in cooperation with the Fish and Wildlife Service to benefit the El Segundo blue butterfly. The Chevron Corporation established a sanctuary for the El Segundo blue butterfly on the grounds of its USA Refinery in 1983 and is currently managing the habitat for the butterfly's protection.

Bibliography

Arnold, R. A., and A. E. Goins. 1987. "Habitat Enhancement Techniques for the El Segundo Blue Butterfly: An Urban Endangered Species." In Adam and Leedy, eds., *Integrating Man and Nature in the Metropolitan Environment*. National Institute for Urban Wildlife, Columbia, Maryland.

U.S. Fish and Wildlife Service. 1978. "Sensitive Wildlife Information System—El Segundo Blue Butterfly." Report. U.S. Fish and Wildlife Service, Washington, D.C.

Contact

Regional Office of Endangered Species
U.S. Fish and Wildlife Service
Lloyd 500 Building, Suite 1692
500 N.E. Multnomah Street
Portland, Oregon 97232

Smith's Blue Butterfly

Euphilotes enoptes smithi

Richard A. Arnold

Status	Endangered
Listed	June 1, 1976
Family	Lycaenidae (Gossamer-Winged Butterfly)
Description	Small butterfly; males are bright blue above, females brown.
Habitat	Coastal sand dunes.
Host Plant	Buckwheat.
Threats	Habitat loss and disturbance.
Region 1	California

Description

Smith's blue butterfly is slightly less than 2.5 centimeters (1 in) across. The male's upper wings are a lustrous blue with wide black borders; females are brown above with a band of red-orange marks across the hind wings. Both sexes have prominent checkered fringes on the fore and hind wings. Smith's blue butterfly can be distinguished from other subspecies by a light undersurface ground color and prominent overlying black markings with a faint black terminal line. Smith's blue was formerly classified as *Shijimiaeoides enoptes smithi*.

Behavior

Adult butterflies feed, rest, sun, and mate on several species of buckwheat (*Eriogonum*), never straying far from host plants. Males perch on flowers, sometimes seeming to watch for approaching females to court. Females deposit eggs individually on buckwheat flowers. Larvae hatch four to eight days later and go through five instars (intermediate stages) before pupating in flower heads or in the sand and litter at the base of the plants.

Pupation occurs between mid-August and early September, and pupae hang in place until adults emerge the following year. Males tend to emerge first; females follow about a week later, at which time courtship and copulation occur. The adult flight period from mid-June to early September corresponds with the blooming of the buckwheat plants. Each adult lives for only about one week, but individual emergences are staggered over the extended flight period.

Habitat

Smith's blue butterfly is found on coastal and inland sand dunes, which support buckwheat and associated species, such as Ben Lomond wallflower, California poppy, bicolor lupine, and ponderosa pine. The butterfly is also found on cliffside coastal sage scrub and serpentine grassland, where dominant grasses are intermixed with buckwheat and other forbs.

Historic Range

The Smith's blue butterfly is an endemic California subspecies, found primarily along the coast from the mouth of the Salinas River to Del Rey Creek.

Current Distribution

The current distribution of Smith's blue butterfly includes coastal portions of Monterey County. Although there is no current population estimate, the butterfly is now considered more abundant than at the time of federal listing due to the discovery of several new populations.

Conservation and Recovery

The Smith's blue butterfly's coastal habitat has suffered a number of disturbances. Dunes are threatened by proposed housing developments, road construction, beach recreation, and off-road vehicles. Some dunes have been invaded by the non-native iceplant and Holland dunegrass, which displace buckwheat. Sand dunes at Fort Ord have been damaged by military activities, and large dunes in the Seaside-Marina dune system have been destroyed by sand mining. Sand mining is also occurring in the Del Monte Forest.

In 1986 the Marina city council prepared a habitat conservation plan for the coastal dunes that lie between Fort Ord and the Salinas River in Monterey County. In 1977 the Army established a butterfly preserve at Fort Ord, and the Youth Conservation Corps has removed non-native plants and attempted to reestablish native plants there.

In 1987 Smith's blue butterfly was confirmed in remnant habitat at Sand City in Monterey County. Some of this dune area has been zoned for housing development, but the city agreed to complete a conservation plan before work proceeds.

Bibliography

Arnold, R. A. 1983. "Ecological Studies on Six Endangered butterflies (Lepidoptera: Lycaenidae): Island Biogeography, Patch Dynamics, and the Design of Habitat Preserves." *University of California Publications in Entomology* 99:1-161.

Langston, R. L. 1963. "*Philotes* of Central Coastal California." *Journal of the Lepidopterists' Society* 17:210-223.

U.S. Fish and Wildlife Service. 1984. "Smith's Blue Butterfly Recovery Plan." U.S. Fish and Wildlife Service, Portland.

Contact

Regional Office of Endangered Species
U.S. Fish and Wildlife Service
Lloyd 500 Building, Suite 1692
500 N.E. Multnomah Street
Portland, Oregon 97232

Bay Checkerspot Butterfly

Euphydryas editha bayensis

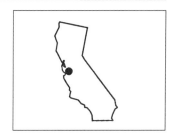

Noel LaDue

Status	. . . . . Threatened
Listed	. . . . . September 18, 1987
Family	. . . . . Nymphalidae (Brush-Footed Butterfly)
Description	. . . Medium-sized butterfly with bright red and yellow spots on upper forewing.
Habitat	. . . . . Grasslands associated with outcrops of serpentine.
Host Plants	. . . Plantain, owl's clover.
Threats	. . . . . Urbanization, drought, over-grazing, fire.
Region 1	. . . . . California

Description

The bay checkerspot is a medium-sized butterfly with a wingspan of 4 to 5.6 centimeters (1.5 to 2.25 in). The upper forewing surfaces have bright red and yellow spots and black bands along the veins. Its appearance is more decidedly checkered than other subspecies of *Euphydryas editha*. It is darker than *E. e. luestherae* and lacks a dark red outerwing band. It has brighter red and yellow coloration than *E. e. insularis*.

Behavior

The bay checkerspot lays eggs on its larval host plants—an annual plantain (*Plantago erecta*) and the hemiparasitic annual owl's clover (*Orthocarpus densiflorus*). The larvae then pupate in leaf litter at the base of the host plants. Both plants seem to be essential for completing the butterfly's life cycle.

Habitat

The host plants grow together in serpentine soils that outcrop throughout the range. Where these soils appear, the supported blend of native herbs and grasses provides preferred habitat. The butterfly thrives only on outcrops larger than about 325 hectares (800 acres), a size that allows the population to survive periods of drought. Smaller outcrops support "satellite" populations that thrive in years of favorable climate.

Historic Range

The bay checkerspot ranges around and south of the San Francisco Bay in San Mateo, western Santa Clara, Alameda, San Francisco, and Contra Costa counties, California. In this area, four large serpentine outcrops and dozens of smaller ones probably supported populations of the bay checkerspot in the recent past. At least 26 satellite bay checkerspot colonies have been documented, but many have been lost to drought, overgrazing, or urbanization.

The largest outcrop occurs near Morgan Hill (Santa Clara County) in a narrow band extending 26 kilometers (16 mi) from Heller Canyon to Anderson Lake. Two large outcrops in San Mateo County were fragmented by construction of Interstate Highway 280. A population historically known from San Leandro (Alameda County) is now extinct. A small population on San Bruno Mountain has not been observed since a 1986 wildfire.

Current Distribution

The largest surviving population of bay checkerspot is at Morgan Hill, but the best-studied colony is at Stanford University's Jasper Ridge Biological Preserve east of Searsville Reservoir. The drought of 1976 and 1977, combined with overgrazing, greatly reduced the Jasper Ridge population.

The second largest population, located in San Mateo County, is threatened by the proposed addition of a golf course and recreation area to Edgewood Park. If implemented, this construction would eliminate 65 percent of the remaining habitat and decimate a population that—because of urbanization and adverse weather conditions—has already declined from 100,000 in 1981 to only about 1,000 in 1987. A larger population in Redwood City was fragmented by urbanization and reduced to satellite

status. A colony near Mt. Diablo (Contra Costa County) was thought to have expired with the last severe drought, but bay checkerspots were found there again in 1988.

Conservation and Recovery

Urban development, highway construction, drought, fire, and livestock grazing have eliminated habitat or altered the composition of local plant communities. When host plants are removed or replaced by other species, the bay checkerspot cannot survive.

A conservation agreement was recently forged between the Fish and Wildlife Service (FWS) and a corporate landowner—Waste Management Inc.—to protect 30 percent of the Morgan Hill site. The FWS believes that this agreement will decrease the overall threat to the species, even though it requires sacrificing 10 percent of the land area to a landfill. For its part, Waste Management agreed to support conservation activities at the site for ten years. As a result, the FWS downlisted the species from Endangered to Threatened.

Bibliography

Ehrlich, P. R., et al. 1975. "Checkerspot Butterflies: A Historical Perspective." *Science* 188:221-228.

Murphy, D. D., and P. R. Ehrlich. 1980. "Two California Checkerspot Butterfly Subspecies: One New, One on the Verge of Extinction." *Journal of the Lepidopterists' Society* 34:316-320.

Contact

Regional Office of Endangered Species
U.S. Fish and Wildlife Service
Lloyd 500 Building, Suite 1692
500 N.E. Multnomah Street
Portland, Oregon 97232

Kern Primrose
Sphinx Moth
Euproserpinus euterpe

John DeLeon, Natural History Museum of Los Angeles County

Status	. . . . . . Threatened
Listed	. . . . . . April 8, 1980
Family	. . . . . . Sphingidae (Sphinx Moth)
Description	. . . Thick-bodied moth with white hind wings with dark margins.
Habitat	. . . . . . Sandy washes, alluvial soils.
Host Plant	. . . . Evening-primrose.
Threats	. . . . . . Collectors, egg-laying on wrong plant.
Region 1	. . . . . California

Description

The thick-bodied Kern primrose sphinx moth is one of three species of the genus *Euproserpinus*. It has white hind wings with dark margins, white underwings, and abruptly hooked antennae. It can be distinguished from the similar phaëton sphinx moth by a marginal band on the hind wing that bows inward rather than running straight along the wing.

Behavior

The flight period of the Kern primrose moth extends from late February to early April. Adults emerge from pupae in the morning, expand their wings, and fly by mid-morning. In the early part of the day, the moth basks on bare patches of soil, dirt roads, or ground squirrel and gopher mounds to warm its flight muscles. Individuals live for one or two weeks.

Mating usually occurs before noon. The female then flies low to the ground and deposits one or two eggs on the underside of the evening-primrose (*Oenothera contorta epilobioides*), the moth's only larval host plant. The larvae develop in the spring, pupate in the soil, and remain inactive until the following spring, when they emerge as adults. Some remain in the pupal stage for several years.

Habitat

The Kern primrose moth is found in Walker Basin, an area 1,470 meters (4,851 ft) above sea level surrounded by the Greenhorn and Piute mountains, which are over 2,000 meters

(6,600 ft) in elevation. The dominant plants on the sandy alluvial soils are filaree, baby blue-eyes, rabbit brush, gold fields, and Brome grass. The surrounding mountain slopes are dominated by juniper, oak, rabbitbrush, sagebrush, and pine. Winter rains in the basin end by mid-April, and summers are dry and hot.

From the moth's perspective, the most important plant in the habitat is the evening-primrose, which grows in dry, disturbed areas, along sandy washes, or adjacent to fallow fields. The plant germinates in February and March, grows quickly, and by mid-June has set seed and dried out.

Historic Range

The Kern primrose sphinx moth is endemic to the Walker Basin in Kern County, California.

Current Distribution

This species is considered the rarest sphinx moth in North America. It was thought extinct until rediscovered in 1974 in a barley field on a privately owned cattle ranch in the Walker Basin. The site remains its only known locality. Field surveys from 1975 to 1979 yielded very low numbers, but in 1979 the population increased dramatically, probably as a result of several years of inactive pupae emerging in response to favorable climatic conditions.

Conservation and Recovery

Land use practices have posed a major threat to the population. The site was repeatedly plowed, disced, and planted from 1962 until the drought of 1975. Since then, cattle have grazed the site, a use that does not seem harmful to the moth or its larval food plant.

A more serious threat to this sphinx moth is the filaree (*Erodium cicutarium*), a plant introduced centuries ago by Spanish explorers. The filaree is widely distributed throughout the area, and egg-laying females often mistake it for the evening-primrose. Eggs deposited on filaree hatch, but larvae cannot digest the plant and do not survive. This rare sphinx moth also suffers at the hands of collectors, who often take the slower-flying females. Federal law now prohibits taking specimens for sale to collectors.

Although the habitat site is on privately owned land, a 1983 survey of the Walker Basin found the site to support more potential habitat than previously believed. At least three additional colonies need to be established to prevent extinction. Developing propagation techniques, however, may take several years.

Bibliography

Tuskes, P. M. and J. F. Emmel. 1981. "The Life History and Behavior of *Euroserpinus euterpe* (Sphingidae)." *Journal of the Lepidopterists' Society* 35:27-33.

U.S. Fish and Wildlife Service. 1984. "The Kern Primrose Sphinx Moth Recovery Plan." U.S. Fish and Wildlife Service, Portland.

Contact

Regional Office of Endangered Species
U.S. Fish and Wildlife Service
Lloyd 500 Building, Suite 1692
500 N.E. Multnomah Street
Portland, Oregon 97232

Palos Verdes Blue Butterfly

Glaucopsyche lygdamus palosverdesensis

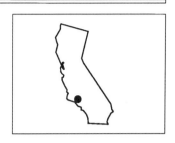

Richard A. Arnold

Status	Endangered (possibly extinct)
Listed	July 2, 1980
Family	Lycaenidae (Gossamer-Winged Butterfly)
Description	Small, silvery blue butterfly with narrow black wing margins.
Habitat	Cool, fog-shrouded slopes.
Host Plant	Locoweed.
Threats	Urbanization, low numbers.
Region 1	California

Description

The Palos Verdes blue butterfly is a small lycaenid butterfly with a wingspan of about 25 millimeters (1 in). It belongs to a species commonly called the "silvery blue butterfly" because of its color. Both sexes are pale gray to dark brownish-gray below, with narrow black margins in the male and diffuse wide dark margins in the female. The Palos Verdes blue is similar in appearance to the common blue and the Reakirt's blue.

Behavior

The Palos Verdes blue butterfly lays eggs on the locoweed (*Astragalus trichopodus* var. *lonchus*). The larvae emerge in seven to ten days and feed on the seeds. When mature, the larvae crawl down the stems to pupate in dried leaf litter around the plant's base or in the seed pods. Adults emerge during the flowering period of the locoweed from mid-February to the end of March.

Habitat

The Palos Verdes blue's larval host plant, the locoweed, grows on well-drained clay or gravelly soils and is frequently found on rocky slopes, especially along the coast.

Historic Range

This species is restricted to the cool, fog-shrouded, seaward side of the Palos Verdes Hills in Los Angeles County, California. The foodplant occurs as far north as Santa Barbara.

Current Distribution

A single known population occupied a large vacant lot near the intersection of Los Verdes Drive and Hawthorne Boulevard in Los Angeles. This site was subsequently cleared for a housing development. Several smaller colonies were discovered nearby, but the present status of the species is in doubt. Some experts feel that this butterfly is already extinct, as it has not been observed in recent years.

Conservation and Recovery

Urbanization has been the main cause of decline of the Palos Verdes blue butterfly. The city and suburbs of Los Angeles have expanded to encompass the butterfly's entire historic range. Weed control practices have all but eliminated the locoweed in and around the city. At remnant habitat sites, the Palos Verdes blue must compete with the more common Western tailed blue butterfly, which also feeds on the locoweed.

The three small habitat areas on the Palos Verdes Peninsula, where the butterfly was last seen, have been designated as Critical Habitat: Agua Amarga Canyon; Frank Hesse Park; and a section along Palos Verdes Drive in the city of Rancho Palos Verdes.

Bibliography

Arnold, R. A. 1980. "Status of Proposed Threatened or Endangered California Lepidoptera." Contract Report to California Department of Fish and Game, Sacramento.

Arnold, R. A. 1987. "Decline of the Endangered Palos Verdes Blue Butterfly in California." *Biological Conservation* 40(1987):203-217

Perkins, E. M., and J. F. Emmel. 1977. "A New Subspecies of *Glaucopsyche lygdamus* from California." *Proceedings of the Entomological Society, Washington* 79:408-71.

U.S. Fish and Wildlife Service. 1984. "The Palos Verdes Blue Butterfly Recovery Plan." U.S. Fish and Wildlife Service, Portland.

Contact

Regional Office of Endangered Species
U.S. Fish and Wildlife Service
Lloyd 500 Building, Suite 1692
500 N.E. Multnomah Street
Portland, Oregon 97232

Schaus Swallowtail Butterfly

Heraclides aristodemus ponceanus

Thomas C. Emmel

Status	. . . . . . Endangered
Listed	. . . . . . August 31, 1984
Family	. . . . . . Papilionidae (Swallowtail Butterfly)
Description	. . . Large, dark brown butterfly; tail bordered in yellow.
Habitat	. . . . . . Hammock vegetation.
Host Plants	. . . Torchwood, wild lime.
Threats	. . . . . . Habitat destruction; loss of larval food plant.
Region 4	. . . . . Florida

Description

Also known as the Keys swallowtail butterfly, Schaus swallowtail is a large (10-13 cm; 4-5 in), dark brown butterfly with dull yellow markings. Its dark tail is bordered in yellow. The black antennae have yellow knobs and black tips. It is easily confused with the giant swallowtail (*Heraclides cresphontes cramer*), which is found in portions of the same habitat. The giant swallowtail is larger than the Schaus and has deeper coloration—bright yellow on coal black.

The Schaus swallowtail is considered one of five subspecies of *Heraclides aristodamus,* a species endemic to the Antilles that tends to vary in appearance according to geographical region. Some taxonomists believe that the Schaus swallowtail is a distinct species. It has

also been scientifically classified as *Papilio aristodemus ponceanus* or *Papilio ponceana.*

Behavior

The Schaus swallowtail emerges from its chrysalis in May and June and feeds on the nectar of guava, cheese shrub, and wild coffee blossoms. It perches on the torchwood plant to bask in the sun. The male is territorial and patrols by circling slowly around intruding males. Schaus swallowtails do not migrate as a group, although individuals sometimes fly across the open water between islands. Adults live about two weeks.

During courtship, the male hovers above and behind the female, who is positioned on the ground with flattened, vibrating wings and a raised abdomen. After fertilization, the female deposits single eggs on the leaves of torchwood and wild lime, the larval host plants. The larvae hatch after three to five days and go through four successive molts. The caterpillar feeds on tender, new growth. After about 20 days, the caterpillar attaches itself to a branch and weaves a thick chrysalis, which can remain dormant for one or two years before the adult butterfly emerges.

Habitat

The Schaus swallowtail lives on hardwood hammocks, which are areas of mature hardwood forest with deep, humus-rich soil typically found in subtropical regions of the southern U.S.

Historic Range

In the past, this swallowtail was found in Florida from the South Miami area (Dade County) to the Lower Matecumbe Key (Monroe County). The last known mainland specimen was collected at Coconut Grove in 1924.

Current Distribution

The Schaus swallowtail now occurs only in the Florida Keys (Monroe County) and is most numerous where host plants are abundant. The population at Elliot Key in 1986 was estimated at between 750 and 1000, with smaller colonies inhabiting several neighboring islands.

Conservation and Recovery

With the urbanization of south Florida, the Schaus swallowtail lost much of its original habitat and suffered the effects of pesticide use. During the 1970s it was found only in Key Biscayne National Park and on north Key Largo. It was declared Threatened in 1976 but because of a decline in numbers was reclassified as Endangered in 1984.

The outlook is encouraging for the survival of the Schaus swallowtail on Key Largo and the islands that make up the Biscayne National Park. Habitats within the park are well managed, and larval host plants are abundant. The Fish and Wildlife Service (FWS) recovery team recommends reestablishing colonies elsewhere within the historic range.

Successful control of pesticide spraying within the swallowtail's range has reduced one of its greatest immediate threats. Since 1980 the FWS has been acquiring lands on north Key Largo for the Crocodile Lake National Wildlife Refuge—an area within the historic range of the butterfly. These efforts may afford the swallowtail an opportunity to increase its numbers in an expanded habitat.

Bibliography

Brown, C. H. 1976. "A Colony of *Papilio aristodemus ponceanus* in the Upper Florida Keys." *Journal of the Georgia Entomological Society* 11:117-118.

Covell, C. V. 1976. "The Schaus' Swallowtail: Threatened Species." *Insect World Digest* 3:21-26.

General Accounting Office. 1988. "Endangered Species: Management Improvements Could Enhance Recovery Program." General Accounting Office, Washington, D.C.

U.S. Fish and Wildlife Service. 1982. "Schaus Swallowtail Butterfly Recovery Plan." U.S. Fish and Wildlife Service, Atlanta.

Contact

Regional Office of Endangered Species
U.S. Fish and Wildlife Service
Richard B. Russell Federal Building
75 Spring Street, S.W.
Atlanta, Georgia 30303

Pawnee Montane Skipper

Hesperia leonardus montana

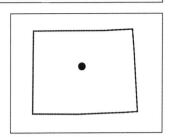

Paul Opler

Status . . . . . . Threatened
Listed . . . . . September 25, 1987
Family . . . . . Hesperiidae (Silver-Spotted Skipper)
Description . . . Small, brownish yellow butterfly.
Habitat . . . . . Mountain pine woodlands.
Host Plant . . . . Blue grama grass.
Threats . . . . . . Limited numbers.
Region 6 . . . . . Colorado

Description

The adult Pawnee montane skipper is a brownish yellow butterfly with a wingspan slightly over 2.5 centimeters (1 in). Distinct, yellowish spots occur near the outer margins of the upper surface of the wings; there are one to four tan or off-white spots on the lower (ventral) surface. Ventral spots are larger on the hindwings and are generally whiter in females.

Behavior

Pawnee montane skipper females deposit single eggs directly on leaves of blue grama grass (*Bouteloua gracilis*), the only known larval host plant. Larvae overwinter; pupation lasts 13 to 23 days. Adult males emerge in late July, followed by females up to ten days later.

Adults feed principally on the nectar of the prairie gayfeather. The musk thistle is also an important nectar source. Adults live until the first strong frost.

Habitat

The Pawnee montane skipper inhabits a rugged mountainous region of plateaus cut by deep canyons and narrow river valleys. The skipper is found in dry, open, ponderosa pine forests on outcrops of Pikes Peak granite where soils are thin, unstable, and susceptible to water erosion. Slopes are moderately steep with a south, west, or east aspect. The understory is very sparse, generally with less than 30 percent ground cover.

Blue grama grass occurs in clumps across the hot, open slopes inhabited by skippers but actually covers only about 5 percent of the surface area. Prairie gayfeather occurs in patches throughout the ponderosa pine woodlands.

Historic Range

The Pawnee montane skipper is endemic to habitat associated with the Pike's Peak Granite Formation in the South Platte River drainage, Colorado, and has probably always had a very limited range.

Current Distribution

This species is found in four Colorado counties directly southwest of Denver: Teller, Park, Jefferson, and Douglas. Within these counties, the skipper is restricted to the South Platte River drainage in a band roughly 40 kilometers (25 mi) long and 8 kilometers (5 mi) wide.

Conservation and Recovery

Sections of the current range are managed by the Forest Service, the Bureau of Land Management, Denver Water Department, county governments, and private landowners. Currently, the skipper's limited numbers threaten its survival more than do environmental factors. If, however, plans to construct the Two Forks Dam on the South Platte River are implemented, a portion of the butterfly's habitat would be eliminated. Residential development of the area would probably accelerate if the reservoir were built.

The prairie gayfeather, which provides nectar for adult skippers, appears to grow in areas subject to occasional fire or logging, and the skipper does not recolonize these areas for several years after such disturbances. Government lands within the butterfly's range are already managed to conserve the species. Control of logging leases and burn-

ing may allow the skipper to expand to additional sites.

Bibliography

ERT Company. 1986. "1986 Pawnee Montane Skipper Field Studies." Prepared for the Denver Water Department, Denver.

Scott, J. A., and R. E. Stanford. 1982. "Geographic Variation and Ecology of *Hesperia leonardus* (Hesperiidae)." *Journal of Research on the Lepidoptera* 20(1):18-35.

Contact

Regional Office of Endangered Species
U.S. Fish and Wildlife Service
P.O. Box 25486
Denver Federal Center
Denver, Colorado 80225

Mission Blue Butterfly

Icaricia icarioides missionensis

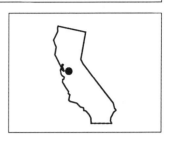

Richard A. Arnold

Status	Endangered
Listed	June 1, 1976
Family	Lycaenidae (Gossamer-Winged Butterfly)
Description	Small butterfly; male silver-blue to violet above; female completely brown.
Habitat	Grasslands and coastal scrub.
Host Plant	Lupine.
Threats	Habitat loss, encroaching non-native vegetation.
Region 1	California

Description

The Mission blue butterfly measures about 2.5 to 3.5 centimeters (1 to 1.4 in) across the wingtips. The male is silver-blue to violet-blue above, with dark wing margins; the female is completely brown above or with blue restricted to wing bases. Beneath, both sexes are silver-gray or brownish with black spots on the front wing. This species has also been referred to as *Plebejus icarioides missionensis*.

Behavior

Adults begin to emerge from pupae in late March and fly until mid-June. They have an average life span of ten days. Females are fertile throughout their life, depositing single eggs on the leaves, stems, flowers, and seed pods of the host plant—one of several species of lupine. Eggs hatch in four to seven days, but the larvae overwinter in leaf litter at the base of the host plants. In spring, the larvae resume feeding, then pupate.

Parasitic wasps attack and lay their eggs inside the mission blue's larvae, but often the larvae are tended by ants, which provide some protection from wasp parasites and other predators. In exchange, the larvae secrete honeydew for the ants.

Habitat

The Mission blue inhabits grasslands and coastal scrub. It is also found along the borders of dunes or tidal marshes. Spring and summer climate is relatively cool, windy, and cloudy. Maximum summer temperatures average less than 21 degrees C (70 degrees F). Winter temperatures seldom fall below freezing. Three perennial lupine species serve as larval host plants (*Lupinus albifrons, L. formosus,* and *L. variicolor*).

Historic Range

The Mission blue butterfly is endemic to the San Francisco peninsula and Marin County, California. This subspecies was first collected in 1937 on Twin Peaks in the Mission District of San Francisco.

Current Distribution

Except for small colonies in the Mission District of San Francisco and at Ft. Baker in Marin County, other colonies of Mission blue butterflies were known to occur on about 810 hectares (1,500 acres) of grassland at San Bruno Mountain south of San Francisco. Several populations were recently discovered in northern and central San Mateo County.

Conservation and Recovery

Loss of habitat to urban San Francisco and related residential development is the major cause for decline of the Mission blue butterfly. Its habitat has also suffered from industrial and agricultural development, quarrying, and encroachment of non-native plant species that crowd out the lupine host plants. The Ft. Baker colony near the north end of the Golden Gate Bridge is afforded protection by the Golden Gate National Recreation Area.

The Mission blue butterfly's host plants grow in a plant community that depends on periodic disturbances, such as rock slides, mud slides, and fires, to establish seedlings. Preserving the Mission blue butterfly will require maintaining sufficient tracts of lupine, which, in turn, depends on sustaining the natural succession of vegetation by inducing periodic disturbance.

A development company, Visitacion Associates, donated 121 hectares (298 acres) of habitat on San Bruno Mountain to the San Mateo County Parks and Recreation Department. The San Bruno Mountain Habitat Conservation Plan has been developed to maintain several hundred acres of open habitat while allowing residential development to continue in other parts of the historic habitat area. The long-term outlook for the mission blue is guardedly optimistic.

Bibliography

Arnold, R. A. 1983. "Ecological Studies of Six Endangered Butterflies: Island Biography, Patch Dynamics, and Design of Habitat Preserves." *University of California Publications in Entomology* 99:1-161.

Arnold, R. A. 1987. "The Mission Blue Butterfly." *Audubon Wildlife Report 1987.* National Audubon Society.

McClintock, E., W. Knight, and N. Fahy. 1968. "A Flora of the San Bruno Mountains, San Mateo County, California." *Proceedings of the California Academy of Science* 32:587-677.

San Bruno Mountain Habitat Conservation Plan Steering Committee. 1982. "San Bruno Mountain Area Habitat Conservation Plan." San Mateo County Planning Department, Redwood City.

U.S. Fish and Wildlife Service. 1984. "Recovery Plan for the San Bruno Elfin and Mission Blue Butterflies." U.S. Fish and Wildlife Service, Portland.

Contact

Regional Office of Endangered Species
U.S. Fish and Wildlife Service
Lloyd 500 Building, Suite 1692
500 N.E. Multnomah Street
Portland, Oregon 97232

Tooth Cave Spider

Leptoneta myopica

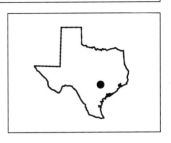

Robert and Linda Mitchell

Status	Endangered
Listed	September 16, 1988
Family	Leptonetidae (Cave Spider)
Description	Tiny arachnid; pale colored, with relatively long legs; reduced eyes present.
Habitat	Cave-dwelling.
Food	Insects.
Threats	Residential development, habitat degradation.
Region 4	Texas

Description

The Tooth Cave spider has a very small, pale-colored body—up to 1.6 millimeters (0.1 in) in length—with relatively long legs. Although it lives in near-total darkness, reduced eyes are present.

Behavior

This arachnid is highly sedentary, spinning webs from the ceiling and walls of Tooth Cave. It feeds on insects that inhabit the cave or happen to enter it. The spider's reproductive biology has not been well studied.

Habitat

Tooth Cave was carved from the Edwards Limestone formation by a flowing underground stream. Entered through a small opening, the cave reaches back into the hillside for about 30 meters (100 ft). Once connected to a large cavern system, this passage was isolated from other caves when stream channels cut through the overlying limestone to lower rock layers. Twenty-one caves and open sinkholes are known from this region and more are presumed to exist.

Tooth Cave contains a selection of species more diverse than any other cave in Texas. At least 48 species have been identified, including highly adapted soil forms that have yet to be described. Other federally listed species present in the cave include the Bee Creek Cave harvestman (*Texella reddelli*), the Tooth Cave ground beetle (*Rhadine persephone*), and the Kretschmarr Cave mold beetle (*Texamaurops reddelli*). The Tooth Cave blind rove beetle (*Cylindropsis sp.*) also inhabited the cave, but may now be extinct.

Historic Range

The Tooth Cave spider is endemic to Tooth Cave, which is located northwest of Four Corners in Travis County near the city of Austin, Texas.

Current Distribution

The number of Tooth Cave spiders is unknown. While only a few specimens have ever been collected, this may reflect the limited size of the habitat rather than a declining population. Tooth Cave is the sole known habitat for this arachnid.

Conservation and Recovery

The area surrounding Tooth Cave has undergone increased development activity in recent years as the Austin suburbs spread further into Travis County. Preliminary land clearing has already begun in the immediate vicinity of Tooth Cave, which could be weakened by the vibrations of heavy equipment. The Tooth Cave spider depends on some infiltration of groundwater, and a disruption of flow due to development would pose an immediate threat. Likewise, the seepage of urban runoff into the ground is likely to degrade water quality.

A proposed pipeline from Lake Travis to supply Austin with water was recently routed (on paper) directly across Tooth Cave. Even if the cavern is ultimately bypassed, as now seems probable, digging and blasting for the pipeline may well cause the cave to collapse. To ensure the survival of cave endemics, a wide easement will need to be secured around the cave. The entrance should also be secured against vandalism.

Because the federally listed Endangered black-capped vireo (*Vireo atricapillus*) nests in the area around Tooth Cave, the cave spider will be treated in the vireo's Recovery Plan by the Fish and Wildlife Service.

Bibliography

Gretsch, W. J. 1974. "The Spider Family Leptonetidae in North America." *The Journal of Arachnology* 1:145-203.

Reddell, J. R. 1984. "Report on the Caves and Cave Fauna of the Parke, Travis County, Texas." Unpublished Report to the Texas System of Natural Laboratories.

Contact

U.S. Fish and Wildlife Service
Regional Office of Endangered Species
500 Gold Avenue, S.W.
Albuquerque, New Mexico 87103

Lotis Blue Butterfly

Lycaeides argyrognomon lotis

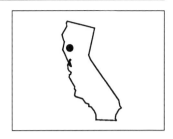

Richard A. Arnold

Status	Endangered
Listed	June 1, 1976
Family	Lycaenidae (Gossamer-Winged Butterfly)
Description	Small butterfly; males are violet-blue, females brown.
Habitat	Wet meadows and sphagnum-willow bogs.
Host plants	Coast trefoil.
Threats	Habitat destruction.
Region 1	California

Description

The lotis blue butterfly, one of the largest of its species, has a wingspan of 1.5 to 3.2 centimeters (0.6 to 1.3 in.). The upper wing surfaces are a deep violet-blue in the male with a black border and fringe of white scales along the outer wing margins. In the female, the upper wing surface is brown, sometimes bluish brown, with a wavy band of orange on both forewings and hindwings. The lotis blue is one of twelve subspecies of *Lycaeides argyrognomon* in North America.

Behavior

The life history of the lotis blue butterfly is not well studied, but some information can be extrapolated from closely related species. The larval host plant is most likely the coast trefoil (*Lotus formosissimus*). Females lay eggs on the host plants during the adult flight season, and newly hatched larvae begin feeding immediately on leaves, flowers, and seed pods.

Larval diapause (the resting stage during larval development) is broken sometime during the following spring, and larvae complete their development four to six weeks later. The pupal stage probably lasts no more than a few weeks.

Habitat

The lotis blue butterfly is found in wet meadows or poorly drained sphagnum-willow bogs, where soils are waterlogged and highly acidic. This habitat has a dense undergrowth of shrubs, including California huckleberry, western Labrador tea, salal, wax myrtle, California rose-bay, western hemlock, and Sitka spruce.

Historic Range

The lotis blue butterfly appears to be a naturally rare insect with low population densities. In the past, it was found at seven coastal localities in Mendocino, northern Sonoma, and possibly northern Marin counties in California. A site near Point Arena (Mendocino County) has not been populated by the butterfly since the 1940s. The limited number of specimens in museum collections and limited field observations make any assessment of the historic range of this butterfly difficult.

Current Distribution

Since 1977, the lotis blue butterfly has been found only at a single 2-hectare (5-acre) site north of the town of Mendocino. Between 1977 and 1981 only 16 adult specimens were seen in 42 days of field searching at the site. This may make the lotis blue the rarest butterfly in the continental U.S.. Natural factors and human intrusion may have played a role in the lotis blue's scarcity.

Conservation and Recovery

Because of its low numbers and limited distribution, the lotis blue butterfly is extremely vulnerable to further loss of habitat, and a number of potential threats exist, such as logging, peat mining, powerline corridor maintenance, herbicide and pesticide application, and alterations of water regimes.

Fire suppression may affect distribution and abundance of the host plants. Drought during 1976 and 1977 caused the sphagnum bog to dry out, and no lotis blue butterflies were observed in 1977.

The only known population site is on private land. The Fish and Wildlife Service has attempted to negotiate a conservation agreement with the landowner to arrange maintenance of vegetation at the site to limit and use of pesticides and herbicides. If the current extant population is ever deemed large enough, several adults may be removed to other breeding locations within the historic range. Captive breeding may also be considered.

Bibliography

Arnold, R. A. 1978. "Survey and Status of Six Endangered Butterflies in California." Report. California Department of Fish and Game, Sacramento.

Arnold, R. A. 1981. "A Review of Endangered Species Legislation in the USA, and Preliminary Research on Six Endangered California butterflies." *Beih. Veröff. Naturschutz Landschaftspflege Bad.-Würh.* 21(1981):79-96.

Tilden, J. W. 1965. *Butterflies of the San Francisco Bay Region.* University of California Press, Berkeley.

U.S. Fish and Wildlife Service. 1985. "Recovery Plan for the Lotis Blue Butterfly." U.S. Fish and Wildlife Service, Portland.

Contact

Regional Office of Endangered Species
U.S. Fish and Wildlife Service
Lloyd 500 Building, Suite 1692
500 N.E. Multnomah Street
Portland, Oregon 97232

Tooth Cave Pseudoscorpion

Microcreagris texana

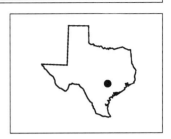

(Vachonium kauae) Kaua blind cave pseudoscorpion

Robert and Linda Mitchell

Status	Endangered
Listed	September 16, 1988
Family	Neobisiidae (Pseudoscorpion)
Description	Tiny scorpion-like arachnid, lacking a stinger.
Habitat	Cave-dwelling.
Food	Small insects and arthropods.
Threats	Development, exotic predators.
Region 2	Texas

Description

The Tooth Cave pseudoscorpion is an arachnid that resembles a tiny scorpion, reaching about 4 millimeters (0.2 in) in length. It lacks a stinger. The unpigmented pseudoscorpion is eyeless. This Species is currently being reclassified as *Tartarocreagris texana.*

Behavior

The Tooth Cave pseudoscorpion preys on small insects and other cave-dwelling arthropods. Its biology is largely unknown.

Habitat

This species is endemic to caves and sinkholes of the Edwards Limestone formation.

Once interconnected, these caves were separated when streams cut through the layers of limestone to harder underlying strata. The fragmented habitat has encouraged the development of a highly localized fauna. Major caves in the system are Amber, Tooth, and McDonald. Other inhabitants of the caves include the blind millipeds *Cambala speobia* and *Speodesmus bicornourus*, and blind isopods of the family Trichoniscidae. Tooth Cave, about 30 meters (100 ft) in length, contains at least 48 species of insects and arachnids.

Historic Range

The Tooth Cave pseudoscorpion is endemic to Tooth, Amber, and possibly McDonald caves in Travis and Williamson counties near Austin, Texas. The pseudoscorpion is not known to exist elsewhere.

Current Distribution

The number of Tooth Cave pseudoscorpions in Amber and Tooth caves has not been estimated, but surveys have only uncovered a single specimen from each cave. Because of the size of the available habitat and the small size of the pseudoscorpion, these survey figures are not thought to indicate actual numbers, although the total population is certainly not large.

Conservation and Recovery

Located adjacent to a developing urban area, the caves inhabited by this pseudoscorpion are threatened by land clearing and residential construction. Tooth Cave lies along a proposed route for a water pipeline and, even if bypassed by construction equipment, could suffer from nearby blasting. Residential development of the area will also contribute to the degradation of groundwater. Recovery options include acquiring, through purchase or donation, wide easements around caves to protect them from ground disturbance and water pollution. Cave entrances will probably be grated to prevent unauthorized entry and vandalism.

Because the black-capped vireo (*Vireo atricapillus*) nests in the region, the Fish and Wildlife Service will treat the pseudoscorpion in the vireo's Recovery Plan and afford additional protection and oversight.

Bibliography

Muchmore, W. B. 1969. "New Species and Records of Cavernicolous Pseudoscorpions of the Genus *Microcreagris* (Arachnida Chelonethida, Neobisiidae, Ideobisiinae)." *American Museum Novitate* 2932:21.

Reddell, J. R. 1984. "Report on the Caves and Cave Fauna of the Parke, Travis County, Texas." Unpublished Report to the Texas System of Natural Laboratories.

Contact

Regional Office of Endangered Species
U.S. Fish and Wildlife Service
500 Gold Avenue, S.W.
Albuquerque, New Mexico 87103

American Burying Beetle

Nicrophorus americanus

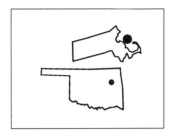

USFWS

Status	Endangered
Listed	June 12, 1989
Family	Silphidae (Carrion Beetle)
Description	Large, shiny black beetle with distinctive orange and red markings.
Habitat	Virgin woodlands, maritime scrub and grasslands.
Food	Carrion.
Threats	Low numbers.
Region 2	Oklahoma
Region 5	New England

Description

Also known as the giant carrion beetle, the shiny black American burying beetle is identified by two pairs of scalloped red spots on the wing covers (elytra), red antenna stems with orange clubs, and large orange-red pronotal disk (segment behind the head). It is the largest member of its genus, measuring from 2.5 to 3.6 centimeters (1 to 1.4 in).

Behavior

A nocturnal beetle, it is attracted to carrion by smell. A number of beetles fight among themselves over a carcass until one pair—usually the largest male and female—takes possession. They then bury it, constructing a brooding chamber at the same time. The female lays eggs on the carrion, and both parents remain with the eggs until they hatch to tend the larvae. The larvae do not survive without this parental attention. Larvae emerge as adults after about 50 days, and parents and young disperse. Adults burrow in the soil to overwinter. Occasionally, burying beetles capture live insects.

Habitat

Scientists speculate that the American burying beetle prefers mature, virgin forests, but its present New England habitat includes maritime scrub thickets, coastal grasslands, and pasture. The availability of deep humus and top soils suitable for burying carrion is essential. Further research is needed to clarify habitat requirements.

Historic Range

This species was once found in 32 states and three Canadian provinces. Its range extended from Nova Scotia and Quebec south to Florida, and west to Texas and the Great Plains.

Current Distribution

The American burying beetle is currently known from only two populations, one on a New England island, the other in eastern Oklahoma. Wildlife officials have intentionally left the location of the New England population vague to deter collectors. Although no population estimate has been attempted, the species is considered to have experienced one of the most disastrous declines ever recorded for an insect species.

Conservation and Recovery

The cause of the precipitous decline of the range of the American burying beetle is unknown, although contamination by DDT and other pesticides is one possibility. In addition, the black lights on "bug-zappers" are thought to attract and electrocute males. Because they participate in brood-rearing, burying beetle males are not considered surplus population, unlike those of many other beetle species. Although scientists fully expect to discover remnant populations in other states, the status of the species is considered critical.

Bibliography

Anderson, R. S. 1982. "On the Decreasing Abundance of *Nicrophorus americanus* in Eastern North America." *Coleoptera Bulletin* 36(2):362-365.

Kozol, A. J., *et al.* 1987. "Distribution and Natural History of the American Burying Beetle." Report. Eastern Heritage Task Force of The Nature Conservancy.

Schweitzer, D. F., and L. L. Master. 1987. "American Burying Beetle: Results of a Global Status Survey." Report. U.S. Fish and Wildlife Service, Newton Corner, Massachusetts.

Contact

Regional Office of Endangered Species
U.S. Fish and Wildlife Service
P.O. Box 1306
Albuquerque, New Mexico 87103

Regional Office of Endangered Species
U.S. Fish and Wildlife Service
One Gateway Center, Suite 700
Newton Corner, Massachusetts 02158

Tooth Cave Ground Beetle

Rhadine persephone

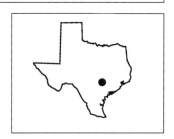

Robert and Linda Mitchell

Status	Endangered
Listed	September 16, 1988
Family	Carabidae (Ground Beetle)
Description	Tiny reddish brown beetle with rudimentary eyes.
Habitat	Caves.
Food	Cave cricket eggs.
Threats	Residential development.
Region 2	Texas

Description

The reddish brown Tooth Cave ground beetle attains a maximum length of only 8 millimeters (0.35 in). This cave-adapted species has only rudimentary eyes.

Behavior

The Tooth Cave ground beetle is suspected to feed on cave cricket eggs. The beetle's reproductive biology is unknown.

Habitat

The Tooth Cave ground beetle is endemic to two caves in the Edwards Limestone formation. Tooth Cave is up to 30 meters (100 ft) in length and contains a greater diversity of fauna than any other cave in Texas. Over 48 species have been identified, and other highly adaptive cave fauna no doubt remain to be discovered.

The other known habitat of this beetle is Kretschmarr Cave, which is about 15 meters (50 ft) deep. Fauna present in Kretschmarr Cave include the blind millipede *Cambala speobia* and several species of beetles. An associated insect, the Kretschmarr Cave mold beetle (*Texamaurops reddelli*), is also federally listed as Endangered.

Historic Range

This species is a highly localized example of the fauna endemic to caves in the Edwards Limestone formation in Travis County, Texas.

Current Distribution

The Tooth Cave ground beetle, first discovered in 1965, is only known from Tooth and Kretschmarr caves. Exact population figures are not known. Few individuals of this species have ever been collected, and although its habitat area is large in comparison to its body size, the total population is probably small.

Conservation and Recovery

The spreading suburbs of Austin have overrun Travis County and continue to threaten the caves that constitute the habitat for the Tooth Cave ground beetle and other highly specialized fauna.

Tooth and Kretschmarr caves are in an area slated for residential development; ground clearing and trenching for sewer lines has already begun. Limestone caves are highly susceptible to collapse caused by blasting or digging, and it is feared that some caves have already collapsed or had their entrances buried.

Cave species are dependent upon a regular infiltration of groundwater. Disruption of fresh water or introduction of effluent containing pollutants such as sewage, pesticides, or fertilizer residues could severely disrupt the habitat that supports this beetle.

Creation and preservation of easements around the caves and installation of gates to prevent vandalism would benefit the endemic fauna. Because the region surrounding Austin also supports the black-capped vireo (*Vireo atricapillus*), the Tooth Cave ground beetle will be included in the Fish and Wildlife Service Recovery Plan for the vireo.

Bibliography

Barr, T. C., Jr. 1974. "Revision of *Rhadine* LeConte (Coleoptera, Carabidae); Vol I. The Subterranean Group." *American Museum Novitates* 2359.

Reddell, R. R. 1984. "Report on the Caves and Cave Fauna of the Parke, Travis County, Texas." Unpublished Report to the Texas System of Natural Laboratories.

Contact

Regional Office of Endangered Species
U.S. Fish and Wildlife Service
500 Gold Avenue, S.W.
Albuquerque, New Mexico 87103

Oregon Silverspot Butterfly

Speyeria zerene hippolyta

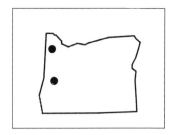

Richard A. Arnold

Status . . . . . Threatened
Listed . . . . . . July 2, 1980
Family . . . . . Nymphalidae (Brush-Footed Butterfly)
Description . . . Orange and brown butterfly with silver spots on under-wings.
Habitat . . . . . Coastal salt spray meadows coastal dunes.
Host Plant . . . . Western blue violet.
Threats . . . . . Residential and recreational development, suppression of fire.
Region 1 . . . . . Oregon, Washington

Description

The Oregon silverspot butterfly is a medium-sized orange and brown butterfly with black veins and spots on the hindwings, and a yellowish band and bright metallic silver spots on the forewings. It has a fore-wing length of about 2.9 centimeters (1.1 in); females are typically slightly larger than males.

The species *Speyeria zerene* consists of 15 subspecies, divided into five major groups. The Oregon silverspot belongs to the *bremnerii* group consisting of five subspecies. The Oregon silverspot is slightly smaller and darker at the base of the wings than its rela-tives, adaptive traits derived from its persis-tently windy and foggy environment.

Behavior

Adult butterflies emerge from early July to early September. Mating occurs during adult flights, and females deposit 200 or more eggs in the vegetation near the violet host plant in late August or early September. Eggs hatch in about 16 days, and the larvae seek out suitable places for overwintering. In spring, the larvae feed on violet leaves for two months, then enter pupation for two or three weeks.

Habitat

This subspecies is found only in the salt spray meadows along the Pacific coast of Washington and Oregon. The climate is characterized by mild temperatures, heavy rainfall, and fog. The most important feature of the habitat is the presence of the western blue violet (*Viola adunca*), the larval host plant.

Historic Range

The Oregon silverspot was historically found in 17 different locations between Rock Creek and Big Creek, about 24 kilometers (15 mi) north of Florence along the central Oregon coast, and in the vicinity of Westport, south of Grays Harbor, Washington which is the northern extent of the range.

Current Distribution

Currently, there are four known Oregon populations: Rock Creek and Big Creek (Lane County); Mount Hebo and Cascade Head (Tillamook County); and a recently discovered population at Clatsop Plain (Clatsop County). There are no current population estimates. Two other populations—at Tenmile Creek (Lane County), Oregon, and at Loomis Lake (Pacific County), Washington—are considered near extirpation.

Conservation and Recovery

The main threats to this butterfly are increased housing development and recreational use of the coast. Natural fire patterns have been suppressed, allowing non-native plants to intrude and change the mix of plants in the habitat. There have also been rapid successional changes in the native plant community.

In the summer of 1986 the Fish and Wildlife Service began negotiations with the Clatsop County government and a local developer then promoting a housing development and golf course that would have affected the Clatsop Plain breeding area. The three parties reviewed options and cooperated in the preparation of a Habitat Conservation Plan. The Gearhart Ranch Development, also on Clatsop Plain, has had an impact on the silverspot's range but at the same time has stimulated local interest in preserving the butterfly's habitat.

Critical Habitat was designated for an area in Lane County, Oregon, where a healthy population of the butterfly exists. Control of brush and sapling trees invading the meadows will give stands of the larval host plant a chance to expand. Transplantation of the violet to other sites may also be attempted.

Bibliography

Arnold, R. A. 1988. "Ecological and Behavioral Studies on the Threatened Oregon Silverspot Butterfly." Report. U.S. Fish and Wildlife Service, Olympia, Washington.

Hammond, Paul C., *et al.* 1980. "Ecological Investigation Report: Oregon Silverspot Butterfly (*Speyeria zerene hippolyta*) Mt. Hebo Supplement." U.S. Forest Service.

Howe, W. H. 1975. *The Butterflies of North America*. Doubleday, Garden City.

U.S. Fish and Wildlife Service. 1982. "The Oregon Silverspot Butterfly Recovery Plan." U.S. Fish and Wildlife Service, Portland.

Contact

Regional Office of Endangered Species
U.S. Fish and Wildlife Service
Lloyd 500 Building, Suite 1692
500 N.E. Multnomah Street
Portland, Oregon 97232

Kretschmarr Cave Mold Beetle

Texamaurops reddelli

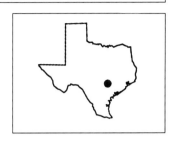

Robert and Linda Mitchell

Status	. . . . . Endangered
Listed	. . . . . September 16, 1988
Family	. . . . . Pselaphidae (Mold Beetle)
Description	. . . Dark, short-winged, eyeless beetle with elongated legs.
Habitat	. . . . . Caves.
Food	. . . . Fungus.
Threats	. . . . . Residential development.
Region 2	. . . . . Texas

Description

The tiny Kretschmarr Cave mold beetle is less than 3 millimeters (0.15 in) in length. Eyeless, its body is dark with short wings and elongated legs. According to James Reddell, who first collected this beetle in 1963, it is the most highly cave-adapted species of its family in Texas and among the more unusual species of cave-dwelling beetles in the United States.

Behavior

It is believed that this species is omnivorous but depends on fungus for the bulk of its diet. Little is known about its reproductive biology.

Habitat

The mold beetle inhabits caves in the Edwards Limestone formation. Caves in the area were once joined into a vast subterranean network but were separated and fragmented when stream channels cut through overlying limestone to lower rock layers.

One habitat—Tooth Cave—supports a greater diversity of species than any cave in Texas, including varieties of pseudoscorpions, blind spiders, and several species of soil forms that have yet to be described. The total depth of the cave is under 30 meters (100 ft).

A second cave—Amber Cave—is over 12 meters (40 ft) deep and, in addition, supports a newly discovered spider in the genus *Cicurina*, a blind cambalid millipede (*Cambala speobia*), a blind polydesmid millipede (*Speodesmus bicornourus*), blind isopods of the family Trichoniscidae, and several other unusual species. Kretschmarr Cave, the beetle's namesake, reaches 15 meters (50 ft) deep and supports fauna similar to Amber Cave.

Historic Range

This species is an example of the highly localized fauna of the caves in the Edwards Limestone formation, Texas. It occurs nowhere else.

Current Distribution

This mold beetle is known from Kretschmarr, Amber, Tooth, and Coffin Caves in Travis and Williamson counties. Recent attempts to locate Coffin Cave have been unsuccessful because residential development in the area has destroyed landmarks and collapsed or concealed the entrance. The size of the Kretschmarr Cave mold beetle population is not known.

Conservation and Recovery

Expansion of the metropolitan area of Austin, threatens to permanently alter the environment surrounding the Edwards Limestone caves. The area around Kretschmarr, Amber, and Tooth caves is slated for development, and preliminary digging and clearing has already begun. Proposed water pipeline construction threatens Tooth Cave. Scientists fear that surface activity could collapse or weaken caves. Landmarks for locating many caves have already been destroyed by construction, and boulders have been piled at the entrance to Kretschmarr Cave. As the area is developed, sewage, pesticide, or fertilizer residues could seep down into the caves, disturb the fragile ecological balance, and extirpate the species.

The creation of wide easements around the caves and the installation of gates at the entrances to prevent human visitation would benefit the endemic fauna. The black-capped vireo (*Vireo atricapillus*) nests in the area, and the Fish and Wildlife Service Recovery Plan for that species will include recommendations for protecting the cave fauna.

Bibliography

Barr, T. C. and H. R. Steeves, Jr. 1963. "*Texamaurops*, A New Genus of Pselaphids from Caves in Central Texas (Coleoptera: Pselaphidae)." *The Coleopterists' Bulletin* 17:117-120.

Mitchell, R. W. 1968. "Food and Feeding Habits of the Troglobitic Carabid Beetle *Rhadine subterranean.*" *International Journal of Speleology* 3:249-270.

Reddell, J. R. 1984. "Report on the Caves and Cave Fauna of the Parke, Travis County, Texas." Unpublished Report to the Texas System of Natural Laboratories.

Contact

Regional Office of Endangered Species
U.S. Fish and Wildlife Service
500 Gold Avenue, S.W.
Albuquerque, New Mexico 87103

Bee Creek Cave Harvestman
Texella reddelli

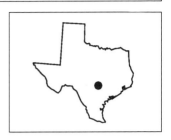

Robert and Linda Mitchell

Status	Endangered
Listed	September 16, 1988
Family	Phalangodidae (Harvestman)
Description	Pale yellow-brown, eyeless arachnid.
Habitat	Caves and sinkholes.
Food	Probably insects.
Threats	Urbanization.
Region 2	Texas

Description

The eyeless Bee Creek Cave harvestman has a pale yellow-brown body, barely 2 millimeters (0.13 in) in length, with relatively long legs. It is similar in appearance to the common "daddy long-legs." It uses its two front legs, which are longer than the others, to feel its way through its lightless habitat.

Behavior

Little is known of this cave dweller's behavior and reproductive activity. It is probably predatory, feeding on other insects.

Habitat

The Bee Creek Cave harvestman is restricted to limestone caves and sinkholes of the Edwards Limestone Formation in central Texas. These caves can be very shallow or as deep as 60 meters (200 ft) and support a greater diversity of endemic species than any other cave system in Texas. The limestone formation has not been fully explored and may contain many other caves and sinkholes supporting highly specific fauna.

Historic Range

This harvestman is an example of a localized cave fauna found in Travis and Williamson counties, Texas. It has been collected from five caves in the region and is suspected to occupy a sixth.

Current Distribution

The size of the Bee Creek Cave harvestman population has not been estimated, but Fish and Wildlife Service (FWS) biologists believe that the species may be more limited in numbers than previously thought. This spider has been collected from Tooth, Bee Creek, McDonald, Weldon, and Bone caves. In 1984, it was reported from Root Cave in Travis County, but its presence there has not been confirmed.

Conservation and Recovery

In recent years, the suburbs of the city of Austin have expanded into Travis and Williamson counties, causing the loss of many caves and natural sinkholes. Land-clearing, digging, and blasting have caused collapsed caves or buried the entrances. Weldon Cave—site of a past biological survey—lay along the path of a recent road expansion and may no longer exist. Coffin Cave also appears to have succumbed to bulldozing in 1988. New roads in the area have stimulated construction of subdivisions closer to the main caves of the system—Tooth, McDonald, and Root caves. The subdivisions are expected to alter drainage patterns and degrade the quality of the groundwater on which the cave species depend.

If built according to plan, a proposed water pipeline running from Lake Travis into Austin would cross Tooth Cave. Even if the pipeline ultimately bypasses the cave, nearby blasting and digging associated with the project could trigger a roof collapse.

Protection of the harvestman would require the creation of sufficient easements around the caves to prevent physical disturbance or pollution of groundwater. Entrances should be secured to prevent human intrusion and habitat disturbance. Protection of endemic cave species will be considered in the FWS Recovery Plan for the black-capped vireo (*Vireo atricapillus*), which nests in the area.

Bibliography

Goodnight, C. J., and M. L. Goodnight. 1967. "Opilionids from Texas Caves (Opiliones Phalangodidae)," *American Museum Novitates* 2301.

Reddell, J. R. 1984. "Report on the Caves and Cave Fauna of the Parke, Travis County, Texas." Unpublished Report to the Texas System of Natural Laboratories.

Contact

Regional Office of Endangered Species
U.S. Fish and Wildlife Service
500 Gold Avenue, S.W.
Albuquerque, New Mexico 87103

Newly Listed Species
August, September, and October 1989

Pygmy Sculpin
(Cottus pygmaeus)

The pygmy sculpin is a small fish, which occurs only in Coldwater Spring and its associated outflow stream in Calhoun County, Alabama. The groundwater has been contaminated with trichloroethylene, which poses a threat to the small, surviving population. The spring is owned by the city of Anniston, which has not yet made a commitment to conserve the fish. This member of the Minnow Family (Cyprinidae) was listed as Threatened in a final rule published in the Federal Register on September 28, 1989.

Virgin River Chub
(Gila robusta seminuda)

The silvery, medium-sized Virgin River chub is native to the Virgin River in northwest Arizona, southeast Nevada, and southwest Utah. Its distribution is currently limited to 80 kilometers (50 mi) of the Virgin River between Mesquite, Nevada, and La Verkin Creek near Hurricane, Utah. It is threatened by habitat alteration, floods, disease, and competition with introduced fishes. This member of the Minnow Family (Cyprinidae) was listed as Endangered in a final rule published in the Federal Register on August 24, 1989.

Cracking Pearly Mussel
(Hemistena lata)

The cracking pearly mussel was once widespread in the Ohio, Cumberland, and Tennessee river basins but is presently confined at a few shoals in the Clinch, Powell, and Elk rivers (Hancock and Lincoln counties, Tennessee, and Scott and Lee counties, Virginia). Small populations possibly survive in the Green River (Hart and Edmonson counties, Kentucky) and in the Tennessee River below the Pickwick Dam (Hardin County, Tennessee). The species' distribution has been restricted by the construction of dams and reservoirs throughout the historic range. This freshwater mussel (formerly classified as Lastena lata) was listed as Endangered in a final rule published in the Federal Register on September 28, 1989.

Ring Pink Mussel
(Obovaria retusa)

The ring pink mussel, formerly named the golf stick pearly mussel, occurred historically in the Ohio River and its larger tributaries in Pennsylvania, West Virginia, Ohio, Indiana, Illinois, Kentucky, Tennessee, and Alabama. It is currently known from small populations in the Green and Tennessee rivers in Kentucky (Edmonson, Hart, Livingston, Marshall, McCracken counties) and in the Tennessee and Cumberland rivers in Tennessee (Hardin, Wilson, Trousdale, and Smith counties). None of the populations appears to be reproducing, apparently because of large-scale alteration of its habitat caused by the construction of dams and reservoirs. Unless existing populations can be stimulated to reproduce or other reproducing populations are discovered, the species will become extinct in the near future. This freshwater mussel was listed as Endangered in a final rule published in the Federal Register on September 29, 1989.

Most of this area falls within the Monongahela National Forest. Surviving populations are small, geographically isolated from each other, and threatened by timbering, mining, and recreational use of the habitat. This amphibian was listed as Threatened in a final rule published in the Federal Register on August 18, 1989.

Roanoke Logperch
(Percina rex)

The Roanoke logperch is endemic to Virginia where it now occurs in four widely separated populations in the upper Roanoke River (Roanoke and Montgomery counties), Pigg River (Pittsylvania and Franklin counties), Nottoway River (Sussex and Dinwiddie counties), and Smith River (Patrick and Henry counties). The most vigorous population is found in the Roanoke River where it is threatened by urbanization, industrial development, and flood control projects. Other populations are threatened by low densities and siltation caused by agricultural runoff. This member of the Perch Family (Percidae) was listed as Endangered in a final rule published in the Federal Register on August 18, 1989.

Cheat Mountain Salamander
(Plethodon nettingi)

The Cheat Mountain salamander occurs in portions of Pendleton, Pocahontas, Randolph, and Tucker counties, West Virginia, above an elevation of 915 meters (3,000 ft).

Shenandoah Salamander
(Plethodon shenandoah)

The Shenandoah salamander is known from three tiny populations on isolated talus slopes in the Shenandoah National Park in Madison and Page counties, Virginia. Its survival is threatened by its restricted range and competition from the more common red-backed salamander (Plethodon cinereus). This amphibian was listed as Endangered in a final rule published in the Federal Register on August 18, 1989.

Independence Valley Speckled Dace
(Rhinichthys osculus lethoporus)

The Independence Valley speckled dace is currently restricted to a single, small spring in northeastern Nevada (Elko County). It is threatened by irrigation practices, which have altered spring flows, and by the introduction of predatory trout and bass. This member of the Minnow Family (Cyprinidae) was listed as Endangered in a final rule published in the Federal Register on October 10, 1989.

Clover Valley Speckled Dace

(Rhinichthys osculus oligoporus)

The Clover Valley speckled dace is known in low numbers from three small springs in northeastern Nevada (Elko County). It is threatened by irrigation practices, which have altered spring flows, and the introduction of non-native fishes, which prey upon the dace. This member of the Minnow Family (Cyprinidae) was listed as Endangered in a final rule published in the Federal Register on October 10, 1989.

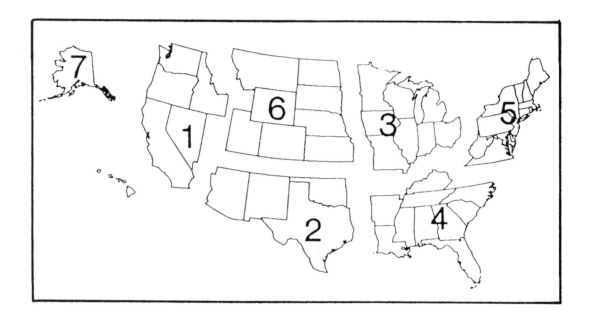

U.S. Fish and Wildlife Service Regions

Appendix I
Offices of the U.S. Fish and Wildlife Service

WASHINGTON OFFICES

Fish and Wildlife Enhancement
Department of the Interior, Room 3024
Washington, D.C. 20240
(202) 343-4646

Division of Endangered Species &
  Habitat Conservation
400 Arlington Square
18th & C St.s, N.W.
Washington, D.C. 20240
(703) 358-2161

National Wetland Inventory
9720 Executive Center Drive
Monroe Building, Suite 101
St. Petersburg, FL 33702
(813) 893-3624

REGION ONE:
**California, Hawaii, Idaho,
Nevada, Oregon, Washington,
and Pacific Territories**

Regional Office
Lloyd 500 Building, Suite 1692
500 N.E. Multnomah St.
Portland, OR 97232
(503) 231-6150

Boise Field Station
4696 Overland Road, Room 576
Boise, ID 83705
(208) 334-1931

Honolulu Field Station
300 Ala Moana Boulevard, Room 6307
Box 50167
Honolulu, HI 96850
(808) 541-2749

Laguna Niguel Field Station

Federal Building, 2400 Avila Road
Laguna Niguel, CA 92677
(714) 643-4270

Lewiston Suboffice
Box 174
Lewiston, CA 96052
(916) 778-3536

Moses Lake Suboffice
Box 1157
Moses Lake, WA 98837

Olympia Field Office
Fish and Wildlife Enhancement
2625 Parkmont Lane, S.W., Building B
Olympia, WA 98502
(206) 753-9440

Pacific Area Office
300 Ala Moana Boulevard, Room 5302
Box 50167
Honolulu, HI 96850
(808) 546-5608

Portland Field Station
727 N.E. 24th Avenue
Portland, OR 97232
(503) 231-6179

Reno Field Station
4600 Kietzke Lane, Building C
Reno, NV 89502
(702) 784-5227

Sacramento Field Station
2800 Cottage Way, Room E-1803
Sacramento, CA 95825
(916) 978-4866

Ventura Endangered Species Recovery Office
2291-A Portola Road, Suite 300
Ventura, CA 93003
(805) 644-1766

REGION TWO:
Arizona, New Mexico, Oklahoma, and Texas

Regional Office
500 Gold Avenue, S.W.
Box 1306
Albuquerque, NM 87103
(505) 766-2324

Albuquerque Field Office
3530 Pan American Hwy., N.E., Suite D
Albuquerque, NM 87107
(505) 883-7877

Clear Lake Field Office
17629 El Camino Real, Suite 211
Houston, TX 77058
(713) 750-1700

Corpus Christi Field Office
Corpus Christi State University, Campus Box 338
6300 Ocean Drive
Corpus Christi, TX 78412
(512) 888-3346

Fort Worth Field Office
819 Taylor St., Room 9A33
Fort Worth, TX 76102
(817) 334-2961

Phoenix Field Office
3616 West Thomas, Suite 6
Phoenix, AZ 85019
(602) 261-4720

Tulsa Field Office
222 South Houston, Suite A
Tulsa, OK 74127
(918) 581-7458

REGION THREE:
Illinois, Indiana, Iowa, Michigan, Minnesota, Missouri, Ohio, and Wisconsin

Regional Office
Federal Building, Fort Snelling
Twin Cities, MN 55111
(612) 725-3276

Bloomington Field Office

718 North Walnut St.
Bloomington, IN 47401
(812) 334-4364

Columbia Field Office
Division of Ecological Services
Box 1506
Columbia, MO 65202
(314) 875-5377

East Lansing Field Office
302 Manly Miles Building
1405 South Harrison Road
East Lansing, MI 48823
(517) 337-6629

Environmental Management Technical Center
575 Lester Drive
Onalaska, WI 54650
(608) 783-7550

Green Bay Field Office
University of Wisconsin/Greenbay
Wood Hall, Room 480
2420 Nicolet Drive
Greenbay, WI 54311
(414) 465-2682

Marion Suboffice
Route 3, Box 328
Marion, IL 62959
(618) 997-5491

Reynoldsburg Field Office
6950-H Americana Parkway
Reynoldsburg, OH 43068
(614) 469-6923

Rock Island Field Office
1830 Second Avenue
Rock Island, IL 61201
(309) 793-5800

South Dakota State Office
Federal Building, Room 227
Box 986
Pierre, SD 57501
(605) 224-8693

St. Paul Field Office
Park Square Court, Suite 50

400 Sibley St.
St. Paul, MN 55101
(612) 290-3131

REGION FOUR:
Alabama, Arkansas, Florida, Georgia, Kentucky, Louisiana, Mississippi, North Carolina, South Carolina, Tennessee, Puerto Rico, and the U.S. Virgin Islands

Regional Office
Richard B. Russell Federal Building
75 Spring St., S.W., Suite 1276
Atlanta, GA 30303
(404) 331-3580

Asheville Field Office
100 Otis St., Room 224
Asheville, NC 28801
(704) 259-0321

Brunswick Field Office
801 Gloucester St.
Federal Building, Room 334
Brunswick, GA 31520
(912) 265-9336

Caribbean Field Office
Box 491
Boqueron, PR 00622
(809) 851-7297

Charleston Field Office
Box 12559
217 Fort Johnson Road
Charleston, SC 29412
(803) 724-4707

Cookeville Field Office
Box 845
Cookeville, TN 38503
(615) 528-6481

Jackson Field Office
300 Woodrow Wilson Avenue, Suite 316
Jackson, MS 39213
(601) 965-4900

Jacksonville Field Office
3100 University Boulevard South, Suite 120
Jacksonville, FL 32216

(904) 791-2580

Lafayette Field Office
Box 4305
103 East Cypress St., Room 102
Lafayette, LA 70502
(318) 264-6630

Panama City Field Office
1612 June Avenue
Panama City, FL 32405
(904) 769-0552

Raleigh Field Office
Box 25039
Raleigh, NC 27611
(919) 856-4520

Vero Beach Field Office
Box 2676
1360 U.S. Route 1 South, Suite 5
Vero Beach, FL 32961
(407) 562-3909

Vicksburg Field Office
Thomas Building, Room 235
900 Clay St.
Vicksburg, MS 39180
(601) 638-1891

REGION FIVE:
Connecticut, Delaware, District of Columbia, Maine, Maryland, Massachusetts, New Hampshire, New Jersey, New York, Pennsylvania, Rhode Island, Vermont, Virginia, and West Virginia

Regional Office
One Gateway Center, Suite 700
Newton Corner, MA 02158
(617) 965-5100

Absecon Field Office
705 White Horse Pike
Box 534
Absecon, NJ 08201
(609) 646-9310

Annapolis Field Office
1825 Virginia St.

Annapolis, MD 21401
(301) 269-5448

Cortland Field Office
100 Grange Place, Room 202
Cortland, NY 13045
(607) 753-9334

Elkins Suboffice
Department of Agriculture Building
Sycamore St., Room 311
Box 1278
Elkins, WV 26241
(304) 636-6586

Gloucester Suboffice
Box 480
Mid-County Center, U.S. Route 17
White Marsh, VA 23183
(804) 693-6694

Long Island Field Office
Brookhaven National Laboratory
Building 179
Upton, NY 11973
(516) 282-3300

New England Field Office
Ralph Pill Marketplace, Suite 400
22 Bridge St.
Concord, NH 03301
(603) 225-1411

State College Field Office
Suite 322, 315 South Allen St.
State College, PA 16801
(814) 234-4090

REGION SIX:
Colorado, Kansas, Montana, Nebraska, North Dakota, South Dakota, Utah, and Wyoming

Regional Office
Box 25486
Denver Federal Center
Denver, CO 80225
(303) 236-7398

Bismarck Field Office
North Dakota/South Dakota Field Office

1500 Capitol Avenue
Bismarck, ND 58501
(701) 250-4402

Grand Junction Fish and Wildlife Enhancement
529-25 1/2 Road, Suite B-113
Grand Junction, CO 81505
(303) 243-2778

Golden Fish and Wildlife Enhancement
730 Simms St., Suite 292
Golden, CO 80401
(303) 236-2675

Manhattan Fish and Wildlife Enhancement
Kansas State University
Division of Biology, Ackert Hall
Manhattan, KS 66506
(913) 532-7320

Helena Fish and Wildlife Enhancement
Box 10023
Federal Building & U.S. Courthouse
301 S. Park, Room 464
Helena, MT 59626
(406) 449-5225

Billings Fish and Wildlife Enhancement
1501 14th St., West, Suite 230
Billings, MT 59102
(406) 657-6750

Missoula Fish and Wildlife Enhancement
HS 105D, University of Montana
Missoula, MT 59812
(406) 329-3223

Grand Island Fish and Wildlife Enhancement
2604 St. Patrick, Suite 7
Grand Island, NE 68803
(308) 381-5571

Pierre Fish and Wildlife Enhancement
Box 986, Federal Building
335 S. Pierre, Room 227
Pierre, SD 57501
(605)224-8693

Salt Lake City Fish and Wildlife Enhancement
2078 Administration Building
1745 West 1700 South
Salt Lake City, UT 84104

(801) 524-4430

Cheyenne Fish and Wildlife Enhancement
Wyoming State Office
2120 Capitol Avenue, Room 7010
Cheyenne, WY 82001
(307) 772-2374

REGION SEVEN:
Alaska

Regional Office
1011 East Tudor Road
Anchorage, AK 99503
(907) 786-3467

Anchorage Field Office
411 West 4th Avenue
Anchorage, AK 99501
(907) 271-2888

Fairbanks Fish and Wildlife Enhancement Field
  Office
101 12th Avenue, Federal Building, Box 20
Fairbanks, AK 99701
(907) 456-0203

Juneau Fish and Wildlife Enhancement
Federal Building, Room 417
Box 021287
Juneau, AK 99802
(907) 586-7240

Ketchikan Fish and Wildlife Enhancement
103 Main St.
Box 3193
Ketchikan, AK 99901
(907) 225-9691

Petersburg Fish and Wildlife Enhancement
Box 1108
Petersburg, AK 99833
(907) 772-3866

Sitka Fish and Wildlife Enhancement
4 Lincoln St., Room 216
Sitka, AK 99835
(907) 747-8882

Kenai Fishery Assistance Office
Box 5089

Kenai, AK 99611
(907) 262-9863

King Salmon Fishery Assistance Office
Box 277
King Salmon, AK 99613
(907) 246-3442

REGION EIGHT
Research and Development
Nationwide

Regional Office/Research and Development
U.S. Fish and Wildlife Service
Washington, D.C. 20240
(703) 358-1710

Appendix II
Offices of the National Marine Fisheries Service

Washington Headquarters

National Marine Fisheries Service
National Oceanic and
   Atmospheric Administration (NOAA)
Department of Commerce
1825 Connecticut Avenue, N.W.
Washington, D.C. 20235
(202) 427-2333

REGIONAL OFFICES

Northeast Region
(Connecticut, Delaware, Indiana, Illinois,
Maine, Massachusetts, Michigan, Minnesota,
New Hampshire, New Jersey, New York,
Ohio, Pennsylvania, Rhode Island, Vermont,
Virginia, West Virginia, Wisconsin)

National Marine Fisheries Service
14 Elm St.
Federal Building
Gloucester, MA 01930
(617) 281-3600

Southeast Region
(Alabama, Arkansas, Florida, Georgia, Iowa,
Kansas, Kentucky, Louisiana, Mississippi,
Missouri, Nebraska, New Mexico, North
Carolina, Oklahoma, South Carolina,
Tennessee, Texas)

National Marine Fisheries Service
9450 Koger Boulevard
St. Petersburg, FL 33702
(813) 893-3141

Northwest Region
(Colorado, Idaho, Montana, North Dakota,
South Dakota, Oregon, Utah, Washington,
Wyoming)

National Marine Fisheries Service
7600 Sand Point Way, N.E.
BIN C15700
Seattle, WA 98115
(206) 526-6150

Southwest Region
(Arizona, California, Hawaii, Nevada)

National Marine Fisheries Service
300 S. Ferry St.
Terminal Island, CA 90731
(213) 514-6197

Alaska Region

National Marine Fisheries Service
Box 1668
Juneau, AK 99802
(907) 586-7221

Appendix III
State Heritage Programs

Alabama Natural Heritage Program
Department of Conservation and Natural
  Resources
Division of Lands
Folsom Administration Building
64 N. Union St., Room 752
Montgomery, AL 36130
(205) 261-3007

Arizona Heritage Program
Arizona Game and Fish Department
2222 W. Greenway Rd.
Phoenix, AZ 85023
(602) 942-3000

Arkansas Natural Heritage Inventory
The Heritage Center, Suite 200
225 E. Markham
Little Rock, AR 72201
(501) 371-1706 ext. 501

California Nongame-Heritage Program
The Resources Agency
Department of Fish and Game
1416 9th St., 12th floor
Sacramento, CA 95814
(916) 322-2493

Colorado Natural Areas Inventory
Department of Natural Resources
1313 Sherman St., Room 718
Denver, CO 80203
(303) 866-3311

Connecticut Natural Diversity Database
Natural Resources Center
Department of Environmental Protection
State Office Building, Room 553
165 Capitol Avenue
Hartford, CT 06106
(203) 566-3540

Delaware Natural Heritage Program
Division of Parks and Recreation
89 Kings Highway
Dover, DE 19903
(302) 736-5285

Florida Natural Areas Inventory
254 E. 6th Avenue
Tallahassee, FL 32303
(904) 224-8207

Georgia Natural Heritage Inventory
Department of Natural Resources
Route 2, Box 119D
Social Circle, GA 30279
(404) 557-2514

Hawaii Heritage Program
1116 Smith St. #201
Honolulu, HI 96817
(808) 537-4508

Idaho Natural Heritage Program
Department of Fish and Game
600 S. Walnut St., Box 25
Boise, ID 83707
(208) 334-3402

Illinois Natural Heritage Inventory
Department of Conservation
Division of Natural Heritage
524 S. 2nd St.
Springfield, IL 62706
(217) 785-8774

Indiana Heritage Program
Division of Nature Preserves
605B State Office Building
Indianapolis, IN 46204
(317) 232-4052

Iowa Natural Areas Inventory
Bureau of Preserves and Ecological Services
Department of Natural Resources
Wallace State Office Building
Des Moines, IA 50319
(515) 281-8524

Kansas Natural Heritage Program
Kansas Biological Survey
The University of Kansas
Raymond Nichols Hall
2291 Irving Hill Drive-Campus West
Lawrence, KS 66045
(913) 864-3453

Kentucky Heritage Program
Nature Preserves Commission
407 Broadway
Frankfort, KY 40601
(502) 564-2886

Louisiana Natural Heritage Program
Department of Wildlife and Fisheries
Box 98000
Baton Rouge, LA 70898
(504) 765-2821

Maine Natural Heritage Program
Office of Comprehensive Land Use Planning
Dept. of Economic and Community Develop-
    ment
State House Station 130
219 Capitol Avenue
Augusta, ME 04333
(207) 289-6800

Maryland Natural Heritage Program
Department of Natural Resources
B-2, Tawes Building
Annapolis, MD 21401
(301) 974-2871

**Massachusetts Natural Heritage and En-
    dangered Species Program**
Division of Fisheries and Wildlife
100 Cambridge St.
Boston, MA 02202
(617) 727-9194

Michigan Natural Features Inventory
Mason Building, 5th Floor
Box 30028
Lansing, MI 48909
(517) 373-1552

Minnesota Natural Heritage Program
Department of Natural Resources
500 Lafayette Rd.
St. Paul, MN 55155
(612) 296-4284

Mississippi Natural Heritage Program
111 N. Jefferson St.
Jackson, MS 39201
(601) 354-7303

Missouri Natural Heritage Inventory
Missouri Department of Conservation
Box 180
Jefferson City, MO 65102
(314) 751-4115

Montana Natural Heritage Program
State Library Building
1515 E. 6th Avenue
Helena, MT 59620
(406) 444-3009

Nebraska Natural Heritage Program
Game and Parks Commission
2200 N. 33rd St.
Box 30370
Lincoln, NE 68503
(402) 471-5421

Nevada Natural Heritage Program
Department of Conservation and Natural
    Resources
Division of State Parks
Capitol Complex, Nye Building
201 S. Fall St.
Carson City, NV 89710
(702) 885-4370

New Hampshire Natural Heritage Inventory
Department of Resources and Economic
    Development
Box 856
Concord, NH 03302
(603) 271-3623

New Jersey Natural Heritage Program
Office of Natural Lands Management
501 E. State St. CN404
Trenton, NJ 08625
(609) 984-1339

New Mexico Natural Resources Survey Section
Villagra Building
Santa Fe, NM 87503
(505) 827-7862

New York Natural Heritage Program
Wildlife Resources Center
Delmar, NY 12054
(518) 439-7488

North Carolina Natural Heritage
Department of Natural Resources and Community Development
Division of State Parks and Recreation
Box 27687
Raleigh, NC 27611
(919) 733-7701

North Dakota Natural Heritage Inventory
Parks and Recreation Department
1424 W. Century Ave., Suite 202
Bismarck, ND 58501
(701) 224-4887

Ohio Natural Heritage Program
Division of Natural Areas and Preservation
Fountain Square, Building F
Columbus, OH 43224
(614) 265-6453

Oklahoma Natural Heritage Inventory
Oklahoma Biological Survey
Sutton Hall, Room 303
625 Elm St.
Norman, OK 73019
(405) 325-1985

Oregon Natural Heritage Program
Oregon Field Office
1205 NW 25th Avenue
Portland, OR 97210
(503) 229-5078

Pennsylvania Natural Diversity Inventory-East
Bureau of Forestry
Department of Environmental Resources
34 Airport Dr.
Middletown, PA 17057
(717) 783-1712

Pennsylvania Natural Diversity Inventory-West
Western Pennsylvania Conservancy
Natural Areas Program
316 Fourth Ave.
Pittsburgh, PA 15222
(412) 288-2774

Rhode Island Heritage Program
Department of Environmental Mgmt.
Division of Planning and Development
83 Park St.
Providence, RI 02903
(401) 277-2776

South Carolina Heritage Trust
Wildlife and Marine Resources Department
Box 167
Columbia, SC 29202
(803) 734-3893

South Dakota Natural Heritage
Department of Game, Fish and Parks
Wildlife Division
445 E. Capitol Ave.
Pierre, SD 57501
(605) 773-4227

Tennessee Department of Conservation
Ecological Services Division
701 Broadway
Nashville, TN 37203
(615) 742-6545

Texas Natural Heritage Program
Texas Parks and Wildlife Department
4200 Smith School Road
Austin, TX 78744
(512) 389-4586

Utah Natural Heritage Program
3 Triad Center, Suite 400
Salt Lake City, UT 84180
(801) 538-5524

Vermont Natural Heritage Program
Agency of Natural Resources
Center Building
103 S. Main St.
Waterbury, VT 05676
(802) 244-7340

Virginia Natural Heritage Program
Department of Conservation and Historic Res-
    toration
203 Governor St., Suite 402
Richmond, VA 23219
(804) 786-7951

Washington Natural Heritage Program
Department of Natural Resources
Mail Stop EX-13
Olympia, WA 98504
(206) 753-2448

Appendix IV
Bureau of Land Management Offices

Washington Headquarters

Bureau of Land Management
U.S. Department of the Interior
18th and C Sts., N.W.
Washington, D.C. 20240
(202) 653-9202

State Offices

Alaska
Bureau of Land Management
701 C St., Box 13
Anchorage, AK 99513
(907) 271-5555

Arizona
Bureau of Land Management
Box 16563
Phoenix, AZ 85011
(602) 241-5504

California
Bureau of Land Management
Federal Building
2800 Cottage Way, E-2841
Sacramento, CA 95825
(916) 978-4746

Colorado
Bureau of Land Management
2850 Youngfield St.
Lakewood, CO 80215
(303) 236-1700

Denver Service Center
Denver Federal Center, Building 50
Denver, CO 80225
(303) 236-0161

Eastern States Office
Bureau of Land Management
Eastern States Office
350 South Pickett St.

Alexandria, VA 22304
(703) 274-0190

Idaho
Bureau of Land Management
3380 Americana Terrace
Boise, ID 83706
(208) 334-1771

Montana (MT, SD, ND)
Bureau of Land Management
222 North 32nd St.
Billings, MT 59107
(406) 657-6655

Nevada
Bureau of Land Management
Box 12000
Reno, NV 89520
(702) 784-5311

New Mexico (KS, NM, OK, TX)
Bureau of Land Management
Montoya Federal Building
South Federal Place
Santa Fe, NM 87504
(505) 988-6316

Oregon (OR, WA)
Bureau of Land Management
825 N.E. Multnomah St.
Box 2965
Portland, OR 97208
(503) 231-6274

Utah
Bureau of Land Management
324 South State St.
Salt Lake City, UT 84111
(801) 524-5311

Wyoming (WY, NE)
Bureau of Land Management
2515 Warren Avenue
Cheyenne, WY 82003
(307) 772-2111

Appendix V
National Forest Service Offices

Washington Headquarters

Forest Service-USDA
Box 96090
Washington, D.C. 20013
(202) 447-3957

Regional Offices

Region One (Northern): northern Idaho, Montana, and northwestern North Dakota
Federal Building
Box 7669
Missoula, MT 59807
(406) 329-3511

Region Two (Rocky Mountain): Colorado, Kansas, Nebraska, southern South Dakota, and eastern Wyoming
11177 West 8th Ave.
Box 25127
Lakewood, CO 80225
(303) 236-9427

Region Three (Southwestern): Arizona and New Mexico
Federal Building
517 Gold Ave., SW
Albuquerque, NM 87102
(505) 842-3292

Region Four (Intermountain): southern Idaho, Nevada, Utah, and western Wyoming
Federal Building
324 25th St.
Ogden, UT 84401
(801) 625-5183

Region Five (Pacific Southwest): California, Guam, Hawaii, and Pacific Islands
630 Sansome St.
San Francisco, CA 94111
(415) 556-4310

Region Six (Pacific Northwest): Oregon and Washington
319 S.W. Pine St.
Box 3623
Portland, OR 97208
(503) 221-3625

Region Eight (Southern): Alabama, Arkansas, Georgia, Kentucky, Louisiana, Mississippi, North Carolina, Oklahoma, Puerto Rico, South Carolina, Tennessee, Texas
1720 Peachtree Rd., N.W.
Atlanta, GA 30367
(404) 347-4177

Region Nine (Eastern): Connecticut, Delaware, Illinois, Indiana, Iowa, Maine, Maryland, Massachusetts, Michigan, Minnesota, Missouri, New Hampshire, New Jersey, New York, Ohio, Pennsylvania, Rhode Island, Vermont, West Virginia, Wisconsin
310 West Wisconsin Ave.
Room 500
Milwaukee, WI 53203
(414) 291-3693

Region Ten: Alaska
Federal Office Building
Box 21628
Juneau, AK 99802
(907) 586-8863

Appendix VI
National Wildlife Refuges

Alabama
Bon Secour, Box 1650, Gulf Shores, AL 36542
Choctaw, Box 808, Jackson, AL 36545
Eufaula, Route 2, Box 97-B, Eufaula, AL 36027
Wheeler, Box 1643, Decatur, AL 35602

Alaska
Alaska Maritime Headquarters 202 W. Pioneer
  Ave., Homer, AK 99603
Aleutian Islands Unit, Box 5251, FPO Seattle,
  WA 98791
Alaska Peninsula, Box 277, King Salmon, AK
  99613
  Becharof
Arctic, 101-12th Ave. Box 20, Fairbanks, AK
  99701
Innoko, Box 69, McGrath, AK 99627
Izembek, Box 127, Cold Bay, AK 99571
Kanuti, 101-12th Ave., Box 20, Fairbanks, AK
  99701
Kenai, Box 2139, Soldotna, AK 99669
Kodiak, 1390 Buskin River Rd., Kodiak, AK
  99615
Koyukuk, Box 287, Galena, AK 99741
Nowitna, Box 287, Galena, AK 99741
Selawik, Box 270, Kotzebue, AK 99752
Tetlin, Box 155, Tok, AK 99780
Togiak, Box 270, Dillingham, AK 99576
Yukon Delta, Box 346, Bethel, AK 99559
Yukon Flats, 101-12th Ave., Box 20, Fairbanks,
  AK 99701

Arizona
Buenos Aires, Box 106, Sasabe, AZ 85633
Cabeza Prieta, Box 418, Ajo, AZ 85321
Cibola, Box AP, Blythe, CA 92225
Havasu, Box A, Needles, CA 92363
Imperial, Box 72217, Martinez Lake, AZ 85364
Kofa, Box 6290, Yuma, AZ 85364
San Bernardino, RR#1, Box 228R, Douglas, AZ
  85607

Arkansas
Felsenthal, Box 1157, Crossett, AR 71635
Holla Bend, Box 1043, Russellville, AR 72801
Wapanocca, Box 279, Turrell, AR 72384

Big Lake, Box 67, Manila, AR 72442
  Cache River
White River, Box 308, 321 W. 7th St., De Witt,
  AR 72042

California
Cibola, Havasu, Imperial (See Arizona)
Kern, Box 670, Delano, CA 93216
Klamath Basin Refuges, Route 1, Box 74,
  Tulelake, CA 96134
  Clear Lake
  Lower Klamath
  Tule Lake
Modoc, Box 1610, Alturas, CA 96101
Sacramento Valley Refuges, Route 1, Box 311,
  Willows, CA 95988
  Colusa
  Delevan
  Sacramento
  Sutter
Salton Sea, Box 120, Calipatria, CA 92233
  Coachella Valley
  Tijuana Slough
San Francisco Bay, Box 524, Newark, CA 94560
  Antioch Dunes
  Humboldt Bay
  Salinas River
  San Pablo Bay
San Luis, Box 2176, Los Banos, CA 93635
  Kesterson
  Merced

Colorado
Alamosa, Box 1148, Alamosa, CO 81101
  Monte Vista
Arapaho, Box 457, Walden, CO 80480
Browns Park, 1318 Hwy. 318, Maybell, CO 81640

Connecticut
Salt Meadow, Box 307, Charlestown, RI 02813
Stewart B. McKinney, 910 Lafayette Boulevard,
  Room 210, Bridgeport, CT 06604

Delaware
Bombay Hook, Route 1, Box 147, Smyrna, DE
  19977

Prime Hook, Route 1, Box 195, Milton, DE 19968

Florida
Arthur R. Marshall Loxahatchee, Route 1, Box 278, Boynton Beach, FL 33437
   Hobe Sound
Chassahowitzka, Box 4139, Homosassa, FL 32647
   Cedar Keys
   Crystal River
   Egmont Key
   Lower Suwannee
   Passage Key
   Pinellas
J.N. "Ding" Darling, 1 Wildlife Drive, Sanibel, FL 33957
   Caloosahatchee
   Florida Panther
   Island Bay
   Matlacha Pass
   Pine Island
Lake Woodruff, Box 488, DeLeon Springs, FL 32028
Merritt Island, Box 6504, Titusville, FL 32780
   Pelican Island
National Key Deer, Box 510, Big Pine Key, FL 33043
   Crocodile Lake
   Great White Heron
   Key West
St. Marks, Box 68, St. Marks, FL 32355
St. Vincent, Box 447, Apalachicola, FL 32320

Georgia
Eufaula (See Alabama)
Savannah Costal Refuges, Box 8487, Savannah, GA 31412
   Blackbeard Island
   Harris Neck
   Savannah (Georgia and South Carolina)
   Tybee
   Wassaw
   Wolf Island
Okefenokee, Route 2, Box 338, Folkston, GA 31537
Piedmont, Round Oak, GA 31038

Hawaii
Hawaiian and Pacific Islands Refuges, Box 50167, Honolulu, HI 96850
   Hawaiian Islands
   James C. Campbell

   Kakahaia
Kilauea Point, Box 87, Kilauea, Kauai, HI 96754
   Hanalei

Idaho
Deer Flat, Box 448, Nampa, ID 83653-0448
   Snake River Islands
Kootenai, HCR 60, Box 284, Bonners Ferry, ID 83201
Southeast Idaho Refuges, 250 S. Fourth Ave., Pocatello, ID 83201
Bear Lake, 370 Webster, Box 9, Montpelier, ID 83254
Camas, HC 69, Box 1700, Hamer, ID 83425
Grays Lake, HC 70, Box 4090, Wayan, ID 83285
Minidoka, Route 4, Box 290, Rupert, ID 83350
   Oxford Slough

Illinois
Chautauqua, Route 2, Havana, IL 62644
Crab Orchard, Box J, Carterville, IL 62918
Mark Twain, 311 N. 5th St., Suite 100, Quincy, IL 62301
Batchtown Division, Box 142, Brussels, IL 62013
Calhoun Division, Box 142, Brussels, IL 62013
Gardner Division, Box 88, Annada, MO 63330
Gilbert Lake Division, Box 142, Brussels, IL 62013
Keithsburg Division, Rt. 1, Wapello, IA 52653
Upper Mississippi River Wildlife and Fish Refuge (See Minnesota)
Savanna District, Post Office Building, Savanna, IL 61074

Indiana
Muscatatuck, Route 7, Box 189A, Seymour, IN 47274

Iowa
DeSoto, Route 1, Box 114, Missouri Valley, IA 51555
Mark Twain (See Illinois)
Big Timber Division, Rt. 1, Wapello, IA 52653
Louisa Division, Rt. 1, Wapello, IA 52653
Union Slough, Route 1, Box 52, Titonka, IA 50480
Upper Mississippi River Wildlife and Fish Refuge, (See Minnesota)
Mcgregor District, Box 460, McGregor, IA 52157

Kansas
Flint Hills, Box 128, Hartford, KS 66854
Kirwin, Route 1, Box 103, Kirwin, KS 67644

Quivira, Route 3, Box 48A, Stafford, KS 67578

Louisiana
Bogue Chitto, 1010 Gause Boulevard, Building
936, Slidell, LA 70458
Catahoula, Drawer LL, Jena, LA 71342
D'Arbonne, Box 3065, Monroe, LA 71201
Upper Ouachita
Delta-Breton, Venice, LA 70091
Lacassine, Route 1, Box 186, Lake Arthur, LA
70549
Sabine, MRH 107, Hackberry, LA 70645
Tensas River, Route 2, Box 295, Tallulah, LA
71282

Maine
Moosehorn, Box X, Calais, ME 04619
Cross Island
Franklin Island
Petit Manan, Box 279, Milbridge, ME 04658
Rachel Carson, Route 2, Box 751, Wells, ME
04090

Maryland
Blackwater, Route 1, Box 121, Cambridge, MD
21613
Eastern Neck, Route 2, Box 225, Rock Hall, MD
21661

Massachusetts
Great Meadows, Weir Hill Rd., Sudbury, MA
01776
Oxbow
Parker River, Northern Boulevard, Plum Island,
Newburyport, MA 01950
Monomoy
Nantucket

Michigan
Seney, Seney, MI 49883
Shiawassee, 6975 Mower Road, Route 1,
Saginaw, MI 48601

Minnesota
Agassiz, Middle River, MN 56737
Big Stone, 25 NW 2nd St., Ortonville, MN 56278
Minnesota Valley, 4101 E. 80th St., Bloomington,
MN 55420
Minnesota Wetlands Complex, Route 1, Box 76,
Fergus Falls, MN 56537

Morris WMD, Route 1, Box 208, Morris, MN
56267
Detroit Lakes WMD, Route 3, Box 47D, Detroit
Lakes, MN 56501
Fergus Falls WMD, Route 1, Box 76, Fergus
Falls, MN 56537
Litchfield WMD, 305 N. Sibley, Litchfield, MN
55355
Rice Lake, Route 2, Box 67, McGregor, MN 55760
Sherburne, Route 2, Zimmerman, MN 55398
Tamarac, Rural Route, Rochert, MN 56578
Upper Mississippi River Wildlife and Fish
Refuge, 51 E. 4th St., Winona, MN 55987
Winona District

Mississippi
Mississippi Sandhill Crane, Box 699, Gautier,
MS 39553
Noxubee, Route 1, Box 142, Brooksville, MS
39739
Yazoo, Route 1, Box 286, Hollandale, MS 38748
Hillside
Morgan Brake
Panther Swamp

Missouri
Mark Twain (See Illinois)
Clarence Cannon, Box 88, Annada, MO 63330
Mingo, Route 1, Box 103, Puxico, MO 63960
Squaw Creek, Box 101, Mound City, MO 64470
Swan Lake, Box 68, Sumner, MO 64681

Montana
Benton Lake, Box 450, Black Eagle, MT 59414
Bowdoin, Box J, Malta, MT 59538
Charles M. Russell, Box 110, Lewistown, MT
59457
Lee Metcalf, Box 257, Stevensville, MT 59870
Medicine Lake, HC 51, Box 2, Medicine Lake,
MT 59247
National Bison Range, Moiese, MT 59824
Red Rock Lakes, Monida Star Route, Box 15,
Lima, MT 59739

Nebraska
Crescent Lake, HC 68, Box 21, Ellsworth, NE
69340
Fort Niobrara, Hidden Timber Route, HC 14,
Box 67, Valentine, NE 69201
Valentine

Rainwater Basin Wetland Management District, Box 1686, Kearney, NE 68848

Nevada
Desert National Wildlife Range, 150 North Decatur Boulevard, Las Vegas, NV 89108
  Ash Meadows
  Pahranagat
Ruby Lake, Ruby Valley, NV 89833
Sheldon, Box 111, Room 308, U.S. Post Office Building, Lakeview, OR 97630
Stillwater, Box 1236, 1510 Rio Vista Rd., Fallon, NV 89406
  Fallon

New Hampshire
Wapack, Weir Hill Rd., Sudbury, MA 01776

New Jersey
Edwin B. Forsythe, Box 72, Oceanville, NJ 08231
  Brigantine
Barnegat, Box 544, Barnegat, NJ 08005
Great Swamp, Pleasant Plains Rd., RD 1, Box 152, Basking Ridge, NJ 07920

New Mexico
Bitter Lake, Box 7, Roswell, NM 88201
Bosque del Apache, Box 1246, Socorro, NM 87801
Sevileta, General Delivery, San Acacia, NM 87831
Las Vegas, Route 1, Box 399, Las Vegas, NM 87701
Maxwell, Box 276, Maxwell, NM 87728

New York
Iroquois, Box 517, Alabama, NY 14003
Montezuma, 3395 Route 5/20 East, Seneca Falls, NY 13148
Wertheim, Box 21, Shirley, NY 11967
  Morton
  Target Rock

North Carolina
Alligator River, Box 1969, Manteo, NC 27954
  Currituck
  Pea Island
Mackay Island, Box 31, Knotts Island, NC 27950
Mattamuskeet, Route 1, Box N-2, Swanquarter, NC 27885
  Cedar Island

  Pungo
  Swanquarter
Pee Dee, Box 780, Wadesboro, NC 28170

North Dakota
Arrowwood, Rural Route 1, Pingree, ND 58476
Long Lake, Moffit, ND 58560
Valley City Wetland Management District, Rural Route 1, Valley City, ND 58072
Audubon, Rural Route 1, Coleharbor, ND 58531
Lake Ilo, Dunn Center, ND 58626
Des Lacs, Box 578, Kenmare, ND 58746
Crosby Wetland Management District, Box 148, Crosby, ND 58730
Lostwood, Rural Route 2, Box 98, Kenmare, ND 58746
Devils Lake Wetland Management District, Box 908, Devils Lake, ND 58301
  Lake Alice
Sullys Hill National Game Preserve, Fort Totten, ND 58335
J. Clark Salyer, Box 66, Upham, ND 58789
Kulm Wetland Management District, Box E, Kulm, ND 58456
Tewauken, Rural Route 1, Box 75, Cayuga, ND 58013
Upper Souris, Rural Route 1, Foxholm, ND 58738

Ohio
Ottawa, 14000 W. State Route 2, Oak Harbor, OH 43449

Oklahoma
Little River, General Delivery, Broken Bow, OK 74962
Salt Plains, Route 1, Box 76, Jet, OK 73749
Sequoyah, Route 1, Box 18A, Vian, OK 74962
Tishomingo, Route 1, Box 151, Tishomingo, OK 73460
Washita, Route 1, Box 68, Butler, OK 73625
  Optima
Wichita Mountains, Route 1, Box 448, Indiahoma, OK 73552

Oregon
Hart Mountain National Antelope Refuge, Post Office Building, Lakeview, OR 97630
Klamath Basin Refuges, Route 1, Box 74, Tulelake, CA 96134
  Bear Valley
  Klamath Forest

Lower Klamath
Upper Klamath
Malheur, Box 245, Princeton, OR 97721
Umatilla, Box 239, Umatilla, OR 97882
    Cold Springs
    McKay Creek
Western Oregon Refuges,
    Finley Refuge Rd., Corvallis, OR 97333
    Ankeny
    Bandon Marsh
    Baskett Slough
    Cape Meares
    William L. Finley
Willapa (See Washington)
    Columbian White-tailed Deer
    Lewis and Clark

Pennsylvania
Erie, RD 1, Wood Duck Lane, Guy Mills, PA
    16327
Tinicum National Environmental Center, Suite
    104, Scott Plaza 2, Philadelphia, PA 19113

Puerto Rico
Caribbean Islands, Box 510, Carr. 301, KM 5.4,
    Boqueron, PR 00622
    Buck Island (Virgin Islands)
    Cabo Rojo (Puerto Rico)
    Culebra (Puerto Rico)
    Desecheo (Puerto Rico)
    Green Cay (Virgin Islands)
    Sandy Point (Virgin Islands)

Rhode Island
Ninigret, Shoreline Plaza, Route 1A, Box 307,
    Charlestown, RI 02813
    Block Island
    Sachuest Point
    Trustom Pond

South Carolina
Cape Romain, 390 Bulls Island Rd., Awendaw,
    SC 29429
Carolina Sandhills, Route 2, Box 330, McBee, SC
    29101
    Pinckney Island
Santee, Route 2, Box 66, Summerton SC 29148

South Dakota
Lacreek, HWC 3, Box 14, Martin, SD 57551

Lake Andes, Rural Route 1, Box 77, Lake Andes,
    SD 57356
    Karl E. Mundt
Madison Wetland Management District, Box 48,
    Madison, SD 57042
Sand Lake, Rural Route 1, Box 25, Columbia, SD
    57433
Waubay, Rural Route 1, Box 79, Waubay, SD
    57273

Tennessee
Cross Creeks, Route 1, Box 229, Dover TN 37058
Hatchie, Box 187, Brownsville, TN 38012
    Chickasaw
    Lower Hatchie
Reelfoot, Route 2, Hwy 157, Union City, TN
    38261
    Lake Isom
Tennessee, Box 849, Paris, TN 38242

Texas
Anahuac, Box 278, Anahuac, TX 77514
    McFaddin
    Texas Point
Aransas, Box 100, Austwell, TX 77950
Attwater Prairie Chicken, Box 518, Eagle Lake,
    TX 77434
Brazoria, Box 1088, Angleton, TX 77515
    Big Boggy
    San Bernard
Buffalo Lake, Box 228, Umbarger, TX 79091
    Grulla
Muleshoe, Box 549, Muleshoe, TX 79347
Hagerman, Route 3, Box 123, Sherman, TX 75090
Laguna Atascosa, Box 450, Rio Hondo, TX 78583
Santa Ana, Route 1, Box 202A, Alamo, TX 78516
    Rio Grande Valley

Utah
Bear River Migratory Bird Refuge, Box 459,
    Brigham City, UT 84302
Fish Springs, Box 568, Dugway, UT 84022
Ouray, 1680 W. Hwy. 40, Room 1220, Vernal,
    UT 84078

Vermont
Missisquoi, Route 2, Swanton, VT 05488

Virginia
Back Bay, 4005 Sandpiper Rd., Box 6286, Vir-
    ginia Beach, VA 23456

National Wildlife Refuges

Chincoteague, Box 62, Chincoteague, VA 23336
Eastern Shore of Virginia, RFD 1, Box 122B,
  Cape Charles, VA 23310
Great Dismal Swamp, Box 349, Suffolk, VA
  23434
Mason Neck, 14416 Jefferson Davis Highway,
  Suite 20A, Woodbridge, VA 22191
Presquile, Box 620, Hopewell, VA 23860

Washington
Columbia, 44 S. 8th Ave., Drawer F, Othello,
  WA 99344
Nisqually, 100 Brown Farm Rd., Olympia, WA
  98506
Dungeness, Box 698, Sequim, WA 98382
San Juan Islands, 100 Brown Farm Rd., Olympia,
  WA 98506
Ridgefield, 301 N. Third, Box 457, Ridgefield,
  WA 98642
Conboy Lake, Box 5, Glenwood, WA 98619
Turnbull, Route 3, Box 385, Cheney, WA 99004
Umatilla, Box 239, Umatilla, OR 97882
McNary, Box 308, Burbank, WA 99323
Toppenish, Route 1, Box 1300, Toppenish, WA
  98948
Willapa, Ilwaco, WA 98624
  Columbian White-tailed Deer
  Lewis and Clark (See Oregon)

Wisconsin
Horicon, W. 4279 Headquarters Rd., Mayville,
  WI 53050
Necedah, Star Route West, Box 386, Necedah,
  WI 54646
Upper Mississippi River Wildlife and Fish
  Refuge (See Minnesota)
La Crosse District,   Box 415, La Crosse, WI 54601
Trempealeau, Route 1, Trempealeau, WI 54661

Wyoming
National Elk Refuge, Box C, Jackson, WY 83001
Seedskadee, Box 67, Green River, WY 82935

Appendix VII
Canadian Agencies

Canadian Wildlife Service

Main Office
Ottawa, Ontario K1A 0H3
(819) 997-1301

Regional Office (Atlantic)
31 West Main St.
Box 1590
Sackville, N.B. E0A 3C0
(506) 536-3025

Regional Office (Ontario)
1725 Woodward Drive
Ottawa, Ontario K1A 0E7
(613) 998-4693

Regional Office (Pacific and Yukon)
5421 Robertson Road
Box 340
Delta, B.C. V4K 3Y3
(604) 946-8546

Regional Office (Québec)
1121 Route de l'église
Box 10100
Sainte-Foy, Québec G1V 4H5
(418) 648-3914

Regional Office (Western and Northern)
Twin Atria No.2
4999-98 Avenue
Edmonton, Alberta T6B 2X3
(403) 468-8919

Canadian Parks Service

Main Office
Ottawa, Ontario K1A 0H3
(819) 997-9525

Regional Office (Western)
220 Fourth Avenue, SE
Box 2989, Station M
Calgary, Alberta T2P 3H8
(403) 292-4444

Regional Office (Prairie)
457 Main St.
Winnipeg, Manitoba R3B 3E8
(204) 983-2127

Regional Office (Ontario)
111 Water St. E
Cornwall, Ontario K6H 6S3
(613) 938-5866

Regional Office (Québec)
3 Rue Buade
C.P. 6060, Haute-Ville
Québec City G1R 4V7
(418) 648-4042

Regional Office (Atlantic)
Historic Properties
Upper Water St.
Halifax, Nova Scotia B3J 1S9
(902) 426-3405

Fisheries and Oceans

Main Office
200 Kent St.
Ottawa, Ontario K1A 0E6

Appendix VIII
State by State Occurrence

OCEANIC

Mammals
Right whale	*Balaena glacialis*
Bowhead whale	*Balaena mysticetus*
Sei whale	*Balaenoptera borealis*
Blue whale	*Balaenoptera musculus*
Finback whale	*Balaenoptera physalus*
Grey whale	*Eschrichtius robustus*
Humpback whale	*Megaptera novaeangliae*
Sperm whale	*Physeter catodon*

Reptiles
Loggerhead Sea Turtle	*Caretta caretta*
Green Sea Turtle	*Chelonia mydas*
Leatherback Sea Turtle	*Dermochelys coriacea*
Hawksbill Sea Turtle	*Eretmocheyls imbricata*
Kemp's Ridley Sea Turtle	*Lepidochelys kempii*
Olive Ridley Sea Turtle	*Lepidochelys olivacea*

ALL CONTIGUOUS STATES

Birds
American peregrine falcon	*Falco peregrinus anatum*
Bald eagle	*Haliaeets leucocephalus*

ALABAMA

Plants
Little amphianthus	*Amphianthus pusillus*
Alabama leather flower	*Clematis socialis*
Mohr's Barbara button	*Marshallia mohrii*
American hart's-tongue fern	*Phyllitis scolopendrium* var. *americana*
Harperella	*Ptilimnium nodosum* (=*P. fluviatile*)
Green pitcher plant	*Sarracenia oreophila*
Alabama canebrake pitcher plant	*Sarracenia rubra ssp. alabamensis*
Relict trillium	*Trillium reliquum*

ALABAMA, cont.

Mammals
Gray bat	*Myotis grisescens*
Alabama beach mouse	*Peromyscus polionotus ammobates*
Perdido Key Beach mouse	*Peromyscus polionotus trissyllepsis*

Birds
Red-cockaded woodpecker	*Picoides borealis*
Bachman's warbler	*Vermivora bachmanii*

Reptiles
Eastern indigo snake	*Drymarchon corais couperi*
Gopher tortoise	*Gopherus polyphemus*
Alabama red-belied turtle	*Pseudemys alabamensis*
Flattened musk turtle	*Sternotherus depressus*

Amphibians
Red Hills salamander	*Phaeognathus hubrichti*

Fishes
Pygmy sculpin	*Cottus pygmaeus*
Slackwater darter	*Etheostoma boschungi*
Watercress darter	*Etheostoma nuchale*
Boulder darter	*Etheostoma* sp.
Spotfin chub	*Hybopsis monacha*
Snail darter	*Percina tanasi*
Alabama cavefish	*Speoplatyrhinus poulsoni*

Mussels
Yellow-blossom pearly mussel	*Epioblasma florentina florentina*
Penitent mussel	*Epioblasma penita* (=Dysnomia)
Turgid-blossom pearly mussel	*Epioblasma turgidula* (=Dysnomia)
Fine-rayed pigtoe	*Fusconaia cuneolus*
Shiny pigtoe	*Fusconaia edgariana*
Pink mucket pearly mussel	*Lampsilis orbiculata*
Alabama lamp pearly mussel	*Lampsilis virescens*
White wartyback pearly mussel	*Plethobasus cicatricosus*
Orange-footed pearly mussel	*Plethobasus cooperianus*
Curtus' mussel	*Pleurobema curtum*
Marshall's mussel	*Pleurobema marshalli*
Rough pigtoe	*Pleurobema plenum*
Judge Taits's mussel	*Pleurobema taitianum*
Cumberland monkeyface pearly mussel	*Quadrula intermedia*
Stirrup shell	*Quadrula stapes*
Pale lilliput pearly mussel	*Toxolasma cylindellus* (=Carunculina)

ALABAMA, cont.

Crustaceans
Alabama cave shrimp   *Palaemonias alabamae*

ALASKA
Plants
Aleutian shield fern   *Polystichum aleuticum*

Birds
Aleutian Canada goose   *Branta canadensis leucopareia*
Arctic peregrine falcon   *Falco peregrinus tundrius*
Eskimo curlew   *Numenius borealis*

ARIZONA

Plants
Arizona agave   *Agave arizonica*
Kearney's blue star   *Amsonia kearneyana*
No common name   *Carex speculicola*
Cochise pincushion cactus   *Coryphantha robbinsorum*
Arizona cliffrose   *Cowania subintegra*
Nichol's Turk's head cactus   *Echinocactus horizonthalonius* var. *nicholii*
Arizona hedgehog cactus   *Echinocereus triglochidiatus* var. *arizonicus*
Brady pincushion cactus   *Pediocactus bradyi*
Peebles Navajo cactus   *Pediocactus peeblesianus peebles*
Siler pincushion cactus   *Pediocactus sileri*
San Francisco Peaks groundsel   *Senecio franciscanus*
Tumamoc globeberry   *Tumamoca macdougalii*

Mammals
Sonoran pronghorn   *Antilocapra americana sonoriensis*
Ocelot   *Felis pardalis*
Jaguarundi   *Felis yagouaroundi tolteca*
Sanborn's long-nosed bat   *Leptonycteris sanborni (=yerbabuenae)*
Hualapai vole   *Microtus mexicanus hualpaiensis*
Mt. Graham red squirrel   *Tamiasciurus hudsonicus grahamensis*

Birds
Masked bobwhite   *Colinus virginianus ridgwayi*
Northern aplomado falcon   *Falco femoralis septentrionalis*
Yuma clapper rail   *Rallus longirostris yumanensis*
Thick-billed parrot   *Rhynchopsitta pachyrhyncha*

Reptiles
Desert tortoise   *Gopherus (=Xerobates) agassizii*

ARIZONA, cont.

Fishes

Desert pupfish	Cyprinodon macularius
Humpback chub	Gila cypha
Sonora chub	Gila ditaenia
Bonytail chub	Gila elegans
Yaqui chub	Gila purpurea
Virgin River chub	Gila robusta seminuda
Yaqui catfish	Ictalurus pricei
Little Colorado spinedace	Lepidomeda vittata
Spikedace	Meda fulgida
Beautiful shiner	Notropis formosus
Woundfin	Plagopterus argentissimus
Gila topminnow	Poeciliopsis occidentalis
Yaqui topminnow	Poeciliopsis occidentalis sonoriensis
Colorado squawfish	Ptychocheilus lucius
Apache trout	Salmo apache
Gila trout	Salmo gilae
Loach minnow	Tiaroga cobitis

ARKANSAS

Plants

Geocarpon	Geocarpon minimum
Pondberry	Lindera melissifolia

Mammals

Gray bat	Myotis grisescens
Ozark big-eared bat	Plecotus townsendii ingens

Birds

Red-cockaded woodpecker	Picoides borealis
Least tern	Sterna antillarum
Bachman's warbler	Vermivora bachmanii

Fishes

Ozark cavefish	Amblyopsis rosae
Leopard darter	Percina pantherina

Snails

Magazine Mountain shagreen	Mesodon magazinensis

Mussels

Pink mucket pearly mussel	Lampsilis orbiculata

ARKANSAS, cont.

Speckled pocketbook mussel — *Lampsilis streckeri*
Fat pocketbook pearly mussel — *Potalimus (=Proptera) capax*

Crustaceans
Cave crayfish — *Cambarus zophonastes*

CALIFORNIA

Plants
San Mateo thornmint — *Acanthomintha obovata* ssp. *duttonii*
Large flowered fiddleneck — *Amsinckia grandiflora*
McDonald's rock-cress — *Arabis mcdonaldiana*
Presidio (Raven's) manzanita — *Arctostaphylos pungens* var. *ravenii*
San Benito evening-primrose — *Camissonia benitensis*
San Clemente Island Indian paintbrush — *Castilleja grisea*
Spring-loving centaury — *Centaurium namophilum*
Slender-horned spineflower — *Centrostegia leptocerus*
Salt marsh bird's-beak — *Cordylanthus maritimus* ssp. *maritumus*
Palmate-bracted bird's-beak — *Cordylanthus palmatus*
Santa Cruz cypress — *Cupressus abramsiana*
San Clemente Island larkspur — *Delphinium kinkiense*
Santa Barbara Island liveforever — *Dudleya traskiae*
Santa Ana wooly star — *Eriastrum densifolium* ssp. *sanctorum*
Loch Lomond coyote thistle — *Eryngium constancei*
Contra Costa wallflower — *Erysimum capitatum* var. *angustatum*
Ash Meadows gumplant — *Grindelia fraxinopratensis*
San Clemente Island broom — *Lotus dendroideus* var. *traskiae*
Truckee barberry — *Mahonia sonnei (=Berberis s.)*
San Clemente Island bush-mallow — *Malacothamnus clementinus*
Ash Meadows blazing star — *Mentzelia leucophylla*
Amargosa niterwort — *Nitrophila mohavensis*
Eureka Valley evening primrose — *Oenothera avita* ssp. *eurekensis*
Antioch Dunes evening-primrose — *Oenothera deltoides* ssp. *howellii*
San Diego mesa mint — *Pogogyne abramsii*
Pedate checker-mallow — *Sidalcea pedata*
Eureka Dunegrass — *Swallenia alexandrae*
Slender-petaled mustard — *Thelypodium stenopetalum*
Solano grass — *Tuctoria mucronata (=Orcuttia m.)*

Mammals
Guadalupe fur seal — *Arctocephalus townsendi*
Morro Bay kangaroo rat — *Dipodomys heermanni morroensis*

CALIFORNIA, cont.

Giant kangaroo rat	*Dipodomys ingens*
Fresno kangaroo rat	*Dipodomys nitratoides exilis*
Tipton kangaroo rat	*Dipodomys nitratoides nitratoides*
Stephens' kangaroo rat	*Dipodomys stephensi*
Southern sea otter	*Enhydra lutris nereis*
Amargosa vole	*Microtus californicus scirpensis*
Vaquita	*Phocoena sinus*
Salt marsh harvest mouse	*Reithrodontomys raviventris*
San Joaquin kit fox	*Vulpes macrotis mutica*

Birds

San Clemente sage sparrow	*Amphispiza bellis clementeae*
Aleutian Canada goose	*Branta canadensis leucopareia*
California condor	*Gymnogyps californianus*
San Clemente loggerhead shrike	*Lanius ludovicianus mearnsi*
Brown pelican	*Pelecanus occidentalis*
Inyo brown towhee	*Pipilo fuscus erempphilus*
Light-footed clapper rail	*Rallus longirostris levipes*
California clapper rail	*Rallus longirostris obsoletus*
Yuma clapper rail	*Rallus longirostris yumanensis*
California least tern	*Sterna antillarum browni (=albifrons)*
Least Bell's vireo	*Vireo bellii pusillus*

Reptiles

Blunt-nosed leopard lizard	*Gambelia (=Crotaphytus) silus*
Desert tortoise	*Gopherus (=Xerobates) agassizii*
San Francisco garter snake	*Thamnophis sirtalis tetrataenia*
Coachella Valley fringe-toed lizard	*Uma inornata*
Island night lizard	*Xantusia riversiana*

Amphibians

Santa Cruz long-toed salamander	*Ambystoma macrodactylum croceum*
Desert slender salamander	*Batrachoseps aridus*

Fishes

Modoc sucker	*Catostomus microps*
Shortnose sucker	*Chasmistes brevirostris*
Desert pupfish	*Cyprinodon macularius*
Owens pupfish	*Cyprinodon radiosus*
Lost River sucker	*Deltistes luxatus*
Unarmored threespine stickleback	*Gasterosteus aculeatus williamsoni*
Mohave tui chub	*Gila bicolor mohavensis*
Owens tui chub	*Gila bicolor snyderi*
Bonytail chub	*Gila elegans*

CALIFORNIA, cont.

Colorado squawfish	*Ptychocheilus lucius*
Little Kern golden trout	*Salmo aquabonita whitei*
Lahontan cutthroat trout	*Salmo clarki henshawi*
Paiute cutthroat trout	*Salmo clarki seleniris*

Crustaceans

Shasta crayfish	*Pacifasticus fortis*
California freshwater shrimp	*Syncaris pacifica*

Insects

Lange's metalmark butterfly	*Apodemia mormo langei*
San Bruno elfin butterfly	*Callophrys mossii bayensis*
Valley elderberry longhorn beetle	*Desmocerus californicus dimorphus*
Delta green ground beetle	*Elaphrus viridis*
El Segundo blue butterfly	*Euphilotes battoides allyni*
Smith's blue butterfly	*Euphiltes enoptes smithi*
Bay checkerspot butterfly	*Euphydryas editha bayensis*
Kern primrose sphinx moth	*Eurposerpinus euterpe*
Palos Verdes blue butterfly	*Glaucopsyche lygdamus palosverdesensis*
Mission blue butterfly	*Icaricia icariodes missionensis*
Lotis blue butterfly	*Lycaeides argyrognomon lotis*

COLORADO

Plants

Mancos milk-vetch	*Astragalus humillimus*
Osterhout milk-vetch	*Astragalus osterhoutii*
Spineless hedgehog cactus	*Echinocereus triglochidiatus* var. *inermis*
Clay-loving wild-buckwheat	*Eriogonum pelinophilum*
Penland beardtongue	*Penstemon penlandii*
North Park phacelia	*Phacelia formosula*
Uinta Basin hookless cactus	*Sclerocactus glaucus*
Mesa Verde cactus	*Sclerocactus mesae-verdae*

Birds

Whooping crane	*Grus americana*
Least tern	*Sterna antillarum*

Fishes

Humpback chub	*Gila cypha*
Bonytail chub	*Gila elegans*
Greenback cutthroat trout	*Salmo clarki stomias*
Pawnee montane skipper	*Hesperia leonardus* (=*pawnee*) *montana*

CONNECTICUT

Plants
Sandplain gerardia   *Agalinis acuta*
Small whorled pogonia   *Isotria medeoloides*

Birds
Piping plover   *Charadrius melodus*
Roseate tern   *Sterna dougalli dougalli*

DELAWARE

Plants
Swamp pink   *Helonias bullata*

Mammals
Delmarva Peninsula fox squirrel   *Sciurus niger cinereus*

Birds
Piping plover   *Charadrius melodus*

DISTRICT OF COLUMBIA

Crustaceans
Hay's Spring amphipod   *Stygobromus hayi*

FLORIDA

Plants
Crenulate lead-plant   *Amorpha crenulata*
Four-petal pawpaw   *Asimina tetramera*
Florida bonamia   *Bonamia grandiflora*
Brooksville bellflower   *Campanula robinsiae*
Fragrant prickly-apple   *Cereus eriophorus fragrans*
Key tree-cactus   *Cereus robinii*
Pygmy fringe tree   *Chionanthus pygmaeus*
Florida golden aster   *Chrysopsis floridana*
Beautiful pawpaw   *Deeringothamnus pulchellus*
Rugel's pawpaw   *Deeringothamnus rugelii*
Garrett's mint   *Dicerandra christmanii*
Longspurred mint   *Dicerandra cornutissima*
Scrub mint   *Dicerandra frutescens*
Lakela's mint   *Dicerandra immaculata*

FLORIDA,cont.

Snakeroot	*Eryngium cuneifolium*
Deltoid spurge	*Euphorbia deltoidea* ssp. *deltoidea*
Garber's spurge	*Euphorbia garberi*
Small's milkpea	*Galactia smallii*
Harper's beauty	*Harperocallis flava*
Highlands scrub hypericum	*Hypericum cumulicola*
Cooley's water-willow	*Justicia cooleyi*
Scrub blazing star	*Liatris ohlingerae*
Scrub lupine	*Lupinus aridorum*
Papery whitlow-wort	*Paronychia chartacea*
Tiny polygala	*Polygala smallii*
Wireweed	*Polygonella basiramia*
Scrub plum	*Prunus geniculata*
Chapman rhododendron	*Rhododendron chapmanii*
Miccosukee gooseberry	*Ribes echinellum*
Cooley's meadowrue	*Thalictrum cooleyi*
Florida torreya	*Torreya taxifolia*
Wide-leaf warea	*Warea amplexifolia*
Carter's mustard	*Warea carteri*
Florida ziziphus	*Ziziphus celata*

Mammals

Florida panther	*Felis concolor coryi*
Gray bat	*Myotis grisescens*
Key Largo woodrat	*Neotoma floridana smalli*
Florida Key deer	*Odocoileus virginianus clavium*
Key Largo cotton mouse	*Peromyscus gossypinus allapaticola*
Choctawhatchee beach mouse	*Peromyscus polionotus allophrys*
Southeastern Beach Mouse	*Peromyscus polionotus niveiventris*
Anastasia Island beach mouse	*Peromyscus polionotus phasma*
Perdido Key Beach mouse	*Peromyscus polionotus trissyllepsis*
West Indian Manatee	*Trichechus manatus*

Birds

Cape Sable seaside sparrow	*Ammodramus maritimus mirabilis*
Florida grasshopper sparrow	*Ammodramus savannarum floridanus*
Florida scrub jay	*Aphelocoma coerulescens coerulenscens*
Wood stork	*Mycteria americana*
Red-cockaded woodpecker	*Picoides borealis*
Audubon's crested caracara	*Polyborus plancus audubonii*
Florida snail kite	*Rostrhamus sociabilis plumbeus*
Roseate tern	*Sterna dougalli dougalli*

FLORIDA, cont.

Reptiles

Loggerhead sea turtle	*Caretta caretta*
Green sea turtle	*Chelonia mydas*
American crocodile	*Crocodylus acutus*
Leatherback sea turtle	*Dermochelys coriacea*
Eastern indigo snake	*Drymarchon corais couperi*
Hawksbill sea turtle	*Eretmochelys imbricata*
Blue-tailed mole skink	*Eumecers egregius lividus*
Gopher tortoise	*Gopherus polyphemus*
Kemp's (Atlantic) Ridley sea turtle	*Lepidochelys kempii*
Sand skink	*Neoseps reynoldsi*
Atlantic salt marsh snake	*Nerodia fasciata taeniata*

Fishes

Okaloosa darter	*Etheostoma okaloosae*

Snails

Stock Island snail	*Orthalicus reses*

Insects

Schaus swallowtail butterfly	*Haraclides aristodemus ponceanus*

GEORGIA

Plants

Little amphianthus	*Amphianthus pusillus*
Hairy rattleweed	*Baptisia arachnifera*
Swamp pink	*Helonias bullata*
Black-sporded quillwort	*Isoetes melanospora*
Mat-forming quillwort	*Isoetes tegetiformans*
Pondberry	*Lindera melissifolia*
Mohr's Barbara button	*Marshallia mohrii*
Canby's dropwort	*Oxypolis canbyi*
Harperella	*Ptilimnium nodosum (=P. fluviatile)*
Michaux's sumac	*Rhus michauxii*
Green pitcher plant	*Sarracenia oreophila*
Large-flowered skullcap	*Scutellaria montana*
Florida torreya	*Torreya taxifolia*
Persistent trillium	*Trillium persistens*
Relict trillium	*Trillium reliquum*

Birds

Wood stork	*Mycteria americana*

GEORGIA, cont.

Red-cockaded woodpecker — *Picoides borealis*

Reptiles
Loggerhead sea turtle — *Caretta caretta*
Green sea turtle — *Chelonia mydas*
Eastern indigo snake — *Drymarchon corais couperi*
Kemp's (Atlantic) Ridley sea turtle — *Lepidochelys kempii*

Fishes
Shortnose sturgeon — *Acipenser brevirostrum*
Spotfin chub — *Hybopsis monacha*
Yellowfin madtom — *Noturus flavipinnis*
Amber darter — *Percina antesella*
Conasauga logperch — *Percina jenkinsi*
Snail darter — *Percina tanasi*

Mussels
Penitent mussel — *Epioblasma penita (=Dysnomia)*

HAWAII

Plants
Ko'oloa'ula — *Abutilon menziesii*
Achyranthes (No common name) — *Achyranthes rotundata*
Ahinahina — *Argyroxiphium sandwicense*
Cuneate bidens — *Bidens cuneata*
Ewa Plains 'akoko — *Euphorbia skottsbergii* var. *kalaeloana*
Na'u (Hawaiian gardenia) — *Gardenia brighamii*
Hillebrand's gouania — *Gouania hillebrandii*
Honohono — *Haplostachys haplostachya* var. *angustifolia*
Kauai hau kuahiwi — *Hibiscadelphus distans*
Cooke's kokio — *Kokia cookei*
Koki'o — *Kokia drynarioides*
Lipochaeta (No common name) — *Lipochaeta venosa*
Uhiuhi — *Mezoneuron kavaiense*
Carter's panicgrass — *Panicum carteri*
Lanai sandalwood or iliahi — *Santalum freycinetianum* var. *lanaiense*
Dwarf naupaka — *Scaevola coriacea*
Diamond Head schiedea — *Schiedea adamantis*
Stenogyne — *Stenogyne angustifolia* var. *angustifolia*
Hawaiian vetch — *Vicia menziesii*

HAWAII, cont.

Mammals

Hawaiian hoary bat	*Lasiurus cinereus semotus*
Hawaiian monk seal	*Monachus schauinslandi*

Birds

Nihoa millerbird (old world warbler)	*Acrocephalus familiaris kingi*
Laysan duck	*Anas laysanensis*
Hawaiian duck (koloa)	*Anas wyvilliana*
Hawaiian hawk	*Buteo solitarius*
Hawaiian crow ('alala)	*Corvus hawaiiensis (=tropicus)*
Hawaiian coot (alae keo keo)	*Fulica americana alae*
Hawaiian common moorhen	*Gallinula chloropus sandvicensis*
Kauai nukupu'u (honeycreeper)	*Hemignathus lucidus*
Kauai akioloa (honeycreeper)	*Hemignathus procerus*
Akiapolaau (honeycreeper)	*Hemignathus wilsoni*
Hawaiian stilt (ae'o)	*Himantopus mexicanus knudseni*
Palila	*Loxioides bailleui*
Maui akepa	*Loxops coccineus ochraceus*
Hawaii akepa	*Loxops coccineus ssp.*
Po'ouli (honeycreeper)	*Melamprosops phaeosoma*
Kauai 'O'o	*Moho braccatus*
Molokai thrush (oloma'o)	*Myadestes laniensis rutha*
Large Kauai thrush	*Myadestes myadestinus*
Small Kauai thrush (puaiohi)	*Myadestes palmeri*
Hawaiian goose	*Nesochen sandvicensis (=Branta)*
Hawaii creeper	*Oreomystis (=Loxops) mana*
Crested honeycreeper ('akohekohe)	*Palmeria dolei*
Molokoi creeper	*Paroreomyza flammea*
Oahu creeper	*Paroreomyza maculata*
Maui parrotbill	*Pseudonestor xanthophrys*
o'u (honeycreeper)	*Psittirostra psittacea*
Hawaiian dark-rumped petrel	*Pterodroma phaeopygia sandwichensis*
Newell's Townsend's shearwater	*Puffinus auricularis*
Laysan finch	*Telespyza cantans*
Nihoa finch	*Telespyza ultima*

Snails

Oahu tree snails	*Achatinella* sp.

IDAHO

Plants

MacFarlane's four o'clock	*Mirabilis macfarlanei*

IDAHO, cont.

Mammals
Woodland caribou   *Rangifer tarandus caribou*
Brown bear or grizzly bear   *Ursus arctos horribilis*

Birds
Whooping crane   *Grus americana*

ILLINOIS

Plants
Mead's milkweed   *Asclepias meadii*
Decurrent false aster   *Boltonia decurrens*
Lakeside daisy   *Hymenoxys acaulis* var. *glabra*
Prairie bush-clover   *Lespedeza leptostachya*
Eastern prairie fringed orchid   *Platanthera leucophaea*

Birds
Least tern   *Sterna antillarum*

Mussels
Higgin's eye pearly mussel   *Lampsilis higginsi*
Orange-footed pearly mussel   *Plethobasus cooperianus*

INDIANA

Plants
Mead's milkweed   *Asclepias meadii*
Pitcher's thistle   *Cirsium pitcheri*
Running buffalo clover   *Trifolium stoloniferum*

Mammals
Indiana bat   *Myotis sodalis*

Mussels
White cat's paw pearly mussel   *Epioblasma sulcata delicata*
Fat pocketbook pearly mussel   *Potalimus (=Proptera) capax*

IOWA

Plants
Northern wild monkshood   *Aconitum noveboracense*
Mead's milkweed   *Asclepias meadii*
Prairie bush-clover   *Lespedeza leptostachya*
Eastern prairie fringed orchid   *Platanthera leucophaea*

IOWA, cont.

Western prairie fringed orchid — *Platanthera praeclara*

Snails
Iowa Pleistocene snail — *Discus macclintocki*

Mussels
Higgin's eye pearly mussel — *Lampsilis higginsi*

KANSAS

Plants
Mead's milkweed — *Asclepias meadii*
Western prairie fringed orchid — *Platanthera praeclara*

Birds
Least tern — *Sterna antillarum*

KENTUCKY

Plants
Cumberland sandwort — *Arenaria cumberlandensis*
White-haired goldenrod — *Solidago albopilosa*
Short's goldenrod — *Solidago shortii*
Running buffalo clover — *Trifolium stoloniferum*

Mammals
Gray bat — *Myotis grisescens*
Indiana bat — *Myotis sodalis*
Virginia big-eared bat — *Plecotus townsendii virginianus*

Birds
Bachman's warbler — *Vermivora bachmanii*

Fishes
Blackside dace — *Phoxinus cumberlandensis*

Mussels
Tubercled-blossom pearly mussel — *Epioblasma torulosa torulosa*
Tan riffle shell — *Epioblasma walkeri*
Cracking pearly mussel — *Hemistena lata*
Pink mucket pearly mussel — *Lampsilis orbiculata*
Ring pink mussel — *Obovaria retusa*
Little-wing pearly mussel — *Pegias fabula*

KENTUCKY, cont.

Orange-footed pearly mussel	*Plethobasus cooperianus*
Rough pigtoe	*Pleurobema plenum*
Cumberland bean pearly mussel	*Villosa trabalis*

Crustaceans
Kentucky cave shrimp   *Palaemonias ganteri*

LOUISIANA

Birds

Brown pelican	*Pelecanus occidentalis*
Red-cockaded woodpecker	*Picoides borealis*
Bachman's warbler	*Vermivora bachmanii*

Reptiles

Gopher tortoise	*Gopherus polyphemus*
Ringed sawback turtle	*Graptemys oculifera*
Kemp's (Atlantic) Ridley sea turtle	*Lepidochelys kempii*

Mussels
Louisiana pearl shell   *Margaritifera hembeli*

MAINE

Plants

Small whorled pogonia	*Isotria medeoloides*
Furbish lousewort	*Pedicularis furbishiae*
Eastern prairie fringed orchid	*Platanthera leucophaea*

Birds

Piping plover	*Charadrius melodus*
Roseate tern	*Sterna dougalli dougalli*

Fishes
Shortnose sturgeon   *Acipenser brevirostrum*

MARYLAND

Plants

Sandplain gerardia	*Agalinis acuta*
Swamp pink	*Helonias bullata*
Small whorled pogonia	*Isotria medeoloides*
Canby's dropwort	*Oxypolis canbyi*

MARYLAND, cont.

Harperella   *Ptilimnium nodosum (=P. fluviatile)*

Mammals
Delmarva Peninsula fox squirrel   *Sciurus niger cinereus*

Birds
Piping plover   *Charadrius melodus*

Fishes
Maryland darter   *Etheostoma sellare*

MASSACHUSETTS

Plants
Sandplain gerardia   *Agalinis acuta*
Small whorled pogonia   *Isotria medeoloides*

Birds
Piping plover   *Charadrius melodus*
Roseate tern   *Sterna dougalli dougalli*

Reptiles
Plymouth red-bellied turtle   *Pseudemys rubriventris bangsii*

Insects
American burying beetle   *Nicrophorus americanus*

MICHIGAN

Plants
Pitcher's thistle   *Cirsium pitcheri*
Dwarf lake iris   *Iris lacustris*
American hart's-tongue fern   *Phyllitis scolopendrium* var. *americana*
Eastern prairie fringed orchid   *Platanthera leucophaea*
Western prairie fringed orchid   *Platanthera praeclara*
Houghton's goldenrod   *Solidago houghtonii*

Mammals
Gray wolf   *Canis lupus*

Birds
Piping plover   *Charadrius melodus*
Kirtland's warbler   *Dendroica kirtlandii*

MINNESOTA

Plants
Minnesota trout-lily	*Erythronium propullans*
Prairie bush-clover	*Lespedeza leptostachya*

Mammals
Gray wolf	*Canis lupus*

Birds
Piping plover	*Charadrius melodus*

Mussels
Higgin's eye pearly mussel	*Lampsilis higginsi*

MISSISSIPPI

Plants
Pondberry	*Lindera melissifolia*

Birds
Mississippi sandhill crane	*Grus canadensis pulla*
Red-cockaded woodpecker	*Picoides borealis*

Reptiles
Eastern indigo snake	*Drymarchon corais couperi*
Gopher tortoise	*Gopherus polyphemus*
Ringed sawback turtle	*Graptemys oculifera*

Fishes
Bayou darter	*Etheostoma rubrum*

Mussels
Penitent mussel	*Epioblasma penita (=Dysnomia)*
Curtus' mussel	*Pleurobema curtum*
Marshall's mussel	*Pleurobema marshalli*
Judge Taits's mussel	*Pleurobema taitianum*
Stirrup shell	*Quadrula stapes*

MISSOURI

Plants
Mead's milkweed	*Asclepias meadii*
Decurrent false aster	*Boltonia decurrens*
Geocarpon	*Geocarpon minimum*

MISSOURI, cont.

Missouri bladder-pod — *Lesquerella filiformis*
Pondberry — *Lindera melissifolia*
Western prairie fringed orchid — *Platanthera praeclara*

Mammals
Indiana bat — *Myotis sodalis*
Ozark big-eared bat — *Plecotus townsendii ingens*

Fishes
Ozark cavefish — *Amblyopsis rosae*
Niangua darter — *Etheostoma nianguae*

Mussels
Curtis' pearly mussel — *Epioblasma florentina curtisi*
Higgin's eye pearly mussel — *Lampsilis higginsi*
Pink mucket pearly mussel — *Lampsilis orbiculata*

MONTANA

Mammals
Gray wolf — *Canis lupus*
Brown bear or grizzly bear — *Ursus arctos horribilis*

Birds
Piping plover — *Charadrius melodus*
Least tern — *Sterna antillarum*

NEBRASKA

Plants
Blowout penstemon — *Penstemon haydenii*
Western prairie fringed orchid — *Platanthera praeclara*

Birds
Piping plover — *Charadrius melodus*
Whooping crane — *Grus americana*
Eskimo Curlew — *Numenius borealis*
Least tern — *Sterna antillarum*

NEVADA

Plants
Ash Meadows milk-vetch — *Astragalus phoenix*

NEVADA, cont.

Spring-loving centaury	*Centaurium namophilum*
Ash Meadows sunray	*Enceliopsis nudicaulis* var. *corrugata*
Steamboat buckwheat	*Eriogonum ovalifolium* var. *williamsiae*
Ash Meadows gumplant	*Grindelia fraxinopratensis*
Ash Meadows ivesia	*Ivesia eremica*
Ash Meadows blazing star	*Mentzelia leucophylla*
Amargosa niterwort	*Nitrophila mohavensis*

Reptiles
Desert tortoise	*Gopherus (=Xerobates) agassizii*

Fishes
Cui-ui	*Chasmistes cujus*
White River springfish	*Crenichthys baileyi baileyi*
Hiko White River springfish	*Crenichthys baileyi grandis*
Railroad Valley springfish	*Crenichthys nevadae*
Devil's Hole pupfish	*Cyprinodon diabolis*
Ash Meadows Amgrosa pupfish	*Cyprinodon nevadensis mionectes*
Warm Springs pupfish	*Cyprinodon nevadensis pectoralis*
Pahrump killifish	*Emptrichthys latos*
Desert dace	*Eremichthys acros*
Bonytail chub	*Gila elegans*
Pahranagat roundtail chub	*Gila robusta jordani*
Virgin River chub	*Gila robusta seminuda*
White River spinedace	*Lepidomeda albivallis*
Big Spring spinedace	*Lepidomeda mollispinis pratensis*
Moapa dace	*Moapa coriacea*
Woundfin	*Plagopterus argentissimus*
Colorado squawfish	*Ptychocheilus lucius*
Independence Valley speckled dace	*Rhinchthys osculus lethoporus*
Ash Meadows speckled dace	*Rhinichthys osculus nevadensis*
Clover Valley speckled dace	*Rhinichthys osculus oligoporus*
Lahontan cutthroat trout	*Salmo clarki henshawi*

Insects
Ash Meadows naucorid	*Ambrysus amargosus*

NEW HAMPSHIRE

Plants
Jessup's milk-vetch	*Astragalus robbinsii* var. *jesupi*
Small whorled pogonia	*Isotria medeoloides*
Robbins' cinquefoil	*Potentilla robbinsiana*

NEW HAMPSHIRE, cont.

Birds
Piping plover	*Charadrius melodus*
Roseate tern	*Sterna dougalli dougalli*

NEW JERSEY

Plants
Swamp pink	*Helonias bullata*
Small whorled pogonia	*Isotria medeoloides*

Birds
Piping plover	*Charadrius melodus*

Fishes
Shortnose sturgeon	*Acipenser brevirostrum*

NEW MEXICO

Plants
Sacramento prickly poppy	*Argemone plelacantha* ssp. *pinnatisecta*
Mancos milk-vetch	*Astragalus humillimus*
Sacramento mountains thistle	*Cirsium vinaceum*
Lee pincushion cactus	*Coryphantha sneedii* var. *leei*
Sneed pincushion cactus	*Coryphantha sneedii* var. *sneedii*
Kuenzler hedgehog cactus	*Echinocerus fendleri* var. *kuenzleri*
Rhizome fleabane	*Erigeron rhizomatus*
Gypsum wild-buckwheat	*Eriogonum gypsophilum*
McKittrick pennyroyal	*Hedeoma apiculatum*
Todsen's pennyroyal	*Hedeoma todsenii*
Knowlton cactus	*Pediocactus knowltonii*
Mesa Verde cactus	*Sclerocactus mesae-verdae*

Mammals
Sanborn's long-nosed bat	*Leptonycteris sanborni* (=*yerbabuenae*)
Mexican long-nosed bat	*Leptonycteris nivalis*

Birds
Northern aplomado falcon	*Falco femoralis septentrionalis*
Whooping crane	*Grus americana*
Least tern	*Sterna antillarum*

Reptiles
New Mexican ridge-nosed rattlesnake	*Crotalus willardi obscurus*

NEW MEXICO, cont.

Fishes

Pecos gambusia	*Gambusia nobilis*
Chihauhau chub	*Gila nigrescens*
Beautiful shiner	*Notropis formosus*
Pecos bluntnose shiner	*Notropis simus pecosensis*
Gila topminnow	*Poeciliopsis occidentalis*
Colorado squawfish	*Ptychocheilus lucius*
Gila trout	*Salmo gilae*
Loach minnow	*Tiaroga cobitis*

Crustaceans

Socorro isopod	*Thermoshpaeroma (=Exosphaeroma)* *–thermophilus*

NEW YORK

Plants

Northern wild monkshood	*Aconitum noveboracense*
Sandplain gerardia	*Agalinis acuta*
Swamp pink	*Helonias bullata*
Small whorled pogonia	*Isotria medeoloides*
American hart's-tongue fern	*Phyllitis scolopendrium* var. *americana*

Birds

Piping plover	*Charadrius melodus*
Roseate tern	*Sterna dougalli dougalli*

Fishes

Shortnose sturgeon	*Acipenser brevirostrum*

Snails

Chittenango ovate amber snail	*Succinea chittenangoensis*

NORTH CAROLINA

Plants

Small anthered bittercress	*Cardomine micranthera*
Swamp pink	*Helonias bullata*
Dwarf-flowered heartleaf	*Hexastylis naniflora*
Mountain golden heather	*Hudsonia montana*
Heller's balzing star	*Liatris helleri*
Pondberry	*Lindera melissifolia*
Rough-leaved loosestrife	*Lysimachia asperulaefolia*

NORTH CAROLINA, cont.

Canby's dropwort	*Oxypolis canbyi*
Harperella	*Ptilimnium nodosum (=P. fluviatile)*
Michaux's sumac	*Rhus michauxii*
Bunched arrowhead	*Sagittaria fasciculata*
Mountain sweet pitcher plant	*Sarracenia rubra* ssp. *jonesii*
Blue Ridge goldenrod	*Solidago spithamaea*
Cooley's meadowrue	*Thalictrum cooleyi*

Mammals
Red wolf	*Canis rufus*
Eastern cougar	*Felis concolor cougar*
Carolina northern flying squirrel	*Glaucomys sabrinus coloratus*
Virginia big-eared bat	*Plecotus townsendii virginianus*
Dismal Swamp southeastern shrew	*Sorex longirostris fisheri*
West Indian Manatee	*Trichechus manatus*

Birds
Piping plover	*Charadrius melodus*
Red-cockaded woodpecker	*Picoides borealis*

Reptiles
Loggerhead sea turtle	*Caretta caretta*
Green sea turtle	*Chelonia mydas*

Fishes
Shortnose sturgeon	*Acipenser brevirostrum*
Spotfin chub	*Hybopsis monacha*
Waccamaw silverside	*Menidia extensa*
Cape Fear shiner	*Notropis mekistocholas*

Snails
Noonday snail	*Mesodon clarki nantahla*

Mussels
Tar River spinymussel	*Elliptio steinstansana*

NORTH DAKOTA

Plants
Western prairie fringed orchid	*Platanthera praeclara*

Birds
Piping plover	*Charadrius melodus*
Least tern	*Sterna antillarum*

OHIO

Plants

Northern wild monkshood	*Aconitum noveboracense*
Lakeside daisy	*Hymenoxys acaulis* var. *glabra*
Eastern prairie fringed orchid	*Platanthera leucophaea*
Running buffalo clover	*Trifolium stoloniferum*

Fishes

Scioto madtom	*Noturus trautmani*

Mussels

White cat's paw pearly mussel	*Epioblasma sulcata delicata*
Pink mucket pearly mussel	*Lampsilis orbiculata*

OKLAHOMA

Plants

Western prairie fringed orchid	*Platanthera praeclara*

Mammals

Ozark big-eared bat	*Plecotus townsendii ingens*

Birds

Least tern	*Sterna antillarum*
Black-capped vireo	*Vireo atricapillus*

Fishes

Ozark cavefish	*Amblyopsis rosae*
Leopard darter	*Percina pantherina*

Insects

American burying beetle	*Nicrophorus americanus*

OREGON

Plants

Bradshaw's lomatium	*Lomatium bradshawii*
MacFarlane's four o'clock	*Mirabilis macfarlanei*
Malheur wire-lettuce	*Stephanomeria malheurensis*

Mammals

Columbian white-tailed deer	*Odocoileus virginianus leucurus*

OREGON, cont.

Birds
Aleutian Canada goose

Branta canadensis leucopareia

Fishes
Warner sucker
Shortnose sucker
Lost River sucker
Hutton tui chub
Borax Lake chub
Foskett speckled dace

Catostomus warnerensis
Chasmistes brevirostris
Deltistes luxatus
Gila bicolor ssp.
Gila boraxobius
Rhinichthys osculus ssp.

Insects
Oregon silverspot butterfly

Speyeria zerene hippolyta

PENNSYLVANIA

Plants
Small whorled pogonia

Isotria medeoloides

Mammals
Delmarva Peninsula fox squirrel

Sciurus niger cinereus

RHODE ISLAND

Plants
Sandplain gerardia
Small whorled pogonia

Agalinis acuta
Isotria medeoloides

Birds
Piping plover

Charadrius melodus

SOUTH CAROLINA

Plants
Little amphianthus
Swamp pink
Dwarf-flowered heartleaf
Black-spored quillwort
Pondberry
Canby's dropwort
Harperella
Miccosukee gooseberry

Amphianthus pusillus
Helonias bullata
Hexastylis naniflora
Isoetes melanospora
Lindera melissifolia
Oxypolis canbyi
Ptilimnium nodosum (=*P. fluviatile*)
Ribes echinellum

SOUTH CAROLINA, cont.

Bunched arrowhead	*Sagittaria fasciculata*
Mountain sweet pitcher plant	*Sarracenia rubra* ssp. *jonesii*
Persistent trillium	*Trillium persistens*
Relict trillium	*Trillium reliquum*

Mammals
West Indian Manatee	*Trichechus manatus*

Birds
Wood stork	*Mycteria americana*
Red-cockaded woodpecker	*Picoides borealis*
Bachman's warbler	*Vermivora bachmanii*

Reptiles
Loggerhead sea turtle	*Caretta caretta*
Eastern indigo snake	*Drymarchon corais couperi*

Fishes
Shortnose sturgeon	*Acipenser brevirostrum*

SOUTH DAKOTA

Birds
Piping plover	*Charadrius melodus*
Least tern	*Sterna antillarum*

TENNESSEE

Plants
Cumberland sandwort	*Arenaria cumberlandensis*
Tennessee purple coneflower	*Echinacea tennesseensis*
American hart's-tongue fern	*Phyllitis scolopendrium* var. *americana*
Ruth's golden aster	*Pityopsis ruthii* (=Chrysopsis)
Large-flowered skullcap	*Scutellaria montana*
Blue Ridge goldenrod	*Solidago spithamaea*

Mammals
Carolina northern flying squirrel	*Glaucomys sabrinus coloratus*
Gray bat	*Myotis grisescens*

Fishes
Slackwater darter	*Etheostoma boschungi*
Boulder darter	*Etheostoma* sp.

TENNESSEE, cont.

Slender chub	*Hybopsis cahni*
Spotfin chub	*Hybopsis monacha*
Smoky madtom	*Noturus baileyi*
Yellowfin madtom	*Noturus flavipinnis*
Amber darter	*Percina antesella*
Conasauga logperch	*Percina jenkinsi*
Snail darter	*Percina tanasi*
Blackside dace	*Phoxinus cumberlandensis*

Snails
Painted snake coiled forest snail	*Anguispira picta*

Mussels
Birdwing pearly mussel	*Conradilla caelata*
Dromedary pearly mussel	*Dromus dromas*
Yellow-blossom pearly mussel	*Epioblasma florentina florentina*
Green-blossom pearly mussel	*Epioblasma torulosa gubernaculum*
Tubercled-blossom pearly mussel	*Epioblasma torulosa torulosa*
Turgid-blossom pearly mussel	*Epioblasma turgidula (=Dysnomia)*
Tan riffle shell	*Epioblasma walkeri*
Fine-rayed pigtoe	*Fusconaia cuneolus*
Shiny pigtoe	*Fusconaia edgariana*
Cracking pearly mussel	*Hemistena lata*
Pink mucket pearly mussel	*Lampsilis orbiculata*
Alabama lamp pearly mussel	*Lampsilis virescens*
Ring pink mussel	*Obovaria retusa*
Little-wing pearly mussel	*Pegias fabula*
White wartyback pearly mussel	*Plethobasus cicatricosus*
Orange-footed pearly mussel	*Plethobasus cooperianus*
Rough pigtoe	*Pleurobema plenum*
Cumberland monkeyface pearly mussel	*Quadrula intermedia*
Appalachian monkey face pearly mussel	*Quadrula sparsa*
Pale lilliput pearly mussel	*Toxolasma cylindellus (=Carunculina)*
Cumberland bean pearly mussel	*Villosa trabalis*

Crustaceans
Nashville crayfish	*Orconectes shoupi*

TEXAS

Plants
Large-fruited sand-verbena	*Abronia macrocarpa*
Tobusch fishhook cactus	*Ancistrocactus tobuschii*

TEXAS, cont.

Texas poppy-mallow	*Callirhoe scabriuscula*
Nellie cory cactus	*Coryphantha minima*
Bunched cory cactus	*Coryphantha ramillosa*
Sneed pincushion cactus	*Coryphantha sneedii* var. *sneedii*
Chisos Mtn. hedgehog cactus	*Echinocereus chisoensis* var. *chisoensis*
Lloyd's hedghog cactus	*Echinocereus lloydii*
Black lace cactus	*Echinocereus reichenbachii* var. *albertii*
Davis' green pitaya	*Echinocereus viridiflorus davisii*
Johnston's frankenia	*Frankenia johnstonii*
McKittrick pennyroyal	*Hedeoma apiculatum*
Slender rush-pea	*Hoffmannseggia tenella*
Texas bitterweed	*Hymenoxys texana*
White bladderpod	*Lesquerella pallida*
Lloyd's Mariposa cactus	*Neolloydia mariposensis*
Hinckley oak	*Quercus hinckleyi*
Navasota ladies'-tresses	*Spiranthes parksii*
Texas snowbells	*Styrax texana*
Ashy dogweed	*Thymophylla tephroleuca*
Texas wildrice	*Zizania texana*

Mammals

Ocelot	*Felis pardalis*
Jaguarundi	*Felis yagouraroundi cacomitli*
Mexican long-nosed bat	*Leptonycteris nivalis*

Birds

Northern aplomado falcon	*Falco femoralis septentrionalis*
Whooping crane	*Grus americana*
Eskimo Curlew	*Numenius borealis*
Brown pelican	*Pelecanus occidentalis*
Red-cockaded woodpecker	*Picoides borealis*
Least tern	*Sterna antillarum*
Attwater's greater prairie chicken	*Tympanuchus cupido attwateri*
Black-capped vireo	*Vireo atricapillus*

Reptiles

Green sea turtle	*Chelonia mydas*
Kemp's (Atlantic) Ridley sea turtle	*Lepidochelys kempii*
Concho water snake	*Nerodia harteri paucimaculata*

Amphibians

Houston toad	*Bufo houstonensis*
San Marcos salamander	*Eurycea nana*
Texas blind salamander	*Typhlomolge rathbuni*

TEXAS, cont.

Fishes
Leon Springs pupfish	*Cyprinodon bovinus*
Comanche Springs pupfish	*Cyprinodon elegans*
Fountain darter	*Etheostoma fonticola*
Big Bend gambusia	*Gambusia gaigei*
San Marcos gambusia	*Gambusia georgei*
Clear Creek gambusia	*Gambusia heterochir*
Pecos gambusia	*Gambusia nobilis*

Insects
Tooth Cave spider	*Leptonida myopica*
Tooth Cave pseudoscorpion	*Microcreagris texana*
Tooth Cave ground beetle	*Rhadine persephone*
Kretschmarr Cave mold beetle	*Texamaurops reddelli*
Bee Creek Cave harvestman	*Texella reddelli*

UTAH

Plants
Dwarf bear-poppy	*Arctomecon humilis*
Welsh's milkweed	*Asclepias welshii*
Heliotrope milk-vetch	*Astragalus limnocharis* var. *montii*
Rydbergh milk-vetch	*Astragalus perianus*
Jones cycladenia	*Cycladenia humilis* var. *jonesii*
Spineless hedgehog cactus	*Echinocereus triglochidiatus* var. *inermis*
Purple-spined hedghog cactus	*Echinocerus engelmannii* var. *purpureus*
Maguire daisy	*Erigeron maguirei* var. *maguirei*
Toad-flax cress	*Glaucocarpum suffrutescens*
San Rafael cactus	*Pediocactus despainii*
Siler pincushion cactus	*Pediocactus sileri*
Clay phacelia	*Phacelia argillacea*
Maguire primrose	*Primula maguirei*
Autumn buttercup	*Ranunculus acriformis* var. *aestivalis*
Uinta Basin hookless cactus	*Sclerocactus glaucus*
Wright fishhook cactus	*Sclerocactus wrightiae*
Last Chance townsendia	*Townsendia aprica*

Mammals
Utah prairie dog	*Cynomys parvidens*

Birds
Whooping crane	*Grus americana*

UTAH cont.

Reptiles
Desert tortoise   *Gopherus (=Xerobates) agassizii*

Fishes
June sucker   *Chasmistes liorus*
Humpback chub   *Gila cypha*
Bonytail chub   *Gila elegans*
Virgin River chub   *Gila robusta seminuda*
Woundfin   *Plagopterus argentissimus*

VERMONT

Plants
Jessup's milk-vetch   *Astragalus robbinsii* var. *jesupi*
Small whorled pogonia   *Isotria medeoloides*

VIRGINIA

Plants
Shale barren rock cress   *Arabis serotina*
Virginia round-leaf birch   *Betula uber*
Swamp pink   *Helonias bullata*
Peter's Mountain mallow   *Iliamna corei*
Small whorled pogonia   *Isotria medeoloides*
Eastern prairie fringed orchid   *Platanthera leucophaea*

Mammals
Eastern cougar   *Felis concolor cougar*
Virginia northern flying squirrel   *Glaucomys sabrinus fuscus*
Virginia big-eared bat   *Plecotus townsendii virginianus*
Delmarva Peninsula fox squirrel   *Sciurus niger cinereus*
Dismal Swamp southeastern shrew   *Sorex longirostris fisheri*

Birds
Piping plover   *Charadrius melodus*

Amphibians
Shenandoah salamander   *Plethodon shenandoah*

Fishes
Slender chub   *Hybopsis cahni*
Spotfin chub   *Hybopsis monacha*
Yellowfin madtom   *Noturus flavipinnis*

VIRGINIA, cont.

Roanoke logperch — *Percina rex*

Snails
Virginia fringed mountain snail — *Polygyriscus virginianus*

Mussels
Birdwing pearly mussel — *Conradilla caelata*
Dromedary pearly mussel — *Dromus dromas*
Green-blossom pearly mussel — *Epioblasma torulosa gubernaculum*
Tan riffle shell — *Epioblasma walkeri*
Fine-rayed pigtoe — *Fusconaia cuneolus*
Shiny pigtoe — *Fusconaia edgariana*
Cracking pearly mussel — *Hemistena lata*
Little-wing pearly mussel — *Pegias fabula*
James (=James River) spinymusel — *Pleurobema (=Canthyria) collina*
Cumberland monkeyface pearly mussel — *Quadrula intermedia*
Appalachian monkey face pearly mussel — *Quadrula sparsa*

Crustaceans
Madison cave isopod — *Antrolana lira*

WASHINGTON

Mammals
Columbian white-tailed deer — *Odocoileus virginianus leucurus*
Woodland caribou — *Rangifer tarandus caribou*
Brown bear or grizzly bear — *Ursus arctos horribilis*

Birds
Aleutian Canada goose — *Branta canadensis leucopareia*

WEST VIRGINIA

Plants
Shale barren rock cress — *Arabis serotina*
Harperella — *Ptilimnium nodosum (=P. fluviatile)*
Running buffalo clover — *Trifolium stoloniferum*

Mammals
Eastern cougar — *Felis concolor cougar*
Virginia northern flying squirrel — *Glaucomys sabrinus fuscus*
Virginia big-eared bat — *Plecotus townsendii virginianus*

WEST VIRGINIA, cont.

Amphibians
Cheat Mountain salamander   *Plethodon nettingi*

Snails
Flat-spired three-toothed snail   *Triodopsis platysayoides*

Mussels
Tubercled-blossom pearly mussel   *Epioblasma torulosa torulosa*
Pink mucket pearly mussel   *Lampsilis orbiculata*
James (=James River) spinymusel   *Pleurobema (=Canthyria) collina*

WISCONSIN

Plants
Northern wild monkshood   *Aconitum noveboracense*
Mead's milkweed   *Asclepias meadii*
Pitcher's thistle   *Cirsium pitcheri*
Dwarf lake iris   *Iris lacustris*
Prairie bush-clover   *Lespedeza leptostachya*
Fassett's locoweed   *Oxytropis campestris* var. *chartacea*
Eastern prairie fringed orchid   *Platanthera leucophaea*

Mammals
Gray wolf   *Canis lupus*

Mussels
Higgin's eye pearly mussel   *Lampsilis higginsi*

WYOMING

Mammals
Black-footed ferret   *Mustela nigripes*
Brown bear or grizzly bear   *Ursus arctos horribilis*

Amphibians
Wyoming toad   *Bufo hemiophrys baxteri*

Fishes
Humpback chub   *Gila cypha*
Bonytail chub   *Gila elegans*
Colorado squawfish   *Ptychocheilus lucius*
Kendall Warm Springs dace   *Rhinichtys osculus thermalis*

PUERTO RICO

Plants

Palo de Ramon	*Banara vanderbiltii*
Vahl's boxwood	*Buxus vahlii*
Palo de Nigua	*Cornutia obovata*
Higuero de Sierra	*Crecentia portoricensis*
Elfin tree-fern	*Cyathea dryopteroides*
Daphnopsis (No common name)	*Daphnopsis hellerana*
Beautiful goetzea or matabuey	*Goetzea elegans*
Cook's holly	*Ilex cookii*
Wheeler's peperomia	*Peperomia wheeleri*
Erubia	*Solanum drymophilum*
Bariaco	*Trichilia triacantha*
St. Thomas prickly-ash	*Zanthoxylum thomassianum*

Mammals

West Indian Manatee	*Trichechus manatus*

Birds

Yellow-shouldered blackbird	*Agelaius xanthomus*
Puerto Rican parrot	*Amazona vittata*
Puerto Rico nightjar	*Caprimulgus noctitherus*
Puerto Rican plain pigeon	*Columba inornata wetmorei*
Roseate tern	*Sterna dougalli dougalli*

Reptiles

Culebra Island giant anole	*Anolis roosevelti*
Mona ground iguana	*Cyclura stegjnegeri*
Puerto Rican boa	*Epicrates inornatus*
Mona boa	*Epicrates monensis monensis*
Hawksbill sea turtle	*Eretmochelys imbricata*
Monito gecko	*Sphaerodactylus micropithecus*

Amphibians

Golden coqui	*Eleutherodactylus jasperi*
Puerto Rican toad	*Peltophryne lemur*

CANADA

Plants

Pitcher's thistle	*Cirsium pitcheri*
Lakeside daisy	*Hymenoxys acaulis* var. *glabra*
Dwarf lake iris	*Iris lacustris*
Small whorled pogonia	*Isotria medeoloides*

CANADA, cont.

American hart's-tongue fern	*Phyllitis scolopendrium* var. *americana*
Eastern prairie fringed orchid	*Platanthera leucophaea*
Western prairie fringed orchid	*Platanthera praeclara*
Houghton's goldenrod	*Solidago houghtonii*

Mammals

Wood bison	*Bison bison athabascae*
Vancouver Island marmot	*Marmota vancouverensis*
Woodland caribou	*Rangifer tarandus caribou*
Northern swift fox	*Vulpes velox hebes*

Birds

Piping plover	*Charadrius melodus*

Fishes

Shortnose sturgeon	*Acipenser brevirostrum*

Glossary

Aquatic: living in water.

Adaptation: the features of an animal that enable it to survive in its environment.

Adult: sexually mature individual.

Aerial: activities in birds and insects that occur in flight.

Algae: microscopic, single-celled plants.

Alternate: leaves that do not grow opposite one another on the stem.

Amphibian: animal capable of living in both water and land habitats.

Animal: a generically used term to designate all species other than plants.

Antennae: head appendages in invertebrates.

Anterior: to the front.

Arachnid: a class of species that includes spiders, scorpions, mites and ticks.

Arthropod: an invertebrate with an exo-skeleton and paired jointed limbs.

Association: group of species that are dependent on one another.

Axil: the angle between the stem and leaf of a plant.

Baleen: plates located in the upper jaws of whales that filter plankton from sea water.

Barbel: a sensory organ on the head of some aquatic animals.

Bask: behavior in animals of absorbing sunlight for extended periods.

Bill/Beak: the appendage birds use to gather food.

Bivalve: in mollusks, the protective shell composed of two hinged halves.

Blowhole: the breathing hole located on the head of a whale.

Blubber: a thick layer of fat beneath the skin of a whale.

Bracts: leaves that bracket the flower of a plant.

Breaching: leaping of a whale from the water.

Brood: offspring raised together.

Brood parasitism: when a bird of one species lays eggs in the nest of a different species to the detriment of the host bird's own young.

Brood pouch: gill structure in freshwater mussels that is modified to store developing glochidia.

Browsing: feeding by plant-eating animals.

Calcareous: composed of calcium carbonate.

Cannibalistic: the practice among some animals of eating the flesh of their own species.

Carapace: a hard structure covering all or part of the body, such as a turtle's shell.

Caudal fin: the tail fin of a fish.

Caudal peduncle: a narrowing of the body in front of the caudal fin.

Climax: fully developed stage in an ecosystem.

Cloud forest: high-altitude forest with a dense undergrowth of dwarf trees, ferns, mosses, and other plants that grow on the trunks of the trees.

Clutch: the number of eggs laid in one breeding.

Cocoon: the tough protective covering wherein insect larvae pupate.

Colonize: to establish a population in a new territory.

Colony: a group of the same kind of plants or organisms living and growing together.

Community: a group of plant species that grow in stable association.

Competition: the interaction between different species vying for the same ecological niche.

Compound leaf: composed of separate, smaller leaflets.

Coniferous forest: comprised primarily of evergreens, usually located in cool, dry climates.

Copulation: the process by which sperm is transferred from the male to the female.

Corolla: the inner portion of a flower.

Courtship: behavior in animals prior to mating.

Covey: group of birds, usually applied to gamebirds such as quail.

Crest: a tuft or ridge on the head of a bird or other animal.

Crustaceans: invertebrates that include shrimps, crabs and other small marine species.

Cycle: a series of events that occurs repeatedly in the same sequence.

DDT: a pesticide that causes eggshell thinning in birds.

Decapod: ten-legged arthropods.

Deforestation: the process of clearing forests.

Depressed: the body form of a reptile that is flattened laterally.

Desert: habitat with low rainfall and sparse vegetation.

Desiccation: the process of drying out.

Detritus: decomposing organisms that serve as a food supply to many species.

Disk: the round center of a ray flower, such as a daisy, around which petals are arranged.

Dispersal: migration of individuals from their home range.

Display: a pattern of behavior that serves as communication between species, such as mating rituals.

Diversity: the number of differing species in a habitat.

Dorsal: situated at the rear of an animal, such as the dorsal fin in a fish.

Ecology: the study of the relationship of plants and animals to each other and to their habitats.

Ecosystem: a community of organisms that interact with each other and their environment.

Embryo: an organism in the early stages of development; unhatched.

Endemic: species that are native to a specific region.

Entire: leaves without lobes or teeth.

Entomology: the study of insects.

Environment: all the conditions that affect the growth and sustenance of organisms.

Environmental stress: caused by the dwindling of resources necessary to sustain an organism's survival.

Estrus: the period in which female animals are receptive to mating.

Exotic: a plant or organism that is not endemic to a region; non-native, introduced.

Extinct: a species that has no surviving individuals.

Extirpate: to eliminate a population.

Family: the category below Order and above Genus.

Fauna: animal life.

Fertilization: the union of a sperm and egg that stimulates growth of the embryo.

Filter feeding: in marine life, the process of filtering food from water through a siphoning organ.

Fin: that portion of a fish's body that propels it or assists in swimming.

Fish ladder: a device constructed by people that assists spawning fish to pass an obstruction, usually a dam.

Fledgling: stage of development in birds when flight feathers are developed.

Flora: plant life.

Food chain: interdependence of feeding organisms in a plant and wildlife community.

Fossil: an impression or cast of a plant or animal preserved in rock.

Fostering: when young of one species are raised by parents of a related species.

Frog: a smooth-skinned amphibian, usually aquatic or semi-aquatic.

Frontal shield: area covering the forehead of birds.

Genetic: pertaining to characteristics that are passed by chromosomes from one generation to the next.

Genus: used with species to denote a basic taxonomic identity to a plant or animal.

Gestation period: amount of time developing young are carried within the body of the mother.

Gill slits: the openings in the gill that permit water to enter.

Gills: the principal respiratory organ of a fish.

Glochidia: mussel larvae.

Habitat: the locality and conditions which support the life of an organism.

Hacking: to release a captive-bred bird into the wild.

Hatchling: a young animal that has just emerged from its shell.

Helper: a bird without young of her own that assists in the nurturing of other young.

Herbicide: a chemical used to kill plants.

Herbivore: species that feed mainly on plants.

Hexapod: six-legged arthropods.

Home range: an area defined by the habitual movements of an animal.

Host fish: a fish on which mussel larvae reside until they are capable of surviving on their own.

Hybrid: an offspring produced by parents that are not genetically identical.

Immature: juvenile; in insects, the larval stage of development.

Incubation: keeping eggs warm until they hatch.

Individual: a single member of a population.

Inflorescence: flower cluster.

Insectivore: an organism that feeds primarily on insects.

Instar: the stage between molts in insects.

Introduced: a plant or animal that has been brought in from outside a region; exotic, non-native.

Invasion: the migration of a species into a new area, usually to the detriment of organisms already living there.

Invertebrate: animals lacking a backbone.

Isolated: a portion of a breeding population that is cut off from the rest of the population.

Keel: a prominent ridge on the back of an animal.

Krill: small marine creatures that serve as an important food supply to fish, whales, and birds.

Larva: a pre-adult form of a species that does not resemble the adult.

Lateral: pertaining to the side of an animal.

Life cycle: the sequence of events in the progression of an organism from birth to death.

Linear leaf: long, narrow leaf, characterized by parallel veins.

Live-bearing: giving birth to fully-developed young; ovoviviparous.

Lobed leaf: characterized by rounded projections.

Localized: found within a limited geographic area.

Mammal: vertebrates that possess hair and nourish their young on the mother's milk.

Mandible: the skeleton of the lower jaw; one of the two jaws of a bird that comprise the bill.

Mangrove: a tropical tree with exposed roots forming an interlocking mass.

Metabolism: chemical process within an organism to release energy.

Metamorphosis: development from one stage of maturity to the next, usually with marked change in appearance.

Microclimate: the conditions immediately surrounding an organism, often differing significantly from the environment as a whole.

Migration: the seasonal movement of animals from one territory to another.

Mollusk: animals that have a muscular foot and a dorsal shell, such as snails and mussels.

Molt: to shed the outer covering.

Monotypic: the only member of its genus.

Montane forest: forest located at the middle altitude of a mountain.

Native: endemic.

Nectar: secretion from plants that attracts pollinators.

Niche: the adaptive position of a species within the ecosystem.

Nocturnal: active at night.

Non-native: not endemic to an area.

Nutrient: food substance that promotes growth.

Omnivore: a species that eats a large variety of foods.

Opportunistic: a species that adapts its feeding habits to the most available food source.

Order: taxonomic category below Class and above Family.

Overgrazing: occurs when animals feed too long in one area, causing destruction of vegetation.

Ovoviviparous: eggs are hatched within the mother and young are born alive.

Pair bond: a long-term relationship between a male and a female.

Palmate leaf: divided so as to radiate from one point like a hand.

Parasite: an organism that extracts nutrients from another host organism.

Pelagic: ocean-dwelling.

Petal: a segment of the corolla of a flower.

Phylum: taxonomic category above Class.

Phytoplankton: aquatic, microscopic plants.

Pinnate leaf: compound leaf with leaflets arranged in pairs along a stem.

Plastron: the ventral portion of a turtle's shell.

Pollination: the process by which pollen is transported to the female parts of a flower.

Pollution: the disruption of an ecosystem by contaminants.

Population: a group of individuals within a defined area that is capable of interbreeding.

Posterior: the rear or tail of an animal.

Predator: an animal that hunts other animals for food.

Prey: animals that are hunted by predators.

Pronotum: plates covering the first segment of the thorax in insects.

Pupa/pupal stage: the non-feeding period when larval tissues are reformed into adult structure inside a cocoon.

Radio tracking: using an affixed transmitter to follow the movements of an animal.

Range: geographical area wherein a species resides.

Raptor: a bird of prey.

Rays: the flat blades that encircle a flower disk.

Relict: a localized species or population that has survived from an earlier epoch.

Salamander: type of amphibian characterized by a tail.

Savanna: dry, scrub-dominated grassland with areas of bare earth.

Scavenger: an animal that feeds on dead animals it did not kill.

Scrape: a shallow depression that serves as a nest.

Scrub: a plant community characterized by scattered, low-growing trees and shrubs, interspersed with herbs, grasses, and patches of bare soil.

Solitary: individual that lives alone.

Spawning: laying and fertilizing of fish eggs, often involving migration to stream headwaters.

Specialization: evolution of a species so that it occupies a narrow place or niche in the community.

Glossary

Species: a group of organisms with distinct characteristics that is capable of interbreeding and producing like offspring; the basic taxonomic category.

Spike: a long flower cluster arranged along a stem.

Spiracle: a secondary gill slit positioned in front of the primary gill slits.

Subspecies: a subgroup that is physically distinguishable from the rest of the species.

Substrate: composition of stream bed.

Subtropical: regions bordering on the tropics.

Succession: progressive changes in the composition of a plant community.

Tadpole: the larva of a frog or toad.

Taxonomy: the science of classifying organisms.

Terrapin: a type of freshwater turtle.

Terrestrial: living on land.

Territory: an area that an animal will defend against intruders.

Toad: a warty-skinned, land frog.

Tolerance limit: physical extremities beyond which a species cannot survive.

Torpor: a state of inactivity.

Tortoise: a land turtle.

Troglobitic: cave-dwelling.

Tubercle: in mussels a small raised area that limits water loss and prevents entry by microorganisms.

Tundra: an area found at higher latitudes that is too cold for trees to grow.

Turtle: any shelled reptile.

Umbel: an umbrella-like flower cluster.

Variety: a closer taxonomic relationship than subspecies.

Vent: the anal opening of the body.

Ventral: located at the lower side of a fish or bird.

Vertebrate: an animal with a backbone.

Viviparous: a species that produces live offspring from the mother.

Wetlands: marshes.

Whorl: three or more leaves radiating from a single point.

Volume 2 Index

A

A'a, 645
Accipitriidae (Eagles and Hawks), 584, 624, 694
Achatinella apexfulva, 1041
Achatinella bellula, 1041
Achatinella buddii, 1041
Achatinella bulimoides, 1041
Achatinella byronii, 1041
Achatinella concavospira, 1041
Achatinella curta, 1041
Achatinella decipiens, 1041
Achatinella fulgens, 1041
Achatinella fuscobasis, 1041
Achatinella juncea, 1041
Achatinella lehuiensis, 1041
Achatinella leucorraphe, 1041
Achatinella lila, 1041
Achatinella lorata, 1041
Achatinella mustelina, 1041
Achatinella papyracea, 1041
Achatinella pulcherrima, 1041
Achatinella pupukanioe, 1041
Achatinella sowerbyana, 1041
Achatinella spaldingi, 1041
Achatinella swiftii, 1041
Achatinella taeniolata, 1041
Achatinella thaanumi, 1041
Achatinella turgida, 1041
Achatinellidae (Hawaiian Tree Snails), 1041
Acipenser brevirostrum, 801
Acipenser oxyrhynchus, 801
Acipenseridae (Sturgeon), 801
Aconitum noveboracense, 1047
Acrocephalus familiaris familiaria, 561
Acrocephalus familiaris kingi, 561
Ae'o, 634
Agelaius phoenicus, 563
Agelaius xanthomus, 563
Agelaius xanthomus monensis, 563
Agelaius xanthomus xanthomus, 563
Akepa
    Hawaii, 640
    Maui, 640
Akialoa
    Kauai, 632
Akiapolaau, 630
Akohekohe, 662
Alabama Cave Shrimp, 1031
Alabama Cavefish, 950

Alabama Lamp Pearly Mussel, 989
Alabama Red-Bellied Turtle, 768
Alae Ke'o Ke'o, 610
Alae'ula, 613
Alala, 599
Aleutian Canada Goose, 581
Alligator
    American, 727
Amargosa Niterwort, 933
Amargosa Pupfish
    Ash Meadows, 827, 933
Amazona agilis, 565
Amazona ventralis, 565
Amazona vittata, 565
Amber Darter, 915, 917
Amber Snail
    Chittenango ovate, 1056
Amblema torulosa, 972
Amblyopsidae (Cavefish), 803, 950
Amblyopsis rosae, 803
Amblyopsis spelea, 803
Ambrysus amargosus, 933, 1061
Ambystoma macrodactylum croceum, 783
Ambystomidae (Salamander), 783
American Burying Beetle, 1093
American Crocodile, 727
American Peregrine Falcon, 607
American Toad
    dwarf, 789
Ammodramus maritimus mirabilis, 568
Ammodramus savannarum floridanus, 570
Ammospiza maritimus mirabilis, 568
Amphipod
    Hay's Spring, 1035
Amphispiza belli clementeae, 572
Anas laysanensis, 574
Anas oustaleti, 576
Anas wyvilliana, 576
Anatidae (Ducks and Geese), 574, 576, 656, 581
Anguispira cumberlandiana, 1044
Anguispira picta, 1044
Anole
    Culebra Island giant, 719
Anolis roosevelti, 719
Antrolana lira, 1023
A'o, 683
Apache Trout, 938
Aphelocoma coerulescens coerulescens, 579
Aplomado Falcon
    northern, 604

Exosphaeroma thermophilum, 1039

olive, 760
Riffle Shell
    tan, 976
Ring Pink Mussel, 1103
Ringed Sawback Turtle, 755
Rio Grande Shiner, 907
River Springfish
    White, 884
Roanoke Logperch, 1104
Roseate Tern, 703
Rostrhamus sociabilis levis, 694
Rostrhamus sociabilis major, 694
Rostrhamus sociabilis plumbeus, 694
Rostrhamus sociabilis sociabilis, 694
Rough Pigtoe Pearly Mussel, 1005
Roundtail Chub, 877, 901
Roundtail Chub
    Pahranagat, 883

S

Sage Sparrow
    San Clemente Island, 572
Salamander
    Cheat Mountain, 1104
    desert slender, 785
    Red Hills, 797
    San Marcos, 793, 841, 857
    Santa Cruz long-toed, 783
    Shenandoah, 1104
    Texas blind, 799
Salmo apache, 938
Salmo aquabonita whitei, 940
Salmo clarki henshawi, 812, 942
Salmo clarki seleniris, 944
Salmo clarki stomias, 946
Salmo gilae, 948
Salmo seleniris, 944
Salmonidae (Trout), 938, 940, 942, 944, 946, 948
Salt Marsh Snake
    Atlantic, 764
Salvin's Pigeon, 597
Sambucus, 1067
San Bruno Elfin Butterfly, 1065
San Clemente Island Loggerhead Shrike, 636
San Clemente Island Sage Sparrow, 572
San Francisco Garter Snake, 776
San Marcos Gambusia, 841, 857
San Marcos Salamander, 793, 857
Sand Skink, 745, 762
Sandhill Crane, 615
Sandhill Crane
    Mississippi, 618
Sandpiper, 658

Santa Cruz Long-Toed Salamander, 783
Sawback Turtle
    ringed, 755
Scaptochelys agassizii, 750
Schaus Swallowtail Butterfly, 1081
Scincidae (Skink), 745, 762
Scioto Madtom, 913
Scolopacidae (Sandpiper), 658
Scrub Jay
    Florida, 579
Sculpin
    pygmy, 1103
Sea Turtle
    green, 724
    hawksbill, 743
    Kemp's ridley, 757
    leatherback, 733
    loggerhead, 721
    olive ridley, 760
Seaside Sparrow
    Cape Sable, 568
Sedum spathulifolium, 1065
Shagreen
    Magazine Mountain, 1050
Shasta Crayfish, 1029
Shearwater
    Newell's manx, 683
    Newell's Townsend's, 683
Shell
    stirrup, 1016
    tan riffle, 976
Shenandoah Salamander, 1104
Shijimiaeoides battoides allyni, 1071
Shijimiaeoides enoptes smithi, 1073
Shiner
    beautiful, 879, 903
    Cape Fear, 905
    Pecos bluntnose, 907
    red, 904
    Rio Grande, 907
Shiny Pigtoe Pearly Mussel, 981
Shortnose Sturgeon, 801
Shortnose Sucker, 809
Shrike
    San Clemente Island loggerhead, 636
Shrimp
    Alabama cave, 1031
    California freshwater, 1037
    Kentucky cave, 1031, 1033
Silphidae (Carrion Beetle), 1093
Silverside
    Waccamaw, 899
Silverspot Butterfly
    Oregon, 1097